**Institute for
Research on
Public Policy**

*Institut de
recherche
en politiques
publiques*

F OUNDED IN 1972, THE INSTITUTE FOR RESEARCH ON Public
Policy is an independent, national, nonprofit organization.

IRPP seeks to improve public policy in Canada by generating research, providing insight and sparking debate that will contribute to the public policy decision-making process and strengthen the quality of the public policy decisions made by Canadian governments, citizens, institutions and organizations.

IRPP's independence is assured by an endowment fund, to which federal and provincial governments and the private sector have contributed.

F ONDÉ EN 1972, L'INSTITUT DE RECHERCHE EN politiques
publiques (IRPP) est un organisme canadien, indépendant et sans but lucratif.

L'IRPP cherche à améliorer les politiques publiques canadiennes en encourageant la recherche, en mettant de l'avant de nouvelles perspectives et en suscitant des débats qui contribueront au processus décisionnel en matière de politiques publiques et qui rehausseront la qualité des décisions que prennent les gouvernements, les citoyens, les institutions et les organismes canadiens.

L'indépendance de l'IRPP est assurée par un fonds de dotation, auquel ont souscrit le gouvernement fédéral, les gouvernements provinciaux et le secteur privé.

The Art of the State IV

Northern Exposure: Peoples, Powers and Prospects in Canada's North

Frances Abele,

Thomas J. Courchene,

F. Leslie Seidle and

France St-Hilaire, editors

Printed in Canada
Dépôt légal 2009

National Library of Canada
Bibliothèque nationale du Québec

LIBRARY AND ARCHIVES CANADA CATALOGUING IN
PUBLICATION

Northern exposure: peoples, powers and prospects in
Canada's North / edited by France Abele ... [et al.].

(The art of the state; IV)
Proceedings of the conference The art of the state IV,
held in Montebello, Québec, Oct. 25-27, 2007.

Includes bibliographical references.
ISBN 978-0-88645-205-6

1. Canada, Northern. I. Abele, Frances II. Institute for
Research on Public Policy III. Series: Art of the
state (Montréal, Québec) IV

FC3956.N676 2009   971.9'04   C2009-901920-5

PROJECT DIRECTORS
F. Leslie Seidle and France St-Hilaire

COPY EDITOR
Mary Williams

PROOFREADER
Barbara Czarnecki

EDITORIAL COORDINATOR
Francesca Worrall

COVER DESIGN AND INTERIOR DESIGN
Schumacher Design

COVER ILLUSTRATION
Normand Cousineau

PHOTO COVER
Canadian Press

PRODUCTION AND LAYOUT
Chantal Létourneau

PUBLISHED BY
The Institute for Research on Public Policy (IRPP)
l'Institut de recherche en politiques publiques
1470 Peel Street, Suite 200
Montreal, Quebec H3A 1T1

Contents

T HIS IS THE FOURTH VOLUME IN THE INSTITUTE FOR RESEARCH ON PUBLIC POLICY'S
The Art of the State series. The papers and commentaries presented here
originated at a conference entitled "Northern Exposure," which was held in
Montebello, Quebec, in October 2007. As the project was being developed, we
received helpful advice and suggestions from a number of people, including
Nellie Cournoyea, Terry Fenge, Bernie Funston, Franklyn Griffiths, David Hik,
Doug McArthur, Jim Moore, Thierry Rodon and Harley Trudeau. The editors and
the IRPP wish to thank all these colleagues for their contributions.

The IRPP would like to express its sincere appreciation to the Walter and
Duncan Gordon Foundation for the generous grant it provided for what was a
truly memorable conference. The following also provided financial assistance: the
Department of Indian Affairs and Northern Development (DIAND); the
Department of Foreign Affairs and International Trade; the governments of
Quebec, the Northwest Territories, Nunavut and Yukon; and the Canadian
Association of Petroleum Producers.

Several people played an important role at different stages of the project.
At the IRPP, Suzanne Lambert coordinated the extensive travel and other conference arrangements with her customary effectiveness; she was assisted by Virginie
Leduc and Chantal Létourneau. Suzanne Ostiguy McIntyre managed the production process for the volume, Chantal Létourneau was responsible for the layout,
and Francesca Worrall coordinated the editorial process with a steady hand and
a rigorous eye.

Mary Williams copy-edited the volume, and Barbara Czarnecki proofread
the manuscript. Jenny Schumacher developed the design of the cover and the
interior of the volume. Senada Delic, Jean-Simon Farrah, Grant Holly, Hugh
Meighen, Laura O'Laughlin, Patrick Lemieux, Jerry Sabin and Brett Smith provided research assistance at various stages of the process.

Patrick Lemieux provided invaluable research support during the drafting
of the concluding chapter, and Chris Burn, Stephanie Irlbacher-Fox, James
Feehan, Mark Salvo, Brett Smith, Harley Trudeau, Thierry Rodon, Richard Van
Loon and Graham White provided helpful comments on drafts of that chapter.
The following people assisted us greatly in finding/making maps: Adam Lewis,
Cartographic Services, Nunavik Research Centre, Makivik Corporation; Cherie
Northon, Mapping Solutions; Kyle Rentmeister, Centre for Geomatics,
Government of the Northwest Territories; Gerry Perrier, Information Management

and Technology, Yukon Department of Environment; and Caroline Sarazin-Normand, DIAND. We are most grateful to all these collaborators.

We are indebted to all of the authors in this volume for their insights and their important contribution to knowledge and ongoing debates about the future of Canada's North. The papers and commentaries presented here reflect a wide variety of views and perspectives, including those of northerners from various regions and backgrounds. We wish to express our appreciation to all of the contributors for their cooperation throughout the process and their openness to the editorial committee's comments and suggestions.

Finally, we would like to express our appreciation to Mel Cappe, President of the IRPP. In numerous ways, his leadership and suggestions enriched both the Northern Exposure research project and this publication.

Introduction and

Overview

C ANADA'S NORTH HAS ALWAYS BEEN AN IMPORTANT PART OF THE COUNTRY'S IDENTITY, but this reality is taking on a new light as melting polar ice transforms the Arctic into the epicentre of new global economic and geopolitical interests. Although in some senses many Canadians still see the North as a frontier, enormous change has already taken place as a result of the push for more resource development and new forms of governance. At the same time, northerners are facing unprecedented challenges as the effects of broad geopolitical, environmental and economic forces converge on their regions and communities. These developments are already commanding greater attention from political leaders, policy-makers and researchers.

Almost unnoticed in the rest of Canada, recent generations of northerners have devised a distinctive and innovative political regime. These new institutions are quite varied — they include the economically driven Aboriginal corporation of the Inuvialuit; the flexible and decentralized self-government regimes of Yukon; the regional Aboriginal governments in Dene, Cree and Labrador Inuit territories; and the hybrid and public government arrangements developed in Nunavut and by Inuit in northern Quebec. Taken together, they represent an impressive flowering of democratic innovation within the Canadian federation that also reflects and safeguards the constitutionally protected rights of Canada's Aboriginal peoples. A new and complex regulatory structure has also emerged as a result, one that provides considerable opportunity for power-sharing and public engagement. Nonetheless, these arrangements are incomplete. The initial designs must now be refined based upon experience and changing circumstances, and emerging difficulties need to be addressed.

The remarkable political innovations of the last generation have not settled major questions about the North's economic future. It remains for northerners to consider how their economies (local, regional and territorial) should be structured, given existing — and continually evolving — circumstances. Understandably, northern residents seek province-like control over their societies and economies, the better to manage the inevitable challenges and to benefit from the gathering opportunities. At the same time, it remains for Canada as a whole to consider how to ensure that northerners can shape their future, while taking into account the very high national stake in northern economic decisions. The threats to the integrity of northern ecosystems from global warming and international demand for northern resources are of a scale and complexity that make them of national, if not international, importance.

Part of the urgency many northerners feel about gaining control over the levers of economic development is related to a desire for a greater say in the large changes that will come to their region and directly affect their lives. Another part is a matter of revenue capacity. Northern societies face severe — and interrelated — deficits in infrastructure (housing, transportation, public facilities) and in health, education and social well-being. There is no question that many northern communities are struggling with serious and growing social problems that contribute to low educational attainment and often poor health outcomes. New and more comprehensive measures are needed to address these deficits. Yet the necessary interventions will be most appropriately and effectively carried out by trained northerners who understand their own situations best and are able to work with the necessary cultural and linguistic competence. In that sense, capacity building may be the most urgent challenge of all.

Overshadowing all moves to improve social development in the North is the impact of climate change. Global warming is certainly creating economic opportunity in the North but it also presents difficulties, even dangers, for all human endeavours. Melting sea ice is opening northern waters to international traffic on a scale never seen before. This development, in concert with intensifying global interest in the vast oil, gas and mineral resources of the circumpolar basin, puts the regulation of Arctic shipping, the establishment and policing of boundaries and the management of potentially substantial offshore drilling on the policy agenda. At the same time, the negative impacts on local ecosystems and traditional activities such as hunting require greater attention from policy-makers, and there is a need for measures to help northerners adapt to the changes already being felt.

A gainst this backdrop, the Institute for Research on Public Policy launched an ambitious multidisciplinary research project titled "Northern Exposure." The overall goal of the project was to inform public debate on northern issues and to increase public awareness of their importance and complexity beyond the climate change and sovereignty issues that so often occupy the headlines. Because of the similar challenges they face and the innovative forms of governance that have emerged in Nunavik (in northern Quebec) and in the Nunatsiavut settlement area in Labrador, it was decided that the project would cover these regions along with the three territories. An advisory group provided valuable assistance during the scoping of the project and initial planning for the fourth Art of the State conference held at Montebello, Quebec, in October 2007. The conference was structured around the following themes:

- Canada in the circumpolar world — environmental, scientific, foreign policy and governance dimensions
- Public, First Nations and Inuit governance
- Northern enterprise — sustainable development, economies and communities
- Sustaining people — education and human capital
- Northern policy for the future

The Montebello conference brought together some 60 presenters and participants from northern and southern Canada, including northern-based academics, present and former practitioners and community activists. Inuit leaders, including Sheila Watt-Cloutier and Mary Simon, shared their rich experience and visions of the future, as did a number of First Nations representatives. A highlight of the conference was a panel of six young northerners who are already making a mark in their communities. Under the theme "Voices of the New Generation — Aspirations for the Future," they presented distinctive, often passionate, perspectives on their region's future. Paul Okalik, then premier of Nunavut, and four former territorial premiers attended, as did officials from the federal government and the government of each of the territories.

In large measure, this volume flows directly from the Northern Exposure conference. However, as the revision of the conference papers and commentaries proceeded, the editors decided to commission some additional research in order to expand the coverage of northern public policy issues. It was also decided that, in order to situate the various texts in a broader historical, constitutional and public policy context, the book should be anchored by a background chapter.

Frances Abele agreed to take on this important assignment. In "Northern Development: Past, Present and Future" she examines three major challenges: (1) the continuing effort to adapt the governing arrangements in various regions of the North to the purposes and needs of northerners; (2) the limitations of an approach to northern economic development focused too narrowly on non-renewable resources and large infrastructure expenditures; and (3) securing the well-being of the residents of all of the North's small and large communities. Abele provides an account of the political and economic development of the North dating from the late nineteenth century and the major changes that came about after 1970 in the three territories, Labrador and northern Quebec. She suggests that the next 30 years will bring into focus problems of economic development, environmental change, and health and social well-being. Her assessment is that federal programs and territorial and local initiatives related to community health and well-being have been insufficient. For Abele, a concerted and comprehensive policy response is needed, "one that puts community and family well-being at the centre of the policy problem definition."

It is appropriate to begin the volume with a contribution from Sheila Watt-Cloutier, who was nominated for a Nobel Peace Prize in the same year as the Montebello conference. As in her numerous interventions on the world stage, Watt-Cloutier underlines the deep significance of climate change for Canada's Arctic regions, notably the potential for the "complete transformation of the northern ecosystem." She is critical of the federal government's policy stance on climate change and contends that "we must mainstream climate change, mitigating it and adapting it to all of our planning processes." Commenting on the Harper government's interest in a stronger defence of Canada's Arctic sovereignty, Watt-Cloutier suggests this goal can also be furthered by "providing the tools for Arctic communities to succeed and thrive," including high standards of culturally appropriate education, investment in community infrastructure and "respectful stewardship of the land" through natural resource comanagement bodies.

In the first of two chapters on sovereignty, Rob Huebert reviews past and ongoing disputes related to Canada's territorial claims in the Arctic. These differences risk becoming more significant because, partly as a result of climate change, "the Arctic is about to become a much busier place." He argues that Arctic sovereignty is a means to ensure greater national security and is of the view that Canada must substantially increase its spending in the North and develop its "capacity to stand up to those who challenge and oppose Canadian interests." He evaluates two options: addressing disagreements through bilateral negotiations and developing an international regime that would coordinate certain activities in the Arctic. Huebert favours a multilateral approach as the most effective way to manage environmental and resource development issues, although he warns this option might require that Canada withdraw some long-held unilateral claims.

Franklyn Griffiths proposes a somewhat different approach, which he refers to as stewardship: "locally informed governance that not only polices but also exhibits respect and care for the natural world." According to Griffiths, Canada must recognize that its internal waters claim owes much to Inuit occupancy; as such, sovereignty should be about more than military presence, surveillance or enforcement. It should also address a wide range of matters relating to the Arctic environment, including health, social and economic development, human resources and circumpolar affairs. This approach should also inform Canada's relations with its Arctic neighbours. For example, Griffiths calls for Canada and the United States to act not only as joint stewards, but also as neighbours determined to proceed with practical cooperation on priority issues.

Violet Ford comments on Huebert's and Griffiths's chapters. She suggests that, in his analysis, Huebert could have taken greater account of the Inuit and their presence in the Canadian Arctic — for example, by discussing the implications of land claims agreements for the way Canada may proceed on challenges to its maritime borders. Ford makes a similar point about Griffiths's chapter, stressing that indigenous rights are gaining greater recognition under international law. She suggests that Griffiths could have mentioned the role played by Canadian Rangers, many of them Inuit, as "the first line of defence in the Canadian High Arctic surveillance system." Ford concludes: "Inuit are centrally placed in the region. They are the key players, and they are the most affected by the Arctic sovereignty processes and by the outcomes and solutions Canada proposes."

In light of the current and potential impacts of climate change on northern ecosystems and communities, it is not surprising that governments in Canada and elsewhere in the Arctic have made scientific research a higher priority. In his chapter, Michael Bravo reviews recent developments in Arctic science, focusing in particular on the federal government's commitment in the 2007 Speech from the Throne to construct a world-class Arctic research station. Although he supports this initiative, he argues that the promise "should be understood as a recognition of the value of a long-term commitment to Arctic science rather than as an example of boom-and-bust spending." Bravo also calls for greater involvement of stakeholders and Aboriginal people in such scientific endeavours. He concludes that the real challenge for the Canadian Arctic research station is "to marshal science and technology to build partnerships, a knowledge base and a regulatory environment that secures and maintains the integrity of Canada's Arctic."

For her part, Hanne Petersen, a senior Danish scientist, explains that Arctic research "encompasses both basic and applied research, and...creates important linkages among communities, industry representatives and policy-makers." She describes how science cooperation in the region has grown, through the work of the Arctic Council and the International Conference on Arctic Research Planning, among other organizations. The latest International Polar Year (IPY) (which also covered the Antarctic) led to the launch of scientific and related activities on an ambitious scale, with more than 60 countries involved. In contrast to the three previous IPYs, the social and life sciences were included in the latest one. Petersen notes that, although a good deal of the research will not be completed for years, it will be a challenge "to maintain the legacy of the initiative — to keep up the momentum and make use of the results."

The next section of the book addresses the complex and fascinating developments in northern governance during the past three decades. The first chapter, by Doug McArthur, provides a detailed account of changes to governance in Yukon and the Northwest Territories (NWT) in the context of larger political, economic and social developments. The author examines some of the problems and challenges associated with developing the new governance arrangements. McArthur's central argument is that "a new constitutional settlement in form and substance" has emerged. However, "formidable obstacles" stand in the way of its completion, including the role of First Nations in relation to development proposals outside settlement lands, the federal government's cap on the amount of resource revenues territorial governments may retain and the related question of territorial and First Nations governments' high dependence on transfer payments from the federal government.

Next, Stephanie Irlbacher-Fox and Stephen Mills examine treaty implementation and institutional development in the NWT and Yukon. On the first issue, they make the following statement: "Indigenous peoples generally view treaties with Canada as agreements about decolonizing state-indigenous relationships and improving the lives of indigenous peoples." They are critical of the way

a number of modern treaties have been implemented; in some cases, implementation approaches have created what the authors describe as a "disabling environment." Drawing on international development literature, Irlbacher-Fox and
Mills call for a less legalistic approach, one that reflects Aboriginal peoples' view
that "treaties mark a beginning — the beginning of a better life for beneficiaries
and their communities and of a new relationship with Canada."

George Braden, a former NWT premier (1980-84), comments on the chapters by McArthur and Irlbacher-Fox and Mills. Starting with the latter, Braden
agrees that frustrations have arisen from the implementation of most land claims
agreements in the territories and that "the North is not receiving the coordinated
attention it deserves within the federal system." He is more skeptical about the
proposal to develop a *national* treaty implementation policy because "it would likely compel northern Aboriginal parties, with their unique circumstances and challenges, to compromise in order to accommodate the resolution of the claims
implementation issues of southern Aboriginal nations." As for McArthur's chapter,
Braden expresses the view that, although the federal government may be comfortable with how governance dynamics have been evolving (as McArthur suggests),
some changes may nevertheless be necessary because of growing concern about
land-use and resource regulation in the NWT and Nunavut. Braden concludes
with an eye to the future: "If Aboriginal governments at the community and
regional levels assume all, or nearly all, of the jurisdiction available to them, will
there be enough left for territorial assemblies and administrations in Whitehorse
and Yellowknife to govern exclusively without first securing the consent or participation of Aboriginal governments?"

Danny Gaudet, a Deline self-government negotiator, tells how his community near Great Bear Lake (NWT) is being affected by climate change and
other factors that are having an impact on their traditional lifestyle. He notes that
Aboriginal peoples in the North have much to offer in shaping public policy and
sees self-government agreements as creating "a long-term relationship...with the
territorial and federal governments." In this regard, he adds: "We expect governments to...ensure that if we're going to spend all this energy and time negotiating these wonderful agreements, we must build enough capacity for the
community to be able to have an impact on the entire system." In closing, Gaudet
also calls for Canada to give greater recognition to the North, including northerners' contribution to protecting sovereignty in the Arctic.

The next chapter on governance, by Graham White, examines the important political and institutional developments that have taken place in Nunavut and the Inuvialuit Settlement Region (ISR) — in particular the land claims agreements, the land claims organizations empowered by the claims and the challenges facing governments in the two regions. His assessment is that, even though self-government remains a goal rather than reality, the Inuvialuit have had considerable success in developing and operating their institutions of governance. As for Nunavut, White observes that the territorial government "is struggling to develop capacity and to provide effective governance." One of his conclusions is that the organizations representing the claims beneficiaries — Nunavut Tunngavik Incorporated (NTI) and the Inuvialuit Regional Corporation (IRC) — "will be key players in long-term political developments." However, White adds, what their actual role will be is less clear: "Thus far, the experience of the land claims organizations in Nunavut and the ISR points to a future of partnership rather than to one of parallel governments, but it is not hard to imagine this changing."

The survey of governance developments continues with a chapter by Thierry Rodon and Minnie Grey on the path to self-government for the Inuit of Nunavik and Nunatsiavut. As they recount, Nunavik, in the northernmost part of Quebec, gained a certain degree of administrative autonomy from the 1975 James Bay and Northern Quebec Agreement. For more than three decades, the Inuit in the region campaigned for greater autonomy. This led to an agreement in principle signed in late 2007 that will establish a system of regional public government. The inhabitants of Nunatsiavut in Labrador, the southernmost Inuit, launched a land claim in 1978. Negotiations did not progress significantly until tensions rose with regard to the Voisey's Bay project (a mining venture on land claimed by the Labrador Inuit). A final agreement was ratified in 2005, and institutions of self-government are now in place. Rodon and Grey discuss some of the social and environmental challenges that lie ahead in both regions. They conclude: "We must measure the success of these innovative governance models by their capacity to meet such challenges, but in the case of Nunavik and Nunatsiavut, it is still too early to do so."

John Zoe discusses the most recent modern treaty signed in the North, the Tlicho Agreement (which came into effect in 2005). Zoe writes about the history and some of the stories of his people, who reside principally in four communities north of Great Slave Lake in the NWT. He explains that the importance of coexistence with nature has been used to guide Tlicho positions on development and notes that two diamond mines are in operation on Tlicho territory and a third is under construction. He provides a detailed account of the process that led to the Tlicho Agreement and the challenges being faced during the implementation phase. Zoe closes on an optimistic note: "Our language, culture and way of life have been immortalized in the Agreement and in its implementation."

The section on Aboriginal and public governance concludes with a chapter by James Feehan on the important question of natural resource devolution. Yukon, which he describes as "the most 'devolved' territory," acquired control over Crown lands and natural resources in 2003 (onshore oil and gas were devolved earlier, in 1998). In the NWT, devolution of natural resources other than forestry has not yet occurred even though a framework agreement was signed in 2004. As for Nunavut, Feehan notes that little progress has been made. He then provides a detailed account of the recently reformed Territorial Formula Financing program, by which the federal government provides a large share of the territorial governments' revenues, and describes the challenges that remain. Feehan's view is that natural resource devolution to the NWT and Yukon would allow them to become less dependent on federal transfers and more self-reliant. He nevertheless concludes that, in light of sovereignty and environmental concerns and the potentially significant value of offshore oil and gas resources, it will be important to strike a balance between the interests of northern residents and those of Canada as a whole.

Prospects of rapid economic development in Canada's North bring to the fore a range of issues and differing perspectives. These are analyzed in the four texts that constitute the next section of this book. Terry Fenge begins with an overview of the context, challenges and opportunities associated with resource development based on available evidence of the potential riches beneath the lands and waters of Canada's North. He identifies four factors that will affect the scale and pace of development: world demand and high prices for energy and minerals; supportive infrastructure; a stable political and public policy environment; and a skilled, educated and motivated workforce. Fenge describes the changed governance and regulatory landscape that all players must contend with as development proceeds. He closes with a discussion of human resources and capacity issues, underlining the fact that "social, cultural and educational policy...will, in part, determine the achievement of economic development goals and objectives."

Next, Nellie Cournoyea writes about economic, environmental and social change in the Inuvialuit community. She states that the Mackenzie Valley gas pipeline is needed, in part to create wealth for the inhabitants of the ISR. On the question of regulatory complexity, Cournoyea states: "We continue to work together to improve our regulatory system and our capacity to effectively participate in the development of the economy and social conditions." Like a number of the other contributors to this volume, Cournoyea is concerned about human resource capacity issues and believes "it is urgent that the territorial and federal governments accept responsibility for investing in public services such as health, education and social services." She calls on the federal government to play a larger role in the NWT than south of the 60th parallel and for northern economic development to be "addressed at a more senior level in the bureaucracy and in government."

The section continues with two private-sector perspectives on economic development. First, Tom Hoefer, a former senior executive with Diavik Diamond Mines, provides a first-hand account of the development of diamond mining in the NWT. The industry grew quite rapidly following discovery of the first diamond-bearing deposits in 1991; by 2006, diamond mining and related activities accounted for half of the gross domestic product of the NWT. Hoefer recounts how, early on in the process, Diavik launched extensive community consultations and negotiated "special agreements" with five Aboriginal groups who traditionally used the lands in the Lac de Gras region. Before construction of the mine was approved, Diavik also developed a Northern Business Participation Policy. The "most significant move," according to Hoefer, was to contract local companies to perform much of the work at the mine site. He adds that in 2007 about half the mine's work was outsourced, the majority with Aboriginal firms. Hoefer concludes that diamond mining in the NWT "has generated significant and valuable local benefits and levels of inclusion, especially for Aboriginal communities, through training, employment and business."

To conclude this section, Gordon Erlandson addresses the impact of regulatory requirements in the North on the petroleum sector. He first addresses the various factors that determine the region's real potential for development based on nonrenewable resources — oil, natural gas and minerals. In his judgment, even before the recession that began in 2008, the petroleum industry's activity in the North was relatively low (in 2003, only 36 wells were drilled in the whole of the NWT compared to more than 17,000 in Alberta). Erlandson links this situation to the risk assessment the industry carries out before embarking on such projects and the uncertainty involved. He observes: "Whether the project involves major drilling or digging a soil pit from which to take samples for an environmental quality survey, the applicant cannot be sure when the decision will be made, what terms will be offered or even whether the project will be approved at all." As for what should be done, Erlandson calls for greater coordination, at a senior level, across all federal departments and agencies involved in resource management and decision-making.

In order to realize the evident potential for enhanced economic development in Canada's northern regions and ensure that territorial and Aboriginal governments and community leaders can play an effective role in defining the region's future, a larger proportion of the local populations must acquire the necessary education and skills. In this regard, the important questions of education and human capital are now addressed. In the first chapter of the section, Greg Poelzer begins by noting that rates of literacy, high school completion and university degree attainment in the North are "not close to being on a par" with those in the rest of Canada. He then provides an overview of the education policy and funding environment in the North, noting that, unlike all the other circumpolar states, Canada does not have a university in its Arctic region. He goes on to describe a number of post-secondary programs that operate in the North through partnerships with southern-based universities — in professional fields such as education, nursing and social work, and in other areas (including public administration and law). One promising initiative is the University of the Arctic, a consortium of more than 100 universities, colleges and Aboriginal organizations around the circumpolar North founded in 2001. Poelzer concludes by recommending that a university (possibly with multiple campuses) be built in the North as an investment in "building strong and effective northern territorial and Aboriginal governments and dynamic, competitive northern economies."

Following up on Frances Abele's overview of the severe social problems that persist in many northern communities, particularly among Aboriginal people, Jack Hicks's paper focuses on the most tragic of these: the dramatic increase in suicide rates. Hicks presents findings from a major research project he has been carrying out on suicide in Nunavut. He begins by recounting that Inuit societies traditionally had low rates of suicide. However, they all experienced a marked increase in its incidence, starting in Alaska in the late 1960s, followed by Greenland and Canada (in the latter case, in the late 1980s through the 1990s). Hicks reports that, during the first nine years of Nunavut's existence, all but three of the 247 suicides were by Inuit, and 56 percent were by men younger than 25. Hicks next explores the factors behind these trends, focusing on what are termed "adverse childhood experiences" and social determinants — in particular, the degree to which young men have the opportunity "to grow up seeing — and being parented by — adult men who are happy and successful." In conclusion, Hicks states that, although experience from Alaska and Greenland demonstrates that effective suicide intervention and prevention are possible, the Nunavut government took no action to develop a suicide prevention strategy until quite recently. In Hicks's view, immediate action also needs to be taken to reduce poverty and improve living conditions in Nunavut communities.

One of the goals of the IRPP in initiating this project and organizing the Northern Exposure conference was to focus on the voices and perspectives of northerners. We believe this is one of the strengths of this collection. The section "Voices of the New Generation" comprises six texts that are rich in personal experience — in this case, that of six young northerners who are making a mark in their communities and who participated in a panel discussion in the opening session of the conference. Their vision of the future is one that favours preserving the North's unique environment, cultures, languages and traditions, while embracing the opportunities that lie ahead.

- Udloriak Hanson, who chaired the panel, sees northern youth as the "next generation" — one that has inherited the land claims and treaties across the North negotiated by their parents. She emphasizes that northerners are very adaptive in nature and that the challenge is "to determine how to maintain the social fabric of decision-making and community processes" in a world that has changed considerably. In this regard, Hanson adds, northern youth envision a future "where fundamental beliefs are cherished and stand the test of time and change." Among these are "the preservation of language, education, culture and the environment."

- Elaine Alexie begins by stating that living in the Arctic presents "strong challenges" for indigenous people. In particular, "there is conflict and the uncertainty of trying to find a balance between living in the present and maintaining the traditional cultural practices of our ancestors in the past." Alexie goes on to address the question of language loss and why it matters so much. She reports that within her language group the Teetl'it Gwich'in dialect is spoken by less than 5 percent of the community and suggests the language could disappear in a generation or two. She adds: "I personally feel that our own leadership really needs to focus on the importance of and the need for protection of our languages and to practise them."

- George Berthe draws a contrast between the past, when the basic priority for Inuit was survival, and the present situation where the cash-based economy has gained importance. He believes it is time "to unlock the success instinct we have as Inuit." This means getting rid of attitudes he terms "successphobia" — resentment within the community toward those who do well. Berthe is also concerned that the transition "from a survival-based society to a success-based society" is being undermined by "rampant violence: verbal, physical and psychological lashing-out within our own people."

- The impact of climate change on Inuit culture and traditions is one of Laura MacKenzie's main concerns. In her words: "If polar bears no longer exist for hunting, then my sons are in danger of losing their culture...I want my sons to be able to understand their culture and to experience the hunt." She is also worried about the survival of the Inuktitut language and calls on the Nunavut government to make this a top priority.

- Natan Obed describes the implementation of land claims agreements as "a slow and frustrating process." He claims that the federal government often acts "as an adversary of its land claims partners" and is critical of the high turnover rate of the federal public servants involved in this area. He also calls on Inuit organizations to become more responsible and to find ways "to involve and empower the majority of beneficiaries." In closing, Obed calls for changes to the education system: "To be successful, school systems in Inuit regions must operate from the Inuit perspective, instead of the current reality where Inuit society and culture are considered add-ons to the curriculum and even a barrier to success."

- In the last of this series of commentaries, Aynslie Ogden focuses on some of the tangible impacts of climate change in the North. She reports that drought, wildfires, insects and outbreaks of diseases are projected to become more frequent and severe across the boreal forest, with consequences for northern forest-dependent communities. She then presents a series of conceptual approaches to adaptation in the forest sector and underscores the need for planners to gain knowledge from experience in evaluating alternative adaptation options. In this regard, she adds that "local values, local experiences and the implications of decision-making about adaptation to climate change for local futures make it essential that these choices be made locally."

In the final section, three highly experienced practitioners present their observations on northern policy for the future. Mary Simon, president of Inuit Tapiriit Kanatami and former Canadian ambassador for circumpolar affairs, first addresses the human dimension of climate change. With reason, she is concerned about the impact on the health of Inuit and of wildlife and ecosystems. Steps need to be taken, she writes, to decrease the "stovepiping" of this issue within several federal government departments; all parties, including the Inuit, should be brought together to coordinate actions and improve collaboration on this front. Simon then turns to what she describes as "an issue that must be moved to the front burner": education and the preservation of the Inuit language. Citing comparative research on the link between indigenous children's educational success and the length of time they receive instruction in their first language, Simon states: "We should be viewing access to education in Inuktitut as a human right."

Next, Richard Van Loon, a former associate deputy minister of Indian affairs and northern development,[1] explores the wide-ranging challenges and expectations facing the North. Among the former, he discusses climate change, the relative youth of northern governments, human resources and education for Aboriginal people, economic development and infrastructure, cultural diversity and culture shock, social pathologies and expected population growth. He devotes particular attention to the implementation of land claims settlements, noting that Aboriginal groups are gaining beneficial experience by participating in processes that protect the rights of those they represent. At the same time, they face difficulties because the procedures the new bodies follow are most often those of non-Aboriginal governments and the working languages may be second or third languages for Aboriginal participants. As for expectations, Van Loon is critical of territorial governments' high level of dependence on federal transfers and states: "We must…ensure that support is provided in ways that permit territorial governments to make their own decisions and take full responsibility for them, while at the same time encouraging these governments to do everything possible to increase their own-source revenues and economic development." In other areas, including infrastructure and housing, he calls for increased investment by the federal government. He concludes that people in the south can and must help northerners develop "a new way of life in a difficult environment," although "in the end it will be northerners themselves who decide their own futures."

The last of the forward-looking essays is by Tony Penikett, a former premier of Yukon (1985-92). He begins by pointing out that resource development prospects led to a renewed interest in negotiating treaties with Aboriginal peoples (an avenue governments had abandoned after 1921). In light of the resulting Aboriginal ownership of tens of thousands of square kilometres of land and large monetary settlements, Penikett believes "the treaties negotiated across the Canadian North in the late twentieth century are huge improvements over the [earlier] numbered treaties." He is nevertheless critical of the time it has taken to negotiate some of them and "inconsistent federal policies" on their implementation. Penikett notes the development of circumpolar institutions such as the Arctic Council and the University of the Arctic, and adds: "These emerging institutions still seem rich with potential." On climate change, he calls for the media and others, often so concerned about the plight of polar bears, to focus more on the impacts on the Arctic's human population. Penikett concludes with a number of proposals to make the federal government's promised integrated northern strategy more effective, calling on governments to "negotiate devolution agreements based on the legal boundaries of the territories, the right of citizens to enjoy the benefits of resource revenues earned from their lands and waters, and the benefits to Canada of building capacity through jurisdictional transfers and cooperative management regimes."

The editors conclude this volume with a chapter titled "The New Northern Policy Universe." They begin with a discussion of the factors that explain the current level of "renewed" attention to the region — climate change, sovereignty and resource development — and their impact (current and potential) on northerners and their way of life. The authors note that the federal government has made a number of significant commitments since 2007 as part of its northern strategy but call for the approach to be broadened through the pursuit of "balanced and participatory development." They then examine a series of policy options that they believe require serious attention — steps to improve the living conditions and adaptive capacity of northerners and their communities, rethinking the federal government's approach to treaty implementation, streamlining the regulatory process in the North and completing the devolution process. The editors conclude that, above all, a new northern policy universe should focus more clearly on the future well-being of northerners and their communities and ensuring they have greater control over their own destinies.

Note

1   The Department of Indian Affairs and
Northern Development (DIAND) is the
legal name of this department and Indian
and Northern Affairs Canada (INAC) is its
corporate name, in accordance with the
federal government's Federal Identity
Program. The legal name DIAND appears
in legislation, proclamations, orders-in-
Council, land claims, self-government
agreements, etc. The corporate name
(INAC) appears in all departmental communications (most departmental publications, news releases, Internet site, and on
letterhead).

Northern Development:
Past, Present and Future

T HE CANADIAN NORTH IS THE SITE OF IMPRESSIVE AND SOMETIMES DARING SOCIAL
and political innovation. It is also, increasingly, the focus of gathering international economic and political pressure, as well as new economic opportunity.
Northern development will be an increasingly important aspect of Canadian
political, social and economic vitality, and it should be a priority for public discussion and debate.

This chapter explains the historical sources of what might seem today
immutable conditions but are in fact the result of yesterday's purposes and decisions. The various new governing institutions, the wage economy based upon
nonrenewable resource development, the gathering social and health crisis in
many places in the North and the current foreign policy landscape all have their
roots in the pattern of northern development and relations between Aboriginal
peoples and the Government of Canada established in the nineteenth and early
twentieth centuries.

Three challenges face Canada in the North. The first is making the new
governing arrangements work. Despite the normal intergovernmental tensions,
there has emerged a widely shared commitment to adapting the governing
arrangements in various regions of the North to the purposes and the needs of
northerners so that they will have adequate means to make decisions and to
implement them in ways that benefit all residents. However, while a number of
new institutions have been put into place, it is not clear that these institutions will
be able to meet the demands of citizens *and* respond to the new demands of federal and international systems. It is not clear, either, that federal institutions are
optimally organized to support this process.

The second challenge arises from Canada's allegiance to an old and limited approach to northern economic development, one that focuses most attention upon mineral exploitation by means of large-scale projects and large infrastructure expenditures — with only awkward and occasional reference to the needs of the people living in the North. The challenge for all orders of government, including Aboriginal government, and for Aboriginal organizations is to work through the new institutional framework to chart a balanced and sustainable economic path.

The third, related challenge is to secure the well-being of the people living in all of the North's small and large communities. Their well-being depends upon two things: the wise selection and exploitation of a range of future economic opportunities; and judicious investment in local institutional and infrastructure development. It is imperative that urgent action be taken to find ways to create meaningful opportunities for young people to lead productive and satisfying lives and to cope with the enormous wave of change that seems poised to wash over northern societies in the twenty-first century as they respond to the many consequences of global warming and the growing international accessibility of Canada's North.

For better or worse, we Canadians will confront our northern future on the basis of a set of political and economic institutions and embedded practices developed initially to express the purposes of national government without reference to the aspirations of northerners. These institutions have been modified over the last 30 years in a complex process of political development led by northerners themselves. Northern expectations and Canadian understanding of the North reflect this history. It is the basis upon which we will all face Canada's northern future.

Canada's Historical Approach to Northern Development

CANADA'S NORTHERN REGIONS SAW THE EARLIEST CANADIAN CONTACT BETWEEN Europeans and Aboriginal peoples. In these regions, until relatively recently, those contacts did not involve the massive displacement of Aboriginal peoples that characterized the settlement of the Canadian south (McGee 2004; Fossett 2001; Dick 2001; Bennett and Rowley 2004).

The long-standing societies of the Canadian North encountered Europeans in significant numbers beginning over a thousand years ago. Vikings, Basques and later Russians and other Europeans came to the eastern and western Arctic coasts seeking a livelihood from whales, fish and fur, as well as religious converts and a trade network. The newcomers established some shoreline settlements but did not attempt to take control of interior lands (Armstrong, Rogers and Rowley 1978, chap. 3; Hanrahan 2003). By the mid-nineteenth century, though, in many dispersed northern locations, fur traders and missionaries had established themselves. State presence was limited to the occasional sponsored voyage or expedition, and after Canadian jurisdiction was established, small numbers of police were stationed in the region (Grant 1988, 2002; Coates 1985, 1991; Coates and Morrison 1992).

By all accounts, Aboriginal peoples were well able to accommodate or control visitors and sojourners during the long years of the early contact period. Often, local groups of Aboriginal peoples found that it was to their advantage to establish trade relations with the incomers and sometimes to engage in occasional paid labour.[1] In general, they treated the Europeans they encountered during this period much as they treated neighbouring groups of other Aboriginal peoples, establishing diplomatic relations by following the practices they had traditionally used with other societies. These practices were a combination of various trade customs, socialization and the exchange of cultural activities, intermarriage and the occasional conflict in defence of territory (Hanrahan 2003; Bennett and Rowley 2004; Dick 2001; Fossett 2001; Forest and Rodon 1995; see also Abele and Rodon 2007).

Generally, the European voyagers conformed to whatever the local authorities required.[2] For Aboriginal peoples, there were clearly commercial and other advantages in many of these early contacts. The most serious negative impact was the importation of diseases for which they had not developed immunity, a scourge that was to persist well into the twentieth century.

The Initial Pattern of Development

Intensified contact between Aboriginal peoples and newcomers often came as a result of mineral discoveries, and this contact in turn prompted the negotiation of treaties and the establishment of public institutions. The Klondike gold rush of the 1890s drew thousands of gold seekers to the Yukon. Many of the newcomers were American, and fears for Canadian sovereignty led directly to the establishment of the Yukon Territory in 1898. The disruptive pressure of large numbers of miners travelling northwest through Canada to the Klondike encouraged Dene along their route to seek a treaty with the Crown; Treaty 8 was signed in 1898 (Coates 1991; Fumoleau 1973). The 1920s and 1930s saw increased mineral exploration in many parts of the North, including the Mackenzie Basin, Yukon, Labrador and northern Quebec. When oil seeping to the surface at Norman Wells came to the attention of business interests, Treaty 11 (1921) was negotiated. An oil production facility was established at Norman Wells just as some mines were opened — for example, gold mining commenced at Yellowknife on Great Slave Lake in the 1930s. These initiatives did have considerable local impact, but the migrant populations of prospectors, miners and those who provided services to them remained relatively small and relatively isolated.[3] In most parts of the North, Aboriginal people could live much as they had always done, choosing the degree of contact they would have with newcomers and with the global economy.

Dominion northern policy during the years from Confederation to the Second World War did not differ in principle from Dominion policy with respect to all of the lands west and north of the original four colonies that confederated in 1867. Of prime importance was the assertion of Crown sovereignty and control of territory. This entailed, first, the negotiation of treaties with Aboriginal peoples and, in southern Canada, their eventual settlement on reserves, with the aim of opening lands for agricultural and other development.[4] Second, it entailed vigorous measures to protect the northwest region from annexation by the United States. These included the creation of the Yukon Territory, the extension of provincial boundaries, the construction of a transcontinental railway and the addition of the new provinces of British Columbia and Manitoba to the federation in the 1870s.

The vision for the economic development of the new country of Canada was embodied in what came to be called the National Policy of 1879, and it applied equally to the northlands and the West. Broadly, the terms of this policy were designed to support the development of an industrial base in central Canada, an agricultural hinterland in the West and an internal trading system in the country as a whole. Protective tariffs sheltered central Canadian industries. The agricultural base in the West was to form a market for central Canadian goods and provide export crops. The building of a transcontinental railway strengthened Canadian sovereignty by linking the former colony of British Columbia to the rest of Canada and opening the western plains to both policing and agricultural settlement.[5] The railway was fundamental to the process by which control of the plains was taken from the Métis and the Aboriginal nations, as it provided transport for soldiers, police and settlers. Métis relations with Canada involved two consequential "rebellions" or resistances,[6] while, under pressure, treaties with the Crown were negotiated by western Aboriginal nations between 1873 and 1921.

An important practical operating principle of the 1879 National Policy was that the Crown would grant the rights to private development of common (Crown) resources in exchange for the activity of development itself. Thus, for example, land was granted to homesteaders on the condition that they work it. The first regulations created for mineral development in the West, after the discovery of oil at Turner Valley in 1914, followed the same principles. In exchange for development activity, economic interests were given the right to develop the resource (Martin 1973).

Dominion policy with respect to the northern regions of the West applied the same principles. There was no prospect of agricultural settlement in most of the North, but mineral development was encouraged for similar reasons and under regulations similar to those applied in the agricultural West.

As for the rest of Canada during this period, employment protection, social provision and health care were not understood to be Dominion government responsibilities, but rather they were considered to fall within the ambit of families, charities and, minimally, local governments. This attitude prevailed even in the territories where Dominion government authority was the only governmental presence. There were minimal efforts to provide education for the residents of the northern lands, and the education that was provided was offered by religious schools. Health care was provided with extreme economy, even though through contact with newcomers, the North's Aboriginal peoples suffered epidemics of smallpox, measles, influenza and tuberculosis (Coates 1991; Rea 1968).

Dominion policy for the Aboriginal peoples of northern Quebec was slighter, though the principle was the same (Gourdeau 2003; Desbiens 2007).

The *Act of Union*, which brought Newfoundland into Confederation, makes no mention of Aboriginal peoples, an omission that was to have consequences for the quality and availability of services reaching well into the late twentieth century (Hanrahan 2003).

Resource Frontier and Aboriginal Homeland (1941 to the 1970s)

Until the middle of the twentieth century, the federal presence in the northern regions was relatively slight. There was a territorial government in Yukon, though outside the capital, Whitehorse, its reach was not substantial. Although federal responsibility for Inuit in northern Quebec had been established in 1939 by Supreme Court reference,[7] this did not result in an active federal presence. Almost everywhere in the North, Aboriginal people could avoid most contact with outside institutions if they chose; and, certainly, their contact with the federal state was minimal, even when they were in need of medical care or relief. Resident non-Aboriginal northerners were in a similar position, though many were supported by the institutions that had sponsored their journeys to the North.

The Second World War changed this situation forever. Concern for sovereignty and security, the postwar expansion of the welfare state and its extension into the North, and increased demand for northern energy and other resources all led to a much greater state presence in all parts of the North. During the war, anticipation of the opening of a North American Pacific front prompted the American and Canadian governments to develop the Northwest Staging Route, a chain of airfields extending from the south to Fairbanks, Alaska. In very short order, armed forces personnel and civilians constructed the Alaska Highway through the territories of numerous Aboriginal peoples to create an overland route to Alaska and to supply the airfields. They also constructed the Canol Pipeline to bring oil from Norman Wells on the Mackenzie River through a refinery in Whitehorse to the Alaskan Pacific front. This effort led to the construction of a number of all-weather and winter roads and greatly increased traffic on the Mackenzie River. Pitchblende that had been discovered on the shores of Great Bear Lake in 1929 provided material for atomic weapons research and development. Aboriginal people were among the civilians and armed forces personnel who worked on these ventures, and Aboriginal communities in their path bore the impact (Coates and Morrison 1992). In the northeast, armed forces personnel constructed a network of airfields to be used for ferrying aircraft to Europe and for returning the wounded. Airfields were built at The Pas, Churchill, Coral Harbour, Frobisher Bay (now Iqaluit), Fort Chimo (now Kuujjuaq) and Goose Bay.

After the Second World War, the armed forces did not leave. With the advent of the Cold War between the United States and the Soviet Union (and their respective allies), the North attained ever-more-strategic importance.[8] Fear of a Russian bomber attack on the United States over the pole (and perhaps, rather unrealistically, fear of a Russian invasion through the Arctic) led to an extensive US presence, joint Canada-US defence-related research programs and the construction of three early-warning radar lines stretching in parallel across the North, more airfields and communications sites related to the Distant Early Warning (DEW) Line.

The continued heavy construction and military activity had a significant impact on Aboriginal people's way of life in many parts of the North. Some were drawn to the sites of activity by employment opportunities or by the huge amounts of discarded *matériel*. In turn, greater contact with outsiders led to more health problems (related to infectious diseases and the availability of alcohol), and also to greater southern awareness of Aboriginal people's living conditions, which in some cases were very poor. It is important to recognize that many people did still manage to control their relations with the outsiders who were now stepping into certain regions with much heavier feet — they simply stayed away from the places where activities were concentrated.[9] But this strategy for remaining in control of relations with outsiders could not provide insulation against the next large presence to appear: the Canadian welfare state.

Dominion government concerns about sovereignty occasioned by the large American presence, and recognition of the visibly difficult living circumstances of some Aboriginal peoples, demanded some form of state intervention. Universal social programs such as Old Age Security and social assistance were expanded in southern Canada and were extended to the North, carried along on a wave of post-war enthusiasm for the positive potential of social engineering and the possibilities of state-led "modernization" — that is, a broad process of social transformation that would supersede traditional practices unsuited to modern economies.[10]

In the two decades after the end of the Second World War, state-led changes to northern life included settlement and resettlement of the Aboriginal population in communities where social housing was provided; the relocation of a number of settlements; the extension of medical care; the introduction of compulsory education as well as the extension of residential school education; and the introduction of social transfer payments such as Old Age Security and social assistance.[11] Besides efforts to encourage and sometimes coerce people to leave the land for settlements where services could be more easily provided, there were a number of forced relocations across great distances, undertaken for external purposes; with these, there were significant failures in execution.[12] Taken together with attempts to regulate harvesting, these initiatives amounted to a massive transformation of Aboriginal peoples' way of life. Health care and educational opportunities were welcomed by many, but they led to the (sometimes permanent) separation of family members, as some were sent south for treatment and others to residential schools for education. The introduction of social housing into the communities, along with increasingly available new technologies such as snowmobiles and more sophisticated guns, meant changes in land use and patterns of hunting.[13] There were also state-led efforts to introduce local government and economic associations in the form of hamlet councils and federated community cooperatives (Bean 1977; Mitchell 1996; Damas 2002).

Accompanying and exacerbating the effects of military and other state activities was accelerated interest in the development of northern resources. Greater Canada-US cooperation in defence and northern research during the Second World War and in the immediate postwar period increased economic integration (Grant 1988). The US economy had expanded rapidly during the war, a boom that was to continue in the postwar period. Many of the resources and some of the energy needed to sustain this boom came from the Canadian mid-North. In the two decades after the war, timber, nickel, iron, tungsten and precious metals were mined in new operations in many locations in the mid-North, while energy was supplied domestically and for export by hydroelectric power developments in Quebec, Labrador, Manitoba and British Columbia, and by petroleum development in Alberta after the discovery at Leduc in 1947. These developments were of enormous import for the whole Canadian economy, orienting it more firmly to staples export to the burgeoning US industrial base. In 1957, when future prime minister John Diefenbaker announced a new "northern vision" and a new federal commitment to "Roads to Resources," he was giving political focus to a process of economic change that was already under way (Rea 1968; Grant 1988; Coates

1985; Zaslow 1988). Similar visions captured political imaginations in several Canadian provinces for the same reasons.[14]

For the North's Aboriginal peoples, northern resource development often meant disruption, relocation and the loss of lands important for subsistence and for spiritual well-being. The opening of mines and associated roads and airstrips further reduced the isolation of Aboriginal communities. Settlements were relocated to make way for these projects, while hunting and trapping was disrupted in many more areas (INAC 1996a). Employment opportunities drew some local interest, but an anticipated new northern Aboriginal labour force on the model of that of southern Canada did not emerge.

As with the introduction of the welfare state, the changes brought by accelerated development of northern resources were driven by forces outside the North and controlled in distant centres. The self-sufficient and independent Aboriginal peoples of the northland made certain choices concerning residency and such things as the education of their children, while maintaining their customary economic activities. They were not hapless victims of these events. In retrospect, though, it is plain that the sheer magnitude, scope and pace of the externally driven changes undermined local control and a sense of efficacy in many communities.[15] By the mid-1960s, there had been multifaceted pressure for two or three generations on long-established social norms and economic practices in Aboriginal societies. By the mid-1960s, Aboriginal peoples were beginning to formulate a collective response. They encountered an energized and newly centralized federal administration and, in the provinces of Quebec and Newfoundland, provincial governments eager to accelerate northern resource development in the service of general provincial economic development (Dorion 1971; Morantz 2002).

As federal activity in the North continued to grow, the apparatus of northern administration was altered. Prime responsibility for the North was transferred from the Department of the Interior to the new Department of Northern Affairs and National Resources (DNANR) in 1953. The growing need for coordination led to the creation of the initially high-level Advisory Committee on Northern Development (ACND) (Abele and Dosman 1981). After a special study of Canada's northern responsibilities, the 1966 Glassco Commission on government organization recommended the creation of the Department of Indian Affairs and Northern Development (DIAND), which would be formed out of the old DNANR and the "registered Indians" offices at Citizenship and Immigration Canada. Also in 1966, an advisory commission on Northwest Territories government reported; it recommended gradual movement toward more province-like government and recommended against division of the Northwest Territories (NWT) at that time (Advisory Commission on the Development of Government in the Northwest Territories 1966).

Responsible and Representative Governments

The 1960s were the halcyon years of the new federal department responsible for northern affairs. With a strong research and policy capacity, a growing budget, much to do in the North and an initially commanding presence on the ACND, the department moved to implement gradual progress toward representative government in the North, on the southern model, and a northern development policy essentially modelled on the National Policy of 1879. By these means, Canada would incorporate the northern territories more fully and more equitably into the federation, while countering the challenge to Canadian sovereignty presented by growing US interest in exploiting Arctic offshore oil and natural gas reserves.

By the mid-1960s, the centrepiece of DIAND's economic development plan was the construction of a pipeline through Canadian territory to transport US oil and gas as well as anticipated Canadian discoveries (Dosman 1975). Federal promotion of what was to become the Mackenzie Valley gas pipeline proposal was the flashpoint that eventually led to the full mobilization of northern Aboriginal peoples and a radical revision of DIAND's capacity to plan northern economic development. The spark may have been lit in the Mackenzie Valley, but fuel for the fire was found across the North. The reasons for this lie in recent Canadian and northern history.

As noted earlier, treaty making halted in 1921, with Aboriginal rights over large parts of Canada, and the Crown's legal claim to these lands, unresolved. Areas not covered by treaty in 1921 included parts of every province and almost all of British Columbia, the eastern NWT, Quebec and Yukon. With the exception of some adhesions (a process through which First Nations groups could join an existing treaty), no more treaties were negotiated until 1975.

During much of the period from 1921 to 1975, the *Indian Act* regulated the lives of "registered Indians."[16] In most of Canada, they were confined to reserves — small tracts assigned to them by treaty or by administrative action.

Canadian Northern Development: A Select Chronology

1870   Britain transfers jurisdiction over Rupert's Land and the Northwest to Canada

1880   Canada is granted sovereignty over the Arctic islands

1898   The Yukon Territory is created; Treaty 8 is signed

1902   Yukon is given parliamentary representation

1912   The northern boundaries of Manitoba, Ontario and Quebec are extended

1921   Treaty 11 is signed

1927   The Judicial Committee of the Privy Council sets the boundary between Canada and Newfoundland

1949   Newfoundland joins Canada

1952   The Northwest Territories is given parliamentary representation

1967   Yellowknife is declared the capital of the NWT; the seat of government is moved there

1968   USS *Manhattan* sails through the Northwest Passage, challenging Canadian sovereignty

1973   Federal policy recognizes Aboriginal interest in lands not covered by treaty

1974-77 The Mackenzie Valley Pipeline Inquiry is conducted

1975   The Northwest Territories gets the first fully elected territorial council; the first modern treaty, the James Bay and Northern Quebec Agreement, is signed

1979   Yukon is granted responsible government

1983-85 The first oil pipeline is constructed, running south from Norman Wells in the NWT

1984   The first modern treaty north of 60, the Inuvialuit Final Agreement, is signed

1993   The Nunavut Land Claims Agreement is signed; the Council for Yukon Indians Umbrella Final Agreement and agreements with four individual First Nations are signed

1998   The first northern diamond mine opens

1999   The Northwest Territories is divided to create two new territories: the Northwest Territories and Nunavut

2005   In Labrador, the Nunatsiavut self-government agreement and modern treaty are signed

2005   The Tlicho Agreement is signed

On reserves, they were closely supervised by a federal Indian agent, who effectively controlled the key aspects of reserve life. The *Indian Act* outlawed certain First Nations' traditional spiritual and political practices, and, after 1927, it also made it illegal for registered Indians to raise funds for the purposes of common legal representation. Administrative authority over their lives was exercised with virtually no democratic control. During this period, First Nations communities were reorganized or moved and reserve lands were taken, all under the authority of the *Indian Act*. Status Indians were not permitted to vote in federal elections until 1960; gender discrimination in the *Indian Act* (it contained a provision by which Indian women, but not Indian men, lost status if they married a nonstatus person) was not addressed until 1985.

Largely for reasons of geography and transportation infrastructure, most northern Aboriginal peoples — First Nations, Inuit and Métis — were somewhat outside the ambit of the heavy administrative control exercised in southern Canada. Although treaties were signed by Dene living in the western NWT, bringing them under the *Indian Act*, no reserves were established in the territorial north until the 1970s, when one was established at Hay River, NWT. Historically, policy affecting Inuit was animated by philosophies of protection and control, though no treaties were attempted and no reserves were ever created. Indeed, officials in Ottawa initially sought to create the conditions under which Inuit could continue to live, as much as possible, as they had always done. Northern nonstatus Indians and Métis did not register at all as a federal responsibility.

In Canada, as in many parts of the circumpolar basin, the Second World War breached the relative stability and isolation of northern Aboriginal societies. The changes brought by the war itself significantly tested their adaptability — but, probably more importantly, the war set in motion a pattern of interaction that was to prevail for the next 50 years. In earlier contacts with incomers, Aboriginal people met individual representatives of distant authorities (such as the trading companies and the churches) whose ability to survive in the North without substantial assistance from Aboriginal peoples was very limited and whose interests, for the most part, depended upon developing good relations with the locals. During the Second World War, this pattern changed forever. Larger groups of newcomers arrived with massive amounts of *matériel*, more powerful technologies and seemingly endless replacements for people and equipment. They had (often unexpressed) purposes of their own. They required

little from northern Aboriginal peoples other than that they get out of the way.
As the effects of this were felt across the North, people began to consider the
ways in which they could regain some of their historic capacity for self-sufficiency and self-determination.

Political and Economic Reforms after 1970

The proposal to build a natural gas pipeline in the Mackenzie Valley — and thus
to open the northwest to development — was of a piece with decades of federal
northern development policy. The future was understood to lie in the development of northern natural resources, which would provide industrial stimulation,
employment for local people and eventually public revenue. There had been little local resistance to previous development projects, and so it was a political
shock when Dene, Métis and Inuvialuit in the Mackenzie Valley, Mackenzie Delta
and Beaufort Sea area organized to press their land rights and to object to the construction of the pipeline or any other development in their territory before land
rights were confirmed.[17]

Aboriginal people across the North found similar reasons to organize.[18]
The modernizing Quebec state turned its attention to northern hydroelectric
potential, commencing construction of a series of dams in the Cree territories. As
did the Dene and Métis of the NWT, the Cree organized to resist this incursion
politically and through the legal system. In 1975, working under pressure but
supported by a court decision, they negotiated the first modern treaty: the James
Bay and Northern Quebec Agreement (JBNQA) (Dorion 1971; Morissonneau
1978; Feit 1979; Morantz 2002; Desbiens 2007). In Yukon, the Yukon Native
Brotherhood (later the Council of Yukon First Nations) was founded in 1968 to
press for a treaty negotiated on the basis of never-ceded Aboriginal rights, releasing its first land claims statement, *Together Today for Our Children Tomorrow*, in
1973 (Council for Yukon Indians 1973). In the same five-year period, the
Committee for Original People's Entitlement was created in the Mackenzie Delta-
Beaufort Sea area in response to the intensive oil and gas exploration that had
begun; by 1984, Inuvialuit had signed the second modern treaty, after the
JBNQA. Similar organizations were formed in Labrador: the Labrador Inuit
Association and the Innu Nation.

In a very short span of time (approximately 1968 to 1973), all of the northern Aboriginal peoples formed organizations for political self-representation.[19]

They began to use political representation and court actions to assert their citizenship and land rights and to obstruct development projects that threatened to undermine their societies. While they were not usually successful in halting such projects permanently, they did, in almost every case, wring better terms for local people from the proponents. In several cases, such as the inaugural conflict over the James Bay hydroelectric project in northern Quebec, they were able to use their legal and political leverage to negotiate recognition of their land and Aboriginal rights. In the course of this political work, in concert with Aboriginal peoples in other parts of Canada, they succeeded in compelling the federal government to reopen treaty negotiations for those parts of Canada where these negotiations had not been completed.[20] The modern treaties have made a permanent change in the northern balance of political and economic power. Another consequence of Aboriginal peoples' activism was the entrenchment, in 1982, of "existing Aboriginal and treaty rights" in the Canadian Constitution. This has forced the government to make alterations to federal policy, and now new political arrangements are being imagined, negotiated and established. A series of high court decisions, rendered both before and after patriation, established that Aboriginal peoples did have land and other rights in Canadian law (Indian and Northern Affairs Canada 1996b; Henderson 2006).

An important consequence of northern Aboriginal peoples' activism and their engagement with non-Aboriginal coresidents has been the redesign of northern political boundaries and institutions. Through the modern treaties, they have delineated the lands that will be theirs alone, in perpetuity, and they compelled the creation of a new subnational jurisdictions through the 1999 division of the NWT.[21] The modern treaties and the self-government negotiations conducted in their context have in different degrees altered the institutions and practices of public government in northern Canada. In the process, they changed the very nature of federalism itself. Each northern region has found a somewhat different institutional solution as governments and citizens have navigated the very complex and necessary process of rebalancing. In each region, another product of the decades of political activism and institutional innovation has been a distinctive regulatory system in which some institutions are constitutionally protected and others are a matter of practice and policy; in this context, high expectations for substantial levels of public participation and deliberation are created.

The mobilization of northern Aboriginal people and their political rep-
resentations concerning their lack of political and economic control of their
lands, along with a series of court actions, led to important institutional
changes. These were reinforced by legal decisions in cases brought by
Aboriginal peoples elsewhere in Canada. Federal policy changed radically in a
generation. Aboriginal land rights were recognized, and a negotiating process
was offered, then revised numerous times by federal authorities aware that
both jurisprudence and political pragmatism demanded change. At the same
time, support was provided for the renegotiation of public government institutions, producing, within about 20 years, new and innovative political
arrangements in northern Canada.

In contrast to the new constitutional principles that shape northern governing arrangements, the principles that underlie the federal approach to the
development of northern resources are little changed from the National Policy
days. Public investment (in the form of direct infrastructure and other subsidies
or tax expenditures) is used to attract private sector development; access to publicly held natural resources is exchanged for the activity of development. It is
expected that this strategy will eventually lead to the creation of a regional economy offering employment and public revenue. To a large extent, territorial governments appear to have accepted these principles. These governments, along
with northern beneficiary organizations, now have some purchase on northern
economic development decisions.

In 2001, the Yukon and federal governments negotiated devolution of
lands and natural resources development to the territory, and a system for
resource-revenue sharing.[22] In the NWT and Nunavut, these basic powers are
still under federal control. The regulatory process, along with decision-making about economic development in general, has been constrained and complicated by the negotiation of modern treaties, each of which contains
provisions to establish comanagement boards and principles that aim to
increase local control over the pace and direction of development (Rodon
2003). The resulting system, though it is entrenched in the treaties and so constitutionally protected, may be seen as transitional, since northerners must
find ways to make it meet their goals of balanced development and since the
division of powers between federal and territorial governments remains a matter of contention (Hodge, Stauch, and Taggart 2007; Papillon 2008).

Labrador and northern Quebec have undergone similar processes of change, fuelled by Aboriginal political activism and pressure for resource development. This has led to institutional innovation and changes in the role of provincial governments. Each province has moved from largely ignoring or denying Aboriginal rights to active collaboration and acceptance. Quebec, the site of the first modern treaty (the JBNQA of 1975), was also the first province to recognize an Aboriginal right of self-government, in 1984; and, as others in this volume argue, the province continues to be an active site of innovation. In Labrador, after a slow start, a modern treaty and self-government agreement was negotiated by Inuit, and with it, the beginnings of a new institutional relationship with both the provincial and federal governments (Desbiens 2007; Feit 1979; Morantz 2002).

The New Northern Landscape
Plainly, the dramatic transformation of the institutions of northern political life in the latter third of the twentieth century has created a new landscape for policy-making in the twenty-first. The new institutions are well described by other authors in this volume. They write about the 10 modern treaties negotiated in the northern regions since 1975, along with 11 self-government agreements pursuant to the Umbrella Final Agreement in the Yukon, self-government agreements that are part of the Labrador Inuit Land Claims Agreement and the Tlicho Agreement in the NWT, the free-standing Nunavik self-government agreement in northern Quebec and the negotiated creation of the new territory of Nunavut. Each region of the North now features a new set of political institutions, most of them constitutionally protected.[23] There are multiple new arrangements for internal governance of Aboriginal nations and peoples, and an array of regulatory and intergovernmental collaborative institutions governing resource use and ordering service provision.

Each northern region has developed distinctly different new arrangements. In Labrador, Inuit have created the Nunatsiavut government, and Innu will likely negotiate a distinctive form of self-government as well. These Aboriginal governments will interact regularly with provincial and federal institutions. The Government of Quebec will interact with the Cree Regional Authority (specific to the Crees) and the Nunavik government (a form of public government). Aboriginal peoples in both provinces — Quebec and Newfoundland and Labrador — also have (or eventually will have)

Treaties in the Five Northern Regions

Historic treaties

Treaty 8	1899	Alberta, British Columbia, Northwest Territories, Saskatchewan
Treaty 11	1921	Yukon, Nunavut

Modern treaties (final comprehensive land claims agreements)

James Bay and Northern Quebec	1975	Quebec
Northeastern Quebec	1978	Quebec
Inuvialuit	1984	Northwest Territories
Gwich'in	1992	Northwest Territories
Nunavut	1993	Nunavut
Sahtu Dene and Métis	1994	Northwest Territories
Council for Yukon Indians Umbrella Final Agreement	1993	Yukon
Vuntut Gwitchin First Nation	1993	Yukon
First Nation of Na-Cho Nyak Dun	1993	Yukon
Teslin Tlingit Council	1993	Yukon
Champagne and Aishihik First Nation	1993	Yukon
Little Salmon/Carmacks First Nation	1997	Yukon
Selkirk First Nation	1997	Yukon
Trondëk Hwëch'in	1998	Yukon
Ta'an Kwäch'än Council	2002	Yukon
Kluane First Nation	2003	Yukon
Kwanlin Dun First Nation	2004	Yukon
Carcross/Tagish First Nation	2005	Yukon
Tlicho	2005	Northwest Territories
Labrador Inuit	2005	Newfoundland and Labrador
Nunavik Inuit	2008	Quebec

Source: St. Germain and Sibbeston (2008).

significant economic resources in the form of capital received as compensation for lands surrendered and natural resources on their lands. Nunavut is governed by a public, territorial government and is home to over 25,000 beneficiaries of the Nunavut agreement, who administer their common affairs through Nunavut Tunngavik Incorporated. In the NWT, the situation is even more complex, as negotiations for regional claims, negotiations for self-government and negotiations concerning shared jurisdiction over resources are creating a variety of regional Aboriginal organizations and governments.[24] These control substantial capital, and each has somewhat different governance arrangements. The Government of the Northwest Territories remains the public government for the whole territory. The overall working relationship among all these governing bodies is a work in progress. The same is true in Yukon, where a single umbrella agreement provides significant autonomy for the individual First Nations who united to negotiate it.[25] All of these groups benefit from capital reserves transferred in compensation for surrendered lands, and all are empowered to choose from a wide array of self-governing powers. In all three territories, the role of federal institutions and federal funding is still very important. In short, there are new governing institutions in each of the northern regions, with numerous lines of cooperation (and probably simplification) under development.

One of the most interesting strands of Canadian political development over the next several decades will be the successful implementation of the modern treaties and the refinement of the public and Aboriginal governing institutions that have been put in place. There are currently significant problems with federal government treaty implementation (Dacks 2004; Irlbacher-Fox and Mills in this volume). It will also likely be necessary to work out the implications for territorial and provincial administrations of the evolving Aboriginal governments (Northwest Territories, Commission on Constitutional Development 1992).

For the federal government, the northern scene is remarkably complex, especially when one takes into account the reality that federal authority over northern resource development in the NWT and Nunavut remains strong. Federal discretion is mediated by the new treaty-based resource management institutions, though constitutionally the power remains at the federal level. In provincial jurisdictions, as others have shown (Rodon and Grey in this volume; Papillon 2008), working arrangements through which development decision-making can take place are being tried.

What will the future federal role be? As in the past, federal northern policy will balance three dynamically interacting imperatives. It will respond to the initiatives of northerners with measures influenced by changes in federal-Aboriginal relations in the country as a whole. It will respond to economic opportunities and imperatives, probably following the long-established path of public subsidy of private development and complex regulation. And it will continue to take steps to protect Canadian sovereignty (ss Huebert's and Griffiths's chapters in this volume).

The Northern Economy Today: Finding the Balance?

THE CANADIAN NORTH, AS IT IS DEFINED IN THIS VOLUME, COMPRISES ABOUT HALF THE area of Canada, but it is home to fewer than 115,000 people (see table 1). This population embodies a great diversity of cultures old and new. About 55 percent are members of Aboriginal nations and peoples — descendants of societies that were established in the North when the Europeans arrived. The rest are immigrants who came to Canada in different periods from every continent in the world. They live in about 140 small communities ranging in size from fewer than 100 people to 22,000 people — the latter is the population of Whitehorse, the region's largest city, although it is still small by national standards. While all but one

Table 1
Aboriginal and Non-Aboriginal Population in the Three Territories, Nunatsiavut and Nunavik, Canada, 2006

	Total population[1] (N)	Aboriginal population (N)	Aboriginal as a % of total population
Yukon Territory	30,372	7,580	25.0
Northwest Territories	41,464	20,635	49.8
Nunavut	29,474	24,915	84.5
Nunatsiavut	2,414	2,200	91.1
Nunavik	10,784	9,650	89.5
All regions	114,508	64,980	56.7

Source: Statistics Canada, Census 2006 (http://www.statcan.gc.ca).
[1] Census population.

Table 2
Employment in the Three Territories, Aboriginal and Non-Aboriginal Populations, by Industry, 2006 (Percent)

	Yukon Territory	
	Aboriginal population	Non-Aboriginal population
Goods		
Agriculture and other resource-based industries[1]	6.4	4.8
Construction	8.6	6.5
Manufacturing	0.8	2.4
Services		
Wholesale trade	0.9	2.0
Retail trade	6.9	11.0
Finance and real estate	1.9	3.1
Health care and social assistance	6.2	9.9
Educational services	5.6	7.1
Business services[2]	13.5	15.5
Public administration	34.7	21.3
Other[3]	14.1	16.2
Total experienced labour force (15 years and over)	3,770	15,115

Source: Statistics Canada, Census 2006 (http://www.statcan.gc.ca).
[1] Resource-based industries include forestry, fishing and hunting; mining and oil and gas extraction; and utilities.
[2] Business services include transportation and warehousing; information and cultural services; professional, scientific and technical services; management of companies and enterprises; and administrative and support, waste management and remediation services.
[3] Other services include the arts, entertainment and recreation; and accommodation and food services.

community in Yukon may be reached by road, many northern centres are accessible only by air, by ice road and, in summer, by water. Telecommunications are improving rapidly; broadband Internet connections are available to most people. Northern economic development planning and decision-making occur under unique circumstances.

Northwest Territories		Nunavut	
Aboriginal population	Non-Aboriginal population	Aboriginal population	Non-Aboriginal population
13.4	6.4	6.0	2.0
8.9	5.5	6.5	4.8
1.1	1.8	1.6	0.4
1.3	1.8	0.7	1.0
8.3	10.1	13.6	6.8
3.9	3.6	3.8	4.1
9.6	8.8	9.1	9.2
5.8	8.0	11.5	16.0
13.0	21.6	11.4	14.5
24.1	20.0	25.6	31.8
10.8	12.3	10.3	8.9
9,130	14,315	8,640	3,440

Although few in number, Canada's northern residents are central to the country's future — or, at least, it is important to Canada's future that people continue to be able to live well in the North. Their presence establishes and preserves Canadian sovereignty. They maintain the centres of population upon which northern economic development turns. As I noted earlier, they are innovators in the area of multi-ethnic democratic government, particularly when it comes to tackling the question of how to provide high-functioning modern institutions that also embody the core values of the original societies of the North. How can northern residents, with their

Table 3
Employment in the Aboriginal Population in Nunatsiavut and Nunavik, by Industry, Canada, 2006 (Percent)

Goods	Nunatsiavut	Nunavik
Agriculture and other resource-based industries[1]	16.4	5.1
Construction	7.6	1.9
Manufacturing	7.0	0.4
Services		
Wholesale trade	0.0	0.4
Retail trade	8.2	10.8
Finance and real estate	0.0	1.4
Health care and social services	14.0	25.2
Educational services	7.0	14.5
Business services[2]	8.8	11.8
Other services[3]	30.4	28.2
Total experienced Aboriginal-identity labour force (15 years and over)	855	3,615

Source: Statistics Canada, Census 2006 (http://www.statcan.gc.ca).
[1] Resource-based industries include forestry, fishing and hunting, mining and oil and gas extraction, and utilities.
[2] Business services include transportation and warehousing; information and cultural services; professional, scientific and technical services; management of companies and enterprises; and administrative and support, waste management and remediation services.
[3] Other services include notably arts, entertainment and recreation; accommodation and food services; and public administration.

numerous small communities, flourish? What policy choices are required to make these communities prosper?

The economic base of northern society, upon which community well-being depends, is composed of the natural gifts of the land, in the form of either food and materials or mines and minerals. Economic decision-making must take into account the special dynamics of these gifts. Although the public sector provides, overall, the most jobs, and although tourism, the commercial fishery, and some small art and boutique-product enterprises are important and lively, decisions made about the mineral and harvesting sectors (whose viability sometimes interacts) will determine much of the economic future of the Canadian North (see tables 2 and 3). These decisions will be made by Aboriginal and non-Aboriginal northerners — jointly, in many instances, with federal officials and politicians — working through the new governance institutions that have been created over the last 30 years. Given the pressures on contemporary northern societies, these institutions will be tested most stringently.

Opportunities and Constraints: Natural Resource Extraction

For nearly a century, it has been clear that Canada's North — indeed, the northern two-thirds of the country — holds enormous mineral wealth.[26] Climate, distance and the lack of infrastructure have kept developmental costs relatively high; and, generally, mineral development has not proceeded except where there has been substantial public subsidy in the form of favourable taxation regimes and infrastructure support. Recently, the NWT has been experiencing boom conditions (now slowing with the global recession) fed mainly by diamond mining. There are no mines currently operating in Yukon, though there is a small placer-gold-mining sector. In the NWT, the gold mines at Yellowknife are closed. There is one tungsten mine in the southwest of the territory, as well as two operating diamond mines and three prospective ones, all north of Great Slave Lake. Another diamond mine opened in the same geological region, just over the border in Nunavut, but it is now closed, perhaps temporarily. There are presently no active mines in Nunavut, though exploration for a variety of minerals continues.[27] On the north coast of Nunavik, the Raglan nickel mine is in operation; while in Labrador, iron ore (Wabush and Labrador City) and nickel (Voisey's Bay) mines are in operation.

Uranium prospecting and exploration continues in the NWT and Yukon. There are closed uranium mines at Port Radium, on Great Bear Lake; Rayrock, north of Great Slave Lake; and Uranium City, on the Saskatchewan-NWT border. Potential new mines are located near Baker Lake, in Nunavut, and near Post Hill and Makkovik, in Labrador. Uranium mining is controversial in the North, as elsewhere, and decision-making about these possible new mines will be a significant test of the regulatory apparatus that has been put in place by modern treaty negotiations.

Petroleum exploration and development has, for decades, been an important area of economic activity. For the last several years, the Mackenzie gas pipeline project, which would bring natural gas from the Mackenzie Delta to pipelines in northern Alberta, has been under regulatory review. A panel report is expected in fall 2009. If the Mackenzie Gas Project goes ahead, a new transportation corridor will open in the Mackenzie Valley, and exploration and development work in the whole vast region will be accelerated. There are large oil or natural gas reserves in Lancaster Sound and in the southern Mackenzie Valley. Given the new working relationships developed between the Quebec government and the Cree and Inuit, hydroelectric and other northern development ventures in the near future are a certainty.

There has been substantial conflict over the terms of major project development, and over mining development, regulation and responsibility for site remediation. The Auditor General of Canada and northern interest groups have criticized federal resource revenue practices. Nearly 20 years ago, the Auditor General noted, "Revenues from mineral activities are well below their potential. Rates for mining fees and rentals have not changed for over 60 years" (1990, 105-7). Similar issues were raised by the Canadian Arctic Resources Committee in 1999, which noted that the NWT's "combined royalty and taxation regimes will remain among the lowest in Canada and the world," despite a 1995 commitment by DIAND to raise resource revenue rates (O'Reilly 1998-99, 1).

Warming northern waters, spiking international commodity prices and growing demand for raw materials in the rising Asian economies in the early twenty-first century led many to predict that the North was finally about to become the busy resource development frontier envisioned by successive federal governments throughout the previous century. The current global recession, falling commodity prices and decline in demand have once again dampened expectations. It seems inevitable, though, that in the long run, northern mineral resources will be developed. The terms of this development, and the timing, are unknown. It is clear that when the mineral sector revives, it will have the potential to generate substantial wealth. It will also continue to be subject to boom-and-bust cycles, and there will continue to be environmental costs associated with production and significant costs associated with decommissioning old mines.

The Mixed Economy of the North

If the nonrenewable resource development sector in the North is marked by volatility, there is another aspect of the northern economy that is characterized by resilience and relative stability. This is the mixed economy — an adaptation of traditional productive practices of the original northern societies to evolving modern conditions.[28]

The mixed economy is found in many communities where a substantial proportion of food and other necessities of life is taken from the land. Its dynamic is somewhat similar to that of the family farm — or, for that matter, to that of the traditional family, which pools paid and unpaid labour. In the heuristic model of the northern mixed economy, the basic unit of analysis is not the individual worker (as is the case in much economic theory), but rather the household or extended family. The household may consist of two or three generations of related people who tend to pool their income (particularly income in kind), and who may or may not share a single dwelling. Households exist as part of a network of kin and exchange relationships that order the sharing of, particularly, harvested food and the labour of harvest. Cash income is important in these households, because on-the-land production depends upon certain commodities that only money can buy: snowmobiles, outboard motors for boats, gasoline and the like. In addition, cash is required to buy foodstuffs not available from the land, to pay rent or mortgages, and to pay for utilities and consumer goods. Sources of cash include wages, universal social transfer payments, small-business income, and income from art or craft production and sales. Generally, all household members contribute their labour. While all members of the group are expected to be versatile and able to perform most essential tasks, there is customarily a division of labour based on both gender and age.

All of this describes the basic operating principles of the mixed economy heuristically and at a high level of abstraction. The mixed economy exists — in locally various forms — in all of the polar countries. For example, comparative data from the Survey of Arctic Living Conditions (SLiCA) demonstrate the interaction of wage employment and subsistence activities, both of which are important to livelihood. In Canada, 58 percent of Inuit adults reported having worked (for wages) in the week immediately preceding the survey, while 59 to 69 percent engaged in activities necessary to harvesting. Employment status, however, seemed to have relatively little impact upon whether individuals had been involved in subsistence production: regardless of whether respondents had worked during the previous week or the previous year, they reported a mean number of 2.6 to 2.9 "subsistence activities" in the preceding week.

Table 4

Domestic Economy in Inuit Communities in Alaska, Canada, Greenland and Chukotka (Percent)

	Alaska	Canada	Greenland	Chukotka
a) Adult Inuit Participation in Wage Economy				
Wage employment status				
Worked last week	50	58	67	66
Worked full time last year but not in last week	10	20	6	15
Worked part time last year but not in last week	15	10	7	7
Did not work last year, (probably unemployed)	8	6	6	6
Not in labour force due to health, family responsibilities	3	0	4	3
Respondent is 65 or older	14	6	9	3
Estimated total (N)	10,787	18,100	37,391	19,042
b) Adult Inuit Participation in Subsistence Activities				
Activity				
Fished in last 12 months	77	69	69	88
Prepared or packed for hunting, fishing or camping trip	71	73	44	84
Made and repaired equipment or did household repairs	51	48	73	64
Hunted waterfowl in last 12 months	44	59	40	26
Manufactured native crafts for sale	23	18	7	12
Trapped in last 12 months	11	11	4	15
Estimated total (N)	10,547	22,090	35,240	17,547
c) Participation in Subsistence Activities, by Wage Employment Status (Mean of Five Subsistence Activities[1])				
Wage employment status				
Worked last week	3.8	2.9	3.0	3.1
Worked full time last year but not in last week	3.5	2.9	3.2	3.7
Worked part time last year but not in last week	3.5	2.6	2.7	2.8
Did not work last year (probably unemployed)	2.9	2.7	2.4	3.2
Not in labour force due to health, family responsibilities	2.8	n/a	2.1	1.8
Respondent is 65 or older	2.1	2.5	2.0	2.2
Estimated total (N)	10,786	22,100	37,392	16,255

Source: Poppel et al. (2007, tables 2-4).

[1] Hunting, herding, gathering, processing, and indigenous art activities.

Similar patterns appear in each of the four northern regions (see table 4) (Poppel et al. 2007).

Where the mixed economy flourishes, cash income buys desirable consumer items, but it also, importantly, subsidizes hunting, fishing, gathering and trapping. The gifts of the land are shared within households and among households. Those who share the fruits of the harvest enjoy the highest-quality food available in the North. Other harvested products — such as fur, hides or bark — are made into items that can be sold for cash. Furthermore, while going into the bush is physically arduous, intellectually taxing and sometimes risky, it is not typically understood as work — rather, it is seen as a very valuable activity that enhances the physical, emotional and mental well-being of participants and their communities.[29]

There are some important patterns to bear in mind. First, the mixed economy is surely much more important in the smaller, predominantly Aboriginal communities than it is in the major wage centres. Its vitality in both types of community likely varies substantially. Second, although some non-Aboriginal people have integrated into the mixed economy, it is sustained on the basis of Aboriginal participation, skills and traditions. Its importance extends beyond subsistence to cultural continuity. Third, the essence of the mixed economy is that the individuals and households within it rely for their livelihood not upon a single source, but rather upon several. The mixed economy may include small-business activity; wage employment; gathering, hunting and trapping; domestic care; or community service. The characteristics of this way of living are resilience, adaptability, practicality and social stability. It nurtures both spirit and body.

The mixed economy serves as a buffer in that it provides some protection to its participants from the boom-and-bust cycles of the resource frontier. Where the mixed economy survives, people who lose or leave their jobs have other options: they can shift to essential nonwage activities, such as hunting, fishing, gathering, food preservation or making products based on the gifts of the land.

The mixed economy also plays a role in preserving northern cultural continuity. It provides a means for the continued exercise of traditional knowledge and skills and for the expression of traditional cultural values. It supports language retention. Very importantly, it provides an opportunity for intergenerational transmission of the place-specific knowledge upon which successful on-the-land production and living depends (Council of Yukon First Nations 2006; Cruikshank 2002; Asch 1977; Wenzel 1981, 1991).

The adaptive, practical aspects of the mixed economy mean that entrenching Aboriginal values in northern political institutions and practices will not be an empty exercise. The continued need for knowledge and skills in the mixed economy means that Aboriginal ideas about human values, the cosmos and humankind's place in it are less likely to be preserved in freeze-dried form — on recordings and in books. Instead, the mixed economy, in its persistence, can support a less abrupt evolution of social ideas, knitting the knowledge of the past into the new circumstances of each generation, and in the process sustaining a sense of meaning and vitality. The potential benefit here is great, and it should be reason enough to sustain and encourage the mixed economy.

These factors may help to explain some of the reluctance with which northern Aboriginal individuals have left traditional productive activity for full-time wage employment. Their importance is also recognized in such collective measures as modern treaty provisions designed to support on-the-land production and protect its material base. The social values embedded in the older ways of living are highly valued by Aboriginal people, who now manage their collective affairs through modern bureaucracies, whether these are public governments, Aboriginal organizations, First Nations governments or comanagement institutions. Such measures as the NWT traditional knowledge policy of the 1990s, and the current Inuit Qaujimajatuqangit (roughly translated as "the Inuit way of doing things") policy of the Government of Nunavut indicate a degree of support for creating a kind of mixed government to balance the mixed economy. Furthermore, support for affirming and elaborating the older values and Aboriginal languages in the contemporary context appears to be strong among both Aboriginal and non-Aboriginal northerners (Timpson forthcoming).

The Fiscal and Structural Imperatives of Northern Development

Both the natural resources sector of the economy and the mixed economy require a favourable policy framework and a substantial subsidy, though the mixed economy will receive less sustained policy attention and, in all probability, a smaller subsidy. There have, though, been some important initiatives and suggestions for improving the economic environment for the mixed economy. The 1975 JBNQA inaugurated a program that provides cash support to active hunters (Papillon 2008). Long-standing programs of the NWT and Nunavut governments subsidize on-the-land activity with the aim of making up the cash deficits that inevitably result from the production of goods in kind. There have been innovative proposals to use social welfare expenditures to support hunting (as part of a broader program to adapt labour force programs of general application to northern conditions) (Irwin 1989). A detailed proposal for an integrated strategy to support the mixed economy in the NWT was prepared for a special legislative committee (Usher and Weihs 1989). But the recommendation for a mixed-economy strategy that was integral to overall economic development planning was never implemented. Indeed, support for the mixed economy has never been a central plank of state economic development policy in any of the northern regions. There are likely a number of reasons for this, both structural and practical.

First, it is important to remember the pattern of state-led development in all regions of the North. As I argued earlier, northern development policy followed the general pattern of Canadian economic development policy. It has depended upon federal or provincial advocacy and funding of private nonrenewable resource development in the expectation that this would eventually generate wealth for the larger Canadian economy and create jobs and business opportunities for northern residents. Northern governments have generally followed this path — maybe this is a matter of path dependency, but it is certainly motivated by practical concerns as well. Despite its many virtues, the mixed economy does not generate a taxable cash surplus, and therefore it cannot sustain northern public expenditures, be they social or economic. Priority has been given to industrial development projects that seem likely to generate employment opportunity and taxable income.

Public expenditures, through direct transfers and favourable taxation regimes, have played an important role in the northern economy from the beginning. Public subsidy was essential to the establishment of the northern mining sector, and it has also directly created the public sector jobs that have, for the last 20 years, been the most stable (and, in several regions, the largest) source of employment for northerners (see table 2).

Today, the three territorial governments have a combined annual expenditure budget of over $3 billion, making the distribution of government expenditures and jobs an extremely important part of each regional economy. Further stimulus has been provided by capital transfer provisions of the modern treaties themselves, which have brought several billion dollars into the northern economies since 1984.

A striking feature of all economic activities in northern Canada, with the partial exception of hydroelectric power generation, is the limited contribution that these activities make to public revenue. The mixed economy generates virtually no taxable cash income; much nonrenewable resource development has been heavily subsidized, in part through favourable royalty regimes and tax expenditures — and, in any case, net revenues accrue in part or in whole to the federal government. Public revenue from personal and small-business taxation is necessarily low, due to the small number of employed people and the fact that some of the employed reside outside the northern regions where their income is generated. In short, government in the North is expensive, and the current arrangements for taxation of economic activity do not create the possibility of sufficient own-source revenues. This situation is reflected in the budgets of the three northern territories, all of which rely substantially on federal transfers (see table 5).

The northern territories' small and dispersed populations, the high costs these territories incur and their lack of direct access to resource revenues prohibit territorial participation in the Equalization Program that applies to all provinces; instead, the mechanism of Territorial Formula Financing (TFF) was developed to provide federal transfers to the territories and enable them to offer public services that are reasonably comparable to those available in the rest of the country. While these transfer arrangements have changed from time to time (most recently in 2007) since they were introduced in the 1980s, the amounts each territory receives annually are still determined by a formula based on the difference between expenditure needs (a gross expenditure base that takes into account population growth and past expenditures) and revenue means (a portion of territorial own-source revenues). As James Feehan reports in this volume, the latest TFF reforms have not resolved long-standing issues related to the disincentive effects of own-source revenue clawbacks built into the formula and the future treatment of resource revenues for Nunavut and the NWT, and even for Yukon, where such revenues have already been devolved (see also Feehan 2006).[30]

In Quebec and Labrador, public expenditure needs are similar to those in the territories. People live in widely dispersed communities in a high-cost

region where there are very few roads. The provision of public services is
expensive. Both federal and provincial governments have responsibilities to the
Aboriginal peoples who constitute the majority of the population of the northern provinces. In the 30 years since the negotiation of the first modern treaty,
in northern Quebec, much energy has been expended in sorting out responsibilities among the two orders of government. Recent developments — for
example, the Paix des Braves socio-economic agreement between the provincial
government and northern indigenous people, and the agreements in the
Labrador Inuit modern treaty concerning resource revenue sharing and self-
government — have created a new landscape. Direct provincial expenditures
will remain important, as will provincial development strategies, but the new
agreements ensure that Aboriginal people in each province have much more
leverage and control than ever before.

In all parts of the North, then, public governments, Aboriginal governments and beneficiary organizations face similar policy choices. Neither governments nor organizations can be sustained, or sustain their services to members,
without substantial continuing cash revenues. All have an interest in balancing

Table 5
Territorial Government Expenditures and Transfer Revenues, 2007-08

	Total expenditures ($ millions)	Federal cash transfers[1] (Territorial Formula Financing) ($ millions)	Federal cash transfers (Territorial Formula Financing) (% of expenditures)
Yukon	908	577	64
		(544)	(60)
NWT	1,220	880	72
		(843)	(69)
Nunavut	1,117	929	83
		(893)	(80)
TOTAL	3,245	2,585	80
		(2,280)	(70)

Source: Finance Canada (2008, 2009).
[1] Federal transfers also include those for health and social services.

the need for revenue generation with the need to ensure that modern versions of the traditional, harvest-based way of life flourish. The most ready source of suffi-cient cash revenue is the nonrenewable natural resources sector, with all its potential for boom-and-bust cycles and environmental and social disruption. These tensions have been played out in successive public debates, often over major nonrenewable resource development projects, since the mid-1970s.[31]

With the resolution of land ownership issues in treaty settlements (and con-sequent alleviation of the deep concern that resource development would erase Aboriginal title), there are some signs that northern Aboriginal public opinion about mineral development is changing. Strong opposition to uranium mining may be attenuating, with, for example, Nunavut Tunngavik's 2006 reversal of its policy refusing all uranium development.[32] There are now beneficiaries on each side of the uranium-mining issue. The Baffinlands iron ore mine on northern Baffin Island is a project that will disrupt traditional productive activity in the hamlet of Igloolik (and so disadvantage the community), but it appears likely that some town residents will support the project anyway out of the need for jobs, especially for young people. The fate of the Mackenzie gas pipeline proposal is not yet known, but the regulatory hearings into the project revealed that there is less unanimous community opposition to such a project than there was during similar hearings in the 1970s — and the Aboriginal organizations through whose territo-ries the pipeline would run are part of the consortium of pipeline proponents.

These shifts in public opinion indicate that the debate over the future of the northern economy and society will occur not between Aboriginal people and the forces of development originating outside, as was the case 30 years ago, but among Aboriginal and non-Aboriginal northerners, who must determine the wisest response to the challenges and opportunities presented by external interest in northern resources. They will require a reliable framework for economic and social development that recognizes all aspects of the northern economy and the very subtle patterns of interdependency that must be balanced in order for the unique requirements of northern viability to be maintained. This will likely necessitate some institutional development (to ensure that deliberations based upon solid and accessible research are conducted), some experimentation with various policy instruments and a determined shift to a more balanced and far-sighted framework for policy development — one that recognizes the full complexity of northern economies.[33]

Social Dimensions of Healthy Northern Societies

T HESE CONSIDERATIONS WILL LOOM LARGE FOR NORTHERN PEOPLE AND THEIR communities as they adapt to large external forces like climate change and the increasing global demand for energy and other resources. The need for healthy, vibrant communities and an educated population has never been greater, yet the task ahead is considerable.

The linked issues of balanced economic development and community well-being will be high on the agenda of all northern governments and beneficiary organizations for the foreseeable future — and therefore they will command federal and provincial attention as well. While employment choices are necessary to the future well-being of northern youth, so are an adequate education system, a healthy environment that will consistently support on-the-land learning and activity, and a public infrastructure suited to northern needs in a changing climate. The new northern institutions of government face formidable challenges quite unlike those faced by previous generations.

Most northern communities are desirable places to live, with their clean air and water, near-pristine landscapes, and a culture of mutual support and community. Both Aboriginal and non-Aboriginal northerners enjoy these assets to a degree that is quite rare in most parts of Canada. Although it is difficult to generalize across the North, a helpful way of thinking about community health has been developed by the Council of Yukon First Nations (2006). Its holistic framework evaluates spiritual, mental, emotional and physical determinants of well-being based on empirical indicators. It identifies a number of benefits enjoyed by Yukon First Nations communities — such as strong family ties, a sense of cultural continuity and generally good health — as well as some problems they face. Problems include psychological difficulties related to past traumas (such as residential school experiences), lower-than-desirable levels of educational attainment and employment, and the recent arrival of crystal meth. The general analysis that emerges from this study depicts basically strong, vital and sustaining community cultures under pressure from shortfalls in service, the present consequences of past traumas and problems related to substance abuse.

There are other signs that well-being in some northern communities is being eroded. For example, a high proportion of the Inuit whose views were captured in the Survey of Living Conditions in the Arctic (SLiCA) expressed concerns about social problems such as unemployment, alcohol and drug abuse, suicide, family violence and sexual abuse (Poppel et. al 2007). As table 6 indicates, these concerns are shared by Inuit in the entire circumpolar basin. A study based upon the last two Aboriginal Peoples Surveys shows some deterioration in perceived healthiness among Inuit adults and persistence in the incidence of child hunger due to parents' inability to provide food (Tait and O'Donnell 2008).[34]

SLiCA researchers found that across all countries, engagement in either full-time employment or subsistence activities was associated with more positive reported levels of life satisfaction (Poppel et al. 2007), a finding similar to that of some other studies (see, for example, Council of Yukon First Nations 2006). The availability of meaningful work or the possibility of engaging in other productive activities appears to be a precondition for healthy northern community life. Another would seem to be having the means to deal with the intergenerationally transmitted social and psychological effects of past traumas related to, for example, relocation, social dislocation or residential schools (Palacios and Portillo 2009; Richmond and Ross 2009). Although there is a need for more research and careful development of place-specific explanations, it seems likely that the very high suicide rate in northern Aboriginal communities is both symptom and cause of social and personal distress for several generations of Aboriginal northerners. In Canada as a whole, the age-standardized mortality rate of suicide is 11.3 per 100,000 people. In Yukon and the NWT, the rate is just under double this (18.5 and 20.8, respectively), while in Nunavut, it is a catastrophically high 80.2 per 100,000 people. Northern suicide statistics indicate a social emergency. While suicide has been addressed by policies in each territory, there has been to date little or no effect on the distressing rate of death (Young and Bjerregaard 2008).[35]

A minority of northern individuals report that they abuse alcohol, but alcohol abuse has led to the birth of children affected to various degrees by fetal alcohol syndrome. These children are handicapped for life by an inability to focus, to reflect and to empathize. Relatively recently, crack cocaine and crystal meth have reached even the most isolated northern communities (Council of Yukon First Nations 2006; NWT Health and Social Services 2006). Most users of these drugs are young, and they are disproportionately male.

Northerners are much more likely than other Canadians to smoke tobacco: while 22.9 percent of Canadians are smokers, 27.5 percent of Yukoners, 36.6 percent

Table 6
Social Problems and the Percent of Inuit Adults Who Perceive Them as
Such, Alaska, Canada, Greenland and Chukotka

Social problem	Alaska	Canada	Greenland	Chukotka
Unemployment	83	87	84	100
Alcohol abuse	84	78	79	100
Suicide	60	70	67	98
Drug abuse	71	79	68	72
Family violence	50	69	63	91
Sexual abuse	34	60	58	89
Estimated total (N)	10,393	16,870	37,026	20,456

Source: Poppel et al. (2007, table 9).

of NWT residents and 64.7 percent of Nunavut residents smoke. Although the
North's cancer rates are not yet higher than those of the rest of Canada — due in part,
perhaps, to the North's more youthful population — it seems likely that cancer rates
will climb. On the positive side, the percentage of northerners who are overweight or
obese is the Canadian average (48 percent), or just slightly higher (though the
Canadian average is hardly the gold standard for good health). It is encouraging that
heart disease and diabetes are still less common in all parts of the North than they are
in the rest of Canada. This effect is particularly marked in Nunavut, where the rate of
diabetes is about a third that of the rest of Canada. Again, the relative youthfulness of
the population is probably important to this outcome, but perhaps some protection
from these diseases may derive from the healthy country-food diet that is still found
in many northern Aboriginal communities (see table 7) (Tait and O'Donnell 2008;
Council of Yukon First Nations 2006).

There are increasingly worrying aspects to the general health statistics in
northern Canada. Life expectancy in Nunavut, for example, is 11 years below the
Canadian average. Infant mortality is higher in all three territories than it is in
Canada as a whole, but in Nunavut it is particularly alarming — three times the
Canadian rate. Tuberculosis remains a largely invisible northern scourge. And the
incidence of lifestyle diseases such as diabetes and heart disease, though now rel-
atively low, is expected to rise as a result of smoking and higher rates of obesity
(Deering et al. 2009; Bjerregaard and Young 1998).

Table 7
Selected Health and Well-Being Indicators, Nunavut, NWT, Yukon, Canada

	Yukon	NWT	Nunavut	Canada
General				
Life expectancy at birth (years)				
Male	75.0	73.7	66.6	77.1
Female	80.5	78.1	70.0	82.1
Infant mortality rate				
(per 100,000 live births)	6.6	7.6	15.0	5.3
ASMR,[1] all causes (per 100,000)	768.6	816.3	1,183.3	605.2
Infectious diseases				
Incidence of tuberculosis				
(per 100,000)	5.2	21.1	108.0	5.2
Chronic diseases				
Diabetes (age-standardized				
prevalence, %)	3.8	4.0	1.3	4.8
ASMR ischemic heart disease				
(per 100,000)	117.3	95.9	79.7	111.2
ASMR stroke (per 100,000)	61.9	76.2	111.7	48.7
Age-standardized incidence				
of all primary cancers				
(per 100,000)				
Male	324.1	339.4	359.6	456.2
Female	297.1	323.4	500.3	347.9
Injuries				
ASMR unintentional injury				
(per 100,000)	59.3	53.6	62.4	25.6
ASMR suicide (per 100,000)	18.5	20.8	80.2	11.3
Health determinants				
Age-standardized prevalence				
of overweight and obesity (%)	50.5	53.7	48.6	48.2
Prevalence of current smoking (%)	27.5	36.6	64.7	22.9

Source: Young and Bjerregaard (2008, 47).
[1] ASMR = age-standardized mortality rate.

As table 8 indicates, Aboriginal people in the North continue to face more crowded housing conditions than do non-Aboriginal people, to have less access to paid employment and to leave school earlier. Although no doubt some unemployment is voluntary (some choose to earn at least part of their living by hunting), it is clear that some is not. There is a gap between the general level of skills in the Aboriginal population and the skills required for the new jobs in the changing territorial economy. While there are federal programs and territorial and local initiatives focused on the question of community health and well-being, it seems clear from the available data that efforts to date have been insufficient. As Jack Hicks argues in his chapter in this volume, and as others have pointed out as well, a concerted policy response is needed — one that puts community and family well-being at the centre of the policy problem definition.

Table 8
Some Indicators of Aboriginal and Non-Aboriginal Economic Well-Being in Northern Canada, 2006 (Percent)

	Aboriginal population	Non-Aboriginal population
Northwest Territories		
More than one person per room	15.9	4.1
Income – $29,999 and less[1]	68.5	36.0
Certificate, diploma or degree	45.3	85.9
Unemployed	20.1	4.0
Yukon		
More than one person per room	5.8	1.8
Income – $29,999 and less[1]	71.0	49.3
Certificate, diploma or degree	58.7	82.7
Unemployed	21.9	6.2
Nunavut		
More than one person per room	38.4	5.3
Income $29,999 and less[1]	76.9	25.3
Certificate, diploma or degree	31.3	88.8
Unemployed	20.1	3.5

Source: Statistics Canada, 2006 Census (http://www.statcan.gc.ca).
[1] 2001 Census

Without idealizing the past, we must recognize that both the original economies of northern Aboriginal peoples and the mixed economy to which they adapted over the years provided a substantial safety net — and not merely in terms of material survival. The net of social obligations and social expectations rooted in generalized reciprocity and cooperation contributed to this; it reduced anxiety and created meaning and a sense of worth. So did the intergenerational transmission of knowledge and values rooted in the landscape and what people did there.[36] A balanced approach to northern development must both build upon and nurture the mixed economy.

Concluding Thoughts

O VER 30 YEARS AGO, EDGAR DOSMAN PUBLISHED A STUDY OF CANADIAN NORTHERN development entitled *The National Interest: The Politics of Northern Development 1968-75*. In it, he documented the "striking failure of the [federal] government in relations with business" to protect Canada's national interest in the North. He concluded that

> the responsible development of the North and Arctic basin offers a unique opportunity for Canada in the international community. Yet there has been neither the insight nor the will to face a responsibility that geography and history have allocated to this country. A great deal of concern has been centred on the jurisdictional issue; almost no intelligent action has been taken to link that issue with the pattern of resource development to be encouraged in the North...[P]ipelines are only part of a broader issue: The objective of balanced growth North of 60 in which the people and environment of the Arctic are not subordinated to profit maximization. (1975, 222-3)

As this chapter shows, much has occurred since 1975, when Dosman issued this challenge — most particularly, the land issue in the North has been settled almost entirely; the regulatory regime has been revised; and a variety of governing institutions, both public and ethnically specific, have been developed and staffed. The most fateful decisions will increasingly be taken by all northern residents working through the new institutions, as they negotiate and interact with still-powerful federal officials and politicians. All face the important challenge of devising economic and social strategies capable of securing the well-being of northerners living in the small and large communities of the North. Despite the ancient tenure of Aboriginal peoples in this region, current northern communities and societies are very new. The new northern societies represent the most daring social experiment our country has undertaken, an experiment rich in opportunity and fraught with risk. In this chapter, I have argued, as Dosman did, that we must take a balanced approach to northern economic development: we must advance the well-being of northern communities while promoting resource development to fund the public sector and provide jobs.

The extent to which either the mixed economy or truly hybrid (or mixed) governments are compatible with the resource-based development of the northern economies or the elaboration of modern, democratically governed public institutions is unknown. It is unclear also whether such measures can address what might become mutually reinforcing spirals of substance abuse, violence and loss of meaning. It does seem clear, though, that for material reasons of economic stabilization and for psychological reasons of cultural continuity, supporting continued efforts toward economic and political hybridization is a valuable goal. Somehow, this must be balanced with equally compelling pressures for revenue generation and job creation related to resource development, and for the modern institutions necessary to interact with Canadian and global institutions.

Balanced northern development will not be an automatic or even planned side effect of major project decisions; rather, it will require a new way of thinking about northern economic and social development, one that is keyed to the unique strengths and dynamics of the northern economy in all its aspects. This is in the true national interest, for if Canada does not develop healthy northern societies, then it will have failed in its great northern venture.

In facing this task, Canada is not alone. All of the circumpolar nations have strong, growing and relatively youthful Aboriginal populations, a resource frontier created in response to the needs of the greater economy, and an interest in building vital, healthy northern societies in which Aboriginal and non-Aboriginal people can live satisfying lives. But it is increasingly clear that the circumpolar nations share more than this. As others in this volume argue, they also share the imperative to manage their increasingly complex common interests in the circumpolar basin with foresight and prudence.

Notes

I am grateful to Mel Cappe, Tom Courchene, Jack Hicks, Stephanie Irlbacher-Fox, Mike Prince, Thierry Rodon, Mark Salvo, Leslie Seidle, Deborah Simmons, Ron Sparks, France St-Hilaire, Mary Ellen Thomas, Harley Trudeau and Graham White, whose advice on various versions made this chapter much better. I thank also Senada Delic, Patrick Lemieux, Laura O'Laughlin, Jerry Sabin and Brett Smith, excellent research assistants all, and, as ever, I thank George Kinloch for rich contributions in kind and in conversation.

1   Aboriginal people in many parts of the North worked as whalers and guides; they also performed work related to transport provision and resupply.

2   There were some instances of murder and some of kidnapping (Harper 1986; McGee 2004).

3   The major historical exception to this generalization is the Klondike gold rush of the 1890s. There were minor "rushes" in other areas, but none was as large, and none lasted more than a few years. On this period in general, see Zaslow (1959) and Funston (2007).

4   Conventionally, three periods of Crown treaty making are identified in Canadian history: the "peace and friendship" pre-Confederation treaties negotiated by European authorities with the Aboriginal peoples they encountered in the course of exploration; the so-called numbered treaties (1 through 11) negotiated by the Dominion government before 1921; and, finally, the modern treaties, negotiation of which commenced in the mid-1970s after a hiatus of over 50 years. See Indian and Northern Affairs Canada (1996b) for a comprehensive overview. Although reserves were created in all provinces — even in British Columbia, where no Dominion government treaties were negotiated — the only reserves in the territories are in the extreme south, in the Northwest Territories.

5   The rate structure on the transcontinental railway encouraged industrial development in central Canada and agricultural development in the West.

6   The Red River Rebellion and the establishment of the provisional government in what is now southern Manitoba led to the province's entry into Confederation; the North-West Rebellion of 1885 was fuelled by Métis resistance to the extinguishment of the buffalo and the imposition of Dominion control over land (see Dickason and McNab [2002, 247-52, 286-96]).

7   See Diubaldo (1985) and Nungak (2003). The Supreme Court reference was related to a dispute between the governments of Quebec and Canada over which of them was responsible for reimbursing the Hudson's Bay Company for the relief it had paid to Inuit in Nunavik. The Supreme Court concluded that the responsibility lay with the federal government.

8   For details, see Armstrong, Rogers, and Rowley (1978, chap. 3).

9   During this period, though, there were a number of cases of involuntary relocation due to the requirements of defence personnel or other state personnel (see INAC [1996a, 411-66]).

10 For example, see Robertson (1960); Gordon Robertson was then deputy minister in the Department of Indian Affairs and Northern Development.

11 Rea (1968) and Damas (2002) both provide very detailed accounts of the expansion of state presence into the territorial North in the 1950s and early 1960s. For a comparative discussion, see Abele (2000).

12 See Royal Commission on Aboriginal Peoples (1994) and INAC (1996a, 411-544).

13 It is difficult to generalize about experiences over such a wide area as the Canadian North; regional differences in how all of these changes were felt are pronounced (see Damas [2002]). For a view of the changes from the northern Mackenzie Valley, see Snowshoe (1977).

14 See, for example, Morissonneau (1978) and Quiring (2004).

15   The North is immense. During the period discussed here, the peoples' responses varied, as did the intensity of the different pressures. These generalizations do not hold true for every place. For various perspectives on the changes, see Quassa (2008); Ittinuar (2008); Brody (1975); Watkins (1977); Cruikshank (1990).

16   A registered Indian is now, as then, an individual whose name appears on a register maintained by federal authorities. Registration entitles the individual to services provided through federal agencies. Most registered Indians are descendants of treaty signatories.

17   Opposition to the Mackenzie Valley pipeline led to the appointment of Thomas Berger to head an inquiry into its construction. The Berger Inquiry hearings provided a well-publicized forum for public discussion of concerns over the direction and pace of northern economic and political development.

18   See for example, Amagoalik (2007) and MacGregor (1989).

19   These included the Committee for Original People's Entitlement (COPE); the Council for Yukon Indians and the Yukon Native Brotherhood (later combined to form the Council of Yukon First Nations); the Indian Brotherhood of the Northwest Territories (later the Dene Nation); the Métis Association of the Northwest Territories; Inuit Tapirisat of 'Canada; the Innu Nation; and the Grand Council of the Crees, among others.

20   They also managed to get negotiations reopened in parts of Canada where such negotiations had not been completed with legitimacy, as was the case with Treaty 11 (see Fumoleau 1973).

21   The first case of Aboriginal activism leading directly to the creation of a new subnational jurisdiction occurred in the nineteenth century, with the creation of the original boundaries of the Province of Manitoba.

22   The only limit on this is that the federal government retains technical ownership of Crown lands in Yukon.

23   The Yukon self-government agreements are excepted from constitutional recognition.

24   The main organizations for the four Aboriginal peoples of the NWT who have signed modern treaties are the Inuvialuit Regional Corporation, the Gwich'in Tribal Council, the Sahtu Secretariat Incorporated and Sahtu Dene Council, and the Tlicho government. The Dehcho First Nations and the Akaitcho Treaty 8 Tribal Corporation are not currently negotiating treaties; the former is seeking an alternative arrangement to protect Dehcho lands, and the latter is seeking enforcement of existing treaty rights. Métis are included in the Sahtu treaty, and the Northwest Territory Métis Nation (whose members are descendants of pre-1921 settlers in the region south of Great Slave Lake) is in negotiations with the federal and territorial governments concerning a negotiating process. See Irlbacher-Fox and Mills, Braden, and McArthur in this volume.

25   They are Carcross/Tagish First Nation, Champagne and Aishihik First Nation, Ehdiitat Gwich'in Council, First Nation of Na-Cho Nyak Dun, Gwichya Gwich'in Council, Kluane First Nation, Little Salmon Na-Cho Carmacks First Nation, Nihtat Gwich'in Council, Selkirk First Nation, Ta'an Kwach'an Council, Teslin Tlingit Council, Trondëk Hwëch'in First Nation, Teetl'it Gwich'in Council and White River First Nation.

26   All of the information about mines in this section is drawn from Natural Resources Canada (2008). A thorough and enthusiastic review of prospects in Nunavut appears in Cope (2000).

27   In the 1970s, two lead-zinc mines were opened in Nunavut (Nanisivik, near Rankin Inlet, and Polaris, on Little Cornwallis Island). Both closed in 2002. After a period of spiking exploration activity, the number of mining exploration permits and the level of mining expenditures in Nunavut dropped sharply in 2008.

28   Anthropologists use a variety of terms to describe the mixed economy, including the

"domestic economy" and the "mixed-subsistence market economy" (see Burch and Ellanna [1994]). Canadian scholars who have documented and analyzed the dynamics of the mixed economy include Asch (1977); Quigley and McBride (1987); Usher and Weihs (1989); Nahanni (1992); Usher, Duhaime, and Searles (2003); Jarvenpa (2004); and Wenzel (1981, 1991).

29 One indication of the degree to which the mixed economy is valued is the persistence with which people retain their attachment to harvesting and to the communities where it is still heavily practised (see tables 5 and 6).

30 For a discussion of current conditions in each territory and analysis of what could be achieved with new thinking on resource development revenues, see Irlbacher-Fox and Mills (2007) and Hodge, Stauch, and Taggart (2007).

31 While regulatory review of major projects is essential, these review processes are not ideal venues for development policy deliberation. First, the focus is not on overall, balanced and longer-term economic health, but on the specific benefits and risks associated with a particular project. Second, hearings typically generate courtroom-like debates between "proponents" and "intervenors," who may be either for or against the project. Even governments tend to be drawn into the polarized discussion. Such discussion may be essential when a clash of interests must be debated, but it does not encourage searching and imaginative economic and social policy development. Third, despite requirements that cumulative effects be taken into account, given the timelines and the guidelines provided for regulatory review, it is virtually impossible to consider overall economic development goals as part of project-based recommendations. And, finally, in this setting, it is not surprising that the particular dynamics, strengths and requirements of the northern mixed economy tend to be marginalized, however much the proponents and others

are enjoined to take into account traditional knowledge.

32 In 2008, the Nunatsiavut government placed a three-year moratorium on all uranium development.

33 For example, it would be helpful if infrastructure projects were planned and assessed on the basis of overall economic need rather than approached as adjuncts to major natural resource projects, and if community-based monitoring systems of the sort tested in the West Kitikmeot/Slave Study in the NWT were developed, refined and provided with stable funding (see Fonda and Anderson [2009]).

34 Tait and O'Donnell note that the proportion of Inuit adults (living in the NWT, Nunavut, Nunavik and Nunatsiavut) who report good health fell from 56 percent to 50 percent between 2001 and 2006, while nearly one-third of parents reported that their children had experienced hunger (2008).

35 See Hicks's chapter in this volume. Each northern territory and region has developed suicide prevention programs. The Government of Nunavut and Nunavut Tunngavik Incorporated have announced a new suicide alertness and intervention training program: Uqaqatigiiluk!

36 Richmond and Ross argue that all of the determinants of health in northern Aboriginal communities (balance, life control, education, material resources, social resources and environment-culture connection) are diminished by "environmental dispossession" — severed ties to the physical environment (2009; see also the references the authors cite in this article).

References

Abele, Frances. 2000. "Small Nations and Democracy's Prospects: Indigenous Peoples in Canada, Australia, New Zealand, Norway and Greenland." *Inroads* 10:137-49. Accessed March 28, 2009. http://www.inroadsjournal.ca/archives/inroads_10/Inroads_10_Abele.pdf

Abele, Frances, and E.J. Dosman. 1981. "Interdepartmental Coordination and Northern Development." *Canadian Public Administration* 24 (3): 428-51.

Abele, Frances, and Thierry Rodon. 2007. "Inuit Diplomacy in the Global Era: The Strengths of Multilateral Internationalism." *Canadian Foreign Policy* 13 (3).

Advisory Commission on the Development of Government in the Northwest Territories. 1966. *Summary Report of the Advisory Commission on the Development of Government in the Northwest Territories.* Ottawa: Queen's Printer.

Amagoalik, John. 2007. *Changing the Face of Canada: The Life Story of John Amagoalik.* Edited by Louis McComber. Life Stories of Northern Leaders. Iqaluit: Nunavut Arctic College.

Armstrong, Terence, George Rogers, and Graham Rowley. 1978. *The Circumpolar North: A Political and Economic Geography of the Arctic and Sub-Arctic.* London: Methuen.

Asch, Michael. 1977. "The Dene Economy." In *Dene Nation: The Colony Within,* edited by Mel Watkins. Toronto: University of Toronto Press.

Auditor General of Canada. 1990. "Department of Indian Affairs and Northern Development: Northern Affairs Program." Chap. 19 of *1990 Report of the Auditor General of Canada.* Ottawa: Office of the Auditor General of Canada. Accessed March 29, 2009. http://209.71.218.213/internet/English/parl_oag_199011_19_e_8014.html

Bean, Wilf. 1977. "Colonialism in the Communities." In *Dene Nation: The Colony Within,* edited by Mel Watkins. Toronto: University of Toronto Press.

Bennett, John, and Susan Rowley, eds. 2004. *Uqalurait: An Oral History of Nunavut.* McGill-Queen's Native and Northern Series 36. Montreal and Kingston: McGill-Queen's University Press.

Bjerregaard, Peter, and T. Kue Young. 1998. *The Circumpolar Inuit: Health of a Population in Transition.* Copenhagen: Munnksgaard.

Brody, Hugh. 1975. *The People's Land: Eskimos and Whites in the Eastern Arctic.* Harmondsworth: Penguin.

Burch, Ernest S., and Linda J. Ellanna, eds. 1994. *Key Issues in Hunter-Gatherer Research.* Oxford, UK, and Providence, RI: Berg Publishers.

Coates, Kenneth. 1985. *Canada's Colonies: A History of the Yukon and Northwest Territories.* Toronto: James Lorimer.

———. 1991. *Best Left as Indians: Native-White Relations in the Yukon Territories, 1840-1973.* Montreal: McGill-Queen's University Press.

Coates, Kenneth, and W.R. Morrison. 1992. *The Alaska Highway in World War II: The U.S. Army of Occupation in Canada's Northwest.* Norman: University of Oklahoma Press.

Cope, Louis W. 2000. "Nunavut: A New Frontier." *Engineering and Mining Journal* 201 (2).

Council of Yukon First Nations. 2006. *Reclaiming the Well-Being of Our People: Yukon Regional Longitudinal Health Report.* Whitehorse: Council of Yukon First Nations.

Council for Yukon Indians. 1973. *Together Today for Our Children Tomorrow: A Statement of Grievances and an Approach to Settlement by the Yukon Indian People,* January. Whitehorse: Council for Yukon Indians; Brampton, ON: Charters Publishing. Accessed March 28, 2009. http://www.eco. gov.yk.ca/pdf/together_today_for_our_children_tomorrow.pdf

Cruikshank, Julie. 2002. *Do Glaciers Listen? Local Knowledge, Colonial Encounters and Social Imagination.* Vancouver: UBC Press.

Cruikshank, Julie, in collaboration with Angela Sidney, Kitty Smith, and Annie Ned. 1990. *Life Lived Like A Story: Life Stories of Three Yukon Native Elders.* Lincoln: University of Nebraska Press, and Vancouver: University of British Columbia Press.

Dacks, Gurston. 2004. "Implementing First Nations Self-Government in Yukon: Lessons for Canada." *Canadian Journal of Political Science* 37 (3): 671-89.

Damas, David. 2002. *Arctic Migrants, Arctic Villagers: The Transformation of Inuit Settlement in the Central Arctic.* Montreal and Kingston: McGill-Queen's University Press.

Deering, Kathleen H., Lisa M. Lix, Sharon Bruce, and T. Kue Young. 2009. "Chronic Diseases and Risk Factors — Canada's Northern Populations: Longitudinal and Geographic Comparisons." *Canadian Journal of Public Health* 100 (1): 14-17.

Desbiens, Caroline. 2007. "'Water All Around, You Cannot Even Drink': The Scaling of Water in James Bay/Eeyou Istchee." *Area* 39 (3): 259-67.

Dick, Lyle. 2001. *Muskox Land: Ellesmere Island in the Age of Contact*. Calgary: University of Calgary Press.

Dickason, Olive, and David T. McNab. 2002. *Canada's First Nations: A History of the Founding Peoples from Earliest Times*. 4th ed. Toronto: Oxford University Press.

Diubaldo, Richard. 1985. *The Government of Canada and the Inuit, 1900-1967*. Ottawa: Indian and Northern Affairs Canada.

Dorion, Henri. 1971. *Rapport de la commission d'étude sur l'intégration de territoire de Québec*. Quebec: Commission d'étude sur l'intégrité du territoire du Québec.

Dosman, Edgar J. 1975. *The National Interest: The Politics of Northern Development 1968-75*. Toronto: McClelland and Stewart.

Feehan, James. 2006. "Territorial Formula Financing." In *A Fine Canadian Compromise: Perspectives on the Report of the Expert Panel on Equalization and Territorial Funding Financing*, edited by Paul Boothe and François Vaillancourt. Edmonton: Institute for Public Economics, University of Alberta; Montreal: CIRANO, University of Montreal. Accessed March 28, 2009. http://www.uofaweb.ualberta.ca/ipe//pdfs/A-Fine-Canadian-Compromise-Perspectives-on-the-Report-of-the-Expert-Panel-on-Equalization-and-Territorial-Funding-Financing.pdf

Feit, Harvey. 1979. "Political Articulations of Hunters to the State: Means of Resisting Threats to Subsistence Production in the James Bay and Northern Quebec Agreements." *Études/Inuit/Studies* 3 (2): 37-52.

Finance Canada. 2008. *Fiscal Reference Tables*. Accessed April 6, 2009. http://www.fin.gc.ca/toc/2008/frt08_-eng.asp
———. 2009. *Federal Support to Provinces and Territories*. Accessed April 6, 2009. http://www.fin.gc.ca/fedprov/mtp-eng.asp.

Fonda, Marc, and Erik Anderson. 2009. "Diamonds in Canada's North: A Lesson in Measuring Socio-economic Impacts on Well-Being." In *Journeys of a Generation: Broadening the Aboriginal Well-Being Research Agenda*, edited by Dan Beavon and Daniel Jetté. Special issue of *Canadian Issues/Thèmes Canadiens*.

Forest, Pierre-Gerlier, and Thierry Rodon. 1995. "Les activités internationales des autochtones du Canada." *Études internationales* 26 (1): 35-58.

Fossett, Renée. 2001. *In Order to Live Untroubled: Inuit of the Central Arctic 1550-1940*. Winnipeg: University of Manitoba Press.

Fumoleau, Rene. 1973. *As Long as This Land Shall Last: A History of Treaty 8 and Treaty 11, 1870-1939*. Toronto: McClelland and Stewart.

Funston, Bernard W. 2007. "Canada's North and Tomorrow's Federalism." In *Constructing Tomorrow's Federalism: New Routes to Effective Governance*, edited by Ian Peach. Winnipeg: University of Manitoba Press.

Gourdeau, Eric. 2003. "Genesis of the James Bay and Northern Quebec Agreement." In *Regard sur la Convention de la Baie-James et du Nord québécois/Reflections on the James Bay and Northern Quebec Agreement*, edited by Alain-G Gagnon and Guy Rocher. Montreal: Quebéc Amérique.

Government of Yukon. 2008. "Operations and Maintenance Estimates, 2007-2008."

Grant, Shelagh. 1988. *Sovereignty or Security?: Government Policy in the Canadian North, 1936-1950*. Vancouver: UBC Press.
———. 2002. *Arctic Justice: On Trial for Murder, Pond Inlet, 1923*. McGill-Queen's Native and Northern Series 33. Montreal: McGill-Queen's University Press.

Hanrahan, Maura. 2003. *The Lasting Breach: The Omission of Aboriginal People from the Terms of Union between Newfoundland and Canada and Its Ongoing Impacts*, March. Report prepared for the Government of Newfoundland and Labrador, Royal Commission on Renewing and Strengthening Our Place in Canada. Accessed March 28, 2009. http://www.gov.nl.ca/publicat/royalcomm/research/Hanrahan.pdf

Harper, Ken C. 1986. *Give Me My Father's Body: The Life of Minik, the New York Eskimo.* Frobisher Bay: Blacklead Books.

Henderson, James Youngblood. 2006. *First Nations Jurisprudence and Aboriginal Rights: Defining the Just Society.* Saskatoon: Native Law Centre.

Hodge, R. Anthony, James Stauch, and Ingrid Taggart. 2007. *Freedom to Choose: Natural Resource Revenues and the Future of Northern Communities. Report of the 2007 Northern Policy Forum, "Power, Revenue and Benefits — Ensuring Fairness Now and across Generations."* Toronto: Walter and Duncan Gordon Foundation. Accessed March 30, 2009. http://www.gordonfn.ca/resfiles/FREEDOM_TO_CHOOSE.pdf

Indian and Northern Affairs Canada (INAC). 1996a. "Relocation of Aboriginal Communities." In *Looking Forward, Looking Back.* Vol. 1 of *Royal Commission Report on Aboriginal Peoples.* Ottawa: INAC. Accessed March 28, 2009. http://www.ainc-inac.gc.ca/ap/pubs/sg/cg/cg11-eng.pdf

————. 1996b. "Treaties." In *Restructuring the Relationship.* Vol. 2 of *Royal Commission Report on Aboriginal Peoples.* Ottawa: INAC. Accessed March 28, 2009. http://www.ainc-inac.gc.ca/ap/pubs/sg/cg/ch2-eng.pdf

Irlbacher-Fox, Stephanie Irlbacher, and Stephen J. Mills. 2007. *Devolution and Resource Revenue Sharing in the Canadian North: Achieving Fairness across Generations.* Toronto: Walter and Duncan Gordon Foundation. Accessed March 28, 2009. http://www.gordonfn.ca/resfiles/Forum_ DiscussionPaper.pdf

Irwin, Colin. 1989. "Lords of the Arctic, Wards of the State: The Growing Inuit Population, Arctic Resettlement, and Their Effects on Social and Economic Change." *Northern Perspectives* 17 (1): 2-12.

Ittinuar, Peter Freuchen. 2008. *Teach an Eskimo How to Read.* Arctic College Publications, vol. 5. edited by Thierry Rodon. Iqaluit: Arctic College.

Jarvenpa, Robert. 2004. "Silot'ine: An Insurance Perspective on Northern Dene Kinship Networks in Recent History." *Journal of Anthropological Research* 60 (2): 153-78.

MacGregor, Roy. 1989. *Chief: The Fearless Vision of Billy Diamond.* Markham, ON: Viking.

Martin, Chester. 1973. *Dominion Lands Policy.* Edited and with an introduction by Lewis H. Thomas. Toronto: McClelland and Stewart. (Orig. pub. 1938.)

McGee, Robert. 2004. *The Last Imaginary Place: A Human History of the Arctic World.* Toronto: Key Porter.

Mitchell, Marybelle. 1996. *From Talking Chiefs to a Native Corporate Elite: The Birth of Class and Nationalism among Canadian Inuit.* McGill-Queen's Native and Northern Series 12. Montreal and Kingston: McGill-Queen's University Press.

Morantz, Toby. 2002. *The White Man's Gonna Getcha: The Colonial Challenge to the Crees in Quebec.* McGill-Queen's Native and Northern Series 30. Montreal and Kingston: McGill-Queen's University Press.

Morissonneau, Christian. 1978. *La terre promise: le mythe du Nord québécois.* Montreal: Hurtubise.

Nahanni, Phoebe. 1992. "Dene Women in the Traditional and Modern Northern Economies, Denendeh, Northwest Territories." Master's thesis, McGill University.

Natural Resources Canada (NRC). 2008. *Mineral and Metal Commodity Reviews.* Ottawa: NRC. Accessed March 29, 2009. http://www.nrcan-rncan.gc.ca/mms-smm/busi-indu/cmy-amc/com-eng.htm

Northwest Territories (NWT). Commission on Constitutional Development, James Bourque, Chair. 1992. *Working toward a Common Future.* Government of the Northwest Territories, Yellowknife.

_____. Health and Social Services. 2006. "The 2006 Addictions Report." NWT Health and Social Services, Yellowknife.

Nungak, Zebedee. 2003. "When the Inuit Became Just Another Tribe." *Windspeaker*, May 1. Accessed March 30, 2009. http://www.articlearchives.com/law-legal-system/trial-procedure-litigation/867356-1.html

O'Reilly, Kevin. 1998-99. "Staking Our Claim: Reform of Northern Mining Law." *Canadian Arctic Resources Committee Northern Perspectives* 25 (3): 1-3. Accessed March 29, 2009. http://www.carc.org/pubs/v25no3/1.htm

Palacios, Janelle F., and Carmen Portillo. 2009. "Understanding Native Women's Health." *Journal of Transcultural Nursing* 20 (1): 15-27.

Papillon, Martin. 2008. *Aboriginal Quality of Life under a Modern Treaty: Lessons from the Experience of the Cree Nation of Eeyou Istchee and the Inuit of Nunavik.* Montreal: Institute for Research on Public Policy. *IRPP Choices* 14 (9).

Poppel, Birger, Jack Kruse, Gérard Duhaime, and Larissa Abryutina. 2007. *Survey of Living Conditions in the Arctic: Results.* Anchorage: Institute of Social and Economic Research, University of Alaska Anchorage. Accessed April 13, 2009. http://www.chairecon ditionautochtone.fss.ulaval.ca/en/PDF/SLICA_Int%20results_March%2007.pdf.

Quigley, N.C., and N.J. McBride. 1987. "The Structure of an Arctic Micro-Economy: The Traditional Sector in Community Economic Development." *Arctic* 40 (3): 204-10.

Quassa, Paul Aarlulaaq. 2008. *We Need to Know Who We Are.* Life Stories of Northern Leaders Series, edited by Louis McComber. Iqaluit: Arctic College Publications, Nunavut Arctic College.

Quiring, David. 2004. *CCF Colonialism in Northern Saskatchewan.* Vancouver: UBC Press.

Rea, Kenneth J. 1968. *The Political Economy of the Canadian North.* Toronto: University of Toronto Press.

Richmond, Chantelle A.M., and Nancy L. Ross. 2009. "The Determinants of First Nation and Inuit Health: A Critical Population Health Approach." *Health and Place* 15:403-11.

Robertson, Gordon. 1960. "Administration for Development in Northern Canada: The Growth and Evolution of Government." *Canadian Public Administration* 3 (4): 354-62.

Rodon, Thierry. 2003. *En partenariat avec l'Etat: Les experiences de cogestion des Autochtones du Canada.* Quebec: Les Presses de l'Université Laval.

Royal Commission on Aboriginal Peoples. 1994. *The High Arctic Relocation: A Report on the 1953-55 Relocation.* Ottawa: Ministry of Supply and Services.

Snowshoe, Charlie. 1977. "A Trapper's Life." In *Dene Nation: The Colony Within,* edited by Mel Watkins. Toronto: University of Toronto Press.

St. Germain, The Honourable Gerry, and the Honourable Nick Sibbeston. 2008. *Honouring the Spirit of Modern Treaties: Closing the Loopholes.* Standing Senate Committee on Aboriginal Peoples. Senate of Canada.

Tait, Heather, and Vivian O'Donnell. 2008. *Aboriginal Peoples Survey 2001 — Initial Findings: Well-Being of the Non-Reserve Aboriginal Population.* Cat. no. 89-589-XIE. Ottawa: Statistics Canada. Accessed March 30, 2009. http://www.arcticliving conditions.org/

Timpson, Annis May. Forthcoming. "Reconciling Indigenous and Settler Language Interests: Language Policy Initiatives in Nunavut." *Journal of Canadian Studies.*

Usher, Peter J., Gérard Duhaime, and Edmund Searles. 2003. "The Household as an Economic Unit in Arctic Aboriginal Communities, and Its Measurement by Means of a Comprehensive Survey." *Social Indicators Research* 61:175–202.

Usher, Peter J., and Fred Weihs. 1989. *Towards a Strategy for Supporting the Domestic Economy of the Northwest Territories.* Background study prepared for the Northwest Territories Legislative Assembly (Special Committee on the Northern Economy). Yellowknife: Government of the Northwest Territories.

Watkins, Mel, editor. 1977. *Dene Nation: The Colony Within*. Toronto: University of Toronto Press.

Wenzel, George. 1981. *Clyde Inuit Adaptation and Ecology: The Organization of Subsistence*. Ottawa: National Museum of Man.

————. 1991. *Animal Rights, Human Rights, Ecology, Economy, and Ideology in the Canadian Arctic*. Toronto: University of Toronto Press.

Young, T. Kue, and Peter Bjerregaard, eds. 2008. *Health Transitions in Arctic Populations*. Toronto: University of Toronto Press.

Zaslow, Morris. 1959. "A Prelude to Self-Government: The Northwest Territories, 1905-1939." In *The Canadian Northwest: Its Potentialities*, edited by Frank Underhill. Toronto: University of Toronto Press.

————. 1988. *The Northward Expansion of Canada 1914-1967*. Toronto: McClelland and Stewart.

SOVEREIGNTY, ENVIRONMENTAL CHANGE AND SCIENCE

A Principled Path

IN THE ARCTIC, WE ARE IN THE MIDST OF A HISTORIC TRANSFORMATION. IN 2007 alone, we witnessed entire landscapes and icescapes on the move or disappearing because of climate change.[1]

Contrary to what some have said, I am not alarmist. I base what I say on the traditional knowledge and Western-based science available — as all those interested in public policy must do.

What I have been hearing and reading of late, whether scientific accounts or traditional knowledge, is worrying me more than ever.

Every day, I wake hoping to hear that this year's trend was not as bad as was projected. It seems that every day, however, we learn that the most alarming projections, made just a few years ago, now appear too conservative. For example, in 2004, the Arctic Climate Impact Assessment saw an ice-free summer by 2050. The following year, that time frame was revised to 2040. And this year, after the tremendous melt, the most alarming estimates show a new, seasonal sea at the top of our world within a decade. More than ever, I have a real sense of urgency.

What does this transformation mean for citizens of the Arctic? What does it mean for Canada? For the world?

How will we reduce absolute greenhouse gas concentrations in the atmosphere? How will we transform the world economy into a low-carbon-intensity economy? How will we adapt to the inevitable changes?

In this age of globalization and ever-increasing connectivity, we must strive to answer these questions while recognizing how the global affects the local and the local affects the global.

The Big Picture

T HERE IS NO AVOIDING THE BIG PICTURE: TO SLOW DOWN THE WELL-DOCUMENTED transformation of the Arctic brought about by climate change, there must be an absolute reduction in global greenhouse gases in the atmosphere. We must not just stall the progress of greenhouse gas emissions; we must reverse it if we are to avoid a rapid and wholesale transformation of the Arctic ecosystem.

Yet the Government of Canada has not made policy choices and taken actions that will ensure leadership toward this reversal. Ottawa supports intensity-based targets for greenhouse gas emissions.

Intensity-based targets will, at best, slow down the rate of growth of emissions. Using intensity-based targets will *not* bring about an absolute reduction in greenhouse gases.

By choosing intensity-based targets, our government is doing nothing less than sacrificing the Arctic and its peoples. By choosing intensity-based targets over hard caps on the amount of emissions, the Canadian government is making a decision to heed entrenched economic interests at the expense of the human rights of its citizens. The frenzied development of the oil sands of Alberta, without full consideration of the impacts, is a good example.

The national decision to embrace intensity-based targets also has international implications. You will have noted that the 2007 Speech from the Throne declared that Canada will not abide by its international legal obligations under the Kyoto Protocol.

As we step away from our reputation as a nation of decency and principle, our legitimacy in influencing global matters is lost. How can we expect developing nations such as Brazil, China or India to forgo needed short-term economic progress, to protect human rights, to be good global citizens if we, a developed nation, do not take our international obligations seriously?

By refusing to meet its international obligations under Kyoto, Canada is undermining the one global instrument to reduce greenhouse gas emissions. If the Kyoto Protocol fails to deliver the necessary first steps toward a global reduction in greenhouse gas concentrations, many peoples and cultures around the world, not just in Canada, will be endangered.

Canada's actions are serving to turn the Arctic from the planet's climate stabilizer — a sort of cooling system for the world — into a great destabilizer that may endanger humankind's prosperity, and perhaps even its survival. As more of the white

Arctic ice, which reflects the sun's rays back into space, melts, the dark land and water underneath it is exposed. These dark surfaces absorb more light and heat and make the whole warming process move faster. In addition, as all of the land-based ice, like the Greenland ice cap, melts, the water flows into our oceans, disrupting natural currents and increasing the sea level around low-lying and small island states.

Don't just take my word for it. The UN Office for the Coordination of Humanitarian Affairs had issued 13 emergency flash appeals by October 2007 — three more than in 2005, which held the previous record. In 2005, only half the international disasters had anything to do with the climate; two years later, all but one of the UN's emergency appeals were climate related.

What Can Canada Do?

THIS MAY SEEM LIKE A GREAT DEAL OF RESPONSIBILITY TO PLACE ON A NATION LIKE Canada. After all, we contribute only 2 percent of global emissions. But principles and ethics matter in a world that too often teeters on the edge of chaos. As a wealthy nation with a privileged history, we have a responsibility to lead in this world. But in not acting on climate change in a principled, ethical manner, we are failing to fulfill that responsibility; ultimately, we are failing the world.

What does this mean for us locally in the Canadian Arctic? When it comes to mitigating climate change, we do not contribute a great deal to greenhouse gas emissions because of our small numbers. However, if we apply the same reasoning to ourselves as we do to Canada, we must do much better. There is, I submit, an obligation even on the part of our communities, those who are most affected by climate change, to take a principled stance and to lead the Canadian fight to develop a low-carbon economy. Our economic decisions must reflect our reality as the most affected communities. Because of our low numbers, we do not wield great political clout. Our influence springs from our ethical authority. If we lose that moral high ground, we will lose our influence.

I am not saying that Inuit ought to return to the past and live as our ancestors did. I am saying that we must assume real control over our economic development by insisting that every opportunity be analyzed against its impact on our world — meaning the greenhouse gases it will emit, the unsustainable cycles it will feed and the lasting impact it will have on our delicate landscape.

I am convinced that Inuit — indigenous people that we are, who have adapted to survive and thrive in some of the harshest conditions in the world — have the ingenuity to develop an economy that will care for both our planet and ourselves. But we will only be able to do so if we make the conscious decision to lead and not follow.

We must mainstream climate change, mitigating it and adapting it to all of our planning processes. By doing so, we will become better able to strategically direct investments and actions in the face of the resource extraction boom that, due to climate change, is hurtling our way.

We have experienced all this before. After all, it was the exploration boom of the 1970s that pushed Inuit to demand the settlement of land claims. That strategic decision has enabled Inuit to better face this new resource exploration and extraction boom. As the world is once again attracted to the Arctic's resources, our government again feels the need to defend its sovereignty. And again those decisions are affecting Inuit.

As the Northwest Passage sea-ice coverage is lost, Canada is pressed to defend its sovereignty over the fabled passage. Inuit already know that defending Canada's sovereignty in the Arctic exacts a heavy price. Just ask those who were relocated to communities in the High Arctic. For us, Mr. Harper's "Use it or lose it" statement about the Arctic is strange, to say the least. We have always used and occupied the Arctic, including the passage and the ice, in particular. Mary Simon, President of Inuit Tapiriit Kanatami, reiterated this in a recent speech (Simon 2007).

As Inuit know, the sea ice, including the land-fast ice that covers much of the passage, has offered our hunting culture a stable platform for untold generations. That ice is the best defence against ships attempting the faster Northwest Passage route. In other words, slowing down climate change would be the best long-term solution to the problem of how to enforce Canada's Arctic sovereignty.

Instead of aggressively facing climate change and becoming an influential international leader, however, Canada has decided that the best way to defend its sovereignty from foreign ships running the passage is with the military and icebreakers.

Canada, a peaceful nation, will now "defend" the Arctic. We will posture and even threaten those who attempt a free passage through our islands. As it makes these plans, the government states that a primary concern is the increased risk of ecologically dangerous spills once the shipping lane is ice-free.

Our government, sadly, is putting the cart before the horse. Ottawa is willing to be a climate change laggard, allowing the complete transformation of the northern ecosystem, but then it commits to defending the Arctic environment against environmental disasters brought on by foreign ships. We must recognize that an ice-free Northwest Passage is an environmental disaster.

The irony is rich, and unfortunately it only gets richer. To defend the Northwest Passage against environmental damage, our government is loosening its own rules and allowing our navy to discard waste overboard.

A Principled Approach

C ANADA SHOULD TAKE ANOTHER APPROACH. A MORE PRINCIPLED AND HUMAN-CENTRED approach would be to fully implement the solemn promises it has made to its indigenous peoples. In the case of the Arctic, that means fully implementing the basic expression of human rights as expressed in the land claims agreements.

Our government could go a long way toward defending our Arctic sovereignty by providing the tools for Arctic communities to succeed and thrive. This would include making a dedicated effort to ensure the highest standards of culturally appropriate education; investing in community infrastructure, not just the military; and undertaking respectful stewardship of the land through natural resource comanagement bodies.

We must insist that Canada's investments for sovereignty be directed first to people and communities.

My preference — and, I imagine, that of most of the world — is to avoid creating yet another region where relationships between nations are marked by strife and fear. The Arctic is one of the last peaceful and pristine places in the world. How can Canada ensure and monitor that peace and also allow respect for human rights to radiate from the circumpolar North?

By the way, this line of thinking is certainly not new for Inuit. In 1992, the Inuit Circumpolar Conference (ICC), through the dedicated efforts of Mary Simon, released a document, called *Principles and Elements for a Comprehensive Arctic Policy*, that makes for very interesting reading even today. For example, in this set of principles one can find the following statement: "The Arctic must not be viewed as a frontier or battleground for East-West competition or conflict. Rather, it is first and foremost the ancestral homeland of Inuit and other northern peoples. In order to achieve real and lasting security in the Arctic, northern peoples should encourage the development of new notions of common security that do not lead to militarization. Such new concepts of security should be based on the promotion of human rights and international cooperation on economic trade, cultural exchanges, environmental protection, circumpolar research, arms control, and other peaceful initiatives" (Inuit Circumpolar Conference 1992).

I propose taking an old idea and revitalizing it with a made-in-Canada notion that was born with our northern land claims.

The old idea is known as the "Arctic Treaty." It has had many forms. In October 1987, for example, Soviet leader Mikhail Gorbachev made a speech in Murmansk outlining a plan for peaceful international cooperation in the development of the North. His plan included a nuclear-weapons-free zone, the restriction of naval activity, cooperation in the exploitation of resources, collaborative scientific study and cooperation in environmental protection.

The made-in-Canada notion that could revive the old idea of the Arctic treaty is that of comanagement — the claims-based institution that Canada and its Arctic indigenous peoples have jointly created. Our contribution to peaceful international regional governance could be the comanagement model.

Recognizing the importance of the Arctic for the whole of the planet, and the historical stewardship of indigenous peoples of the Arctic ecosystem, consider an Arctic treaty that charges circumpolar indigenous peoples with the stewardship, through comanagement, of the Arctic for the continued benefit of humankind.

These proposed international comanagement boards, on which the indigenous peoples of the Arctic would be guaranteed majority representation, would integrate traditional and scientific knowledge to ensure sound and peaceful management of the Arctic's natural resources.

If we in Canada believe in the merits of such an approach, why not seek to export it to the whole world? Why not export our successes? Through ICC, Inuit have been doing so: for instance, ICC has undertaken comanagement and institution-building projects in Belize and Russia.

The international community is receptive to such an approach. After all, the Declaration on the Rights of Indigenous Peoples, which was recently adopted in the United Nations General Assembly by an overwhelming majority of states, recognizes the contribution of indigenous peoples to sustainability and peace. The preamble to the document reads: "Recognizing that respect for indigenous knowledge, cultures and traditional practices contributes to sustainable and equi-table development and proper management of the environment...[and] Emphasizing the contribution of the demilitarization of the lands and territories of indigenous peoples to peace, economic and social progress and development, understanding and friendly relations among nations and peoples of the world" (United Nations 2007).

Furthermore, the Arctic is internationally recognized as the bellwether of the planet's health and as a delicate and fragile environment.

Rather than engaging in more military posturing, why not declare the Arctic to be what it is — a fragile ecosystem that needs the protection that its indigenous inhabitants can continue to provide?

I would like to conclude by citing a portion of a 2007 op-ed piece I wrote for the *Ottawa Citizen*: "As a nation, we have wandered from our principles. We have allowed the language of economics and inconvenience to dissuade us from our duties to other nations, to our natural world, and to one another. It is time for Canada to find its way again, to once more follow a path of purpose. Our own peo-ple demand this, and the world waits for our leadership" (Watt-Cloutier 2007).

Those words apply not only to our country but also to our international alliances and institutions. And because, as I stated earlier, the global affects the local and the local affects the global, we must continuously remind ourselves in our own regions not to stray from our principled path.

Particularly now, as we face difficult choices in our hunger for economic development, we must ensure economic justice. We must not move toward los-ing our culture through our economic choices at home while we seek to defend our cultural rights internationally. The way forward in these times of rapid change will test our wisdom and our clarity of vision.

In the end, I remain an optimist. I look forward as well to the wealthy, developed nations that surround the Arctic behaving with care and foresight as they determine the new uses of the new sea. As they do so, I urge them to remember that we Inuit are not far from the poles, and that we rely on the ever-migrating animal populations and the delicate ecosystems that make the Arctic their home. Let us be courageous and innovative and make the peaceful, coop-erative, sustainable management of the Arctic a model for the globe, a shining example at the top of the world of how nations can overcome their differences and come to a shared vision of sustainability in the Arctic and on the planet.

Note

1   This is the text of the keynote presentation
     by the author at the Northern Exposure
     Conference in October 2007.

References

Inuit Circumpolar Conference (ICC). 1992.
     *Principles and Elements for a Comprehensive
     Arctic Policy*. Ottawa: ICC.
Simon, Mary. 2007. "Inuit and the Canadian
     Arctic: Sovereignty Begins at Home."
     Speech presented at the Canadian Club,
     October 23, 2007, Ottawa.
United Nations. 2007. *Declaration on the Rights of
     Indigenous Peoples*, September 7, 61st ses-
     sion, agenda item 68. New York: United
     Nations General Assembly. Accessed April
     22, 2008. http://www.iwgia.org/graphics/
     Synkron-Library/Documents/International
     Processes/DraftDeclaration/07-09-13
     ResolutiontextDeclaration.pdf
Watt-Cloutier, Sheila. 2007. "Canada's Way."
     Ottawa Citizen, August 29. Accessed April
     22, 2008. http://www.canada.com/
     ottawacitizen/news/opinion/story.html?id
     =b92d96f2-18d3-4456-a74f-79e160cf
     3578&p=1

Canada and the Changing
International Arctic:
At the Crossroads of
Cooperation and Conflict

D URING THE 2006 FEDERAL ELECTION, STEPHEN HARPER SURPRISED MANY BY
making Canadian Arctic sovereignty and security one of his core campaign
issues. After becoming leader of a minority government, in January 2006, he took
steps to deliver on his electoral promises. His government committed to the construction of between six and eight Arctic offshore patrol vessels, the establishment
of a northern military training base in Resolute Bay and the conversion of a
retired mining site into a refuelling base in Nanisivik. The Stephen Harper government also made the protection of Arctic sovereignty and security a priority and
promised to build a world-class research station in the Canadian North in its
Throne Speech of October 16, 2007 (Government of Canada 2007). In recent
budgets, it followed up on several of these promises with substantial spending
commitments — including the construction of a $720-million icebreaker.

As the Canadian government developed its plan, it was clearly motivated
by the fact that the Arctic is transforming rapidly. The Arctic is a hot topic. Arctic-
related stories are constantly showing up as major news items. One day we read
a story about the impact of climate change on the ice caps; the next day, it's a story
about the port of Churchill's historically active shipping season, or endangered
polar bears, or the resumption of polar overflights by the Russian air force. The
Arctic has become critically important for Canada. The factors that are now combining to raise the profile of the North have been developing for a long time. A
perfect storm is brewing, and it's prompting the Canadian government to act.

Canadian policy-makers have long insisted that Ottawa enjoys complete
jurisdiction over all of the country's Arctic land, water and ice. However, while successive Canadian governments have talked boldly, they have allocated few resources

to the North. This is not to suggest that certain Arctic initiatives of previous Canadian governments — such as the creation of the Arctic Council — have not been important and innovative. It's just that most have been done on the cheap. Until very recently, the Arctic climate has allowed Canadian leaders the luxury of spending very little to secure the region — the North was inaccessible to all but those willing to expend great effort to get there. Now, however, climate change, resource development and geopolitical realities are gradually opening the Arctic to the world.

Perhaps the greatest challenge facing Canadian policy-makers is related to the uncertain future of this increasingly busy region. All three of Canada's Arctic neighbours — Russia, the United States and Denmark/Greenland — are re-examining and redeveloping their policies and activities in their respective sections of the Arctic. The four Arctic nations must deal with the rapid transformation of the Arctic, a process that none can fully understand. Complicating this situation is the absence of a tradition of international cooperation in the North. The Cold War effectively prevented the development of multilateral cooperation; it was only when it ended that the first steps toward international cooperation were taken. But these initial steps were tentative and underfunded.

Canada and the other Arctic states face a developing set of choices in responding to the new realities of the Arctic. On the one hand, they can elect to build on the rudimentary beginnings of an international cooperative regime. This would mean that all Arctic countries — Canada included — would need to scale back or abandon some of their unilateral objectives and develop a multilateral framework for new governance. On the other hand, these countries could decide that they are unable to sacrifice any of their unilateral objectives. The Arctic is at a crossroads, and Canada has some hard decisions to make.

In exploring these hard decisions, I will examine three main issues. First, I will briefly assess the Arctic's overall changing nature — physical, social, economic, political and strategic — in an attempt to understand what it means for Canada's North. Second, I will focus on Canadian efforts to cooperate in the Arctic. The severity of the climate combined with the advent of the Cold War had all but eliminated international cooperation and interaction in the Arctic; not until the collapse of the USSR and the end of the Cold War were the first tentative steps toward collaboration taken. Led by Canada and Finland, the eight Arctic states plus three northern Aboriginal organizations (labelled "permanent participants") created the Arctic Environmental Protection Strategy (AEPS),

which later became the Arctic Council (several additional permanent participants joined the initiative at this point). However, as important as this body has
been, its success has been limited. While it has acted to determine the scientific
nature of the environmental problems facing the region, it has been unable to
formulate a regionally acceptable set of policy actions to respond to these problems. Third, I will examine the sources of existing and potential conflicts for
Canada in the Arctic by focusing on sovereignty and on boundary disputes
between Canada and its immediate neighbours. In this context, I will look at the
status of Arctic waterways, existing maritime boundary disputes, developing
maritime boundary disputes and land disputes. What are the stakes involved,
and how do they impact on Canada?

The Changing North

TRADITIONALLY, THE ARCTIC HAS BEEN SEEN AS A REGION OF EXTREME COLD. ITS
harsh climate was a major deterrent to incursions from the south. However,
the increasing level of industrial greenhouse gas emissions in the south is changing that. Over the last decade, it has become clear that the Arctic is warming. And
warming means greater accessibility. The Canadian North is about to become
much busier.

The Arctic Council (a body that was very much a Canadian creation) has
been instrumental to our understanding of the problems posed by climate
change. In 2000, as changes became apparent, the council commissioned two of
its working groups — the Arctic Monitoring and Assessment Programme (AMAP)
and Conservation of Arctic Flora and Fauna (CAFF) — and the International
Arctic Science Committee (IASC) to undertake an extensive and exhaustive study
of the impact of climate change on the Arctic. Four years later, the Arctic Climate
Impact Assessment (ACIA) was released. The assessment — a peer-reviewed scientific document produced by the world's leading experts and a more concise
summary document — starkly outlines the enormity of the threat to the Arctic
region and the entire world (Hassol 2004, 34-45). The ACIA's key findings are:

- The Arctic climate is now warming rapidly, and greater changes are
  projected. Annual average Arctic temperatures have increased at almost
  twice the rate they have in the rest of the world over the past few

decades; increasing precipitation, shorter and warmer winters, and substantial decreases in ice and snow cover will likely persist for centuries; and unexpected and larger shifts and fluctuations are possible.

◆ Arctic warming and its consequences have worldwide implications. These include the melting of highly reflective snow and ice cover, which will in turn lead to a greater warming of the planet; an increase in glacial melt and river runoff, which will result in rising sea levels; and the possible slowing of the world's ocean-current circulation system.

◆ Animal species' diversity, ranges and distribution will change. Reduction in sea ice will drastically shrink marine habitat for species such as polar bears, ice-inhabiting seals and some seabirds; species' ranges will shift northward, bringing new species to the Arctic and limiting some already present; and some marine fisheries will become more productive, while freshwater fisheries are likely to decline.

◆ Many coastal communities and facilities face increasing exposure to storms. Severe coastal erosion will continue to be a problem as rising sea levels and the reduction of sea ice allow higher waves and storm surges to reach the shore; some coastlines will face increased permafrost melt, adding to their vulnerability; the risk of flooding in coastal wetlands may increase; and some communities are already facing significant threats to their coastlines.

◆ Reduced sea ice is very likely to increase marine transport and access to resources. Continued reduction of sea ice is likely to lengthen the navigation season and increase access to the Arctic's marine resources; reduced sea ice is likely to increase offshore oil and gas extraction projects; and sovereignty, security and safety issues, as well as social, cultural and environmental concerns, are likely to arise as marine access increases.

◆ Ground thawing will disrupt transportation-related building and other infrastructure. Transportation and industry on land, including that related to oil and gas extraction, will increasingly be disrupted as the periods during which ice roads and tundra are frozen sufficiently to allow travel get shorter. This could mean a greater shift to marine transport; as frozen ground thaws, many buildings, roads and so on will become destabilized, creating a need for substantial maintenance and rebuilding;

and permafrost degradation will impact natural ecosystems by collapsing ground surface, draining lakes and wetland areas and toppling trees.

- Indigenous communities are facing major economic and cultural impacts. Many indigenous peoples depend on food sources that are now threatened; and changes in species ranges and availability, access to these species and perceived and real changes in travel safety because of changing ice and weather conditions will create serious challenges to human health and food security.

- Elevated ultraviolet (UV) radiation levels will affect people, plants and animals. The stratospheric ozone layer over the Arctic is not expected to improve for at least a few decades, largely due to the effect of green-house gases on stratospheric temperatures; the current generation of Arctic young people is likely to receive a lifetime dose of UV that is 30 percent higher than any prior generation has received; elevated UV levels can disrupt photosynthesis in plants and have detrimental effects on the early life stages of fish and amphibians; and risks to some Arctic ecosystems are likely, as the largest increases in UV occur in spring, when sensitive species are most vulnerable.

- Multiple influences interact to impact on people and ecosystems. Changes in climate are occurring in the context of many other stresses, including chemical pollution, overfishing, land-use changes, habitant fragmentation, human population increases and economic changes. These stresses can combine to amplify impacts on human and ecosystem health and well-being. In many cases, the total impact is greater than the sum of its parts. For instance, the changes in sea ice are affecting the algae that live on the bottom of the ice; this, in turn, affects the entire Arctic food chain. A decreased ice cover in the Arctic will result in drastic changes in the region, from the microscopic to the international. (Hassol 2004, 10-11)

These changes are occurring now, and they will transform the entire Arctic in ways that we cannot yet fully appreciate. And, as if this were not enough, the impacts of climate change are coinciding with a renewed and vastly increased interest in the resources of the Canadian North.

Canada, a country that had never produced diamonds, has now become the world's third-largest diamond producer on the basis of three new northern mines; more will come online in the future (Natural Resources Canada 2008). In 1985, depressed oil and gas prices ended almost all exploration for these commodities in the North. Soaring prices led to a powerful expansion of exploration both on land and offshore (Jones 2007). The Beaufort Sea is the main focus of current exploration, though there is some speculation that the High Arctic may also contain reserves of oil and gas. While exploration companies are not releasing reports on their findings to the public, the fact that their level of activity has increased so dramatically over the last four years strongly suggests that they are confident enough of success to dedicate substantial resources to exploration (Gregoire 2007).

Canada and International Cooperation and Conflict in the Arctic

T HE HISTORY OF INTERNATIONAL COOPERATION IN THE CANADIAN ARCTIC IS fragmented, yet brief. The region has been inhabited by several groups of indigenous people for thousands of years, but southerners have only just begun to understand their interactions and their histories. When John Cabot's son Sebastian sailed into Hudson Strait in 1508, he may have been the region's first European visitor; while it is possible that Viking voyagers arrived even earlier, there is no conclusive evidence to prove it. After Cabot, the Europeans pressed westward and northward in the region. Some were driven by the pursuit of knowledge, but most were in quest of resources. Members of the Hudson's Bay Company sought animal pelts, and farther north a succession of explorers looked for access to the Orient via the Northwest Passage.

These Europeans tended to ignore the knowledge that the indigenous population offered of the land and its climate, and many perished needlessly. In the 1800s, explorers such as Franklin undertook voyages in particularly harsh climatic conditions, with tragic results. By the time Canada had begun to gain some independence from Britain, the drive to explore the Arctic was dissipating. The Hudson's Bay Company was retreating from its focus on northern trade, and Canada was looking east-west rather than north-south. The one exception to this focus shift was the Yukon gold rush of the 1890s, but as the goldfields were emptied, interest in the North waned.

Britain officially transferred the northern territories to Canada in 1880, but the region's borders were not well defined. The Americans had bought Alaska from Russia in 1867, and a dispute developed between Canada and the United States over the land boundary between Alaska and the Yukon. In 1903, an arbitration tribunal was established to resolve the dispute. It was composed of three Americans, two Canadians and one Briton. The United Kingdom, concerned about Germany's increasing world power, wanted to cultivate the goodwill of the US, so the British tribunal member supported the Americans.

The next major international event in the region occurred in 1906, when Norwegian explorer Roald Amundsen became the first to successfully navigate the Northwest Passage. Economic activity in the Canadian North continued to develop as various mining operations were established, but the region's role in the international sphere remained very limited. It was not until the Second World War that policy-makers began to appreciate that the North's harsh climate and geographic isolation could no longer protect it from foreign incursions. The Japanese invaded the Aleutian islands of Attu and Kiska in 1942, and it has recently been confirmed that the Germans had at least one secret weather station in northern Labrador (Dege 2003, appendix IV). On the Soviet side of the Arctic, the German auxiliary cruiser *Komet* reached the Pacific Ocean via the Northeast Passage (now the Northern Sea Route) across the top of Siberia before the German-Soviet nonaggression pact had been broken. Each of these events was minor, but together they demonstrated that the Arctic was no longer completely isolated from the outside world.

New technologies developed during the war combined with the growth of hostilities between the USSR and the Western democracies would soon make the Arctic one of the most important strategic locations in the world. The development of the atomic bomb, the long-range bomber delivery systems and the inter-continental-range missile meant that the USSR and the US, locked in an escalating conflict, would clash over the Arctic region — the shortest route between the USSR and the US was over the North Pole.

The Soviet threat was very real to Canada, a close ally of the western European states and the United States — a nuclear-armed USSR posed the biggest danger to Canadian security in the postwar era. There was never a question of Canada being neutral in the developing conflict, but when it came to the Arctic, Canadian policy-makers were faced with a serious problem: they had to confront the growing Soviet threat and at the same time prevent the Americans, in their response to the same threat, from undermining Canada's control over its Arctic territories (Grant 1988). To defend itself against Soviet bomber attacks, the US wanted to build a network of fighter bases and radar sites that would range from western Alaska across Canada to Greenland. When the main delivery system for nuclear weapons shifted from manned bombers to missiles, the US would use these sites to support its core defensive policy of mutually assured destruction, the foundation of its deterrence policy. The sites would provide warning of a Soviet nuclear missile attack, thereby allowing American nuclear weapons to also be fired. Ultimately, it was the knowledge that this capability existed that was to deter the Soviets from launching in the first place. Canadian officials wanted the US to shoulder the cost of building these sites, but they were not prepared to hand full control of the network over to their southern neighbours. During the construction of the Distant Early Warning (DEW) Line, some American officials suggested that since they were taking responsibility for the bulk of the construction and paying for it, they should retain control over the installations and the land they occupied; but once the sites became operational, they were given to Canada to control.

In 1968, a new issue related to Canada-US control over the Arctic arose when a very large deposit of oil was discovered on the Alaska North Slope (Dosman 1976). The problem at hand was to determine the best means of transporting the oil to American markets, and two options were identified: build a north-south pipeline through Alaska; or use oil tankers. In 1969, in order to test the viability of the second option, Humble Oil outfitted a large tanker, the *Manhattan*, for a test run through the Northwest Passage. This sparked an international crisis. The Americans refused to seek Canada's permission for the voyage, insisting that since in their view the passage was an international strait, permission was not required. Canada countered that the passage was an internal stretch of water, not an international one. Ultimately, Canada granted permission, even though the US had not requested it, and the *Manhattan* took its test run. The Canadian Coast Guard sent an icebreaker to assist the tanker and its American icebreaker escort. This was fortuitous — due to severe ice conditions, the coast guard's help was needed.

The dispute prompted Canada to develop several initiatives to advance its claim for control. These included passage of the *Arctic Waters Pollution Prevention Act, 1985* and pursuit of international support for its position. In 1985, the

American icebreaker *Polar Sea* went through the Northwest Passage without asking permission from the Canadian government,[1] and Brian Mulroney's Conservative government vowed to take major steps to reinforce and protect Canadian Arctic sovereignty. Six initiatives were announced by External Affairs Minister Joe Clark, though of these, only the ones that did not require substantial new funds were ever implemented. A promise to build a Polar-8-class icebreaker was abandoned within a couple of years of its announcement, as was a plan to purchase 10 to 12 nuclear-powered submarines.

The onset of the Cold War froze all international relations in the Arctic. Canada, the United States, Iceland, Norway and Denmark cooperated closely as NATO allies, but they had no meaningful relationship with the USSR except as potentially deadly adversaries. Sweden remained neutral, and Finland, while nominally neutral, was closely connected with the USSR. These divisions ensured that there would be little development of international cooperation in Canada's Arctic region. The one exception was the 1973 Agreement on the Conservation of Polar Bears, a response to the concern that hunters were decimating the polar bear population. However, this could also be seen as a confidence-building measure in the context of USSR-NATO relations: while the drafters of the treaty were concerned about the polar bears, they were also attempting to show that cooperation was possible by forging an agreement on a politically minor issue.

There was little follow-up to the polar bear agreement, and not much changed in the Arctic until Mikhail Gorbachev, who had become leader of the Soviet Union in 1985, called upon all Arctic nations to join together to make the Arctic a zone of peace (Scrivener 1989). Initially, this proposal — delivered on October 1, 1987 — was either greeted with suspicion or dismissed. However, as it became evident that Gorbachev was serious about reforming his country, some Western leaders saw an opportunity to improve their relations with the USSR. In November 1989, Prime Minister Brian Mulroney, while visiting Leningrad, proposed that the Arctic nations create a council (Canadian Arctic Resources Committee 1991), which would hold regular high-level meetings to discuss issues of common interest. At the time, Mulroney's proposal was not well received by the other Arctic nations, and the initiative appeared to be stillborn, but the need for some form of multilateral organization remained. Finnish officials, recognizing that change within the USSR needed to be supported, maintained that some form of organization that supported cooperative action in the Arctic could also serve to keep the Soviets from backsliding. But what was the best way to create such an organization?

After consulting with Canadian officials and others, the Finns decided to make the Arctic environment their focus. This was the period in which the World Commission on Environment and Development — the Brundtland Commission, which published its report in 1987 — made the world aware of the growing danger of international environmental degradation. While the Arctic had long been considered environmentally pristine (because it was so far removed from heavy industrial activity), studies released at the end of the 1980s contradicted this view. In 1989, the Finnish launched their initiative, known as the Rovaniemi process, which led to the creation of the Arctic Environmental Protection Strategy (AEPS) in 1991. Under the terms of the strategy, the eight Arctic nations — Canada, Russia, the US, Denmark, Sweden, Norway, Iceland and Finland — would create a body dedicated to studying and responding to environmental threats to the Arctic. This body would be based on four working groups: the Arctic Monitoring and Assessment Programme (AMAP), Protection of the Arctic Marine Environment (PAME), Conservation of Arctic Flora and Fauna (CAFF) and Emergency Prevention, Preparedness and Response (EPPR). Each would examine the environmental problems covered by its mandate. The AEPS has done an excellent job in bringing together scientists and officials from the eight nations as well as representatives of northern Aboriginal organizations; it has also succeeded in defining the environmental problems facing the North. It has not done as well in developing policy responses.

Although the strategy was the result of what is referred to as the "Finnish initiative," Canadian officials were instrumental in the formation of the AEPS. The final agreement is very similar to a Canadian domestic policy document that addressed Arctic environmental pollution and was developed for Canada's Green Plan — the Arctic Environmental Strategy (AES). A comparison of the AEPS and the AES suggests that the two documents were developed by the same officials (Huebert 1998, 37-58).

The AEPS was an important first step toward a cooperative Arctic regime, but Canadian policy-makers still believed that a stronger multilateral organization was necessary. After Mulroney delivered his 1989 proposal, an independent panel of Canadian Arctic experts convened to examine the potential of a council and to consider its possible structure. The panel then made a series of trips to the Canadian Arctic and drafted a preliminary model. In October and November of

1990, panel members met with Canadian federal and territorial government officials to elaborate their position. They claimed that now that the Cold War had
ended, Canada needed to show leadership and utilize its multilateral negotiation
skills to improve multilateral cooperation.[2] The idea that northern Aboriginal
groups should have greater participation in such initiatives can also be traced to
this panel (Scrivener 1996, 19-20). Panel members maintained that the council
should be composed of delegations from the eight Arctic nations, a ninth delegation from the Arctic indigenous organizations and a tenth delegation from the
Arctic territorial governments. All ten delegations were to operate as equals.

On November 28, 1990, Secretary of State for External Affairs Joe Clark
announced that he would be bringing the proposal for an Arctic council to the
attention of the other Arctic nations. Progress was slow, primarily because of
American concerns about the scope of such a council. Two meetings of international experts were held — one in May 1992 and another a year later. At the May
1993 meeting, all of the Arctic nations except the US agreed to a draft declaration
and terms of reference for the council. The declaration listed these objectives: the
council would promote cooperation between the eight states; recognize the unique
contribution of indigenous peoples to the Arctic; advance Arctic interests; and
review, support and complement existing international Arctic initiatives. The
council's terms of reference were to include all eight Arctic states as core members;
they would also recognize the three main Arctic indigenous groups — the Inuit
Circumpolar Conference (ICC), the Saami Council and the Association of
Aboriginal Peoples of Northern Russia (now the Russian Association of Indigenous
Peoples of the North) — as permanent participants in the council. These groups
would have the right of full participation in the council's proceedings.

The United States had attended these initial meetings only as an observer,
but Canadian officials pressed the Americans for their support throughout the talks.
In January and February of 1995, consultations were held between the Canadian
foreign affairs minister, André Ouellet, and the American secretary of state, Warren
Christopher, and the US finally agreed to support the initiative. While this was
occurring, the Americans were also conducting a review of their own Arctic policy,
prompted by the end of the Cold War and domestic concerns about the growing
environmental degradation of the Arctic region. The resulting revised policy, completed in June 1994, placed a much higher degree of importance on regional cooperation in protecting the environment; the policy also noted that the end of the

Cold War and the breakup of the USSR had diminished American security concerns in the Arctic (Arctic Research Policy Committee 1994, 125).

American support for the council was publicly noted in Canada in February 1994 at an Ottawa conference held to examine Canadian northern foreign policy. At this conference, Minister of Foreign Affairs André Ouellet made two important announcements: the US had expressed its support for an Arctic council, and Canada would create the position of ambassador for circumpolar affairs. The new ambassador's major focus would be to develop and promote the council. Mary Simon, who would be appointed to this position, had been a member of the independent panel that had initiated the concept of the council and had served as president of the ICC. After her appointment, in the fall of 1994, Ambassador Simon conducted an extensive series of meetings, finally convincing the Americans to offer their full support for the council's initiatives. In early 1995, President Bill Clinton formally announced that the US would participate in the Arctic Council. In March 1995, following discussions, officials from all of the eight Arctic nations and indigenous organizations decided to convene a June meeting of senior officials to finalize a draft agreement that had been prepared by Canadian officials (Foreign Affairs and International Trade Canada 1995a, 2). Several important topics were considered at that meeting: the objectives of the council, its relationship with other Arctic initiatives, its structure, its financial organization and its legal status.

While the Canadian government pushed for the creation of an Arctic council, it also actively supported the inclusion of northern indigenous peoples (especially the Inuit), primarily through the ICC, which was formed in 1977 to provide a stronger political voice for the Inuit. The ICC has four divisions: ICC Canada, ICC Alaska, ICC Greenland and ICC Chukotka. Government support has allowed the ICC to strengthen its role in the development of the circumpolar world. Both the ICC and ICC Canada have had a major part in building global support for a range of international initiatives and treaties — particularly some environmentally focused ones. The ICC played a key role in drafting and in developing political support for the 2001 Stockholm Convention on Persistent Organic Pollutants, which banned the use of certain pollutants transported from southern locations to the Arctic. The ICC also helped to demonstrate the human face of the impacts of these pollutants (Downie and Fenge 2003). In addition, the ICC made an important contribution to the drafting of the 2004 Arctic Climate Impact Assessment (ACIA) and teaching the ACIA's southern-based researchers about the applicability of traditional knowledge in confronting climate change. The ACIA was thus one of the first international studies to place traditional knowledge on an equal footing with Western science.

ICC leaders such as Mary Simon and Sheila Watt-Cloutier have shown the world what global warming means to the people of the Arctic regions and their way of life. Watt-Cloutier and Al Gore shared a Nobel Peace Prize nomination for their joint battle against climate change. The ICC's success is largely due to the hard work of its leaders and members, but they have been ably assisted by successive Canadian governments. Since the end of the 1980s, the federal government has recognized the importance of giving the Inuit and other northern indigenous peoples a voice in determining government responses to the environmental degradation of the North. Representatives of northern indigenous groups were included in the development of the Northern Contaminants Programme of the Arctic Environmental Strategy. This proved so successful that when the Finnish government approached them to assist in the development of the Arctic Environmental Protection Strategy, Canadian officials simply transplanted the AES into the international arena. They made it clear that the involvement of northern indigenous peoples was now a necessity. Some countries, such as the US, were not initially in favour of this approach, but Canadian government lobbying overcame their opposition. Ultimately, the partnership between the Government of Canada and northern indigenous organizations (the ICC, in particular) has been very successful for everyone involved.

Canada's role in the creation of the Arctic Council was pivotal. Conservative and Liberal governments gave their strong support to the creation of this multilateral body to facilitate cooperation in the Arctic. Canadian diplomats showed great initiative and foresight in helping to develop a new means of governance. Their insistence on including northern Aboriginal representation was both inspiring and forward thinking. However, since the creation of the council, successive Liberal and Conservative governments have gradually reduced their support. The Harper government even went as far as to eliminate the position of circumpolar ambassador in 2006.

Despite its excellent track record, the Arctic Council has been unable to marshal support for its actions against the problems that are afflicting the North. And Canada is no longer playing a leadership role among the Arctic nations. While the Department of Foreign Affairs and International Trade did develop the Northern Dimension of Canada's Foreign Policy and select support for the Arctic

Council as one of its four main pillars, there has been little evidence that such support has been given to any significant degree. A four-year, $10-million allocation was approved, but this fund also had to cover support for the University of the Arctic and a program to improve relations with Russia.

There are now signs that the Harper government is about to embark on a circumpolar diplomatic initiative. Foreign Affairs Minister Lawrence Cannon gave two speeches — in Whitehorse on March 11, 2009, and in Montreal on March 27, 2009 — in which he underlined Canada's commitment to working with its circumpolar neighbours. He also affirmed Canada's intention to strengthen the Arctic Council. However, the speech did not explain how this was to be done (Foreign Affairs and International Trade Canada 2009a, b). As I will show in the next section, this country is facing a wide range of international challenges in the Arctic. To confront them, it will need to reapply the strategies that have proved successful in the past.

Existing and Potential Conflicts for Canada in the Arctic

PERHAPS THE GREATEST CHALLENGE CANADA FACES IS RELATED TO THE FACT THAT THE Arctic is about to become a much busier place, and Canada cannot agree with its Arctic neighbours as to how its maritime borders should be drawn. As long as no one was going to the Arctic, such disagreements could be ignored, but in an era when access is increasing and resource development is beginning to reshape the region, Canada must work to resolve such issues.

While most Canadians believe that our national claim is incontestable, the reality is that Canada is embroiled in numerous international disputes over various aspects of control over its Arctic region, and other such disputes may arise (see map on page 97). The immediacy of these disputes varies, and some may not erupt for some time, but the fact that there are so many is troubling. Three are with the United States and another seems likely; soon there will be one with Russia; and there are two, possibly three, with Denmark. While these disputes are either potential or on hold, they may have a serious cumulative effect on Canada's overall claim of control in the region. Should some or all of them have unfavourable results for Canada, the international community may come to view Canadian claims of sovereignty with skepticism.

The Northwest Passage: Canada versus the United States

Canada claims that the Northwest Passage is an internal Canadian waterway (Franckx 1993, 65-108). This would mean that Canada has the right to unilaterally pass legislation and impose regulations on all Canadians and foreigners on the passage's ice and waters. The United States, the European Union and possibly Japan do not accept this claim (Huebert 1995). In their view, the passage may be used for international navigation — Canada does not have unilateral control over the region's waterways and cannot pass laws governing international shipping via the Northwest Passage.[3] The Northwest Passage dispute is strictly limited: the issue of sovereignty in the passage concerns only the regulatory regime governing international shipping. Canada has a sovereign right over all living and nonliving resources in the subsoil (for example, oil and gas) and the water column (fish) up to 200 miles from its coastline. It also has the right to control all maritime research in this zone (Rolston and McDorman 1988). The attractiveness of the passage for international shipping is twofold. First, it makes travel between the eastern US and Asia or Europe much shorter and therefore far more economical. Second, the passage can serve substantially larger vessels than the Panama Canal. In 1969, the *Manhattan*, an ice-strengthened supertanker weighing 155,000 tonnes, sailed through the passage; the Panama Canal cannot accommodate vessels of more than 70,000 tonnes (McRae 1987, 98-114; Mitchell 2000; Nickerson 2000).[4]

In 2007, ice cover in the passage reached its lowest level ever, and speculation is growing that shipping in the passage will increase accordingly. The dispute over access to the Northwest Passage is thus a direct result of the decrease in Arctic ice cover, which, in turn, has been caused by what leading scientific research bodies have identified as an unprecedented rise in Arctic temperatures due to global warming (Hassol 2004). There is some debate as to the exact cause of the ice cover decrease; and some see it as a short-term transformation, others as a long-term trend. However, the majority view in the scientific community is that the trend is real, and that over the next 15 to 40 years the shipping season in the Canadian Arctic will lengthen substantially (Hassol 2004, 82-5).

The bulk of the increase in shipping in the Northwest Passage will likely be related to the development of the Canadian Arctic, not transpolar shipping. The Russian side of the Arctic is melting more quickly than the Canadian side, so it will probably be used initially as the main transpolar route. There are numerous reasons for this: prevailing ocean currents, the location of the islands of the archipelago and the impact of the Greenland ice sheet. Furthermore, of the three Arctic regions that could serve as a link between the Pacific and Atlantic oceans — the Northern Sea Route, the Arctic Ocean and the Northwest Passage — the passage will be the last to become ice-free for extended periods and hence will probably be the last to be used as a transpolar route. But even this is not certain, so its impact on Canada also remains uncertain.

Ultimately, however, Canada's policy challenge will be to develop the shipping regime that will best serve Canadian interests — one that will adequately protect the environment; maintain the highest vessel safety standards; guarantee that ships entering the icy Arctic waters are built to the highest technical standards; and ensure that Canadians, particularly those living in the North, share in the economic benefits of increased shipping. However, Canadian policy-makers must confront two uncertainties. The first pertains to the rate of warming in the Northwest Passage. If the temperature increases of the last 30 years represent only a temporary trend, then there is little likelihood that the passage will open for shipping; even if the majority of scientists are correct, and the warming trend is permanent, we still do not know what its full impact will be. Furthermore, there is evidence that a warming Arctic would also mean *more* ice in the Northwest Passage, at least temporarily, because as the passage's ice cover melts, thicker ice from the polar ice cap will flow southward into the passage.

The second uncertainty that policy-makers face is that if Canada does not establish its sovereignty over the Northwest Passage and climate change makes the passage more accessible, then Canada is unlikely to win a challenge in the International Court of Justice (ICJ) or any other such juridical body (Pharand 1988). But even if Canada does make a tremendous effort to bolster its surveillance and enforcement capability in the Arctic, there is still no guarantee that it would win such a challenge. In its 1949 Strait of Corfu judgment, the ICJ defined an "international strait" as a body of water that joins two international bodies of water and is used by international shipping interests.[5] The Northwest Passage does join two international bodies of water, but ice conditions have often prevented its use as a shipping lane. If climate change alters this situation, then it would seem that Canada would lose any legal claim to sovereignty, especially since the ICJ tends to be conservative in its judgments (Kindred et al. 1987, 254).

Ultimately, any resolution of this dispute will depend upon the ability of Canada and the United States to come to an understanding over the status of these waters. The US does not want to set a precedent with the Northwest Passage case that could be used against it should a similar situation arise on another international waterway. Although the official position of the US government is that the passage is an international strait, and thus open to all, former US ambassador to Canada Paul Cellucci has suggested that it would be in the interest of US national security to have Canada control it (Struck 2006). One approach Canada could take to resolving the dispute would be to convince the US government that permitting Iranian or North Korean vessels to use the Northwest Passage would indeed pose a security risk. While it is unlikely that the US would publicly endorse this view, it could agree not to contest Canada's claim — given, of course, that Canada could actually control the region.

But if international shipping does commence on the passage, then Canadian policy-makers must find ways to ensure that it is conducted in a manner that protects and promotes the national interest. Canada can afford to lose the right to refer to the Northwest Passage as internal waters, but it cannot afford to lose control over the regulation of the ships that sail on it.

The Americans complicated this possibility with the release of a new Arctic policy in the dying days of the George W. Bush administration. A National Security Presidential Directive and Homeland Security Presidential Directive explicitly states that the US views the Northwest Passage as a strait used for international navigation. The document states that "(p)reserving the rights and duties relating to navigation and overflight in the Arctic region supports our ability to exercise these rights throughout the world, including through strategic straits" (US National Security Presidential Directive 2009). While this is not a change of the American position it is perhaps one of the most stark statements of it. This will make any effort to reach an accommodation with Canada that much more difficult. Any new administration must now explain why it is breaking with this policy if it does attempt to work with Canada in reaching an agreement.

The Maritime Boundary between Alaska and the Yukon (Beaufort Sea): Canada versus the United States

The second debate between Canada and the US is over the maritime boundary between Alaska and the Yukon. In 1825, Russia (which then controlled what is now Alaska) and the United Kingdom signed a treaty that established a land boundary between Canada and Russia. Canada maintains that the Canada-US maritime boundary should be a direct continuation of that land boundary; the US insists that it should be drawn at a 90-degree angle to the coastline (Kirkey 1995). The US version of the boundary extends in a more easterly direction than the Canadian version. At the heart of the dispute is a wedge of marine territory in the Beaufort Sea that has been created by this disparity in the two countries' positions.

At stake are the region's oil and gas resources — during the 1970s, there was considerable speculation that these could be extensive. But, as substantial as the reserves may be, the severity of the climate may make their extraction (especially due to their offshore location) economically unfeasible. It is therefore not surprising that when oil prices collapsed in the 1980s, the boundary dispute seemed to disappear; neither Canada nor the US pursued commercial development in the disputed zone, and even exploration was contained.

The Bush administration had signalled its intent to develop its northern oil and gas reserves. Bush's efforts to develop the oil and gas potential of the protected land region of northeast Alaska were ultimately defeated by Congress. The Obama administration has not made its position clear on this question. Testifying before Congress recently, Obama's interior secretary Ken Salazar stated that the administration was not opposed to production in the offshore but intends to include oil drilling as part of a well-deliberated, long-term energy plan (Garber 2009). At the same time, Obama repeatedly suggested during the election campaign that he was not in favour of developing new oil and gas sites in Alaska. Therefore it is too soon to know for certain what the new American government will do.

However both Secretary of State Hillary Clinton and Canadian Foreign Affairs Minister Lawrence Cannon have begun to discuss Arctic issues. They discussed the Arctic on February 24, 2009, and then again on April 6, 2009, in Washington. While the particulars of the discussions are not yet known, it is assumed they addressed the issues surrounding the Arctic continental shelf claims, the status of the Northwest Passage and the Beaufort Sea boundary dispute. If so, it is hoped that possible means of resolving these differences were considered.

A possible solution could be the development of a joint management scheme. Such a venture does not seem improbable: after all, the North American Free Trade Agreement created a shared energy market, and there are numerous international examples of such arrangements.

The Maritime Boundary between Nunavut and Greenland (Lincoln Sea): Canada versus Denmark

A very minor disagreement exists between Canada and Denmark over the division of the Lincoln Sea. In 1974, the two countries agreed on the maritime boundary along the coasts of the Northwest Territories (what is now Nunavut) and Greenland, but later, in establishing Exclusive Economic Zones, they extended the boundary northward into a region not covered by the 1974 agreement. The disputed territory is small — 65 square miles — so the problem should be relatively simple to rectify.

The Continental Shelf: Canada versus Russia, Denmark and the United States

In the summer of 2007, there was considerable interest in Russia's bid to assert control over what it claimed was its Arctic continental shelf. The northern continental shelf sections of Canada, the United States and Russia join in the High Arctic, and overlapping claims thus seem inevitable. The United Nations Convention on the Law of the Sea (UNCLOS) contains a means of determining a coastal state's maritime zones, including its continental shelf. Such a state can claim rights over the seabed and subsoil of its shelf to an offshore distance of 350 nautical miles — sometimes even further. This gives the state the right to the resources found on the seabed and in the subsoil, including oil and gas deposits.

Under the terms of the UNCLOS, a state must determine the limits of its continental shelf within 10 years of ratifying the convention. Once it has done so, it submits the specifics of its claim to an international panel — the United Nations Commission on the Limits of the Continental Shelf (UNCLCS) — for scientific review. When this process is completed, and if there are no counterclaims from neighbouring states, the claim is granted. Russia ratified the convention in 1997, and it is now preparing to submit its claim, of which its Arctic interests are a part (an earlier submission was returned with a request for improvement). Denmark ratified the convention in 2004, and it has until 2014 to submit its claim.

The United States has not ratified or acceded to the convention. President George W. Bush attempted unsuccessfully to build the necessary Senate support for American accession to it. The Obama administration has clearly indicated that it intends to complete the job. Secretary of State Hillary Clinton stated on April 9, 2009, that the US is committed to ratifying the UN Convention on the Law of the Sea, "to give the United States and our partners the clarity we need to work together smoothly and effectively in the Arctic region" (Alberts 2009).

Canada ratified the convention in 2003. The 2004 budget allocated $65 million to map the Canadian claim. In 2008 an additional $40 million was granted for this work. Over three-quarters of this funding is earmarked for determining the Arctic continental shelf (the remainder is allocated for work in the Atlantic). Canada has agreed to work with both the Americans and the Danes in order to share resources to accomplish this task. We do not yet know whether Canada's claim to its continental shelf in the Arctic region will overlap those of Russia, the US or Denmark. For a long time, the issue of which nation could claim sovereignty over which portion of the shelf did not present much of a problem, but now Russia's movements in the Arctic are putting pressure on Canada to act. This pressure will only increase if, further down the road, climate change permits development of the region's resources.

The Russians and the Swedes mounted a three-ship Arctic expedition in 2004. Stationing a drill ship at the North Pole, they took ice core samples and thus proved that it is technologically possible to drill at the highest latitudes.[6] Further technological developments may allow for under-ice resource exploration in this area. The Russian government has even considered refitting a Typhoon-class nuclear submarine to carry oil under the ice cap (Kurdrik 2003). It is already possible to build an extraction system under the ice — albeit at considerable expense. Whether the Typhoon proposal is serious or not, many believe that it will take this type of innovative thinking to achieve a breakthrough in Arctic resource development.

The challenges facing Canada are significant. It has to submit its claim by 2013, but it must conduct the necessary research without the assistance of a nuclear-powered submarine. It is the only Arctic nation without such a tool at its disposal; the US and Russia have their own submarines, and Denmark has an agreement with the UK to use one of its fleet. Considerably more work is needed, and meeting the deadline will be difficult. Equally daunting is that even once Canada has submitted its claim, there are no clear procedures for resolving territorial overlaps. The UNCLCS will pass judgment on the technical merits of each country's submission and suggest possible dispute resolution processes, but it will be up to the four states involved to work out their differences. Complicating this already difficult situation is the fact that the US is not party to the convention. However, in May 2008 the Danish government invited the other four Arctic states that have extended continental shelf claims (including Norway) to meet in Illulissat, Greenland. The Danes claimed that this was necessary to ensure that all countries concerned follow existing international rules. After the meeting, the five states

Arguing Over the Top of the World[1]

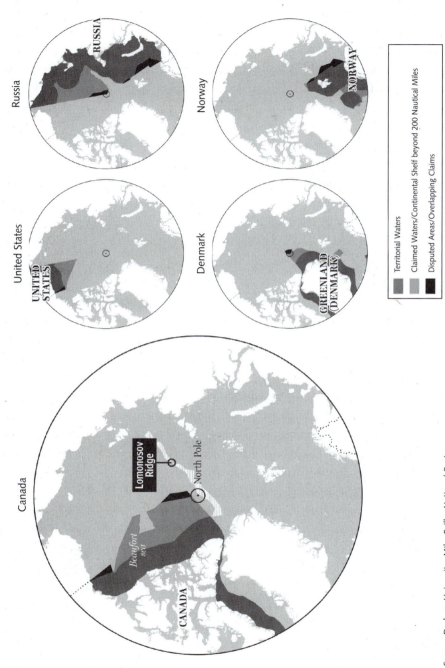

Source: Durham University; Mike Faille, *National Post.*

[1] British researchers have unveiled a new map illustrating the various competing national claims.

issued a declaration that no further international treaties were needed, and that they all would abide by the existing rules. Absent in the declaration was any mention that the United States has not yet ratified UNCLOS, and therefore is not a member of the most important set of rules.

Hans Island: Canada versus Denmark

Canada faces only one land dispute. It is over Hans Island, located in the Kennedy Channel of Nare Strait between northern Ellesmere Island and Greenland. Not much larger than a rock, the island appears to have no resources, and ownership of this tiny territory will not affect the maritime boundary between Canada and Greenland — according to a 1974 maritime boundary agreement between Canada and Denmark, that line extends to the southern tip of the island and recommences at the northern tip (Bankes 1987). However, in the summer of 2002, the Danish government sent an ice-strengthened frigate to assert its claim over Hans Island (Huebert 2005). In response, the Canadian minister of defence, Bill Graham, visited the island in the summer of 2005. These actions brought the Hans issue to the public's attention, and the two countries eventually agreed to discuss their differences at the United Nations. The result of these discussions has not yet been made public.

Illegal Fishing: Canada versus Greenland and the Faeroe Islands

There is a dispute developing between Canada and fishers from Greenland and the Faeroe Islands in the waters between Greenland and Baffin Island. Canadian Coast Guard officials believe that these fishers have been illegally entering Canadian waters, although, due to Canada's weak surveillance capability, this has not yet been confirmed. The draw is a growing market for shrimp and turbot. NORDREG, the regulatory body supporting the *Arctic Waters Pollution Prevention Act*, does not require vessels — either foreign or Canadian — to report their presence in or near Canadian northern waters; it only requests that they do so.[7] Concern is mounting that foreign fishers are ignoring this request and going undetected. The Canadian Forces have cut down on their flights of long-range maritime patrol aircraft in this region due to budget reductions and aging equipment, and Canada has only a limited satellite surveillance system. RADARSAT-1 can be used for some surveillance tasks but has trouble detecting smaller fishing vessels. When RADARSAT-2, launched in December 2007, becomes fully operational, its more advanced resolution capability may improve Canada's ability to detect these vessels.

Canada needs to improve its surveillance and enforcement capability in all regions of the Arctic, but the suspected illegal fishing makes the eastern Arctic a region of special concern. If Canada fails to redevelop its long-range maritime patrol aircraft capability, it will be unable to catch the foreign fishers who are entering its waters illegally. Replacement craft should be ordered and the operational budget of the air force increased to allow for more deployments over the eastern Arctic. The follow-up to RADARSAT-2 must be begun as soon as possible and surveillance of Canadian Arctic regions made a priority mission. Canada will also need to increase its fleet of icebreakers and ice-strengthened vessels. When it has sufficiently strengthened its surveillance and enforcement capability, Canada must then make the NORDREG reporting system mandatory.[8] Only by taking this step can it demonstrate to the international community that it is serious about its claim to the Arctic.

Canada faces challenges of every magnitude along its Arctic maritime borders. Since it no longer has the luxury of ignoring these problems, how should it proceed? One option would be to tackle problems on a case-by-case basis, treating each as a separate, bilateral issue. The advantage of this approach is that foreign affairs officials would probably be most comfortable with it, and it would be the simplest to pursue — bilateral negotiations are generally easier to conduct than multilateral ones. Its main disadvantage is that it would put Canada in the weaker position when dealing with such powerful nations as Russia and the United States. It could also result in Canada offending a neighbour. For example, by entering into direct negotiations over the continental shelf with Russia, Canada could easily cause the US to feel slighted; or if Canada were to negotiate with the US and Denmark, the Russians could interpret it as an instance of NATO allies ganging up on them. Furthermore, this approach would not fully address many of the developing issues. Continental shelf claims need to be resolved by all four claimant states, just as the problems of increased shipping in the Northwest Passage and environmental risks to the Arctic Ocean should be resolved multilaterally. Bilateral solutions would give rise to a patchwork of shipping regulations and environmental standards, which would be unworkable.

Another option would be to develop an international regime to coordinate activity in the Arctic. Issues like climate change and resource development would be managed most effectively via an international approach. However, if Canada is to convince the other Arctic nations to accept this approach, it must give up some of its own short-term interests. Would Canadians be willing to accept the Northwest Passage as an "international strait" if there was an international regime in place to protect the environment and the interests of northern Canadians? Would they support a Beaufort joint-management scheme with the US, despite the fact that they consider the region Canadian? These are, of course, hard questions. In considering them, we must recognize that multilateral options always carry an element of political risk and are much more difficult to coordinate than unilateral actions. And, especially given the complexity of the issues facing the Arctic states, the negotiations would take substantial time and effort.

Current Canadian Action

C ANADA NOW FINDS ITSELF AT A CROSSROADS, AND IT IS UP TO THE GOVERNMENT TO choose a direction. In its October 2007 Throne Speech, the Harper government made a wide range of promises — some of which were outlined in the first paragraph of this chapter — and referred to Arctic defence as one of its primary initiatives. It also noted that a massive transformation is occurring in the Arctic and restated its commitment to the region; it went on to announce the creation of a "world-class research centre" in the Arctic, a plan to improve the living conditions of northern First Nations and Inuit peoples, and a plan to finish mapping the Arctic continental shelf (Government of Canada 2007). These commitments and promises exceeded those made by any preceding Canadian government. If carried out, they would constitute a very important victory in the fight to protect Canadian Arctic sovereignty — specifically, these measures would substantially improve Canada's ability to act in its Arctic territory.

The Harper government also made some important funding decisions related to the Arctic. Its February 26, 2008, budget included $34 million over two years for geological mapping in support of economic development; the extension of the Mineral Exploration Tax Credit for another year; $8 million for the construction of a commercial harbour in Pangnirtung, Nunavut, in support of northern fisheries; an additional $20 million for mapping the northern continental shelf; and, most surprising of all, $720 million to replace the Canadian Coast Guard vessel *Louis S. St- Laurent*, Canada's oldest and largest icebreaker. This budget also reconfirmed the government's commitment to build six to eight Arctic offshore patrol vessels and a deepwater port ($7.4 billion); improve national coastal protection and surveillance, including in the North ($62 million); expand protected areas in the Northwest Territories ($15 million); and improve northern housing ($300 million). There is no question that this was one of the largest budget allocations for northern expenditures in Canadian history (Finance Canada 2008). In the 2009 budget, the government added even more funding for housing and various infrastructure projects, as well as a feasibility study for the Arctic Research station (Finance Canada 2009). Currently the government has a Bill before Parliament to extend the *Arctic Waters Pollution Prevention Act* from its current limit of 100 nautical miles to 200 nautical miles. In conjunction with the new Bill, the government has also stated its intention to make the NORDREG reporting system within these waters a mandatory requirement for all domestic and international shipping.

At the same time, there are several areas in which no progress has been made. The Harper government chose not to appoint a new circumpolar ambassador since it terminated the mandate of the serving ambassador in 2006, a decision it never fully explained. Given the increased level of international activity in the North, this is a disturbing situation: there is currently no Canadian official in a position to lead a multilateral effort to resolve Arctic issues, suggesting that the government places a low priority on relations with its northern neighbours. The government also does not appear to believe that it is necessary to produce a specific document outlining Canada's policy direction for the North. It seems to prefer to let its actions speak for themselves. The preceding administration, Paul Martin's Liberal government, produced policies related to the country's role in the North and issued them in *Canada's International Policy Statement*. In order to provide a coordinated policy framework, the Martin government released four subdocuments — one each on diplomacy, defence, development and commerce — as well as an overview paper. The role of Canada's Arctic in the international system figured prominently in the overview, defence and diplomacy policy books. The two main themes were support of the Arctic Council and defence of Canadian Arctic sovereignty (Government of Canada 2005). The Martin government also attempted to develop a corresponding domestic policy, entitled "The Arctic Strategy," but it failed to complete the task before it was defeated in the 2006 federal election. The Harper government has stated that its Integrated Northern Strategy has been articulated in the 2007 throne speech and substantiated in the following budgets.

Among the troubling recent developments was the tentative sale of the space division of MacDonald Dettwiler (MDA) to an American company, Alliance. MDA designed and built both RADARSAT satellites, which have been crucial to Canada's capacity to monitor what is happening in the North; using a Canadian-designed, radar-based imaging system, the satellites can detect an object as small as a fishing boat in darkness or under cloud cover. The potential sale of the MDA division raised serious questions about Canada's ability to continue to control the operation of its RADARSATs and could have undermined its plans to develop the next generation of satellites. If it had been permitted, Canadian northern surveillance would undoubtedly have been weakened. Ultimately, the minister of industry, Jim Prentice, did step in to suspend the sale.

The Harper government has shown that it is thinking seriously about improving Canada's ability to act in its northern areas. If its promises are kept, Canada will have acquired substantially improved means to do so effectively. Yet whether there is a commitment to applying multilateral approaches in the Arctic, to coordinating Canada's actions with those of its neighbours or developing the necessary policy framework for such actions remains to be seen. Canadian officials attended meetings devoted to northern issues when invited, but the Harper government seemed content to allow others to organize such initiatives. This ultimately suggests that it intended to proceed in a unilateral fashion.

Conclusion

CANADA IS AN ARCTIC NATION. IT HAS ALWAYS PROCLAIMED ITSELF AN IMPORTANT Arctic presence in an international context. However, the region's harsh climate, sparse population and limited opportunities for economic activity have kept Canada from dedicating real resources to it. This is about to change. Climate change and resource development are transforming the Arctic from a backwater into a region of major international importance. The United States, Russia and Denmark are all engaged in the Arctic, and the nature and location of their activities will have a great impact on Canada. Canadian policy-makers are now compelled to act.

While building its capacity to monitor activities in its northern regions, Canada must also work with the countries that have important Arctic interests that potentially overlap with its own. It is imperative that Canada have frank discussions with all of its Arctic neighbours focused on minimizing their differences and maximizing their shared interests. Canada also needs to decide what it wants from its Arctic region. Declarations of the need to protect Canadian Arctic sovereignty will always garner media attention, but sovereignty alone is meaningless if it is not used for an end. So what end does Canada want to pursue? The answer must be national security, but this has to be established with special attention to the needs of the people who call the North home and who have developed a way of life there over centuries. And critical to this security is an uncompromised natural environment. While many effects of climate change may be irreversible, Canadian leaders must ensure that everything possible is done to mitigate those effects. They must also ensure that new northern economic activity has minimal environmental impacts.

Complicating such policy initiatives is the fact that Canada's northern region has the youngest population in the country. There is a dire need to ensure that young Arctic residents have the same opportunities as their counterparts in southern Canada, and this means that the quality of the educational and social services they receive must be greatly improved. Young northerners must be educated and trained to partake in the new economic opportunities that the forces of globalization are bringing to the North. And Canada faces the enormous challenge of harnessing the benefits of these opportunities while minimizing their costs.

Canada cannot do any of this alone. It must find a way to work with those whose interests coincide with its own while developing its capacity to stand up to those who challenge and oppose Canadian interests. This will be an extremely difficult balancing act, but failing to attempt it will amount to a surrender of national sovereignty. Canadian policy-makers have certainly made an innovative start. Canada's role in the creation of AEPS and the Arctic Council is a source of great pride. But now, as well as coming up with good ideas, Canada must substantially increase its spending in the North and accept that its participation in cooperative international ventures will probably require it to sacrifice some long-held interests and unilateral claims. The time in which Canada could dabble in the art of international politics in the Arctic is ending.

Notes

1   There is reason to believe that this was not actually an act of defiance on the part of the US government. In fact, the US Coast Guard needed the icebreaker to resupply the US air force base at Thule, Greenland, and to provide research support in northern Alaskan waters. When an East-Coast-based icebreaker was found unfit for duty following its annual inspection, the *Polar Sea* was assigned to serve in its territory as well; to accommodate the time frames of its two missions, the *Polar Sea* had to use the Northwest Passage.

2   The Arctic Council Panel members were Franklyn Griffiths, Rosemarie Kuptana, John Amagoalik, William Erasmus, Cindy Gilday, Stephen Hazell, John Lamb and Mary Simon (see Griffiths et al. 1991).

3   I have had a lively debate with Franklyn Griffiths, my discussant on this issue, but I believe that our differences are not actually so great. See Griffiths (2003, 2004) and Huebert (2003, 2004).

4   However, ice can be a complicating factor. Due to poor ice conditions, the *Manhattan* needed the assistance of two icebreakers to complete its transit (Kirton and Munton 1987).

5   *Corfu Channel Case (Merits) (United Kingdom v. Albania)* [1949] I.C.J. Rep. 4.

6   See the expedition's Web site for more information about the project: http://www.marum.de/English/Arctic_ Coring_Expedition_2004.html%20

7   *Arctic Waters Pollution Prevention Act*, R.S.C. 1970, c.2 (1st supp.).

8   In August 2008 Prime Minister Harper announced that NORDREG would no longer be a voluntary system but would be a mandatory requirement for all vessels entering Canadian Arctic waters. However, this change was not implemented in September 2008 when a general election was called. This issue is to be addressed by the current Parliament.

References

Alberts, Sheldon. "Obama Committed to Resolving Arctic Disputes — Clinton." *Montreal Gazette*, April 9, 2009. Accessed April 15, 2009. http://www.montrealgazette.com/Travel/ Obama+committed+resolving+Arctic+ disputes+Clinton/1470347/story.html

Arctic Environmental Protection Strategy (AEPS) Working Group. 1991. *Arctic Environmental Protection Strategy: Declaration of the Protection of the Arctic Environment*, June 14. Rovaniemi, Finland: AEPS. Accessed May 19, 2008. http://portal.sdwg.org/ media.php?mid=623&xwm=true

Arctic Research Policy Committee. 1994. "Report of the Interagency Arctic Research Policy Committee." *Arctic Research of the United States* 8. Arlington, VA: National Science Foundation.

Bankes, Nigel. 1987. "Forty Years of Canadian Sovereignty Assertion in the Arctic, 1947-87." *Arctic* 40: 285-91.

Canadian Arctic Resources Committee. 1991. "Pondering an Arctic Council." In "Arctic Council: Canada Prepares for a New Era in Circumpolar Relations." Special issue, *Northern Perspectives* 19 (2). Accessed May 19, 2008. http://www.carc.org/pubs/v19no2/1.htm

Dege, Wilhelm. 2003. *War North of 80: The Last German Arctic Weather Station of World War II*. Calgary: University of Calgary Press.

Dosman, E.J. 1976. "The Northern Sovereignty Crisis, 1968-70." In *The Arctic in Question*, edited by E.J. Dosman. Toronto: Oxford University Press.

Downie, David Leonard, and Terry Fenge, eds. 2003. *Northern Lights against POPs: Combatting Toxic Threats in the Arctic*. Montreal and Kingston: McGill-Queen's University Press.

Franckx, Erik. 1993. *Maritime Claims in the Arctic: Canadian and Russian Perspectives*. Dordrecht, Boston and London: Martinus Nijhoff Publishers.

Finance Canada 2009. *Budget 2009: Canada's Economic Action Plan*. Ottawa: Finance

Canada. Accessed April 20, 2009. http://www.budget.gc.ca/2009/plan/bptoc-eng.asp.

———. 2008. *Budget 2008: Responsible Leadership*, February. Ottawa: Department of Finance Canada. Accessed May 23, 2008. http://www.budget.gc.ca/2008/plan/table-eng.asp

Foreign Affairs and International Trade Canada (DFAIT). 2009a. "Canada's Arctic Foreign Policy." Notes for an address by the Honourable Lawrence Cannon, Minister of Foreign Affairs, on March 11. Accessed April 20, 2009. http://w01.international.gc.ca/minpub/Publication.aspx?isRedirect=True&publication_id=386933&language=E&docnumber=2009/11

———. 2009b. " Our Sovereignty in the Arctic: A Priority for the Government of Canada." Notes for an address by the Honourable Lawrence Cannon, Minister of Foreign Affairs, to the Montreal Council on Foreign Relations on March 27. Accessed April 20, 2009. http://w01.international.gc.ca/minpub/Publication.aspx?isRedirect=True&publication_id=386986&Language=E&docnumber=2009/14

———. 1995a. "The Arctic Council: Objectives, Structures and Program Priorities," May. Ottawa: DFAIT.

———. 1995b. "Canada's Proposal to Establish an Arctic Council of the Eight Arctic Nations," April. Ottawa: DFAIT.

Garber, Kent. 2009 "Oil Drilling Debate Rages on, 20 Years after the Valdez Spill." *US News and World Report*, April 19.

Government of Canada. 2005. *Canada's International Policy Statement: A Role of Pride and Influence in the World*. Ottawa: Government of Canada. Accessed May 14, 2008. http://www.international.gc.ca and http://www.forces.gc.ca

———. 2007. *Strong Leadership. A Better Canada. Speech from the Throne, October 16, 2007*, 39th Parliament, 2nd sess. Ottawa: Government of Canada. Accessed May 14, 2008. http://www.sft-ddt.gc.ca/grfx/docs/ sftddt-e.pdf

Grant, Shelagh. 1988. *Sovereignty or Security? Government Policy in the Canadian North, 1936-1950*. Vancouver: University of British Columbia Press.

Gregoire, Lisa. 2007. "River of Money." *Canadian Geographic*, September-October.

Griffiths, Franklyn. 2003. "The Shipping News: Canada's Arctic Sovereignty Not on Thinning Ice." *International Journal* 58 (2): 257-82.

———. 2004. "Is Canada's Arctic Sovereignty Threatened?" *WWF Arctic Bulletin* 1.04: 15-16. Accessed May 26, 2008. http://assets.panda.org/downloads/ab0104.pdf

Griffiths, Franklyn, Rosemarie Kuptana, John Amagoalik, William Erasmus, Cindy Gilday, Stephen Hazell, John Lamb, and Mary Simon. 1991. "To Establish an International Arctic Council: A Framework Report." In "Arctic Council: Canada Prepares for a New Era in Circumpolar Relations." Special issue, *Northern Perspectives* 19 (2). Accessed May 19, 2008. http://www.carc.org/pubs/v19no2/2.htm

Hassol, Susan Joy. 2004. *Impacts of a Warming Arctic: Arctic Climate Impact Assessment*. Cambridge: Cambridge University Press. Accessed May 26, 2008. http://www.amap.no/acia/

Huebert, Rob. 1995. "Polar Vision or Tunnel Vision: The Making of Canadian Arctic Waters Policy." *Marine Policy* 19 (4): 343-63.

———. 1998. "New Directions in Circumpolar Cooperation: Canada, the Arctic Environmental Protection Strategy and the Arctic Council." *Canadian Foreign Policy* 5 (2): 37-58.

———. 2003. "The Shipping News Part II: How Canada's Arctic Sovereignty Is on Thinning Ice." *International Journal* 58 (3): 295-308.

———. 2004. "The Coming Arctic Maritime Sovereignty Crisis." *WWF Arctic Bulletin* 2.04: 22-4. Accessed May 26, 2008. http://assets.panda.org/downloads/ab0204.pdf

———. 2005. "Return of the Vikings." In *Breaking Ice – Renewable Resource and Ocean Management in the Canadian North*, edited by Fikret Berkes, Rob Huebert, Helen Fast, Micheline Manseau and Alan Diduck. Calgary: University of Calgary Press and Arctic Institute of North America.

Jones, Jeffery. 2007. "Beaufort Crawl." *National Post*, October 25.

Kindred, Hugh M., Jean-Gabriel Castel, William C. Graham, Ivan A. Vlasic, Donald J. Fleming, Armand L.C. de Mestral, and Sharon A. Williams. 1987. *International Law Chiefly as Interpreted and Applied in Canada*. 4th ed. Toronto: Emond Montgomery Publications.

Kirkey, Christopher. 1995. "Smoothing Troubled Waters: The 1988 Canada-United States Arctic Co-operation Agreement." *International Journal* 50 (2): 401-26.

Kirton, John, and Don Munton. 1987. "The *Manhattan* Voyages and Their Aftermath." In *Politics of the Northwest Passage*, edited by Franklyn Griffiths. Montreal and Kingston: McGill-Queen's University Press.

Kurdrik, Igor. 2003. "Typhoon Subs to Ship Oil and Gas," May 15. Oslo: Bellona. Accessed May 26, 2008. http://www.bellona.no/en/international/russia/navy/northern_fleet/vessels/29577.html

McRae, Don. 1987. "The Negotiation of Article 234." In *Politics of the Northwest Passage*, edited by Franklyn Griffiths. Montreal and Kingston: McGill-Queen's University Press.

Mitchell, Alanna. 2000. "The Northwest Passage Thawed." *Globe and Mail*, February 5.

Natural Resources Canada. 2008. *Canada: A Diamond-Producing Nation*, April 17. Accessed May 15, 2008. http://www.nrcan-rncan.gc.ca/mms/diam/index_e.htm

Nickerson, Colin. 2000. "Girding for a Sea Change: With Ice Thinning, Canada Claims a Northwest Passage." *Boston Globe*, March 21.

Pharand, Donat. 1988. *Canada's Arctic Waters in International Law*. Cambridge: Cambridge University Press.

Rolston, Susan, and Ted McDorman. 1988. "Maritime Boundary Making in the Arctic Region." In *Ocean Boundary Making: Regional Issues and Developments*, edited by

Douglas M. Johnston and Phillip M. Saunders. Vancouver: University of British Columbia Press.

Scrivener, David. 1989. *Gorbachev's Murmansk Speech: The Soviet Initiative and Western Response*. Oslo: Norwegian Atlantic Committee, 1989.

———. 1996. *Environmental Cooperation in the Arctic: From Strategy to Council*. Security Policy Library 1. Oslo: Norwegian Atlantic Committee.

Struck, Doug. 2006. "Dispute over Northwest Passage Revived." *Washington Post*, November 6.

US National Security Presidential Directive 66/Homeland Security Presidential Directive 25. 2009. "Arctic Region Policy." The White House of President George W. Bush. Accessed April 20, 2009. http://www.fas.org/irp/offdocs/nspd/nspd-66.htm

Canadian Arctic Sovereignty: Time to Take Yes for an Answer on the Northwest Passage

T HOSE OF US WHO FOLLOW ARCTIC AFFAIRS HAVE BEEN HEARING OF A WIDENING array of threats to Canadian sovereignty for several years now.[1] Such threats tend to be framed as challenges to Canadian Arctic possession. What's ours and what might be lost to Denmark in the offshore delimitation of the water column and seabed in the Lincoln Sea will be known only to the most attentive. More familiar is our disagreement with the United States over our maritime boundary and therefore who owns what in, and under a part of, the Beaufort Sea. Virtually everyone who's been following the news will have heard of Hans Island, a small piece of rock in the strait between Greenland and Ellesmere Island whose ownership is contested by Canada and Denmark. And now we've begun to witness an international scramble for the resources of the outer continental shelf under the Arctic Ocean — a rush for riches that, many believe, could see us lose out if we fail to stand up for what's ours. But it's the Northwest Passage that continues to tower above all other of our Arctic sovereignty concerns. It does so by virtue of the direct connection between the passage and the Canadian identity. It does so because of the proven ability of perceived challenges to possession, principally by the United States, to mobilize real passion among the great southern majority of Canadians. This chapter therefore focuses on the Northwest Passage as prototypical of Canadian thinking and practice on matters of Arctic sovereignty. It calls for a radical reconsideration of how we southerners imagine the Arctic and what needs doing there.

Let us rid ourselves of the apprehension and self-doubt that surround the discussion of sovereignty over the passage and the need to assert it in an era of global warming and easier international navigation in Arctic waters. The facts are different. We do not merely claim but have unquestioned possession of the islands, waters, seabed and subsoil of the Canadian Arctic Archipelago. The United States agrees that this is the situation but also insists that the varied waterways that make up the Northwest Passage are in the ensemble an international strait through which the government and private vessels of all countries have rights of unencumbered passage. We say the passage consists of internal waters, which are open, or closed, to foreign navigation as mandated by the will, laws and regulations of Canada. Accordingly, if we have a serious problem in the Northwest Passage, it has to do not with possession but with foreign transit through waters that are incontrovertibly our own.

A problem does indeed arise, because the sovereign needs not only to possess but to control the space that's hers. Even on this account, however, things are going our way. Due largely to our own efforts and partly to processes not of our making, we are in a position to exercise rights of exclusive jurisdiction over the Northwest Passage and to make that jurisdiction fully effective for foreign *private* vessels. When it comes to the sovereignty challenge posed by the merchant ships of other countries, the outlook is getting better for Canada, not worse. As I will show, there is reason here for congratulation and good cheer.

As to the exclusion or admission of foreign *government* ships, the situation is less promising. This is largely because naval vessels, unlike merchant ships, can fight. Canada, I will argue, is unable alone to prevent unauthorized entry and transit of the archipelago either by foreign nuclear submarines throughout the year at present, or by conventional submarines and warships in the course of a lengthening and ultimately a wholly ice-free summer. Simply put, we are not going to risk nuclear contamination of the Northwest Passage in pursuit of sovereignty over it. But then we are not without prospects where foreign navies are concerned. We have allies. With them, we already seem to operate according to arrangements that provide for some degree of authorized entry into the passage and that circumvent differences of opinion on its status in international law. And in future consultation with them, we can create common security arrangements that give us assured authority and backing to police the archipelago against unauthorized naval activity in peacetime — which is ordinarily most of the time, and could be all of the time if the ice states are able to build new structures of cooperation and arms control against a remilitarization of the Arctic as a region.

Aided by our own actions, circumstances are conspiring to give us virtually all the privileges and benefits of sovereignty over the government and private vessels of other countries wishing to traverse or enter the Northwest Passage. Going with a favourable flow of events, we should now be dealing directly with the United States, which has quietly been saying yes to unilateral Canadian action and multilateral initiatives that are consistent with exclusive Canadian jurisdiction. In a word, we ought now to take yes for an answer in a set of cooperative arrangements that deepen and widen the Canada-US agreement to disagree on the Northwest Passage. With worries over the Northwest Passage diminishing, we should be able to move forward with confidence and vigour into the Arctic region that's now opening before us.

All of this runs directly against the grain of contemporary Canadian discourse. It needs explaining, to say nothing of justification. I will therefore first consider the problem of the Northwest Passage as typically understood in this country. Thereafter I will elaborate on the solution as I see it. Finally, I will ask how Canada might best make the transition from a what's-mine-is-mine stance governed by fear of loss to a dynamic pursuit of gain through an active engagement in circumpolar affairs.

The Problem as Currently Understood

SOVEREIGNTY IS THE ABILITY OF THE STATE TO EXERCISE RECOGNIZED RIGHTS OF exclusive jurisdiction within a territorially delimited space. There is a lot packed into these few words. But it comes down to the capacity to do two things: to secure recognition of one's rights, and to act on or enact these rights. Recognition and enactment — the latter understood not as legislation but as performance — are interconnected. The more secure the recognition of one's rights or claims to exclusive jurisdiction, the more effective their enactment will be; the more potent one's ability to act on the same rights or claims, the greater the likelihood they will be acknowledged by others.

In its approach to Arctic sovereignty, Canada has until recently favoured recognition over enactment. When not a lot was happening in the waters of the Canadian Arctic Archipelago, and not a lot was therefore required by way of on-site action, we endeavoured to persuade others to accept our claims and subsidiary arguments without giving them compelling reasons to believe we could and would enforce them. Nevertheless, the United States and the member states of the European Union have continued to regard the passage as an international strait through which the vessels and aircraft of all countries have very considerable rights of transit under the 1982 United Nations Convention on the Law of the Sea (UNC-LOS). In our view, the waters of our Arctic Archipelago are internal to Canada, bereft of any foreign right of transit and fully open to foreign navigation in accordance with Canadian law and Canadian regulations, all in keeping with the law of the sea (McRae 2007).

Though it's impossible to predict how the Canadian position might be constructed if ever the issue went to law, we seem likely to argue that the waters that make up the Northwest Passage (see map on following page) are as internal to Canada as those of Lake Winnipeg. Being internal, they are subject to the sovereign will of Canada and to that will alone. These waters are internal by virtue of historic title transferred to us from Britain, transferred from Inuit who are now Canadian and have occupied them since time immemorial, and by virtue of decades of effective Canadian occupation and control. The waters in question were not so much enclosed as delimited in 1986, when we, following generally accepted legal practice, drew straight baselines from headland to headland around the entire archipelago to make clear where our internal waters end and the 12-mile territorial sea begins. Although UNCLOS article 234 allows us to regulate commercial and other private vessels for purposes of pollution prevention out to 200 miles beyond the baselines, the authority granted here has no direct bearing on Canada's internal waters claim (though clearly it does assist in controlling the approaches to the passage). In short, Canada claims and indeed has the unfettered historic right to permit and deny access to foreign government (naval, coast guard, oceanographic) and private (commercial, adventurer, pleasure) vessels wishing to transit or merely enter the Arctic Archipelago.

The United States, for its part in a future court proceeding, could well dispute Canada's historic waters claim, together with the length and other features of the baselines we have drawn. But the main burden of the US argument would surely go to show that, in keeping with the convention, the channels of the Canadian Arctic Archipelago constitute an international strait in that they join two high-seas areas and are used for international navigation. The geography

Potential Intercontinental Shipping Routes

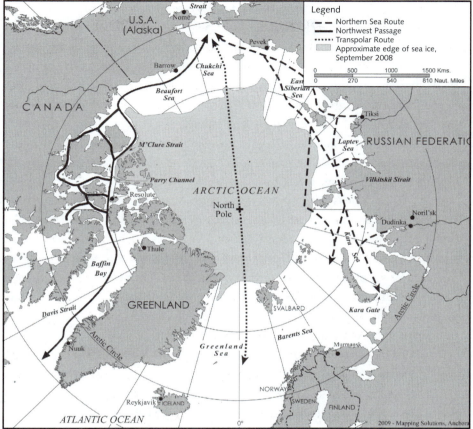

being what it is, the key contentions in the US case could revolve around the number of transits required to constitute international use, the number of transits that have been made, and the number of transits made not in conformity with Canadian regulations but in disregard and defiance of them. How the deliberation on questions such as these might unfold is anyone's guess. But the United States could have a case, especially if we start to experience conflicted transits in the years ahead.

Sovereignty conflicts often come down to a struggle for possession. But not where the Northwest Passage is concerned. When we consider the legalities, our dispute with the United States and other maritime powers is about terms of transit, not about ownership or possession, which is assured under the law of the sea.

Both Canada and the United States take the passage to be open for international navigation. At issue is the nature and extent of coastal state control and maritime state freedom to proceed. Knowledgeable Canadians tend to believe that coastal state control over foreign vessels would be substantially less under a straits regime than when the waters concerned are treated as internal to Canada. The principal issues here are pollution of the marine environment and the vulnerability of Inuit to economic and cultural deprivation. There is truth to this view, but rather less than we might expect, as we will see in a moment.

Meanwhile, I take it to be the general opinion of Canadians that the Northwest Passage and all it stands for cannot and must not be surrendered if Canada is fully to pursue a destiny of its own on the continent of North America. "Use it or lose it" has become the watchword. Many of us seem to believe we could actually lose the passage to other states — indeed, to the United States. The premise is misguided. The slogan should be stricken from our vocabulary. Canadians should know that they have not been, and continue not to be, informed of the realities by a succession of federal governments only too pleased to talk the talk of an imperilled Arctic sovereignty. Nor has the Canadian public been made aware of an evolution in the ability of Canada and the United States to manage their Arctic waters differences to mutual advantage.

Pursuing international recognition of our right to prevent pollution in the passage, Canada's diplomats achieved a triumph in securing US assent in 1982 to UNCLOS article 234 (McRae 1987). In so doing, they made consensual Canada's *Arctic Waters Pollution Prevention Act, 1970 (AWPPA)*, which was enacted unilaterally in the wake of the intrusive voyages of the US supertanker *Manhattan* in 1969-70. Then, following the unauthorized transit of the US icebreaker *Polar Sea* in 1985, a further Canadian initiative resulted in the Arctic Cooperation Agreement of 1988, which sidestepped the dispute in allowing the two coast guards to collaborate in the Arctic waters of North America without prejudice to the legal position of either party. Net effect as of the late 1980s, and indeed today: agreement to disagree, which enables both countries to work together on matters of mutual interest despite our dispute on the law. And then, in the 1990s, an awareness of climate change came upon the scene.

As of about 2000, Arctic sovereignty became directly linked to a growing awareness of global warming that no right-minded Canadian could ignore. Thus was born the sovereignty-on-thinning-ice thesis: in melting Arctic sea ice, global warming promised to open the Northwest Passage to high volumes of intercontinental commercial shipping, which could not but result in a US, or a US-backed, legal challenge to Canada's sovereignty claim based on flag-state objections to Canadian regulatory action. Note that when climate change is accentuated in the way we frame our sovereignty problem, attention is biased toward surface vessels — the comings and goings of nuclear-powered submarines not being greatly affected by ice conditions. Although public opinion and the media might also have been exercised by the imminence of foreign ice-capable surface naval ships in Canada's Arctic waters, proponents of the thinning-ice thesis chose to focus on the prospect of new intercontinental commercial navigation and how it might play into the Canada-US dispute over the passage (Huebert 2002, 2003, 2004, 2007; Byers and Lalonde 2006; Byers 2006b, 2007c). All along, I disagreed (Griffiths 2003, 2004, 2006).

The scenario as it first appeared was one that confronted us with a challenge of steadily growing urgency: the more rapidly the passage is emptied of ice, the greater its allure to commercial shipping firms, which stand to save their container ships and bulk carriers travelling between Asia and the North Atlantic thousands of miles, as they will not have to resort to the Suez or Panama canal. In turn, the greater the volume of transits, the more likely it is that one firm or another will sail as though the passage were an international strait — which is to say, without proper regard for Canadian regulations. Accordingly, and in a lengthening chain of argument, we are faced with a greater likelihood of a flag-state legal challenge in the event we take enforcement action; Canadian inaction, which would work strongly against the Canadian claim; or direct intervention by the United States to ensure Canada was brought to court, where we could face an adjudicated loss of sovereignty. All of this is quite alarming, especially when accompanied by expert talk of an "inevitable showdown" with the United States (Harris 2007).

Today, the extent and thickness of sea ice in the Arctic Ocean and within the Canadian Arctic Archipelago continue to diminish with extraordinary rapidity. The focus of sovereignty-on-thinning-ice discourse has, however, shifted from the coming armada of high-value merchantmen to a few tramp ships or rust-bucket tankers, even a single rogue ship, whose illicit or improper voyage — any day now — could gravely weaken Canada's claim if uncontested, or could again prompt us into regulatory action that risks a hostile court ruling.

Leaving aside the potential for pollution, drug and human smuggling, and the landing of terrorists and weapons of mass destruction — all of which those most worried about Canadian Arctic sovereignty are inclined to cite — we can say that climate-related and commercial shipping variables in the sovereignty-on-thinning-ice scenario have boiled down to a fear of imminent legal proceedings stemming from the wayward activities of the occasional small operator. Whether the small operator is to be regarded as a major threat to Arctic sovereignty or a challenge to Canadian law and law enforcement, there should be no question of Canada's need for the hardware to cope with vagrant shipping. Getting the threat right is nevertheless a precondition for getting the hardware together over the course of procurement processes likely to last many years.

The niceties of Arctic threat assessment tend not to be well captured by the attentive, much less by the general public. Quite the contrary: climate-related fear for sovereignty over the Northwest Passage shows signs of morphing into a pervasive concern that the entire High Arctic may be lost. Consider the following from an editorial in the *Winnipeg Free Press*:

> At the moment, the Northwest Passage is not good for much except history lessons and romantic fancies. But if global warming is a long-term reality that leads to even partial melting of the Arctic ice, it will become a hot spot as other nations deny not just this country's claim to the passage, but to the islands around it as well.
>
> This is already happening, to a degree. The Danish claim to Hans Island may seem frivolous, but it possibly forebodes other American and European claims to many other larger and more important islands.
>
> If those claims were pressed, Canada might find itself hard-pressed to refute them. This country's claim to sovereignty over the archipelago is considered by rivals to be only tenuously based — some of the islands were actually discovered by Americans, Danes and Norwegians; others were ceded to Canada by Britain before they had been discovered.

The editorialist ends up saying that with "half the world" waiting to use an open Northwest Passage, for Canada "losing the waterway could mean losing the islands as well" ("Our Arctic" 2007; also, more broadly, Struzik 2007; White 2007).

Meanwhile, the government ships of other countries add a dimension to our Arctic sovereignty problem that is even less well appreciated by the Canadian public. Actually, this is what drew Prime Minister Stephen Harper's attention when first he addressed the theme of Arctic sovereignty.

Speaking in December 2005 in the course of the federal election, the future prime minister declared it intolerable that the submarines of other states should enter the Arctic waters of Canada without Canadian consent. No longer would we acquiesce to the unauthorized naval operations of others — above all, the United States — within Canada. On the contrary: we would acquire new military means to secure respect for Canadian sovereignty.

> The single most important duty of the federal government is to defend and protect our national sovereignty. And now there are new and disturbing reports of American nuclear submarines passing through Canadian waters without obtaining the permission of — or even notifying — the Canadian government.
>
> It's time to act to defend Canadian sovereignty. A Conservative government will make the military investments needed to secure our borders. You don't defend national sovereignty with flags, cheap election rhetoric, and advertising campaigns. You need forces on the ground, ships in the sea, and proper surveillance. And that will be the Conservative approach.
>
> As Prime Minister, I will make it plain to foreign governments — including the United States — that naval vessels travelling in Canadian waters will require the consent of the government of Canada. (Harper 2005)

Clearly, Harper was determined to change the way the Government of Canada spoke and acted on the matter of Arctic sovereignty. Indeed, he went on to commit a Conservative government to installing submarine sensing devices in the passage, procuring and deploying several heavy naval icebreakers, establishing a training base in the High Arctic, building a deepwater seaport and so on.

There was no sign here of the lawyerly interest in international recognition of Canada's right to exercise exclusive jurisdiction over the Northwest Passage. Nor was commercial shipping the threat. Instead, the problem lay in the dereliction of duty on the part of Liberal governments, which had failed to enforce Canada's sovereign rights against foreign naval vessels. Prime Minister Harper entered office firmly prepared to change Canada's sovereignty conversation from recognition to enactment and from the commercial to the naval dimension of the problem.

For interested southerners, the enactment of Arctic sovereignty comes down to surveillance and enforcement. International recognition is not, however, to be ignored. On the contrary, in generating new means for Canada to act in sovereign fashion, Harper might have expected to improve our negotiating position if and when it came time to address the issue of the Northwest Passage directly with the United States. Let us therefore briefly consider what's happened under the headings of surveillance, enforcement and negotiation since the federal election of January 2006. Let us also distinguish between the surface and subsurface waters of the passage.

Surface surveillance has traditionally been performed by the polar ice-breakers of the Canadian Coast Guard. Able to go readily where neither commercial nor naval vessels have yet been able to venture, the polar fleet is aging rapidly and needs to be replaced. I am told that recapitalization of the fleet is well in hand — which is to say, well understood by the Harper government and proceeding as expected through the federal apparatus. Indeed, the February 2008 budget provides $720 million for a new Polar-class icebreaker (El Akkad 2008). Meanwhile, surveillance is being improved with the first Arctic deployment of a Victoria-class Canadian submarine, HMCS *Corner Brook*, and with the launch of RADARSAT-2 in December 2007. During sovereignty operation Nanook, in August 2007, the *Corner Brook* demonstrated a capacity to exercise covert surveillance of vessels of interest in the eastern approaches to the passage (Canuel 2007). As to RADARSAT-2, a commercial venture in which the government has been participating through the Department of National Defence and its Project Polar Epsilon (Taylor 2007), it is soon to give us Arctic surface imagery at about 90-minute intervals, together with follow-on surveillance technology for effective High Arctic governance in coming years.

And then we have the eight naval patrol vessels that are to be acquired and deployed beginning in 2012 (Office of the Prime Minister 2007). Though the doctrine governing the use of these ships is to be determined in the course of a two-year project definition phase, it's clear they will have gun armament and likely they will have no capability for active antisubmarine warfare. They will conduct armed surveillance of the surface. Possibly equipped with an on-board helicopter, they will assist other government departments in the boarding, arrest and detention of private ships deemed to be in violation of Canadian regulations or to present a security threat. This they will do in our internal waters, and out to the end of the exclusive economic zone and beyond, on all three coasts, in the course of a 25-year service life. In the Arctic, they will be active during the months in which private vessels (such as merchant and fishing vessels) are likely to approach and venture into the Arctic Archipelago. Costing $3.1 billion to build and $4.3 billion to sustain, and dedicated to the performance of constabulary tasks for which the coast guard is better suited, these new vessels will be financed from the existing capital allocation for the navy. What navy, I ask, will persevere in championing an acquisition that not only obliges it to break ice in its own internal waters but also comes out of its own hide?

Irrespective of what happens to the naval patrol vessel program, it's fair to say that Canada's ability to exercise surveillance over the surface waters of the Northwest Passage has improved since January 2006, and this should stand us in good stead in responding to modest increases in the level of foreign commercial and other surface-ship activity in the years ahead. Might the same be said of the subsurface?

Through NORAD, if not NATO as well, we would seem to have some awareness of nonallied submarine activity around and within North American waters, notwithstanding continued formal rejection of our Arctic sovereignty claim by our allies. This inference follows from the fact that for many years we operated extremely silent diesel submarines and are now doing so again. An implication: within NATO and NORAD, we may for years have participated in allied Arctic maritime surveillance on the basis of without-prejudice "agree-to-disagree" arrangements, on which the 1988 Canada-US cooperation agreement could also have been patterned. A further implication: if allied intelligence sharing is what it should be, the new national submarine sensor system that was Harper's first promise in his sovereignty speech of December 2005 is not a necessity. But now we learn that Canada is to test and report on available submarine sensing technologies by 2010 (Defence Research and Development Canada 2008).

Whatever the reasons for this announcement — fulfillment of a campaign pledge, preliminaries for an independent Canadian contribution to NORAD maritime domain awareness — it gives rise to a question: What do we intend to do when the sensors are deployed and we detect a foreign submarine voyaging in the passage without our say-so? No way would we take ourselves to court by contesting the legal right of the state concerned to voyage in our waters. Nor would we confine ourselves to public protest: in advertising unauthorized naval activity, we would help to establish an international practice that contravened our claim. Instead, the sensor announcement implies Canadian readiness to establish and defend the archipelago as a keep-out zone for unauthorized naval vessels. This brings us to the enforcement of Canadian jurisdiction.

There's really not a lot to say here. Whether we do or don't end up with a small fleet of modestly Arctic-capable naval patrol vessels, it's my view that coast guard icebreakers already suffice and will likely continue to do so in providing for effective law enforcement with regard to private-vessel activity in the archipelago. Others, anticipating a surge of intercontinental commercial shipping or an increase in the frequency of voyages by accident-prone and ill-intentioned tramp ships, are sure to disagree. They may well be representative of prevailing opinion when it comes to our enforcement capabilities in maintaining sovereignty over the Northwest Passage. Meanwhile, there has been virtually no public discussion of how Canada might enforce its will in denying access to the subsurface waters of the archipelago to foreign submarines making unauthorized voyages. Nor, beyond the exploration of submarine-sensing technologies, has the federal government hinted at how we might defend our claim with armed force, as proposed by Harper in December 2005. And yet it's just such things that would be front and centre if we were somehow to enter a negotiation with the United States.

The idea in negotiating is that since the events of September 2001, US national security interests have changed sufficiently to warrant a new Canadian approach to Washington on the status of the Northwest Passage in international law (Byers and Lalonde 2006, 34). Specifically, the United States no longer gains from a position that treats the passage as an international strait and thereby gives ready entry to foreign vessels, which may be carrying terrorists, weapons of mass destruction and the like into northernmost North America for transfer southward. Meeting with President George Bush at the North American Leaders' Summit at Montebello in August 2007, Prime Minister Harper reportedly suggested something like this, only to be told that whereas the United States supported greater Canadian defence preparedness in the Arctic, there was no change in the US position on the passage as strait (Foot and Greenaway 2007; Freeman 2007). Although for now the Prime Minister shows no signs of readiness to pursue things beyond the exchange at Montebello, some in Canada have favoured formal negotiation (Byers 2006a; Pharand 2006; New Democratic Party of Canada 2007).

If advice in favour of negotiating wth the United States were taken, we would no doubt stay focused on the Arctic sovereignty theme over the next two or three years. By holding one or more informal Canada-US consultations on the matter, we might possibly familiarize Congress, the executive and American influentials outside of government with the issues. Either a coalition of the willing would be built in the United States, or the president would be persuaded of the wisdom of a Northwest Passage in Canadian hands. In any event, talks would be ordered. The two sides would sit down and work out an exchange in which US recognition of our claim was traded for assured US transit though the passage and fully effective Canadian suppression of terrorist and other asymmetrical security threats that might appear in the archipelago.

The main problem here is that, from an American point of view, international law already gives the US the right of transit through a Northwest Passage that has never been — nor is ever likely to be — well secured by Canada. I am reminded of my days as a keen defender of endangered Canadian Arctic sovereignty in the early 1970s, when I said to a senior US naval officer that the American position on the passage opened our waters to Soviet nuclear submarine operations, only to be told, "Don't you worry, we'll look after those subs." Back then, I took the remark as a sign of US presumption and readiness to intrude. But it could as well have been heard as a statement of readiness to assist in something we were not equipped to handle alone.

Be this as it may, commentators on Canadian Arctic sovereignty continue to focus on the civil and commercial dimensions of our problem. Specifically, it's proposed that Canada and the United States work out a transit management system for the Northwest Passage, modelled perhaps on the St. Lawrence Seaway and the International Joint Commission (Byers 2007a; Flemming 2007). It's also thought that Canada should actively promote and support intercontinental navigation by foreign firms on Canadian terms (Byers 2007c). As of early 2008, formal negotiation with the United States for a binational Northwest Passage seaway is yet to be excluded as a route to US acceptance of our internal waters claim.

Viewing the entirety of our sovereignty problem, I suggest that we've talked ourselves into believing we are challenged more severely in the Northwest Passage than actually we are. In reality, the issue is not possession but the conditions under which foreign vessels will sail into and through the Canadian Arctic Archipelago. The public has come to believe that considerably more is at stake than this. Academic purveyors of polar peril bear some of the responsibility for this state of affairs. But the sovereignty-on-thinning-ice scenario and the focus on foreign commercial ships would not have been received the way they have been if the media and the public at large weren't already disposed to a discourse of fear and apprehension over sovereignty and possession. Nor would thinning-ice worries have deflected public interest from the naval dimension of our problem. Nearly 40 years after the first of the *Manhattan* voyages, the great majority of southern Canadians are still caught up in what's-ours-is-ours Arctic thinking from behind the lines of sovereign authority. Such is our stance at a time when the entire circumpolar North is coming alive.

The Solution

I N OFFERING A SOLUTION TO OUR ARCTIC WATERS DILEMMA, I WILL CONSIDER FIRST THE commercial shipping threat to our internal waters claim and its enactment, and then the naval dimension of our situation — all with our principal adversary in mind. Where merchant vessels are concerned, we need to address the economics of intercontinental shipping through the Northwest Passage; comparative ice conditions; US continental security interests in light of the events of September 2001; and the evolving legal context as it relates to the status of, and Canadian rights over, the waters of the Arctic Archipelago.

For the first time in recorded history, the Parry Channel was almost clear of ice and easily navigable from one end to the other in September 2007. Sea ice is indeed retreating in the Arctic Ocean and in the archipelago. Barring the appearance of nonlinear effects, the Northwest Passage shipping season will continue to lengthen. Some of us are sure to entertain new illusions of a Canadian Arctic throughway that cuts thousands of kilometres off the sailing distance between Asia and the North Atlantic. Let us therefore rehearse the realities likely to be met by the shipping firm that would begin to use the Northwest Passage for reliable intercontinental navigation in the course of the next couple of decades. These realities came to the fore in July 2007 at a conference in Washington, DC, on the effects of an ice-diminished Arctic on naval and maritime operations. Sponsored by the US Navy and attended by Canadian ice scientists, who participated actively, the gathering produced a valuable update on conditions and prospects for Arctic navigation (Falkingham 2007). I'll comment and elaborate on the proceedings as they relate to the Northwest Passage, in particular.

Variability of ice conditions continues to be "extreme." Formed in the dark and cold of winter, seasonal sea ice can be absent or very challenging in the course of the summer months. From one year to another, and within the archipelago from one location to another, new ice also varies in extent and thickness. But in its difficulty and danger it pales in comparison with the old ice that will persist in the passage until it has disappeared entirely from up in the archipelago and out in the ocean. This old sea ice has lost its salt. Hard as concrete, it is lethal to the vessel not strengthened against it.

International shipping is conducted as a year-round liner business in which every day lost risks scheduling disasters and financial losses. When it encounters high seas, fog, twilight and old ice, a thin-skinned ship cannot expect to run the passage at speeds allowed in temperate waters. Ice-condition variability and the continued presence of old ice also negate predictable and therefore regular use of the passage by high-value vessels sailing on tight schedules. Add the necessity to ice-strengthen in order to steam with greater assurance and speed during the summer months, add the need to amortize the cost of strengthening a ship that sails the greatest part of the year in ice-free waters, add insurance expenses, including the inevitable deductibles — and the economic advantage in using the Northwest Passage to move cargo between the Atlantic and the Pacific all but vanishes.

Major messages arising from the July 2007 gathering on Arctic operations are that "ship traffic will be overwhelmingly destinational and dominated by the development of natural resources and tourism," and that "ocean to ocean transit shipping will not develop significantly for a long time" (Falkingham 2007, 2). In short, the Northwest Passage will see an increase in commercial shipping, but it will move in and out of sites in Arctic North America and not between the Atlantic and Pacific in volume any time soon. And yet there's something more that needs saying about intercontinental Arctic shipping before we turn to the sovereignty threat of destination voyages.

Let us imagine an Arctic region that's totally free of ice in the summer months. Let us also find someone with the software required to determine the length of alternative shipping routes and then ask who might sail where between Asia and the North Atlantic — actually, between Yokohama and Rotterdam or New York. Right away, it becomes clear that the shortest trade route between Yokohama and Rotterdam is right over the pole: 12,074 kilometres, as opposed to 14,759 kilometres via the Parry Channel, the straight-through Northwest Passage route between M'Clure Strait and Baffin Bay (see the map on page 111). Barring other variables that might compel liner ships to take longer routes, the passage — a 14,111-kilometre Yokohama-New York trade route — will be the route of choice for vessels sailing only between Asian markets and ports on the eastern seaboard of North America. By the same token, Russa's northern sea route will be favoured for shipping between Asian and northern ports. This suggests that development of an intercontinental passage through the Arctic waters of North America — for instance, the generation of infrastructure and management rules for safe and efficient navigation — would in essence be a joint Canada-US enterprise. But how much should Canada pay and indeed charge to help move cargo between US and Asian ports? Meanwhile, there's still plenty of ice, and there's also the Panama Canal. Widened to accommodate the largest of container ships, the canal could prove more attractive than the Northwest Passage for destinations south of New York (Somanathan, Flynn and Szymanski 2007).

As for foreign ships sailing to and from Canadian Arctic locations, they will of necessity conform to Canadian regulations. They therefore pose no challenge to Canadian authority. Destination shipping that might offer a challenge is confined to the movement of US bulk cargo and equipment in and out of the Beaufort Sea and North Slope. Here the US interest in conflict avoidance may come into play. The events of September 2001 would seem to have altered the politics of the Northwest Passage in the United States by adding to the force of pre-existing agree-to-disagree considerations (Griffiths 2003). Dictates of the global war on terror have made the US government not only less likely to act on its view of the passage as a strait, or to welcome third-party efforts to straiten the archipelago, but also more likely to value Arctic cooperation with Canada.

Even though the American people and their leaders seem to know even less about the Arctic than they do about Canada, advisers on Canadian affairs are sure to report that an active US effort to impose a straits regime on the Northwest Passage would create a furor in Canada. Canadians would turn in rage and humiliation against the United States at a time when continental security requires ever more intimate and effective cooperation. Best, therefore, for Washington to steer clear of confrontation. And while this is inference on my part, there's fact as well. US officials — for example, Admiral Thad Allen, Commandant of the US Coast Guard; Commander James Kraska, oceans policy adviser to the Joint Chiefs of Staff; and Mead Treadwell, Chair of the US Arctic Research Commission — have been signalling an interest in Canada-US Arctic waters cooperation that's inconsistent with prevailing Canadian conceptions of inflexible US opposition.

To be specific, Admiral Allen is strongly in favour of extending Canada-US cooperation in North Pacific oil spill response and search and rescue into the Arctic. As well, he says, "Now is the time to look for international coordinating mechanisms and establish governance models that can help us all develop whatever is going to go on in the Arctic in terms of policy, presence and national interests in a way that benefits us all in a world that we all share together" (Allen 2007, 7). To the extent that the Commandant speaks for the US government, his is a recipe for working it out, getting along and finding a way together, including through Canada-US Arctic relations. Kraska, who cannot but be in the loop, makes no bones about the Northwest Passage being an international strait. Nevertheless, he would not override the Canadian view; instead, he speaks of opportunities for Canada to "attract support for appropriate measures to protect the Arctic ecosystem, ensure Canadian security and sovereignty, and promote safe navigation through designated routes through the vast northern expanse" (Kraska 2007, 59). To these ends, he proposes that Canada consider an International Maritime Organization (IMO)-led multilateral straits management model, such as the one already used for the Straits of Malacca and Singapore. For his part, Treadwell favours not just an IMO-multilateral approach but an Arctic regime similar to the one the US and Canada share in the St. Lawrence Seaway and the Great Lakes, "where coordinated investment and joint action has made operational issues across national borders virtually seamless." The St. Lawrence Seaway being a binational operation in which Canada has complete authority over what occurs on the Canadian side, he seems willing to countenance a Northwest Passage management regime in which, irrespective of differences over the law, the two parties each assume exclusive responsibility for what goes on in their respective areas. Citing UNCLOS article 234 as a means of "conflict avoidance," he also refers to "sovereign-type control in an area in which sovereignty is under dispute" (Treadwell 2008, 4, 12).

None of this is to say there's zero risk of another *Manhattan*. But the basis for getting along together is wider now. Given stated US preferences, the likelihood of a confrontation is in decline. Furthermore, a third party wishing to contest Canadian jurisdiction in the passage will now find it difficult to secure US backing. Foreign vessels that pose an environmental, social or security threat to Canada can expect to be at the mercy of Canadian law and law enforcement. They are therefore likely to desist from a challenge.

Barring serious error on the part of Canadian and US policy-makers, the United States will exercise restraint in furthering its legal position, Canada will exercise Canadian jurisdiction in regulating foreign shipping, and what might be called the rustbucket threat to Canadian Arctic sovereignty will very largely disappear. We are not going to be taken to court as we monitor and respond to the actions of small private operators in the archipelago. Nor do we face an onrush of intercontinental shipping between the North Atlantic and North Pacific. Nor, as we were reminded at Montebello, is the United States going to surrender its position on the status of the Northwest Passage in international law. Canada and the United States seem set on agree-to-disagree as the best they can do in the management of foreign shipping in the Arctic waters of North America.

At first sight, agree-to-disagree is likely to be viewed as an inferior and even unworthy solution to our Arctic sovereignty problem, which must be resolved with general and complete acceptance of our claim. But, as I see it, agree-to-disagree arrangements, propelled by the Canadian side, represent very real progress in the two parties' handling of their Arctic waters differences. What we have here is a proven way of coping that could be extended from the icebreakers to the commercial and indeed the naval vessels of both countries. It would allow us to move, if we wished, from agree-to-disagree on one class of ship to a wider, without-prejudice arrangement whereby cooperative activity in waters claimed by Canada to be internal would proceed under Canadian authority. This kind of formula has in fact arisen in Canada-US security cooperation — for example, in planning for the renewal and expansion of NORAD. The awkward passage reads, "Being able to control what goes on above and under the waters within Canadian and US jurisdiction requires mechanisms that facilitate critical capabilities to...[f]ulfill the responsibilities implicit in claiming jurisdiction over certain bodies of water" (Bi-national Planning Group 2004, 37-8). There is no reason why wording like this should not be extended to US destination shipping eastward through the passage from the North Slope of Alaska.

In Canada, the thought of shipping to and from American locations in Arctic North America is sure to be associated with the *Manhattan* episode and the necessity to avoid a repetition of it. US opposition to Canada's internal waters claim does not, however, signify indifference to the risk of pollution in the passage. Quite the contrary — US commercial vessels would need to sail the Northwest Passage in accordance with Canada's *Arctic Waters Pollution Prevention Act*, or themselves proceed without the backing of the US government. In the 1992 issue of the Limits in the Seas series entitled *United States Responses to Excessive National Maritime Claims*, the State Department refers in passing to the *AWPPA*:

> "The United States continues to object to the application of the law in so far as it purports to apply to sovereign immune vessels. The United States believes that internationally agreed standards should be developed to replace many of the unilateral provisions. However, the United States considers U.S. commercial vessels subject to this law. The United States has agreed to consult with Canada in the development of standards and operational procedures to facilitate commercial navigation in the Arctic." (United States Department of State 1992, 73).

This US government position is not widely known in Canada. It means that article 234 applies in the Northwest Passage when the latter is taken to be an international strait. It should now be reaffirmed by the State Department (Borgerson and Griffiths 2007).

Unless the US government has changed its mind, US merchant ships in transit through the Northwest Passage may be expected to conform, as others already do, to Canada's pollution prevention regulations under the *AWPPA*. Commercial vessels that are US-owned or carrying US cargo would be unlikely to challenge any reasonable application of our regulations. If they did, they could not rely upon the US government, which does not wholly oppose Canada on the matter and even gives effect to the Canadian legislation. Furthermore, if and when US commercial vessels are seen to comply in moving oil and liquefied natural gas eastward from the Beaufort Sea, the merchant ships of other states will be less likely to contest Canadian regulations and their enforcement.

With few third-party intercontinental transits in the offing and the prospect of US compliance with Canadian pollution prevention legislation governing merchant vessels in destination mode, the notion of deep-seated Canada-US conflict over what is to transpire in the Northwest Passage starts to melt away. Thinking in terms of internal waters and strait status as the two possible outcomes of the dispute begins to yield to the idea of an intermediate solution in which there's little to bar Canada from the nondiscriminatory exercise of sovereign rights to regulate foreign commercial shipping. Strongly influenced by the practicalities of the Canada-US relationship, this development also owes something to the collapse of the distinction between internal waters and international strait where the Northwest Passage is concerned.

With the negotiation of article 234, Canada normalized the provisions of the *AWPPA* by entering them into the international consensus on the law of the sea. The regulations issued by Canada pursuant to the *AWPPA* were, however, a different matter in that the particular standards applied by Canada were ahead of the consensus and difficult to update unilaterally in light of changing polar ship technology and design. Now, as a consequence of a lengthy Canadian initiative, the *AWPPA* regulations (AWPPR) have also been normalized. They became consensual when, in March 2008, the member societies of the International Association of Classification Societies (IACS) completed their ratification of a new set of uniform requirements for polar ship construction, equipment, operations and environmental protection (International Association of Classification Societies 2006). This they did as mandated by the IMO, pursuant to the latter's 2002 Guidelines for Ships Operating in Arctic Ice-Covered Waters (Brigham 2000; International Maritime Organization 2002). Both the IMO guidelines and the IACS uniform requirements have the support of the United States.

Canadian regulations for ship safety and pollution prevention in ice-covered waters that we regard as internal to Canada have now become pretty well synonymous with the "generally accepted regulations, procedures and practices" governing the duties of ships in what might otherwise be regarded as an international strait under article 39 of UNCLOS. Actually, the new international standards constructed with Canadian leadership are superior to the AWPPR, which have not been revised since they were issued, in 1972. Be they applied by Canada in what we take to be our internal waterways or in Canadian waters that another state regards as an international strait, the standards we employ in regulating commercial activity in the Northwest Passage are now harder than ever to dispute. As such, they are less likely to be contested by flag states large or small. Meanwhile, in its support for Canadian-led IMO/IACS guidelines, the United States tacitly endorses Canadian regulation of commercial traffic in the Northwest Passage.

The very question of whether the Northwest Passage is an international strait or an international waterway wholly subject to Canadian jurisdiction is becoming less consequential. In effect, and as arrived at via a different route by Professor Donald McRae of the Faculty of Law at the University of Ottawa, "although it would widely be perceived as a significant sovereignty loss, [a determination] that the Northwest Passage constituted an international strait would have little effect on Canada's legal authority to regulate commercial shipping" (McRae 2007, 18). And yet, I'd add, there's little likelihood of any such outcome. Though the United States and others will continue to claim that the passage is a strait, we are not going to encounter serious resistance in acting on our rights. On the contrary: we already meet with tacit assent when it comes to foreign commercial navigation. Exclusive jurisdiction is well in hand for foreign commercial and other private ships. Can the same be said of naval vessels?

The ends-means fit between exclusive jurisdiction and armed force is by no means an easy one for a stand-alone Canada that would have all other states treat the Northwest Passage as internal Canadian waters. In first committing a Conservative government to the armed defence of sovereignty, back in December 2005, Harper promised that no foreign submarine, American or otherwise, would enter or transit our Arctic waters without our authorization. To my mind, 100 percent effective solo Canadian control over foreign naval activity in the passage cannot be achieved. The military means required and the likely consequences of their use would force us either to build a nuclear navy or to deter foreign intrusion by promising devastation within the archipelago in the name of Arctic sovereignty. All the while, we could be responding to one, two or no intrusions per year in the 2010s. As with inter-continental commercial voyages, the appeal of the passage for submarines could turn out to be small — indeed, small enough to obviate the need for expensive counter-measures. Or, depending on the strategic naval development of the Arctic as a region, the threat of intrusion could one day be substantial.

A middle way must be found between the desire for complete naval con-trol and the fear of none, between premature commitment to complete mastery and failure to take the first steps toward capabilities with long lead times to acqui-sition. Discovery of the *via media* begins with a glance at a map of the Canadian High Arctic and a consideration of the diverse channels it presents for north-south as well as east-west voyages by foreign submarines and, we assume increas-ingly, surface naval vessels in a less icy region.

Basically, there are three ways to deny the archipelago to naval vessels pro-ceeding without Canadian authorization. The first, of which no more need be said, is to be liberal with our authorizations. The others entail a defence that is either archipelagic or oceanic. As recommended some years ago by the late David Cox, an archipelagic defence would see Canada not merely install underwater sensors but also mine the Northwest Passage in order to deter illicit naval opera-tions and yet allow legitimate civil navigation to proceed. Two or three sites — Barrow Strait, Jones Sound and possibly one other — could suffice for the emplacement of bottom-mounted torpedo devices that would launch on receipt of the appropriate acoustic signature. In what would amount to an act of unilat-eral arms control, Canada would thereby make the archipelago into a "peacetime submerged vessels keep-out zone" for all states. In a crisis situation, however, the United States would be given unfettered access to Canadian Arctic waters. Washington, for its part, would accept a keep-out zone in exchange for Canadian contributions to US security in the form of peacetime surveillance, crisis stability and denial of the archipelago to third parties (Cox 1986).

Whatever we might think of the negotiability of a peacetime keep-out zone now, Cox was writing in 1986. No way today is the leader of the global ban on land mines going to lay mines in its pristine Arctic domain in the name of sovereignty. Nor will Inuit and other northern residents, to say nothing of southern Canadians, fail to object vehemently to a defence that involves radioactive contamination of the archipelago. And if Canada were to undertake to defend with mines in territorial waters seaward of the baselines in Lancaster Sound and the Beaufort, Canadian Inuit would surely be joined by their counterparts in Greenland and Alaska. In short, if Canada is to explore an archipelagic defence of Arctic sovereignty, means will have to be found to deter unauthorized transits without great risk of destroying a nuclear submarine in the Northwest Passage. Even then, deterrence that fails to face a violator with fateful consequences may well be unsuccessful.

The alternative is an oceanic defence, which would see us acquire and deploy a fleet of nuclear attack submarines such as we considered in the late 1980s. These and other antisubmarine warfare (ASW) assets would allow us to operate under ice in monitoring, countering and, if necessary, engaging foreign submarines and, in due course, warships bent on unauthorized transit through or entry into Canadian Arctic waters. All this we would endeavour to accomplish seaward of the archipelago. But it's obvious that little or none of it could be done unilaterally. In practice, we would surely set the exercise of Arctic sovereignty aside and join the United States and other allies in the exercise of a common naval strategy for the Arctic Ocean, and indeed the world oceans. This we would do if not only the United States but also other of our allies continued to reject our claim of exclusive jurisdiction. An oceanic defence of exclusive jurisdiction over foreign naval vessels in the archipelago would therefore see us replicate our present situation at vastly greater expense and opportunity cost.

A cost-effective unilateral defence of Canadian Arctic sovereignty by military means is not on. When it comes to foreign naval vessels — and to submarines, in particular — the binary option of no sovereignty and general and complete sovereignty yields to a choice between more and less. We cannot secure our Arctic sovereignty against foreign naval activity without the military cooperation of those who oppose us — which is to say, first of all, the United States, the most favourably disposed of the states that reject Canada's internal waters claim. In other words, it's not all states but only hostile states that must be constrained in their access to the Canadian Arctic Archipelago. Harper pointed us in this direction when, at the end of the North American Leaders' Summit in Montebello, he cited the continuing need for Canada and the United States to manage their Arctic differences (Freeman 2007). But how to manage our differences with the United States in a way that makes it easier to handle hostile foreign navies seeking to use the archipelago?

Intelligence comes first. Not only the federal government but also the Canadian public need to know what's happening by way of submarine traffic in the passage from year to year. Public knowledge gained with a national Arctic sensor system is essential if in the long haul we are to avoid a disproportionate military response. Again, there may be so little going on that for now we ought to confine ourselves to extending surveillance and scientific research into the high archipelago in anticipation of an increasing need to exercise control as sea ice is reduced in the years ahead. At the same time, we should today be seeking out ways of bringing our allies into common security arrangements whereby they may more readily support Canadian control over the Northwest Passage.

To this end, I propose that we consider what might be accomplished if Canada, without prejudice to its right to exclusive jurisdiction over the waters of the Arctic Archipelago, chose to govern the Northwest Passage *as though* it were an international strait. Since the outlook is good for Canadian control over foreign private vessels, I will for now confine discussion of this "as though" proposition to warships.

Under the law of the sea, states bordering an international strait are entitled to channel foreign vessels along designated sea lanes. Ships so proceeding must do so in a continuous and expeditious manner. Refraining from all activity other than that incident to sailing without delay, they must in no way threaten the sovereignty, integrity or political independence of the bordering state, or in any manner violate the principles of international law as embodied in the charter of the United Nations. As well, they are to comply with generally accepted international standards, and corresponding bordering-state regulations, for safety at sea and environmental protection (United Nations 1983, 12-14). If the Northwest Passage were an international strait, Canada would need, under UNCLOS article 41, to refer its sea lane proposals for adoption by the IMO. But the passage is not an international strait. We are, however, free unilaterally to make use of the elements of a straits regime, if that's what best meets our needs in managing the waters of the archipelago and in providing allies with reason to support our actions.

Applied without prejudice by Canada, provisions of the law relating to international straits could see us confine all foreign submarine transits of our internal waters to a single route through Parry Channel, unless permission were given to proceed otherwise. Warships appearing as ice conditions allowed would be channelled, as required, along alternative routes. There would be no deviation, no dallying, no ASW activity, no reconnaissance for alternative passages, no exercising to find sites for sanctuary in a crisis, no coming ashore — only direct and expeditious transit. Any departure from these rules would be met with countervailing Canadian enforcement action backed up by allied support as necessary. Allies would support Canada in pursuit of common security requirements to limit and deny hostile use of the archipelago. They would do so even as they persisted in their denial of Canada's internal waters claim. Net effect: vastly simplified, less expensive and more effective policing and control over foreign naval activity than could be achieved by a stand-alone Canada bent on denying all unauthorized activity.

The Arctic interaction of Canada and the United States is marked by a steady elaboration of agree-to-disagree, in which we proceed not to settle but to set aside our disagreement in favour of coordinated action without prejudice to our positions in law. We take the initiative, and the United States responds. There is a repeated "yes" in the US acceptance of article 234, in the negotiation of the Arctic Cooperation Agreement of 1988, in the State Department's going on record that US commercial vessels will conform to Canada's *AWPPA*, in persistent shows of middle-level US support for getting along as distinct from putting Canada's internal waters claim to the test, in US endorsement of IMO Arctic guidelines that make Canadian regulatory standards the international norm for ship construction and operation. And then, in what may be the biggest US "yes" of all, at Montebello in August 2007, President Bush endorsed Prime Minister Harper's unilateral commitment to defend Canadian Arctic sovereignty with armed force. Washington has been telling us that the issue of the status of the Northwest Passage in international law need not hold us back from security cooperation nor prevent self-help of the kind Canada wishes to pursue.

It's time for us to take yes for an answer from the United States. We have the sovereignty we need. Let us exercise it unilaterally and in cooperation with our allies, as circumstance requires. We are in a strong position as new space opens up before us in the Arctic. No longer needing to hunker down behind our straight baselines, we ought to be moving out into the region. We should engage.

Beyond   Sovereignty

SOUTHERN CANADIANS WHO LOOK TO THE ARCTIC CANNOT BE EXPECTED TO YIELD
their obsession with sovereignty and possession any time soon. New thinking will take hold in the course of a transition that carries forward some of the
old — especially the felt need to control, police and exclude. While we do need
to move forward, we will have differing ideas of what lies beyond sovereignty as
an animating impulse. For me, it is stewardship: locally informed governance that
not only polices but also exhibits respect and care for the natural world. A great
deal might be said about stewardship, but not here. Instead, let us briefly imagine how something like it might shape our conduct as and when we southerners
come out of our shell and actively engage our own North and, foremost, Canada's
Inuit; the United States on Arctic issues; and the awakening circumpolar region.
In drawing this chapter to a close, I consider Inuit first.

Everything I have said thus far will appear to some degree disrespectful and
offensive to Inuit in its unexamined southern assumptions of the need to rely on
hardware and law in maintaining control over a prized but distant domain that's
essentially uninhabited. Inuit — what they might wish as fellow Canadians on site
in the Arctic, and what they might be able to contribute to the Canadian enterprise
— have been excised from the discussion. This is quite in keeping with the observation of Inuit that to us down south they are invisible. There should be no more of
it. Paul Okalik, Premier of Nunavut, has pointed the way ahead: "But sovereignty is
not just about military presence, surveillance and enforcement. From a Nunavut perspective, sovereignty would be enhanced by fulfilling the opportunities to build
capacity in the North and to create a vision of Canadian Arctic stewardship in which
Nunavummiut play a significant role for Canada" (Okalik 2006).

As well as capacity building, the agenda here is one that calls for the use
of existing and new institutions to address a host of matters relating to the Arctic
environment, health, social and economic development, human resources and
circumpolar affairs. Aside from recognizing that Canada's internal waters claim
owes much to Inuit occupancy, the agenda is also one that would see us shift from
sovereignty to stewardship in approaching the Arctic.

Inuit do have something to tell the rest of Canada about stewardship.
Consider the mix of meanings that attend the Inuit word *aulatsigunnarniq*. Used
to translate "sovereignty" into Inuktitut, *aulatsigunnarniq* is a compound word

meaning "to run things" and "being able to." The "sovereign" in Inuit culture is not, however, the free-standing, self-realizing individual typical of European civilization. On the contrary — he or she is doubly embedded, in community and in nature. She watches, keeps, takes care of and provides for in the running of things. As such, she has much in common with the steward, though not in the European sense of managing a stand-apart environment.

If the Canadian imagination is heading north — as it must with the greater accessibility brought on by climate change — a new dialogue between southerners and northerners about who we are, what we seek and how we ought to conduct ourselves is indispensable. *Aulatsigunnarniq* may well be of use to us down south as we endeavour to understand the Arctic not so much as an expression of our identity, but as it is. Inuit, too, may have something to learn in deploying their own understandings of the world, as distinct from relying upon European conceptual frameworks. A Canadian *aulatsigunnarniq* might therefore inform our actions as keepers of the Northwest Passage — and by "keepers" I mean those who take care of and protect, not those who have avoided becoming losers. But if there's new thinking to be done as Canada surrenders its fixation on sovereignty, as yet there is no north-south process for policy-related consensual learning. Given that existing forums are suffused in and unable to get free of old-think, new means of Canadian Arctic governance are required.

A commitment to establish a new body already exists, but it has yet to be acted on. It's to be found in the Nunavut Land Claim Agreement of 1993 — specifically, in the call for a marine council to advise and recommend to government agencies on marine matters in the settlement area, which embraces by far the greater part of the Arctic Archipelago. Enlarged to include Beaufort-Delta representation, the marine council could become the key Canadian forum for priority setting and analytical input into federal government policy on High Arctic issues and for our participation in the Arctic Council. Focusing on marine matters to begin with, it could serve as the domestic Canadian equivalent of the Arctic Council, establishing priorities for Canadian action in the archipelago and providing guidance and backup for Canadian participation in the Arctic Council. Proceeding by consensus and including nongovernmental participation, the marine council ought to be equipped with a secretariat and located in Resolute Bay, given that there is a Canadian Armed Forces training facility there. Obliging southern officials and private persons to travel, if not also relocate, to the archipelago, a fully instituted marine council would support a northward transfer of the Canadian imagination and political purpose.

Northern Exposure: Peoples, Powers and Prospects in Canada's North

As to engaging the United States, Canada needs to act on commonalities that have been slighted in the mutual leeriness that's arisen from our dispute over the Northwest Passage. Fully aware of the Arctic region's opening to cooperation as well as conflict, Canada and the United States ought to recognize and base their collaboration on unexploited opportunities for joint stewardship in Arctic North America.

The range of bilateral hands-on cooperation strategies open to our two countries is very large. The majority should be undertaken with the direct participation of Canadian and US Arctic indigenous peoples. The list includes maritime domain awareness and, in due course, maritime command under NORAD; ocean stewardship under the Security and Prosperity Partnership of North America; coast guard cooperation in search and rescue operations, including in the event of a cruise ship fire or grounding; cooperation between other agencies of our two countries if there is a major air disaster; improved capabilities for oil spill cleanup in ice-covered waters; protection of Arctic ice and snow albedo against black soot through the joint imposition of commercial vessel smokestack emission controls; joint marine environmental monitoring and study of marine ecosystems especially vulnerable to climate change; fisheries management and response to invasive species in Arctic waters; reduction of greenhouse gas emissions and increasing reliance on renewable energy sources for small Arctic communities; reconsideration of measures to protect the Porcupine Caribou herd; further harmonization of navigational practices and ice information classification, involving Denmark/Greenland as well; and an invitation to the United States and Denmark/Greenland to comment as Canada proceeds to bring the *AWPPA* regulations up to date.

All of the foregoing, and more, could readily be addressed by Canada and the United States acting not only as joint stewards, but also as neighbours determined to proceed with practical cooperation on priority issues. Where the larger strategic interests of the two countries are concerned, climate change also raises the prospect of naval and commercial developments, which we should plan for without delay.

Given what I take to be the limits on Canada's ability to mount an Arctic oceanic defence, to say nothing of our interest in peaceful change, we should be opening a discussion with the United States that, from the start, emphasizes regional cooperation to reduce the likelihood of tension, crisis and thereby loss of control over what happens in Canadian Arctic waters. In so doing, we would necessarily address the potential for renewed geopolitical rivalry in the region, and the need to begin positioning ourselves now for advantage later. We Canadians, northerners and southerners alike, should therefore be considering alternative futures for naval inter-action and arms control in the circumpolar region, identifying means of steering the region's development toward a preferable future and discussing the implications with the United States. In any such discussion, it will be hard to avoid considering what lies ahead for Arctic resource development and marine transportation.

Actually, when it comes to resources and transportation, what might Canada's ambitions be for its High Arctic and the circumpolar region beyond? Do we want, and will we therefore go to the trouble and expense of inducing, a high volume of intercontinental shipping in the Northwest Passage? Are foreign mer-chant vessels to be capable of independent navigation, as Canada has long required, or are we now to provide icebreaker services for them? Are we to charge transit fees, and what might this do to the competitiveness of the passage relative to Panama? What might Inuit say about transiting ships that generate no local revenue and yet produce black soot and adverse effects on marine mammals? What might their position be when it comes to destination shipping in the Arctic waters of North America? And beyond matters such as these, what might Canada contribute to the construction of a region-wide regime for safe and efficient marine transportation?

The time has come for Canada not merely to engage in the affairs of a part of the world long frozen in the standoff of the Cold War but to take the lead in resolving its problems. For many years, we southerners played in the Arctic principally with political-military cards, in deterrence mode and without reference to indigenous peo-ples. Today, we and the seven other ice-state members of the Arctic Council, along with representatives of the region's indigenous peoples, are beginning to draw on a full deck. We are dealing with a host of issues related to, among other things, geopolitical mat-ters, resource extraction, legal questions, marine transportation, environmental protec-tion, climate and indigenous peoples — all of which are interrelated. Putting surety of possession in its proper place, we in Canada must rise to the occasion. Whether it's a Canadian *aulatsigunnarniq* or another vision of stewardship that is to move us, we need to create an array of new relationships and to work out new means of Arctic gover-nance. This we must do within Canada, with the United States and by contributing to the work of the Arctic Council far more actively than we have in recent years.

Like nostalgia, sovereignty ain't what it used to be. Along with the sea ice, our Arctic sovereignty problem in the Northwest Passage is melting away. Before us lies a beckoning region in which we have much to give and much to gain. With others, we should now move forward into the Arctic not as possessors but as stewards.

Note

1   A version of this paper was presented to
Foreign Affairs and International Trade
Canada (DFAIT) on October 18, 2007, in the
context of the Deputy Minister Presents
series. The opinions and recommendations
expressed are the personal views of the author
and do not necessarily represent the views,
policies or positions of DFAIT or those of the
Government of Canada. The paper was completed in spring 2008 and released in the fall
of that year. As of April 2009, nothing had
happened to alter the judgments made here.

References

Allen, Thad. 2007. Presentation to the IFPA-
Fletcher National Security Conference,
September 26-27, Washington, DC. Accessed
February 29, 2008. http://www.ifpafletcher-
conference.com/oldtranscripts/Allen.pdf

Bi-national Planning Group. 2004. *Interim Report on
Canada and United States (CANUS) Enhanced
Military Cooperation*, October 13. Patterson
AFB, CO: Bi-national Planning Group.

Borgerson, Scott, and Franklyn Griffiths. 2007.
"This Is No Time for Chest Thumping."
International Herald Tribune, September 10.

Brigham, Lawson. 2000. "The Emerging
International Polar Navigation Code: Bi-
polar Relevance?" In *Protecting the Polar
Marine Environment: Law and Policy for
Pollution Prevention*, edited by Davor Vidas.
Cambridge: Cambridge University Press.

Byers, Michael. 2006a. "Canada Must Seek Deal
with the U.S." *Toronto Star*, October 27.

_____. 2006b. "Canadian Government
Cannot Afford to Dither on Arctic
Sovereignty." *Hill Times*, October 16.

_____. 2007a. "Build an Arctic Gateway for
the World." *Globe and Mail*, November 26.

_____. 2007b. "Sovereignty Will Solve the
Northwest Passage Dispute." *Globe and
Mail*, August 11.

_____. 2007c. "Unfrozen Sea: Sailing the
Northwest Passage." *Policy Options* 28 (5):
30-3. Montreal: Institute for Research on
Public Policy.

Byers, Michael, and Suzanne Lalonde. 2006.
"Who Controls the Northwest Passage?"
Discussion paper for the conference
"Canada's Arctic Waters in International
Law and Diplomacy," June 14, Ottawa.
Accessed March 8, 2008.
http://www.ligi.ubc.ca/sites/liu/files/
Publications/7Jun2006ArcticWaters
DiscussionPaper.pdf

Canuel, Hugues. 2007. "Nanisivik Refuelling
Facility Will Enable Naval Presence." *Hill
Times*, August 20.

Cox, David. 1986. *Trends in Continental Defence: A
Canadian Perspective*. Ottawa: Canadian
Institute for International Peace and Security.

Defence Research and Development Canada
(DRDC). 2008. *Northern Watch: A Window
into Canadian Arctic Surveillance*, February.
Ottawa: DRDC. Accessed February 24,
2008. http://www.drdc-rddc.gc.ca/
newsevents/spotlight/spotlight_e.asp

El Akkad, Omar. 2008. "Large Chunk of Security
Measures Aimed at Foreigners." *Globe and
Mail*, February 27.

Falkingham, John. 2007. Presentation notes for
the National Ice Center and United States
Arctic Research Commission conference
"Impact of an Ice-Diminishing Arctic on
Naval and Maritime Operations," July 10-
11, Washington, DC.

Flemming, Brian. 2007. "Northwest Passage: A
Voyage Canada and the U.S. Can Take
Together." *Globe and Mail*, December 18.

Foot, Richard, and Norma Greenaway. 2007. "Bush
Praises Mission." *National Post*, August 22.

Freeman, Alan. 2007. "Troops Doing 'Fabulous
Job,' Bush Says." *Globe and Mail*, August 22.

Griffiths, Franklyn. 2003. "The Shipping News:
Canada's Arctic Sovereignty Not on Thinning
Ice." *International Journal* 53 (2): 257-82.

_____. 2004. "Pathetic Fallacy: That Canada's
Arctic Sovereignty Is on Thinning Ice."
Canadian Foreign Policy 11 (3): 1-16.

_____. 2006. "Our Arctic Sovereignty Is Well
in Hand." *Globe and Mail*, November 8.

Harper, Stephen. 2005. Remarks on Canadian
Arctic sovereignty. Accessed March 7, 2008.

http://www.cs.queensu.ca/home/skill/
election/10.txt

Harris, Kathleen. 2007. "Our True North Strong
and Free?" *Ottawa Sun*, February 23.

Huebert, Rob. 2002. "Climate Change and
Canadian Sovereignty in the Northwest
Passage." *Isuma* 2 (4): 86-94.

————. 2003. "The Shipping News Part II: How
Canada's Arctic Sovereignty Is on Thinning
Ice." *International Journal* 58 (3): 295-308.

————. 2004. "The Coming Arctic Maritime
Sovereignty Crisis." *WWF Arctic Bulletin*
2.04: 22-4. Accessed June 26, 2008.
http://assets.panda.org/downloads/ab0204.pdf

————. 2007. "Warming Likely to Trigger Cold
War." *London Free Press*, February 23.

International Association of Classification
Societies (IACS). 2006. *Unified Requirements
for Polar Ships*. London: IACS. Accessed
February 29, 2008. http://www.iacs.org.uk/
document/public/Publications/Unified_
Requirements/PDF/UR_I_pdf647.pdf

International Maritime Organization. 2002.
*Guidelines for Ships Operating in Arctic Ice-
Covered Waters*. Ottawa: Transport Canada.
Accessed February 29, 2008.
http://www.tc.gc.ca/marinesafety/CES/Arctic/
menu.htm

Kraska, James C. 2007. "The Law of the Sea
Convention and the Northwest Passage." In
Defence Requirements for Canada's Arctic,
edited by Brian MacDonald. Vimy Paper
2007. Ottawa: Conference of Defence
Associations Institute. Accessed June 26,
2008. http://www.cda-cdai.ca/Vimy_Papers/
Defence%20Requirements%20for%20
Canada's%20Arctic%20online%20ve.pdf

McRae, Donald. 1987. "The Negotiation of
Article 234." In *Politics of the Northwest
Passage*, edited by Franklyn Griffiths.
Kingston and Montreal: McGill-Queen's
University Press.

————. 2007. "Arctic Sovereignty? What Is at
Stake?" *Behind the Headlines* 64, no. 1. Toronto:
Canadian Institute of International Affairs.

New Democratic Party of Canada (NDP). 2007.
"Jack Layton's Letter to Prime Minister

Stephen Harper on Arctic Sovereignty,"
August 6. Ottawa: NDP. Accessed February
28, 2008. http://www.ndp.ca/page/
5580?refer=more

Office of the Prime Minister. 2007.
"Backgrounder — Strengthening Canada's
Arctic Sovereignty — Constructing Arctic
Offshore Patrol Ships," July 9. Ottawa:
Office of the Prime Minister. Accessed
March 5, 2008. http://pm.gc.ca/eng/
media.asp?id=1743

Okalik, Paul. 2006. "Nunavut Needs 'Provincial-
Like' Authority to Help Manage Canada's
Arctic Sovereignty." *Hill Times*, August 21.

"Our Arctic, Their Desire." 2007. *Winnipeg Free
Press*, February 19.

Pharand, Donat. 2006. "Our Sovereignty Is
Melting." *Ottawa Citizen*, August 23.

Somanathan, Saran, Peter C. Flynn, and Josef K.
Szymanski. 2007. "Feasibility of a Sea Route
through the Canadian Arctic." *Maritime
Economics and Logistics* 9 (2): 324-34.

Struzik, Ed. 2007. "Who's Guarding Our Back
Door?" *Toronto Star*, November 18.

Taylor, Paul. 2007. "A Hawkeyed Addition to
Canada's Arctic Arsenal." *Globe and Mail*,
December 10.

Treadwell, Mead. 2008. Remarks on US Arctic
policy to the United States Arctic Research
Commission, January 9, Washington, DC.

United Nations (UN). 1983. *United Nations
Convention on the Law of the Sea*. New York:
UN. Accessed June 26, 2008.
http://www.un.org/Depts/los/convention_
agreements/texts/unclos/unclos_e.pdf

United States Department of State. 1992. *United
States Responses to Excessive National
Maritime Claims*, March 9. Limits in the
Seas 112. Washington, DC: Office of Ocean
Affairs, Bureau of Oceans and International
Environmental and Scientific Affairs.
Accessed February 25, 2008.
http://www.state.gov/documents/
organization/58381.pdf

White, Marianne. 2007. "'Frightening' Projection
for Arctic Melt." *Gazette* (Montreal),
November 16.

The Inuit and Issues ·of Arctic Sovereignty

T HE CHAPTERS IN THIS VOLUME BY ROB HUEBERT AND FRANKLYN GRIFFITHS UNDER-
line the new Arctic reality in Canada, and both chapters focus attention on
the North. They also remind us that a good deal has been happening, even
though the public may not be aware of it. Although the two authors present differing options related to Arctic sovereignty, they make positive contributions to
the discussion on this important issue.

My principal concern about their chapters is that in them the Inuit and their
presence in the Arctic are hardly mentioned. To me, this is very disappointing. In addition, the North could be better defined to include Nunavik and Nunatsiavut, the two
sub-Arctic regions where Inuit face the same challenges as those living north of 60.

Huebert brings to the attention of the readers the changes and new realities of the Arctic. He states that Canada has always had an unclear policy on the
Arctic and that it has been influenced by outside forces, particularly the United
States, and by other Arctic countries, such as Russia and Finland. In the opening
paragraphs of his chapter, he states that Canada has jurisdiction over the Arctic.
He could have strengthened this by commenting on the jurisdiction that Inuit
now have as a result of land claims agreements and other political realities,
including the creation of the Nunavut territory 10 years ago. Huebert neglects to
mention that Canadian Inuit have relations with Inuit in other Arctic regions,
such as Alaska. A fuller discussion of these points would have provided a broader perspective on the challenges and realities of the present-day Arctic, which
should be reflected in a new Arctic foreign policy. The future of the Arctic is crucial to the Inuit, who have lived there for millennia. They have the most to gain
or lose from future northern policy.

With regard to the Arctic Council, the potential value of the council to Arctic indigenous peoples is not to be taken lightly. Although Huebert acknowledges the role of the Inuit and other indigenous peoples in the council's formation, it would have been useful if he had considered the Inuit's views on the value of the Arctic Council, including its emerging role in environmental governance.

Finally, Huebert suggests ways for Canada to address the challenges to its maritime borders. One of these ways is to discuss this issue with the Inuit who have been managing these borders for millennia. They could play a key role in any jurisdiction that results from Inuit land claims.[1]

Griffiths's chapter makes a twofold contribution: it reminds the reader that Arctic sovereignty entails more than military presence and it outlines solutions many may not have considered; and it states that Inuit views should be considered in any approach to the sovereignty question. However, Griffiths does not pursue much further the potential Inuit role. He could have discussed the role that the Canadian Rangers play in Arctic sovereignty matters. During the Cold War, Inuit Rangers were given some training by the military. While hunting and carrying out their daily activities in the Arctic, they were, in essence, acting as the first line of defence in the Canadian High Arctic surveillance system.

Griffiths usefully reminds the reader that sovereignty entails securing the recognition of rights and acting on those rights. From an Inuit viewpoint, it would have been helpful if he had explored how existing Inuit rights could be strengthened, and how Canada will have to act on Inuit rights that have been established through land claims processes and, broadly speaking, through the Canadian Constitution. Griffiths states correctly that Inuit concerns relate to economic and cultural deprivation and marine pollution. But his point would have been strengthened if he had addressed how Inuit have legal rights under land claims agreements. In fact, he could have integrated discussion of the role the Inuit might play in strengthening Canada sovereignty throughout the chapter, not just mentioned it at the end.

Griffiths also notes that the public and the media have been responding to the climate change/ice thinning thesis, arguing that the media has contributed to public fear. He adds that the focus has been on surface vessels, whose activities have caused disputes over who controls the Northwest Passage. He refers to Canada's recent efforts to strengthen its negotiating position by increasing surveillance and demonstrating interest in the subsurface. In this context, it is important to note that international law is evolving and beginning to recognize indigenous rights. This is also becoming part of the Arctic sovereignty debate.

In summing up, the Inuit are, and expect to remain, the permanent majority population of the Arctic. Inuit are centrally placed in the region. They are the key players, and they are the most affected by the Arctic sovereignty processes and by the outcomes and solutions Canada proposes.

Note

1   Duane Smith, vice-chairman of the pan-Arctic Inuit Circumpolar Council, said that Prime Minister Stephen Harper "doesn't seem to know that working together with us could be very beneficial to him and all the goals of Canadians" ("Inuit Leader" 2007).

Reference

"Inuit Leader Demands Input on Arctic Sovereignty" 2007. CBC.ca, August 22. Accessed March 11, 2009. http://www.cbc.ca/canada/north/story/2007/08/22/north-arctic.html.

Arctic Science,

Nation Building

and Citizenship

I N THE OCTOBER 2007 SPEECH FROM THE THRONE, THE GOVERNMENT OF CANADA
signalled its intention to renew Canada's commitment to the North.[1] This
could be seen as a response to the widespread perception, at home and abroad,
that the Canadian government was sleepwalking into the present, seemingly
oblivious to the growing interest of other nations in gaining access to the waterways and offshore resources of territory traditionally believed by Canadians to be
their own. The Throne Speech signalled very publicly the government's intention
to develop a new integrated northern strategy, its purpose to reassert Canada's
sovereignty over its Arctic waters and resources. The key elements include a new
"world-class Arctic research station," a survey capacity for a "comprehensive mapping of Canada's Arctic seabed" and expanded surveillance by land, sea and air-
space to "guard Canada's Far North and the Northwest Passage" (Government of
Canada 2007, 3-4).

The basic logic of this strategy is straightforward. Its essential components
are scientific knowledge to understand what's there; surveys to demarcate national territory and, implicitly, resources; and surveillance to monitor the national
integrity of the space and to regulate and enforce Canadian jurisdiction. Science
and technology are implicated and entangled in different ways in each component, and each component needs to be planned in relation to the northern strategy as a whole.

In matters of sovereignty and national identity, the symbolic significance
of technologies is often no less important than their utility. Just as in environmental politics, where there are iconic species (like polar bears), in sovereignty
politics there are iconic technologies.[2] The scientific research station is one such

iconic technology. In the 1920s and 1930s, aviation and aerial surveys came to symbolize national feelings of power and progress in expanding science and commerce into the circumpolar North. During the International Geophysical Year (1957-58), the proliferation of research stations on the polar peripheries (Arctic and Antarctic) — like Canada's Polar Continental Shelf Project, initially based at the Joint Arctic Weather Station at Isachsen — came to represent the possibilities of peaceful science and international cooperation. Starting around that time, research stations were also popularized in science fiction as sites of Cold War secret knowledge and espionage.

In the 1970s, geostationary satellites, land claims maps and video broadcasting were the technologies that reconfigured Canada's North, enabling its peoples to look outward on their own terms and to access the cultures of southern Canada and the rest of the globe. Telecommunications played a significant though understated role in enabling northerners to develop distinct grassroots political voices, presaging political devolution. In these examples of iconic technologies, there is an implicit technological determinism that gives them a certain mythological power. What, then, might be the canonical technologies for the present moment in Arctic politics? Is it the floating platform of the icebreaker, which demonstrates symbolic mastery over navigation and the oceans — ironically, just at the moment that the sea ice is becoming an endangered habitat? Is it perhaps a return to the era of the International Geophysical Year (IGY), when prestigious new research stations were brought into the compass of exciting new buildings inspired by architectural modernism? Or is the technology that best captures the need for connectivity in the early twenty-first century the social and material network? And, if so, where does the research station belong in this genealogy of Arctic technologies?

The main purpose of this chapter is to explore how a future High Arctic research station could contribute to the sovereignty and stewardship of the Arctic. Scholarship that goes to the heart of this relationship between science and international politics is still in its early days. Even though there is a growing body of literature on imperial history and the history of science about science, internationalism and colonialism, political scientists have been shy about teasing out the complex relations between epistemology and political theory. These are, of course, big issues to tackle. My approach here is to open up the question of science and sovereignty in two ways: first, through a historically informed discussion of international science as an instrument of nationalism; and second, through an examination of how the context and uses of the field sciences have been transformed by the participation of nonstate actors. Historians have demonstrated that there are many instances in which scientific expeditions have been undertaken to satisfy nationalist or geopolitical motives, and the history of the polar regions has some of the best examples. So we can confidently assert that science and sovereignty have a history of entanglement.

I am indebted to the recent work of political scientists who have tried to theorize how sovereignty today is enacted or constructed in ways that differ significantly from the original Westphalian model while retaining important antecedents. At the heart of the Westphalian model is the premise that sovereignty belongs only to autonomous states with territory and is predicated on mutual recognition of their boundaries. The model of the nation-state, where national and state boundaries coincide, is still largely intact, but it is no longer so autonomous in a world where transnational flows of capital, goods and people around the globe are only partly controlled by individual states. Add to this Canada's own historical and constitutional political history, and the result is a highly complex set of subnational, national, transnational and international structures — all of which appeal to expertise, often scientific and technological expertise, for their legitimacy. Science, I would suggest, is not outside Canada's political complexity but, rather, thoroughly imbricated in it. In Arctic Canada, scientific research plays a vital role in assessments that mediate between multinational industries (which develop capital-intensive science and technology but also sponsor an enormous amount of highly local research) and indigenous groups with self-governing powers (those, for example, that participate in impact and benefit agreements), as well as with transnational groups (for example, the Inuit Circumpolar Council, which has made extensive use of the Arctic Climate Impact Assessment). If we consider the political and economic context, it is very difficult to make simple generalizations about science and sovereignty.

The Arctic may be in transition from a traditional Westphalian model to a post-Westphalian model (Shadian, forthcoming). That is to say that the Arctic, far from being a laboratory stripped down and insulated from the rest of the world, is actually highly permeable and connected — both physically, through global energy flows (oceans and atmosphere as well as mineral extraction) and politically, through a growing number of highly mobile, sophisticated stakeholders.

The notion that Arctic science is a bounded activity defined simply by what Arctic scientists do is a pernicious fallacy because it undervalues the importance of science and makes an understanding of its political significance impossible. The early pioneers of the Polar Continental Shelf Project (PCSP) — Fred Roots and, later, George Hobson — sought to overcome potential insularity with their project design.[3] Implicit in the claim made by scientists that the Arctic is a sensitive barometer for the rest of the globe is the idea that the Arctic is tightly coupled to other regions. Behind this claim lies another truth: the Arctic is becoming politically and economically much more tightly connected. Evidence of this is the growing importance of human rights, indigenous peoples' rights and environmental rights, all areas of international law where the common good of individuals and collectives transcends, or is even at odds with, national interests. In the Arctic, these third-generation rights are closely bound up with political devolution, land claims, human rights, sustainable development and environmental stewardship (Shadian, forthcoming). Scientific research is an instrument used by many stakeholders, unequally and for different purposes. How, then, does this affect the status of science as an instrument of public policy?

My argument begins with the simple observation that sovereignty does not flow directly from having a research station and doing science. It depends upon who is doing the science. In a Westphalian world that privileges states, nonstate actors can achieve many goals by doing science, but becoming a sovereign state isn't one of them. However, sovereign states can demonstrate their sovereignty by providing concrete demonstrations of governance throughout their territory. State-sponsored research stations that provide reliable information about national territory are a historically recognized means of demonstrating governance. This is why Canada, with its network of Arctic research stations, is able to make a strong show of sovereignty — it already has. Just as individual states can devolve governance to subnational levels, such as provincial and territorial, so too can they devolve responsibilities for science and technology. For example, in Arctic Canada, the federal government negotiated the transfer in 1988 of three of its research stations (Inuvik, Igloolik and Iqaluit) to the Government of the Northwest Territories, which subsequently transferred the latter two to the Government of Nunavut.

Nonstate actors, however, carry out science on behalf of themselves or others, and usually not the state, although they often contribute knowledge to the public sphere and share knowledge with the state. These actors are as diverse as the Inuit

Tapiriit Kanatami of Canada, which has had scientists on staff; the Inuit Circumpolar Council, which has collaborated with scientists internationally as well as in Canada; and private sector companies that employ a wide range of knowledge experts in order to satisfy their public duties, particularly in relation to environmental standards and impact assessments. These very wide-ranging stakeholders can provide some of the most persuasive demonstrations of Canada's stewardship of the Arctic, but they can also create ambivalence because they exert influence through scientific networks in which the Canadian state is only one player among many.

The demonstrations of sovereignty that derive from science are not a priori different in kind from other activities. However, the idea that science is disinterested — that it simply purports to describe the laws of nature (through, for example, climate change research and monitoring) — gives it a special authority in relation to stewardship of the Arctic and distinguishes it from other forms of state-sponsored presence. My conclusion is that state-sponsored science makes a valuable contribution by demonstrating good governance — provided that its claims remain just and coherent in the complex context of Canada's northern polity.

Background

THE NATURE OF THE GLOBAL DEMANDS ON CANADA'S ARCTIC IS RAPIDLY CHANGING. After decades of underfunding (England, Dyke and Henry 1998), spending money to update Arctic infrastructure has moved up the federal government's list of priorities. However, spending simply to compensate for decades of underspending will not be enough to secure full participation in the management of Canada's Arctic. The conventional framing of the problem with Canadian science has itself changed. Once seen as the problem of how to prevent the loss of science expertise in a region of special importance to the construction of nationhood, it has become the problem of how to prevent the breakdown of the spatial integrity of Arctic Canada itself. The way feelings of loss of control and powerlessness affect the national psyche when part of the nation's imagined "geo-body," once taken for granted, suddenly seems in jeopardy has been recognized by some political geographers (Thongchai 1994).

The new conventional framing of Canada's Arctic malaise is that the dramatic global rise in commodity prices, together with the rapid decline in multiyear Arctic sea-ice concentration, is suddenly making Arctic Canada's maritime arteries accessible to everyone (in fact, the ice has not vanished, though there are signs that the previously linear decline of multiyear sea-ice concentrations has recently accelerated). The rising cost of fuel means that mobility in the Arctic — in Russia as much as in Canada — is reduced, creating new levels of poverty and geographical isolation. Thus Arctic Canada is becoming inaccessible to its citizens just when commodity prices and economies of scale are causing the emergence of a new neo-liberal geographical space that may be controlled by multinational corporations that will use it for resource extraction and international shipping. Consequently, the benefits to be derived from investing in new technological infrastructures — like research stations, ground- and space-based radars, and icebreakers — depend on how these infrastructures serve the interests of multiple parties. This means that the calculus of science policy is complex and contingent on Canada's geography, politics, environment and resources.

Canada's Arctic environment comprises most of the Arctic's ecosystems, each of which is changing in different ways not adequately captured by the general term "climate change." For example in the High Arctic, the Ward Hunt and Ayles ice shelves on the northwest coast of Ellesmere Island show signs that they are disconnecting and breaking up, no longer fed by the land-based glaciers that created them. Contaminants from around the globe arrive and accumulate in the Arctic. As they rise in the food chain, they become toxic to people, fish and mammals (Hassol 2004). Canada has almost no capability to clean up the greatest contamination threat: a major oil spill in one of its High Arctic waterways. Farther south, almost unnoticed, the massive peatlands of the mainland Arctic contain some of the world's largest stores of methane and carbon, which look set to release very large quantities of carbon dioxide into the atmosphere. This will have major feedback effects on the global climate.

Even to the casual observer in the Canadian south, the poor condition of the refitted CCGS *Louis S. St-Laurent* and CCGS *Amundsen* and the largely run-down or closed-down federal research stations and sporadically distributed environmental monitoring sites are all shocking in light of the obvious national and economic importance of this rapidly changing landscape. We imagine the Arctic landscape as unchanging and pristine, but this is largely myth. The commercial pursuit of fish and whales decimated populations, while the Hudson's Bay Company, which created an empire based on animal pelts, was once one of the largest companies in the world. The idea that the Arctic is isolated from the rest of the world by virtue of its high-latitude geography has long been obsolete. Many Canadians still find it convenient to imagine that the purity of the Arctic environment makes it special for science, but I would argue that the truth is rather different. Reading about the latest discoveries in Arctic science in *Nature* is fascinating precisely because new research reveals unexpected ways in which the Arctic environment — what the Inuit call "sila" — is intricate, diverse and sometimes unstable through many, many processes that connect the Arctic to the rest of the globe.

The federal government recognizes that a research station cannot by itself provide the scientific capacity to understand and monitor the Arctic and sub-Arctic. In reality, the Canadian Arctic Research Initiative (CARI, coined by the independent expert panel convened by the Council of Canadian Academies commissioned by Indian and Northern Affairs Canada [INAC]) accurately describes the coordinated system of scientific research and monitoring of Canada's Arctic that has been adopted. The system can better be seen as a social and material network of human capital and infrastructure tasked with carrying out sustained monitoring of Canada's Arctic ecosystems and solving key problems identified as research priorities. CARI is, for the government, a concrete instrument for demonstrating governance in the Arctic. However, it is also a policy instrument the federal government can use in thinking through the future organization and structure of its relationship to its Canadian and international partners as joint custodians of the Arctic regional environment.

The development of these knowledge partnerships is a key ingredient in designing shared stewardship of the regional and global environments — and by being seen to exercise its sovereignty responsibly, establishing mutual recognition with other sovereign states, the federal government reassures the Canadian public. Whether northern Canadians feel that this strengthens their sense of citizenship is an intriguing question, one to which I shall return later. It suffices to say that a much stronger federal presence will be problematic if it is not consonant with the political changes in the Arctic that in recent decades have strengthened Canada as an inclusive nation.

Thinking of CARI as an isolated, remote station on an outcrop overlooking the Arctic Ocean is evocative, but misleading. CARI should adopt a structure that will enable it to connect to the stakeholders on whose behalf it is acquiring expert knowledge, starting with Canada's northern citizens, while of course recognizing that territorial and federal agencies and departments, universities and industries will also play a significant role in the governance and use of this knowledge. The proposed research station(s), as part of a distributed knowledge network, could comprise a number of Arctic research stations of different sizes and capabilities, flexibly designed for the different ecosystems or communities. The fact that monitoring subregional ecosystems is a challenge only drives home the point that the institutional and geographical architecture of a network, not just a single outpost, is what is at stake.

It is helpful, if unconventional, to think of a research station as a technology of travel. What defines a research platform in general is the mobility it provides for observation and measurement. Fixed land-based stations depend for their effectiveness on other forms of transportation — like helicopters, Ski-Doos, and all-terrain vehicles — to extend their range of field sites and scientific support. But they are not the only important research platforms in an Arctic environment. Maritime counterparts, like the CCGS *Amundsen*, are equally important; without them there would be no comprehensive coverage of the region. Ships offer a practical means of bringing medical laboratory equipment to coastal communities — air transport would be costly, time-consuming and impractical. Some ships carry sophisticated precision hydrographic and seismic instruments for seabed surveyors to map geological profiles, identify resources and delineate the limits of the continental shelf. Remotely piloted drone aircraft may soon come of age for meteorological monitoring and forecasting.

These technological platforms, though in some respects independent of each other, require integration using common standards and sophisticated communications technology for real-time data transmission in a fully functional coordinated system. The price tag for such systems can easily run to billions of dollars, not including operations and maintenance costs. How the structure of a research network could be made integral to the planning and design of a research station is a topic I will address later.

A key question for public policy-makers is how these technologies translate into political currency and capability. Examining concepts of stewardship, for example, allows us to explore how communities value their surroundings; what they consider to count as resources, sustenance and shelter; and how they conceive of their obligations and duties and regulate their conduct. However, if we want to explore further how communities square their obligations as stewards with enactments of state sovereignty, we should consider changing constructions of citizenship alongside stewardship.

This question could, admittedly, be the subject of an entire research program, but I want to draw attention to one particular line of argument: global change science (exemplified by the Arctic Climate Impact Assessment) can be seen as constructing a new form of Arctic regional citizenship by bridging the people of the Arctic across state boundaries and recognizing their agency, while also making space for new local voices (Martello 2004, 41). The argument could be developed much further, but it suggests that "Arctic citizenship" coconstructed with "Arctic science" can provide a transnational political account that bridges notions of stewardship, which vary greatly from state to state, across very diverse cultures and ecosystems. In other words, regional citizenship can add political coherence to stewardship at the transnational and the subnational levels simultaneously. This argument extends the shared ground occupied by the Arctic Council into a more explicitly political realm.

What makes technologies like stations and scientific survey vessels familiar, yet makes some Arctic inhabitants uneasy, is that besides being instruments of environmental research, these technologies enact on behalf of sovereign states certain rituals of possession — from conducting seabed surveys, with their implicit territorial meanings to planting flagpoles, a more theatrical gesture (Greenblatt 1991; Seed 1995). Technological demonstrations by states have an intrinsic rhetorical quality that has been well documented by historians of technology. In the twentieth century, nuclear weapons were the most poignant sign of the complex political calculus surrounding the possession and display of a state-owned technology. The Kennedy administration was famously frustrated by the difficulty of translating nuclear weapons into political power, in spite of the prestige associated with possessing those weapons (Roberts 1981). The belief that technological supremacy can secure the political and territorial integrity of a nation is part of the "rhetoric of the technological sublime," a term that originates in nineteenth-century visions of the railway and nation building (Nye 1994). If the railway played a key role in the practical and imaginary political integration of western Canada, so too has the development of northern landscapes been instrumental in constructing a close relationship between ideas of nordicity and Canadian nationhood (Powell 2004, 67).

Some conceptions of nationhood, like that promoted by the strident Canada First movement of the late nineteenth century, have been far from benign, so now is a good moment to ask what relationships between North and nation the discourse of icebreakers and research stations is constructing. Would the impact of acquiring a set of integrated Arctic technologies today be akin to the impact of completing the Canadian Pacific Railway over a century ago? The answer lies in the most contemporary of technologies: the social and material networks in which these more visible technological complexes are situated. Discussion of these networks is of practical importance, because if Canada is going to commit billions of dollars to implementing an integrated complex of technological systems, how can government ministers be assured of a political return on investment? To show how an integrated approach can deliver a political return, I want to turn to the historical role of environmental science as an instrument of diplomacy.

Science, Internationalism and the International Geophysical Year

S TATES HAVE BEEN USING THE LANGUAGE OF INTERNATIONALISM TO PRESENT SCIENCE as a disinterested activity — one that rises above the interests of nations — for over 200 years. For example, British gentlemen of science and French savants continued to correspond, sharing scientific results, in the aftermath of the French Revolution (1789-99) and the Napoleonic Wars (1800-15). Internationalism as a political ethos of sharing and collaborating in science emerged most clearly in the period 1860 to 1914 (Crawford, Shinn and Sörlin 1993). Regional or global studies in geophysics and biogeography, which involved increasingly specialized professional, coordinated networks of scientific labour, necessitated access to international territory. This entailed scientific diplomacy; scientific leaders negotiated standardized procedures for calibrating precision instruments, measuring natural phenomena, sharing data and publishing in a common scientific community. This diplomacy sometimes served national goals within the international political arena, while at other times scientists sought cooperation in a climate of international tensions. The pattern of negotiating synergies and competitive tensions between national and international advantage characterized the forces that gave birth to the four International Polar Years (1882-83, 1932-33, 1957-58 and 2007-08), and it continues to inform international partnerships in science.

Although international initiatives in science have often been simultaneously competitive and collaborative, they have produced prestige and a body of shared public knowledge — this is far more than a zero-sum game. Following the Great Exhibition of 1851 in London, nations vied to host international congresses in science and industry because these bestowed prestige upon their hosts. Various nations invested great energy in demonstrating their ranking in the scientific and technological worlds, all the while espousing internationalism as an ideology that understood science to be a transnational activity serving interests beyond those of the state. Many internationalists also embraced an ethos of tolerance and freedom. For them, science seemed to hold out the promise of world peace. In truth, internationalism coexisted in tension with nationalism, simultaneously serving national interests and disavowing them.

Throughout the period 1870 to 1920, the transformation of scientific research was closely linked to the advent of new research institutions, particularly laboratories and national museums. International sharing and exchange could take many forms. For instance, colonial scientific expeditions routinely brought back to museums copious specimens, including dozens of duplicates, which were then traded with other national museums to develop the breadth of all the collections. A nation that lacked colonial access could rely on private travellers or exchanges between museums. At the same time, decisions about whether to publish scientific surveys for international dissemination, keep them secret or present them for international adjudication were frequently decided on pragmatic grounds. Because scientific internationalism in the polar regions was embraced in various guises by Russia, the United States, Denmark, Sweden, Norway, France and Germany, it occupied a particular kind of shared epistemic space.

Scientific research stations, field stations or bases were the counterparts in the geographical peripheries of the laboratories and museums in metropolitan centres during this period of "High Empire" (Cunningham and Williams 1992; Kohler 2002a; Bravo and Sörlin 2002). As outposts ostensibly dedicated to peaceful ends, though sometimes used for surveillance or espionage, research stations were seen by politicians as an effective means of establishing a nonthreatening state presence at relatively little cost. No less important from the perspective of scientists, they also made possible new kinds of field experiments, bringing new kinds of precision scientific apparatus to distant regions for the first time (Kohler 2002c). Whereas labs were designed to be "placeless places," stripped of their locality to create a setting where results could be universalized, research stations in the field were more often sites where direct and sometimes long-term experience with, and knowledge of, human, plant and animal communities and their surroundings were held in productive tension with universalist goals (Kohler 2002b).

In some contexts (like Antarctica, prior to the Antarctic Treaty), research stations were simultaneously sites of national scientific presence and places explicitly linked to territorial claims. However, they were also markers that projected a geopolitical presence beyond their immediate surroundings, although the logic and source of that power was rarely spelled out publicly. The political ambiguity inherent in having stations that stood for claims to larger territories mirrored the ambiguity arising from their roles as both local sites of access to field observations and experiments and powerful, placeless signifiers of the production of universal scientific laws.

Antarctica, following the Antarctic Treaty (1961), is today the most famous example (though it is by no means the first) of a colonized region evoked by colonizing language as the "continent for peaceful science" and the "heritage of all mankind." Putting aside for a moment the innovative character of the treaty, it is useful to recall the important tradition of colonial natural history writing, in which non-European landscapes were viewed as depopulated, their resources in need of being described and classified rationally or scientifically and then wisely managed (Pratt 1992; Drayton 2000).

Shrouded in mythology, Antarctica presents a romantic, modernist, even utopian vision of the world; it is a vast and fragile landscape where human presence pales to insignificance. This spawns the oft-repeated trope of Antarctica as uninhabited — which is, of course, quite false, since the ice-capped continent has towns and stations populated by scientists and support workers. However, the notion of Antarctica as "empty continent" tells us something important about the exceptionalism of research stations — it's as though the objectivity of scientific research effaces the stations' presence in the landscape. The absence of a native population is, however, no accident; it is a product of Antarctica's recent climate and still more recent legal regime.

During the International Geophysical Year (1957-58), many research stations were rapidly constructed in Antarctica. Under the banner of "a continent devoted to peace and science," the stations created a geopolitical presence by proxy. In time, human settlements became communities — in some cases, tiny camps; in others, miniature science cities. Recent research has, for example, begun to explore the construction of identity among the civilian workers who provide support services to the National Science Foundation research station at McMurdo. Local citizens identify themselves as Americans, but they also see themselves as a community of Antarcticans (Dozier 2007); at the Chilean research station on the Antarctic Peninsula, a number of babies have been born, presumably lending credence to the idea that the peninsula is part of the nation and home to its people.[4] These are just two examples of how people living at research stations play a role in constructing geopolitical meanings.

The construction in the mid-1950s of joint American-Canadian military mega-infrastructure, like the Distant Early Warning (DEW) Line of radar stations spanning the Arctic coast from Alaska to Baffin Island, heralded a period of massive technological development in the North. For many southern Canadians, the arrival of so many foreign servicemen — albeit allies — was a source of unease. The 1957 launch of the Sputnik satellites, which took geopolitical tensions into space, as well as the transit of the submarine USS *Nautilus* across the Arctic Basin, drew further attention to remote strategic spaces like the Arctic. With its rapidly increasing strategic importance, Canada came under pressure from the US to carry out more defence-related scientific research (Powell 2004, 77; Powell 2008).

Up until that time, a significant proportion of Canada's state-funded Arctic scientific research (as opposed to the Geological Survey of Canada) had been initiated by the Defence Research Board, which envisaged the Arctic as a remote strategic theatre separating and protecting North America from the Soviet Union. The questions posed by defence research projects were typically more concerned with understanding the physiological effects of cold and exposure on the human body. Indigenous health was interesting to them insofar as northern peoples seemed better adapted to the extreme conditions than southerners, but understanding the everyday health care needs and epidemiology of northern peoples would have to wait for the arrival of social medicine and the reorganization of Arctic research funding in a way that would recognize that indigenous health was a legitimate state responsibility.

In his study of the Polar Continental Shelf Project (PCSP), historical geographer Richard Powell makes the persuasive argument that a distinctly national program of Arctic science was developed in order to protect Canada's sovereignty during this period of heightened strategic focus on the Arctic. The Diefenbaker government's role in the demise of the Avro Arrow project and its "divisions over continental defense policy" led historians to "neglect both the northern policies introduced during the early years" of the government and "the impact of the [northern] vision on the public servants tasked with its implementation" (Powell 2004, 75). Excessive attention was instead focused on the government's later Roads to Resources campaign, which was linked to Diefenbaker's re-election and spearheaded by Alvin Hamilton. This undertaking also reflected a concern with the resource potential of Canada's northern provinces as well as the activities of the Soviets and Americans in the Polar Basin, but this phase of implementing a northern vision was preceded by the creation of the PCSP (Powell 2004, 77). Recognizing the significance of establishing sovereignty for future resource claims, the federal government took action to secure knowledge relevant to hydrocarbon deposits on the continental shelf. To that end, Canada had a relatively large proportion of its IGY projects (26 out of 76) based in the Arctic.

One of the lessons learned from Canada's Arctic IGY is that a network of research stations and camps — based on a hub-and-spokes model, with the PCSP at the centre — enabled the Canadian government to use the PCSP's scientific practices (scientific surveys, structured measurements and experiments) in this particularly critical High Arctic geographical space to demonstrate a national sovereign presence in the Arctic (Powell 2007). This program of science was also sufficiently autonomous from military institutional interests that Canadian polar science could be clearly recognized as a peaceful contribution to the international community, for all that it was also based on a degree of national self-interest (Powell 2004). Under the leadership of its first coordinator, Fred Roots, the PCSP was established at the Joint Arctic Weather Station at Isachsen in 1959 as a field site because of its proximity to the continental shelf. It later operated out of Mould Bay, and then Tuktoyaktuk, but for much of its existence it remained true to Roots's vision of a "footloose research organization without owning its infrastructure, undertaking a lot of excellent science."[5]

Judging the success of the PCSP is a complex task. It depends upon context and time frame. The PCSP built a reputation for itself, attracting a dedicated, highly skilled and — when required — adventurous new generation of Arctic scientists. While it produced hydrographic and seismic information that was of practical value to those promoting Canadian sovereignty and those engaged in resource mapping, it also helped to resolve research problems concerning the behaviour of glaciers, sea ice, ocean circulation and navigation (Powell 2004). Seen over the longer term, the separation of a large chunk of the Ward Hunt Ice Shelf from Ellesmere Island in July 2008 was anticipated thanks in part to long-term glaciology and telecommunications research (the space-based photographs of this event were provided by Canada's RADARSAT-2) that has its origins in the IGY period. Seen from the standpoint of international law, the mapping of the continental shelf also has to be judged in the context of the successive negotiations in the three conferences of the United Nations Convention on the Law of the Sea (UNCLOS), the first of which began in 1956, and the last of which entered into force in 1994 (see Rob Huebert's chapter in this volume). Nevertheless, some of the continental shelf areas, besides falling within nations' 200-mile exclusive economic zones, are inhabited and subject to customary or traditional use (by, for example, the northern indigenous peoples of Canada, the United States, Norway or Russia). Other bodies of international agreements governing coastal regions, particularly those related to environmental law and human rights, may also come to be seen in hindsight as important to Canada's understanding of science and governance.

Several key political precedents related to the way that international science is governed were established during the IGY; these are crucial to our understanding of the significance of today's international polar research stations and networks, and of their limitations. When the World Meteorological Organization (WMO) was created, in 1950, it was widely seen as an opportunity to add "an important new component to international science by establishing and coordinating joint scientific research agendas" (Miller and Edwards 2001, 198). Drawing on a longer history of cooperation in international research, with its roots in nineteenth-century networks of geophysical surveys, the WMO extended to the newly emerging IGY networks established practices of standardization: training in experimental techniques; calibration of precision instruments; and implementation of shared standards of metrology, uniform record-keeping formats and centres for long-term storage. Many of these practices have their origins in early-nineteenth-century magnetic networks formed around key magnetic observatories like Carl Friedrich Gauss's in Gottingen (1833) or Edward Sabine's at Kew (circa 1842) (Cawood 1979). The IGY defined the principal inherited features of nineteenth-century scientific geophysical networks by adopting a distributed model of international funding where scientific agendas were "organised, funded, and implemented by national scientific agencies" (Miller and Edwards 2001, 201).

Behind the scientific idealism of the IGY and the special status afforded to Antarctica were the growing international political divisions created by the Cold War climate. The Eisenhower administration supported the building of scientific bridges across political boundaries by encouraging the sharing of scientific knowledge. Using its economic and political clout, the United States promoted the idea of building new research stations and situating them with an eye to enhancing global coverage (Miller and Edwards 2001, 203). However, the separation of science in the spirit of international peace from military research was always contingent on the political organization of research. American scientists worked to solve a range of problems connected to global atmospheric circulation that seemed unrelated to military concerns, but the American scientific administration recognized that this work was highly relevant to military issues, such as ballistic missile trajectories (Miller and Edwards 2001, 203).

Sovereignty in the Arctic, and in other parts of the world, was bound up with the IGY and growing international divisions in ideology, security and wealth. With the onset of the Cold War and the emergence of the Third World group of countries, world politics were by no means entirely conducive for building international scientific cooperation. The Eisenhower administration decided that it needed to engage with other countries to promote its own ideology of freedom, and that it also needed to play a leading role in creating the mechanisms and rules governing how science and technology were used as international instruments to share knowledge, promote dialogue and deliver aid to less-developed countries. It was deemed that the best way to maintain American influence, encourage the growth of democracy abroad and prevent the balkanization of the Third World was to take the lead in funding and promoting the sharing and transfer of knowledge. In negotiating who could participate in the IGY, the US was forced to confront the problem that the participation of the People's Republic of China, accepted by the IGY, could imply international (and therefore American) recognition of its sovereignty, something that the US was at great pains to avoid.

Yet withdrawing from the IGY would run strongly against American political interests, and excluding China and other unrecognized regimes would seriously hinder the effort to achieve global coverage in new scientific models. In response, the International Council for Science (ICSU) at the end of the IGY adopted an American-led resolution with considerable long-term implications, affirming "the right of scientists of any country or territory to adhere to or to associate with international scientific activity without regard to race, religion or political philosophy" (Miller and Edwards 2001, 167) while also stating that "such adherence or association has no implications with respect to recognition of the country or territory concerned" (218). In one sense, this had the intended impact of injecting some distance between international science and issues of sovereignty.

Seen more critically, the constraints placed on the relationship between science and sovereignty also drew attention to new possibilities of using international science as a political instrument in situations where sovereignty is contested. The Antarctic Treaty (1961) is an example of precisely this. The establishment of research stations that would offer logistical support for scientific field experiments provided a legal basis for states to maintain a national presence in Antarctica while placing their sovereignty claims in abeyance in the name of peaceful science. Political geographers have debated the political significance of the Antarctic Treaty, and they don't necessarily agree to what extent the treaty used science to mask geopolitics by other means. Nevertheless, what I want to draw attention to here is the idea of the research station as an emblematic institution that simultaneously represents a national presence and disavows its political role. It is able to do so partly by virtue of the Antarctic Treaty's prestige but also through the rhetoric of disinterest attached to subnational scientific institutions and agencies operating at arm's length from the military. It is therefore no accident that Canada achieved its most conspicuous presence in the IGY by building an Arctic research station, and that the Canadian government seeks to replicate this achievement today through a federally coordinated plan, albeit in changing circumstances.

Can Arctic Science
Bridge the Great
Divides?

I N THE 2007-08 IPY, MOST SCIENTISTS LOOK BACK ON THE RESEARCH QUESTIONS, instruments and techniques of the IGY as an early and distant chapter in the field sciences, but the model of coordinating science top-down through umbrella organizations like the WMO and the ICSU, and devolving the identification of priorities and funding to nations, persists. This has resulted in a division of responsibilities between international bodies that provide the sanction and coordination for international scientific programs and national bodies that create research policies, define research priorities and locate funding agencies. International research programs — like the IPY of the WMO and the ICSU — are mechanisms whereby science representatives of various states can structure and coordinate shared international research priorities. The agreement of the eight Arctic countries to establish the Arctic Monitoring and Assessment Programme in 1991 under the aegis of the Arctic Environmental Protection Strategy is an important example of a critical, ongoing science program whose success depends on the individual country electing to fund participation over the long term.

The announcement of Canada's intention to commit to the IPY roughly $150 million, a sum considerably in excess of those offered by most other states, caused stakeholders at home and abroad to sit up and take notice, as did the decision that climate change and health and well-being would be the primary focuses of Canada's IPY research efforts. Seen from abroad, this appeared to be a statement of Canadian policy — it was as if Canada were saying to its fellow Arctic Council member states, "This time we are serious: we are going to prove that we no longer deserve our reputation for talking up the importance of Arctic governance without spending." The response abroad has been both positive and cautious; observers are waiting to see whether the funding materializes, and what kinds of research investment might follow. On the one hand, the significance of Canada's IPY commitment depends on whether it leads to a sustained, long-term strategy for investment in Arctic science. On the other hand, governments and international planners of IPYs see the planning of a legacy as an integral part of the IPYs.

Histories of "Big Science" programs tend not to be typical legacy stories — those that identify a particular heroic genius as the focal point of discovery. Similarly, they do not usually identify a single historical moment, like a crucial experiment, as a turning point to justify the importance, even dominance, of an international research program like an IPY. Instead, they tend to focus on institution building and recognize specific norms that are integral to scientific partnerships. Observation networks (for example, Sustaining Arctic Observation Networks [SAON] in this IPY) that can generate large calibrated and standardized data sets are traditionally the measure by which IPY success is judged (which may explain why IPYs do not figure prominently in hagiographies hinging on the genius of individuals). Broadly defined, research stations are institutions that encompass all sites — whether on land or at sea, large or small, manned or unmanned — that support sustained observation and experiment, though the term often conjures up the romantic image of a building with laboratories in a pristine location.

The Throne Speech promise of an Arctic research station should be understood as a recognition of the value of a long-term commitment to Arctic science rather than as an example of boom-and-bust spending, which is often the downside of IPY-type international events. In other words, CARI can be a vehicle for transforming a brief burst of coordinated scientific activity into a long-term program. The resonance between the promise of CARI in the 2007-08 International Polar Year and the inauguration of the Polar Continental Shelf Project in the IGY is unmistakable. And we should not be surprised, as some critics have been, that the Harper government invoked Diefenbaker's rhetoric of a northern vision in the Throne Speech; the current government may see itself in a similar position — confronting a new sense of vulnerability and seeking to secure the nation's territory, boundaries and resources. The research station is, therefore, an expression of a political desire for a stronger demonstration of a technologically modern and sovereign scientific presence. In this sense, CARI does resonate with the founding of the PCSP.

One fundamental fact that distinguishes the structure of Canada's IPY from that of its IGY is that Canada is a very different country from the one it was 50 years ago. Today's Arctic Canada has been redefined by a series of political agreements involving a far more complex range of stakeholders, partnerships and science needs. For some Arctic citizens, the day-to-day federal presence, which once felt overwhelming, still feels excessive. However, many southern Canadians concerned about sovereignty perceive the Arctic as lacking an adequate federal presence. This highlights a serious fault line in north-south relationships that mirrors and inverts the global north-south divide. For northerners, science is a source of development or aid; but for federal government officials and university researchers, science and technology are powerful instruments for producing knowledge that facilitates better rational governance (Bravo 2006).

This asymmetric perception of science and technology reflects the economic history of core-periphery relationships in Canada and should not be lightly dismissed. The political challenge for federal northern science and technology policy is to foster research that can help to reduce domestic north-south inequalities and build a northern research capacity while meeting international obligations to provide more research into, and monitoring of, processes and issues that affect the entire Arctic, if not the globe. Although north-south political differences may be difficult to resolve, a northern science and technology strategy built on strong partnerships would present a real opportunity to find shared ground for northern and southern interests.

Complicating the design of the government's northern strategy is the distribution of responsibility across a horizontal hierarchy of stakeholders. Within the federal government, responsibility for scientific research in the Arctic is divided between several departments: Natural Resources Canada, Fisheries and Oceans Canada, Environment Canada, Foreign Affairs and International Trade, National Defence, Health Canada, Industry Canada, Parks Canada and INAC. Add to this the Canadian Polar Commission (a departmental corporation), the Canadian Space Agency (a statutory agency) and the International Polar Year Secretariat (part of INAC but at arm's length). The profound challenge of overcoming interdepartmental divisions and historical rivalries is faced by most governments, but it is particularly difficult in cases where science activity is not coordinated by a central agency. The small team of federal officials with INAC's Northern Affairs Program charged with developing CARI has commissioned scoping papers from a number of federal departments. The Canadian Polar Commission has also published an evaluation of the state of Canada's Arctic research infrastructure. The Canadian IPY Secretariat and ArcticNet have each made a significant contribution to a policy assessment of Canada's Arctic research needs, as has Inuit Tapiriit Kanatami on behalf of Inuit. After holding several consultations with Arctic science stakeholders from government, academia, the private sector and Aboriginal organizations, INAC produced "Defining Science Priorities for Canada's New Arctic Science Station" (Council of Canadian Academies 2008). All these reports, taken together, demonstrate that an enormous amount of work has been undertaken to determine scientific priorities and assess what demands these will make on CARI.

Building a consensus is an essential but time-consuming task, and it is complicated by the fact that stakeholder science policy entails various approaches and stages of development. The devolution of responsibility from international scientific organizations to the state gives a key role in Arctic science to federal government departments, as well as to universities, whose scientific research funding depends on government-funded research councils (and on private sector interests). The IPY is a federal initiative in the sense that it is federally funded and administered by an arm's-length secretariat with support from the Natural Sciences and Engineering Research Council of Canada. Applications for funding have not been restricted to government departments and universities — though to date, they have submitted most of the applications.

In principle, nothing prevents the federal government from devolving some responsibility for the IPY to subnational governments and nonstate actors. After all, the devolution of political responsibility through land claims and self-government agreements in northern Canada was matched by the devolution of federal research station assets at Inuvik, Igloolik and Iqaluit to the Northwest Territories in 1988 — though not the PCSP, which remained under federal control. A big challenge for CARI that won't be met overnight is to recognize the difference between those areas where research needs should be reintegrated into nationally funded and administered research programs (for example, persistent organic pollutants, or POPs), and those better suited to a coordinated model of devolved funding (for example, the health of Aboriginal youth). This means that CARI could explore a new kind of social contract between science and its stakeholders for particular areas of research. The IPY model of research, built into the creation of a semi-autonomous secretariat, could form part of that model, but it is unlikely to meet all of the needs of northern citizens.

Architecture and Community Collaboration with CARI

IN PRACTICAL TERMS, PLANNING AN ARCTIC RESEARCH STATION FOR A NEW INTEGRATED northern strategy requires clear answers to these questions: Where should the station be located? In what form should it be constructed? For whom should it be built? The government is currently exploring all options. Given the current concern over regulating sea traffic, one might anticipate that CARI will need access to a deepwater port near the Northwest Passage. A hub-and-spokes model of science, perhaps with a distributed network of smaller hubs, also seems sensible, as it would ensure that CARI has access to all of the Arctic's ecosystems — though, given the large capital expenditure required, CARI may initially have to be a centralized research station. In other words, a request for proposals would likely require a singular design to be built to high specifications corresponding to multiple geographical and logistical requirements.

Architectural contracts for designing polar research stations of this kind are prestigious and normally awarded through competition and tenders. The new British research station in Antarctica, Halley VI, designed by Faber Maunsell and Hugh Broughton Architects, is an excellent example. The high-spec design meets demanding logistical requirements for accommodation, transportation, laboratory space and transportation to the field; the station stands on hydraulic legs and can be relocated periodically to avoid the fate of most Antarctic stations — being buried in the perennially thickening ice sheet. Marrying form and function to provide services to a range of Canada's High Arctic workers in different ecosystems and communities that see great seasonal variations presents some new architectural challenges. A station that could meet such challenges would not be an off-the-shelf product. The government will likely commission a design that is striking in appearance and sublime in the way that it integrates geography, environment and functionality.

A number of modernist schemes for science cities, research stations and schools have been designed for northern Canada (for example, early designs for the Iqaluit and Igloolik research centres). Of those built, none is sufficiently recent or successful to serve as a relevant model for the innovative architecture being discussed. The research station, like most major new commissions, would constitute an Arctic experiment in its own right — an experiment in creating and managing expert knowledge. Done right, the project would allow the federal government to demonstrate that its commitment to science is serious and long term. This would represent a departure from decades of short-term planning and be a credible response to the theatrical planting of titanium flagpoles, which characterizes the race for resources.

Successful partnerships between researchers and local institutions show us the enormous potential such a project would hold for addressing local and regional problems — but only if there is a restructured model for the governance of research. For instance, the Aurora Research Institute, with the support of Nellie Cournoyea, Chair and CEO of the Inuvialuit Regional Corporation, is advocating the development of wind farms to meet some of the local energy demand, which is currently met by hydrocarbons. However, the Aurora Research Institute inherited the federal government's model, in which northern research is carried out on a small scale and oriented toward fact-finding for federal policies. Such research is conducted at a distance from those who make decisions about finance and investment, and it is largely disconnected from northern resource development.

In drawing lessons about northern partnerships for CARI from previous partnerships between research stations and communities, it is helpful to start from the perspective of the late 1960s and early 1970s, when there was a growing indigenous political consciousness in northern Canada. As grassroots movements for land claims and devolution emerged, the authority of Western science came under close scrutiny. Its status as sole arbiter of truth was challenged not only in Canada but also in many regions of the globe, where indigenous groups were renegotiating the legal meanings and conditions of sovereignty and aboriginal title. The utilitarian notion that science promoted the common good (unlike medicine, which was widely understood to provide a direct social benefit) had little impact on northern peoples. Research stations were perceived by northern communities as southern institutions serving southern interests and offering local employment to, at best, a handful of people; those perceptions persist.

In 1969, departing from the Cold War practice of building research stations near Inuit communities in order to provide the benefits of local employment without the social impact, the federal government changed its policy and decided to construct a temporary research laboratory in Igloolik. Although a fire destroyed it before it could be used, the laboratory was designed for visiting scientists working in the International Biological Program who intended to undertake biological and medical studies on members of the community.[6] Four years later, the government announced plans to build a full-fledged research station in Igloolik. The Inuit Tapirisat of Canada (ITC; now called Inuit Tapiriit Kanatami) wrote to the Department of Indian and Northern Affairs questioning whether the station would actually serve Inuit interests. ITC proposed instead a new community cultural centre extending the network of the Inuit Cultural Institute, which would have stronger local support and be more useful. This example illustrates how, early in the formation of a new grassroots indigenous political movement, a research station became a site for contesting the status of expert knowledge with an eye to promoting community development (Bravo 2006).

Nellie Cournoyea recognizes the fundamental importance of marrying instruments of regional investment with access to advanced scientific and industrial research and development, and she has therefore invited the federal government to locate Canada's new Arctic research station near Tuktoyaktuk. Exploring how a regional development corporation could work in partnership with a well-funded federal research institute — and, presumably, private sector industries — could represent a significant departure from past federal models for research stations. The Canadian IPY Secretariat has tried to involve Canada's northern peoples and their representatives, though the institutional structure of IPY militated against this. However, the institutional model of public engagement used throughout most spheres of international science remains the deficit model, and it divides citizens into two groups. Those with qualifications in science and technology and who do the research are deemed experts; while members of a large lay public, who do not possess such qualifications, participate as the recipients of outreach initiatives. This model has been widely challenged, and it is giving way to a variety of new approaches to public engagement (land claims mapping is an extremely important example). Yet the deficit model persists, in spite of the fact that it is totally unsuited to situations of devolved governance, particularly in cultures where local expertise does not necessarily imply the exclusion of others' viewpoints.

Conclusion

THE INCLUSION OF A SPECIAL SIXTH THEME DEDICATED TO THE HUMANITIES AND social sciences in the framework for the 2007-08 IPY distinguished it from the IGY and all previous IPYs. It could be argued that the late addition of this theme — "The Human Dimension" — to the set of five natural science themes provided the warrant for Canada's approach to the IPY: a focus on climate change and health. While that may be true, Canada's human dimension focus was more narrowly conceived than the IPY humanities theme for reasons that are worth reflecting upon. Initially, it looked as though the IPY would be strictly limited to the natural sciences. Some members of the International Arctic Social Sciences Association were dismayed at the prospect of launching a full-blown IPY to study the Arctic without making any attempt to involve the people living in the region (Krupnik et al. 2005; Hovelsrud and Krupnik 2006). As my colleague

Igor Krupnik remarked, it seemed a throwback to the early days of the IGY, before Alaska had been granted statehood. The IPY's sixth theme was "to investigate the cultural, historical, and social processes that shape the sustainability of circumpolar human societies, and to identify their unique contributions to global cultural diversity and citizenship" (International Council for Science International Polar Year Planning Group 2004, 7). This explicit statement linking the importance of citizenship to research was a landmark — the first time an IPY's scope had ever been defined in terms that recognized the role and contribution of circumpolar societies. In its interpretation of the "human dimension," a term that has acquired currency in earth systems science, Canada referred to "climate change" and "health" primarily as they related to the impact of natural processes on northern populations.

The IPY, whatever its virtues, is widely perceived in northern Canada as a program imposed on northern citizens by the federal government rather than as an opportunity created with the participation of those citizens. This perception is by no means groundless. At a time when the social contract between science and its public is being renegotiated in many leading industrialized nations and a new ethical consensus on the management of research into emergent technologies like nanotechnology and biotechnology is being sought, the position of Canada (and, to a large extent, other Arctic nations) in relation to Arctic research looks less than adventurous. Canada's decision to involve northern societies to a lesser extent than, say, the public of Ontario in debates about nanotechnology is, however, no accident; rather, it demonstrates that the federal university-funding institutions take a relatively conservative approach to framing and understanding their role as experts in relation to the people and institutions of the North.

CARI could be Canada's best opportunity to integrate the sixth theme, citizenship and humanities/human dimension, into its mandate instead of remaining content to see the benefits of expert science reach the public through a diffusion or trickle-down effect. The polity must promote citizenship by providing mechanisms to allow citizens to shape the policies that have an impact on their welfare. When it comes to expert knowledge like science and medicine, this would give citizens a voice in deciding to what end expert knowledge was marshalled and how expert interventions, including research, would be regulated. The early signs are that CARI will take citizenship more seriously, possibly out of a sense of justice, but almost certainly because the CARI mandate will involve the private sector, which (in some industries) has regulatory procedures for environmental impact assessments and impact benefit agreements with built-in principles of citizenship. These procedures need significant strengthening, and here scientists will have a major opportunity to make a contribution by providing systematic environmental baseline data.

For many scientists, focused on their research programs, discussions of citizenship are irrelevant — or, at least, best left until the day's work has been completed. But fundamental questions must be addressed about the public's trust in scientists, particularly in the Arctic, where public institutions have not always been as disinterested as they have purported to be. These issues are complex, but the way forward is clear: we must explore new kinds of partnerships across old and new institutional boundaries. Many of the building blocks are in place. Many northerners are already highly trained in mobilizing expert knowledge in everyday life, and some northern leaders have made distinguished contributions to global citizenship. The stakes are high. The excessive dependence of northern citizens on a powerful federal government ironically underscores that government's limited ability to act on behalf of those who inhabit the perimeter of its territory. However, the growing capacity of northern citizens to use expert knowledge and intellectual capital to sustain their livelihoods and environment is the clearest demonstration of Arctic stewardship. The real challenge for CARI is to marshal science and technology to build partnerships, a knowledge base and a regulatory environment that secures and maintains the integrity of Canada's Arctic.

Notes

1   I would like to thank this volume's editors
     for the encouragement they gave me as I
     shaped the argument of this chapter. I owe a
     particular debt to Richard Powell for availing
     me of his encyclopedic knowledge of the
     history of twentieth-century Arctic science in
     Canada. For his understanding of interna-
     tional law, sovereignty and human rights, I
     am also indebted to Timo Koivurova. For
     numerous conversations that introduced me
     to the importance of international relations
     in understanding Arctic science, I have a
     debt of gratitude to Jessica Shadian. Danielle
     Labonté, Nick Xenos and Georgina Lloyd of
     INAC all offered helpful critical comments
     and clarifications, as did Steven Bigras of the
     Canadian Polar Commission.

2   The idea of exploring the relationships
     between iconic species and iconic technolo-
     gies was proposed in a roundtable discus-
     sion on conservation and development to
     which I contributed with Christina
     Sawchuk; the discussion was entitled
     "Heading North, Heading South: Arctic
     Social Sciences Research in a Global
     Dialogue," and it was held at the Max
     Planck Institute for Anthropology, Halle,
     Germany, in March 2008.

3   Richard Charles Powell, conversation with
     the author, June 23, 2008.

4   Juan Salazar, personal communication with
     the author, May 4, 2008.

5   Richard Charles Powell, conversation with
     the author, June 23, 2008.

6   Very little research has been carried out on
     the history of the International Biological
     Program.

References

Bravo, Michael. 2006. "Science for the People:
     Northern Field Stations and
     Governmentality." In "Governance, Culture
     and Identity in Contemporary Canada,"
     edited by Susan Hodgett and Stephen A.
     Royle. Special issue, British Journal of
     Canadian Studies 19 (2): 78-102.

Bravo, Michael, and Sverker Sörlin. 2002.
     Narrating the Arctic: A Cultural History of
     Nordic Scientific Practices. Canton, MA:
     Science History Publications.

Cawood, John. 1979. "The Magnetic Crusade:
     Science and Politics in Early Victorian
     Britain." Isis 70:493-518.

Council of Canadian Academies (CCA). 2008.
     "Visioning Workshop: Defining Science
     Priorities for Canada's New Arctic Station."
     In Vision for the Canadian Arctic Research
     Initiative: Assessing the Opportunities, appen-
     dix A. Ottawa: CCA

Crawford, Elisabeth T., Terry Shinn, and Sverker
     Sörlin, eds. 1993. Denationalizing Science:
     The Contexts of International Scientific Practice.
     Dordrecht: Kluwer Academic Publishers.

Cunningham, Andrew, and Perry Williams, eds.
     1992. The Laboratory Revolution in Medicine.
     Cambridge: Cambridge University Press.

Dozier, Ann. 2007. "Getting the Science Done:
     An Ethnography of Science in Antarctica."
     Paper presented at the International Polar
     Year Field Stations meeting, Scott Polar
     Research Institute, January 3-4, Cambridge.

Drayton, Richard H. 2000. Nature's Government:
     Science, Imperial Britain, and the
     "Improvement" of the World. New Haven:
     Yale University Press.

England, John, Arthur S. Dyke, and Greg H.
     Henry. 1998. "Canada's Crisis in Arctic
     Science: The Urgent Need for an Arctic
     Science and Technology Policy; Or, 'Why
     Work in the Arctic? No One Lives There.'"
     Arctic 51 (2): 183-90.

Government of Canada. 2007. Strong Leadership.
     A Better Canada. Speech from the Throne,
     October 16, 2007, 39th Parliament, 2nd
     sess. Ottawa: Government of Canada.

Greenblatt, Stephen. 1991. Marvellous Possessions:
     The Wonder of the New World. Oxford:
     Clarendon.

Hassol, Susan Joy. 2004. Impacts of a Warming
     Arctic: Arctic Climate Impact Assessment.
     Cambridge: Cambridge University Press.
     Accessed May 26, 2008.
     http://www.amap.no/acia/

Hovelsrud, Grete, and Igor Krupnik. 2006. "IPY 2007–08 and Social/Human Sciences: An Update." *Arctic* 59 (3): 341-8.

International Council for Science (ICSU) International Polar Year Planning Group. 2004. *A Framework for the International Polar Year 2007-2008*. Paris: ICSU. Accessed 31 July 2008. http://classic.ipy.org/development/framework/framework.pdf

Kohler, Robert E. 2002a. *Landscapes and Labscapes: Exploring the Lab-Field Border in Biology*. Chicago: University of Chicago Press.

————. 2002b. "Labscapes: Naturalizing the Lab." *History of Science* 40 (4): 473-501.

————. 2002c. "Place and Practice in Field Biology." *History of Science* 40 (2): 189-210.

Krupnik, Igor, Michael Bravo, Yvon Csonka, Grete Hovelsrud, Ludger Müller-Wille, Birger Poppel, Peter Schweitzer, and Sverker Sörlin. 2005. "Social Sciences and Humanities in the International Polar Year 2007-2008: An Integrating Mission." *Arctic* 58 (1): 91-7.

Martello, M.L. 2004. "Global Change Science and the Arctic Citizen." *Science and Public Policy* 31 (2): 107-15.

Miller, Clark A., and Paul N. Edwards. 2001. *Changing the Atmosphere: Expert Knowledge and Environmental Governance*. Cambridge: MIT Press.

Nye, David E. 1994. *American Technological Sublime*. Cambridge: MIT Press.

Powell, Richard Charles. 2004. "Intemperate Spaces: Field Practices and Environmental Science in the Canadian Arctic, 1955-2000." Ph.D. diss., University of Cambridge.

————. 2007. "The Rigours of an Arctic Experiment: The Precarious Authority of Field Practices in the Canadian High Arctic, 1958-1970." *Environment and Planning A* 39 (8): 1794-811.

————. 2008. "Science, Sovereignty and Nation: Canada and the Legacy of the International Geophysical Year 1957-58." *Journal of Historical Geography* 34: 618-38.

Pratt, Mary Louise. 1992. *Imperial Eyes: Studies in Travel Writing and Transculturation*. London: Routledge.

Roberts, Alan. 1981. "Preparing to Fight a Nuclear War." *Arena* 57:45-93.

Seed, Patricia. 1995. *Ceremonies of Possession in Europe's Conquest of the New World, 1492-1640*. Cambridge: Cambridge University Press.

Shadian, Jessica. Forthcoming. "Revisiting Politics and Science in the Poles: IPY and the Governance of Science in Post-Westphalia." In *Legacies and Change in Polar Science: Historical, Legal and Political Reflections on the International Polar Year*, edited by Jessica Shadian and Monica Tennberg. Aldershot: Ashgate Press.

Thongchai, Winichakul. 1994. *Siam Mapped: A History of the Geo-body of a Nation*. Honolulu: University of Hawaii Press.

The Arctic: A Model for
Science Cooperation?

I N MY OFFICE, I HAVE A MAP SHOWING THE ARCTIC REGION WITH THE NORTH POLE AT the centre and the Arctic countries surrounding it. It surprises many of my visitors — they are used to seeing the Arctic as a remote white blot in the map's extreme upper left-hand corner. But on my map the North Pole is the centre of the world and the Arctic countries are clearly neighbours. Until 10 years ago, most people outside the Arctic — decision-makers and laypersons alike — saw the Arctic as a very distant place of interest mostly to its own inhabitants plus a handful of nerds and geeks. Now, after a revolution in technological communication and in light of a rising awareness of the impacts of climate change, this perception has changed dramatically. The North Pole is suddenly as central as it appears on the circumpolar map. We must take advantage of this new interest in the Arctic and capitalize on the increase in research, knowledge and awareness of Arctic issues in ways that will benefit the people who live in the region.

There is a long tradition of science collaboration in the Arctic, and a considerable number of international scientific polar organizations have been established in the region. Through an examination of examples of cooperation in various international forums, I will illustrate some of the ways in which Arctic science cooperation is unique, how it could be enhanced and what it has to offer.

Arctic research is not a discipline as such, but a collection of themes that, for various reasons, are related to the Arctic. It encompasses both basic and applied research, and it creates important linkages among communities, industry representatives and policy-makers. The Arctic's vastness, remote location and extreme climatic conditions make logistical cooperation — among people, disciplines, regions and countries — all the more attractive, and even necessary. There is, in fact, a long tradition of such cooperation. The 2007 celebration of International Polar Year (the first was in 1882) is one element of this tradition, and it gave rise to interaction between the scientific world and the rest of society at the local, regional and global levels. But science cooperation is an ongoing process, and in the Arctic it still faces substantial challenges.

Today's Arctic is a region characterized by considerable variations in population, climate, culture and community life (Young and Einarsson 2004). The circumpolar North also features an abundance of natural resources — such as marine cultures, wildlife, oil and gas. Many Arctic landscapes are pristine; their flora and fauna are adapted to the cold and are largely undisturbed by human activity, though the area has been shown to be affected by transported contaminants (Conservation of Arctic Flora and Fauna 2001). In other areas, however, there is extensive exploitation of biological and mineral resources. The polar regions are an active and vital component of our planet, and significant changes are occurring there. They harbour information about the Earth's past geological behaviour and have growing economic and geopolitical importance. While the harsh physical conditions and remote location of the polar regions have hampered scientific investigation (Rapley, Bell, Allison et al. 2004), these regions have inspired inhabitants to conduct research of their own and also attracted many researchers from outside the Arctic. The challenge remains to ensure that Arctic inhabitants and visiting researchers continue to communicate and interact, that Arctic inhabitants are involved in the research process and that the polar regions derive maximum benefits from escalating world interest. Considerations such as these make the Arctic a very interesting site for research cooperation.

Science Cooperation through the Arctic Council

I FIRST UNDERSTOOD HOW IMPORTANT SCIENCE COOPERATION IS WHEN I BEGAN WORKING on the Arctic Environmental Protection Strategy (AEPS), which, in 1996, would lead to the formation of the Arctic Council. In 1991, I served as a member of the Arctic Monitoring and Assessment Programme (AMAP), an international organization established to implement components of the AEPS, which would later become one of the Arctic Council's five working groups. AMAP was asked to monitor the levels and assess the effects of selected anthropogenic pollutants in all parts of the Arctic. Our task was to organize sample collection and present research data in a way that would be useful to decision-makers and the public (AMAP 1997). This collaborative effort involved more than 400 scientists and administrators. Based on data derived from national and international monitoring programs within the eight Arctic countries and contributions from non-Arctic countries and international organizations, we produced an assessment of contaminants in the entire Arctic region (AMAP 1998). Since the assessment reflected the reality of all the Arctic countries, its influence was considerable, and it facilitated the 1998 Protocol on Persistent Organic Pollutants (POPs) and the 1999 Protocol to Abate Acidification, Eutrophication and Ground-Level Ozone, both under the United Nations Economic Commission for Europe's Convention on Long-Range Transboundary Air Pollution (LRTAP) (United Nations Economic Commission for Europe 1998, 1999). The purpose of the LRTAP is to reduce, control or prevent transboundary air pollution. This regionally binding agreement and its five related protocols are an appropriate instrument for addressing aspects of Arctic pollution. Its adoption sent a tremendously strong message that Arctic inhabitants living in the traditional way, eating foods native to the region, had the world's highest levels of PCB and mercury — contaminants produced mainly outside the region (AMAP 1998).

The cooperative effort of AMAP also led to the creation of a circum-Arctic network of scientists working on contamination issues who were capable of interpreting results and making science-based recommendations. The assessment process forced the scientists to take an interdisciplinary approach, and this presented them with a communications challenge: How could they provide indigenous peoples with advice that balanced the cultural priority of maintaining a traditional, healthy diet with the urgent need to address the problem of contamination of the local food supply? At the same time, they also had to find a way to make it clear to Arctic inhabitants and the rest of the world that the issue of increasing contaminant levels was a complex one: not every organism in the Arctic was contaminated; on the contrary, many food items remained untainted.

The Arctic Climate Impact Assessment Process

E ARLY OBSERVATIONS OF ARCTIC CLIMATE CHANGE PROMPTED PARTICIPANTS AT THE
2000 Arctic Council Ministerial Meeting to support an Arctic climate impact
assessment. The council requested that its working groups and the International
Arctic Science Committee (IASC) evaluate and synthesize knowledge on climate
variability and change and increased ultraviolet radiation in the Arctic (Arctic
Climate Impact Assessment 2005). The council also requested that the assessment include consequences for human health and social, cultural and economic
impacts (Foreign Affairs and International Trade Canada 2000).

Nilsson points out that in the Arctic Climate Impact Assessment (ACIA), climate change is framed in two different ways: globally, in that the Arctic climate is a
key component of the global climate; and locally, in that regional climate change is
one of the many interrelated factors affecting the Arctic. With regard to the first perspective, the ACIA report emphasizes the physical and biological processes in the
Arctic that are having a significant impact on the global climate system. For example,
as the polar ice melts, freshwater runoff, ocean currents and sea levels increase or alter
in pattern; as the rate of Arctic carbon flux changes, the global carbon budget is affected; and as the Arctic habitats of migratory birds are disrupted, global biodiversity feels
the impact. The global perspective in the ACIA report is reflected in the often-repeat-
ed statement that what occurs in the Arctic as the result of greenhouse gas emissions
in the south is a bellwether for the rest of the planet (Nilsson 2007, chap. 6).

ACIA has adopted this perspective for several reasons. Since 1950, the World
Meteorological Organization (WMO) and the World Climate Research Programme
(WCRP) have promoted and coordinated research that seeks to understand the role of
Arctic processes in the global context. In doing so, they have created global science communities as well as networks of people and technologies to coordinate the Arctic part of
the undertaking. In addition, the United Nations Framework Convention on Climate
Change (UNFCCC) and the Intergovernmental Panel on Climate Change (IPCC) have
set the scene for the global initiative and drawn attention to specific climate change
issues. These developments have also provided the Arctic Council, whose work is based
on regional interests, with the opportunity to present the Arctic as globally important —
in other words, the council has acquired a globally relevant regional identity.

The second, local, perspective is reflected in the attention that ACIA pays to the multiple environmental stressors responsible for physical disturbances in the Arctic's ecosystems. It is also apparent in ACIA's view of human health as subject to a complex of influences emanating from the physical environment, cultural and community contexts, and genetic dispositions (Nilsson 2007). The regional scientific perspective on the impact of climate change on indigenous peoples also created a connection to the area of political rights, and this in turn created a formal role for indigenous peoples throughout the assessment process. The will to ensure the inclusion of indigenous voices has not been common in other climate assessments, and so ACIA represents important progress. The participation of indigenous peoples in the activities of the Arctic Council has meant that new approaches to producing knowledge about Arctic climate change have strengthened the assessment. While indigenous peoples have a power base in the Arctic Council, governments are the only legitimate political actors in the IPCC; ACIA thus illustrates how organizations can influence knowledge production by creating space for new actors in the knowledge production process, as well as by promoting and coordinating research in certain fields and channelling policy demand for knowledge (Nilsson 2007).

It remains to be seen whether the Arctic Council, in conjunction with other regional initiatives, can create new foundations for the promotion and coordination of research and organize the data collection needed to generate knowledge beyond that related to climate change issues. One hopes that such goals can be attained through the power of the Arctic's science community and the knowledge generated by scientists elsewhere. If such mechanisms are successfully formed, it will stand as a legacy of International Polar Year 2007-08.

The ACIA Process as a Basis for Science Cooperation on Adaptation

THE CIRCUM-ARCTIC SCIENCE COOPERATION THAT HAS OCCURRED THROUGH THE ACIA process has improved the basis for studies on adaptation and vulnerability — areas that are expected to receive increasing attention. During climate change discussions over the last decade, vulnerability issues have frequently emerged.

Adaptation issues have received less attention and, in some cases, research on them has even been blocked (Pielke et al. 2007). This may be because many people believe that greater focus on adaptation will undermine the fight to achieve emissions reductions. Indeed, in 1992, former US vice-president Al Gore forcefully declared his opposition to such a focus, claiming that it represented a "kind of laziness, an arrogant faith in our ability to react in time to save our skins" (1992, 240).

However, adaptation is now seen as an essential part of climate policy, alongside greenhouse gas mitigation. This is reflected in *The Economics of Climate Change: The Stern Review* and the IPCC's 2007 report on climate change (Stern 2007; IPCC 2007). One reason for this shift relates to timelines. Whatever actions are taken to decarburize the global energy system, it will take many decades for them to have a marked effect on the climate. Even the most optimistic emissions projections show global greenhouse gas concentrations continuing to rise for the foreseeable future. Furthermore, research has shown that climate change is increasingly affected by factors not directly linked to greenhouse gas emissions, such as rapid population growth along coastlines and in areas with limited water supplies (Pielke et al. 2007).

It is important that we resist seeing adaptation merely as a response to climate change resulting from anthropogenic greenhouse gas emissions. If we view it in a much broader context, it may lead us to develop a range of strategies to make our societies more robust in the face of climate change and other threatening trends. The Arctic countries, with their mixed and dispersed populations, should strive for a balance between perceiving themselves as victims of climate change created by exterior forces and realizing that global warming is only one of many challenges to their well-known ability to adjust to environmental changes. Human societies in the circumpolar North are highly resilient; they have been subjected to severe tests before and have adapted successfully to changing conditions. At the same time, it would be a mistake to assume that Arctic societies can remain resilient in the face of all change — and today they are confronting an unprecedented combination of biophysical and socio-economic stresses (Young and Einarsson 2004).

The increased attention accorded to adaptation has altered the global framing of climate change. There is a growing recognition among scientists that knowledge production focusing only on global-scale processes is not sufficient to address the issue of how society should adapt to climate change. There are, for example, major ongoing efforts to scale down global climate models in order to accommodate national studies of the impact of, and need for, adaptation. The science cooperation that led to the ACIA illustrates how a regional focus can help us to better understand some of the complexities of adaptation. The local approach does not oppose the global, but it does underline a focus shift in climate science and governance (Nilsson 2007).

The International Conference on Arctic Research Planning

T HE INTERNATIONAL CONFERENCE ON ARCTIC RESEARCH PLANNING (ICARP) OFFERS another example of how the Arctic science community is unique. A self-organized regional effort initiated by the International Arctic Science Committee, the ICARP is a comprehensive science planning conference with a 10-year perspective. It involves all Arctic science organizations and demonstrates a high level of commitment to Arctic science cooperation. For two years, 12 working groups composed of leading researchers worked on the development of science plans to improve understanding of the region — how it is changing, and how the changes will affect it and the world. This led to the second International Conference on Arctic Research Planning (ICARP II), which was held in Copenhagen in 2005 (the first was held in New Hampshire in 1995). It brought together scientists, policy-makers, research managers, indigenous peoples and other interested actors.

Between the first and second conferences, there was a shift to a holistic and multidimensional perspective in the Arctic research plans. This perspective includes the human dimension, indigenous insights and recognition that the Arctic, due to its strategic position, is a unique and important part of the planet — environmentally, socially, economically and politically. In what ways is the Arctic changing? What will the region be like in the future? These crucial questions are being asked by policy-makers, land-use managers and people who live in the Arctic. ICARP II gave voice to these questions and developed plans to address them (ICARP II Steering Group and ICARP II Secretariat 2007). The conference also enhanced the long tradition within the Arctic scientific community, Arctic governments and nongovernmental organizations of assessing the current state of scientific understanding and determining future research needs; it produced thoughtful projections related to research initiatives crossing national borders and spanning many disciplines. The ICARP II conference report encompasses a range of ideas, framings and conceptual perspectives on future Arctic research (Bowden 2005). It is noteworthy that a major commitment to reflecting the perspectives of indigenous communities was made during the planning process and the conference itself — a far greater commitment than that made 10 years earlier, during the first ICARP.

International Polar Year

INTERNATIONAL POLAR YEAR (IPY) IS AN INTERNATIONALLY COORDINATED SCIENTIFIC program focused on the Arctic and the Antarctic, but with a global dimension. It is sponsored jointly by the International Council for Science (ICSU) and the World Meteorological Organization (WMO) with the goal of exploiting new technological capabilities and strengthening international research coordination while placing a stronger emphasis on interdisciplinary research involving the physical and social science communities, indigenous communities and educators. The 2007-08 IPY is the fourth: the first three were 1882-83, 1932-33 and 1957-58 (the latter was also designated International Geophysical Year). It has involved more than 200 projects and the participation of thousands of scientists from more than 60 nations who have examined a wide range of physical, biological and social research topics. IPY is motivated by many factors: the polar regions are active, closely interconnected components of the planet; significant changes are occurring there; they harbour unique information about the past behaviour of the planet; they provide us with a unique vantage point for observing a variety of terrestrial and cosmic phenomena; and they have growing economic and geopolitical importance (Rapley, Bell, Allison et al. 2004).

From a science cooperation perspective, the planning process for such an event is interesting to analyze. IPY was born of discussions among various individuals and organizations about having an IPY 50 years after the last International Geophysical Year. One obvious challenge was to find an acceptable umbrella for the event. The ICSU — a nongovernmental organization with a global membership that includes both national scientific bodies (111) and international scientific unions

(29) — was asked to sponsor IPY. It began by forming an IPY planning group and assigning it the task of creating a basic organizational framework for the event. At the same time, the WMO decided to plan its own international polar year. In December 2003, the WMO proposed to the ICSU that they merge their undertakings. The prospect was daunting, but all involved agreed that holding competing events would not be possible. They also realized that a merger would yield several advantages — for example, a merged IPY would enjoy more linkages with other world organizations and governments as well as national science committees and unions. From the beginning, the planning group clearly understood that since logistical cooperation and funding had to be national or regional, it was important to involve national funding agencies and polar organizations continuously in the process. One way to create legitimacy for the initiative was to establish contact with and solicit input from individuals, governments and nongovernmental organizations; endorsement would also be needed from the 32 IPY national committees or national points of contact. In the planning process, discussion and debate took place during a dozen international meetings and two discussion forums hosted by the ICSU and attended by representatives of the IPY national committees and a variety of interested polar organizations. The planning group asked the broad polar science community to offer its ideas on the scientific content of the IPY; it received more than 490 submissions. When the ideas were posted on the IPY 2007-08 Web site, the link received many hits. The substantial interest in the project demonstrated by the science community and the fact that the planning group held open forums for organizations and agencies ensured the acceptance of the IPY program. It was formally adopted by the general assembly of the ICSU in October 2005, and a program office established (Rapley, Bell, Allison et al. 2004).

The research ideas that emerged during the planning phase were arranged according to several broad themes: the status of the polar regions, environmental and social change in the polar regions, global linkages, new frontiers and the poles as vantage point. The human dimension was initially thought to be integral to these themes, but elements in the science community expressed a wish to see that dimension stand as a theme in its own right, so it was added to the list. This theme encompasses investigations of the cultural, historical and social processes that shape circumpolar human societies and of the unique contributions of these societies to global cultural diversity and citizenship. The 2007-08 IPY was the first to include the social and life sciences in its overall strategy —

the others concentrated only on geophysical themes. Such development of IPY themes reflects the fact that polar processes extend across national boundaries, and it addresses the desire for a coordinated approach to maximizing outcomes and cost-effectiveness. Also evident in the 2007-08 IPY is the conviction that outreach is a very important part of the process: much greater attention has been paid to explaining how climate change in the Arctic affects the entire globe and to raising the general level of knowledge about the Arctic.

The Selection of IPY Projects

A s I HAVE SAID, INTEREST IN THE 2007-08 IPY — BUILT UP IN THE COURSE OF THE consultation process — was enormous, and the call for project proposals brought 1,000 responses. The planning group created a set of criteria supporting IPY objectives, to which projects had to adhere in order to be endorsed as IPY projects that might be eligible for funding back home. These criteria included the provision of a viable data access and management plan, an education plan, an outreach and communication plan and a recruitment plan targeting the new generation of polar scientists. The joint committee took responsibility for evaluating the proposals. As proposals were developed — or, in some cases, withdrawn — a valuable matchmaking role was adopted by the IPY's international program office, which conjoined proposals with the aim of making the whole greater than the sum of its parts.

Funding IPY projects was a challenge, because funds have to be provided by a range of individual bodies and worldwide consortiums. Initial expressions of intent filed by those who presented project proposals had to demonstrate an ability to meet the requirements of funding agencies willing to dedicate funds to the IPY program. To date, we know that 2007-08 IPY projects have had varied success in procuring funding; about one-third are substantially funded, and one-third are partially funded, but the final tally has yet to be taken. Although the IPY initiative has not managed to solve the difficulties inherent in coordinating and funding international projects, its success at organizing such a huge number of projects through a bottom-up process has been remarkable. This success is partly due to the long-established tradition of science cooperation in the Arctic and the Antarctic. While the results of the 2007-08 IPY will not be known for years, the initiative has attract-ed the interest of other organizations. For example, the Organisation for Economic Co-operation and Development's Global Science Forum — an advisory committee for governments on science cooperation — has launched a study of the IPY process to determine its potential benefits in other contexts.

Another IPY-related challenge is to maintain the legacy of the initiative — to keep up the momentum and make use of the results. For example, we have learned that the areas of the Arctic where temperature increases are highest also have the highest degree of variability; furthermore, they are widely dispersed and have few observation stations. IPY participants have advocated the establishment of a coop-erative Arctic observation network to allow for more comprehensive measurement.

Challenges and
Possibilities for Future
Cooperation

A LTHOUGH BOTTOM-UP SCIENCE COOPERATION IN THE ARCTIC IS SUBSTANTIAL, THERE is still a lack of science cooperation at the government level. Despite the contribution of the Arctic Climate Impact Assessment, which in turn benefited from research activities that began with the International Geophysical Year half a century earlier, the eight nations with territories north of the Arctic Circle remain too passive in their approach to coordinating polar research. Their benign posi-tion has led, for example, to the gradual deterioration of parts of the network of Arctic meteorological stations. Better baseline support for such monitoring would cost little but would make a huge difference to Arctic researchers in all disciplines ("Coming in from the Cold" 2006).

In Antarctica, a 1959 international treaty obliges signatories to collaborate on scientific research, and this has led to bottom-up cooperation through the Scientific Committee on Antarctic Research (SCAR), logistical cooperation through the Council of Managers of National Antarctic Programs (COMNAP) and a govern-mental framework for cooperation. Government commitment to research funding will give Antarctic research initiatives with long time frames the secure foundation they need. In the Arctic, there is no political framework for collaboration on Arctic research. Although regional issues are discussed in the Arctic Council, there is no formal provision for research cooperation ("Coming in from the Cold" 2006). That said, in 2004, the ministers of education and science and other representatives from the Arctic Council member states signed a declaration at a meeting in Reykjavik. The declaration focuses on increasing and strengthening cooperation with regard to education and research in the North; it also points to the need to increase government involvement. Through the Reykjavik declaration, the ministers have agreed to support intensified international research cooperation in the Arctic region in order to better understand ongoing environmental changes and to explore opportunities for sustainable development. They are encouraging cooperation to improve higher education and research training, and they are promoting increased mobility among researchers and students. A working group is in the process of following up with recommendations for future cooperation between the ministers and research councils in the Arctic countries. This could help build a bridge between scientific bottom-up cooperation and the top-down involvement of government.

Organization of polar research is done in different ways in different countries, and this has an effect on international cooperation. Some countries, both inside and outside the Arctic region, have dedicated institutes for polar research; in others, research undertakings are scattered among various institutions, in small or large units. Some countries have centralized logistical support for research; in others, a case-by-case approach is taken to organizing logistical support. If the necessary logistical support is comprehensive (for example, the research must be conducted in a particularly remote area, or an icebreaker is needed), then the dilemma of how to balance logistical requirements with research requirements arises. Some countries have dedicated funds for polar programs; in others, polar researchers have to compete for funds with those researching other topics. This diversity in arrangements and best practices represents a significant challenge to those working to organize international science cooperation.

The 2002-06 Sixth Framework Programme, the European Union's initiative to fund and promote research and technological development, contains a program to involve all 25 of Europe's major funding agencies in polar research. The goal is for the agencies to share information and facilities, gradually integrate their programs and optimize their combined annual budget (European Polar Consortium 2005). Incorporating links to the United States and Canada would enhance the initiative's effort to establish circum-Arctic cooperation and infrastructure sharing; in fact, a plan for a follow-up project to create links to countries outside the EU is in progress. The Arctic Council has agreed to urge its member countries to maintain and extend long-term monitoring of change in all parts of the Arctic. It has also asked its working groups to join forces with other international Arctic organizations to find ways to build a coordinated Arctic observing network (Arctic Council Secretariat 2007). The Sustained Arctic Observing Networks Initiating Group (SAON-IG) was formed with the mission to develop a set of recommendations on how to organize long-term Arctic-wide observing activities that would provide free and timely access to high-quality data — data that would facilitate the provision of pan-Arctic and global value-added services and yield societal benefits (SAON-IG 2006).

Canada's recently announced northern strategy has scientific knowledge as one of its pillars. It includes a plan to build a sophisticated research station in Canada's High Arctic, and this will put Canada in a position to play an important role in international science cooperation.

Our complex planet, as the only known place in the universe where life exists, challenges our scientific understanding. We may take a reductionist approach to acquiring such understanding — studying Earth's components in increasingly smaller units — but this won't be sufficient. We are starting to realize that if we eliminate confining research silos and focus on working together, we can conduct our investigations on a far broader scale: we will be able to explore both temporal and spatial dimensions; we will gain access to both microscopic and global perspectives; we will achieve insight into processes that play out in seconds or over billions of years (Rapley 2007). We know that the climate is changing, and we know that we have to adapt to and mitigate the effects. However, there are still many fundamental gaps in our scientific knowledge, and it is now more important than ever for the science community to fill those gaps. In its 2007 report, the United Nations Scientific Expert Group on Climate Change and Sustainable Development states: "We must avoid the unmanageable and manage the unavoidable" (Bierbaum et al. 2007). This will require an immediate and major acceleration of our adaptation and mitigation efforts. International science cooperation and coordination are essential, and the Arctic, with its tradition of science cooperation arising from the IPY, has a lot to offer us in our struggle to address the challenges of climate change.

References

Arctic Climate Impact Assessment. 2005. *Arctic Climate Impact Assessment*. New York: Cambridge University Press. Accessed July 15, 2008. http://www.acia.uaf.edu/pages/scientific.html

Arctic Council Secretariat. 2007. *Salekhard Declaration*. Tromsø: Arctic Council Secretariat. Accessed July 21, 2008. http://arctic-council.org/filearchive/SALEKHARD_AC_DECLARATION_2006.pdf

Arctic Monitoring and Assessment Programme (AMAP). 1997. *Arctic Pollution Issues: A State of the Arctic Environment Report*. Oslo: AMAP. Accessed July 21, 2008. http://amap.no/documents/index.cfm?dirsub=/Arctic%20Pollution%20Issues%20-%20A%20State%20of%20the%20Arctic%20Environment%20Report&sort=default

———. 1998. *AMAP Assessment Report: Arctic Pollution Issues*. Oslo: AMAP. Accessed July 21, 2008. http://www.amap.no/documents /index.cfm?dirsub=/AMAP%20Assessment%20Report%20-%20Arctic%20Pollution%20Issues

Bierbaum, Rosina M., John P. Holdren, Michael C. MacCracken, Richard H. Moss, and Peter H. Raven. 2007. *Confronting Climate Change: Avoiding the Unmanageable and Managing the Unavoidable. Executive Summary. Scientific Expert Group Report on Climate Change and Sustainable Development*. New York: United Nations Foundation, Sigma Xi. Accessed July 21, 2008. http://www.unfoundation.org/files/pdf/2007/SEG_ExecSumm.pdf

Bowden, Sara, ed. 2005. *ICARP II: The Arctic System in a Changing World: Conference Proceedings*. Copenhagen: Danish Polar Centre.

"Coming in from the Cold." 2006. *Nature*, May 11.

Conservation of Arctic Flora and Fauna (CAFF). 2001. *Arctic Flora and Fauna: Status and Conservation*. Helsinki: CAFF.

European Polar Consortium. 2005. *Breaking the Ice in Polar Research Coordination*.

Strasbourg: European Polar Consortium. Accessed July 19, 2008. ftp://ftp.cordis.europa.eu/pub/ coordination/docs/europolar_individual_project_sheets_en.pdf

Foreign Affairs and International Trade Canada (DFAIT). 2000. *Barrow Declaration on the Occasion of the Second Ministerial Meeting of the Arctic Council*. Ottawa: DFAIT. Accessed July 15, 2008. http://www.international.gc.ca/polar-polaire/barrow.aspx?lang=en

Gore, Al. 1992. *Earth in the Balance: Ecology and the Human Spirit*. New York: Houghton Mifflin.

Intergovernmental Panel on Climate Change. 2007. *Climate Change 2007*. Geneva: United Nations Environment Programme. Accessed July 16, 2008. http://www.ipcc.ch/ipccreports/ar4-syr.htm

International Conference on Arctic Research Planning (ICARP) II Steering Group and ICARP II Secretariat. 2007. *Arctic Research: A Global Responsibility*. Copenhagen: Danish Polar Centre. Accessed July 18, 2008. http://arcticportal.org/extras/portal/iasc/icarp/ICARP%20overview-0507-4.pdf

Nilsson, Annika E. 2007. *A Changing Arctic Climate: Science and Policy in the Arctic Climate Impact Assessment*. Linköping Studies in Arts and Science 386. Linköping: Department of Water and Environmental Studies, Linköping University.

Pielke, Roger, Jr., Gwyn Prins, Steve Rayner, and Daniel Sarewitz. 2007. "Climate Change 2007: Lifting the Taboo on Adaptation." *Nature*, February 8.

Rapley, Chris. 2007. "Climate Change and the Antarctic: What Next?" Paper presented at the Scientific Council of Antarctic Research, XXX Antarctic Treaty Consultative Meeting, 30 April-11 May, New Delhi. Accessed July 21, 2008. http://www.scar.org/treaty/atcmxxx/Atcm30_ip124_all.pdf

Rapley, Chris, Robin Bell, Ian Allison et al. 2004. *A Framework for the International Polar Year 2007-2008*, November. Paris: International Council for Science. Accessed July 21,

2008. http://classic.ipy.org/development/
framework/framework_short.pdf

Stern, N. 2007. *The Economics of Climate Change:
The Stern Review.* Cambridge: Cambridge
University Press.

Sustained Arctic Observing Networks Initiating
Group. 2006. *Sustained Arctic Observing
Networks Initiating Group (SAON-IG).*
Helsinki: Arctic Observing Networks.
Accessed July 19, 2008.
http://www.arcticobserving.org/images/
stories/saon_doc_final2.pdf

United Nations Economic Commission for
Europe (UNECE). 1998. "Protocol on
Persistent Organic Pollutants." *Convention
on Long-Range Transboundary Air Pollution.*
Geneva: UNECE. Accessed July 15, 2008.
http://www.unece.org/env/lrtap/full%20text/
1998.POPs.e.pdf

————. 1999. "Protocol to Abate Acidification,
Eutrophication and Ground-Level Ozone."
*Convention on Long-Range Transboundary Air
Pollution.* Geneva: UNECE. Accessed July
15, 2008. http://www.unece.org/env/
lrtap/multi_h1.htm

Young, Oran R., and Níels Einarsson. 2004. "A
Human Development Agenda for the
Arctic: Major Findings and Emerging
Issues." In *Arctic Human Development
Report,* edited by Níels Einarsson, Joan
Nymand Larsen, Annika Nilsson, and Oran
R. Young. Akureyri: Stefansson Arctic
Institute.

ABORIGINAL

AND PUBLIC

GOVERNANCE

The Changing
Architecture of
Governance in Yukon
and the Northwest
Territories

C ANADA'S NORTH IS CHANGING, AND SOME OF THE MOST SIGNIFICANT CHANGES ARE
in governance. Until the 1970s, administration in northern Canada was
modelled on the British colonial system. The Aboriginal population was under the
protection and tutelage of a distant government, the region was valued almost
solely for its resources and its contribution to the external economy, and its administration was largely in the hands of a remote national government that viewed it
as a burden on the larger society. The government's main goals were modernization and resource development, which would be achieved through federal management and control. The North was governed through bureaucratic instruments
of the federal government (located in the North and in Ottawa), smaller administrations in Yukon and the Northwest Territories and, to a limited extent, Indian
band councils. Federal legislation set out the form of these administrations, and
federal public servants provided oversight and management. Policy was the
domain of the federal government, and the entire system was accountable to it
through the Department of Northern Development. The deputy minister and minister had final executive power and authority. Over the last 35 years, however,
Canada's northern regions have experienced substantial experimentation and
restructuring: the federal government has surrendered considerable control to
northern governments, and Aboriginal peoples, who make up a majority of the
North's population, have become increasingly active in governance.

This chapter examines changes to governance in the western North in the
context of larger political, economic and social developments. It outlines some of
the problems and challenges associated with developing new governance arrangements in the region. It asks whether a new constitutional settlement is being real-

ized and, if so, what form it is taking. To what extent and in what ways has the institutional balance of power shifted in the North between various levels of government — federal, territorial and local — and between the federal government and Aboriginal peoples? What major issues have emerged during this change?

Twenty-five years ago, a settlement based on governance principles that adhered to Aboriginal systems of government was anathema to federal policy-makers, who believed that governance should be based on civic institutions that were controlled by and accountable to all northern residents, regardless of whether they were of Aboriginal or settler origin. This public government model prevailed until the 1990s, when it underwent considerable erosion, starting in Yukon. Policy-makers had long feared that Aboriginal self-government would be divisive and, in many cases, not economically viable. First Nations resisted this view, and the federal government now accepts their approach to governance. Given that Aboriginal people demand core governance based on internal self-government, federal and territorial governments acknowledge that partnerships and shared administration are necessary to overcome barriers, such as scale and costs, to effective Aboriginal governance.

It is widely accepted that the creation of Nunavut resulted in significant constitutional change in that region. I argue that a new constitutional settlement is likewise unfolding in Yukon and the Northwest Territories (NWT). But the settlement is not in accordance with some grand plan. Rather, it evolved in response to contesting political forces. The federal government played a large role but was not in a position to impose a settlement based on a predetermined policy. Aboriginal groups shaped the new arrangements, and so too did territorial governments. Complex consultations and negotiations have been critical. While much has changed, outcomes are not yet fully complete, and, in some respects, they remain contested. However, many of the critical questions have been addressed, and a new governance infrastructure is taking shape in parts of the region. In Yukon, the territorial government has assumed most of the powers of the provinces and most First Nations governments have acquired self-governing powers on First Nations lands and in First Nations communities. By contrast, in the NWT, where a long-standing belief in the efficacy of public government continues to influence policy-makers, land claims negotiations have taken precedence over self-government negotiations, and an Aboriginal model of governance has been slower to emerge. A model based on Aboriginal governments

on Aboriginal lands and communities, as opposed to public governments at the
regional and community levels, is favoured. In some cases, Aboriginal governments will agree to share the administration of some local and regional activities,
but authority will derive from Aboriginal governments.

As these arrangements fall into place, the system of governance in the
North is taking a shape that differs from that in the rest of Canada. To those not
familiar with recent events in the North, the fundamental and unique constitutional changes taking place there may be surprising. According to our political
leaders, Canadians have rejected constitutional change. Thus it may be difficult
to accept that something fundamentally new in this respect has been happening,
seemingly out of the sight of the majority of Canadians. Nonetheless, major
change has occurred. A new constitutional settlement is in the making, and it
will, I suggest, endure.

Thinking about Northern Governance: A Review of the Literature

OUTSIDE OBSERVERS, INCLUDING ACADEMICS, HAVE STRUGGLED TO KEEP UP WITH
and anticipate governance developments in the North. While these developments have tended to evolve slowly, there have been instances of dramatic
change. Gurston Dacks, writing in 1981, reported that the federal government
and the Yukon Territorial Government (YTG) held the position that Native people should integrate into northern society and participate in the institutions of
the dominant society on the same basis as other Canadians. Policy-makers
believed that this position satisfied the democratic principle that all citizens
should bear the same relationship to the state and society. Dacks observed, however, that Aboriginal peoples preferred to relate to the rest of society through
their own cultural groupings. Dacks thought that the federal government might
be prepared to allow the delivery of certain programs to devolve to First Nations;
beyond that, however, he saw little likelihood of substantial change through
negotiation (1981, 78-9).

A decade later, Mark Dickerson identified decentralization as the primary
force underlying change in the NWT. He observed that Aboriginal people wanted

out from under the heavy hands of Ottawa and Yellowknife and favoured local and regional governments as the means to achieve this objective. He observed that First Nations saw the retention of band councils as the preferred means to achieve their self-government goals: to control land, influence culture and affect economic development. He noted that the Government of the Northwest Territories (GNWT) in 1988 encouraged public government at the local level through the *Charter Communities Act*, which combined band councils and local municipalities into community councils to prepare for the decentralization of selected programs and services delivered by Indian and Northern Affairs Canada (INAC) and the GNWT. Dickerson concluded that, if the federal government's resistance to decentralization could be overcome, the legislation would create local, regional and territorial governing bodies throughout the region, with regional governments acting much like county governments, except that representatives of local councils would make up governing councils (Dickerson 1992, 169-85).

In 1995, Kirk Cameron and Graham White noted considerable divergence between governance developments in Yukon and in the Northwest Territories. In the former, an umbrella final agreement in 1993 settled the shape and form of land claims agreements and provided for self-governing First Nations through individual self-government agreements. The creation of territory-wide management boards, councils and committees, which in most cases included 50 percent Aboriginal representation, gave First Nations an irrevocable role in land and resource management. Cameron and White reported that governance in Yukon had entered a new era, and the next challenge would be to work out the interplay of self-government and public government in the context of uncertain federal financial support. By contrast, they reported, the situation in the Northwest Territories was less settled. First Nations in general had shifted their focus from decentralization to self-government, but attitudes toward governance differed from nation to nation. In the northern part of the territory, Inuit and Gwich'in remained committed to decentralized public government, but in the central part of the territory Sahtu favoured public government for social services, economic development and taxation, and Aboriginal self-government for lands and resources. The Tlicho (known earlier as Dogrib), by contrast, wanted extensive self-government, enhanced community/regional government and direct governing authority over claims settlement lands; however, they also recognized the need for public government and a central territorial government. Further south,

Treaty 8 Dene demanded recognition of sovereignty and the creation of what would amount to a Dene territory in southwestern NWT. Dehcho, located in the southwestern corner of the territory, wanted a new Denendeh territory, which would have a public government with full rights of citizenship for all residents of the territory (Cameron and White 1995, 26-36, 65-76).

Bernard Funston, writing in 2007, found that self-government discussions in the NWT had evolved to include features such as concurrent powers for First Nations and the territorial/provincial government, as is the case in the Yukon and Nisga'a agreements, and the constitutional recognition of self-government agreements as section 35 rights, as is the case in the Nisga'a agreement. As a result, Funston believes, community governments may evolve and come to constrain the territorial government's authority, as occurred following the Yukon and Nisga'a agreements (2007). While he does not say so explicitly, his observations suggest a convergence of developments in the NWT and Yukon, with rights-based First Nations assuming governance authority for their people and lands, while community and regional governance becomes an administrative rather than a public form of government.

Aboriginal Title and Rights

ABORIGINAL TITLE AND RIGHTS ARE THE BASIS FOR LAND CLAIMS AND TREATIES. IN common law, Aboriginal title is an exclusive property interest equivalent to fee simple title, except that it can be owned and alienated only by an Aboriginal community or tribe, and it can be sold only to the federal Crown. Title derives from Aboriginal people's long occupation and use of the land prior to and at the time of settlement and colonization. Although legislatures can extinguish common-law rights, provided that their intent to do so is clear and explicit, section 35 of Canada's *Constitution Act, 1982* protects Aboriginal rights and title from extinguishment. Canadian constitutional law now holds that Aboriginal rights exist in law; they may range from rights not tied intimately to specific land sites, to site-specific rights, to Aboriginal title; they are *territorial*, fact- and group-specific; and they are not absolute and may be justifiably infringed by the Crown. However, rights and title may be extinguished, transferred, modified, placed in abeyance or alienated only with Aboriginal peoples' consent — primarily by treaty. In modern treaty making, potential and actual rights and title within a traditional territory are typically exchanged or substituted for specific treaty rights and title (McNeil 2000).

Some First Nations leaders and lawyers representing Aboriginal groups argue that modern treaties are unacceptable because they require the extinguishment of Aboriginal rights and title. Lawyers have engaged in a rights-based dialogue with the courts through litigation that centres on the extent and limits of Aboriginal rights. The judgments have concluded that Aboriginal rights and title are not absolute: governments have extensive powers to infringe upon them. Some Aboriginal leaders and lawyers therefore believe that infringement with compensation is preferable to treaties because it avoids the extinguishment tangle. Litigation has, however, resulted in a very broad-based definition of permissible infringement and a substantial discounting of the value of Aboriginal rights. Infringement agreements, which are popularly known as "accommodation agreements" (for cosmetic reasons) or "comanagement agreements" (when applied to lands), hold some appeal for governments because they are a workable risk management strategy. Industry and other economic interests are less enthusiastic because these agreements do not resolve property rights and ownership issues. And some First Nations advocate the comanagement approach because it does not require the extinguishment of rights through claims agreements.

Rights and Claims Negotiations, 1899-2007

IN THE LATE NINETEENTH CENTURY, CANADA NEGOTIATED TREATIES WITH INDIAN PEOPLE as settler populations moved westward. Aboriginal peoples north of the 60th parallel were only marginally affected. In 1899, Treaty 8 was extended into the southeastern area of the NWT that bordered Saskatchewan and Alberta, and Treaty 11 was imposed on the Mackenzie Valley region in 1921. In both cases, meaningful negotiation between the government and First Nations was either doubtful or absent, most of the terms were not implemented, and Aboriginal people began to question the legitimacy of the process and the extent to which the treaties had been honoured.

In the early 1970s, southern governments developed considerable enthusiasm for oil and gas exploration and development in the North, ushering in a new era of discussion and negotiation. Policy-makers envisaged pipelines that would stretch from Alaska through Yukon, and from the Beaufort Sea through the Mackenzie Valley. Northern Aboriginal people were less enthusiastic and cited outstanding rights and title claims as an impediment. The Minister of Indian and Northern Affairs, in a 1972 statement on northern pipeline development, stated that "the Government is prepared to discuss with the Indian people north of 60 their land claims and treaty rights," and he proposed the appointment of a senior representative of government to discuss how the "approach to an agreed settlement should be made" (Chrétien 1972).

The federal government, which had experienced a brutal political battle over its rejection of Aboriginal rights and title in its notorious 1969 White Paper on Indian Policy, had reluctantly come to the conclusion that discussion of Aboriginal rights and title claims in the North would be necessary if development was to proceed. But in 1972, policy-makers still believed that Aboriginal rights and title had not been established in the North and, consequently, did not exist. Discussions would simply recognize political reality. Because section 35 of the *Constitution Act* did not yet exist, the discussions could have extinguished Aboriginal rights in the North. However, policy-makers recognized that this outcome would result in national and international opprobrium. The federal government also hoped to avoid costly, time-consuming and unpredictable litigation, and it was experiencing outside pressure to resolve Aboriginal rights and claims in the region through negotiation. The US government under President Richard Nixon had recently negotiated a settlement with Native peoples in Alaska, and the United Nations was drawing attention to the Canadian government's failure in this area. The Government of Quebec, for instance, had reached a negotiated settlement with the James Bay Cree in advance of the federal government.

Canada's courts were also more likely to acknowledge Aboriginal rights and title. In 1972, the Indians of Old Crow in Yukon presented a petition to Parliament concerning oil and gas exploration on their hunting grounds. The following year, the Supreme Court of Canada found in the *Calder* case that Aboriginal title in British Columbia, contrary to the claims of the BC government, could exist in common law. In the same year, Justice Morrow of the NWT recognized the Aboriginal title of the Dene of the Mackenzie River Valley, and

Justice Malouf recognized Cree and Inuit title in Quebec. Although these last two decisions were overturned on appeal, they showed that the courts were giving more weight to the legitimacy of Aboriginal claims.

In 1973, the Yukon Indian Brotherhood presented a formal claim to the federal government based on nonextinguished rights and title. This event and the cases that preceded it convinced the federal government that the discussions started in 1972 must conclude with a commitment to negotiations with Aboriginal peoples on lands and resources in Yukon and the NWT, particularly if pipeline development was to proceed. On August 8, 1973, the federal government established a federal policy for the negotiation and settlement of Aboriginal land claims. The new federal policy confirmed "the responsibility of government to meet its lawful obligations through fulfillment of the terms of the treaties and to negotiate settlements with native groups in those areas of Canada where native rights based on traditional use and occupancy of the land had not been dealt with by treaty or superseded by law" (Indian and Northern Affairs Canada [INAC] 1973). The policy was revised in 1981 to state that the goal was to exchange claims to undefined Aboriginal rights for a package of clearly defined rights and benefits set out in a settlement agreement. Amendments were made to the Comprehensive Land Claims Policy in 1986 to provide for greater flexibility on issues such as land (INAC 1987); and the Inherent Right Policy of 1995 established that self-government arrangements could be negotiated as part of comprehensive claims agreements based on inherent self-government (INAC 1995).

Within the framework of these policies, the slow, grinding, at times unfathomable and often unpredictable process of northern treaty negotiations proceeded. The federal government, for reasons that seem arcane today, has never called these proceedings "treaty negotiations." It prefers the terms "land claims negotiations" and "land claims final agreements," and these terms continue to circulate. Some northern Aboriginal groups also favour this terminology because they do not want to repudiate the historical treaties that extend to their lands. In this chapter, the terms "land claims negotiations" and "treaty negotiations," and "final agreements" and "treaties," are used interchangeably to refer to the treaty process in the North.

Inuit Negotiations

The Inuit were among the first Aboriginal people to actively pursue their rights and claims in the North. In the 1970s, the Inuit of the eastern Arctic and the

Inuvialuit of the Mackenzie Delta in Yukon and the NWT formed an alliance to pursue negotiations. The Inuvialuit, however, broke away from the original alliance and signed a separate final agreement in 1984. This was the first settlement in the North. It is a complex agreement providing lands, cash, renewable resource harvesting and the shared management of lands and resources. The Inuit of the central and eastern NWT concluded the Nunavut agreement in 1993, and a political accord providing for the new Nunavut territory was agreed to at the same time. A substantial portion of the Inuvialuit settlement area remains in the northern region of the NWT, and a smaller part is located on the North Slope of Yukon. The remainder (the much larger part) is in Nunavut. Both of these agreements have huge significance for the North. (A detailed review of the Inuvialuit agreement is contained in the chapter by Graham White, so I will not address it further here.)

Yukon Treaty Negotiations
Treaty negotiations in Yukon commenced in 1973, when the Council for Yukon Indians (CYI) formed to represent 14 Indian bands. Nonstatus Indians joined the council two years later. The CYI presented to the government *Together Today for Our Children Tomorrow*, which proposed settlement through negotiations (CYI 1973). Under the proposal, Yukon First Nations would have specific lands controlled by each First Nation, they would participate in the management of renewable and nonrenewable resources, and they would receive support for economic development through training programs and cash compensation. The settlement would protect traditional values and lifestyle and, at the same time, provide for future political and economic growth.

Discussions were slow and interrupted by pipeline inquiries, but an agreement in principle was achieved in 1984. Yukon First Nations repudiated the agreement, however. Negotiations resumed in 1986, and in May 1987, the federal government developed a new mandate for negotiations. The mandate provided for negotiations between all Yukon First Nations and the YTG under a territory-wide umbrella agreement, which could then be tailored to meet the needs of individual First Nations. At the CYI's insistence, it was agreed that self-government negotiations would proceed as part of overall negotiations. In 1993, the federal government, the YTG and the CYI signed the Umbrella Final Agreement (UFA) and final agreements with the Vuntut Gwitchin, the Na-Cho

Nyak Dun, the Champagne and Aishihik, and the Teslin Tlingit First Nations (see map on following page). The umbrella and individual agreements included self-government chapters, but the federal government insisted that they be excluded from protection under section 35 (INAC 1993b).

Settlement and self-government legislation was introduced in Parliament on May 31, 1994, and it received royal assent on July 7, 1994. Total settlement lands amount to 41,000 square kilometres, 25,900 of which contains mines and minerals. Cash compensation is $242,673,000 (in 1989 dollars), with additional compensation for giving up tax exemptions. Additional terms provide for participation in the management of national parks and wildlife areas, specific rights for fish and wildlife harvesting, and special economic and employment opportunities. Territory-wide boards with First Nations participation are established for water and land-use management. The governments, however, refused to include the right to commercial harvests of renewable resources.

To date, 11 of 14 Yukon First Nations have land claims and self-government agreements. Of the three that remain, the most challenging is the Kaska Dene claim in the southeast, which includes the Liard and Ross River First Nations. In March 2003, Canada suspended its participation in negotiations with both the BC and Yukon Kaska First Nations because of the latter's litigation claims. When the Kaska put their litigation on hold, negotiations in Yukon resumed. There are a number of unresolved issues, including acceptance of the land partition/selection model, tax exemptions, extinguishment and resource management regimes (British Columbia, Ministry of Aboriginal Relations and Reconciliation 2007).

In many respects, the Yukon agreements are quite remarkable. They establish new territory-based governments by partitioning land into First Nations settlement lands and general Yukon lands. This is often called the land selection model. They also create First Nation citizenship for members of each First Nation, allowing Aboriginal people to enjoy status as citizens of a First Nation and as citizens of Canada. The concept of numerous new territorial governments with powers — like provinces, in many respects — and of a new identity and governance relationship in the form of citizenship is controversial among non-Aboriginal people and Aboriginal people alike, but often for quite different reasons. Under the UFA, First Nations in Yukon play an integral role in land and resource management through a series of territory-wide management

Yukon: Traditional Territories of First Nations and Settlement Areas of Inuvialuit and Tetlit Gwich'in

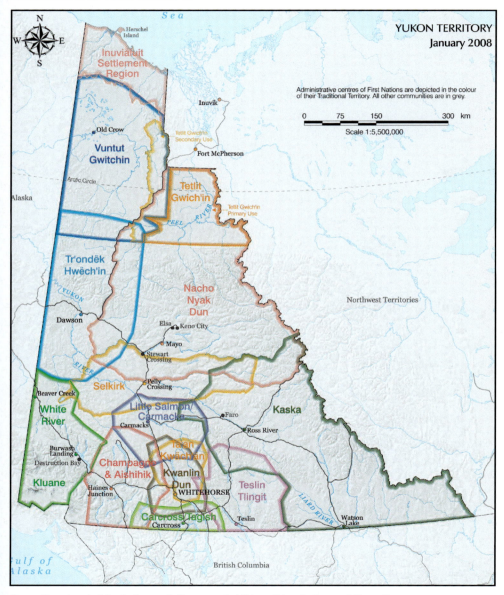

Source: Department of the Environment, Government of Yukon; Yukon Environment Geomatics.

boards, councils and committees, which in most cases include 50 percent First
Nations representation. These bodies are expected to bring about a dramatic
change in the way that land-use planning, resource regulation and management,
and the assessment of developments are undertaken. Public servants and professionals will no longer undertake these activities independent of First Nations.
First Nations representatives are not simply consulted; they have an active and
direct role in decision-making. In numerous communities, governance is complex. Often, First Nations governments exercise local government functions on
properties included in their settlement lands, whereas local municipalities and
the YTG do so on the remainder. Meanwhile, First Nations governments may
regulate and provide social services for First Nations citizen residents on both
types of land. Shared administration is possible through agreements; however,
sharing and common delivery arrangements are dependent on First Nations
assent, and financial considerations often play a role.

First Nations governments have become actively involved in taxation. In
cases where the YTG has agreed to back out of taxing the property of First
Nations occupants, they have assumed responsibility for property taxation. Most
self-governing First Nations have also entered into tax administration agreements
with the federal government to establish a First Nations goods and services tax
(FNGST). The FNGST replaces the GST on supplies made on or delivered to settlement lands. The federal and territorial governments have likewise entered into
personal income tax administration agreements with six self-governing nations.
Under these agreements, the governments share personal income tax room with
First Nations. The taxes are collected and distributed by the federal tax agency.
Participating First Nations receive 75 percent of the federal income tax levy and
95 percent of the Yukon income tax levy on residents of settlement lands, including those who are not citizens.

While it is somewhat early to assess the Yukon treaties and self-government agreements, the evidence suggests progress and success. A five-year review
completed by the Yukon, federal and First Nations governments in 2000 reported that the joint resource management boards, councils and committees had successfully fulfilled their roles. It also reported considerable progress in the
transition from *Indian Act* bands to self-governing First Nations. The list of
accomplishments includes the establishment of new governance structures, the
enactment of new legislation across a wide range of subjects, the creation of

financial management and accountability systems, agreements on transfers of programs and services, and tax transfer agreements (INAC 2000). A subsequent departmental review, in 2003, confirmed these conclusions (INAC 2003).

Yukon First Nations have joined Treaty First Nations from across Canada to extract from the federal government a firm commitment to provide financial resources and to implement measures. First Nations leaders believe that self-government has resulted in significant gains for their citizens, and their expectations for social, economic and political development are substantial. First Nations are now actively developing institutional capacities not possible under the *Indian Act*: First Nations laws have been legislated; responsibility for programs and services to citizens is expanding; First Nations are taxing residents of their lands; and new partnerships with other First Nations, governments and corporations are being strategically pursued to achieve improved development and service delivery. Support for and recognition of self-government, including law-making, is more substantive in Yukon than in any other country or region with a large settler population.

NWT Treaty Negotiations

In 1976, the Dene in the Northwest Territories drafted an agreement in principle that proposed a government for the Northwest Territories under Indian control and with province-like powers. The Métis opposed the idea and, in 1977, they proposed their own settlement based on an east-west division of the territory. The federal government refused to negotiate separate agreements. The Métis agreed to representation by the Dene negotiator, and in 1981 the joint negotiator proposed a model for a Dene- and Métis-controlled government with province-like powers in the western region. This was unacceptable to Canada.

Seven years passed before a comprehensive land claims agreement in principle was reached between Canada, the Dene Nation and the Métis Association of the NWT. In 1990, the parties agreed to a final land, resources and cash deal. The agreement did not address Aboriginal self-government, in part because federal negotiators had no mandate to negotiate self-government in the territory. The federal government's position was that Aboriginal influence should be exercised through local, regional and territorial public governments. Public governments are those in which the right to vote is based on residency, not on membership in an Aboriginal group. These governments provide services on a uniform basis to Aboriginal and non-Aboriginal people alike. Since many communities and regions in the NWT have Aboriginal majorities, to some degree they would be able to establish government processes and programs geared to Aboriginal needs and wants.

A number of the members of the territory-wide association subsequently rejected the land claims agreement. At this point, negotiations in the NWT took a decided turn. Canada refused to renegotiate the initial agreement and discontinued negotiations with the Dene and Métis. In response to requests from the Mackenzie Delta Tribal Council (the Gwich'in) and the Sahtu Tribal Council for regional claims settlements, Canada agreed to negotiate regional settlements on the basis of the April 1990 agreement. It began negotiations with the Gwich'in in November 1990 and with the Sahtu in October 1991, initiating a pattern of regional negotiations that continues today (see map on following page). A Gwich'in agreement, which was based on the agreement rejected in 1990 by the Dene and Métis, was concluded in 1992. It provides for lands, cash and the sharing of resource revenue from the Mackenzie Valley and wildlife harvesting. Throughout their territory, the Gwich'in participate in decision-making bodies dealing with such matters as land-use planning, renewable resource management, environmental review, and water and land-use regulation. The agreement does not address the issue of self-government.

Canada then negotiated a final agreement with Sahtu Dene and Métis in 1993. This agreement covers a large area of the middle and northern portion of the NWT between Yukon and Nunavut that encompasses about 800 kilometres of the Mackenzie River. Its terms are very similar to those of the Gwich'in agreement, although the amount of Sahtu land is about two and a half times larger. It provides for two types of land: Sahtu settlement land and Sahtu municipal land. The latter is land within the existing five communities of the region. Sahtu municipal land may be purchased, while settlement land may not. When municipal land is purchased in fee simple, it is no longer Sahtu land. The Sahtu settlement lands are dispersed in blocks throughout the communities. Close to a dozen land, financial and management corporations manage the land and capital, while Métis have separate corporations. The agreement does not address self-government.

The Tlicho final agreement, which was concluded in 2003, deserves special attention because it is considered state of the art — the template for future settlements in the NWT — largely because it is the first agreement that addresses self-government. It followed the Dogrib agreement in principle of 1999, and it took effect when federal legislation was passed in 2005. The agreement is based on a land partition model, whereby ownership of the traditional territory is divided between the First Nation and government. The agreement establishes four geographic areas: Monwhi Gogha De Niitlee, the Tlicho's traditional use area; a resource management area, which is part of the traditional lands; a geographic area called Tlicho Lands, which the Tlicho own in fee simple; and a geographic area that has historical and cultural importance to the Tlicho but is not owned by them. On these lands, the agreement establishes self-government in accordance with the federal government's policy on the inherent right to self-government. Self-government is integral to the agreement and protected under section 35 of the Constitution — a first in the Northwest Territories. The Tlicho government has authority to control, govern and manage Tlicho lands and assets; to represent Tlicho in various resource comanagement arrangements; to manage benefits; to deliver and regulate social services to members; and to regulate and direct other activities.

Four of the five Tlicho communities are surrounded by the Tlicho Lands block but not included in it. These community lands are neither owned nor governed directly by the Tlicho government. Yellowknife, which is part of the traditional-use area, is among them. As a consequence, the NWT legislation created a new form of community government for these four communities that has features of public government. Within each community, Tlicho residents elect a chief and half the councillors; and all residents, Aboriginal and non-Aboriginal, elect the remainder of the councillors. The Tlicho government has various powers with respect to members but does not have direct control over the community governments. However, the four community chiefs plus a grand chief, elected by all members, make up the executive council. The Tlicho Assembly comprises the grand chief, the four chiefs and two representatives of each community. The assembly sits at least four times per year in one of the communities and is the law-making body of the Tlicho government. The two forms of government, community and public, are thus closely integrated (Government of the Northwest Territories 2003).

The Tlicho agreement has set a precedent for final agreements or treaties yet to be concluded in the NWT. In the southeast, the federal government asked the Akaitcho in 1992 to proceed on the basis of Treaty 8 land entitlement negotiations. The Akaitcho rejected the government's offer of land and cash. Although the Akaitcho suggested settling outstanding issues through coexistence — good faith implementation of the treaty — they signed a framework agreement in 2000 to negotiate land, resource and governance issues without prejudice to Treaty 8 rights

Northwest Territories Land Claim Boundaries, 2009

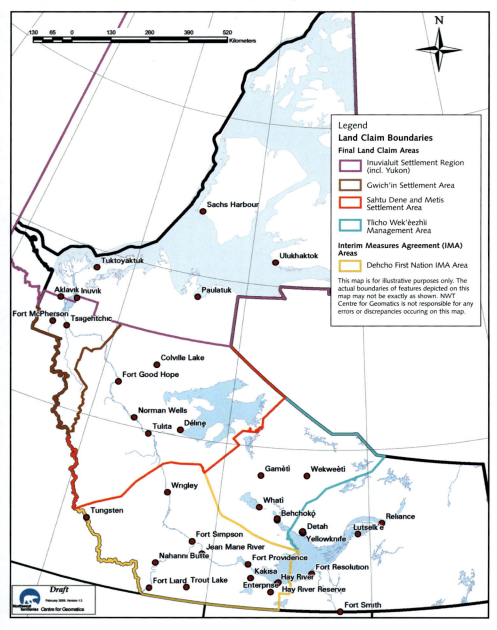

130 65 0   130   260   390   520
Kilometers

N

Legend

Land Claim Boundaries

Final Land Claim Areas

Inuvialuit Settlement Region (incl. Yukon)

Gwich'in Settlement Area

Sahtu Dene and Metis Settlement Area

Tlicho Wek'èezhìi Management Area

Interim Measures Agreement (IMA) Areas

Dehcho First Nation IMA Area

This map is for illustrative purposes only. The actual boundaries of features depicted on this map may not be exactly as shown. NWT Centre for Geomatics is not responsible for any errors or discrepancies occuring on this map.

Sachs Harbour

Ulukhaktok

Tuktoyaktuk

Paulatuk

Aklavik Inuvik

Fort McPherson

Tsiigehtchic

Colville Lake

Fort Good Hope

Norman Wells

Tulita Délįne

Gamètì Wekweètì

Wrigley

Whatì

Tungsten

Behchokǫ̀

Reliance

Detah

Łutselk'e

Yellowknife

Fort Simpson

Jean Marie River

Nahanni Butte Fort Providence

Fort Resolution

Kakisa

Fort Liard Trout Lake

Enterprise

Hay River

Hay River Reserve

Fort Smith

Draft

February 2009, Version 1.3

Northwest Territories Centre for Geomatics

and obligations. One year later, the First Nation reached an agreement to protect lands on an interim basis, and in 2006 the Akaitcho and the GNWT reached a deal to temporarily protect land in and around Yellowknife while negotiations continue. It appears that negotiations will evolve on the basis of the land partition model. Negotiations are also proceeding with Métis in southeastern communities.

In the southwest, the government began negotiations with the Dehcho Dene in 1999. The Dehcho proposed shared ownership and jurisdiction over the whole traditional area. In 2006, after prolonged negotiations, Canada rejected this approach in favour of the land partition model that has been applied in other modern treaty settlements, proposing to partition the traditional territory into three areas: a single block of lands owned by the Dehcho government and over which it would have governance powers; a large wildlife management area; and a still larger resource management area. Canada wants the Dehcho to have the power to make laws on their own lands while maintaining "clear lines of author- ity for the Dehcho, territorial and federal governments," and it has proposed to combine existing Dehcho First Nations and municipal governments into new local governments with law-making powers. These local governments would have guaranteed majority representation for Dehcho Dene, and, according to Canada, governments would acknowledge and respect each other's jurisdictions and share some authority. The Dehcho would exert influence through their par- ticipation in a Dehcho regional government, a Dehcho resource management authority and a Dehcho land-use plan. Thus, the Dehcho First Nations would have law-making powers in a core geographical area, but outside this core their influence would be limited. The Dehcho would set resource royalty rates on their lands and collect 100 percent of royalties. Areas of traditional, cultural, spiritual and economic importance to the Dehcho would be respected, and self-govern- ment powers would be constitutionally protected by treaty (INAC 2006).

Canada's proposal is patterned almost entirely on the Tlicho agreement; however, it is not clear that this agreement will provide the basis for a final settle- ment. The Dehcho have long been committed to the shared ownership model, which Canada adamantly continues to oppose. In November 2006, a Dehcho spe- cial assembly authorized exploratory discussions on Canada's proposed land selection model, and at the 2007 fall leadership meeting and assembly, the Dehcho decided to extend discussions to include the selection of surface and subsurface lands and land selection quantum. An agreement in principle is under discussion, but conflicts and arguments have emerged over land-use planning, extinguish-ment of Aboriginal title and rights, resource revenue sharing, GNWT royalty rates and self-government. The Dehcho continue to favour the comanagement model, with some form of community and regional power sharing between governments.

This continuing gap between Dehcho and government negotiators does not bode well for constitutional settlement in the North. Yet a Dehcho settlement based on infringement agreements rather than on a modern treaty would not be fatal to the overall constitutional settlement project. The Dehcho are part of Treaty 8, and the government could manage uncertainty reasonably well if infringement agreements were supplemented by self-government arrangements along the lines of the Tlicho agreement. The settlement might not be as tidy as some would like, but it is workable, and it appears that it may be more acceptable to the Dehcho.

The Territorial Governments

TERRITORIAL ADMINISTRATIONS ARE A LONG-STANDING FEATURE OF GOVERNANCE IN the Canadian northwest. They originally served as administrative vehicles for the federal government to extend its writ throughout the region. Unlike those in the south, territorial governments (TGs) in the North have taken on adminis-trative responsibilities for services, delivering them to both Aboriginal and non-Aboriginal people. It was not until the last quarter of the twentieth century that major progress was made toward responsible government, culminating with the Epp letter in 1979, in which Minister of Indian and Northern Affairs Jake Epp declared that the Yukon Legislature would be responsible for determining the laws of Yukon and that administrative and executive actions would be based on the advice and consent of the executive council.

Since that time, the legislatures and cabinets of both territories have come to enjoy a certain degree of autonomy, with Westminster-style responsible gov-ernment much like that of the provinces. While the NWT has adopted a consen-sus rather than a party system, both Yukon and the NWT have ministers and cabinet heads with almost exactly the same functions and powers as their provin-cial counterparts. Ministers are part of federal-provincial and interprovincial min-isterial councils, and the leaders are participants in First Ministers' Meetings and members of the Council of the Federation. The TGs derive their powers from federal legislation rather than from the *Constitution Act*. This is of course relevant to stability and certainty. Today, the TGs' powers are approaching those of the provinces in many respects and are greater than those found in many federations: the territories have control over social programs, local governance, property and civil rights, and administration of justice.

The creation of the Nunavut government in 1999 was a significant milestone in the process of weaving the territories into the fabric of governance. The separation of the old NWT into eastern and western parts and the continuation of the old territory in the west signalled the territory's continued acceptance in the northern constitutional fabric. With the creation of Nunavut and substantial progress on Aboriginal claims settlements, the territorial governments now occupy an accepted and settled constitutional space that is no longer vulnerable to parliamentary termination. One robust indicator of this was the enactment of a new *Yukon Act* by Parliament in 2002. The legislation employs contemporary language characteristic of responsible Westminster government to describe the Yukon government. The preamble confirms that the territory's system of responsible government is similar in principle to that of Canada, and the Act renders the relationship between the commissioner and the executive council (cabinet) consistent with the conventions of modern government in Canada.[1]

Today territorial governments are for all practical purposes as much a part of the governance fabric of Canada as the governments of Saskatchewan, Alberta and British Columbia. Territorial government leaders have often expressed a desire to acquire for their territories the same powers as provinces, but the federal government has never fully supported this aspiration. Its focus has been on a process known as devolution and on fiscal arrangements that make devolved governance feasible. In 1987, the federal government developed guidelines for the transfer of federal programs to the territories.

Financing Territorial Governments

With the exception of consumption tax and retail sales tax, northern territorial governments have direct taxation powers much like the provinces', and they collect the standard range of fees and levies. Each territory receives per capita transfers under the Canada Health Transfer and the Canada Social Transfer on the same basis as the provinces, and the territories also receive fiscal transfers that are sometimes called

"Equalization Lite." Own-source revenues make up about 15 percent of the expenditures of the YTG and about 25 percent of the expenditures of the GNWT. Each territory is thus highly dependent on federal transfers.

The Territorial Formula Financing (TFF) transfer is the largest. It was established in 1985 to provide the TGs with an annual block of revenue that they could allocate unconditionally to individual programs and services based on a self-determined set of priorities. Federal policy-makers hoped to enhance northern control over priorities but increase federal control over spending growth by linking federal expenditures to formulaic factors. A formula determines the amount of revenue transferred to the territorial government. The formula was originally intended "to fill the gap between expenditure needs (how much money a territory needs to cover the costs of providing reasonably comparable public services to its citizens) and revenue capacity (how much money a territory can potentially raise from a combination of taxes, fees, and some other federal transfers)" (Expert Panel on Equalization and Territorial Formula Financing 2006). The principle was that the annual transfer would be determined by subtracting the own-source revenue capacity of a territorial government from a measure of its expenditure needs. Because revenue capacity is used, based on representative tax rates, it frees a territorial government to pursue an independent taxation policy. Major taxes count as revenue based on adjusted provincial averages for each tax, whether they are collected or not; consequently, a territory is free to decide whether to reduce a tax rather than increase spending, or vice versa, without penalty. The arrangements are contained in five-year renewable agreements.

The expenditure base is an important variable in the arrangements. It was established in 1985 to allow each TG to provide an annual gross expenditure base (GEB). The GEB is a proxy of the cost of governance and is not tied to any actual expenditure. Since its introduction, the base has been adjusted annually to track average increases in provincial government expenditures and the territories' population growth. However, periodic caps have been placed on GEB growth, and in the mid-1990s the federal government arbitrarily reduced its size. In addition, when responsibilities have been transferred under devolution, the federal government has identified its expenditures for each activity, sometimes topping them up to account for special circumstances. This amount is added to the GEB.

The TFF has thus been an important and integral part of the devolution arrangements. After devolution, the TG determines the actual amount to be spent on the devolved activity and works on the assumption that it has been allocated enough money to maintain the activity at a predevolution level. However, the territories insist that the formula has acted as a disincentive to economic growth. For many years, the amount transferred was reduced by 100 percent and then, from 1995 to 2004, by 80 percent of a territory's own-source revenue capacity increase. This clawback often meant that, after the costs of developing a new mine or other major economic project were accounted for, a territorial government was worse off. The TGs claim that the system impedes their ability to pursue major developments. They also point out that the formula does not take into account higher costs of government and cost increases in the North. Finally, territorial governments claim that the federal government can manipulate the arrangement to ensure that the TGs never retain enough fiscal flexibility to develop self-sufficiency and independence. The rules were written by the federal government to get the result it wants.

This final grievance gained credibility in 2004, when the federal government legislated transfers rather than basing them on five-year agreements. Instead of using a formula, the federal government established a single amount that would be transferred annually for the next 10 years, with an annual population and inflation adjuster of 3.5 percent. Each year, this overall amount was divided, as with a zero-sum pool, among the three territories on the basis of their relative population and own-source revenue growth. Thus, while there was no longer any provision for an own-source revenue adjuster, in terms of the total federal transfer amount, it did play a role in each territory's allocation. The federal government had simply set the amount of transfers to the North after some less than convincing negotiations. This practice was consistent with the "let's-make-a-deal federalism" of the Paul Martin era. Transfers in the territories, much as in the provinces, became highly politicized. The territories objected to this arrangement and demanded new arrangements based on adequacy, revenue-raising incentives, certainty, stability and predictability. Table 1 reports payments made under the TFF since 1993-94 (Finance Canada 2007).

In the winter of 2007, the federal government announced a new TFF arrangement that reinstates transfers to each territory based on separate expenditure bases and own-source revenues. A GEB is based not on each government's costs, but on an expert panel report and a number that will establish (compared to the year previous) a reasonable and equitable increase in the 2007-08 transfer (6.6 percent for Yukon and the NWT, and 8.2 percent for Nunavut) (Expert Panel

2006). The base will be adjusted annually to reflect population growth and rates of increase in provincial, territorial and local spending. Own-source revenue capacity will be deducted from the GEB with 30 percent of a territory's own-source revenue capacity excluded from the deduction. This is to maintain an incentive to increase own-source revenue capacity. The federal government claims that the system is once again "principles-based." The system's greatest attribute, however, may be acceptability. The TGs seem satisfied with the renewed formula-based approach, even though the GEB still understates the costs of comparable services in the North and fails to meet the criterion of adequacy. However, it does go a considerable way toward meeting the other criteria set out. And, from a constitutional perspective, the system appears to provide the kind of certainty and stability related to financing that is needed to support stable and predictable governance.

Table 1
Territorial Formula Financing Entitlements, 1993-94 to 2007-08
(millions of dollars)

Year	Yukon	Northwest Territories	Nunavut	Canada
1993-94	289	861	–	1,150
1994-95	289	892	–	1,181
1995-96	291	906	–	1,197
1996-97	289	908	–	1,197
1997-98	307	921	–	1,229
1998-99	310	935	–	1,246
1999-2000	319	493	520	1,333
2000-01	336	310	566	1,212
2001-02	359	546	613	1,518
2002-03	372	588	656	1,616
2003-04	435	626	692	1,754
2004-05	466	678	756	1,900
2005-06	487	714	799	2,000
2006-07	506	739	825	2,070
2007-08	540	788	893	2,221

The issue of resource revenues has long surrounded discussions of the TFF.
When Yukon assumed responsibility for oil and gas, these revenues were not
included in the TFF. Revenue amounts were instead subjected to a separate clawback (which I will explain in greater detail in my discussion of devolution), with
the rate increasing significantly as revenues increased year after year over a
threshold. This arrangement continues for the YTG. In addition, the federal government confirmed that its 2007 TFF formula for the GNWT will not include
resource revenues. It will, however, include an offset against the TFF grant of 50
percent of resource revenues — up to an overall cap. According to the federal
government, this will provide "a net fiscal benefit and an additional incentive to
develop natural resources" (Finance Canada 2007).

Aboriginal Self-Government

T HE YUKON SELF-GOVERNMENT CHAPTERS — OR SELF-GOVERNMENT AGREEMENTS, AS
they are often called — are unique and innovative and have established a
template for the federal government as it undertakes self-government negotiations with First Nations, particularly in the NWT. The Yukon self-government
and related provisions have the following notable elements:

- For each First Nation, agreements and First Nations governments
  replace the *Indian Act* and band governments.
- Self-government chapters are included in each claims settlement but
  excluded from section 35 protection.
- First Nations governments have the authority of municipalities, with
  many of the powers of provinces and territories.
- First Nations have ownership of and jurisdiction over settlement lands
  and residents.
- First Nations have authority over culture, heritage and social services,
  regardless of residency.
- First Nations powers are concurrent with those of the territorial and
  federal governments, with complex paramountcy and conflict-of-laws
  provisions in a number of cases, and in cases like taxation, all three levels of government share powers.

- First Nations participate jointly in numerous Yukon-wide resource management boards.
- First Nations governments have property taxation powers over occupants of settlement lands.
- First Nations governments have direct taxation powers over citizens on settlement lands; there are provisions for agreements with Canada and Yukon to occupy tax room over noncitizens on settlement lands.
- Canada is committed to negotiating and concluding financial transfer agreements to deliver programs and services and operate governments.
- There is a reduction in transfers based on own-source revenue capacity at a ratio (or tax-back rate) of less than 1:1, with arrangements to be set out in the transfer agreements.

The situation in the Northwest Territories differs starkly from that in Yukon. As recently as four years ago, there were no self-government arrangements, and today only one has been successfully negotiated. The federal and NWT governments have a long-standing preference for public rather than Aboriginal governments at the local and regional levels, and they have been reluctant to include Aboriginal self-government as part of the treaty process. The federal position evolved in the 1990s, however, as the Yukon agreements made it difficult to deny self-government chapters to groups in the NWT (INAC 1993b). Today, there is a common intention on the part of Aboriginal people, the federal government and the territorial governments that self-government agreements be part of governance in the North.

The Gwich'in land claim agreement of 1993 contained a framework agreement on self-government negotiations, and in the Inuvialuit agreement, the government promised to treat the Inuvialuit no less favourably than the Gwich'in. In 1993, the Inuvialuit and Gwich'in proposed to negotiate jointly on governance; they reached an agreement on process in 1996, and in 2001 an agreement in principle, which was signed two years later. Public government structure at the regional and local levels guaranteed 50 percent Aboriginal representation and separate Gwich'in and Inuvialuit governments. Powers and responsibilities would be determined later.

The agreement appeared to represent real progress, but it avoided difficult questions. In January 2006, the Gwich'in Tribal Council board rejected the agreement. In a report on self-government negotiations, it stated, "Departing from the previous focus on development of regional public government structures, the

Gwich'in leadership preferred to emphasize negotiation of an Aboriginal model of government that fully expresses the Gwich'in inherent right to self-government" (Gwich'in Tribal Council 2006). Following renewed discussion on process, negotiations commenced in February 2007, and a process and schedule agreement was reached in July (Government of the Northwest Territories, Gwich'in Tribal Council and Government of Canada 2007).

With the termination of joint negotiations, the Inuvialuit likewise pursued separate negotiations and signed a process and schedule agreement in May 2007. The agreement provides for community public governments that will represent and provide local services to all residents, a regional Inuvialuit government that will provide services only to Aboriginal citizens and a regional service agency that will cooperate with the GNWT to coordinate programs and services for all residents and reduce costs. In the five primarily Inuvialuit communities, Inuvialuit are guaranteed at least half the community council memberships and one-quarter of the memberships in the mixed communities of Aklavik and Inuvik (Inuvialuit Regional Corporation 2007). The prospects for agreement seem to be good, but the timing will be affected by negotiations between the government and the Gwich'in because of shared residency in the two largest communities.

The Sahtu agreement likewise includes a commitment to negotiate self-government. Negotiations are proceeding at the subregional level in the area of the claims agreement, including the communities of Deline, Tulita and Norman Wells, where over 90 percent of the residents are Métis or Dene. To an outsider, the negotiations appear extremely complex. They illustrate some of the challenges of reconciling Aboriginal self-government with public government. In Tulita, Aboriginal negotiators are mandated to jointly represent four separate local bodies: the First Nation, the hamlet, the First Nation Land and Financial Corporation and the Métis Land and Financial Corporation. In Deline, both the Deline Band and the Deline Land Financial Corporation are party to the negotiations. The Deline model of self-government is based on a single community government that will replace the band council and local government. There will be universal suffrage, and all residents will be eligible to stand for office. The new government's powers have yet to be finalized, but they are expected to go well beyond the traditional powers of local municipal governments. In Norman Wells, the total Aboriginal population is about 270, and the total non-Aboriginal population is about 550. The Norman Wells Land Corporation is negotiating self-government on behalf of 70 Métis residents. A framework agreement, which is based on the Deline self-government model but will reflect Métis governance aspirations, was signed in June 2007. The parties plan to reach a final agreement within four years (Government of the Northwest Territories 2007).

Self-government negotiations have not yet commenced in the remaining two Sahtu communities, Fort Good Hope and Colville Lake, and self-government negotiations in the two southern regions of the NWT, which include Yellowknife, are likewise proceeding slowly. This is primarily because land claims and treaty negotiations are progressing slowly. Self-government negotiations are included in the overall negotiations, and by all appearances, the two will proceed in tandem. However, it is clear that individual First Nations and Aboriginal groups have taken control of self-government negotiations. They possess an inherent right to self-government, and governments now acknowledge their authority to determine the units through which that right will be exercised. The federal and territorial governments' preference for public government models is impossible to impose, and, as the Sahtu example suggests, this makes the task of establishing efficient governance in communities that have diverse Aboriginal and non-Aboriginal populations difficult. The public governance model addresses Aboriginal participation as influence rather than control, with influence expressed through voting and proportional numbers on elected bodies. First Nations governments do not have any direct control over the decisions of such bodies. This approach was dealt a near-fatal blow with the collapse of the joint Inuvialuit-Gwich'in negotiations.

The Tlicho agreement has residual public government dimensions, but it too reverts to the principle that the First Nations government controls the decisions of the new community governments; that a First Nations government's jurisdiction is territorial, but its citizens may reside elsewhere. Governance bodies chosen by and accountable only to First Nations members will make decisions and control community governments. Non-Aboriginal people can influence community governments, but control rests with the First Nations government. If one accepts the idea of Aboriginal people's inherent right to self-government, then this model is as expected; and it is similar to the models in the Sahtu, Gwich'in and Inuvialuit agreements, whereby public service agencies are contractually agreed upon, with each Aboriginal government controlling what is included in the contract.

A framework for self-government based on developments in Yukon and acceptable to all parties is taking shape. Within it, the agreement is made with

rights holders rather than government-defined aggregations, and public government becomes an administrative rather than a governance concept. In communities with mixed populations, partnerships and shared arrangements of various
sorts are possible and even encouraged, but these will only be established with
the consent of the entities that possess self-government rights and powers. Core
self-government authority applies to settlement lands, but it extends to citizens
when it comes to social services delivery and matters of importance to identity
and culture. Because decision-making authority resides with the First Nations
and relevant Aboriginal groups, Aboriginal self-government anchored in territorial-based governments with citizenship based on membership in a First Nation as
opposed to residency will be the pattern in the North.

Devolution

ERRITORIAL GOVERNMENT LEADERS HOPE TO EXPAND THEIR POWERS AND OBTAIN
province-like status, if not actual province status. During the 1990s, the powers and responsibilities of the Yukon and NWT governments gradually expanded
through devolution, particularly in the area of health services. Both governments
now provide medicare and health services on the same basis as the provinces and,
in many cases, they provide services to Indians in First Nations communities. Other
transfers have affected matters such as transportation, land title registries, mine safety and fisheries, and the territorial and federal governments agree that control of
onshore resources should be transferred to the territories.

Territorial control over resources has been impeded by three obstacles,
however. First, First Nations and other Aboriginal people have been reluctant to
support a transfer of resources until their claims are settled or they have received
assurances that the TGs will agree to resource transfers and resource revenue
sharing on a basis that will be acceptable in future settlements. Second, First
Nations fear that territorial governments might not transfer to them those
programs and services they want to deliver to their people. Third, the federal government has adopted the position that if lands and resources are transferred, then
it must receive a substantial share of the revenues flowing from resource use and
extraction on nontreaty lands. Conflict over these issues is acute in the NWT,
where First Nations and Aboriginal groups are reluctant to accept devolution

without a guarantee that the newly empowered territories will not frustrate their self-government aspirations.

Notwithstanding these concerns, there has been some progress. In 1988, Canada and the NWT signed a much-heralded Northern Accord agreement in principle. A final agreement proved impossible, however, as the parties disputed revenue shares and authority over offshore resources. Power over oil and gas in the NWT remains with Indian and Northern Affairs Canada. In Yukon, the federal and territorial governments agreed in 1993 upon the Canada-Yukon Oil and Gas Accord, which provided a framework to negotiate the transfer of responsibility for onshore oil and gas resources to the territory. The same year, the Umbrella Final Agreement provided for resource royalty sharing with First Nations. In cases where resource administration is devolved from Canada to Yukon and the Crown royalty exceeds the First Nations royalty, the territorial government must each year pay to the First Nation an amount equal to 50 percent of the first $2 million and 10 percent of any additional amount. However, the amount due to the First Nation in any given year "cannot exceed the amount which, if distributed equally among all Indian Yukon People, would result in an average per capita income for Yukon Indian People equal to the Canadian average per capita income" (INAC 1993b). On April 1, 1993, the federal government began to deposit revenues from the Kotaneelee gas field, and five years later the amount had reached approximately $7.8 million.

In 1998, a devolution agreement between First Nations, Yukon and Canada addressed First Nations' concerns about devolution. The governments assured First Nations that lands identified in outstanding claims would be protected and programs and services would be transferred to First Nations with self-government agreements. Aboriginal rights were shielded from any adverse affects, and the federal fiduciary duty was protected from any derogation, as a result of devolution. In November, the Yukon government assumed responsibility for oil and gas resources under the *Canada-Yukon Oil and Gas Accord Implementation Act*, and one month later it paid $2.1 million from the Kotaneelee fund to seven First Nations with land claims agreements. The remainder, which has now been paid, was held back until the remaining five First Nations reached final settlements (Auditor General of Canada 2003).

Yukon in effect owns and has regulatory authority over oil and gas resources on public lands, it can impose taxes and royalties on them, it is responsible for surface access and permitting, and it is mandated to develop an oil and gas regime in cooperation with First Nations (Yukon, Department of Energy, Mines and Resources 2007). When a treaty comes into effect, the First Nation has the same powers as the territory over lands for which it owns sub-surface rights. First Nations implement their powers by legislating a regime that mirrors that of the Yukon government. The territory's oil and gas revenues are partially offset by a federal tax-back on a portion of revenues. The proportion increases as annual revenues increase. The 1998 accord also committed the federal government to completing a joint offshore management regime and revenue-sharing arrangement in the Beaufort Sea. Three years later, Canada concluded the Yukon Devolution Transfer Agreement, which transferred remaining province-like responsibilities for land, forestry, minerals, onshore water and resource management, and taxation to the territory. In 2003, eight First Nations, with the support of the Council of Yukon First Nations, signed and consented to the Agreement. Although five First Nations argued before Parliament that devolution should not proceed until they had reached land claims and self-government settlements, the transfer took place in 2003 on the basis that the 1998 agreement on devolution, which all First Nations had signed, would protect their interests.

The situation has been quite different in the NWT, where responsibility for forests was transferred in 1987 and responsibility for health and local administrative services in the 1990s. The federal government retains responsibility for oil, gas, minerals, water and land; and the issues of land claims, self-government and revenue sharing have hindered the federal government's efforts to devolve all province-like responsibilities to northern governments. In 2000, the federal minister of Indian and northern affairs, Robert Nault, presented his government's perspective to the NWT Legislative Assembly:

> We have been talking about devolution for 30 years...Today's picture of what devolution can be has evolved...When this discussion started, devolution meant transfer of responsibilities from the federal government to the territorial government. And, along the way, we would negotiate claims and self-government agreements with Aboriginal groups, also transferring jurisdictions to them...Today, when I say devolution I envision a relationship that recognizes linkages to lands and resources in land claim and self-government negotiations. I see Canada transferring responsibilities to appropriate territorial and Aboriginal governments. According to trilateral decisions. (Nault 2000)

In other words, devolution will proceed only with the consent of Aboriginal peoples and the development of Aboriginal governments.

To that end, the federal government established an intergovernmental forum to bring together federal, territorial and First Nations governments to develop a process to deal with the devolution of land and resource management responsibilities. The Aboriginal Summit comprises all Aboriginal groups in the NWT except the Dehcho Dene. The Aboriginal Summit reached a general agreement in May 2001, and the parties agreed to the following objectives: the transfer of legislative powers, programs and responsibilities for land, water, mines, minerals, oil and gas, the environment and archaeological resources to the NWT; the creation of an effective, efficient and coordinated resource management regime; and a fair net fiscal benefit for the territory. A joint statement elaborated on the final objective:

> A transfer of responsibilities for natural resources will result in a financial benefit to the NWT from resource revenues derived from such activities as mining and petroleum...Under devolution, the federal government will transfer to the NWT legislative powers and administrative responsibilities for lands and natural resources including powers to levy and collect resource revenues. Net fiscal benefit discussions will determine how territorial resource revenues received under devolution will impact Territorial Formula Financing...so as to provide the NWT with a "net fiscal benefit." Finance Canada is the department with the mandate to negotiate the net fiscal benefit the NWT will receive. The Government of Northwest Territories and Aboriginal governments have agreed that the net fiscal benefit the territorial government will receive from the Government of Canada will be shared among them. (Intergovernmental Forum 2001)

Formal negotiations for developing a devolution framework agreement began in September 2002, and the three parties reached a framework agreement in 2004. Although they hoped to reach an agreement in principle by 2004 and a devolution agreement by 2005, this has not yet been achieved.

Aboriginal groups own subsurface resources on settlement lands for which their governments or institutions have undisputed access to royalties. Resource revenue is contested in the NWT, however. Although final agreements with First Nations specify revenue-sharing arrangements for each area, the federal government adjusts the cash compensation component of an offer to offset the predicted value of revenue-sharing arrangements. This practice is never stated explicitly, and an outstanding policy question remains: How will resource revenues be divided when the TG assumes responsibilities for and ownership of lands and resources? In principle, this is a matter to be decided between the territorial governments and Aboriginal representatives. However, the matter is complicated by the fact that the territorial governments and Canada lack a revenue-sharing agreement for the same resource.

The federal government's 1993 oil and gas accord with Yukon suggests a possible approach to the problem. Under this agreement, Yukon retains 100 percent of revenues up to $3 million per year for oil and gas as a group, and for revenues exceeding $3 million, it retains a share declining from 40 to 20 percent (INAC 1993b). However, the 2003 devolution accord, which deals with other resources, includes a radically different arrangement. The accord divides other resources into four groups — forestry, minerals, lands and water; for each group, Yukon receives all revenues up to $3 million per year, and no share above $3 million. Resource revenues are not included in Territorial Formula Financing, but tax-back amounts are deducted from the TFF transfer as a charge against resource revenues. The net amount of resource revenues realized by Yukon is referred to as the "net fiscal benefit," and it must be shared with First Nations under the UFA. Under the agreement, if Yukon were to collect annual revenues of $8 million from oil and gas and $3 million or more from each of the other groups, its net fiscal benefit per capita would be about $500. If First Nations collected royalties of $6 million from their resources, the net fiscal benefit per capita to the YTG would be about $400.

The NWT does not have a similar resource-revenue-sharing agreement, but the federal government has indicated that the issue will be part of devolution discussions. In May 2007, the GNWT reached a resource-revenue-sharing agreement in principle with the Inuvialuit, Gwich'in, Sahtu and Métis. Under this agreement, Aboriginal parties will receive 25 percent of the territory's net fiscal benefit from any resource revenue sharing between the NWT and Canada, and under self-government, these amounts will not be clawed back as own-source revenue. If this agreement holds and devolution proceeds, resource revenues will be shared between the three parties as follows: First Nations and Aboriginal groups, up to 12.5 percent; the GNWT, up to 37.5 percent; and Canada, up to at least 50 percent. First Nations will also get a share, set out in their individual agreements, of revenues from their traditional territories.

It is uncertain whether this agreement will prevail, however. Although the agreement in principle was forwarded by the GNWT to the appropriate federal officials with a recommendation that it be adopted as the basis for a final agreement within a year, the Tlicho, Dehcho and Akaitcho refused to sign the deal — in fact, they are actively opposing it. On May 28, 2007, Tlicho chief George Mackenzie stated, "When you don't have confidence, you cannot agree with the proposal." Mackenzie said that the GNWT had not fulfilled its commitments under the 2005 settlement (Thompson 2007). Earlier that month, Akaitcho chiefs had accused the Premier of "sabotaging their land claims process, lying to their people, and going behind their backs to make the deal," and Dehcho chief Herb Norwegian condemned the deal as amounting to crumbs that would not sustain his people (Unrau 2007). The Dehcho added that the territory's royalty regime was inadequate and, they believe, designed to pressure them to reach land claims and pipeline agreements (Dehcho First Nations 2007).

It is difficult to assess what amounts of resource revenues will eventually be distributed to the GNWT and First Nations and Aboriginal groups. Proportionate shares before the cap continue to be a source of conflict; interestingly, there seems to be little debate or discussion of the cap that the federal government intends to apply to the amounts of resources that remain in the territory, whether it be with the GNWT or Aboriginal governments. This is a more significant issue than the proportionate shares — if the cap tracks Yukon, it would limit revenue sharing with the NWT to $500 per capita per year. Total revenues retained by NWT governments would be about $22 million, which is less than 10 percent of the $260 million in annual royalties from diamonds.

Further progress in land and resource devolution in the NWT is important to any final settlement on the North's constitutional structure. Resource-revenue-sharing agreements, unsettled land claims and self-government negotiations could impede progress and will centre on the conditions under which the federal and territorial governments will be prepared to proceed with the devolution of resources. From the federal government's perspective, the question is what degree of Aboriginal consent is necessary for Canada to transfer responsibility for resources to the GNWT. For the GNWT, the more important question is whether an acceptable revenue-sharing agreement can be reached with the federal government. Following the 2007 budget, the NWT's newly elected premier, Floyd Roland, said in his first public statement, "A prime goal of this government will be to win province-like powers over the territory's natural resources...It is time the federal government took seriously the North's desire to control and benefit from its own resources. I do believe we need to take a stronger approach" (Weber 2007).

It is not clear whether the GNWT wants a better deal or whether the Premier is simply trying to accelerate the pace of devolution within the parameters that have been established. It is possible that his goal is to pressure Canada to accept Aboriginal support for the 2007 agreement as sufficient to proceed. For the First

Nations who have not yet agreed to land claims and revenue-sharing agreements —
the Akaitcho and the Dehcho, in particular — two questions remain: What kind of
agreements can we reasonably expect to achieve? And how much influence can we
exert over devolution and resource revenue sharing? Canada and the GNWT may
proceed with devolution and revenue sharing on the basis of the budget, the Yukon
precedent and the NWT's revenue-sharing agreement in principle.

Northern Pipelines

UNDER THE CANADIAN CONSTITUTION, THE FEDERAL GOVERNMENT IS RESPONSIBLE
for interprovincial and international trade and commerce; as a result, the
National Energy Board is responsible for international and interprovincial
pipelines. The federal body known as the Northern Pipeline Agency, under the
minister of natural resources, is responsible for the coordination and development of pipeline projects. Two major pipeline projects (the Mackenzie Gas Project
[MGP] and the Alaska Highway Pipeline Project [AHPP]) have been proposed to
transport natural gas from the Mackenzie Delta and Prudhoe Bay, Alaska, to
southern Canada and the United States.

Northern pipelines have once again become a subject of intense negotia-
tion. The Aboriginal Pipeline Group (APG) has been formed to participate in the
MGP, which is on a fast-track development schedule. The group's president, Bob
Reid, said in 2005:

> By June of 2001, APG negotiated a memorandum of understanding with the
> Mackenzie Delta Producers Group that provided for a one-third interest in the
> Mackenzie Valley pipeline. In June of 2003, APG negotiated an enhanced deal
> that brought funding from TransCanada Pipelines, the Delta Producers, and the
> federal and territorial governments. We are now focussing on arranging the
> long-term financing needed to support our ownership position, loans that will
> be repaid from our share of revenue from the pipeline...Once the loans are
> repaid, *dividends could be as much as $100-million per year.* These very signifi-
> cant dividends will be distributed according to pipeline distance through each
> Aboriginal region to those groups that have formally joined the APG, current-
> ly the Gwich'in, the Inuvialuit and the Sahtu. We have an open invitation to
> the Dehcho, but they have indicated that their land claim and self-government
> initiative — the Dehcho Process — remains their priority. I am optimistic that
> they will recognize the significant benefits available to them — based on the
> length of pipeline through Dehcho lands, they could earn more than one-third
> of the total annual dividends. (Reid 2005)

Aboriginal community groups and governments are also negotiating separate benefits agreements. The Dehcho, not having a land claim agreement, are in a position to negotiate an accommodation agreement that will permit the federal government to infringe their title and rights in the course of the development. The Dehcho First Nations (DFN) have opposed the proposed Mackenzie pipeline, saying it wants a land agreement and taxation rights before any development goes forward. In 2004, the Dehcho mounted a legal challenge to block progress on the pipeline review, but one year later they reached an agreement with the federal government that included, among other things, the federal government's agreement to consult on the pipeline's impact on rights and title, its commitment to keep a large amount of public land from being leased or sold for development unless it has the First Nations' consent, and its promise to provide over $30 million in funds. However, the Minister of Indian Affairs and Northern Development subsequently said that Dehcho consent is not needed for the pipeline to proceed.[2]

The 2005 agreement repeatedly references the Dehcho process, which is described by Canada as "a step-by-step approach" in which the DFN seeks a final agreement based on land management, not land selection. The process differs "from a traditional 'comprehensive claim,' and is new to land and resource negotiations in the Northwest Territories" (INAC 2006). Land claims, self-government, resource revenue sharing and pipeline issues have melded into one new process, and it is difficult to predict how quickly the process will move forward and whether it can successfully integrate all of the issues. Given that their territory spans almost one-third of the southern section of the MGP, the Dehcho have considerable leverage, but the federal and territorial governments are unlikely to veer from established settlement patterns, if for no other reason than to avoid alienating those groups. There will be intense pressure on all sides to reach a compromise; if they fail, the federal government will likely let the status quo prevail. It could, if necessary, use its powers of infringement to force the DFN to accept the pipeline and allow the *Indian Act* framework to prevail for any matters that remain.

This outcome would not be fatal to the overall settlement between the federal government and other First Nations and Aboriginal groups. The new arrangements and distribution of powers can operate without the participation of the Dehcho. A similar argument applies to the Kaska in southeastern Yukon. Now that the courts have recognized extensive infringement powers, it is not essential to the federal and Yukon governments that the Kaska participate in the overall settlement. Infringement arrangements will permit governments to realize their development goals, and the Kaska can continue to use the *Indian Act* as the framework for land management and governance.

Is a Constitutional Settlement Imminent?

ALTHOUGH THERE IS LOTS OF ROOM FOR DEBATE OVER DEFINITIONS OF constitutional change, it is certain that any new constitutional settlement will promote changes in governance that will alter long-established structures; empower new independent governing authorities; assign meaningful scope and powers to the governing authorities; and refine the character of citizenship. The changes in governance must also be credible, stable, sustainable and irreversible, and they must provide fiscal autonomy. Has a constitutional settlement been established — or is one at least in the making — in Canada's northwest? Based on the criteria I have listed, my tentative answer is yes.

In the case of land claims, a standard model (which might be called the "Yukon model") has emerged that is based on land selection and the partition of traditional territories, cash compensation, wildlife and traditional harvests, and resource revenues and management. In the case of Aboriginal self-government, the framework for settlements has likewise been established. The model recognizes the right to self-government of First Nations and Inuit based upon their historical control and occupation of traditional lands. Self-government agreements will thus be made with the rights holders rather than with government-defined aggregations, and public government will become an administrative rather than a governance concept. In communities with mixed populations, partnerships and shared administrative arrangements will be made and encouraged, but only with the consent of the entities that possess self-government rights and powers. Self-government authority will apply on First Nations settlement lands, and it will extend to citizens more generally for matters important to identity and culture and for social services delivery. Aboriginal governments will have broad-based taxation powers and the authority to deliver many services now provided by the federal and territorial governments. They will be supported by fiscal arrangements with Canada that are based on the existing finances allocated to the programs and services by Canada or the TGs, and transfers will be reduced over time as the own-source revenue capacity of Aboriginal governments increases.

Territorial governments, based on almost the same governance model as the provinces, are now permanent fixtures in the North's constitutional framework, and relationships with First Nations and Aboriginal governments are now settled. Devolution will soon make this relationship a reality in the Northwest Territories. Territorial services and institutions, including local governments, will serve noncitizens and nonresidents, and various service arrangements and partnerships will be established for their joint delivery and coordination. First Nations and Aboriginal group representatives will participate in territorial governments through panels and committees and, in some cases, make decisions about land-use planning; the management of wildlife, water, surface rights and parks; and certain other functions.

The basic formula for financing the territorial and First Nations and Aboriginal governments has also been settled. TFF has proven resilient and can be expected to be a permanent part of the region's governance architecture. The issue of disincentives appears to be settled, with an acceptance that 30 percent of own-source revenue capacity will be excluded from the fiscal capacity of territorial governments. Because the expenditure base in the formula will not be reassessed to reflect actual costs, it will continue to be based on past numbers. Resource revenues will remain a contested feature of the arrangements, but it is clear that the federal government is prepared to share resource revenues with the territories up to a cap that ensures that the largest part of such revenues will be retained by the federal government if the amounts become significant. The federal government insists that territorial governments seek the approval of a majority of First Nations and Aboriginal groups before sharing in net resource revenues, but it is clear that the TGs will proceed with resource devolution without the consent of all First Nations and Aboriginal groups. Aboriginal governments will be able to impose direct taxes within their territories, and they will be expected to tax in accordance with their fiscal capacity. Federal transfers will be based on past government expenditures for programs and services, with capped annual adjusters. Own-source revenues will be partially taxed back. While the current rate of 50 percent is high, given the degree to which Aboriginal communities lag behind the larger society in terms of social and economic status, there is room to achieve an improved system of self-government financing through negotiation and discussion.

Challenges   to   Finalizing
the   Architecture   of
Governance

THE FACT THAT MANY OF THE ELEMENTS OF GOVERNANCE CAN NOW BE PREDICTED IN specific terms does not mean that all the challenges to settlement implementation have been overcome. The claim that a stable constitutional settlement is in the making can be challenged on the grounds that it is still not complete and that formidable obstacles stand in the way of completion.

Surrendering Rights in Modern Treaties
According to the federal government's theory of modern treaties, First Nations exchange claims to undefined Aboriginal rights for a package of clearly defined rights and benefits set out in a settlement agreement. Many First Nations, who view Aboriginal rights as inherent and inalienable, reject this approach on the grounds that a treaty thus requires a First Nation to surrender, or extinguish, its traditional rights. Most First Nations leaders view the extinguishment issue as an obstacle to the Kaska and Dehcho negotiations. In an artful dodge, government negotiators have made alternative arrangements, through which First Nations can agree not to exercise traditional rights after a treaty is signed, and they have assured First Nations that future court-determined self-government rights will be recognized — even if a treaty has been concluded. This strategy has proven to be unacceptable in negotiations to date, and it is doubtful that similar strategies will be well received in future.

The Land Selection Model
Modern settlements have at their core the land selection and partition model, which has been an obstacle to the Kaska and Dehcho negotiations. First Nations have proposed joint ownership and comanagement of lands and resources in traditional territory as an alternative that addresses the obstacles of extinguishment and the land selection model simultaneously. It is not clear whether the government sees it the same way, but there is an obvious relationship between the two obstacles.

Powers off Settlement Lands
A subject of some intense discussion in treaty negotiations has been whether First Nations must be consulted before major developments can proceed outside of

settlement lands. The government position has been that treaties are full and final commitments, and that the powers they describe extend only to the things they contain. First Nations are assured environmental assessments in advance of such developments and are provided a role in the process, but they are not included in permitting or final approval processes. Some First Nations object on the grounds that the honour of the Crown creates a continuing common-law duty to consult First Nations and accommodate their interests throughout their traditional territories, regardless of whether the lands are First Nations lands under the treaty. Representatives of the federal and territorial governments claim that if the First Nations' position is true, then the governments' authority to control and use non-First-Nations lands is compromised, and the governance of those lands is still in some sense shared, which is contrary to the terms of modern treaties.

The Little Salmon Carmacks First Nation recently took the Yukon government to court over the approval of a land-use application, claiming that there is a continuing common-law duty to consult and accommodate First Nations. In October 2007, a judge of the Yukon Supreme Court ruled that the duty to consult and accommodate arises from the concept of the honour of the Crown and applies to every treaty as a matter of common law.[3] On the face of it, this dealt a major blow to the governments' position on the finality and certainty of treaty terms; however, it is not clear how general the obligation will be and what remedies might be required. In this particular case, the land-use application was not reassessed: the government was simply directed to consult with the First Nation before finalizing the permit. The decision will also be appealed by the Yukon government with the support of the federal government. The uncertainty flowing from the case could slow progress on treaty negotiations now under way.

Resource Revenue Cap for Territorial Governments

One issue that remains unsettled regarding the financing of the territorial governments is what share of resource revenue will be retained by the federal government. While Yukon has an agreement, the NWT does not. The federal position is that the amounts going to the TGs will be capped. If the cap is as low as the $500 per capita suggested in this study, and if resource revenues grow as substantially in the North as expected, such a low cap will not be sustainable. The proposed cap signals the federal government's unwillingness to loosen the purse strings of northern governance; it suggests, in one important way, that colonial relationships persist in the modern era. Northern governments will not accept this, and they will likely demand an arrangement similar to those between the provinces and the federal government, including the Atlantic Accord. Lack of agreement on this issue could impede the progress of devolution in the North. Perhaps the federal government is concerned that the northern governments will become unduly rich. However, given their current dependence on transfers, this is far-fetched. The federal government is also concerned that the NWT will realize greater revenues than Yukon, creating a horizontal fiscal gap in the North. Even if this is the case, a low cap on resource revenues would be an ineffective way to address the problem, and a fair and workable solution to resource revenue sharing appears to be elusive.

Fiscal Relations with First Nations

The federal and territorial governments' fiscal relationship with First Nations has three problems. In the NWT, three First Nations claims groups — including the Tlicho, who already have a treaty — have contested the fairness of their share of the net fiscal benefit from the territorial government's resource revenues. The issue's resolution will likely depend on whether the federal government believes that the agreement of northern and northwestern claimant groups is sufficient to proceed with the devolution of resources. The other two problems pertain to the form of fiscal agreement the federal government enters into with self-governing First Nations. First, the formula's expenditure base bears no relationship to the cost of services but is rather arbitrarily set at current expenditures on the services. These expenditures are, without doubt, well below the costs of either comparable services or needs-driven services. With such a paucity of funds, First Nations cannot take the measures necessary to build capacity and pursue self-sufficiency. Second, the federal government's clawback rate on own-source revenues or revenue capacity would be reasonable if it kicked in after First Nations reached a level of development comparable to modern developed communities; however, the application of this rate at a time when communities are underfunded and underdeveloped seriously threatens the overall project of development. Funds needed for development are taken out of the communities at a time when First Nations can use them to realize the dual goals of development and service provision at a level already experienced by other citizens. This issue has been brought to the attention of the federal government on many occasions, and the government has responded with an obstinacy that is perverse and puzzling. However, given the government's slow but nevertheless substantial movement on other issues over the years, one can hope for similar movement on this important matter.

Fiscal Dependency

Some people question whether stable constitutional development is possible when the governance entities are dependent on transfer payments to the degree that is the case in the North. Currently, territorial and First Nations governments receive from 75 to 95 percent of their revenue as transfer payments. Under such conditions, critics argue, accountability is compromised and the quality of government is undermined. Supporters of the new northern governance argue that autonomous governments with adequate transfers will create the conditions for growth and development needed to reduce the dependence on transfers. They believe that northern resource development will accelerate the shift from dependency, provided that northern governments can access resource revenues, including offshore resources, on the same basis as the provinces. While some critics believe that resource revenue dependency can likewise distort good governance, Alberta's situation provides an awkward counterargument. Finally, supporters of northern governance argue that the gains from decentralized government far outweigh academic concerns about the effects of fiscal dependency.

Section 35 Protection of Self-Government Agreements

The federal government has not, to date, agreed to provide section 35 recognition and protection to Yukon self-government agreements. However, it has done so with the Tlicho agreement in the NWT. Some argue that the overall settlement in the North will never be considered stable and legitimate until every self-government agreement falls under the protection of section 35. This is a legitimate position, and it seems unthinkable that the federal government will not soon commit to constitutional protection and recognition of all self-government agreements, including those in Yukon. Yet even if that commitment is not forthcoming, Yukon self-government agreements will be protected by custom and practice, and they will most likely be recognized as deserving of legal protection because of their status as agreements between governments and First Nations. In the final analysis, it may not matter whether the federal government has accorded them section 35 status.

Constitutional Certainty

Just as some argue that Aboriginal self-government should be constitutionally protected, others argue that the new territorial governments must be provided for in the Constitution if they are to be stable and secure. One problem is the

absence of a mechanism as readily available as section 35 to recognize and
protect territorial governments: a formal constitutional amendment would be
necessary. While it is unlikely that the provinces would object to the territories having provincial status conferred upon them, federal politicians fear that
Quebec (and perhaps other provinces bordering the territories) would see the
opening of the Constitution and boundary discussions as a chance to fulfill its
own aspirations. Whatever the reality, politicians are reluctant to accommodate the territories by opening the Constitution. In the meantime, the territorial governments have achieved much of the informal constitutional status
they seek. Their existence is accepted as permanent, they have a full and complete role in interprovincial and federal-provincial forums and arrangements.
Their status as province-like creatures is well established, and their place is
unlikely to be seriously compromised.

Conclusion: The New North Is Here to Stay

A NEW CONSTITUTIONAL SETTLEMENT IS FALLING INTO PLACE IN THE NORTH. ITS
implementation is far from complete, but its architecture is identifiable. It
is unlikely that there will be substantial variation from the form and structure that
has evolved over the last quarter century. Some issues and problems will have to
be resolved, but the direction is clear, and some variation in the outcome of outstanding issues will not fatally alter the overall pattern. There will need to be
some improvements to certain aspects of the settlement if good and effective governance is to be achieved, but this will be feasible over time. These accommodations will require the federal government to either modify its long-standing policy
positions or take action on issues it has been avoiding.

There is a new North. It has been shaped and developed through much
effort and great perseverance on the part of northerners. The voice of the south
— the federal government — has had to change and adapt to realities that would
have been unthinkable 25 years ago. The result is indeed a new constitutional settlement in form and substance. It is true that not everyone is yet fully part of it,
and there are still some battles to fight and win, but a final settlement is inevitable
and irreversible. The North will never be the same.

Notes

1   *Yukon Act*, S.C. 2002, c.7.
2   "Ottawa Offer Could Clear Major
    Stumbling Block to Mackenzie Pipeline,"
    CBCnews.ca, May 31, 2006.
    http://www.cbc.ca/canada/north/story/2006/
    05/31/dehcho05312006.html (accessed
    July 22, 2008).
3   *Little Salmon/Carmacks First Nation v. The
    Government of Yukon (Minister of Energy,
    Mines and Resources)*, 2007 YKSC 28.

References

Auditor General of Canada. 2003. *Report of the
    Auditor General to the Yukon Legislative
    Assembly for 2002-2003*. Ottawa:
    Government of Canada.
British Columbia. Ministry of Aboriginal
    Relations and Reconciliation. 2007. "Kaska
    Nation." Victoria: Government of British
    Columbia. Accessed November 7, 2007.
    http://www.gov.bc.ca/arr/firstnation/kaska_
    nation/default.html
Cameron, Kirk, and Graham White. 1995.
    *Northern Governments in Transition: Political
    and Constitutional Development in the Yukon,
    Nunavut and the Western Northwest
    Territories*. Montreal: Institute for Research
    on Public Policy.
Chrétien, Jean. 1972. "Statement on Northern
    Land Claims Negotiations." Ottawa: Indian
    and Northern Affairs Canada.
Council for Yukon Indians. 1973. *Together Today
    for Our Children Tomorrow: A Statement of
    Grievances and an Approach to Settlement by
    the Yukon Indian People*. Brampton: Charters
    Publishing.
Dacks, Gurston. 1981. *A Choice of Futures: Politics
    in the Canadian North*. Toronto: Methuen.
Dehcho First Nations. 2007. "Dehcho Leader
    Rejects Resource Sharing Agreement In
    Principle as Just Crumbs." Press release,
    May 15. Accessed July 22, 2008.
    http://www.dehchofirstnations.com/archives/
    press_archive.htm
Dickerson, Mark O. 1992. *Whose North? Political
    Change, Political Development and Self-
    Government in the Northwest Territories*.
    Vancouver: University of British Columbia
    Press, Arctic Institute of North America.
Expert Panel on Equalization and Territorial
    Formula Financing. 2006. *Achieving a
    National Purpose: Putting Equalization Back
    on Track*. Ottawa: Finance Canada.
Finance Canada. 2007. "Annex 4: Restoring
    Fiscal Balance for a Stronger Federation."
    Budget 2007. Ottawa: Finance Canada.
    Accessed May 30, 2008. http://www.bud-
    get.gc.ca/ 2007/bp/bpa4e.html
Funston, Bernard. 2007. "Federalism and First
    Nations: In Search of Space." In
    *Constructing Tomorrow's Federalism: New
    Perspectives on Canadian Governance*, edited
    by Ian Peach. Winnipeg: University of
    Manitoba Press.
Government of the Northwest Territories. 2003.
    "Land Claims and Self-Government
    Agreement among the Tlicho, the
    Government of the Northwest Territories,
    and the Government of Canada."
    Yellowknife: Government of the Northwest
    Territories. Accessed November 7, 2007.
    http://www.gov.nt.ca/MAA/agreements/
    tliagr2_e.pdf
———. 2007. "Norman Wells Self-
    Government Framework Agreement."
    Yellowknife: Government of the Northwest
    Territories, Department of Aboriginal
    Affairs and Intergovernmental Relations.
    Accessed July 22, 2008.
    www.daair.gov.nt.ca/what-we-do/
    documents/normanwellssignedframe
    workagreement_13june07.PDF
Government of the Northwest Territories,
    Gwich'in Tribal Council, and Government
    of Canada. 2007. *Process and Schedule
    Agreement*. Inuvik: Gwich'in Tribal Council.
Gwich'in Tribal Council. 2006. *Annual Report*.
    Inuvik: Gwich'in Tribal Council.
Indian and Northern Affairs Canada (INAC).
    1973. "Federal Native Claims Policy."
    Ottawa: INAC.
———. 1987. "Comprehensive Land Claims
    Policy (1986)." Ottawa: Minister of Public
    Works and Services Canada.

_____. 1993a. *Federal Policy for the Settlement of Native Claims*. Ottawa: INAC.

_____. 1993b. *Umbrella Final Agreement between the Government of Canada, the Council for Yukon Indians and the Government of the Yukon*. Ottawa: INAC.

_____. 1995. *Aboriginal Self-Government: The Government of Canada's Approach to Implementation of the Inherent Right and the Negotiation of Aboriginal Self-Government*. Ottawa: INAC.

_____. 2000. *Five-Year Annual Review of the Umbrella Agreement Implementation Plan and Yukon First Nation Agreement Implementation Plans for the First Four Yukon First Nations*. Ottawa: INAC. Accessed November 7, 2007. http://www.ainc-inac.gc.ca/pr/agr/ykn/yua_e.pdf

_____. 2003. *Yukon Land Claims and Self-Government Agreements: 02-03 Annual Report*. Ottawa: INAC. Accessed November 7, 2007. http://www.ainc-inac.gc.ca/pr/agr/ykn/ar02/02-03_e.pdf

_____. 2006. *Backgrounder: Canada's Offer to the Dehcho First Nations*. Ottawa: INAC. Accessed November 7, 2007. http://nwt-tno.inac-ainc.gc.ca/dehcho/news/053006a_e.htm

Intergovernmental Forum. 2001. "Memorandum of Intent on Devolution and Resource Revenue Sharing," appendix 1. *Northwest Territories Lands and Resources Devolution Framework Agreement*. Yellowknife: Government of the Northwest Territories.

Inuvialuit Regional Corporation. 2007. *Self-Government Newsletter*. Inuvik: Inuvialuit Regional Corporation.

McNeil, Kent. 2000. "The Post-Delgamuukw Nature and Content of Aboriginal Title." Unpublished paper. Accessed June 4, 2008. http://courses.forestry.ubc.ca/cons370/documents/McNeil.content.pdf

Nault, Robert D. 2000. "Speaking Notes for the Honourable Robert D. Nault at the NWT Legislative Assembly, Yellowknife, NWT," January 20. Ottawa: INAC. Accessed November 7, 2007. http://www.ainc-inac.gc.ca/nr/spch/2000/ 00j20_e.html

Reid, Bob. 2005. "An Exceptional Deal." Aboriginal Pipeline Group. Accessed July 22, 2008. http://www.mvapg.com/page/page/2501121.htm

Thompson, Roxanna. 2007. "Tlicho Grand Chief Angry over Lack of Consultation." Northern News Services Online, May 21. Accessed November 7, 2007. www.nnsl.com/frames/newspapers/2007-05/may28_07gc.html

Unrau, Jason. 2007. "Handley Brushes Off Akaitcho Demand That He Leave Town." Northern News Services Online, May 21. Accessed July 22, 2007. www.nnsl.com/frames/newspapers/2007-05/may21_07joe.html

Weber, Bob. 2007. "New NWT Premier Promises Assertive Style." *Globe and Mail*, October 18.

Yukon. Department of Energy, Mines and Resources. 2007. "Oil and Gas Resources: Rights." Accessed July 22, 2008. http://www.emr.gov.yk.ca/oilandgas/rights.html

Living Up to the Spirit
of Modern Treaties?
Implementation and
Institutional
Development

T HE INSTITUTIONAL DEVELOPMENT OCCURRING IN THE NORTHWEST TERRITORIES (NWT) and Yukon rests in part on a combination of unique circumstances and legal and policy environments of land claims and self-government implementation. Scholarly analysis of implementation has been generated sparsely, even though implementation has become the foremost practical concern for organizations involved in negotiating and implementing agreements. In our experience, agreements between indigenous peoples and the state are perceived very differently by land claims organizations than by Canada. Indigenous peoples generally view treaties with Canada as agreements about decolonizing state-indigenous relationships and improving the lives of indigenous peoples. In contrast, Canada views modern treaties' primary purpose as achieving certainty of rights, entitlements and obligations.[1]

For land claims organizations, the intrinsic and instrumental value of land claims agreements can be undermined by the conditions in which agreements must function — specifically, when implementation approaches create a disabling environment, preventing the achievement of overall agreement objectives. This is in contrast to an enabling environment, in which conditions are created that promote effective implementation. While we elaborate these concepts later in this chapter, it is important to note here that international development efforts and research into indigenous governance development have indicated that the relationship between emerging (land claims and self-government) governments and established (federal and territorial) governments is one of the most important factors determining the effectiveness of new governments. This is particularly true in cases where established governments have financial and legal obligations affecting the authorities and programs of the emerging governments.[2] Developing viable and effective governing institutions in the North that can cooperate on issues ranging from devolution to economic development initiatives depends in part on the conditions in which these institutions operate. We conclude this chapter by suggesting ways to create the conditions that will enable us to avoid some of the common problems identified with land claims (and, by extension, self-government) implementation to date.

National Problems,
National Policy

UPON COMPLETION OF HER AUDIT OF THE IMPLEMENTATION PROGRESS OF THE GWICH'IN and Nunavut land claims agreements, the Auditor General of Canada concluded that the main agency responsible for implementation, Indian and Northern Affairs Canada (INAC), "seems focused on fulfilling the letter of the land claims' implementation plans but not the spirit. Officials may believe that they have met their obligations, but in fact they have not worked to support the full intent of the land claims agreements" (2003, chap. 8.3).

The 2003 Auditor General's Report, hailed by land claims organizations as a welcome critique of land claims implementation, highlights that relational friction and specific disputes over implementation arise from government efforts to meet legal obligations rather than taking a results-oriented approach to assessing implementation efforts. A results-oriented approach would take into account the outcomes or effects of activities undertaken to fulfill land claims obligations in the context of broad land claims objectives. Currently, in all land claims agreements save that of the Inuvialuit, Canada is not compelled to negotiate or resolve disputes among the parties.[3] A results-oriented approach would require a mechanism within agreements ensuring not only Canada's participation in dispute resolution or a periodic agreement review process, but also its commitment to participate in a way that would bring the dispute to a conclusion in accordance with certain principles, including the honour of the Crown.

Generally, the objective of land claims agreements is to improve the social and material well-being of indigenous peoples in exchange for a combination of surrender and definition of their Aboriginal rights. INAC's response to the Auditor General's charge that it had failed to honour the spirit of the land claims agreements brings into stark relief the difference in the way government and land claims organizations understand what implementation is intended to achieve. This is illustrated by the Auditor General's observation that "while [INAC] agrees with many of our recommendations, it fundamentally disagrees with our view of the way success for implementing land claims should be measured. The Department defines success as fulfilling the specific obligations as set out in the [implementation] agreements and plans. We believe that results matter too, and that the Department should be giving them more attention" (2003, chap. 8.10).

When the 2003 audit was conducted, all land claims organizations in Canada had just formed an alliance called the Land Claims Agreement Coalition (LCAC). The LCAC is now seeking a federal implementation policy to address issues and challenges posed by the current approach to land claims implementation. The coalition has held two major conferences that have attracted hundreds of participants, basing its efforts on commonly held views on the shortcomings that all land claims organizations have experienced in .their implementation relationships with Canada. According to Nellie Cournoyea, chairperson of the Inuvialuit Regional Corporation:

> On the Government of Canada side land claims implementation efforts are governed by a 1986 policy statement that is as thin as it is outdated. This fact is well known. The Auditor General of Canada has noted the deep and chronic defects of the policy on repeated occasions. The first conference organized by the members of the Land Claim Coalition testified to these deficiencies. Thomas Berger's recent report on the implementation shortcomings of the Nunavut Land Claim Agreement provides graphic evidence of the gap between the objectives of the land claim agreements and what is actually happening — and what is not happening — on the ground. His report speaks to the very heavy costs, not just to Aboriginal peoples but to all Canadians, of half-hearted, inadequate implementation efforts. Mr. Berger's report is of course very important for what it says about Nunavut; and even more important in that the problems it addresses in Nunavut exist in various forms with all the other modern land claim agreements. (quoted in LCAC 2006a, 2)

Disputes between Canada and land claims organizations over implementation are inevitable; each party to an agreement brings its own views of legal, institutional and performance obligations and goals, and these sometimes differ. However, land claims organizations, as articulated through the LCAC position paper on a national implementation policy (LCAC 2006b), have frequently experienced frustration with Canada's implementation approaches, and this has prompted them to undertake significant collaborative work on national policy reform. Their efforts have not yet yielded the desired result. We should note that some commentators — for example, former Northwest Territories premier George Braden (see his commentary in this volume) — have pointed out that a national policy may not resolve specific problems with particular agreements, given their varying institutions and contexts. However, a national policy might be a starting point in the process of refining approaches to resolving more localized implementation issues.

Recent developments in Canada's ongoing land claims implementation story include an agreement reached in 2007 between Canada and the Eeyou Istchee (Grand Council of the Crees), which addresses in part the implementation issues arising from the 1975 James Bay and Northern Quebec Agreement (Indian and Northern Affairs Canada [INAC] 2007a). As of late 2007, Canada had still not completed the land transfers and exchanges provided for under the 1984 Inuvialuit Final Agreement (IFA) — issues that had been referred to resolution through arbitration.[4] However, the Nunavut land claims organization, Nunavut Tunngavik Incorporated (NTI), has launched a billion-dollar lawsuit against Canada motivated partly by its sheer frustration with Canada's unwillingness to resolve outstanding disputes through the Nunavut claim's prescribed resolution process. In addition, NTI alleges the nonfulfillment of important aspects of the Nunavut claim — specifically, article 23 of the Nunavut Land Claims Agreement, which addresses proportional Inuit employment in Nunavut's public service (Nunavut Tunngavik Incorporated 2006). Canada has decided to engage in what will likely be a long, drawn-out and expensive court battle rather than attempting to settle the problems through negotiation or through the dispute resolution mechanisms prescribed within the Agreement.

The concepts of "spirit" and "intent" are not neatly wrapped up within the legal provisions of land claims agreements. However, the agreements contain provisions or preambles that speak to the spirit and intent of the claims. The statement of goals included in the IFA provides one example:

> The basic goals expressed by the Inuvialuit and recognized by Canada in concluding this agreement are
> a) to preserve Inuvialuit cultural identity and values within a changing northern society;
> b) to enable Inuvialuit to be equal and meaningful participants in the northern and national economy and society; and
> c) to protect and preserve the Arctic wildlife, environment, and biological productivity. (INAC 1984, 1, 1.a-c)

Spirit and intent inform the principles that permit the existence of land claims and self-government agreements — government policies that seek to change the relationship between the state and indigenous peoples. These include policies such as the 1995 Inherent Right Policy, the 1986 Comprehensive Land

Claims Policy and the 1997 policy Gathering Strength. Such policies speak, individually and collectively, to principles such as the need for agreements to restore dignity, build capacity, establish new and more positive relations between indigenous peoples and the state (INAC 1995, 1997), and establish the certainty necessary for indigenous peoples and the state to function effectively as governments (INAC 1986, 1995).

It is apparent that Canada recognizes that more needs to be done to achieve socio-economic wellness among indigenous peoples struggling against the fallout of colonialism, and that land claims and self-government agreements can help to achieve that goal. However, it is also clear that despite the rhetoric of new relationships and better futures, the implementation of northern land claims is a troubled process. So what does this mean for institutional development in the North?

Canada's response to problems with land claims implementation seems to lack coherence. Indigenous peoples and the state hold fundamentally different views about how implementation should be understood and evaluated, and this presents significant problems for institutional development in the North generally. The state must contend with the reality that land claims organizations are major players in the North — politically, socially and economically. This is due to their land-claims-based authority and responsibilities, not to mention their profound psychological importance and their effect on the material and spiritual well-being of indigenous peoples, as land claims agreements are to some extent a decolonizing force in state-indigenous relations. However, land claims agreements are only one element of the decolonizing effort. Normative dimensions of such agreements, such as implementation, are significant determinants of their efficacy.

Land claims organizations, and new and imminent self-governments, require access to the means and the conditions that will enable them to discharge their obligations in ways that will meet the larger goals of the land claims agreements (Irlbacher-Fox 2008). Canada — and, to an increasing extent, territorial governments as they prepare to take on federally devolved responsibilities — must recognize that land claims should not be seen as purely legalistic, contractual agreements. Rather, they are the basis for ongoing intergovernmental relationships that will evolve over time. Without robust land claims institutions, and without government partners committed to fulfilling land claims obligations in ways that will achieve broader goals related to an agreement's spirit and intent, the groundwork is laid for social conflict, economic uncertainty and political instability. That is not good for the well-being of northerners — social-ly, economically or politically. Neither does it bode well for institutional devel-opment toward greater northern autonomy and local control of northern governance and resources. There may be unanticipated costs for effective land claims implementation, but, as we noted earlier, there are certainly high costs associated with bungling the job. For example, with respect to the Inuvialuit Final Agreement, the Auditor General in 2007 found that although section 16 of the IFA requires Canada to award contracts in the Inuvialuit Settlement Region preferentially to Inuvialuit businesses, adequate systems for informing potential contractees and awarding contracts were not maintained. Contracts to clean up mine or military operations sites, for example, represent a significant economic opportunity for Inuvialuit communities in the region, and in order to obtain them the Inuvialuit have had to resort to arbitration in the past (Auditor General of Canada 2007, sec. 3.31-3.45).

"Modern" Treaties in the Northwest Territories and Yukon

A S NOTED BY MATTHEW COON COME, FORMER ASSEMBLY OF FIRST NATIONS national chief and for many years chief of the Grand Council of the Crees of northern Quebec, modern treaties continue a timeless colonial practice: indigenous peoples' rights are extinguished by treaties that are either not imple-mented or implemented in ways that do not meet treaty promises. Coon Come points out that rights extinguishment and subsequent nonfulfillment of recipro-cal obligations, practices common in the early nineteenth and twentieth cen-turies, have in the modern era been repudiated by the international community as de facto human rights abuses (Coon Come 2006). In this chapter, the term "modern treaties" denotes agreements between indigenous peoples and Canada reached during the 35 years since Canada introduced its Comprehensive Land Claims Policy.[5] Under that policy, Canada negotiates rights, compensation and land ownership; it also determines which indigenous peoples' representative organizations have a legal basis and legitimacy with regard to the negotiated agreements.

Yukon Agreements

The majority of Yukon First Nations — 11 out of 14 — have negotiated land claims and self-government agreements. The land claims agreements were negotiated under the Government of Canada's Comprehensive Land Claims Policy and comply with the definition set out in section 35 of the *Constitution Act, 1982*. The associated self-government agreements are not considered section 35 agreements, as that was the policy of Canada when the framework was negotiated. Although the policy has changed, their status has not.

Negotiated on the basis of a framework known as the Umbrella Final Agreement, the first land claims and self-government agreements came into effect in 1995. The "first four" First Nations — namely, the Vuntut Gwitchin, Na-Cho Nyak Dun, the Teslin Tlingit and the Champagne and Aishihik — celebrated their effective dates on February 14, 1995. They were followed by the Little Salmon/Carmacks and Selkirk First Nations in 1997, the Tr'ondëk Hwëch'in First Nation in 1998, the Ta'an Kwäch'än Council in 2002 and the First Nations of Kluane in 2004, Kwanlin Dun in 2005 and Carcross/Tagish in 2006. Without agreements, the Liard First Nation, the Ross River Dena Council and the White River First Nation remain under the *Indian Act*; no conclusion to their negotiations is anticipated in the near future.

Each First Nation has approached land claims and self-government implementation differently. Some have focused on heritage and cultural programs, while others have emphasized implementation efforts in the areas of land and resource management. There is a marked difference in each First Nation's success in capitalizing on governance, social and economic opportunities.

For example, the Vuntut Gwitchin First Nation has invested heavily in its heritage department, and this has resulted in social and economic capacity building of direct benefit to the community. As noted earlier, land claims and self-government agreements have proved challenging to reach, but Yukon First Nations communities have also benefited from them. Their institutional development has been neither easy nor uniform; First Nations government institutions have followed a steep developmental curve and learned many lessons along the way. Construction began on the Vuntut Gwitchin's visitor reception centre in Old Crow in spring 2008 — a good example of maximizing land-claims-based authorities. Positive economic development outcomes allowed the Vuntut Development Corporation, the economic arm of the Vuntut Gwitchin First Nation, to lead the planning and development of this important infrastructure project. The centre will serve as a gateway to Vuntut National Park, which was established under the final agreement. Years of capacity development within the Vuntut Gwitchin Heritage Department and a thriving filmmaking and cultural industry in the community have given the centre a strong First Nation government component. In addition to offices and research facilities, the building will house a multimedia theatre and an interpretive centre. It is also the first key piece of infrastructure in a strategy to develop Old Crow as a tourist destination. The Vuntut Gwitchin example shows a First Nation drawing upon the strengths of its people, environment and locale and combining them with the resources afforded to it by its land claim agreement. Other First Nations in the Yukon have been able to harness their resources to similar advantage in their own unique contexts.

NWT Agreements

Dene, Métis and Inuvialuit in the NWT have or are negotiating land claims and self-government agreements with Canada. There are three existing land claims agreements — the Inuvialuit (1984), Gwich'in (1992) and Sahtu (1993) — along with one combined land claim and self-government agreement, that of the Tlicho (2003). Currently, the Inuvialuit and Gwich'in, as well as Sahtu communities, including Deline, Tulita, Norman Wells and Fort Good Hope, are at various stages of negotiating self-government agreements. The Dehcho First Nation, like the Northwest Territories Métis Nation, is engaging in a combined land and governance negotiation, and the Akaitcho peoples are negotiating a treaty land entitlement agreement.

Generally, for land claims organizations,[6] implementation has been phased in over several years as the various boards, committees, community organizations and regional infrastructure and human resource capacities have evolved. In most organizations, for several years after the signing date, technical and management positions were often held by nonindigenous employees.[7] Most land claims organizations have taken several years to develop the necessary infrastructure, establish credible and stable management and leadership, and move beneficiaries into technical positions through a combination of employment training, employment and educational incentives. Today, land claims organizations once criticized for employing mostly young, transient, university-educated nonindigenous technocrats now boast staffs consisting mainly of indigenous beneficiaries with significant expertise.

Their qualifications range from university degrees to decades of experience with government and industry; others are valued as indigenous knowledge holders.[8]

Not surprisingly, capacity building is a significant issue for land claims organizations, as the claims themselves are intended to increase employment and employability among beneficiaries. This intent applies in particular to land claims organizations such as comanagement boards and businesses created or purchased with land claims capital, ranging from cultural institutes to construction companies. Land claims organizations have become major players in local and regional economies, and to some extent in territorial ones. The Aboriginal Pipeline Group, a consortium of land claims and indigenous organizations that share ownership of the proposed Mackenzie gas pipeline, is one example of land claims organizations working together to take advantage of a territorial economic opportunity. It also offers an example of land claims organizations and their economic initiatives creating employment and promoting economic development of potential benefit to all northern residents. Land claims organizations' efforts in these areas have been aimed squarely at enlivening the spirit and intent of the land claims agreements, thus providing a windfall for industries seeking new economic opportunities, indigenous and nonindigenous individuals looking for work, and tax-recipient governments. Therefore, when land claims governments lobby the other governments to join them in taking creative and holistic approaches to realizing the spirit and intent of land claims agreements, they do so based on their knowledge of the benefits of such an approach primarily for their beneficiaries, but also for all residents.

The Role of Disabling and Enabling Conditions in Institutional Development

ACTION TAKEN TO ENLIVEN RECOGNIZED RIGHTS GIVES RIGHTS A GREAT MEASURE OF THEIR practical usefulness and meaning (Irlbacher-Fox 2008). In this sense, the function and significance of rights are inseparable from their implementation — a right's meaningfulness relies to some extent upon the actions taken to animate it. In his analysis of the principles of legitimacy of constitutional democracy, philosopher

James Tully notes that the spirit of an agreement must guide its implementation: "This traditional endpoint of normative analysis, even when it is related to practical case studies, leaves the entire field of implementation and review to empirical social sciences, often under the false assumption that implementation is different in kind from justification, simply a technical question of applying rigid rules correctly. There are many ways actors can agree to a settlement...and either avoid or subvert implementation while appearing to follow norms of legitimation" (2002, 227).

We build on this analysis by contending that the legitimacy of an agreement depends in part on the conditions in which it is implemented. Legitimacy requires an enabling atmosphere — one in which the spirit and intent of an agreement can be realized through implementation measures that support land claims organizations in their efforts to achieve broad objectives. The opposite situation is one in which lack of adequate implementation creates conditions that prevent the realization of spirit and intent — that is, a disabling environment. We draw this concept from international research into the development of indigenous governance institutions (Hunt 2005).

Within the context of development work in emerging democracies and developing countries, empirical evidence has shown that an array of factors — institutional, legal and policy-related issues; dominant-subordinate versus equal power relations; and social and financial trends — constitute the environment in which institutional development, including capacity building, takes place. The implementation of modern treaties encompasses measures to ensure that the various provisions of the treaties do the work they are meant to do. This involves constructing buildings, setting up capital assets, hiring and planning. It also includes administering the claims — investing and disbursing large sums of compensation money, managing wildlife and resources, conducting community consultations on various topics and negotiating legal agreements with governments and private industry. These activities require funding and cooperation among various governments; they also involve recruiting and retaining indigenous and nonindigenous staff to work effectively together, often in specialized technical roles. It is apparent that in evaluating implementation, we must look at both what is done and the way it is done — quantitative and qualitative measures matter equally.

In land claims implementation, an enabling environment is one in which obligations are fulfilled in a way that enables institutions to discharge their functions effectively over the long term. A disabling environment is one in which implementation obligations are addressed in a manner that prevents institutions from discharging their functions effectively over the long term. For example, First Nations in Yukon have found that due to the inadequate funding levels established in their agreements, they have been unable to carry out their implementation responsibilities. A review of the agreements confirmed that their implementation funding provisions were inadequate, and now Yukon First Nations are discussing refinancing with the federal government.[9] In enabling environments, the institutions in question work as partners with governments. Funding recipients are not subject to overly restrictive or onerous reporting requirements, and they work to implement sustainable, self-determined priorities. In these environments, relations are predicated on mutual respect and equality and rooted in shared goals; parties are challenged to recognize their differences and to remain flexible in their dealings with one another. The result is that institutions develop a stable capacity over the long term to discharge their obligations in the context of respectful relations with partner governments.

Janet Hunt and Diane Smith have done years of fieldwork in indigenous communities in Australia. They offer insights based on a multisite research approach to uncovering what works and what does not work in indigenous community governance. Their comparison of different governance models and contexts shows that indigenous governance is shaped by various historical, political and cultural factors. Key among these is the extent to which indigenous governments' interactions with, and dependence on, external governments and agencies and funding affect their own operations.[10] For example,

> Strengthening Indigenous governance capacity rests on the preparedness of governments to devolve power and authority to community and regional levels. For example, simplifying and streamlining funding and reporting arrangements could reduce the time Indigenous organisations spend on managing a multitude of complex contracts and free up skilled people to spend time on developing capacity. In essence, capacity development for governance is not a "power neutral" process — it is concerned with the flow of funds, access to resources, the power to make decisions and control assets, etc. It should be a process that actively strengthens Indigenous decision-making and control over their core institutions, goals and identity, and that enhances cultural match and legitimacy. (Hunt and Smith 2006, 56)

Disabling environments are characterized by dominant-subordinate power relations, short-term outlooks with respect to programs and institutional development, and an emphasis on meeting reporting requirements despite the often inflexible conditions set by the donor partner. Such environments lead to ineffective implementation: planning is restricted to the short term; activities are restricted to the discrete, program-oriented variety; and institutions are prevented from building stable and effective capacity over the long term.

In the context of land claims implementation, disabling environments are those in which institutions are inadequately funded, or funding for activities is restricted by the policies and reporting requirements — often determined without reference to the realities of land claims implementation — of donor governments. For example, funding may be available only on a fiscal-year basis, or tied to specific program criteria rather than broad objectives, or subject to an uncertain renewal process.[11] This may be the case, for instance, with funding for land claims comanagement boards, or with core funding for land claims governments' own administration costs. In these situations, the needs, perceptions and practices of the donor government often take primacy over those of the recipient. This may create an environment in which relationship building is undermined by the domination-and-control imperative that has marked relationships under the *Indian Act*. Such practices are based on principles developed without reference to the intergovernmental relationships envisioned in the modern treaties. As a result, frustration and apathy may pervade recipient institutions' dealings with donors; this will have the effect of reinforcing stereotypes and animosity between donors and recipients and fuelling disputes and dissatisfaction on both sides, eventually eroding the potential for communication and cooperation. Recipient governments forced to operate with inadequate or unstable financing may be less able to dedicate staff time to accountability requirements, such as monthly or quarterly report writing. They may also be unable to attract staff with the requisite skills and commitment to perform accountability functions. This may inaccurately be interpreted by donor governments or the public to mean that recipients lack an ethic of accountability. The instability created by inadequate funding will severely impede the development of credible and firmly established institutions that can function as legitimate and representative self-governments.

Disputes over implementation, and to some extent failures in implementation, are inevitable. Such disputes as the current one between Nunavut Tunngavik and Canada over the implementation of the Nunavut claim are not necessarily a product of obligation shirking, ill will or incompetence, but rather the cumulative effect of a series of systemic factors and a lack of capacity on the part of INAC and the Canadian government to reshape partnerships in order to create an enabling environment for land claims implementation and institutional development. In the words of Chief Diane Strand of the Champagne and Aishihik First Nation in Yukon, "We are not *Indian Act* bands, we are self-governing First Nations. The policies of the federal government have to start reflecting that" ("Yukon First Nations" 2008).

It is important to note that capacity must be built within both government and land claims organizations. Implementing land claims requires a different approach from the one used for discharging obligations under the *Indian Act*. Canada has essentially moved to a new system of relations with indigenous peoples without overhauling its bureaucratic or policy apparatuses for implementing land claims agreements and developing post-*Indian Act* relationships. Land claims relationships require that all parties adopt a mutually respectful, government-to-government, reflexive approach. And this is not just the view of land claims organizations — it is reflected in the observations of the Auditor General (2003). Canada's implementation approaches are not tied to the spirit and intent of land claims, they are not tracked on a results basis, and evaluations of impacts of claims have not been undertaken. Despite this critique, Canada clings to the view that it simply has legal obligations to fulfill — a view more appropriate to the discharge of responsibilities under state-imposed colonial legislation than to the development of a decolonizing relationship.

Canada must recognize that its relations with indigenous peoples' governments recognized by land claims and self-government agreements carry obligations that may necessitate new ways of doing business. The implementation of entire agreements cannot be left to a single department — INAC. It requires the participation of all departments with responsibilities bearing on land claims and self-government. Policies of central agencies such as the Treasury Board cannot be applied when they are known to be inadequate simply because they are the only ones available. That is just not good enough. Surely our politicians and bureaucrats are capable of shaping policies and taking actions that will effectively accommodate evolving relationships with domestic governments. Such accommodation could be as straightforward as giving responsibility for revising and integrating relevant policies to existing interdepartmental committees of senior officials, or establishing a deputy-minister-level committee to address land claims implementation served by a dedicated staff with a mandate to assist relevant departments in implementing systems or protocols to ensure smooth transitions to new policy application.

As practitioners, we are often faced with problems caused by inadequate implementation measures. These pose challenges that we must overcome if we are to achieve effective land claims implementation. Such issues inform our work in current negotiations, particularly in negotiating implementation and financing agreements. The first modern treaties were such a new departure that few negotiators anticipated the importance of implementation. That initial lack of emphasis ultimately led to implementation being negotiated alongside the self-government agreements themselves.

Past experience of land claims implementation has taught us that agreements can be significantly undercut by inadequate implementation planning. In current self-government negotiations, for example, the text of agreements describing the authorities of self-governments is viewed by indigenous negotiators as only half the story. That is because we now know that while a self-government could be recognized as having province-like law-making powers in an area such as education, if the financial transfer agreement does not provide for adequate funding — for programs, or for incremental costs, or for anticipated cost increases due to population growth and infrastructure replacement — then that law-making authority cannot be exercised. And what is the point of recommending an agreement for ratification when its potential is hobbled?

In this sense, Canada's track record for implementing agreements with indigenous peoples matters. In negotiations, each party often has to rely on the other's good faith in order to ensure the workability of critical aspects of an agreement. Such aspects might include dispute resolution mechanisms. In current self-government negotiations, all parties must agree to use and be bound by these mechanisms. But no guarantees are provided and no guidelines are set for determining when to engage in dispute resolution. The Auditor General has found that Canada has yet to consent to participate in the dispute resolution process provided for in the Gwich'in and Nunavut land claims agreements (2003, 8.3). Instead, disputes remain unresolved, or, as in the case of the Nunavut claim, they are taken to court. This does not create a climate of confidence for current or future negotiations in which similar dispute resolution mechanisms will be contemplated.

Challenges in
Implementation

Yukon Challenges

YUKON AGREEMENTS HAVE RESULTED IN BENEFICIAL CHANGES TO FIRST NATIONS institutions and had positive impacts on First Nations citizens. With increased control over funding and decision-making, and with an evolving system of self-government that has taxation powers and the power to enact legislation, First Nations have directed beneficial changes at the community level. These changes have been somewhat constrained, for several reasons. A 10-year review of the first four Yukon agreements was conducted by the Governments of Yukon and Canada and the Council of Yukon First Nations. Completed in 2007, it concluded that funding levels for Yukon First Nations are inadequate, and this has slowed their legislative development, limited their ability to meet obligations and forced them to focus too closely on fundraising instead of implementation; and that the policies and practices of the federal government are not consistent with the commitments that it made under the agreements.

Canada's Inherent Right Policy drives its position in negotiations rather than its commitments and obligations under the agreements. Some federal departments have conflicting policies and approaches to implementation that impede the implementation process and the successful transfer of important programs and services. For example, Human Resources and Social Development Canada refused to negotiate program and service transfers for Yukon consistent with the self-government agreements, and this resulted in the first and only utilization of the agreements' dispute resolution provisions.[12]

First Nations have also had occasion to challenge the Yukon government's approach to land claims implementation. The recent *Little Salmon/Carmacks First Nation* case,[13] in which the court found the Yukon government in breach of good-faith consultation principles with First Nations, underscored how important it is for governments to review and revise practices based on principles that do not take into account or foster government-to-government relationships. The First Nation throughout held that despite the provisions of the land claim, the Yukon government's approach to consultation was inadequate. The Yukon government held that since the land claim extinguished First Nation rights on lands adjacent to settlement lands, consultation was not required — despite the proximity of the different types of lands, and the fact that a First Nation member's trapline would likely be disturbed by the proposed new usage. This is but one example not only of the difficulties that arise from governments persisting in practices congruent with dominant-subordinate rather than government-to-government relations, but also of the fact that First Nations are forced to waste energy in resolving disputes through litigation. The results have been varied, but one thing is clear: significant resources are being spent on litigation instead of implementation.

There is a marked difference among First Nations in their capacity to implement their respective agreements. All have struggled to develop their institutional capacity while meeting the land claims obligations and implementation deadlines set out in their agreements, and inadequate funding is a problem common to all the agreements. For example, the much higher governance costs in small communities compared to the Yukon capital of Whitehorse are not reflected in the funding allocations. This creates recruitment challenges, as wages do not match the significantly higher cost of living. Add to this an educational and social support system that has produced low high school and post-secondary graduation rates among First Nations citizens. The result has been an overreliance on transient professionals and thus a lack of continuity and long-term corporate knowledge. The development of a skilled local workforce has been slow, but it is occurring, and it is benefiting the community.

Implementation Challenges in the Northwest Territories

In the NWT, land claims agreements reached prior to 1995 were negotiated separately from self-government agreements. The Inuvialuit, Gwich'in and Sahtu have had a decade or more to implement land claims. Lessons learned during the initial land claims implementation period will serve as a basis for self-government arrangements in these regions. And that experience has resulted in an emphasis being placed on negotiating implementation agreements alongside self-government agreements.

With the exception of the most recently negotiated Tlicho agreement, which is a combined land and self-government agreement, all NWT self-government agreements have yet to be finalized. It is important to note that the Tlicho self-government model includes arrangements by which the Government of the Northwest Territories is contracted to continue to provide many government services on the Tlicho government's behalf for a 10-year period. This has given the Tlicho the ability to develop their governing structures and capacity prior to taking on responsibility for law-making and service delivery in areas such as health and education.

However, we must recognize that each region has unique circumstances and institutional development issues to address. The Inuvialuit have been extremely successful at this: they have used their original settlement compensation of $40 million, along with rights and interests recognized in their land claim, to increase the corporation's value to almost $400 million in assets; the corporation now employs more than 1,100 people in the settlement region and in other areas of the NWT and Canada (Aarviunaa 2004). The Inuvialuit are currently in self-government negotiations that will likely result in the Inuvialuit Regional Corporation exercising authorities for Inuvialuit community governments. One land claims implementation issue for the Inuvialuit has been to secure core funding for their land claims organization; this funding would directly impact capacity building and, as a result, the implementation of land-claims-based initiatives.[14]

In contrast, the Sahtu claim has brought the development of authority and infrastructure within the three district land corporations focusing on local economic, social and political development. A similar emphasis on local control has been replicated in self-government negotiations, which are being conducted on an individual basis with each Sahtu community. Regional authorities or cooperative arrangements will likely be determined after all self-governments have been negotiated. Despite the community-based emphasis suffusing implementation of the Sahtu agreement, communities in the region work cooperatively on projects of territorial importance, such as NWT devolution negotiations. Implementation issues related to the Sahtu claim vary by community. At the regional level, though, such issues are related to funding and to the slow pace of implementation due in part to the processes of other governments. For example, although the Sahtu claim was negotiated in 1993, the region has yet to have a land-use plan approved. Such a plan is a critical tool for overseeing conservation and economic development, but the review and approval process has languished because the claim-based Land Use Planning Board is underfunded and governments are acting so slowly on the initiative.[15]

The Gwich'in have faced implementation issues similar to those encountered by the Sahtu and the Inuvialuit. The Gwich'in Tribal Council (GTC) has focused on developing regional land-claims-based institutions, businesses and social and wellness programs ranging from construction companies to healing camps to a cultural institute. The GTC has expended much effort to create a holistic network of supports for Gwich'in beneficiaries in the region to fulfill its vision of "land, culture, and economy for a better future."[16] However, despite the GTC's efforts to realize the broader objectives of the land claims agreements, there are ongoing disputes with Canada related to implementation. During the late 1990s, a dispute over core funding was settled out of court, but there was no real resolution as to Canada's obligations over the long term (Auditor General of Canada 2003).

Capacity Building: A Shared Concern among Land Claims Organizations and Self-Governments

THE CONTRAST BETWEEN THE SUCCESSFUL EFFORTS OF LAND CLAIMS ORGANIZATIONS to achieve their vision of self-determination as broadly conceived in the land claims and the efforts of government are instructive. Organizations such as the GTC have used land claims capital to build and fund healing facilities and programs. Similarly, land claims organizations in every region have often used cash compensation and income to supplement core organization funding — a strategy that was not anticipated when the agreements were made. However, these organizations are concerned that Canada does not adequately fund public government claims-based organizations (such as resource comanagement boards), which have a significant impact on lands and resources, and consequently on indigenous subsistence lifeways. Thus the frustration experienced by land claims organizations does not arise from having to wait so long for government to act; rather, it comes from seeing their own efforts — backed by their own considerable energy, focus and funding — undermined by the often inadequate approach Canada takes to fulfilling its obligations. Fulfillment of these obligations is essential to realizing the broad objectives of the land claims agreements and, ultimately, to ensuring a better future. The most compelling evidence that more needs to be done to improve the futures of indigenous peoples is the appalling statistics on the social pathologies that persist despite positive developments, such as land claims agreements (Statistics Canada 2001). Land claims implementation presents Canada with an opportunity to partner with credible and legitimate indigenous peoples' organizations that are well placed to address these issues within a framework of self-determination.

This argument was advanced by Thomas Berger in his 2006 conciliator's report. He advocates a bilingual Inuktitut-English education system in Nunavut and asserts that article 23 of the Nunavut land claim, which provides for proportional Inuit employment in Nunavut's bureaucracy, cannot be fulfilled before practical measures aimed at successfully educating Inuit children are undertaken. The Berger Report argues that through the institution of effective educational measures (radically different from those taken to date), not only will the article 23 obligations be satisfied, but also progress will be made toward overcoming the social ills linked to the lack of a bilingual education system (Berger 2006, iv). The Inuvialuit, as evidenced by the Auditor General's audit of the Inuvialuit Final Agreement implementation (Auditor General of Canada 2007), have also argued that the proper implementation of section 16 of their agreement, which relates to the preferential awarding of contracts to Inuvialuit companies, has a direct effect on the employment of Inuvialuit. While such initiatives may not measurably alleviate specific social problems, an increase in the number of well-educated Inuit or gainfully employed Inuvialuit could reasonably be expected to reduce the overall incidence of these problems.

A major problem for those involved in land claims implementation is inadequate support from Canada for capacity building within land claims institutions and governments (Land Claims Agreement Coalition 2006a). Land claims organizations are very different creatures from *Indian Act* bands and other organizations that negotiate on behalf of indigenous peoples. They have unique legal, political, social and economic positions vis-à-vis other governments. For these organizations to be effective locally and in the wider social, political and economic landscape, capacity building is essential. For example, during a recent conference of the LCAC, the LCAC Capacity Building Working Group recommended that "underlying principles and provisions of the implementation policy [that the LCAC was lobbying Canada to develop and implement] must give rise to much needed capacity building and training at all levels to ensure successful governance. This should be a shared, collaborative process with joint responsibility, accountability, and commitment to achieving the spirit and intent of the

Agreement. The policy must provide adequate resources during the pre-implementation period to ensure effective transition and ongoing implementation"
(LCAC 2006a, 2).

The LCAC has undertaken a sustained effort to achieve a national policy
for the implementation of modern treaties. It has articulated four major recommendations to Canada:

> 1.Recognition that the Crown in Right of Canada, not the Department of
> Indian Affairs and Northern Development, is party to our land claims agree-
> ments and self-government agreements.
> 2.There must be a federal commitment to achieve the broad objectives of the
> land claims agreements and self-government agreements within the context of
> the new relationships, as opposed to mere technical compliance with narrow-
> ly defined obligations. This must include, but not be limited to, ensuring ade-
> quate funding to achieve these objectives and obligations.
> 3.Implementation must be handled by appropriate senior level officials repre-
> senting the entire Canadian government.
> 4.There must be an independent implementation audit and review body, sep-
> arate from the Department of Indian Affairs and Northern Development. This
> could be the Auditor General's department, or a similar office reporting direct-
> ly to Parliament. Annual reports will be prepared by this office, in consultation
> with groups with land claims agreements. (LCAC 2006b)

Essentially, the LCAC is seeking a commitment from Canada that is national in scope and comprehensive in application and that once and for all clarifies
the ground rules for the state's approach to land claims implementation. The four
recommendations speak to the need for a qualitative, evaluative approach to
implementing and tracking how obligations are fulfilled by Canada.

Conclusion

NORTHERN SOCIAL, ECONOMIC AND POLITICAL DEVELOPMENT DEPENDS IN PART ON
the ability of land claims organizations to function effectively. While in this
chapter we focus on land claims implementation issues, contexts and relationships, in our suggestions for change we recognize that it is important for all governments to work together in other ways to achieve effective political
development. In his commentary in this volume, George Braden correctly highlights the need for intergovernmental and interagency cooperation; it is critical to
northern development. Institutional development in the North is dependent on
Canada living up to its modern treaty commitments. As our analysis

demonstrates, the difficulties land claims institutions have experienced with respect to implementation stem primarily from the fact that Canada's approach to implementation is tied to a dominant-subordinate relationship that was shaped by the *Indian Act*, a relationship that has allowed Canada to unilaterally determine how it will fulfill its obligations. In this scenario, it is understandable that Canada would defend its record of implementation on the basis that it focuses on meeting legal obligations.

This situation does not arise simply from an overly legalistic turn that Canada has taken in the era of modern treaties, although that is part of the problem. Transforming a relationship of domination and subordination to one of mutual respect takes time and a change of mentality. It also requires a plan. Without a plan, the parties involved will continue to operate with opposing sets of principles and expectations. Canada has shunted most of the government-wide responsibility for implementing modern treaties to one department: Indian and Northern Affairs Canada. INAC's purpose is to fulfill obligations under section 91(24) of the Constitution, guided by its flagship legislative directive, the *Indian Act*. When it comes to implementing land claims, INAC's *Indian Act* relational culture is combined with general Government of Canada policies on funding, reporting and accountability. This creates a disabling environment in which policies and approaches are determined without consideration of the importance of fostering a new government-to-government relationship. As a result, land claims organizations may become underresourced, overburdened by reporting and destabilized by inadequate funding or arrangements that hamper long-term planning and capacity development. Frustrations on both sides grow; the situation continues to breed tension and dissatisfaction. Land claims organizations, to their credit, have attempted to channel their frustrations into creating a dialogue between indigenous peoples and the Canadian state about developing new principles to guide implementation.

Our analysis yields three suggestions. The first is that we view inadequate implementation as a systemic problem arising from policies of central government agencies such as the Treasury Board and departments such as INAC that contribute to a disabling environment. Canada has taken little effective action to remedy the situation. The second suggestion is that Canada develop a plan to resolve implementation issues and in the process move from a dominant-subordinate to a mutually respectful government-to-government relationship with indigenous peoples. The LCAC advocates a plan that would include a national implementation policy. The development of such a policy would require the participation of the LCAC. If lessons from international institutional development and capacity building are applied, then the fundamental difficulties contributing to a disabling environment could be overcome without simply throwing money at the problem. Instead, statewide policies to promote the government-to-government relationship called for in the modern treaties could be revised.

Our final suggestion is that Canada and indigenous peoples work together to establish a shared understanding of the objectives of modern treaties. Canada's approach to modern treaty implementation and negotiation continues to take a legalistic turn. Canada seeks certainty through treaties — certainty of rights, of access to resources, of ownership of lands. Indigenous peoples seek recognition and a basis for achieving psychological, spiritual and material well-being. It seems that for Canada, treaties are an end, a final definition of a relationship, secured by the extinguishment of rights through certainty clauses. For indigenous peoples, treaties mark a beginning — the beginning of a better life for beneficiaries and their communities and of a new relationship with Canada. If the shared goals of Canada and indigenous peoples in forging modern treaties are better quality of life, social stability, a thriving economy and effective institutions, and if both parties maintain a mutual respect, then it will be possible to engage in an ongoing dialogue and so move forward. That forward movement will be beneficial not only for indigenous peoples but also for northerners generally, since northern social, economic and political development will be shaped to a great extent by the land claims governments, businesses and social programs fostered by the effective implementation of land claims and self-government agreements.

Notes

1   See the Canadian Comprehensive Land
     Claims Policy (Indian and Northern Affairs
     Canada [INAC] 1986). INAC describes the
     policy on its Web site: "The 1973
     Comprehensive Claims Policy was reaf-
     firmed in 1981 and its primary thrust was to
     obtain certainty respecting ownership, use
     and management of lands and resources by
     negotiating an exchange of claims to unde-
     fined Aboriginal rights for a clearly defined
     package of rights and benefits set out in a
     settlement agreement" (INAC 2007b).

2   See, for example, Cornell and Kalt (1989);
     Hunt and Smith (2006).

3   For example, one of the main reasons the
     Inuit have chosen to take Canada to court
     over land claims implementation issues is
     that Canada has never consented to be
     party to an arbitration process for disputes.
     Arbitration is one of the prescribed dispute
     resolution mechanisms of last resort within
     the Nunavut land claim (see Nunavut
     Tunngavik Incorporated 2006).

4   For more details on this situation, see the
     audit of the Inuvialuit Final Agreement by
     the Auditor General of Canada (2007).

5   The term "modern treaties" is meant to
     encompass land claims agreements under
     section 35 of the Constitution Act, 1982.
     While the Yukon self-government agreements
     lack constitutional protection under section
     35, we include them for the purposes of this
     chapter as they stem from the Yukon land
     claims agreements and play a significant role
     in Yukon political development.

6   In both the NWT and Yukon, not all indige-
     nous peoples have negotiated modern
     treaties; as a result, those behind institution-
     al development initiatives in these territories
     must contend with what are known as
     "claimant" and "nonclaimant" groups.

7   This observation is based on both authors'
     experiences working for organizations
     resulting from the Inuvialuit, Gwich'in,
     Sahtu and Vuntut Gwitchin agreements
     during the past decade.

8   For example, as of February 2008, the
     Gwich'in Tribal Council Web site indicated
     that 22 of 25 positions at the council's
     office in Inuvik were filled by Gwich'in
     beneficiaries; similarly, the Inuvialuit
     Regional Corporation's directory indicated
     that of 45 positions at its Inuvik headquar-
     ters, approximately 30 were held by
     Inuvialuit beneficiaries.

9   According to a November 2007 CBC News
     article, "Yukon's premier and top First
     Nation leader agreed...to more talks with
     Indian and Northern Affairs Minister
     Chuck Strahl to address a lack of federal
     funding to implement land claims and self-
     government agreements in the
     territory...Premier Dennis Fentie and Grand
     Chief Andy Carvill of the Council of Yukon
     First Nations said they were pleased with
     the progress made during their morning
     meeting with Strahl in Whitehorse. All
     sides discussed a recent review of the
     Yukon's land claim agreements that calls for
     a new federal mandate — and more money
     — to support First Nations governments.
     The Yukon land claim review is being con-
     ducted by the territorial and federal gov-
     ernments, but its contents have not been
     made public. Fentie said its findings paral-
     lel those of federal Auditor General Sheila
     Fraser's office, who has been generally criti-
     cal of how Ottawa has handled aboriginal
     land claims in the North" ("Strahl" 2007).

10   According to Hunt and Smith, "The
     research is indicating that sustained capaci-
     ty for effective governance amongst individ-
     uals, entities and systems requires a
     positive authorising or enabling environ-
     ment. Many governance initiatives are fail-
     ing or not being sustained because they are
     not supported by a wider enabling environ-
     ment. The research findings suggest a criti-
     cal need for top-level support from
     government and provision of integrated
     funding mechanisms, backed by bureau-
     cratic leadership and collaboration. Many
     of the factors that determine the sustain-

ability of Indigenous governance relate to the cross-sectoral context. This includes the adequacy of policy, funding and legal frameworks; the effectiveness of mainstream education and training programs; the extent of service-delivery coordination; the impact of government program guidelines and reporting criteria; the extent of public-sector capacity; political and bureaucratic will; the scope of devolved power and authority; levels of accountability; property rights and so on" (2006, 52).

11 This example is offered for illustrative purposes only — arrangements may differ, depending on the agreement. Under land claims and self-government agreements, the terms and duration of financial transfer arrangements are determined on a case-by-case basis.

12 This assessment is based on one of the authors' experience in implementing Yukon agreements and both authors' experience with Canada's policies (see also INAC 1995a).

13 *Little Salmon/Carmacks First Nation v. The Government of Yukon (Minister of Energy, Mines and Resources)*, 2007 YKSC 28.

14 Bob Simpson, Inuvialuit self-government chief negotiator, conversation with the authors, October 12, 2007.

15 The August 2007 submission by the Deline First Nation and its land corporation to Indian and Northern Affairs Canada regarding the implementation of the Sahtu land-use plan and the Great Bear Lake management plan is a case in point.

16 Visit the GTC Web site for an elaboration of the council's vision and activities: http://www.gwichin.nt.ca

References

Aarviunaa. 2004. "Vision + Leadership = Success: Salute to the Inuvialuit on the 20th Anniversary of the Inuvialuit Final Agreement." *Native Journal*, October 1. Accessed August 25, 2008. http://www.irc.inuvialuit.com/publications/pdf/Inuvialuit%20Celebrations%20October%202004.pdf

Auditor General of Canada. 2003. "Indian and Northern Affairs Canada: Transferring Federal Responsibilities to the North." Chap. 8 of *2003 Report of the Auditor General of Canada*. Ottawa: Office of the Auditor General of Canada, November. Accessed August 5, 2008. http://www.oag-bvg.gc.ca/internet/ English/aud_ch_oag_2003_8_e_12931.html

———. 2007. "Inuvialuit Final Agreement." Chap. 3 in *2007 Report of the Auditor General of Canada*, October. Ottawa: Office of the Auditor General of Canada. Accessed August 5, 2008. http://www.oag-bvg.gc.ca/internet/English/aud_ch_oag_2007_3_e_23827.html#ch3hd5c

Berger, Thomas R. 2006. *"The Nunavut Project." Nunavut Land Claims Agreement: Implementation Contract Negotiations for the Second Planning Period 2003-2013. Conciliator's Final Report*, March 1. Ottawa: Indian and Northern Affairs Canada. Accessed August 25, 2008. http://www.ainc-inac.gc.ca/pr/agr/nu/lca/nlc_e.pdf

Coon Come, Matthew. 2006. Closing remarks at "Achieving Objectives: A New Approach to Land Claims Agreements in Canada" conference. Land Claims Agreement Coalition, Lac Leamy, Quebec, June 29. Accessed October 14, 2008. http://www.consilium.ca/alcc2006/ppt-presentations/Matthew_Coon_Come.pdf

Cornell, Stephen, and Joseph P. Kalt. 1989. *Pathways from Poverty: Development and Institution-Building on American Indian Reservations*. Harvard Project on American Indian Economic Development Project Report Series 89-5. Cambridge: Malcolm Weiner Center for Social Policy, John F. Kennedy School of Government, Harvard University. Accessed August 26, 2008. http://www.hks.harvard.edu/hpaied/docs/PRS89-5.pdf

Hunt, Janet. 2005. *Capacity Development in the International Development Context: Implications for Indigenous Australia*. Centre for Aboriginal Economic Research (CAEPR) Discussion Paper 278/2005. Canberra:

CAEPR, Australian National University.
Accessed August 7, 2008.
http://dspace.anu.edu.au/bitstream/
1885/43047/1/2005_DP278.pdf

Hunt, Janet, and Diane Smith. 2006. *Building
Indigenous Community Governance in
Australia: Preliminary Research Findings.*
Centre for Aboriginal Economic Research
(CAEPR) Working Paper 31/2006.
Canberra: CAEPR, Australian National
University. Accessed August 7, 2008.
http://www.anu.edu.au/caepr/Publications/
WP/CAEPRWP31.pdf

Indian and Northern Affairs Canada (INAC).
1984. *The Western Arctic Claim: The
Inuvialuit Final Agreement.* Ottawa: INAC.
Accessed August 12, 2008.
http://www.ainc-inac.gc.ca/pr/agr/inu/
wesar_e.html

_____. 1986. *Comprehensive Land Claims
Policy.* Ottawa: INAC.

_____. 1995. *Federal Policy Guide: Aboriginal
Self-Government. The Government of Canada's
Approach to Implementation of the Inherent
Right and the Negotiation of Aboriginal Self-
Government.* Ottawa: INAC. Accessed
August 18, 2008. http://www.ainc-
inac.gc.ca/pr/pub/sg/plcy_e.html

_____. 1997. *Gathering Strength: Canada's
Aboriginal Action Plan.* Ottawa: INAC.
Accessed August 18, 2008. http://dsp-
psd.pwgsc.gc.ca/Collection/R32-192-
2000E.pdf

_____. 2007a. *Agreement Concerning a New
Relationship between the Government of
Canada and the Crees of Eeyou Istchee.*
Ottawa: INAC.

_____. 2007b. *General Briefing Note on the
Comprehensive Land Claims Policy of Canada
and the Status of Claims.* Ottawa: INAC.
Accessed August 4, 2008. http://www.ainc-
inac.gc.ca/ps/clm/gbn/index_e.html

Irlbacher-Fox, Stephanie. 2008. "Justice
Authorities in Self-Government
Agreements: The Importance of Conditions
and Mechanisms of Implementation and
Making Structural Changes in Criminal
Justice." In *Moving Toward Justice: Legal

Traditions and Aboriginal Justice*, edited by
John Whyte. Saskatoon, SK: Purich
Publishing.

Land Claims Agreement Coalition. 2006a.
"Capacity Building Working Group
Summary." In *Achieving Objectives: A New
Approach to Land Claims Agreements in
Canada.* Ottawa: Consilium. Accessed
August 25, 2008. http://www.consilium.ca/
alcc2006/main.html

_____. 2006b. *A New Land Claims
Implementation Policy: Discussion Paper.*
Ottawa: Consilium.

Nunavut Tunngavik Incorporated. 2006.
"Statement of Claim: The Inuit of Nunavut
vs. the Queen, December 2006." Unfiled
court document. Accessed August 5, 2008.
http://www.tunngavik.com/publications/
07Why%20is%20NTI%20Suing%20the%
20Government%20of%20Canada/NTI%20
Statement%20of%20Claim.pdf

Statistics Canada. 2001. *Aboriginal Peoples' Survey
2001 — Initial Findings: Well-Being of the
Non-Reserve Aboriginal Population.* Ottawa:
Statistics Canada. Accessed August 25,
2008. http://www.statcan.ca/english/
freepub/89-589-XIE/index.htm

"Strahl, Yukon Leaders Agree to Further Land
Claims Talks." 2007. CBCnews.ca,
November 5. Accessed August 13, 2008.
http://www.cbc.ca/canada/north/story/
2007/11/05/yk-strahl.html

Tully, James. 2002. "The Unfreedom of the
Moderns in Comparison to Their Ideals of
Constitutional Democracy." *Modern Law
Review* 65 (2): 204-28.

"Yukon First Nations Wrap Up Talks with
Federal Ministers." 2008. CBCnews.ca,
February 14. Accessed August 15, 2008.
http://www.cbc.ca/canada/north/story/2008/
02/14/yukon-talks.html?ref=rss

Governance in the Western North

I AM PLEASED TO HAVE THIS OPPORTUNITY TO COMMENT ON THE TWO CHAPTERS IN THIS volume dealing with governance in the western North — Yukon and the Northwest Territories (NWT). I will start with some introductory comments, follow with my thoughts on "Living Up to the Spirit of Modern Treaties? Implementation and Institutional Development," by Stephanie Irlbacher-Fox and Stephen Mills, and conclude with reaction to Doug McArthur's chapter, "The Changing Architecture of Governance in Yukon and the Northwest Territories."

By way of introduction, the authors' work and the profile given to western governance issues at the IRPP's October 2007 Northern Exposure conference are important contributions to our understanding of what has taken place in the western North over the past quarter century and the challenges that Yukon and the NWT will face in the coming years. Aboriginal land rights settlements have fundamentally changed the economic and political dynamics in the two territories, and more change can be expected as other outstanding land rights and self-government agreements are concluded and implemented. Meanwhile, territorial institutions of public government have continued to evolve, assuming — or attempting to assume — more province-like jurisdiction, particularly in the areas of resource management and development.

However, as the authors make evident, there is no grand federal plan for Yukon and the NWT. There has been no grand plan for the negotiation and implementation of Aboriginal land rights settlements over the long term, and there has been no grand plan that provides a framework in which public and Aboriginal institutions of government can evolve in a fashion that provides for strong, united territories that are more than the sum of their regional parts. While it may be accurate to describe the western North as a work in progress, there are already signs that the work and the progress have produced two jurisdictions, numerous Aboriginal institutions and two public governments that are already in need of significant reform if Yukon, the NWT and their Aboriginal nations are to realize their full potential.

In their chapter, Irlbacher-Fox and Mills accurately describe the implementation challenges facing Aboriginal land rights institutions in Yukon and the NWT and the federal and territorial governments. Securing necessary and adequate financial support from the federal government, in particular; establishing and staffing the administrative structures needed to implement settlements; building relationships with various levels of government and industry; and producing results for beneficiaries represent formidable challenges for Aboriginal nations of the western North.

To date, the implementation experiences of most Yukon and NWT Aboriginal land claims institutions have been marked by frustrations, most of which they blame on the federal government in general and Indian and Northern Affairs Canada (INAC) in particular. The authors make a case, supported in part by the Auditor General of Canada, for the federal government taking a more results-oriented approach to implementation of Aboriginal land rights settlements and for creating an "enabling" implementation environment based upon mutual respect. Without improvements, the authors predict, further economic, social, cultural and political development of Yukon and the NWT will be compromised.

One of the improvements Irlbacher-Fox and Mills propose is to create a more government-wide focus on the implementation of land rights settlements rather than maintaining INAC in the lead role within the federal system. Their proposal builds upon recommendations made by the Land Claims Agreements Coalition (LCAC). The concerns of the LCAC are not unique. Like provincial, territorial and Aboriginal governments, as well as nongovernmental organizations and industry, the LCAC must struggle to determine where it has to go in the federal system to have its issues addressed or to find a champion. Confusion even exists within the federal government about where responsibility for northern issues and northern Aboriginal issues resides. It sometimes seems that the INAC mandate for all things northern, including Aboriginal peoples, has become a convenient excuse for other federal departments to use when they do not want to become engaged in these matters. However, when federal departments other than INAC do want to become more active in the North, they have been able to justify their initiatives and expenditures. Unfortunately, for the North in general and Aboriginal land rights institutions in particular, these circumstances clearly demonstrate that there is no federal grand plan — although such a plan would not be all that hard to formulate. The fact that the former Liberal government under Paul Martin was unable to produce a northern strategy, and that the current Conservative government under Stephen Harper has yet to produce its version beyond references in speeches and press releases, demonstrates that the North is not receiving the coordinated attention it deserves within the federal system.

The authors also make the case that the federal agencies responsible for implementation are still operating from an *Indian Act* perspective rather than a government-to-government perspective and not basing their relations with Aboriginal institutions on respect. After almost 25 years of personal experience in the federal-provincial-territorial intergovernmental environment, I am not sure that Aboriginal land rights and self-government institutions should expect that the federal government will undergo the kind of conversion outlined by Irlbacher-Fox and Mills. While there may be some support within the federal system for a more results-oriented and respectful approach to land rights settlement implementation, the reality, as accurately described by the authors, is that there are other, overriding forces and dynamics at play. Unfortunately, it is highly likely that for the foreseeable future the federal government will continue to dictate the terms of relations with Aboriginal institutions in the NWT and Yukon. In defence of the federal government, sometimes these terms respond to Aboriginal objectives and interests, as was apparent in recent decisions concerning the creation or expansion of national parks and protected areas in the NWT.

Another feature of Aboriginal land rights implementation raised by Irlbacher-Fox and Mills concerns public government claims-based regulatory institutions. As the resource base of the western North becomes more accessible, increasing demands will be placed upon the various territorial boards and agencies that have been established to review and make recommendations or decisions on resource development activity. Many of these institutions were established by, or in response to, Aboriginal land rights settlements. While the authors make passing reference to the similar financial and capacity challenges faced by these institutions, it is important to note that the growing dissatisfaction of all parties — government, Aboriginal peoples, industry representatives and environmental groups — with the performance of these institutions, particularly in the NWT, has produced a response from the federal government. A special adviser to the INAC Minister consulted with stakeholders and in 2008 made recommendations to the Minister on reform of the regulatory regimes for northern resource management and development (for further details on the McCrank report, in the concluding chapter).

This reform could entail a combination of actions: improving the capacity of government departments, regulatory agencies and Aboriginal institutions to respond to their mandates; establishing the necessary policy frameworks to guide internal regulatory agency management practices, decisions and relations with various stakeholders; and undertaking the statutory and regulatory change necessary to ensure improved operation over the long term. While all parties to this initiative are understandably cautious, given the challenges involved, they must recognize that the environments in which they operate have changed since the settlements were finalized and implemented, and they will continue to change. Moreover, finding solutions will, in my view, require Aboriginal stakeholders to look beyond their individual settlements and regions and consider how they can contribute to the strength of the territory within which they reside.

Following from this point, while the authors make a number of recommendations for fundamental changes in how the federal government approaches Aboriginal land rights agreement implementation, they do not make many suggestions that would require a similar response from Aboriginal claims institutions. While both parties are likely reluctant to open up legislated agreements, there are some compelling issues — like regulatory reform and climate change — that require immediate attention. Both parties need not only to be more effective in implementing what was negotiated 10 or 20 years ago but also to make the necessary adjustments to deal with new challenges and circumstances.

Finally, the authors are of the view that many of the implementation problems faced by Aboriginal nations in Yukon and the NWT could be addressed through a national implementation policy, as advocated by the LCAC. The problem with this approach — beyond the length of time it would take the federal, provincial and territorial governments and numerous Aboriginal parties from Yukon, the NWT, Nunavut, British Columbia, Quebec, and Newfoundland and Labrador to develop a consensus policy package — is that it would likely compel northern Aboriginal parties, with their unique circumstances and challenges, to compromise in order to accommodate the resolution of the claims implementation issues of southern Aboriginal nations. Their time and energy would be better spent improving how implementation takes place in the western North and Nunavut.

Moving on to McArthur's paper, my primary focus will be on two of the author's "basic questions" dealing with the extent to which control has shifted, or is expected to shift, from public to Aboriginal government institutions in Yukon and the NWT and the major issues that have arisen in the course of change over the past quarter century.

With respect to the former, McArthur provides an excellent overview of how Aboriginal land and self-government settlements have changed or will fundamentally change government structures and the delivery of programs and services in Yukon and the NWT. He accurately describes the incredible scope of municipal- and territorial-level jurisdiction that can be exercised exclusively or concurrently by Aboriginal self-governments that are separate from or merged in some fashion with Aboriginal land claims or public government institutions. McArthur's timely reference to the collapse in 2006 of self-government negotiations in the NWT's Beaufort-Delta region, which might have produced a public-Aboriginal hybrid government system at the community and regional levels, underscores the preference for exclusively Aboriginal government institutions. To the extent that public government will continue to exist outside of major centres like Whitehorse and Yellowknife, McArthur observes, it will "becom[e] an administrative rather than a governance concept" at the community and regional levels.

The author also correctly concludes that there is no grand plan for a constitutional settlement in the western North, although some key features of a plan, such as exclusively Aboriginal government institutions at the community and regional levels, are starting to emerge. However, his observation that the federal government seems to be comfortable with how the governance dynamics are evolving in the western North may need to be reconsidered in view of the concerns, noted earlier, that federal, territorial and Aboriginal governments, land claims institutions, and industry and environmental organizations have expressed with land and resource management regulation in the NWT and Nunavut. The appointment by the INAC Minister of an adviser to make recommendations on how to improve the northern regulatory regime is an indicator that the no-grand-plan approach has some fundamental shortcomings. Moreover, some key features of the no-grand-plan approach, such as agreements on Territorial Formula

Financing and resource revenue sharing, may undergo major changes when federal, territorial and Aboriginal governments realize that the increasing cost of energy will make it extremely difficult for northern government institutions to function, even at current levels, without significant additional subsidies from the federal government or more generous revenue-sharing regimes.

On the matter of the major issues that have arisen over the last 25 years, I expected that in describing and analyzing public government in the western North, McArthur would critically examine whether public government institutions at the territorial level might also be relegated to an administrative rather than a governance concept. While I can support his conclusion that the existence of territorial government institutions is secure in Yukon and the NWT, I have to question whether they will have the jurisdiction and financial resources to effectively advance the collective interests of each territory. If Aboriginal governments at the community and regional levels assume all, or nearly all, of the jurisdiction available to them, will there be enough left for territorial assemblies and administrations in Whitehorse and Yellowknife to govern exclusively without first securing the consent or participation of Aboriginal governments?

Perhaps this question deserves to be examined and answered in another study — one that considers the full impact of Aboriginal land and self-government agreements on public government institutions at the territorial level. Such a study would also need to consider whether the political culture of the western North, after claims and self-government implementation, will express itself through public government institutions or through Aboriginal institutions at the community and regional levels. In the recent past, territorial governments and legislative assemblies effectively represented all of their constituents when solidarity was needed to protect territorial interests. The Meech Lake and Charlottetown constitutional accords are examples. However, given scenarios for the future, I am concerned that there may be insufficient political will for the parts to function as one entity, especially if territorial institutions are largely relegated to an administrative rather than a governance concept. Strong public government institutions are still critical for each territory if it is to respond effectively to the increasing costs of energy and the territory-wide impacts these increased costs will have on the North's economy and quality of life.

So, after a quarter century of building what McArthur describes as a "constitutional settlement" in the western NWT, the no-grand-plan approach has produced some certainty with respect to the existence and direction of Aboriginal institutions at the community and regional levels. As for territorial public institutions, while they are likely to continue to exist, their future relevance and effectiveness needs further consideration. Furthermore, as I have already noted, the federal government is beginning to question some of the public government arrangements — relating to resource management and development — that are or will be the products of Aboriginal land rights and self-government settlements in the western North. Now, at a time when industrial investors, government regulators and territorial residents are requiring some measure of certainty and stability from large resource development initiatives such as the Mackenzie Gas Project, there is a general sense that resource management and development regimes are far from efficient. The NWT, in particular, needs regulatory reform in this predevolution period to ensure that the regime that is eventually transferred to public and Aboriginal governments will operate more efficiently in the interest of all parties. Effective regulatory reform could also reinvigorate public government by encouraging institutions to have a more balanced territorial and regional-Aboriginal perspective on resource management and development.

The western North will continue to face major challenges during the next quarter century. In order to meet these challenges, it will, in my view, require territorial public institutions of government that do not merely exist but also have the internal legitimacy and the resources and jurisdiction to effectively advance territorial interests. Any future constitutional settlement must focus on how this can be achieved at the territorial level while maintaining a balance with the strong community and regional institutions to which Aboriginal people aspire. As governance evolves in the western North, we will likely need to re-examine the foundations and direction of Aboriginal and territorial public government institutions, taking into account the current and future realities of an ever-changing region. Otherwise, the western North will become a balkanized collection of Aboriginal institutions focused exclusively on claims and self-government agreements competing with territorial public governments that do not have the jurisdiction or financial resources to effectively govern in the interest of all territorial residents.

Gonaewo – Our Way of Life

THE TLICHO PEOPLE NEGOTIATED A LAND CLAIM AND SELF-GOVERNMENT AGREEMENT, titled the Tlicho Agreement, with the Governments of Canada and the Northwest Territories. It has been in effect since August 4, 2005. The agreement builds on the Tlicho perspectives on language, culture and way of life, while achieving recognition of land and resource ownership and a governance system. To understand the Tlicho, the Tlicho Agreement and the negotiations, one must understand the historic perspective of the Tlicho world view. It is based on the traditional view of coexistence, respect, collectivity, representation and recognition, and it is also grounded in the requirement to prepare the next generation to ensure the continuance of those perspectives.

Background

THE TLICHO LIVE IN THE NORTHWEST TERRITORIES, IN AN AREA NORTH OF GREAT Slave Lake. The population mainly resides in the four Tlicho communities of Behchokò (population 1,900), Whatì (600), Gamètì (400) and Wekweètì (200). Behchokò is accessible year-round by road, while the other three are fly-in communities accessible in winter by ice road. The largest community, Behchokò, is 110 kilometres northwest of Yellowknife, the capital of the territory and home to the Government of the Northwest Territories.

The Aboriginal peoples of the Northwest Territories began to organize as a collective during the 1960s, as part of the national Indian movement, to demand the recognition of Aboriginal rights and titles. This led to the Mackenzie Valley

Pipeline Inquiry, headed by Justice Thomas Berger, who recommended a 10-year moratorium on pipeline construction until the claims of Aboriginal peoples were addressed. The pressure for resource and economic development was great at this time, and the Aboriginal groups began to organize politically to be at the front line and to give their perspective on these pressing issues.

The Indian Brotherhood of the Northwest Territories was formed in 1970, and the Aboriginal leaders issued a Dene declaration for recognition of Aboriginal rights and title. The brotherhood was later renamed the Dene Nation. The Tlicho are members of the Dene Nation, along with other Indian bands in the Northwest Territories. The Métis of the Northwest Territories also organized as a group. The Dene and Métis agreed to work together to negotiate a land claim with the Government of Canada. The negotiations led to the initialling of the Dene/Métis Final Land Claim Agreement in 1990. Some members of the Dene Nation would not accept the Agreement unless changes were made to it. Canada withdrew from negotiations, resulting in the demise of the Agreement. Some regional groups within the Dene Nation were willing to negotiate a regional claim based on the Agreement. Negotiations of regional land claims were accepted by Canada, and two land claims agreements were concluded by 1993.

After much consultation and discussion among members of their community, the Tlicho agreed to enter into negotiations in 1992. A negotiating team was appointed — and eventually an advisory group of elders — and the negotiations began. The challenge was to ensure that our land claim and self-government agreement was deeply embedded in the foundations of our identity.

Who We Are

FOR CENTURIES, THE TLICHO OF THE NORTHWEST TERRITORIES HAVE RELIED ON THEIR intimate knowledge of the land and wildlife within their traditional use area. The Tlicho lived in a yearly cycle, following traditional trails and waterways in birchbark canoes to the barren lands and to the northeast to harvest caribou. The harvested meat was dried to reduce its weight on return portages. Hide, sinew, bone, antler and other parts of the animal were harvested for the manufacture of shelter, clothing and tools. The Tlicho returned below the treeline in winter to harvest the caribou that migrate south every fall.

In the historic Tlicho world, there was no written language. However, there was an oral tradition, which served as an intergenerational communication system: messages were embedded in the landscape as place names describing significant impacts and events that occurred over time.

Floating Time

WHEREVER CAMPS WERE ESTABLISHED, THE HEARTH BECAME THE HOME. MANY stories were told over the fire. The most popular stories for all generations were those in which animals and people spoke the same language and could switch places — move back and forth between their respective animal and human forms. The stories were told as preparation for the emotional and physical challenges of the day. The stories stirred and exercised every emotion of spirit and body to help strengthen the character of the listener. The stories were timeless and were told over and over so that they became ingrained in the Tlicho psyche.

Some of these stories tell about the gathering of the animals and the people and how they danced together. Afterwards, they determined what form they wanted to retain once and for all. Some of the animals were large, and in time they became predators of the people. The people were now challenged with a threat too great for them to resolve.

Coexistence

THE LANDSCAPE OF THE TLICHO IS FILLED WITH PLACE NAMES THAT TELL OF A cultural hero named Yamozah, who travelled to many places to rid the people of the larger animals and to make the smaller animals understand that they must not be predators of the people. Some of the animals left gifts on the land for the people to use as medicines. The place names of these sites established by Yamozah recognize their own significance, and people make offerings at them in exchange for their visits. Some are also identified by their names as being places where the future of a visitor might be foretold. Other sites of importance offer visitors an opportunity to dream and acquire knowledge through visions, enhancing their capability to survive on their own.

The place name describes the method of harvesting animals in that area and includes messages about the animals' habitat. Natural tools were used, so knowledge of the areas for harvesting using these tools was very important. Many rules for the preparation of animals were preserved in place names and constantly observed. It was understood that if these rules were not followed, the animals would vacate the area, and thus the law of coexistence as set by Yamozah would be breached.

The departure of the animals would make the people venture to the outer reaches of their traditional-use area to harvest. Additional travel in unfamiliar terrain was inherently risky, and there was the added risk of encountering other tribal groups. These early encounters were sometimes brief and brutal, as depicted in some of the overlapping place names of different groups, but stone tools and knowledge were exchanged when encounters with other tribes were friendly. Life did not change much for the early Tlicho.

We rely on this early principle of coexisting in the habitat of the animals to guide us in our environmental impact assessments for projects in our region. We must be very careful to protect the habitats of the animals. We neutralize the passing of visitors on traditional lands so that the animals that inhabit them will continue to sustain us in the environment to which we are all accustomed. We rely on the early coexistence principle, but it is not a threat to development. Rather, it complements development and demonstrates how the environment should be managed in a sustainable way. In fact, we already have large-scale development activity within the Tlicho territory. We have three diamond mines: two are operational, and a third is in the construction phase. We met the challenges that go along with development in the environmental assessments that were carried out.

Respect

WHEN EUROPEANS WERE DISCOVERING NORTH AMERICA, AROUND 1492, IT WAS inevitable that the impact would eventually reach the homeland of the Tlicho. In 1670, the Crown incorporated the Hudson's Bay Company by charter and acknowledged the area of its operation. The fight for Canada escalated until Britain established itself as the authority for land and commercial transactions.

Treaties were made with the Aboriginal groups directly by the British Crown after the Royal Proclamation of 1763.

The threat to the Tlicho of being wiped out and the land becoming empty of people was great. Skirmishes beyond traditional chance encounters with other Aboriginal groups escalated that threat, and new tools introduced by the Europeans made such skirmishes much more dangerous. The Tlicho were not yet familiar with these newly acquired European trade goods.

The Tlicho's leader led them into an isolated area, and they only ventured to their hunting grounds, at great risk, to harvest caribou. The leader's eldest son, Edzo, led the hunting brigade, and by stealth they avoided encounters. On one hunting expedition, in the early 1800s, Edzo decided to turn back from the point of safety to confront their challengers. The confrontation led to peace, and once the peace was made, the groups danced together and the people returned to the fishing holes that they remembered.

It is these principles of respect for others that we have drawn upon to reach agreements with our Aboriginal neighbours on traditional-use overlap in areas described in our oral history and on the land identified in the Tlicho Agreement. It gives us comfort to know that the Tlicho Agreement supports the ongoing rights of our Aboriginal neighbours, and that it will not affect their pursuit of future land agreements.

Collective

OUR HISTORY ALSO LIES IN THE FUR TRADE PERIOD, WHEN WE ACTED COLLECTIVELY TO define the Tlicho's unity as a people and to meet the economic potential that was presented to us. New tools — like nets, guns and axes — gave us an opportunity to explore new areas for harvesting. Place names depicting people with new tools and methods started to appear in newly discovered harvesting areas.

With the establishment of new trading posts in the homeland in the mid-1850s, new leadership methods emerged to deal with the trade. The Tlicho trading chiefs spoke and bartered on behalf of their collective group and its members to achieve a fair trade for the harvest. Dancing followed a successful trading session. The fur traders were quickly followed by representatives of the Christian churches, and within a short time all the Tlicho accepted the Christian faith.

In the late 1970s, we established our first corporation as a tool to foster experience, training and management. The corporation was visualized as an extension of our history, so that the trading chief was now the president and the group members were the shareholders. Using the same principles of trade, in 1993, the Tlicho managed to negotiate an agreement with the NWT Power Corporation, a Crown corporation of the Northwest Territories government. That agreement, which was signed in 1994, allowed the Tlicho to finance and build a 4.3-megawatt hydroelectric dam on one of the rivers within our traditional lands.

Throughout the years, we have gained experience and developed partnerships and relationships with leading businesses and corporations, to our mutual benefit. This has allowed us to develop our human resources — we have made sure that training and jobs are available to our people so that we can participate in economic development in a meaningful way.

The Tlicho have managed to negotiate with the three diamond mines, impact and benefit agreements. Some of these are called "protection and benefit" agreements. As well, we have negotiated environmental and socio-economic agreements with each of the mining companies. In negotiating these agreements, we have had to do much shuffling of schedules to ensure that things are done. Sitting down with industry and interest groups has given us some insight into their sensitivities and provided us with experiences that we have applied to the Tlicho negotiations. We have worked to ensure a level of certainty and comfort for all with respect to development in the North.

Representation

THE CROWN ENACTED THE *BRITISH NORTH AMERICA ACT* IN 1867. THE ACT GAVE recognition to the new Canadian government and delegated to it the administration of land transactions on the Crown's behalf. In response to the expansion of Canada's borders and to the need for more settler lands, the Canadian government embarked on peace treaties known as "historic" and "numbered" treaties. The Tlicho signed Treaty 11 in 1921. The government's version of this treaty called for the Tlicho to cede, release and surrender all their rights and titles to, and interests in, the land. It was to remain in effect for them and for their successors.

Canada started to establish day and residential schools to assimilate Aboriginal children into the new way of life. Meanwhile, Canada acted on its perceived right to open up lands in the Northwest Territories for development of natural resources, which started the full-scale encroachment on traditional Aboriginal lands. These early developments left a legacy of many contaminated sites. The Tlicho's way of life was ignored, and their contributions to this development remain unrecorded in modern history. The economic benefits gained by the Tlicho were minimal.

In 1967, Canada established a territorial government in the North. In time, it devolved to that government programs and services for which Ottawa still had fiduciary obligations. The new territorial government established municipal governments in Aboriginal communities that were completely different from the traditional system of governance. In 1969, Canada introduced the White Paper on Indian Policy to ensure that Aboriginal people were included in the broad term "Canadian" and treated exactly the same as everyone else. The Aboriginal people rose to meet the challenge and opposed the proposed legislated assimilation. The Aboriginal view of the White Paper was that it was a deliberate attempt to deny Aboriginal people recognition of their inherent rights and unencumbered access to their traditional lands.

As they became more organized for business and for resistance, the Tlicho adopted the band council system (an *Indian Act* system) in order to acquire funds and enable communication with the Canadian government. This new structure was a face that the federal government could recognize, and it added credibility and perceived legitimacy to the voice of the Tlicho. The band system appeared to separate the Tlicho; but, beneath the surface, a united First Nation (Tlicho) waited for the right time to demand recognition without that facade.

Our place names tell us of the 1921 treaty that was signed with the Government of Canada by our representative, Monfwi. Our elders talk about the treaty negotiations, in which the Tlicho were represented as an equal partner. This knowledge of equality gave us a strong argument for the legitimate inclusion of the self-government component in the land claim agreement. The understanding was that the relationship of equality would strengthen and continue. The Tlicho version of the treaty, as spoken by Chief Monfwi, embedded for generations the Tlicho interpretation, which was contrary in many respects to the government's. Chief Monfwi wanted to ensure that the history of traditional lands and their usage as described in the landscape would be unchanged. He said: "As long as the sun rises, the river flows and the land does not move, we will not be restricted from our way of life." The people dance on an annual basis to acknowledge our version of the encounter.

The Tlicho continue to keep the words of Chief Monfwi alive; continue to practise their language, culture and way of life; and continue to pass on stories to the next generation. This has become the foundation from which to meet future challenges and to give support and recognition to the inherency of the Tlicho by law.

Recognition

F IRST NATIONS' STRUGGLES, OVER TIME, LED TO THE RECOGNITION OF EXISTING TREATY rights and to the negotiation of new rights that could be accessed through the repatriation of the Constitution to Canada in 1982. The Tlicho, over a 12-year period, have managed to negotiate the Tlicho Agreement within the framework of Canada's laws. The negotiating teams were dedicated to their principles and negotiated in good faith to ensure that their principles, policies and sense of fairness were addressed at the table and in the final agreement.

The parties gave equal respect to the views of all and made every effort to find solutions rather than taking adversarial positions. It was more a matter of finding solutions within our jurisdictions and ensuring that things would be done. That experience gave us the confidence to go beyond cooperative negotiations and ensure that consultations with the people of the North were conducted in a respectful way.

The Tlicho Agreement is the only agreement that was initialled twice. It was initialled the first time to open it up for public consultation. The constructive comments that were made gave us insight and the opportunity to clarify and improve the understanding of the Agreement. The second initialling, done in early 2003, opened the way to ratification. In June 2003, we became the first to ratify the Agreement, with over 90 percent of beneficiaries voting in favour.

The Prime Minister of Canada, Jean Chrétien, came to Behchokò to sign the final agreement in 2003, and it was a real pleasure for many of our elders, who had known him since his first visit, in 1972, when he was the minister of

Indian affairs and northern development. They welcomed him back as an old friend. A tea dance was held to celebrate the signing. The Government of the Northwest Territories also ratified the Agreement through its legislative process with unanimous consent.

The Tlicho negotiation process, from beginning to end, was a long journey. It was accomplished while respecting the parliamentary process for the eventual recognition of the Tlicho Agreement. The senators held a committee hearing prior to the final reading within the Senate chamber, and the committee members heard the Tlicho speak passionately and eloquently about what the Agreement meant to their people. Senator Viola Léger's response best captures the Tlicho negotiation strategy and vision:

> I have witnessed many individual Aboriginal role models here and this is the first time that I am meeting a whole community role model. The fact that so many of you travelled such a great distance speaks louder than words for me. The words are important but your presence here is almost sacred. I saw a vision in what I have heard and you have a vision that comes from your roots. You have strategies, passion and a great deal of courage to continue to take one step at a time. I believe that, based on your historical vision of life, your negotiations were dedicated on principles, which I find are lacking in many cases. I was stunned when you spoke to the agreements with the animals. It demonstrates how true and deep your presence here is. This is a wonderful piece of work, especially the part about ordinary citizens being able to feel, touch and understand the process and the agreement. Congratulations on such lovely work. With the hard work of the chiefs and many people in the small communities, you have now gone one step further towards establishing your own government. It is remarkable. I just commend all of you. (Proceedings of the Standing Senate Committee on Aboriginal Peoples, February 8, 2005)

A historic first tea dance was held in the foyer of the Senate chamber to celebrate the extension of our history that resonated to the beginning of our own time, as we the Tlicho understood it.

Our Future

B ILL C-14 HAS GIVEN RECOGNITION TO THE THINGS THAT WE INHERITED AS TLICHO from our ancestors and has also given recognition to our ability to pass on those rights to future generations. The Tlicho Agreement is a living continuance of our history of concluding agreements and meeting challenges as we encounter them.

While negotiating the Tlicho Agreement, there were a lot of other factors to consider, the main one being that we had to ensure that education for future generations would be strengthened with our language, culture and way of life. We invested in scholarships for those pursuing post-secondary education. The funds for this came from the impact-protection benefit agreements we negotiated with the mining companies. In addition to the traditional non-Tlicho education system, we are sticking to the principles of our elders, like our late chief Jimmy Bruneau, who talked about making sure that our language, culture and way of life are equally maintained.

Since 1995, we have been running what we call "on-the-land canoe programs." Our youth paddle, hunt and fish on our lakes and rivers and along our traditional trails so that they understand their history and are able to read the place names. As an elder has said, "You turn the pages every time you dip your paddle" and recount your history. We encourage our future generations to coexist with the land and be good stewards, to have respect for other people, to act collectively for strength, to represent what has been inherited and to give recognition to other jurisdictions. Our trust is that future generations will be "strong like two people."

Challenges Facing the Tlicho

ON THE EFFECTIVE DATE OF AUGUST 4, 2005, THE NEW TLICHO GOVERNMENT inherited all the assets and liabilities of the four former Indian bands. A starter kit of laws enacted on that date created new governing and administrative bodies. Newly elected leaders took their seats. Three years have passed since we raised the Tlicho flag, and it has become evident that the work of nation building based on historical and traditional principles has its challenges.

Despite these challenges, it is still an exciting and rewarding time for the Tlicho. The primary challenge is to not feel overwhelmed by the implementation of the Agreement and the magnitude of the nation-building task. We must maintain unity and practise the collective responsibility the Tlicho have always had. These are some of the initial issues we have been working on:

- We are setting up the governance system (with elements such as the annual gathering) to ensure that all Tlicho citizens can voice their ideas about where they think their government should be heading. We have been working on the procedures and policies, including those of the assembly sessions, to realize the law-making authority to implement the Tlicho Agreement. Other procedural development is under way in the actual making of laws and the workings of the Chiefs Executive Council — the body that implements the laws of the assembly.

- The assets and liabilities of the four former band councils and the Dogrib Treaty 11 Council, as well as the economic arms, have been transferred to the Tlicho government, and we are working to ensure that amalgamation is ongoing.
- All human resources functions have been absorbed by the Tlicho government, and we are working to set up job descriptions, pay scales and benefits; training plan development for all staff is under way.
- All the corporations from previous regimes have been transferred to the Tlicho government, and they are being reorganized under a new corporate structure to ensure transparency and accountability and to fulfill reporting requirements.
- The Tlicho government now has both surface and subsurface control over 39,000 square kilometres. A land-use planning exercise is under way. Until a land-use plan is completed and approved, the Tlicho government will not allow development of lands.
- The Tlicho government is constantly reviewing the programs and services that it receives from other governments to ensure that the integration of language, culture and way of life is the foundation for the implementation.
- To provide financial transparency and accountability, the Tlicho government develops all its own budgets for each fiscal year and debates and approves them at the assembly sessions. Work on the financial systems is ongoing to meet new challenges as they arise.
- The Tlicho government wants to ensure that the membership list is interactive to meet the needs of the membership for additions and removals; work on the system to monitor and manage this important component is ongoing.
- The Tlicho government wants to ensure that all members are aware of the issues and is developing a system of membership communications.

Conclusion

W E HAVE LEARNED A LOT IN SUCH A SHORT PERIOD, AND THE KNOWLEDGE WE HAVE gained is something that could be shared with other First Nations. It has been an amazing journey through time and process, and when viewed retrospectively, it is exhilarating. Applying ancient principles in the negotiation of a modern agreement and attempting to incorporate the land claim and self-government agreement into our language, culture and way of life instead of the opposite has been a source of immense pride and joy. Our language, culture and way of life have been immortalized in the Agreement and in its implementation. Our journey has also been a source of significant challenge: we are implementing an agreement and building a nation, with partners and within a system, in an era that is changing technologically, culturally and economically at the speed of light.

Self-Government, the
Northern Environment
and Aboriginal Culture

T HE FIRST POINT I WOULD LIKE TO MAKE IS I DON'T THINK ABORIGINAL PEOPLE OR the governments that are emerging in the North intend to undermine the territorial or federal governments. Aboriginal people in the North have a lot to contribute to public policy and legislation that affects us day to day, on the ground. People in Ottawa sit in their offices making legislation and policies, but they have no clue what the impact will be on a small community of 650 people like mine. And it's the same with the territorial and provincial governments.

Every day, northern Aboriginal communities are faced with suicides, drug and alcohol problems, changes in their traditional lifestyles and negative changes to wildlife, the water and the air. We have tried for the last 40 years to use the systems that have been imposed on us to make ourselves heard in order to protect what is affecting us every day. That system doesn't seem to be working, because nobody hears us from Deline, Great Bear Lake.

Great Bear Lake has the freshest water of any lake in Canada. My community is the only one on the lake, and we use the entire lake, some 12,000 square miles, and the surrounding area for different purposes, including fishing and hunting for caribou, moose and bear. We have been forced to start claiming land and developing systems that will allow us to have a role in managing the resources in the area. Our elders have told us that we need to get involved, otherwise we will be a lost people on our own lands. People will come and take over, and push us out. People will forget about us.

If we allow that to happen, there is no future for our people, no future for our culture, no future for our languages. The only way that we, as Aboriginal people, can protect those things is actually to get involved in the public system. The way we can do that is to design processes that will allow our people to speak and get other people to listen, and to make sure these things are constitutionally protected. We also have to deal with wildlife: conservation will have an impact on whether we will be allowed to hunt in the future. We will do whatever we can to make sure these resources last.

One elder from our community who passed away around 1940 talked about global warming. He predicted that the North was going to get hot and the south was going to get cold; and that the south would be destroyed by natural disasters, floods, fires and winds. One of his biggest predictions was that water would become the most valuable resource in the world, and that there would be no more food and water except for the fish and water in Great Bear Lake. It looks as though these predictions are coming true: the North is warming up, fires are happening, and there are floods, tornadoes and hurricanes. Well, maybe it's time we got ready, because one of the elder's predictions was that Great Bear Lake will end up being full of boats side by side around the entire shore.

As an Aboriginal people, we need to protect our culture and beliefs and preserve wildlife. However, nobody seems to care about whether Aboriginal people are doing well. People say, "Negotiate agreements; put the people in their corner, then they'll be happy!" Well, the reality with the Deline agreement is that we're developing a relationship, a long-term relationship, with the territorial and federal government. We're not going to go away. We're going to live there, and we expect you also to not go away. We expect governments to be involved and ensure that we are building capacity; to ensure that if we're going to spend all this energy and time negotiating these wonderful agreements, we must build enough capacity for the community to be able to have an impact on the entire system. This means that policy-makers and legislators have to have raw data so that they're not working blind.

We also need to recognize that people are not the same. Some people live on muskox, some on buffalo and some on caribou. The fortunate ones can live on all of them, but at the end of the day you can't paint everybody with the same brush and say all policies should apply to everyone. The reality is that on the ground we have some serious problems. We are trying to keep our people out of the jails, trying to get our people educated. But every four years there are elections. Policies change, programs change, directors change. This means that, just as 650 people are getting used to a new housing program, someone comes back and says, "Well, that housing program is gone; we're going to develop another one."

I care about this country just as much as everybody else does. I think our forefathers have done lot to preserve and protect Canada. But Canadians need to recognize that we have a role just like you in defending this great country.

For me, it's all about culture. It's not just some myth that if you understand a language, you have a culture. I am hoping that Canada recognizes the North and says to the North, "We need you to get involved in helping us develop legislation; we recognize your contribution to this country; we recognize your contribution to protecting sovereignty in the Arctic."

In my mind, traditional knowledge is the most valuable thing that Aboriginal people have. Aboriginal people are sometimes reluctant to share what they know with researchers. The main reason is that it's probably the only domain they have left that has not been invaded, because it's in their heads. And if somebody can figure out how to get it out of my head without my knowing it, then you can have it all! But as soon as I give that knowledge to researchers, it becomes public information. We need to change policy on how research is carried out in the North, because Aboriginal people need to hold on to their traditional knowledge. It's the last identity they have in terms of who they are.

We have spent a lot of time negotiating agreements. However, Aboriginal groups do not actually know how to get the full benefits of what was negotiated because the capacity is not there. This needs to be corrected. We need to hit the ground running and maximize benefits on day one, not 10, 15 or 20 years down the road. Otherwise, our people will say, "This stuff doesn't work, I'll just stay home and do nothing."

Nunavut and the
Inuvialuit Settlement
Region: Differing
Models of Northern
Governance

I N THE MODERN WORLD, THE NATURE, SCOPE AND QUALITY OF GOVERNANCE ARE everywhere important, but nowhere is government of greater moment than in northern Canada. On a local, human level, government is omnipresent in the North; the services, opportunities and supports it provides loom far larger in people's everyday lives than is the case south of 60. On a wider — indeed, global — scale, the seemingly inexorable advance of global warming is making the North far more accessible to international interests than ever before. Whether this means an ice-free Northwest Passage, which will cut thousands of kilometres off shipping routes between Asia and Europe, or militarization of the Arctic or increased pressure to exploit northern nonrenewable resources, the implications are enormous and the demands on government obvious.

In this chapter, I will look at the governance regimes in two regions of the Canadian North: Nunavut and the Inuvialuit Settlement Region (ISR). Governments in both face heavy demands in response to local problems as well as the prospect of becoming increasingly important players on the international stage. In both Nunavut and the ISR, Aboriginal people are far more numerous than non-Aboriginal people; Inuit make up roughly 85 percent of the population in Nunavut, while in the ISR, approximately 57 percent of the population is Inuvialuit.[1] Moreover, the most important and interesting governance issues in both regions — and, not to put too fine a point on it, some of the most problematic issues — are those relating to governance of and by Aboriginal people. Accordingly, the emphasis in this chapter is on the governance roles and experiences of the Inuit and the Inuvialuit.

The Inuvialuit of the Mackenzie Delta and the western Arctic islands and the Inuit of Nunavut have a common origin: both are descendants of the Thule people who spread across the Arctic islands from present-day Alaska around the start of the first millennium. The Inuit and the Inuvialuit are thus closely related branches of a single Aboriginal family. They share many cultural characteristics, reflecting both their common origin and the similarities of their harsh homelands, and they speak close variants of the same language. The demographic profiles of the Inuit and the Inuvialuit are similar, as are the social and economic challenges they face. Both peoples draw strength from the land and from their close-knit communities. The federal *Indian Act* never applied to the Inuit, so that the often-times artificial distinctions that divide other Aboriginal peoples — status Indian, nonstatus Indian and Métis — have no equivalent among the Inuit of Nunavut and the Inuvialuit.

The original Nunavut land claim, submitted to the federal government by the Inuit Tapirisat in 1976, included the Inuvialuit and their lands. Shortly there-after, however, the Inuvialuit and the Inuit went their separate ways politically. The Inuvialuit pulled out of the Nunavut proposal to pursue their own claim, which was finalized in 1984. The Inuvialuit Settlement Region established by the claim remains a region — albeit a distinctive region — within the Northwest Territories (NWT).[2] The Inuit of Nunavut settled their claim in 1993 and six years later saw the establishment of Nunavut as a separate territory in which Inuit dom-inate numerically and politically.

This combination of shared culture and social structure and divergent political paths raises intriguing questions about governance of northern Aboriginal peoples. I will explore some of these questions by looking at the polit-ical-governmental successes, challenges and prospects experienced by the people of the ISR and Nunavut. Two of the issues that I will consider are the importance of scale (in population and in land mass, Nunavut is several times larger than the ISR) and the implications of autonomy (Nunavut is an autonomous territory with distinct status in the Canadian federation, while the ISR is but one of several regions within the Northwest Territories). Beyond scale and autonomy, other fac-tors examined that affect governance include the provisions of the land claims agreements covering the two regions and the nature of the two organizations rep-resenting beneficiaries of the claims: Nunavut Tunngavik Incorporated (NTI) and the Inuvialuit Regional Corporation (IRC).

In describing and analyzing governance in the two regions, I do draw some midrange comparisons, several of which could well be applied to government regimes in other parts of northern Canada. In terms of broadly applicable conclusions, however, one stands out — not only because of the degree of assurance with which is offered, but also because of its importance for understanding governance in Canada's North. As will become evident, Nunavut and the ISR exhibit a number of commonalities, yet marked differences are also apparent in their governance structures, in their political priorities and approaches, and in their records of success and failure. The lesson is clear: in the North, even two adjacent jurisdictions with seemingly similar cultural, demographic and political features may diverge substantially on key governance dimensions.

After presenting a brief overview of the geography, demographics and economic foundations of the two regions, I provide a broad description of their governance arrangements. A series of more focused discussions follow: on the land claims agreements so central to governance in both the ISR and Nunavut; on the land claims organizations empowered by the claims; and on the experiences of, and challenges facing, governments in the two regions, as well as the political issues of greatest immediate concern. While space limitations permit me to offer only a broad-brush analysis of the experiences of governments in Nunavut and the ISR and the opportunities and challenges that lie before them, I hope that this chapter will spur the detailed analysis that each and every topic I touch on deserves.

The Land and the People

The Inuvialuit

THE ISR, AS DEFINED BY THE INUVIALUIT FINAL AGREEMENT, COVERS SOME 216,000 square kilometres in the Mackenzie Delta, the Yukon North Slope, and several western Arctic islands, most notably Banks Island and part of Victoria Island (see map on the following page). Most of the ISR, like all of Nunavut, lies above the treeline, though the area around Aklavik and Inuvik in the southern delta is lightly forested. The mainland portion of the ISR is mostly flat and low-lying, save for many pingos — ice-cored hills rising directly out of the tundra, a landform unique to the Arctic. A very different geography marks the large islands: high, stark cliffs and wide plains.

By comparison with the adjacent coastal waters off Nunavut, the Beaufort Sea is unusually bountiful, as are the northern reaches of the Mackenzie River.

Accordingly, in pre- and early-contact times, the Inuvialuit had a less precarious existence than their cousins to the east and lived for extended stretches in substantial driftwood-and-sod houses within semipermanent settlements (Morrison 2003).

Today, virtually all the Inuvialuit of the ISR are found in six communities: two (Aklavik and Inuvik) on the Mackenzie River, two (Tuktoyaktuk and Paulatuk) on the coast and two (Sachs Harbour and Ulukhaktok [Holman]) on Banks and Victoria islands. Inuvik is — by northern standards — a substantial centre, with over 3,000 residents, whereas the population of Sachs Harbour barely exceeds 100; the other communities range in size from 300 to 1,000.[3] Only Inuvik enjoys year-round road access (though the Dempster Highway, which serves the town, leads not to the southern NWT but to Yukon); ice roads reach Aklavik and Tuktoyaktuk in the winter. Inuvik is further atypical in that roughly 40 percent of its residents are non-Aboriginal, whereas in all other Inuvialuit communities, save Aklavik, 80 to 90 percent or more of the population is Inuvialuit. Nor are all of Inuvik's Aboriginal residents Inuvialuit, for the town also has a substantial Gwich'in (Dene) presence. The total population of the ISR stands at roughly 5,800 (of whom about 57 percent are Inuvialuit); this constitutes about 14 percent of the NWT population.

A high proportion of Inuvialuit live outside the ISR. Just over 40 percent of Inuvialuit beneficiaries — those officially enrolled under the provisions of the Inuvialuit Final Agreement (IFA) — live in other parts of the NWT or elsewhere in Canada and the world.[4] Each Inuvialuit community is in its own way distinctive, and a certain level of tension exists among these communities; as the largest community with the greatest resources, Inuvik is the prime target of complaint. But regionalism plays little if any role in Inuvialuit society and politics.

Unlike many northern Aboriginal communities, particularly those in Nunavut, Inuvialuit communities are not undergoing rapid population growth. Indeed, although census data must be interpreted with caution because of the possibility of significant population underreporting, the 2006 Census indicates that communities in the ISR, with the exception of Inuvik, have either stable or declining populations. In the four communities for which reliable data are available, the population declined or grew between 2001 and 2006 as follows: -6.5, -6.0, 0.0 and +2.8 percent. Inuvik grew by roughly 20 percent.[5] Nonetheless, the Inuvialuit population is still markedly younger than the Canadian population as a whole. Accordingly, despite a relatively stable population, the number

Nunavut

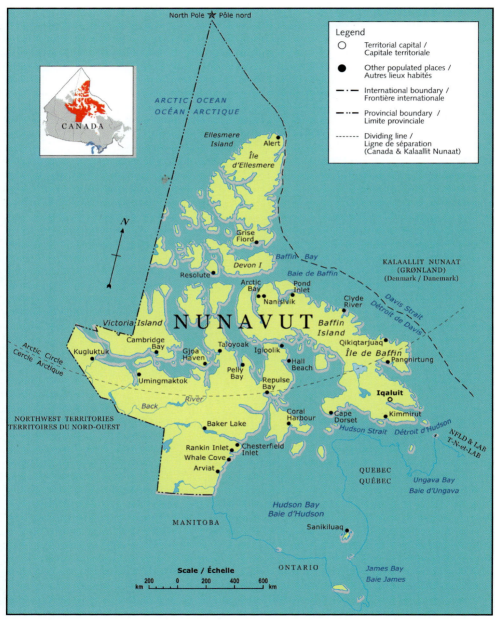

North Pole ★ Pôle nord

Legend

○ Territorial capital /
Capitale territoriale

● Other populated places /
Autres lieux habités

–·– International boundary /
Frontière internationale

—··— Provincial boundary /
Limite provinciale

------ Dividing line /
Ligne de séparation
(Canada & Kalaallit Nunaat)

ARCTIC OCEAN
OCÉAN ARCTIQUE

CANADA

Ellesmere
Island
Alert

Île
d'Ellesmere

N

Grise
Fiord

Baffin Bay

Devon I
Baie de Baffin

Resolute

Arctic
Bay
Pond
Inlet

Nanisivik

KALAALLIT NUNAAT
(GRØNLAND)
(Denmark / Danemark)

Clyde
River

Davis Strait
Détroit de Davis

Victoria Island

NUNAVUT

Baffin
Island

Cambridge
Bay

Taloyoak

Igloolik

Qikiqtarjuaq

Île de Baffin

Arctic Circle
Cercle Arctique

Kugluktuk

Gjoa
Haven

Hall
Beach

Panghirtung

Pelly
Bay

Umingmaktok

Repulse
Bay

Back

River

Iqaluit

NORTHWEST TERRITORIES
TERRITOIRES DU NORD-OUEST

Coral
Harbour

Cape
Dorset

Kimmirut

Baker Lake

Hudson Strait   Détroit d'Hudson

NFLD & LAB
T-N-et-LAB

Rankin Inlet   Chesterfield
Inlet

Whale Cove

Arviat

QUÉBEC
QUÉBEC

Ungava Bay
Baie d'Ungava

Hudson Bay
Baie d'Hudson

MANITOBA

Sanikiluaq

Scale / Échelle

200   0   200   400   600
km   km

ONTARIO

James Bay
Baie James

Source: Natural Resources Canada, reproduced with the permission of the Minister of Public Works and Government Services. www.atlas.gc.ca

of enrolled beneficiaries (who must be 18 or older) continues to rise substantially; in the past decade, it has grown by 35 percent (Inuvialuit Regional
Corporation 2007a, 3).

Both the IRC and the Government of the Northwest Territories (GNWT)
operate programs to encourage the use of Inuvialuktun, but still Inuvialuit familiarity with their language is in steady decline. The 2004 NWT Community Survey
conducted by the NWT Bureau of Statistics showed that barely a quarter of
Inuvialuit beneficiaries over 15 years old speak their language; in all communities, the number of Inuvialuktun speakers was lower — in some cases much
lower — than it had been 20 years earlier.[6]

As is the case throughout the North, the economy of the ISR is heavily
dependent on government for public sector jobs and for transfers to individuals,
such as welfare payments. In no small measure due to the efforts of the IRC to
parlay claims money into economic opportunity, the private sector is, by northern standards, strong and diverse in the ISR. Far fewer Inuit in the NWT (who
are, with few exceptions, Inuvialuit) indicate that government transfers are their
main source of income than do Inuit in Labrador, northern Quebec and Nunavut[7]
(Inuit Tapiriit Kanatami and Research and Analysis Directorate, Indian and
Northern Affairs Canada 2007a, 2007b, 9). Oil and gas exploration and pipeline
preparation activities are the most prominent private sector ventures, but transportation, construction, tourism and other service industries generate important
investment and employment opportunities.[8] The traditional economy — hunting, fishing and trapping — provides little by way of cash income but remains an
important source of low-cost, nutritious "country food" and is of enormous cultural significance. In 2004, more than half the adult (age 15 and over) Inuvialuit
population reported having hunted or fished in the previous year.[9]

Nunavut

At 1.9 million square kilometres, Nunavut would rank as one of the largest countries in the world were it not part of Canada. It would certainly be the most
sparsely populated, with a population, as of the 2006 Census, of just under
30,000. As befits such a huge swath of land, its geography varies widely — from
the flat tundra west of Hudson Bay to the soaring fjords of Baffin and Ellesmere
islands. Though plans have been mooted for all-weather roads from Coronation
Gulf to the resource-rich interior of the Kitikmeot region and up the west side of

Hudson Bay, at present no communities are joined by road (an ice road connects Arviat to Churchill, Manitoba, during the winter).[10] Baker Lake is the only inland Nunavut community; all others are on the sea.

Roughly 85 percent of Nunavummiut (the people of Nunavut) are Inuit; virtually everyone else is non-Aboriginal. Of the 25 communities, Iqaluit is by far the largest, with over 6,000 residents; two (Rankin Inlet and Arviat) have populations slightly larger than 2,000; nearly two-thirds of the other communities have fewer than a thousand residents. Non-Inuit are concentrated in the larger centres such as Iqaluit, Rankin Inlet and Cambridge Bay; in the smaller communities, Inuit typically make up 90 to 95 percent of the population.

Not surprisingly, Nunavut's expansive geography — three time zones wide — fosters a certain regionalism. The Government of Nunavut, NTI and other political and cultural entities formally recognize three regions: the Baffin (Qikiqtani) region in the east, the Kivalliq to the west of Hudson Bay and the Kitikmeot in the far west. While Nunavut is hardly riven by regional political conflict, tensions are never far below the surface. Regional political divisions stem partially from modest cultural and linguistic distinctions but at root reflect competition for government largesse and services. In the Kitikmeot, discontent arising from distributive politics gives rise to a Nunavut variation of that well-known Canadian phenomenon, western alienation. Symbolic and substantive complaints intermingle in this least populous region, which finds itself at the greatest distance from the centre of power, Iqaluit. By way of illustration, Kitikmeot communities such as Cambridge Bay and Kugluktuk have far better transportation links to Yellowknife, in the NWT, than to other parts of Nunavut. Symbols reinforce perceptions of distinctiveness: Inuinnaqtun, the Kitikmeot variation of Inuktitut, is written using Roman orthography, whereas elsewhere in Nunavut syllabics are the norm.

Unlike the Inuvialuit communities, which, save Inuvik, have population figures that are either holding steady or declining, Nunavut continues to experience remarkable population growth. According to the 2006 Census, Nunavut's population grew by 10.2 percent in the five years since the previous census.[11] Three small communities lost population,[12] but most expanded substantially: in nine communities, the population increased by 10 percent or more — often a good deal more — in a mere five years. The other notable related demographic fact about Nunavut is its very high proportion of young people. The 2006 Census demonstrated that whereas the median age of all Canadians is 39.5, with 17.7 percent of the population under 15, in Nunavut it is 23.1 and over a third of the population (33.9 percent) is under 15.[13] The implications of this population pressure for government are enormous: simply keeping pace with what is termed "forced growth" — building schools and hiring teachers, expanding the stock of already overcrowded housing, creating new employment and delivering social services — is a daunting task.

Nunavut's economy is extraordinarily dependent on government. The weakness of the private sector means that in many communities, few jobs exist outside the public sector (which accommodates regular Government of Nunavut [GN] departmental employees, municipal employees, teachers, nurses and RCMP personnel). Prospects for extensive mining activity (most notably diamonds, gold and possibly uranium) are good, with several projects in the planning or development stages, but realization of their economic potential remains some distance away. Sectors such as tourism, arts and crafts, commercial fishing, construction and retail are all relatively small, though some have considerable potential for expansion. Lack of infrastructure — no Nunavut community has a dock suitable for large ships — and low levels of educational attainment are major impediments to economic development, as is the burgeoning population whose need for schools, housing and basic government services leaves little financial room for economic development initiatives, at least on the GN's part. The traditional economy continues to play an essential role in many households, and, as in the ISR, it is a cultural mainstay.[14]

Governance in Nunavut and the ISR: An Overview

WHILE THIS CHAPTER IS ESSENTIALLY A CONTEMPORARY ANALYSIS OF GOVERNANCE in Nunavut and the ISR, it is important to recognize that the past three or four decades have witnessed sweeping political change in both regions (and across the North generally). As Frances Abele's chapter in this volume demonstrates, the emergence of strong Aboriginal political organizations, the development by the federal government of a comprehensive claims policy in the 1970s, the entrenchment of Aboriginal and treaty rights in the *Constitution Act, 1982*, the federal government's acknowledgement of Aboriginal people's inherent right to self-government in the 1990s, the massive devolution of province-like powers from Ottawa to the territorial governments and other landmark political developments have fundamentally transformed the northern political landscape in a remarkably short time.

Government in both Nunavut and the ISR is predominantly public — meaning that all residents are entitled to vote and to hold elected office and that services are offered to all residents, regardless of cultural background. (The alternative is Aboriginal self-government, which may take many forms but involves at least some exclusionary provisions — for example, restricting the right to vote and to hold office to Aboriginal people, or delivering programs only to Aboriginal people.) Elements of self-government are found, to a limited degree, in each region, but they tend to be relatively minor in scope. As I will discuss later, however, the Inuvialuit are actively pursuing a far-reaching self-government regime through negotiations with the federal and territorial governments.

The GN follows the familiar outlines of the British cabinet-parliamentary system, as it operates in Ottawa and the provinces, with certain important variations. The GN is headed by a premier and a cabinet, who hold seats in and are responsible to the 19-member legislative assembly (elected by universal adult franchise), supported by a professional, politically neutral public service. All the tenets of Westminster-style responsible government are operative, despite what might seem to parliamentary purists a heretical aberration: the absence of political parties. All candidates for the assembly run as independents, and the premier and the ministers are selected by a secret vote in which all MLAs participate. Lacking anything like an organized opposition, the system, termed "consensus government," is far less adversarial than the legislative system of southern Canada, though it is also a far cry from the traditional consensus style of Inuit decision-making (White 2006).

This arrangement was inherited from the Northwest Territories, where, despite occasional attempts to replace it with a party system, it has operated for the better part of three decades. The key difference in how consensus government at the territorial level affects the two regions arises from the ISR's position within the NWT. In the 19-member legislative assembly, four MLAs represent ISR communities, though only one of their ridings is entirely within the ISR and has mainly Inuvialuit constituents.[15]

Just as constituency boundaries do not conform to ISR boundaries, the GNWT does not recognize the ISR as an administrative region. Some years ago, the entire NWT was subdivided into administrative districts, each overseen by a regional director (a senior bureaucrat); the Inuvik region encompassed more than the ISR, but at least all GNWT departments were organized along consistent regional lines. Currently, however, each department establishes regional operations according to its own priorities, making for administrative variation across the ISR.

Public government, it is worth noting, is dominant not only at the territorial level, but at the local-municipal level as well. Elements of Aboriginal self-government are evident at the community level: Inuit and Inuvialuit organizations perform governmental functions, providing services (such as promoting economic development) and regulating behaviour (for example, distributing hunting tags and controlling hunting, fishing and trapping activities). However, the vast majority of locally delivered services (water, sewage, garbage collection, road maintenance and the like) and locally administered regulation of behaviour (animal control, speed limits, curfews and so on) are the responsibility of the public, municipal governments. In both Nunavut and the ISR, all municipal governments are organized according to the mayor-and-council model standard throughout Canada (save in certain NWT and Yukon communities) (White 2007). The proposed Inuvialuit government regime contemplates significant self-government elements at the community level.

Public government may be the order of the day in the ISR and Nunavut, but in ways well outside the experience of southern Canadians, the contours of government and politics in the two regions are profoundly shaped by land claims agreements, which are nothing less than modern-day treaties, with far-reaching, constitutionally protected governance provisions. Accordingly, the authority accorded by the claims to the IRC and NTI, the land claims organizations, render them exceptionally powerful political forces. Their clout is far greater than that of any interest group in southern Canada. Indeed, it would be quite wrong to think of them as interest groups, given their deep and extensive roots in the communities, the fact that their legitimacy often eclipses that of the territorial governments and their implicit, if not explicit, engagement in what amount to government activities. In short, they are not simply powerful forces influencing government, they are integral components of the governance regime; they are not parallel governments, but governments they are.

Government, of course, requires money — a good deal of money, especially in the North. How are governments in the ISR and Nunavut financed?
Neither the GN nor the GNWT, which provides the great bulk of government
services in the ISR, has much capacity to generate own-source revenue. Both can
and do levy personal and corporate taxes, but they refrain from imposing sales
taxes other than in hidden form on such traditional cash cows as cigarettes and
liquor. Both governments tap into other minor revenue sources through
licences, fees and the like, but all told they raise only a small proportion of the
monies required — roughly 7 percent in Nunavut and 25 percent in the NWT.
The territorial governments are heavily dependent on federal transfers, mostly
through a formula financing agreement by which Ottawa provides to each a massive, unconditional grant reflecting a mind-numbingly complex set of factors
such as territorial population, territorial revenue-generating potential, inflation
rate and Canada-wide government expenditure trends. The Territorial Formula
Financing payments are far more generous than the Equalization payments
directed to poorer provinces, though, as I will discuss later, all royalties from
nonrenewable resources such as diamonds, gold, oil and gas in the NWT and
Nunavut accrue to federal rather than territorial coffers (in the provinces, royalties flow to the provincial treasuries).

At the local level, most communities in the ISR and Nunavut are what are
termed "non-tax-based municipalities," meaning that taxes on the limited number of privately owned properties are paid to the territorial rather than to the
municipal government. Lacking any significant capacity to raise own-source revenue, municipalities receive most of their funding through a variety of grants and
contribution agreements.

Devolution and revenue sharing are on the political agenda in both the ISR
and Nunavut. Devolution refers to the transfer to the territorial government of the
few remaining important province-like powers — most notably, jurisdiction over
public lands and nonrenewable resources, which is still exercised by Ottawa in
Nunavut and the NWT. (Devolution occurred in Yukon several years ago.)
Revenue sharing, which is intimately intertwined with devolution, involves rejig-
ging the royalty and tax regimes for nonrenewable resources so that the territorial governments reap significant financial benefits from the massive deposits of
diamonds, oil, gas, gold and other minerals within their boundaries.[16]

In Nunavut, negotiations on devolution are in their early stages. Prime

Minister Paul Martin's unrealistic pledge to have a devolution agreement in place for Nunavut by 2008 has given way to the current federal posture: lack of governance capacity is cited to support the argument for a long phase-in of jurisdictional transfer. Nunavut's premier, Paul Okalik, has responded with remarkably forthright language. For example, he described Indian and Northern Affairs Canada in a speech to the Northern Exposure conference as "reviled by most Aboriginal people" and called for Nunavummiut "to exercise the same degree of control over — and benefit from — our resources as do Albertans, Québécois or any other Canadian" (Okalik 2007, 4). Despite, or perhaps because of, such confrontational tactics, the file has not moved forward appreciably. The symbolism of what the Premier terms federal "paternalism" is doubtless significant, but in the short term, agreement with Ottawa on devolution and revenue sharing is thus not as pressing a concern as it is in the NWT. Nunavut does have numerous high-quality mineral deposits, and while exploration and development planning is proceeding apace, at present the territory has only one operating mine (quite recently, it had none); the long-term potential for oil and gas is substantial, but production is many years away. Accordingly, the immediate financial implications for Nunavut of the stalled devolution/revenue-sharing negotiations are significantly smaller than they are for the NWT.

With hundreds of millions of dollars in resource royalties (primarily from diamonds) at stake annually, devolution and revenue sharing have long ranked as prime concerns for the GNWT. Negotiations have been difficult and complex, because the NWT's Aboriginal governments and organizations have insisted that they are entitled to a major share of resource revenues. A framework agreement signed in 2004 has generated little enthusiasm and much criticism, and thus considerable uncertainty surrounds its final disposition. The Inuvialuit, through the IRC, are but one of several groups of players in this complicated process, and while they are no less interested in resolving the matter and tapping into the resulting revenue stream than anyone else, their leverage is limited.

A revenue-sharing deal would not likely result in a massive influx of new monies, since it would be accompanied by a substantial reduction in the formula financing grant from Ottawa, which currently provides the lion's share of the GNWT's revenue. Such a deal would, however, give governments in the NWT — Aboriginal governments as well as the GNWT — control over a highly lucrative revenue source. Among other things, this would give these governments the option, which is not currently open to them, to increase royalty rates, which are among the lowest in Canada. In short, it would substantially reduce dependence, economic as well as political, on the federal government.[17]

A final point of comparison between the two jurisdictions turns on scale. On a national scale, both are very small societies in terms of population. One implication is that a small number of astute, determined, visionary leaders have enormous influence not only in establishing greater autonomy for their peoples through land claims and associated political negotiations, but also in shaping the arrangements that have emerged in the new governance regimes. Among these leaders are Nellie Cournoyea, Agnes Semmler and Andy Carpenter in the ISR; John Amagoalik, Tagak Curley, Peter Ittinuar and Jose Kusugak in Nunavut (to cite only a few in each jurisdiction).

At the same time, the scale of government varies enormously across the North, from the GN to self-governing Yukon First Nations with only 200 to 300 citizens. Although the Inuvialuit are one of the larger northern Aboriginal peoples, a comparison of governance in the ISR and Nunavut underlines just how significant differences in scale can be. To span the vast land mass and the (relatively) large population of Nunavut, an extensive and complex government with political and administrative regions and a full complement of departments is required. (And this applies to NTI almost as much as it does to the GN.) Social and economic problems are magnified by their sheer volume, though economies of scale are sometimes possible. By contrast, politicians and administrators in the ISR can take advantage of the region's relatively small scale: it has only six communities and a population of less than 6,000. Literally, members of the political and economic elites all know one another well, and this permits informal resolution of issues that elsewhere might require less flexible official processes. Additionally, it is possible for the top officials in the IRC and the other Inuvialuit corporations to conduct an annual community tour; they hold public meetings in each Inuvialuit community, during which they recount their activities over the year and respond to questions and concerns. Logistically and financially, such an exercise would simply not be possible in Nunavut.

At the same time, manageable scale is a double-edged sword. It means that a strong leader like Nellie Cournoyea can impose discipline and direction, making for significant, positive change. But it also means that leaders lacking in integrity or competence have fewer checks on their power, and this could cause serious governance problems. Cournoyea's predecessor, for example, ended up in court, along with two of his top officials, facing tax evasion charges stemming from large, questionable bonus payments issued at a time when the IRC was losing tens of millions of dollars annually (Taylor 1997). The susceptibility of governance institutions in relatively small polities such as the ISR to problematic leaders is heightened by the weakness of local media. The CBC radio outlet in Inuvik and the weekly *Inuvik Drum* provide limited news coverage but generally lack the wherewithal or the commitment to aggressively pursue political issues in a manner that would hold politicians to account; by contrast, Nunavut's *Nunatsiaq News* routinely runs long, tough-minded stories critical of the political regime.

The Claims

I N BOTH NUNAVUT AND THE ISR, THE LAND CLAIMS CONSTITUTE THE FUNDAMENTAL underpinning of government and politics. Specifics vary in important ways, but the fundamental components of the two claims are similar. In exchange for giving up Aboriginal title to their traditional lands (but not all Aboriginal rights), the Inuvialuit and the Inuit received substantial cash payments (paid not to individuals but to the IRC and NTI); fee simple ownership of substantial blocks of land, with subsurface rights on a small proportion of these lands (again, owned not individually but communally); hunting, fishing and trapping rights; guaranteed participation in a series of comanagement boards with jurisdiction over wildlife and the environment; and a host of miscellaneous benefits, such as mineral royalties, preferential hiring in government and involvement in the development and operation of national parks. In addition, the claims included undertakings by the federal government on major political governance issues. In Nunavut, this primarily meant a commitment to create a Nunavut territory; in the ISR, it took the form of a pledge that Ottawa would negotiate extensive restructuring of the governance regime.

Significant differences are also evident between the two claims. The 1984 Inuvialuit Final Agreement (IFA) — also known as the COPE (Committee for Original Peoples' Entitlement) claim, named for the Inuvialuit political organization that negotiated it — was the first comprehensive claim settled in the territorial North and only the second nationally, after the 1976 James Bay and Northern

Quebec Agreement. Although only finalized nine years later, the Nunavut Land Claims Agreement (NLCA) reflects important transformations in the approaches and objectives of both Aboriginal leaders and government. Not least of the influences that produced distinctive agreements was a sense among some Nunavut leaders that the Inuvialuit had not secured sufficiently strong guarantees that their claim would adequately protect and advance their interests. To take but one example, key figures in the Tunngavik Federation of Nunavut (TFN), the organization negotiating the claim, believed that the IFA's comanagement boards "lacked teeth."

Compared with subsequent claims, the IFA is relatively short, at 40 pages of text. By contrast, the NLCA runs to 267 pages. It is longer largely because during negotiations both sides insisted upon including extensive detail, not because it covers topics that the IFA does not address. (One might assume that large parts of the NLCA relate to the creation of Nunavut and the organization and powers of its government, but barely a page is devoted to political development in Nunavut, including Ottawa's commitment to creating a Nunavut territory.) At the same time, the NLCA does cover a number of matters not touched on in the IFA — most notably, perhaps, in articles 23 and 24, which detail preferential treatment for Inuit seeking government employment and government contracts.

Though they were signatories to the IFA, the NWT and Yukon governments were very junior players in the negotiations. The GNWT played a far more substantial, albeit secondary, role in the negotiation of the Nunavut claim and was given a far more extensive formal role in implementing the claim. By way of illustration, the IFA defined "government" as the Government of Canada, whereas the TFN claim specified that the term included both the federal and territorial governments.

The Land Claims Organizations

THE INUVIALUIT REGIONAL CORPORATION AND NUNAVUT TUNNGAVIK INCORPORATED are the principal political organizations responsible for representing Inuvialuit and Inuit beneficiaries in dealings with government on land claims implementation. (Claims implementation is, for both government and Aboriginal organizations, an ongoing responsibility: it involves performing routine tasks, such as nominating and appointing comanagement board members; and it entails dealing with major policy issues, such as periodic renegotiation of basic funding arrangements.) Both organizations engage in a range of activities beyond their responsibilities under the claims; some — scholarships, cultural programs and the like — are services that other broadly based organizations typically provide for their members, while others are more in the nature of governmental functions.

The IRC and NTI are legally enshrined in the claims. In formal as well as in substantive terms, they differ somewhat from their predecessor organizations, COPE and TFN, though important continuities are evident as well — not least in leadership. Both are established as corporate entities. The IRC and NTI exhibit many similarities in terms of aims and activities and in administrative structures, but politically they are organized very differently, as are their links to their economic development arms.

The basic building blocks of the IRC are its six community corporations. In each community, Inuvialuit beneficiaries (who must be 18 or over) elect a local chair and six directors to run the community corporation. The six community corporation chairs and the IRC chair, who is elected by the 42 community council directors, make up the IRC board, the effective decision-making body. The chair and the community council directors have two-year terms.

The IRC has four direct subsidiaries (which in turn own all or part of a number of corporations): the Inuvialuit Development Corporation, the Inuvialuit Investment Corporation, the Inuvialuit Petroleum Corporation and the Inuvialuit Land Administration — collectively, the Inuvialuit Corporate Group. Monies from the land claim enabled the development and investment corporations to invest in a range of ventures in real estate, transportation and other service industries, thereby building substantial and profitable portfolios and providing jobs for Inuvialuit (though complaints are occasionally heard about the number and nature of the jobs available to Inuvialuit). The IRC board appoints the boards of the development and investment corporations and provides them with governance guidelines, such as dollar limits on what they can initiate on their own and specification of what has to be approved by the IRC. The IRC chair and the chair of the IDC consult frequently, as do their senior staff (two key staff positions are held by the same person in both organizations — chief legal counsel and chief financial officer), and the IDC board reports to the IRC board quarterly. In short, the operations of the Inuvialuit economic institutions are closely monitored and controlled by the principal Inuvialuit political organization. In recent years, the strong economic performance of the Inuvialuit corporations has permitted the IRC to make annual payments of several hundred dollars to all registered beneficiaries.

Like those of many Nunavut organizations, NTI's structure reflects the territory's vast geography and the importance of regional loyalties. In addition to NTI, the claim recognizes the three regional Inuit associations (RIAs) — the Kitikmeot, Kivalliq and Qikiqtani Inuit associations — as representing Inuit and carrying out certain functions under the claim. The RIAs are funded through NTI and by proceeds from their economic development corporations, which they, rather than NTI, control. NTI's 10-member board of directors includes the elected presidents from each of the RIAs plus one member nominated by each association and the chair of the Nunavut Trust.[18] The president and two other top officials, the first and second vice-presidents, are elected through universal vote by all claim beneficiaries over 16. Accordingly, the president of NTI comes into office with far more direct votes than the premier of Nunavut. In their most recent elections, for example, NTI's president, Paul Kaludjak, garnered 2,224 votes, while Premier Paul Okalik won his Iqaluit riding with 415 votes. Thus far, this discrepancy has been of little consequence, though should a serious confrontation develop between NTI and the GN, especially if it becomes personal between the president and the premier, it could well foster questions about the legitimacy of the GN, or at least its political head.

The IRC has a full-time staff complement of 48, though 10 of these are community positions (mainly child care workers at the community child care centres) retained on the IRC payroll until the communities take over full administrative responsibility for them. Six of the seven Inuvialuit Land Administration employees are located in Tuktoyaktuk, and the IRC's Inuvialuit Cultural Resource Centre has a position based in Ulukhaktok; otherwise, all IRC staff work out of the Inuvik office. The IRC receives small amounts of money for specific projects from government contribution agreements; the bulk of its funding — roughly $6 million annually — comes in the form of management fees from its subsidiaries.

Roughly 100 people work directly for NTI (the RIAs have their own staff); a recent count indicated that some 87 percent were Inuit beneficiaries.[19] The main office of NTI is in Iqaluit, but it also maintains offices in Cambridge Bay, Rankin Inlet and Igloolik, as well as in Ottawa. The lion's share of NTI funding comes from the Nunavut Trust, which invests and manages the money received through the claim; in 2005-06, this amounted to over 90 percent of NTI's total revenue of just over $50 million (in turn, some $13.4 million was transferred directly to the RIAs) (Nunavut Tunngavik Incorporated 2006, 75). NTI gives small monthly payments to elders, but not to other beneficiaries.

Governance Experiences
in the ISR and Nunavut:
An Overview

THE FUNDAMENTAL — AND DAUNTING — CHALLENGES CONFRONTING THE Government of Nunavut have not changed since it opened its doors, on April 1, 1999. The GN must deliver a host of public services and programs critical to Nunavummiut: everything from the timely distribution of welfare cheques, to air ambulance services, to the recruitment of nurses for community health centres, to the design of primary school curricula, to the oversight of municipal budgets, to the provision of fuel to communities. At the same time, it must address a substantial deficit in basic organizational capacity — a lack of the human, financial and organizational resources that large modern governments need to perform their functions adequately.

And not only does the GN need to keep the wheels turning while building the machine, but also, more than most governments in this country, it needs to develop innovative, aggressive new policies to alleviate pervasive social problems: lack of economic development; overcrowded, substandard housing; high rates of suicide and domestic violence; and so on (all compounded by burgeoning population figures). Nor have these tasks been lightened by the expectations — which in hindsight seem unrealistically high — of what the GN could accomplish in its first years. Adding yet another layer of difficulty to an already formidable set of challenges, the GN, strongly encouraged by NTI, committed itself to a governance regime that not only was run by Inuit but also operated according to Inuit culture and values.

As in Nunavut, the basic governance issues in the ISR remain largely the same as they were when the COPE claim was finalized, in 1984, though in important respects the problems of governance in the ISR — and the solutions attempted — differ from those in Nunavut. With most of the essential public services and programs delivered by the GNWT, the political-govern-

mental institutions of the ISR have not been called on to provide basic government functions, as is the GN. (And, given the GNWT's greater organizational maturity and capacity, provision of these functions is less problematic
than it is in Nunavut.) Since the territorial government holds responsibility
for public services, local institutions carry a much lighter load than they otherwise would, but this means that the people of the ISR lack control over policy development and implementation, as key decisions are made at the
territorial level. Thus, for many years, the Inuvialuit have been working
through ideas for self-government and negotiating with the federal and territorial governments. Achievement of self-government remains a central but as
yet unrealized Inuvialuit goal.

While no northern government can ignore the need for capacity building
— or at least capacity maintenance — this has been a less pressing concern in the
ISR than in Nunavut. Nor is significant pressure evident in the ISR to ensure that
governance institutions and processes are congruent with Inuvialuit values, as
opposed to simply serving Inuvialuit interests. Where ISR leaders face pressures
not commonly experienced in Nunavut is in the realm of economic development.
It is not simply that the IFA and its Inuvialuit economic institutions have been in
place for nearly a quarter century and thus are widely expected to have used
claim monies to become mature, big-time economic players — which in important ways they are. More fundamentally, the massive oil and gas deposits in the
region and the ISR's pivotal location should a pipeline be built down the
Mackenzie Valley have created huge economic stakes. As well, shifts in the international economy and the international geopolitical situation have, over the
years, produced repeated booms and busts. In the ISR, these fluctuations greatly
increase the urgency to secure the huge short- and long-term benefits that potential megaprojects are perceived to generate.[20] In Nunavut, the people and their
leaders are certainly eager for nonrenewable resource developments to spur economic growth. The pressures there for quick resolution of resource development
issues, however, are less intense than in the ISR, in part because Nunavut lacks a
history of boom-and-bust cycles, and it has not experienced initiatives like the
all-or-nothing Mackenzie Gas Project.

Finally, in governance, size matters. As I will discuss later, the much smaller scale of government in the ISR produces both advantages and disadvantages in
comparison with Nunavut.

P o l i t i c a l   a n d
G o v e r n a n c e   I s s u e s   i n
t h e   I S R

I N RECENT YEARS, THE INUVIALUIT HAVE LARGELY FOCUSED THEIR POLITICAL ATTENTION
on three key issues: ensuring that the Mackenzie Gas Project (MGP) goes
ahead and that the Inuvialuit are major partners in the project, reaping significant
long-term benefits; pushing the federal government to proceed with devolution
of jurisdiction over nonrenewable resources to the GNWT with a revenue-sharing deal favourable to the Aboriginal governments across the NWT; and pursuing self-government negotiations. (Any number of less far-reaching political
issues have also required attention.) While the first two — especially the MGP file
— are hugely important, and Inuvialuit leaders have been at the forefront of political activity related to them (the IRC's president, Nellie Cournoyea, has been a
central figure in the Aboriginal Pipeline Group, which plays a prominent role in
the financing of and politicking on the pipeline), many other players are also
involved. The self-government negotiations involve only the Inuvialuit and the
federal and territorial governments.

Planning for and discussion about distinctive regional government
arrangements in the Beaufort-Delta region have been under way for decades,
though they have often been relegated to the back burner for extended periods.
No great purpose would be served by reviewing the checkered history of ideas —
such as the proposal to create a western Arctic regional municipality (WARM) —
on regional governance in the ISR and neighbouring areas of the NWT. Two
points are, however, worth noting. First, some schemes, such as the WARM proposal (in which substantial time and energy were invested), were primarily aimed
at establishing public governments. Second, a key provision of the IFA guaranteed that the Inuvialuit were entitled to political-governmental accommodations
equivalent to those that might be negotiated by other Aboriginal groups (the
neighbouring Gwich'in and Sahtu Dene and Métis emerged as the principal
groups in this context).[21]

The current self-government talks effectively date to 1993, when the
Inuvialuit and the Gwich'in began joint negotiations with Ottawa and
Yellowknife. In 1996, the Self-Government Process and Schedule Agreement was
signed, leading to an agreement in principle (AIP) in 2003 between the IRC, the

Gwich'in Tribal Council (GTC), and the federal and territorial governments. The AIP set out understandings on jurisdictions, intergovernmental relations, financing and the like, though important details remained to be settled. However, in early 2005, the GTC confirmed long-standing speculation about Gwich'in unease about the direction the enterprise was taking and announced that it was pulling out of the process. According to one close observer, "While many factors came into play in the [GTC's] decision to pursue separate agreements, issues around representation and uncertainty about the protection of rights through combined Aboriginal/public government had consistently arisen as prominent concerns during community consultations" (Irlbacher-Fox 2007, 164). The Inuvialuit continue to negotiate on their own, and in 2007 they reached a new self-government process and schedule agreement based on the abandoned GTC-IRC negotiations.

Throughout 2006, the IRC's small self-government secretariat conducted a broad consultation, holding community workshops on governance principles and possible models, ranging from an exclusive Inuvialuit government to a largely public government with guaranteed Inuvialuit representation. Late in the year, the IRC board directed its negotiators to pursue exclusive Inuvialuit self-government, with the possibility of guaranteed Inuvialuit seats on the local community councils that would deliver certain programs and services. This mandate recognizes that some aspects of the Inuvialuit self-government regime would likely operate in concert with other governments, most notably the Gwich'in, especially with respect to region-wide programs in health and education, where economies of scale are possible, and in the mixed communities of Aklavik and Inuvik.

As this last point suggests, relations with external governments critically affect the nature of Inuvialuit governance. Dealings with the Gwich'in have sometimes been difficult, but the inescapable reality is that they are neighbours; furthermore, the largest Inuvialuit community, Inuvik, is also the largest Gwich'in community. This makes political and administrative accommodation essential. In addition, of course, governance in the ISR is strongly affected by the approaches and activities of the federal government, the GNWT and — since the ISR includes the Yukon North Slope — the Yukon territorial government. On specific issues, the Inuvialuit may also find themselves dealing with Alaska, the Sahtu Dene and Métis (whose settlement area borders eastern portions of the ISR), and the GN.

One external issue of special import relates to claims implementation. As is evident from the analysis in Stephanie Irlbacher-Fox and Stephen J. Mills's chapter in this volume, land claims such as the IFA may be settled in the sense that an agreement has been accepted by all participants, but the process of implementing the various provisions of the claims is never-ending. Financial arrangements are often subject to dispute, since the federal government is responsible for funding many activities and processes mandated in the claims, and claimant groups often take a different view of appropriate funding levels than does Ottawa. Other issues of jurisdiction, process and policy arise under the rubric of implementation. In the ISR, implementation issues have generally not reached the level of conflict that characterizes such matters in Nunavut, but significant disagreements have occurred. For a period in the 1990s, the intergovernmental mechanism for discussing and reviewing implementation concerns broke down. In 1999, a revamped version of the Inuvialuit Final Agreement Implementation Coordinating Committee was established; it is composed of senior officials from the IRC, the Inuvialuit Game Council, the federal government, the GNWT and the Yukon territorial government, and it has made reasonable progress in managing implementation concerns. Still, Nellie Cournoyea, the IRC chair, did not mince words when responding to a report by the Auditor General of Canada that criticized Ottawa's implementation of the IFA: "[The report] has provided the Parliament and people of Canada with a clear message on the failings of the federal government in meeting their obligations over the past 23 years...The federal government continues to focus narrowly on the letter of its obligations under land claim agreements while refusing to accept any responsibility to work with the respective claimant groups in identifying and implementing measures that would support achievement of the spirit and intent and overall goals of the agreements" (Inuvialuit Regional Corporation 2007b).[22]

Political and Governance Issues in Nunavut

THE GOVERNMENT OF NUNAVUT FACES A PANOPLY OF CHALLENGES RELATED TO developing policies and delivering services to Nunavummiut and to building a government congruent with Inuit culture and values. Social problems are severe: overcrowded housing; limited employment opportunities; low levels of education; and high rates of substance abuse, domestic violence and suicide. These problems are long-standing and of such magnitude as to sometimes seem overwhelming. They are not the GN's doing, but the GN is responsible for reme- dying them. In its attempts to do so, the GN has been hampered not only by financial constraints but also by the difficulty of building and maintaining capac- ity in a way that meaningfully involves Inuit beneficiaries in their government.

Not the least of the governance problems in Nunavut is the fact that the tal- ent pool from which governments can draw is limited. Quite sensibly, many Inuit have no interest in becoming bureaucrats. Of those who do, many lack the requi- site training or credentials for such jobs, despite the GN's willingness to accept equivalencies (real-world experience in place of formal education or training). Inuit who are educated and able are in huge demand, so that in attempting to recruit and retain them, the GN finds itself in competition with land claims organizations, the federal and municipal governments and the private sector. Moreover, the GN is often unable to match the pay and benefits offered by its competitors.

At the political level, Nunavut has an extraordinary number of elected positions — municipal council members, MLAs, officials of NTI and the RIAs, leaders of local hunter and trapper organizations and regional wildlife organiza- tions — and of appointed positions on myriad boards, including the "institutions of public government" established under the claim. All told, the pool of talented Inuit is insufficient to fill the numerous political and administrative positions in Nunavut. The burnout that can afflict able Inuit called on too often to take on governance responsibilities only exacerbates the problem.

A key provision of the NLCA, article 23, requires government — which includes the federal government as well as the GN — to employ representative numbers of Inuit at all levels and in all occupational groupings. "Representative" here means at a ratio equivalent to the Inuit proportion of the population of Nunavut, currently about 85 percent. Article 23 sets out no timelines, though the GN and NTI both rank reaching the target as a high priority.

At start-up in 1999, roughly 44 percent of GN jobs were held by Inuit; within a few years, this figure had declined to 42 percent (Timpson 2006, 523). In 2007, the GN announced that, for the first time, overall Inuit employment exceeded 50 percent, the interim target set by Nunavut leaders shortly before divi- sion (Government of Nunavut 2007). This significant accomplishment is tem- pered by two important qualifications. First, the overall figure masks significant variation across levels of the bureaucracy. While nearly half (46 percent) of the very small executive cadre (38 positions across the GN) was Inuit, only 25 percent of the much larger senior- and middle-management groups (477 positions) was Inuit. A similar proportion of professional positions were staffed by beneficiaries, while in the paraprofessional and administrative support categories, Inuit were dominant (66 percent in the former, 92 percent in the latter).[23] In short, Inuit are concentrated in the lower, less influential ranks of the GN bureaucracy. Second, a remarkable 20 percent of all full-time GN positions were vacant, indicating the difficulty of recruiting and retaining staff and the magnitude of the capacity deficit.

Filling positions — with Inuit — and developing capacity are one facet of the GN's task in building a government for Nunavummiut. Another is ensuring that the government is Inuit in more than just the nominal sense. There is little doubt that the GN will be guided by Inuit politicians, since all MLAs and ministers are Inuit, or that it will have a high proportion of Inuit employees. The GN seeks to go beyond numerical control by incorporating Inuit values in government operations, and has thus committed itself to the principle of Inuit Qaujimajatuqangit (IQ, "that which has been long known by Inuit"). A precise specification of what this entails remains a work in progress, but it involves Inuit principles such as sharing and cooperation as well as an emphasis on flexibility rather than rigid adherence to formal bureaucratic procedures (for example, accepting that when the conditions are good, employees will go hunting or clam picking on a workday and make up the lost time later). IQ coordinators and committees have sprung up across the GN, and if the tangible products of their work are limited, they have clearly fostered a sense of the importance of imbuing the GN with Inuit culture and values (Timpson 2006). At the same time, "the pressure on public servants to prioritize the delivery of services over the development of long-term cultural projects makes it difficult for IQ to be developed in any systematic way" (Timpson 2006, 527).

A key element in the drive to build a truly Inuit government is language. The GN has set 2020 as the target for making Inuktitut the working language of government. On the one hand, this makes good sense, considering the centrality of language to cultural preservation and growth and the high levels of Inuktitut use in Nunavut. The 2006 Census confirmed that Nunavut Inuit continue to exhibit high levels of Inuktitut knowledge and use, though it also revealed perceptible declines in all indicators of language health. Eighty-three percent reported Inuktitut as their mother tongue (the first language they learned and still understood), down from 88 percent in 1996. For 64 percent — down from 76 percent a decade earlier — Inuktitut was the home language (spoken most often at home). Ninety-one percent said they could conduct a conversation in Inuktitut, down three percentage points from 1996 levels.[24]

On the other hand, it is an ambitious objective, given the almost negligible levels of Inuktitut capacity among non-Inuit employees. Language training is available for senior GN officials but has yet to make a perceptible difference in the use of Inuktitut by non-Inuit; the fact that many Inuit staff at lower levels of the bureaucracy have uncertain Inuktitut skills remains unaddressed. Deputy ministers are now given deadlines to acquire genuine Inuktitut fluency, resulting in at least one high-profile resignation of a deputy unable to comply with the policy.

In addition to fostering IQ and demanding language skills, the GN has embarked on another unique initiative to render it a distinctively Nunavut institution. All modern governments are to some degree decentralized by virtue of their networks of regional service delivery offices; the GN, like the GNWT before it, has posted staff to all but the tiniest communities. The designers of the Government of Nunavut sought a far more radical decentralization, however, with extensive headquarters functions — normally located in the capital city — widely dispersed in small communities across the territory. The objectives of this unprecedented plan included sharing the wealth represented by stable, high-wage, white-collar jobs (and associated infrastructure) beyond Iqaluit; rendering the GN more attractive to Inuit unwilling to leave their home communities for middle- and senior-level GN positions; and dispersing political and administrative power to local communities rather than having it concentrated in Iqaluit. Results of the decentralization initiative have been mixed, though on balance it has been at least as successful as the more conventional components of the GN (Hicks and White 2005).

Largely because of Nunavut's status as a territory, the GN's external relations are qualitatively different and significantly more complex than those of governance institutions in the ISR. With several GN departments spanning the remits of two or three departments in southern governments, ministers and senior public servants can find themselves spending inordinate amounts of time and energy preparing for and attending intergovernmental meetings. A recent analysis refers to the "external challenge" facing the GN: "how to maintain this focus [on key

Nunavut priorities] while working successfully within the Canadian federal system to keep Nunavut afloat fiscally and as a participant in federal-provincial-territorial policy deliberations" (Abele and Prince 2007, 183; see also Timpson 2004). As well, though Nunavut lacks what has been termed an "international legal personality," it nevertheless has an interest in, and to a limited degree participates in, international affairs (Loukacheva 2007, 105, chap. 5). Nunavut's links with Greenland are less extensive than one might imagine, given their proximity (scheduled air service between Iqaluit and Nuuk, the capital of Greenland, ceased several years ago), but the GN and several Nunavut organizations are involved in other international activities. NTI, for example, is a major presence in the Inuit Circumpolar Council (ICC, formerly the Inuit Circumpolar Conference) — as indeed is the IRC.

The GN's unique relationship with NTI also warrants mention. NTI does not behave like anything resembling an alternative government, though as the constitutionally mandated representative of some 85 percent of Nunavut's population, it is an undeniable force in Nunavut governance. The unusual nature of the relationship was underlined early in Nunavut's history, when the GN and NTI, with great fanfare, proclaimed their adherence to the Clyde River Protocol, a formal document setting out principles to guide interaction between the two. NTI and the GN often make common cause on important political or policy matters, especially when conflict arises with the federal government, but NTI does not hesitate to criticize the GN vigorously if it believes beneficiaries' interests are at stake.

By a wide margin, Nunavut's most important external relation is with the federal government. Not only is the GN all but totally dependent on Ottawa for revenue through the formula financing arrangement, but its hopes for badly needed infrastructure improvements (or, in most cases, infrastructure creation) also rest largely on the federal government. A major source of conflict has been the failure of negotiations to renew the implementation contract for the claim. Comprehensive land claims agreements are typically supplemented by detailed implementation plans or contracts that assign responsibility for implementing particular elements of the claims to the federal and territorial governments and to the Aboriginal land claims organization. Among the central features of these contracts are the dollar figures that Ottawa has agreed to contribute to specific claim objectives — training, operating the boards discussed in the next section and the like. The 10-year term of the initial NLCA implementation contract was up in 2003, but agreement has yet to be reached on a new contract, despite the fact that no less a personage than politician and jurist Thomas Berger was recruited to mediate the dispute. Interim funding arrangements are in place, but the lack of progress has generated bad feeling on all sides, symbolized by NTI's billion-dollar lawsuit against Ottawa for, in NTI's view, failing to live up to its obligations under the claim.

Claims Boards

N O ACCOUNT OF GOVERNANCE IN THE ISR AND NUNAVUT WOULD BE COMPLETE without reference to the distinctive and powerful comanagement and regulatory boards established under the IFA and the NLCA. These claims boards are neither federal or territorial government agencies nor species of Aboriginal self-government. They exist at the intersection of the three orders of government, guaranteeing Aboriginal participation and influence in what are termed "institutions of public government" (IPGs). Although technically only advisory bodies, they exercise significant power over a wide range of wildlife management issues and over the regulation of environmental processes, including approving or rejecting major resource extraction and infrastructure projects, such as those that involve mines, roads and pipelines.

The formal mandates, funding mechanisms, administrative support arrangements, legislative authorities and linkages with government and land claims organizations differ between the IFA and Nunavut boards, sometimes in minor ways, sometimes in significant ones. Perhaps the most notable illustration is that water licences in Nunavut are the purview of a claim-mandated institution, the Nunavut Water Board, whereas in the ISR they are dealt with by the preclaim NWT Water Board, whose offices are in Yellowknife.

The boards established under the IFA lack some of the formal powers of the Nunavut boards (hence the Nunavut leaders' insistence on holding out for boards "with teeth"), but they have amassed a solid record of competently promoting Inuvialuit interests. The record of the Nunavut IPGs is very mixed. The Nunavut Wildlife Management Board is one of the great Nunavut success stories, whereas others — the Nunavut Planning Commission and the Nunavut Water Board, for example — have experienced debilitating periods of dysfunction and internal strife.

A detailed comparison of the IFA and Nunavut boards is unnecessary here. However, it is important that we recognize that these boards, which have become the norm across the North in the wake of the land claims settlements, are truly distinctive and fundamentally different — in mandate, organization and clout — from anything in southern Canada.

Conclusion

THE CONSTANT AND RAPID CHANGE SUFFUSING NORTHERN GOVERNMENT AND POLITICS is a source of fascination and frustration for those of us attempting to follow them. The current governance regimes in Nunavut and the ISR look almost nothing like those that existed a mere 30 years ago. Over the next 10 years, both will doubtless evolve into something quite different again. Accordingly, conclusions based on the current state of affairs may have a limited shelf life. That said, let us conclude with a few observations based on the foregoing account of governance in the two regions.

Perhaps the most obvious conclusion is that governance in the North is profoundly different from that which is standard south of 60. To be sure, governments everywhere in Canada have many similar problems and opportunities, but (save in the northern parts of British Columbia, Quebec, and Newfoundland and Labrador, where comprehensive land claims have been settled) nowhere in the provinces do organizations enjoy anything remotely similar to the IRC's and NTI's interaction — formal and informal — with government or influence on government. And no government in southern Canada has attempted to imbue its policies and operations with a cultural orientation profoundly different from that of Western bureaucratic governance the way the GN has done with its IQ initiative. I could cite other differences, but the point is surely clear.

Far more than in most parts of Canada, the institutions and processes of governance in the ISR and Nunavut are in flux. Many of the changes under way are sweeping in scope and ambitious in objective, which amounts to nothing less than returning to the Inuvialuit and the Inuit control over their lives and their lands. Little wonder that in both regions the results reflect a mixture of success, failure and delay.

At first blush, it might seem that the Inuvialuit have enjoyed greater success in developing and operating their institutions of governance than the Inuit of Nunavut. On reflection, however, it becomes clear that this is not a straight-forward comparison. The Inuvialuit have had several advantages over the Inuit: a substantially longer time in which to sort out problems (and, to be sure, Inuvialuit governance has had its share of problems); a much smaller popula-tion and geographical territory; better, more readily realized economic prospects; and substantially fewer far-reaching governance responsibilities and challenges. Moreover, if the GN is struggling to develop capacity and to provide effective governance, it at least has the jurisdiction and authority to do so; Inuvialuit self-government, though apparently close to fruition, remains a goal rather than a reality.

Some form of Inuvialuit self-government will likely be realized in the near future. But what are the long-term prospects for governance in Nunavut and the ISR?[25] Much, of course, will depend on the demographic composition of these and other northern regions: will resource extraction ventures and other develop-ments trigger an influx of non-Aboriginal people, significantly diluting or even eliminating Inuit/Inuvialuit numerical domination of their regions, thereby increasing the pressure to establish stronger self-government institutions with wide jurisdictional scope? Possible demographic shifts aside, will self-govern-ment regimes evolve into something very different from the public governments in southern Canada and elsewhere in the North, or will they gradually converge, leaving nothing but a symbolic difference between the two? Once a constitution-al settlement among the peoples and the regions of the Northwest Territories is finally reached, what status will the ISR carve out for itself?

As their prominence throughout this chapter confirms, it is clear that the IRC, NTI and the regional Inuit associations in Nunavut will be key players in long-term political developments. Rather less clear is the role they will play. Will they develop cooperative partnerships with the institutions of public government and self-government, or will they evolve into parallel governments uneasily coex-isting with these institutions? Thus far, the experience of the land claims organi-zations in Nunavut and the ISR points to a future of partnership rather than to one of parallel governments, but it is not hard to imagine this changing. Should, for example, consensus politics in Nunavut and the NWT give way to a system dominated by political parties, the demands on the land claims organizations and the options open to them could change dramatically. Of course, the future gov-ernance roles of the IRC and NTI will, to an important degree, be determined by their access to resources (human as well as financial), their capacity to meet existing challenges and take on new ones, and, of course, their leadership.

Factoring such considerations into any comparison of the relative success or failure of governance in the ISR and Nunavut, either now or several decades down the road, underlines the salience of the fundamental point I made at the outset. Despite being adjacent to one another and being populated by very similar peoples and facing many of the same logistical, demographic, social and economic challenges, the two regions have often exhibited different political priorities and approaches, which, in turn, have produced quite different governance regimes. The lesson is clear: we in the south generalize about northern governance at our peril.

Notes

I wish to thank officials of the Northwest Territories Bureau of Statistics, the Inuvialuit Regional Corporation and Nunavut Tunngavik Incorporated for providing statistical data and other information. None bears any responsibility for my interpretations of the material.

1   The data used are based on the six Inuvialuit communities. Technically, as it lies just outside the boundaries of the ISR, in the Gwich'in Settlement Area, Inuvik is not an ISR community. However, since it contains the largest single concentration of Inuvialuit, not to mention the headquarters of the Inuvialuit political and economic organizations, I have treated it here as part of the ISR. Total population data are taken from the 2006 Census (accessed April 21, 2008, http://www.stats.gov.nt.ca/ Statinfo/ Census/census%2006/CommCounts_ 1981-2006.xls); the number of Inuvialuit is based on unpublished 2006 population estimates for Inuit persons prepared by the NWT Bureau of Statistics (virtually all "Inuit persons" in the ISR are Inuvialuit).

2   The ISR extends into Yukon, but this area has no permanent communities.

3   These data are taken from the 2006 Census; see note 1.

4   These data were provided by IRC officials.

5   This figure must be interpreted with particular caution, since Statistics Canada indicates problems with data reliability.

6   These data were provided by the NWT Bureau of Statistics.

7   In the NWT, 26.4 percent of Inuit 15 years of age and older reported that government transfers were their major source of income, as opposed to between 35.2 and 39.2 percent in Nunavut, Nunavik and Nunatsiavut. Were data available for just the ISR rather than the entire NWT, the difference would not likely be quite so pronounced, since the substantial numbers of Inuvialuit in the NWT living outside the ISR could be expected to have higher than average participation rates in the labour force.

8   For a detailed review of the components of the economy of the ISR, see Imperial Oil Resources Ventures Limited 2004.

9   These data are from the 2004 NWT Community Survey, as provided by the NWT Bureau of Statistics.

10 A 21-kilometre road connects the community of Arctic Bay with Nanisivik, site of an abandoned lead-zinc mine, where the federal government proposes to build Nunavut's first deep-water port.

11 Accessed April 21, 2008, http://www12.statcan.ca/english/census06/ data/popdwell/Table.cfm?T=101

12 In addition, with the closure of the Nanisivik mine, the population of this community declined to zero. As well, the 2006 Census indicates that the population of two tiny outposts, Bathurst Inlet and Umingmaktok, both declined from five to zero; but, given census rounding procedures, apparent changes in these figures have little meaning.

13 Statistics Canada, 2006 Census, cat. no. 97-551-XCB2006005.

14 For an overview of the Nunavut economy, see Conference Board of Canada 2001.

15 The Nunakput riding encompasses the communities of Holman, Paulatuk, Sachs Harbour and Tuktoyaktuk; two MLAs represent the Town of Inuvik; the riding of Mackenzie Delta comprises Aklavik and two Gwich'in communities.

16 The territorial governments already collect corporation taxes and personal income taxes from workers at the mines, oil wells and the like, as well as garnering benefits from spinoff economic activities. These revenues, however, pale by comparison with the monies generated by royalties.

17 For an extended discussion of devolution and revenue sharing in the NWT, see Douglas McArthur's chapter in to this volume.

18 The Nunavut Trust, which exists independently of NTI, is charged with managing and developing the monies received by the Inuit as part of the settlement of their claim.

19 These data were supplied by NTI officials.
20 It is worth bearing in mind that the pipeline is only part of what is termed the Mackenzie Gas Project, which would also include a massive feeder system of wells and pipelines throughout the ISR.
21 "Canada agrees that where restructuring of the public institutions of government is considered in the Western Arctic Region, the Inuvialuit shall not be treated less favourably than any other native group or native people with respect to the governmental powers and authority conferred upon them." "The Western Arctic Claim: The Inuvialuit Final Agreement" (1984), s.4 [3] (accessed April 21, 2008, http://www.ainc-inac.gc.ca/pr/agr/inu/wesar_e.html).
22 For the Auditor General's report, see Auditor General of Canada 2007.
23 These data were either taken or calculated from Government of Nunavut, Department of Human Resources 2007.
24 These data are from the 2006 Census.
25 The reflections in this and the following paragraph were stimulated by James Feehan's insightful comments át the Montebello conference on the ideas presented in this chapter and on Thierry Rodon and Minnie Grey's chapter in this volume.

References

Abele, Frances, and Michael Prince. 2007. "Constructing Political Spaces for Aboriginal Communities in Canada." In *Constructing Tomorrow's Federalism: New Perspectives in Canadian Governance*, edited by Ian Peach. Winnipeg: University of Manitoba Press.

Auditor General of Canada. 2007. "Inuvialuit Final Agreement." Chap. 3 of *Report to Parliament*, October. Accessed March 10, 2008. http://www.oag-bvg.gc.ca/internet/English/aud_ch_oag_2007_3_e_23827.html

Conference Board of Canada. 2001. *Nunavut Economic Outlook: An Examination of the Nunavut Economy*. Ottawa: Conference Board of Canada.

Government of Nunavut. 2007. "Inuit Employment within Government Increases to 50 Percent." Press release, October 1. Iqaluit: Government of Nunavut.

Government of Nunavut, Department of Human Resources. 2007. *Towards a Representative Public Service*. Iqaluit: Government of Nunavut. Accessed March 10, 2008. http://www.gov.nu.ca/hr/site/towardrepps.htm

Hicks, Jack, and Graham White. 2005. "Building Nunavut through Decentralization or Carpet Bombing It into Near-Total Dysfunction?" Paper presented at the annual meeting of the Canadian Political Science Association, June 4, London, ON.

Imperial Oil Resources Ventures Limited. 2004. "Nontraditional Land and Resource Use." In *Socio-economic Baseline*. Vol. 4 of *Environmental Impact Statement for the Mackenzie Gas Project*. [Submitted to the National Energy Board and the Joint Review Panel on the Mackenzie Gas Project.] Toronto: Imperial Oil Limited. Accessed February 29, 2008. http://www.mackenziegasproject.com/gtheProject/regulatoryProcess/applicationSubmission/Documents/MGP_EIS_Vol4_Section_6_S.pdf

Inuit Tapiriit Kanatami and Research and Analysis Directorate, Indian and Northern Affairs Canada. 2007a. "Levels and Sources of Individual and Household Level Income for Inuit in Canada, 1980-2000." Ottawa: Indian and Northern Affairs Canada.

———. 2007b. "Knowledge and Use of Inuktitut among Inuit in Canada, 1981-2001." Ottawa: Indian and Northern Affairs Canada.

Inuvialuit Regional Corporation. 2007a. *Board Summary* 12 (2). Inuvik: Inuvialuit Regional Corporation.

———. 2007b. "Report of the Auditor General: Chapter 3, Inuvialuit Final Agreement," press release, October 31. Inuvik: Inuvialuit Regional Corporation.

Irlbacher-Fox, Stephanie. 2007. "Self-
    Government and Social Suffering."
    Unpublished paper.
Loukacheva, Natalia. 2007. *The Arctic Promise:
    Legal and Political Autonomy of Greenland
    and Nunavut*. Toronto: University of
    Toronto Press.
Morrison, David. 2003. "Ingilraqpaaluk (A Very
    Long Time Ago)." In *Across Time and Tundra:
    The Inuvialuit of the Western Arctic*, edited by
    Ishmael Alunik, Eddie D. Kolausok, and
    David Morrison. Vancouver: Raincoast Books.
Nunavut Tunngavik Incorporated. 2006. "Annual
    Report."
Okalik, Hon. Paul. 2007. Speech presented at
    the IRPP conference "Art of the State IV:
    Northern Exposure," October 27,
    Montebello, QC.
Taylor, Glenn. 1997. "Former IRC Chair under
    Investigation." *News/North* (Yellowknife),
    August 15.
Timpson, Annis May. 2004. "The Challenges of
    Intergovernmental Relations for Nunavut."
    In *Canada: The State of the Federation 2002:
    Reconfiguring Aboriginal-State Relations*, edit-
    ed by Michael Murphy. Kingston and
    Montreal: McGill-Queens University Press.
_____. 2006. "Stretching the Concept of
    Representative Bureaucracy: The Case of
    Nunavut." *International Review of
    Administrative Sciences* 72 (4): 517-30.
White, Graham. 2006. "Traditional Aboriginal
    Values in a Westminster Parliament: The
    Legislative Assembly of Nunavut." *Journal of
    Legislative Studies* 12 (1): 8-31.
_____. 2007. "Local Government in the
    Canadian Territorial North: The Political
    Context." In *Federalism, Power, and the
    North: Governmental Reforms in Russia and
    Canada*, edited by John F. Young. Toronto:
    University of Toronto, Centre for European,
    Russian and Eurasian Studies at the Munk
    Centre for International Studies.

The Long and Winding
Road to Self-Government:
The Nunavik and
Nunatsiavut Experiences

N ORTHERN CANADIAN GOVERNANCE IS EVOLVING VERY RAPIDLY. THE SLOW PROCESS OF
decolonization that started in 1966 in the Northwest Territories with the
Carrothers Report and eventually led to the creation of Nunavut in 1999 has also
spread to provincial northern Quebec and northern Labrador (see Frances Abele's
chapter in this volume), giving birth to some very innovative models of governance.

Northern governments share a number of features: the territories over which
they have jurisdiction are very large and have very small populations; and they are vulnerable to external factors — to name a few, global warming, the opening of the Arctic
to ships, militarization and big projects (again, see Abele's chapter). In spite of this, the
observer is struck by the vast differences between them in governance arrangements.
In fact, from Alaska to Greenland, experiences in northern governance are strongly
shaped by the sociopolitical context of the particular region. Even in the case of
Canada's Inuit people, a population with one cultural and political tradition, the three
self-government experiences in existence or in the making — Nunavut, Nunatsiavut
and Nunavik — have very different institutional designs and political contexts.

In this chapter, we will look closely at two of these experiences in northern governance: in Nunavik, the northern part of Quebec; and in Nunatsiavut,
the northern part of Labrador. Nunavik has enjoyed a certain degree of administrative autonomy since the signing of the James Bay and Northern Quebec
Agreement (JBNQA) in 1975,[1] and it is now negotiating the creation of its own
regional government. The Nunatsiavut government was created in 2005, following ratification of the Labrador Inuit Land Claims Agreement.

Nunavik and Nunatsiavut differ from Nunavut in that they are both
located within provinces. This has an impact on their models of governance;

the territorial model used for Nunavut is not applicable. It also means that their governance arrangements are the result of a tripartite negotiation in which the provinces have most of the jurisdiction and the federal government plays a secondary role. We will focus primarily on the relations between Inuit organizations and provincial governments, since the outcome of the self-government negotiations was greatly dependent on these actors.

First we will look at the similarities. Both the Nunatsiavut and Nunavik projects have developed a non-Westminster model of governance based on an elected executive and on community involvement in the design of the governance model — an element especially strong in Nunatsiavut, but also present in Nunavik. And both are models of Inuit self-government.

However, the similarities stop there. Nunavik is a public government project for 11,000 citizens, while Nunatsiavut is mostly, but not exclusively, based on ethnicity and represents 6,500 beneficiaries. There is also a difference in the size of the territory these governments administer, which is clearly a reflection of the nature of their membership. Nunavik, as a public government, covers 500,000 square kilometres (one-fourth of Nunavut and almost one-third of Quebec), while Nunatsiavut covers only 72,520 square kilometres of land and 48,690 square kilometres of sea rights.

Furthermore, even though both governance models are located within provinces, the provincial contexts are very different. Newfoundland and Labrador did not recognize Aboriginal peoples for a long time, whereas Quebec has moved from a history of neglect to a keen interest. Clearly, the relationship between Nunavik and Quebec can be understood only in light of the sometimes competing, sometimes congruent quest for autonomy. We will explore these elements further.

The Long Road to Self-Government

Nunavik's Road to Self-Government

NUNAVIK IS THE INUIT REGION WHERE THE EARLIEST MODERN LAND CLAIMS TREATY WAS signed. It will be one of the last to obtain some form of self-government, since only an agreement in principle has been signed by the Governments of Canada and Quebec and Makivik Corporation; this took place on December 5, 2007.

The relationship between the Inuit and Quebec has gone through different stages — from neglect to intense interest, culminating in conflicting nationalisms.[2] It has finally settled into what might be called a partnership. Nunavik Inuit have also experienced profound internal dissension, followed by a reconciliation of diverging visions through democratic means. This process has been a vital step on the path to self-government. Finally, the Nunavik Inuit have had the longest experience of administrative autonomy, but at the same time they have had to overcome the very fragmented system of governance established by the JBNQA.

Nunavik is located in the northernmost part of Quebec (see map on following page). It is part of the territory that was added to the province under the *Quebec Boundaries Extension Act, 1912*. The passage of the Act did not have much of an effect on the Inuit, who were not informed of the change (Nungak 1995). In fact, no government wanted to be responsible for the Inuit of northern Quebec, and a quarrel arose between the provincial and federal governments over who should be accountable for their welfare. The dispute was finally settled in 1939 by the Supreme Court of Canada: the Inuit were declared to be Indians for the purposes of section 91(24) of the Constitution, and they therefore came under federal jurisdiction. Once again, the Inuit were not informed of the decision, and since the federal government did not intervene very often in their lives, they did not notice much of a change.

Change occurred during the Second World War with the establishment of military bases in Nunavik and after the war with the extension of the federal social net to the Inuit of northern Quebec. Strong incentives were also offered Inuit to move to permanent settlements (Duhaime 1983); in some cases, this meant relocation to the Far North.[3] These measures were all taken by the federal government — the Government of Quebec was not present during this period.

In fact, the Inuit of Quebec noticed that they were part of the province only in 1963, when René Lévesque, then minister of natural resources, created a government branch to develop this new northern territory: La Direction générale du Nouveau-Québec.[4] This sparked another disagreement with the federal government, which had started to provide schooling and social and medical relief to the Inuit. This period was marked by competition between the two levels of government, and in some villages, Inuit families could choose to send their children to either a provincial- or a federal-government-run school. For the first time, the Inuit became aware that they were part of both Canada and Quebec, and that the

Nunavik

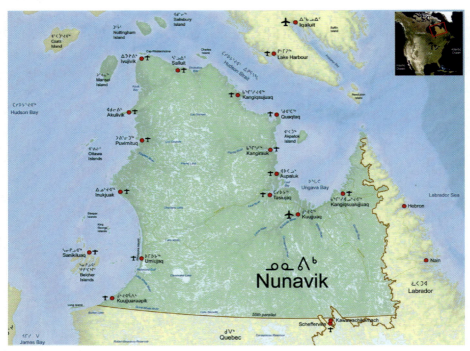

Source: Cartographic Services, Nunavik Research Centre, Makivik Corporation.

two levels of government were in competition with one another. These were confusing times for everybody.

In 1969, the quarrel between Quebec and the federal government led to the creation of a joint federal-provincial body known as the Neville-Robitaille Commission. It was mandated to determine which level of government should provide services to the Inuit. However, the commission's most striking aspect was that, for the first time, it asked the Inuit of what was now called Nouveau-Québec for their opinion. Some of their answers surprised the commissioners: a few Inuit strongly urged a transfer of federal power to their people so that they could establish a form of self-government.

However, two competing visions of self-government emerged. A more radical grassroots organization centred on the co-op movement and especially strong in the Hudson Bay region called for the creation of an Inuit government. A more pragmatic group based in the Ungava region and closer to Indian and Northern

Affairs Canada (INAC) asked only for a continued federal presence and some administrative autonomy. Both propositions went well beyond the Neville-Robitaille Commission's mandate.

The issue of Inuit autonomy resurfaced in 1973, during the negotiation of the JBNQA. The two viewpoints were still present, but the pragmatic vision prevailed. Three regional administrations were created — the Kativik Regional Government (KRG), the Kativik School Board (KSB) and the Nunavik Regional Board of Health and Social Services (NRBHSS) — and they provided a level of administrative autonomy to northern Quebec. The three administrations are still in place. Staffed mainly by Inuit, they have served as a valuable training ground, but they also constitute a fragmented model of governance: each administration has its own board of directors and is responsible to its parent Quebec government department. There is therefore little coordination between them, and this has at times led to conflict.

The proponents of self-government rejected this limited form of autonomy and created a dissident organization called Inuit Tungavingat Nunamini (ITN). Three villages — Puvirnituq, Ivujivik and Salluit — refused to endorse the JBNQA, and the prospect of self-government seemed well out of reach. However, René Lévesque, by then the premier of Quebec, offered renewed hope during a 1983 parliamentary commission on Aboriginal rights. ITN representative Eliyassi Sallualuk asked him, "If all existing groups of Nouveau-Québec decide to work together for the creation of such a government, could you tell them: OK, let's go?" Lévesque replied, "My answer is yes…It is quite simple: if the Inuit unify their approaches in the way of an autonomy within Québec, in order to have better management of their affairs, to pass laws in fields that concern them directly, to organize their life, we would be ready at once to discuss that with them and to accept this consideration. We could negotiate from this base whenever they want…We would be ready anytime but it is up to them to decide" (quoted in Nunavik Commission 2001, 17).

Lévesque's position was hardly surprising, given that his Parti Québécois government was trying to obtain more political autonomy, if not outright separation, from the Canadian federation. The Inuit were keenly aware of this situation, and it created a rapprochement between Quebec and the Inuit of Nunavik.

The dissidents and the organizations stemming from the JBNQA agreed to create a joint working group, called Ujjituijiit,[5] to consult Inuit communities and propose a plan for self-government; they also proposed the amalgamation of the

JBNQA-created institutions. But they could not resolve the differences that existed among them, and subsequently tabled two proposals: the first was that a constitutional committee be elected to develop a strategy for political autonomy. This committee would be funded by voluntary consumption taxes, clearly establishing it as a grassroots democratic initiative. The second proposal was that the committee be constituted of representatives from the different Inuit organizations and funded by those organizations — a more institutional approach to self-government. But no agreement was reached, and the Inuit asked the Quebec government to organize a referendum in Nunavik. The referendum was held in 1987, and the grassroots democracy option was chosen. When it came time to elect the members of the constitutional committee, the proponents of the second option were chosen to implement the first option. To some degree, this ensured the end of the dissension, since the two camps could both claim victory and admit defeat.

The Nunavik constitutional committee visited all communities to hear people's opinions and drafted a proposal for a constitution that was approved in a referendum held in 1991, the third since 1975. The Inuit were now reunited behind a common process, and negotiations could take place. The constitutional proposal was for the creation of a public regional government that would respect both provincial and federal laws. We should also note that it was at this time that Quebec agreed to use the name Nunavik instead of Nouveau-Québec — a very symbolic and significant change. The northern part of Quebec would no longer be considered a "new found" land that had yet to be conquered. Instead, it would be the land of the Inuit of Nunavik, inhabited by the Nunavimmiut (the suffix *miut* means "from" in Inuktitut; a Nunavimmiut is therefore somebody from Nunavik, whether Inuit or non-Inuit).

In 1995, as Quebec prepared for a second sovereignty referendum, the idea of creating a regional government for Nunavik took a back seat in Quebec political circles. The Inuit of Nunavik challenged this: during the referendum campaign, they made it clear that if Quebec could choose to separate from Canada, then Nunavik could choose to separate from Quebec. To assert this right, Makivik organized its own referendum one week before the Quebec referendum; 96 percent of Inuit voted in favour of remaining within Canada in the event of Quebec separation. This was a strong statement. It demonstrated to Quebec sovereignists that they needed Inuit support if they wanted an independent Quebec to include Nunavik.

The sovereignist side lost the referendum, and in 1996 Lucien Bouchard became Quebec premier. The Nunavik negotiations had to be started again from scratch. Finally, in 1997, Bouchard and Zebedee Nungak, the president of Makivik, agreed to set up a commission to study and recommend the establishment of a Nunavik government. The stage was set for yet another round of negotiations, since a policy recognizing Aboriginal people's inherent right to self-government was adopted by the federal government in 1995.[6]

In December 1999, after an agreement had been reached between the federal and Quebec governments and the Nunavik organizations, the Nunavik Commission got to work. Commission members travelled to all the Nunavik communities, and in its final report the commission recommended the creation of a public government in Nunavik. Real negotiations began, and an agreement in principle (AIP) for the creation of a Nunavik regional government was initialled in the summer of 2007 by the negotiators. The three political parties represented in the Quebec National Assembly supported the deal, and the AIP was signed on December 5, 2007.

The Inuit of Nunavik are now very close to reaching a final agreement that would allow them to create a Nunavik regional government. Although Nunavik would remain part of both Quebec and Canada, this is nonetheless a form of the self-government that the Inuit have been seeking since 1969. Throughout this process, they have had to overcome deep internal divisions through very democratic means. Nunavik is the only Inuit region to have resolved open dissension through a democratic process — it has held four referendums since 1975, as well as two public consultations on the self-government project (the Nunavik Constitutional Committee and the Nunavik Commission). The Inuit of Nunavik are creating a new type of jurisdiction in Canada: a regional government inside a province that allows for political decentralization and provides a model for the decolonization of the provincial North. But they have had to contend with the fact that Quebec nationalism has led to a gradual focus shift on the part of the federal government away from the Nunavik project and toward Quebec provincial politics.

Nunatsiavut's Road to Self-Government

The Labrador Inuit have a distinct history. Their first contact was with the Basques, followed by the French traders, but the most influential outsiders were Moravians — members of a Protestant church from central Europe with a strong missionary tradition — who established missions in Labrador Inuit communities in the late eighteenth century and maintained them until the beginning of the twentieth century. These missions provided schooling, medical assistance and trading facilities.

In this way, Labrador's experience is closer to Greenland's than it is to that of other Canadian Inuit regions, where, for a long time, trading company employees and whalers were practically the only foreign presence. When Newfoundland entered the Canadian federation, in 1949, the services provided by the Moravians were taken over by the provincial and federal governments.

The Labrador Inuit are the southernmost Inuit (see map on following page), and the patterns of colonization that occurred in their territory were more intensive than those in the other Inuit regions. They had experienced a great deal of contact with fishermen by as early as 1540. Over time, some of these fishermen settled in Inuit communities, creating a category of non-Inuit or part-Inuit long-time residents. Some of them adopted the ways of the Inuit and were recognized as Kablunângajuit ("partly White men"); some fell outside the Inuit community and were known as Métis or new residents.

Nunatsiavutmiut inhabit a province that for a long time did not recognize the existence of Aboriginal people in its territory. In 1948, when Newfoundland negotiated its terms of union with Canada, it was agreed that no mention of the province's Aboriginal people would be made (Tanner et al. 1994; Hanrahan 2003). This prevented negotiations for self-government. However, the Labrador Inuit were later recognized by the federal government, and their land claim application was accepted in 1978. Newfoundland agreed to sit at the negotiating table in 1980, but only under two conditions: there would have to be a cost-sharing agreement with Ottawa and an extinguishment clause (Haysom 1992). It took another nine years for active negotiations to get under way. Finally, in 1990, the three parties concluded a framework agreement. Negotiations for an AIP got off to a slow start, but the 1994 announcement of the Voisey's Bay project — a mining venture on land claimed by the Inuit of Labrador — greatly sped up the process. At first, the province refused to include the area in the land claim negotiation and quickly approved the application to build roads and airports. The Labrador Inuit and the Innu Nation applied for, and eventually received, a court injunction against the building of mine access roads. In order to avoid stalling the development of the mine, the three negotiating parties agreed to fast-track negotiations (Alcantara 2007). The AIP was signed in 1999 and ratified in 2001, and a final agreement was ratified in 2005. The Nunatsiavut transitional government was put into place in 2005, and the first elections were held in October 2006.

Labrador Inuit Land Claims Agreement

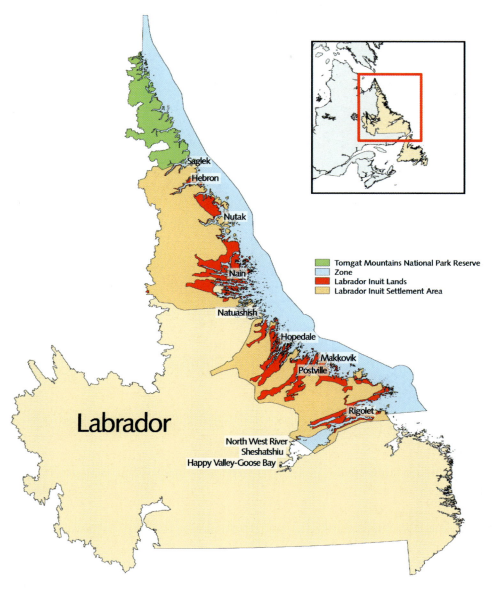

- Torngat Mountains National Park Reserve
- Zone
- Labrador Inuit Lands
- Labrador Inuit Settlement Area

Saglek
Hebron
Nutak
Nain
Natuashish
Hopedale
Makkovik
Postville
Rigolet
North West River
Sheshatshiu
Happy Valley-Goose Bay

Labrador

Source: Indian and Northern Affairs Canada, reproduced with the permission of the Minister of Public Works and Government Services.

During the land claim negotiation, the Labrador Inuit Association decided to work on a constitution for the new government and to allow the Labrador Inuit to participate fully in the process. The constitution was drafted by a small committee and sent to all the Inuit of Labrador. A public consultation was organized, and a second version was drafted, which was sent to everybody for further comment. A final version was submitted to a referendum and approved in 2002.[7]

Governance in Nunavik and Nunatsiavut

WE HAVE SEEN THAT THE INUIT OF LABRADOR AND THE INUIT OF NUNAVIK HAVE different histories and, more importantly, live in different provincial contexts. This has had a direct impact on their self-government arrangements. In this section, we present their governance models — established in the case of Nunatsiavut, and projected in the case of Nunavik.

The Nunavik Model

The JBNQA legacy

The 1975 James Bay and Northern Quebec Agreement was the first modern treaty signed in Canada. In many ways, it is at odds with other land claims agreements, because it was developed when Canadian land claims policy was still in its early stages. In 1973, the federal government had set up the Office of Native Claims and announced its willingness to receive land claims proposals, but the policy was drafted after the signing of the JBNQA. Indeed, in several respects, the JBNQA — with its provisions for economic development, health service delivery and income support for subsistence activities — resembles a collective agreement more than a land claims agreement. It is also very unusual because it encompasses three different Aboriginal groups: the Inuit, the Cree and the Naskapi.

The JBNQA has created a complex governance system centred on three regional public administrations: the Kativik School Board (KSB), the Nunavik Regional Board of Health and Social Services (NRBHSS) and the Kativik Regional Government (KRG). These administrations operate independently. Each has its own board of directors and is responsible only to its parent provincial department. The KRG has the most varied jurisdictions; it constitutes a form of supramunicipal government in charge of economic development, employment and training, public security, renewable resources, scientific research, public works, transportation, telecommunications and recreation. The KSB is in charge of the education system north of the 55th parallel; the NRBHSS is responsible for health care and supervises two regional hospitals. Each administration has its own finance department, human resources department, accounting system and collective agreements with a variety of unions. This is indeed a very fragmented model of governance.

The funding of the administrations is also very fragmented. Each is funded through a series of transfer agreements with its parent department and also receives financial support through special programs. The KRG gets some block funding from the Quebec municipal affairs department, but it finances its activities through multiple funding agreements with various Quebec and federal departments, each with its own reporting requirements. At present, aggregate funding from all levels of government is approximately $400 million, with Quebec contributing 78 percent of the total.

Besides these public governance entities, the JBNQA has created some comanagement boards — notably, for wildlife management and environmental assessment. Each board is composed of an equal number of Aboriginal representatives and government representatives. The wildlife management board — a fairly cumbersome institution in which two levels of government and three Aboriginal groups are represented — has not proven to be a very effective forum (Rodon 2003). The environmental assessment process is slightly better, since Nunavik has its own environmental regime.

Finally, as has occurred with all land claims settlements, an organization has been created to manage the settlement money and defend Aboriginal culture and rights. The Makivik Corporation, as it is called, also acts as an economic development agency and owns two northern airlines. In Nunavik, Makivik is a very powerful actor, politically as well as economically.

The dissident movement is another legacy of the JBNQA. The cooperative movement and the northern Hudson Bay villages have been the dissidents' stronghold. Three of these villages refused to sign the JBNQA in 1975, and one, Puvirnituq, has not yet agreed to land selection.

Nunavik's socio-economic profile

Since Nunavik is a public government, we will mostly present data for all the Nunavimmiut. However, since the Inuit constitute 91 percent of the population, there is not always a significant difference. Nunavik has 10,417 inhabitants living in 14 coastal communities from eastern Hudson Bay to Ungava Bay.[8] The biggest community is Kuujjuaq, which has close to 2,000 residents. Three other communities have more than 1,000 inhabitants: Inukjuak, Puvirnituq on Hudson Bay and Salluit on Baffin Strait.

The population of Nunavik is very young (39 percent are under the age of 14) and growing rapidly. This creates important challenges in terms of education, training and job creation. Like economies everywhere in the North, that of Nunavik is mostly dependent on government activities, which represent 50 percent of the region's domestic product (Duhaime 2007).

The employment structure in Nunavik is composed of 5,500 positions (3,189 of which are full time); 56 percent are held by Inuit (66 percent, if the Raglan mine is excluded from the data). Of these 5,500 jobs, 53 percent are in the public and para-public sector, 37 percent are in the private and cooperative sector and 10 percent are in the nonprofit sector (Kativik Regional Government 2006). Nunavik has a very strong cooperative sector. La Fédération des coopératives du Nouveau-Québec has been an agent for economic development and capacity building in Nunavik communities and is the largest nongovernment employer in Nunavik, with 300 employees, mostly Inuit (99 percent). Other key nongovernment actors are Makivik and its subsidiary companies, which employ a large number of Nunavimmiut. And the Raglan mine is also an important employer, with 550 workers; but only 80 (16 percent) are Inuit, even though the company has trained over 350 Inuit workers. Most of its other workers are from outside the region. In the public sector, Inuit constitute 99 percent of the employees at the local government level and 49 percent at the regional government level (Kativik Regional Government 2006).

Nevertheless, earnings in Nunavik are lower than they are in the rest of Quebec and the other northern territories, especially for the Inuit. In addition, Nunavimmiut support larger families and pay prices that are up to 60 percent higher than paid by people living in the rest of Canada. Hunting and fishing allow them to make ends meet. According to a recent survey, 81 percent of Inuit adults in Nunavik participate in harvesting activities — the highest percentage of all the Inuit regions (Statistics Canada 2001b).

The job creation rate is quite high in Nunavik, but the employment needs of its young population are considerable, so the unemployment rate also remains high. The proportion of women in Nunavik's regular workforce — 42 percent — is on the rise (Kativik Regional Government 2006), as it is in most Inuit jurisdictions.

The cost of public service delivery is high, as it is everywhere in the North, and funding it adequately is always a challenge. This is even more difficult in a context of fragmented governance that does not allow for economies of scale. Here, again, in spite of higher spending per capita on service delivery, the standard of living is not improving (Duhaime 2007).

More than half the population of Nunavik (53.5 percent) has less than a high-school-level education, compared to 23.5 percent of the Quebec population as a whole (Duhaime 2007). However, the proportion of Nunavik inhabitants aged 15 and older attending school is similar to the province-wide proportion, and this is an encouraging statistic. It indicates an interest among the young in staying in school, and it could be a sign that the new generation has a more positive outlook toward formal learning and is on its way to acquiring a better education.

Social problems are fairly prevalent in Nunavik. There is a very high suicide rate — 181 per 100,000 inhabitants (Statistics Canada 2001a), the second-highest rate among Canadian Inuit (see Jack Hicks's chapter in this volume). Drug and alcohol abuse and child abuse are also important problems in the region (Duhaime 2003).

Nunavik has a higher percentage of Inuktitut speakers than any other Inuit region: 99 percent of Nunavik Inuit are able to sustain a conversation in Inuktitut, 97 percent consider it their mother tongue and 94 percent use it at home. These numbers are very strong, but there has been a 1 percent decrease since the 1996 Census in the categories of mother tongue and use at home (Statistics Canada 2006).

The new self-government project

Nunavik self-government is clearly the fruit of many years of intense negotiation, consultation and consensus building. Its parameters have also been shaped by Quebec politics and the province's fear of losing this northern territory. Because the self-government model has had to conform to the JBNQA, it is based on the amalgamation of the three regional administrations (the KSB, NRBHSS and KRG) and the creation of an elected assembly and a responsible Nunavik government. However, unlike the situation in Nunavut, in Nunavik political powers will not stem from an act of

Parliament. Instead, the Quebec Legislative Assembly will create the first regional government within a Canadian province — a first for the Canadian federation.

The AIP creates a process leading to the amalgamation of the three administrations and the election of the first Nunavik assembly and executive council. The transfer of additional powers will then be initiated and a new funding agreement negotiated. An incremental approach has been chosen not only to alleviate the fears of the provincial government but also to overcome resistance to change among the three regional administrations, which have been in place for a long time.

Nunavik's legislative assembly will have at least 21 members: 15 locally elected community representatives (that is, one for each community, plus one for communities over 2,000),[9] one Naskapi representative and five members of the executive elected by all the Nunavimmiut. The leader of the executive will be elected from one list and the other members of the executive from another list. Portfolios for the four members of the executive will be assigned by the leader.

We should make two observations here. First, Nunavik clearly falls outside the Westminster parliamentary model, since its executive is directly elected; nor is it a presidential model, since the executive, including the president, is part of the legislative assembly — a feature of a parliamentary regime. This is therefore an original, hybrid model of governance. Our second observation is that an effort has been made to balance community and regional interests. This is also a departure from the Westminster model, according to which communities have no role in governance. In fact, this model is inspired by the system of governance used by the Makivik Corporation, and so it has the intentional benefit of being familiar to the Nunavimmiut.

Nunavik's assembly will have special advisory bodies, which must be consulted on matters related to their respective fields of expertise. These organizations are already in place: the Avataq Cultural Institute (culture, elders and heritage), Taqramiut Nipingat Incorporated (communication), the Saputiit Youth Association and a set of local education committees.

The Nunavik government will first have jurisdiction over the three amalgamated administrations: health, education and regional affairs. Over time, it will acquire new fields of jurisdiction from the other two levels of government. In the first phase of its implementation, the Nunavik government will inherit the multiple funding agreements. However, negotiations will be held to develop a new funding regime in phase 2 of the implementation. This regime may include some block funding for recurrent programs and services.

Nunavik's strengths and challenges

At present, the Nunavik government is only a project, and it is hard to assess the new model of governance that it will establish, but we can identify its potential strengths and the challenges it faces. Nunavimmiut have a long history of resolving dissension through democratic processes. They have had more political education (four referendums and two consultations) than Inuit in any other region and are therefore well prepared for self-government. Furthermore, they have had extensive experience in managing regional public administrations and in providing services. Fifty percent of Nunavik's public administration is already staffed by Inuit, and their presence is especially strong at the management and executive levels.

Like Nunavut, Nunavik will have a public government. The choice was not an easy one, and some Inuit did express a preference for an ethnic form of governance. However, this was not an option. Quebec has always insisted on a public model of governance because it is inclusive — it avoids making a distinction between two categories of citizen (Duhaime 1992). We should note that like the Inuit of Nunavut, the Nunavimmiut of Inuit descent are also beneficiaries of a land claim agreement and therefore have access to special programs run by Inuit organizations.

The incremental process set up by the AIP — transition (phase 1), amalgamation of the existing public administrations and the election of a legislative assembly and an executive council (phase 2), and the devolution of additional powers (phase 3) — should facilitate the establishment of the new regional government. But the challenges related to this process are numerous. Amalgamating the three regional administrations, with their differing organizational cultures and long histories, will be a difficult task. Relations between the administrations have not always been good, and there is still some mistrust. In order to avoid problems, the first step will be to merge the boards of directors of these three administrations, which will eventually be replaced by the legislative assembly and the Nunavik government. This will leave their internal administrative structures, most of the positions and all of the financial transfer agreements unaffected during the first phase.

Ensuring that Inuit culture is protected will also be an important challenge. The majority of Nunavimmiut are Inuit, and the new governance model has been designed in response to their aspiration for self-government. At present, no problems exist, but the Inuit could lose their majority status due to an influx of southern workers. There is, however, some protection for Inuit rights under the JBNQA and through Makivik. As in Nunavut, there is in Nunavik a need for a public service that

reflects the population it serves. Currently, 50 percent of the Nunavik public service
is Inuit — far from the target of 90 percent. There are two ways to improve this situation: through education, and by making the public administration "Inuit friendly."
We have seen that education levels are not very high in Nunavik, and it is not easy
to attract Inuit to public administration, as shown by the experience in Nunavut.

There will also be challenges directly related to governance. The model
chosen for Nunavik is unusual, but it can work, provided no conflict arises
between the executive and legislative branches. Relations between the new government and Makivik, an organization with extensive political and economic
clout in Nunavik, could also give rise to problems. This situation is very similar to one faced in Nunavut: Nunavut Tunngavik Incorporated and the
Government of Nunavut signed a document — entitled *Iqqanaijaqatigiit:
Working Together* — that looks very much like an intergovernmental agreement
in order to map out their relations (Government of Nunavut and Nunavut
Tunngavik Incorporated 2004). The status of the Nunavik community will also
have to be resolved; that status is determined by provincial legislation,[10] and
only Quebec's Department of Municipal Affairs and Regions can intervene in
the event of mismanagement. This means that the new Nunavik regional government will have no authority over the Nunavik communities, but it will be
able to provide guidance and assistance.

Yet another challenge could be posed by relations with neighbouring First
Nations. Nunavik encompasses a huge tract of land used by the Cree, Naskapi and
Innu. At present, relations between the Nunavimmiut and the Cree are quite good,
and the Grand Council of the Cree supports the creation of Nunavik. However,
relations with the Naskapi community — which includes just 590 people — are
very tense. The Naskapi were not included in the JBNQA negotiations, but in 1978
they signed the Northeastern Quebec Agreement, which gives them hunting rights
on the territory that will be under the Nunavik government's control. They currently have one seat on the KRG council. The AIP grants one seat in Nunavik's legislative assembly to a Naskapi representative and foresees the creation of a bilateral
committee through which Nunavik and Naskapi representatives will advise the
new government on the Naskapi area. However, this has been insufficient to alleviate the Naskapi's fears, and they have started lobbying government to stop the
creation of Nunavik. To date, neither Quebec City nor Ottawa has responded to
their demands, but there is always the threat of a court injunction. This problem

must be resolved, because Naskapi hunting grounds will be encompassed by Nunavik, and the new government will have to find a way to accommodate its Naskapi minority.

The Nunatsiavut Model

The Inuit of Labrador negotiated self-government at the same time as they settled their land claim. They chose an ethnic model of governance — the one originally chosen by Canada's Aboriginal peoples — because the demographic balance did not favour them and a public model would not guarantee them control of the new government. The ethnic model also allows for extraterritorial membership, and since half the Labrador Inuit live outside the settlement area, a public governance model was not practical.

The Labrador Inuit do not have as much experience in administrative autonomy as the Nunavik Inuit, but they have administered a number of programs and services over the years — notably, in post-secondary education and in health through the creation of the Labrador Inuit Health Commission in 1990. The Labrador Inuit are thus experienced in program management and service provision.

The Nunatsiavut government is slowly being put into place. In 2005, just after the signing of the final agreement, a transitional government made up of the former Labrador Inuit board of directors was established. The first local and legislative assembly elections took place in 2006, and a new president will be elected in 2008. The Nunatsiavut government has its own constitution, which was approved by the Labrador Inuit in a 2002 referendum.

Nunatsiavut's socio-economic profile

Nunatsiavut encompasses only five communities. Nain is the largest, with 1,155 people. The others are much smaller: Hopedale has 559 inhabitants; Makkovik, 384; Rigolet, 317; and Postville, 215. The Inuit constitute the vast majority of the populations (averaging 90 percent) of all these communities. There are also sizeable Inuit populations in Happy Valley-Goose Bay (1,095) and Northwest River (195), but both communities are outside Nunatsiavut (Statistics Canada 2001a). This poses a special governance challenge, since half the beneficiaries live outside the settlement area. The Nunatsiavut government provides services to a total of 6,500 beneficiaries. The Labrador Inuit have a different age structure from Inuit in other regions: there are fewer people under 14 and more in the 45-to-64 and the over-65 age categories. Still, the Labrador Inuit population is younger than the Canadian one (Inuit Tapiriit Kanatami and Research and Analysis Directorate 2006a).

In 2000, the major source of individual income was employment, at 57 percent. This is the lowest rate of all the Inuit regions (Inuit Tapiriit Kanatami and Research and Analysis Directorate 2006a). This figure does not take into account the Voisey's Bay project — the percentage is actually much higher, since approximately 110 Inuit are now employed by the project. Government employs 300 people at all levels; more than 80 percent are Inuit. Another 200 to 250 people work in fisheries. The education level among the Labrador Inuit is higher than it is among the Inuit in other regions, according to a survey conducted by Indian and Northern Affairs Canada on Inuit community well-being (Senécal and O'Sullivan 2007).

There is little statistical research on social problems in Nunatsiavut, but the suicide rate is an alarming indicator: at 239 per 100,000, the rate is higher than in any other Canadian Inuit region (Statistics Canada 2001a). This figure should be considered with caution, however, since we are dealing with a very small population.

In terms of language preservation, 27 percent of Labrador Inuit can sustain a conversation in Inuktitut, 22 percent consider it their mother tongue and only 7 percent speak it at home (Statistics Canada 2006). Among all the Inuit regions, Nunatsiavut has one of the lowest percentages of Inuktitut speakers, and if we compare these numbers to those from the 1996 Census, we see that the percentage of Labrador Inuit able to sustain a conversation in Inuktitut remains the same, but there is a two-percentage-point decrease in the two other categories. By comparison, in Nunavut there has been an increase of two percentage points in mother-tongue speakers since the 1996 Census (Statistics Canada 1996). It is too early to relate this to self-government, but this is an encouraging trend, and it could emerge in Nunatsiavut.

The Nunatsiavut governance structure

Community governments constitute the basis of the Nunatsiavut governance model. There are five such governments — in Nain, Hopedale, Makovik, Rigolet and Postville. They have mixed representation, with a maximum of 25 percent of the seats allotted to new residents and the rest to Inuit. Members of a third category, made up of old residents, can choose to vote on either the Inuit list or the new residents list. The AngajukKât ("community leader") has to be Inuit. There are also two Inuit community corporations that represent the interests of Inuit living outside the settlement area, one for Northwest River and one for Happy Valley-Goose Bay.

Nunatsiavut's legislative assembly provides very strong representation for the region's communities. Nunatsiavut is divided into seven constituencies: each of the five villages in the settlement area and, outside the settlement area, Northwest River/Happy Valley-Goose Bay and the rest of Canada.[11] Each constituency has one MLA for every 1,000 voters, up to a maximum of four. The five AngajukKât and the two Inuit community corporation chairmen are also members of the assembly. Thus, each community has at least two representatives; one is elected directly, and the other is the local AngajukKât.

The president of Nunatsiavut is directly elected by all the Nunatsiavutmiut and has to speak Inuttitut,[12] a condition that eliminates 73 percent of the Nunatsiavutmiut. The president is a member of the legislative assembly. The first minister is an ordinary member of the assembly nominated by the assembly and appointed by the president. The rest of the executive is nominated by the first minister from among ordinary members and then appointed by the president. With a directly elected president, we are clearly outside the Westminster model yet again. However, the assembly also has important powers, since it chooses the first minister as a way of avoiding an overly powerful executive.

Nunatsiavut, like Nunavik, has taken an incremental approach to governance. At the time of its creation, the Nunatsiavut government inherited the powers and responsibilities of the former Labrador Inuit Health Commission and the Labrador Inuit Association. In the health sector, the Nunatsiavut government administers seven core programs; these deal with mental health, addictions, community health and communicable disease control, child care and child development, home and community care, environmental health and noninsured health benefits. The land claim agreement has allowed the Nunatsiavut government to assume a greater role in health care, and a review of provincial and federal services and programs is presently under way.

The Nunatsiavut government also has full jurisdiction over the education system in Inuit communities, but at present it administers only the programs inherited from the Labrador Inuit Association (that is, the post-secondary education program and the various training programs aimed at improving the employability of the Labrador Inuit).

Financing Nunatsiavut

The Nunatsiavut government is financed through a $27-million fiscal agreement with the federal government. Additional revenues are generated through property taxes, federal excise and personal income taxes shared by the Government of Canada, business income, investment income and royalties paid by the Voisey's Bay mine. The province does not contribute any funds, but negotiations for a fiscal financing agreement with the province started in 2007.

Nunatsiavut's strengths and challenges

Nunatsiavut is the only Inuit ethnic government in Canada. This is advantageous for the Labrador Inuit in two important ways: it allows them to focus on protecting and advancing their culture and, in terms of governance, it helps them to avoid the kind of tension that typically arises between land claims organizations (such as Nunavut Tunngavik Incorporated or Makivik Corporation) and governments. In fact, the Government of Nunatsiavut has taken over the Labrador Inuit Association and manages the settlement money. This brings more resources to the new government and prevents conflict between rival institutions. It also allows the new government to establish its jurisdiction over the Nunatsiavutmiut living outside the claim area, thus creating a nonterritorial form of governance.

However, ethnic governance also creates challenges. It fosters divisions inside communities, since only beneficiaries can receive government services. In a small community, where many people share a lifestyle, this can be a difficult issue to resolve, and it is compounded by the eligibility rule that bars a non-Inuit spouse from becoming a land claim beneficiary. An effort has been made to take into account the interests of new residents, but only at the community level. One of the most important drawbacks of the ethnic model of governance linked to land claims settlements is that it tends to create beneficiaries instead of citizens. Beneficiaries have rights, while citizens have not only rights but also a duty to their community. This issue is not yet noticeable in Nunatsiavut, but in the long term it could create governance challenges if the ethnic government does not create a sense of citizenship among its constituents.

The other specificity of Nunatsiavut is the strong community representation in its model of governance. In fact, the only regionally elected politician is the president. All other members of the legislative assembly are elected at the community level, with the exception of the representative of Canada, who is elected by Labrador Inuit living outside Labrador. This can be seen as a strength, since Inuit traditional governance has always been locally based, but it might also make it difficult to achieve regional consensus among local and special interests.

Nunatsiavut is very small in terms of both population (6,500) and area (72,250 square kilometres), and the limits on its human and natural resources have posed certain challenges. So far, the incremental approach that the Labrador Inuit have taken to governance has yielded good results, and the opening of the Voisey's Bay mine has created major employment opportunities. However, these jobs will last only as long as the mine, so they might not contribute to long-term development. In that sense, Nunatsiavut, like every small nation, is highly dependent on — and vulnerable to — external factors (Rodon and Forest 1997).

Another challenge facing Nunatsiavut is that more than half its constituents live outside its territory. It has sought to address this by establishing two Inuit corporations to provide services to these constituents and by creating two extraterritorial constituencies to allow them to vote. Still, this is a fairly modest level of representation for such a large proportion of the Labrador Inuit population.

Nunatsiavut has been quite successful at Inuit staffing, with a rate of 80 to 90 percent.[13] While this is undeniably an impressive achievement, it can be explained by two factors: Labrador Inuit have a higher level of education than Inuit in other regions, and the new government has taken over programs formerly administered by the Labrador Inuit Association and the Labrador Inuit Health Commission. But Nunatsiavut faces an important test in the area of language preservation. Use of Inuttitut is very limited among the Labrador Inuit. This is a major problem for the new government; for one thing, since Nunatsiavut's president must speak Inuttitut, the general lack of Inuttitut speakers narrows the field of eligible candidates for the post.

The new government has a good relationship with the Innu Nation of Labrador, and the two communities make an effort to maintain it. The same cannot be said for the Métis, who have challenged the creation of Nunatsiavut in court. This issue is still unresolved.

Conclusion

N UNAVIK AND NUNATSIAVUT HAVE FOLLOWED VERY DIFFERENT PATHS TO INUIT SELF-government. As we have seen, this is due to the diverse historical, political and institutional contexts that characterize these two regions. This observation also applies to the regions of Nunavut and Inuvialuit, and it could even be extended to include Inuit governance in Alaska and Greenland. In many cases, however, the impetus for the settlement of land claims and the subsequent establishment of local forms of governance has been created by resource development projects. Yet, whatever path they have chosen, the Inuit people have shown remarkable adaptability, pragmatism and persistence in their quest for self-government; they have been able to — or are about to — acquire self-government in most of their ancestral territories.

There are some key similarities between Nunavik and Nunatsiavut. Both have chosen an incremental approach to governance: the new government initially exercises only the powers exercised by the former regional administrations, then it gradually acquires additional powers, thus allowing for a smoother transition to self-government. Both regions also take an innovative approach to governance — the architects of their new governments might not have set out to break new ground, but they were compelled to by circumstance. The self-government arrangements put in place in Nunavik and Nunatsiavut have little in common with mainstream governance in Canada or even governance in Nunavut. This capacity for innovation should not be underestimated. It could be fostered in southern Canada to create a more decentralized mode of governance.

The innovator's path is not always an easy one. We will have to wait to see how these new models of governance evolve. There are grounds for optimism: some achievements have already been realized, and the long and very public process of building a new form of government has increased the level of political education among inhabitants of the regions. However, there are also numerous challenges. The northern economies are very dependent on resource development, with its cycles of boom and bust. Nunatsiavut and Nunavik are currently benefiting from mining projects, which have had a significant economic impact, but mining is not a sustainable mode of development. Another challenge will be to raise levels of training and education, although there have been some data showing improvement in this area, especially in Nunavik. Social problems are also prevalent in northern communities, where rates of suicide and substance abuse are alarmingly high. It would be nice to think that self-government could provide a way to effectively address these issues, but we know from the Nunavut experience that it is not that easy.

Global warming and the resultant opening of the Arctic to shipping and competing sovereignty claims present another important challenge. Here, again, it is difficult to predict the role Nunatsiavut and Nunavik will play, but their creation is a signal that Canada and the provinces care about the northern regions and are willing to give the new governments the means to address these challenges in a more efficient way. Northern governments, as Nunavut has shown, can be an effective part of the new Arctic dynamic (Timpson 2002).

Inuit governments have different institutional settings, but they face common problems. Currently, Canada has two established Inuit governments and one in the making. Each has a direct relationship with a higher level of jurisdiction: the federal government for Nunavut; the federal government and the Newfoundland and Labrador government for Nunatsiavut; and the federal and Quebec governments for Nunavik. This gives rise to a form of governance in which lines of communication run primarily north-south. This issue is not limited to Inuit governance; it applies across the board to northern governance where eastern jurisdictions have limited relations with western ones. Given the extent of political activity and innovation in Canada's North, there is a need to establish cooperation and exchange networks on northern policy among the northern governments, which face similar challenges.

We would like to conclude by making a point that is not often raised. All of the new northern governments have been founded on imported models of public administration. Nunavut is an offspring of the Northwest Territories, Nunavik will have a public administration shaped by Quebec bureaucracy, and Nunatsiavut is built on programs and services devolved from Indian and Northern Affairs Canada. These models of governance have been tested in their original milieux, but northern governments are different — in terms of people, land, cultures and institutions. We have stressed that innovation is required to develop northern governance models, but we also recognize that regional public administrations have to abide by provincial and federal rules. Therefore, the challenge is to develop a mode of governance that will be relevant to northern citizens as they face social conundrums and environmental changes. We must measure the success of these innovative governance models by their capacity to meet such challenges, but in the case of Nunavik and Nunatsiavut it is still too early to do so.

Notes

We want to acknowledge the contributions of a number of people to this chapter. Michael McGoldrick (Makivik Corporation) and Chesley Andersen (Government of Nunatsiavut) took the time to explain the intricacies of the self-government arrangements, and Nick Bernard (Centre interuniversitaire d'études et de recherches autochtones) provided very enlightening conversation about Nunavik statistics. We also want to thank Frances Abele, Paul Bussières (Makivik Corporation) and Chesley Andersen for reading the first draft. Finally, we are grateful to James Feehan, the Montebello conference participants and the IRPP staff for their comments and suggestions. If, despite all these contributions, errors of fact or omission are still present, they are our sole responsibility.

1   The JBNQA was the first modern land claims settlement agreement to be signed in Canada. It was negotiated before the creation of a Canadian land claims policy.

2   We should here differentiate the forms of nationalism: Quebec nationalism is a classic form of Western nationalism that strives for the creation of an independent country; the nationalism of the Inuit of Nunavik is grounded in an effort to regain control over their life and territory after a short but intense period of colonization marked by a strong paternalistic attitude at all levels of government.

3   For example, Inuit from Inukjuak were relocated to Grise Fjord and Resolute Bay, thousands of kilometres north of their traditional territories (see Tester and Kulchyski 1994).

4   This was the first time the toponym Nouveau-Québec (New Quebec) was used, and it was a clear indication that the Government of Quebec intended to take over this not-so-new territory, which it claimed had been part of Quebec since 1912.

5   *Ujjituijiit* can be translated as "committee of the wise."

6   Aboriginal rights were recognized in section 35(1) of the *Constitution Act, 1982*, but the federal government did not consider self-government to be an Aboriginal right. However, in 1995, based on the conclusions of the Royal Commission on Aboriginal Peoples, the federal government changed its policy and acknowledged that self-government is an Aboriginal right. This policy change explains why, during the earlier land claims negotiations, no self-government arrangements were made.

7   Chesley Andersen, Government of Nunatsiavut, conversation with the authors, October 2007.

8   According to the 2006 Census, there are 9,565 Inuit in Nunavik — 19 percent of the Inuit of Canada's total population. Nunavik is home to Canada's fastest-growing Inuit population: it has increased by 25 percent since 1996 (Statistics Canada 2006).

9   Kuujjuaq is the only Nunavik community with a population in excess of 2,000.

10 *An Act Respecting Northern Villages and the Kativik Regional Government*, L.R.Q. chap. V-6.1.

11 At present, there are two representatives for Northwest River/Happy Valley-Goose Bay and one for Canada outside Labrador. However, the Labrador Inuit residing outside Labrador are asking to have one more representative.

12 In Nunavik and Labrador, Inuktitut is called Inuttitut.

13 Chesley Andersen, Government of Nunatsiavut, conversation with the authors, October 2007.

References

Alcantara, Christopher. 2007. "Explaining Aboriginal Treaty Negotiation Outcomes in Canada: The Cases of the Inuit and the Innu in Labrador." *Canadian Journal of Political Science* 40 (1): 185-207.

Duhaime, Gérard. 1983. "La sédentarisation au Nouveau-Québec inuit." *Études/Inuit/Studies* 7 (2): 25-52.

_____. 1992. "Le chasseur et le minotaure: itinéraire de l'autonomie politique au Nunavik." *Études/Inuit/Studies* 16 (1-2): 149-77.

_____. 2003. "Nunavik: Political Solutions Expected for Persisting Resources and Social Problems." *The Indigenous World 2002-2003*, edited by Diana Vindig. Copenhagen: International Work Group for Indigenous Affairs.

_____. 2007. *Profil socioéconomique du Nunavik 2006*. Quebec: Chaire de recherche du Canada sur la condition autochtone comparée, Université Laval. Accessed May 13, 2008. http://www.chairecondition autochtone.fss.ulaval.ca/extranet/doc/146.pdf

Government of Nunavut and Nunavut Tunngavik Incorporated. 2004. *Iqqanaijaqatigiit: Working Together*. Iqaluit: Government of Nunavut. Accessed May 13, 2008. http://www.gov.nu.ca/documents/iqqanaijaqatigiit/Iqqanaijaqatigiit_eng.pdf

Hanrahan, Maura. 2003. *The Lasting Breach: The Omission of Aboriginal People from the Terms of Union between Newfoundland and Canada and Its Ongoing Impacts*, March. Report prepared for Government of Newfoundland and Labrador, Royal Commission on Renewing and Strengthening Our Place in Canada. Accessed May 13, 2008. http://www.gov.nl.ca/publicat/royalcomm/research/Hanrahan.pdf

Haysom, Veryan. 1992. "The Struggle for Recognition: Labrador Inuit Negotiations for Land Rights and Self-Government." *Études/Inuit/Studies* 16 (1-2): 179-97.

Inuit Tapiriit Kanatami and Research and Analysis Directorate. 2006a. *Inuit in Canada: Regional Distribution and Demographic Changes from 1981 to 2001*, December. Ottawa: Minister of Public Works and Government Services Canada. Accessed May 13, 2008. http://www.inchr.org/Doc/January2007/Inuit-pop.pdf

_____. 2006b. *Knowledge and Use of Inuktitut among Inuit in Canada, 1981-2001*, March. Ottawa: Minister of Public Works and Government Services Canada. Accessed May 13, 2008. http://www.ainc-inac.gc.ca/pr/ra/kui/kui_e.pdf

Kativik Regional Government. 2006. *Jobs in Nunavik in 2005: Results of a Survey Carried Out with the Nunavik Employers in 2005*. Kuujjuaq, QC: Employment, Training, Income Support and Child Care Department, Kativik Regional Government. Accessed May 13, 2008. http://www.krg.ca/pdf/jobs/ job_survey_eng.pdf

Nungak, Zebeedee. 1995. "Pigatsi Pivugut: You Attain, Therefore We Attain." In *Nunavut: Inuit Regain Control of Their Lands and Their Lives*, edited by Jens Dahl, Jack Hicks, and Peter Jull. IWGIA Document 102. Copenhagen: International Work Group for Indigenous Affairs.

Rodon, Thierry. 2003. *En partenariat avec l'État: les expérience de cogestion des autochtones du Canada*. Quebec: Les presses de l'Université Laval.

Rodon, Thierry, and Pierre Gerlier Forest. 1997. "Autonomie et viabilité des micro-états et territoires: étude comparative avec les projets de gouvernement autochtones au Canada." Unpublished report, Secrétariat aux affaires autochtones du Québec.

Senécal, Sacha, and Erin O'Sullivan. 2007. *The Well-Being of Inuit Communities in Canada*. Strategic Research and Analysis Directorate, Indian and Northern Affairs Canada. Ottawa: Minister of Public Works and Government Services Canada. Accessed May 13, 2008. http://www.aincinac.gc.ca/pr/ ra/cwb/icc/icc_e.pdf

Statistics Canada. 1996. 1996 Census. Ottawa: Statistics Canada. Accessed May 3, 2008. http://www12.statcan.ca/english/census/index.cfm

_____. 2001a. 2001 Census. Ottawa: Statistics Canada. Accessed May 3, 2008. http://www12.statcan.ca/english/census/index.cfm

_____. 2001b. *Harvesting and Community Well-being among Inuit in the Canadian Arctic: Preliminary Findings from the 2001 Aboriginal Peoples Survey — Survey of Living Conditions in the Arctic*. Ottawa: Statistics Canada. Accessed May 3, 2008. http://dsp-psd.pwgsc.gc.ca/Collection/Statcan/89-619-X/89-619-XIE.html

_____. 2006. 2006 Census. Ottawa: Statistics Canada. Accessed May 3, 2008.

http://www12.statcan.ca/english/census/
index.cfm

Tanner, Adrian, John C. Kennedy, Susan
McCorquodale, and Gordon Inglis. 1994.
*Aboriginal Peoples and Governance in
Newfoundland and Labrador*. Report pre-
pared for the Governance Project, Royal
Commission on Aboriginal Peoples.
Ottawa: Indian and Northern Affairs
Canada.

Tester, Frank James, and Peter Kulchyski. 1994.
*Tammarniit (Mistakes): Inuit Relocation in the
Eastern Arctic, 1939-63*. Vancouver:
University of British Columbia Press.

Timpson, Annis May. 2002. "Nunavut and
Intergovernmental Relations." Paper presented at the Institute of Intergovernmental
Relations, Queen's University. November
1-2, Kingston.

Natural Resource
Devolution in the
Territories: Current
Status and Unresolved
Issues

C ANADA'S THREE FEDERAL TERRITORIES ENCOMPASS ALL OF ITS LANDS AND OCEANS
   north of the Arctic Circle and a great deal of area immediately south.[1] These
territories — Yukon, the Northwest Territories and Nunavut — constitute
approximately 40 percent of Canada's total area, covering more than 3.9 million
square kilometres. Additionally, the adjacent Arctic Ocean area, including the
Beaufort Sea, is huge. The territories have about 100,000 residents, approximately half of whom are Aboriginal peoples whose roots there reach back thousands of years. Most other residents have moved there from elsewhere.

Responsibility for the territories and jurisdiction over them rest with the
federal government. They are not like the provinces, which have constitutionally
established jurisdiction and authority in specific areas. Indeed, some provinces
predate the federal government. The founding provinces of Quebec, Ontario,
Nova Scotia and New Brunswick were self-governing political entities prior to
Confederation in 1867. Three that joined later — Prince Edward Island, British
Columbia and Newfoundland — were also separate political jurisdictions prior
to their respective decisions to join the Canadian federation. Since these founding and joining provinces predate the federation, it is not surprising that they
have retained jurisdiction over and ownership of their natural resources.

Canada's three other provinces — Alberta, Manitoba and Saskatchewan —
are a different case. In 1870, Great Britain transferred the geographical area they
now cover (as well as the North and what are now northern Ontario and northern Quebec) to Canada.[2] From some of that area, the federal government created
the three prairie provinces: Manitoba in 1870, and Saskatchewan and Alberta in
1905.[3] Interestingly, the federal government did not initially transfer ownership

of natural resources to the governments of those provinces. This led to two class-es of province: those that owned their resources and those that did not (that is, provinces carved out of federal lands). This was a source of friction between the prairie provinces and the federal government until 1930, when Ottawa trans-ferred natural resource ownership to those provinces. Meanwhile, the remaining territories stayed under the direct authority of the federal government.

Jumping forward to 2008, we see that natural resource jurisdiction is also a matter of contention when it comes to territorial devolution — the transfer of province-like responsibilities and jurisdiction from the federal government to the territorial governments. This process has been ongoing since the mid-1970s. Prior to that, the territories were managed by federally appointed commissioners, who operated with limited input from elected representatives of local residents. However, in the 1970s, there was a shift to responsible government. The com-missioners no longer have executive authority, and the elected territorial govern-ments are responsible for managing those public services that have been delegated to them by the federal government.

While there is some variation across the territories, generally speaking, the territorial governments now do the same sorts of things as provincial govern-ments. The main exception is for natural resources. Given the vast natural resource potential of the North, it is not surprising that this is the most difficult issue to resolve. In addition, there is a related consideration at play. The territor-ial governments are fiscally very dependent on transfers from Ottawa. Perhaps the only substantive way of eliminating that fiscal dependency is to allow those gov-ernments access to a sizeable share of future resource-related public revenues. Resource development also offers the prospect of substantial personal and busi-ness income gains as well as employment opportunities.

Bearing on the issue of natural resource potential are a number of cru-cially important considerations: resource development may involve Aboriginal lands and rights and thus have substantial socio-economic and cultural impacts on long-established communities; the resources with the greatest potential are nonrenewable, and the environmental impacts of their development could be severe; and the federal government is responsible for managing the North in a way that serves the national interest as well as fulfilling specific duties and com-mitments to the region's Aboriginal peoples. While my primary purpose in this chapter is to examine the revenue-related aspects of natural resource devolution, I will address such considerations because they provide the overall context of the discussion.

Next I will outline the process of devolution to 2008, and then I will elaborate on the crucial matter of net fiscal benefits (NFB) arising from devolution — that is, the extent to which territorial natural resource revenues resulting from devolution are offset by corresponding reductions in transfer payments from the federal government. This will be followed by an overview of the people of the territories: it is on their behalf that the territorial governments seek devolution, and therefore it is important to have some idea of their background and needs relative to the geographic scope of the North. I will go on to highlight some broader questions relating to natural resource devolution and then offer some brief conclusions.

The Status of Natural Resource Devolution

THE PROCESS OF DEVOLUTION IS DISTINCT FROM THE PROCESS THAT LED TO THE THREE prairie provinces being carved out of federal lands. Devolution does not involve constitutional change. Rather, it is accomplished by federal legislation. This means that the federal government retains ultimate authority over the territories. Still, the delegation of province-like authority to the territorial governments allows them to operate like provincial governments; they are able to provide much the same public services as provincial governments do and enjoy similar powers of taxation.

Under the Canadian Constitution, the provincial governments own their natural resources. They have exclusive power to tax those resources and apply royalties to them. Such exclusive authority was more thoroughly laid out in 1982 with the addition of section 92A to the *Constitution Act, 1867*.[4] The situation is different in the three territories. There, Canada — as represented by the federal government — has jurisdiction and ownership. How far the Parliament of Canada will go in delegating that authority to territorial governments and how far it ought to go are important questions.

Devolution began in the mid- to late 1970s, and it has proceeded at a varying pace across the territories. Most province-like program areas have been transferred from the federal government (usually from the Department of Indian

Affairs and Northern Development) to the territorial governments. The outstanding exception is jurisdiction over natural resources. Therefore, at this juncture, it is worthwhile to summarize the current situation with respect to natural resources in each territory.

Yukon

Yukon is the most "devolved" territory. In 2001, the federal government and the Yukon territorial government signed the Yukon Northern Affairs Program Devolution Transfer Agreement,[5] a comprehensive agreement that transferred the administration of and control over Crown lands and natural resources to the territorial government. The actual transfer took place on April 1, 2003. It covered forestry resources and all minerals, excluding oil and gas, on those lands. Under this arrangement, the territorial government can exercise the same type of decision-making authority as a provincial government. This includes setting royalties and other fees for the use of lands and resources.

As for oil and gas, province-like authority was devolved in 1998 with the Canada-Yukon Oil and Gas Accord. Since then, Yukon has had the authority to set royalty rates and other fees in relation to oil and gas resources and has collected the resulting revenues. That authority does not extend to offshore areas — that is, the Beaufort Sea. The federal government has retained control there. However, the Accord, which was signed in 1993, did include a commitment to reach a Beaufort Sea resource-revenue-sharing agreement, under which the federal government would share its Beaufort Sea revenues with both Yukon and the Northwest Territories (NWT) as well as establish a shared management arrangement. As of 2008, the Yukon government was still seeking such a management regime, including a revenue-sharing agreement for offshore oil and gas (see Government of Yukon 2008a).

A very important precursor to Yukon's acquisition of authority over natural resources came in 1993 with the Umbrella Final Agreement between the Government of Canada, the Council for Yukon Indians and the Government of Yukon. This agreement is a framework for land claims negotiations, which, in addition to land rights, would include many other substantive matters, including self-government, financial compensation, traditional land use and resource management.[6] Regarding natural resources, the agreement was important because it clarified Aboriginal ownership of land and mineral rights in the territory.

Specifically, it recognized approximately 41,500 square kilometres as settlement lands — that is, about 9 percent of the area of Yukon (Government of Yukon 2007). About two-thirds of that area is category A settlement lands; the remainder is category B. To the former are attached subsurface as well as surface rights. This means that petroleum and other subsurface minerals belong to the relevant Aboriginal community, not to the Crown. As for category B lands, Aboriginal title applies to the surface only.

Thus, this agreement delineated which natural resources could not be devolved (those from lands held under Aboriginal title) and which could be (those from Crown lands). Additionally, the umbrella agreement anticipated natural resource devolution and laid out the formula by which mineral resource royalties accruing to the territorial government would be shared with those Yukon Aboriginal groups with land claims agreements. These groups would receive annually 50 percent of the first $2 million in royalties from mineral resources and 10 percent thereafter. That amount is net of the hypothetical royalty revenue that would be collected by the territory if its royalty applied to category A settlement lands.[7] By mid-2008, 11 of the 14 Yukon First Nations had come to land claims agreements and therefore now have the right to share this revenue.[8]

Despite the extensive agreements on natural resource revenue sharing, there has been relatively little to share. While Yukon has forests, pristine wilderness, freshwater resources and wildlife, these do not generate significant direct public revenues; this is not especially surprising or unique across Canadian jurisdictions. Typically, only certain kinds of nonrenewable natural resources have great revenue-generating potential — for example, oil and gas and various precious metals. Currently, production of such resources in Yukon is very sparse. In 2006, only about 3 percent of Yukon's gross domestic product (GDP) was generated by the mining and petroleum industry (Government of Yukon 2006). According to the territorial government, its oil and gas resource revenues will be $416,000 in 2008-09, and revenues from land and mineral leases and royalties will be $178,000 (Government of Yukon 2008c, 6). These figures are practically negligible in comparison to the territorial government's total anticipated budgetary revenues of about $874 million for that fiscal year (Government of Yukon 2008c, 7).

However, the devolution of authority over natural resources is likely to be of substantial consequence in the future. There is a lot of nonrenewable natural resource potential, and the Yukon government is actively promoting mineral exploration with incentive programs. It is also encouraging investment in oil and gas exploration and development (see Government of Yukon 2008a). In particular, the possibly imminent construction of the Alaska Highway gas pipeline, which would pass through southwest Yukon, could be a catalyst for the development of Yukon's natural gas potential.[9]

The Northwest Territories

The situation in the NWT is quite different. Natural resource development is substantial, but devolution of natural resources other than forestry has not yet occurred (forestry management was transferred to the territorial government in 1987). In 2007, the value of mineral and oil and gas production in the territory was just over $2 billion. Diamond mining accounted for about 70 percent of that total; oil and gas accounted for most of the remainder. Oil and gas have a long history, but diamond mining began only in 1998, and it has been driving the territory's economic growth ever since (see Tom Hoefer's commentary in this volume). Largely due to this sector, the GDP per capita in the NWT in 2008 was close to $110,000, which is much higher than it is in any other territory or province, including Alberta, and more than double the national figure of $46,500.[10] In addition, there are renewed prospects for the construction of the Mackenzie Gas Project. That project entails the development of large pools of natural gas in the Mackenzie Delta in the north of the territory and construction of pipelines down the Mackenzie Valley to carry the gas south. The National Energy Board, the federal government regulatory agency with jurisdiction in this matter, reports that the project will have an estimated cost of more than $16 billion and will tap enormous reserves of natural gas. Since 2004, the board has been assessing applications related to the project (see National Energy Board 2008, 16-17) and although a decision was expected in 2008, there had been no new developments on this front in the spring of 2009.

The authority for management and regulation of these natural resources and the right to levy and collect royalties on them remain with the federal government. That is in spite of the Northwest Territories Lands and Resources Devolution Framework Agreement, which was signed in March 2004 by the federal government, the territorial government and the Aboriginal Summit.[11] This agreement established the process for negotiating an agreement in principle for devolution of authority over onshore lands — including minerals, oil and gas, and bodies of water — to the territorial government. It also set June 2005 as a target date for a final agreement and projected April 2006 as the date it would come into effect. These expectations have not been realized. As of April 2009, the parties had still not reached a final agreement, and one did not appear imminent. Apparently, resource revenue sharing was a key stumbling block in the negotiations.

However, there has been progress in settling Aboriginal land claims. The first settlement came in 1984: the Inuvialuit agreement. As well as providing for self-government, economic development and other important measures, it recognized Inuvialuit title to specific lands, including a portion on which beneficiaries would hold mineral rights (see Graham White's chapter in this volume). Since then, three other Aboriginal organizations have reached land claims agreements.[12] There are still some groups with unsettled claims; negotiations related to these are at various stages.

Nunavut

Nunavut covers a vast area — some 20 percent of Canada. Little natural-resource-related development is taking place there right now, but there is active exploration, and there are high expectations for rich deposits of nonrenewable natural resources, both on land and offshore. There has been a complete resolution of the Aboriginal land claim in Nunavut, but no agreement has been reached with the territorial government on devolution of jurisdiction over lands and natural resources.

There is only one land claim agreement for Nunavut due to the fact that it has a single, homogeneous Aboriginal community — Inuit — whose members constitute the overwhelming majority of the population. In the early 1990s, a comprehensive land claim agreement was reached between the federal government and the Tunngavik Federation of Nunavut, which represented all Inuit in the negotiations. The Government of the Northwest Territories was also party to the agreement, as Nunavut was part of the NWT at the time. The Nunavut Land Claims Agreement, which was ratified by the Inuit in 1992 and signed by the three parties to it in May 1993, provided for the creation of a separate territorial government for Nunavut, which officially came into effect in 1999 (for further details, see Graham White's chapter in this volume). Regarding lands and natural resources, this agreement established Inuit title to some 351,000 square kilometres; on 37,000 square kilometres of this area, title includes mineral rights. It also provided for the sharing with Inuit of mineral royalties from Crown lands in the territory. Specifically, article 25 gives Inuit a right to 50 percent of the first $2 million in government royalties and 5 percent thereafter.

No self-government was created in Nunavut. In the absence of a self-government institution, however, there are land claims institutions. One is the Nunavut Trust, which was created to receive and manage the compensation mandated by the land claim agreement and to use the earnings from those funds.[13] The key operational institution is Nunavut Tunngavik Incorporated (NTI), the successor to the Tunngavik Federation of Nunavut. NTI, which is funded by the Nunavut Trust, is the organization that represents Inuit in the administration and fulfillment of the land claim agreement. It plays a crucial role in representing Inuit in various arrangements established by the agreement; it also supports regional Inuit associations and other Inuit organizations.

While there has been a resolution of the land claim issue, little progress has been made in negotiations with the territorial government on devolution of jurisdiction over Crown lands and natural resources. In December 2004, the federal government indicated that it would proceed with negotiations on devolution, but by the end of 2005 there was still no agreement. So, in early 2006, the federal minister for Indian affairs and northern development appointed Paul Mayer as the senior ministerial representative for Nunavut devolution. His task was to identify the key issues and assess the likelihood for successful negotiations. In June 2007, he submitted his report.

Three elements of Mayer's report are worth emphasizing. First, the report gives important context. At present, there are enormous challenges facing Nunavut beyond the obvious hurdles of distance and climate: several social problems, educational deficiencies, an acute housing shortage, lifestyle and related health problems and insufficient governance capacity. Second, the report highlights what Nunavut is seeking with respect to the devolution of natural resources. It wants devolution to involve offshore areas, which are vast; it wants 100 percent of natural resource revenues, with no offsetting reductions in federal transfer payments for an agreed time, and sharing only when the territory reaches an agreed level of development; and it wants a fund to support access to and assessment of nonnatural renewable resources. Third, the report reaches some conclusions about the prospects for devolution. It suggests that, in light of the need to build more capacity within the territorial government, there should be a "phased approach" to devolution. It also recommends that the "net fiscal benefit" from resource devolution be similar to that in other northern jurisdictions (Mayer 2007).

It seems, then, that devolution in Nunavut may be some time in coming, and it is uncertain how extensive it will be.

Net Fiscal Benefits

E ACH TERRITORIAL GOVERNMENT IS FINANCIALLY DEPENDENT ON OTTAWA. THROUGH its Territorial Formula Financing (TFF) program, the federal government provides each territory with an annual fiscal transfer that reflects the gap between estimated expenditure requirements, known as gross expenditure base (GEB), and some measure of potential own-source revenues. As of 2007, the calculation of the TFF grant for each territory can be represented like this:

$$\text{TFF grant} = [\text{GEB}] - [70 \text{ percent of potential revenue} \qquad (1)$$
$$\text{from seven main revenue sources}]$$

It is worth emphasizing that the amounts on the right-hand side of this calculation are not, respectively, actual expenditures and revenues. The GEB is the federal government's estimate of the funding needed to support territorial programs; and "potential revenue" is an estimate of the amount that could be raised if the territory applied tax rates reasonably comparable to those of the provinces. Also, the 70 percent figure needs some clarification. Essentially, it acts as an incentive for a territory to seek means of improving its revenue potential — for every dollar of potential revenue increase, the TFF grant would decrease by 70 cents, leaving a net gain of 30 cents for the territory. Finally, the "seven main revenue sources" do not include natural resource revenues.

The TFF grants are substantial, as table 1 illustrates. For instance, Yukon received a TFF grant for 2008-09 of approximately $564 million, which, as indicated in the table, works out to just over $18,000 per resident; in Nunavut, the grant is more than $30,000 per resident. These grants largely finance the territorial governments. As the last column of the table shows, Nunavut received more than 80 percent of its revenue and the other two territories obtained about two-thirds of their revenues from the federal transfer.[14]

Directly related to devolution of natural resources is the issue of net fiscal benefit (NFB) from devolution. For the purposes of this chapter, NFB refers to the extent to which territorial natural resource revenues resulting from devolution are offset by reductions in the TFF grant from the federal government. If the TFF grant is reduced for each dollar of natural resource revenue collected by a territory, then there will be no NFB from natural resource devolution unless the resource revenue was large enough to exceed the entire value of the TFF grant.[15] With smaller amounts of natural resource revenue, an NFB is realized only if the TFF grant is reduced at rate that is less than dollar-for-dollar.[16]

Territorial Formula Financing has evolved since it began in 1985. Its present form is quite recent, dating from the 2007 federal budget, and it reflects the recommendations made by the Expert Panel on Equalization and Territorial Formula Financing (2006).[17] At the time the panel was conducting its work, natural resource revenues were not part of the formula. That is probably because most such revenues were then being collected by the federal government, and adjustments for Yukon's revenues were being made outside of the formula. However, as part of its mandate, the panel considered the future treatment of natural resource revenues. Recognizing that the devolution and revenue-sharing negotiations were ongoing, the panel recommended that natural resource revenues continue to be excluded from the TFF formula and addressed outside of it. As well, the panel maintained that natural resource devolution ought to result in net fiscal benefits to the territories, and that such benefits should be similar across the territories.

The federal government accepted the panel's advice to keep natural resource revenues outside of the TFF formula. This has meant that all three territories have their TFF grants calculated according to a common formula — that is, equation 1, cited earlier. After that, the grant is reduced with an adjustment that is specific to each territory. Thus, the actual amount received can be expressed as:

Table 1
Territorial Formula Financing Grants, 2008-09

	Total ($ millions)	$ per capita	Estimated share of total revenue (%)
Yukon	564	18,166	64.5
Northwest Territories	805	18,704	65.4
Nunavut	944	30,265	81.2

Sources: Finance Canada (2008) for total and per capita figures; Government of the Northwest Territories (2008a), Government of Nunavut (2008) and Government of Yukon (2008b) for revenue shares.

Adjusted TFF grant = [TFF grant] – [a territory-specific adjustment   (2)
based on natural resource revenues]

In the case of Yukon, the form of the adjustment is already known. Under the Canada-Yukon Oil and Gas Accord, which became effective in 1998, Yukon's annual TFF grant will not be reduced if oil and gas royalty revenues are $3 million or less. There will be a reduction equal to some fraction of oil and gas revenues in excess of $3 million — for example, if royalty revenues are $4 million, then the TFF grant will be reduced by a fraction of $1 million. The fraction starts at 60 percent and rises progressively to 80 percent. For the other natural resources — that is, those that were part of the 2001 devolution agreement — up to $3 million is allowable before there is a reduction in the annual TFF grant. Beyond that $3-million threshold, the grant is reduced on a dollar-for-dollar basis, despite the potential disincentive effects.[18] Thus, there are two separate and independent adjustments that apply to the Yukon grant. There is no obvious rationale for these separate treatments.

It is important to note that these types of TFF adjustment can have consequences for Aboriginal governments in Yukon. Recall that under the 1993 umbrella agreement, Aboriginal groups with land claims agreements in place are entitled to a portion of the territorial government's natural resource revenues — they share in the territory's natural resource revenues, net of the natural resource revenue adjustments to the TFF grant. More significantly, Aboriginal governments have their own fiscal transfer agreements with the federal government, and these take own-source revenues into account. Therefore, when an Aboriginal government receives its share of territorial resource revenue, its transfer from the federal government may be reduced. This amounts to a double clawback: one on the TFF grant, and another on any part of that amount that is shared by the territorial government with Aboriginal governments.[19]

At present, Yukon's natural resource revenues are modest, so concerns about the magnitude of TFF grant adjustments and the double-clawback phenomenon are more to do with principle than practicality. However, if substantial new resource development occurs, and if an offshore oil and gas agreement is reached, then these issues will surely come into play.

The situation in the NWT is almost the reverse. Before the recent economic downturn, there had been a 10-year resource boom, and massive oil and gas development in the Mackenzie Delta in the near future seems likely. Yet there has been no devolution of nonrenewable minerals or oil and gas. Therefore, any adjustment to that territory's TFF grant would involve a small amount of money — it would perhaps be limited to a deduction related to forestry revenues. Nevertheless, the federal government in its 2007 budget made this proposal for adjusting the NWT's TFF grant in the context of eventual devolution: it would cut the grant by 50 percent of the territorial government's natural resource revenue up to a specified maximum amount, beyond which the grant would be reduced on a dollar-for-dollar basis (Finance Canada 2007, 353).[20] Apparently this measure is still at the proposal stage and is a matter for discussion between federal and territorial officials.

It is not possible to determine how substantially a 50 percent rule would benefit the NWT should devolution be realized. In 2007, the value produced by its diamonds and oil and gas was approximately $2 billion. Also, exploration is active and the Mackenzie Gas Project, if it goes ahead, would add substantially to the value of natural resource production. This suggests that postdevolution royalty revenues could be huge. However, that depends on what royalty regime the territorial government adopts: it could use low royalties to encourage rapid and massive development; or it could adopt higher royalties to capture a larger share of the economic rent.[21] And for a given royalty regime, the extent of the NFB depends not only on the 50 percent reduction but also on where the maximum is set. No doubt these considerations are at the core of devolution negotiations.

Also, the NFB will be of material importance to organizations representing Aboriginal peoples in the territory. In May 2007, in anticipation of a devolution agreement, the Government of the Northwest Territories reached an agreement in principle with Aboriginal groups to share up to one-quarter of its NFB.[22] Through the Aboriginal Summit, these groups are party to devolution negotiations as well.

For Nunavut, the NFB is similarly important, although its importance is less immediate because no major natural resource production is currently taking place. According to the Mayer Report, the Nunavut government wants 100 percent of natural resource revenues with no offsetting adjustment to its TFF grant until the territory has reached an agreed-upon level of development (Mayer 2007, 33). Under the Nunavut Land Claims Agreement, a share of government royalty revenues — whether they are collected by the territorial government or by Ottawa — is paid to the Inuit.[23] The sharing provision of the Agreement does not refer to the NFB; it refers to "resource royalty." One presumes that in the event of devolution, the share would be based on the NFB rather than on the natural resource revenues before any linked reduction in the TFF grant. Negotiators will have to clarify this matter.

In sum, the amount of natural resource revenue that a territory might collect as a result of devolution does not tell us much about the budgetary consequences of this revenue. Offsetting adjustments to the TFF grant could result in an NFB that ranges from nearly zero to the full amount collected. The form that such adjustments will take is far from fully settled. For the sake of consistency and interterritorial equity, a common adjustment formula could be used. However, the process seems to be moving in a different direction: Yukon has an established formula, but those being discussed for the NWT and Nunavut seem quite different from one another and also bear little resemblance to that of Yukon. Moreover, the Yukon formula, with its 100 percent clawback on nonpetroleum revenues in excess of $3 million, cannot serve as a good model for the others.

Who Is the North?

THE TERRITORIES COVER SOME 40 PERCENT OF CANADA, AND PRACTICALLY ALL OF THE natural resources in that immense area — other than where Aboriginal title applies — are owned by the federal government on behalf of all Canadians. Devolution of the management and control of those federal lands and natural resources to the three territorial governments is therefore no small matter. Depending on the design, devolution could give the territories a much greater influence over the future of Canada's North and — possibly — greatly enrich them through NFB arrangements. And the nature and direction of the three territorial governments will be determined by the peoples they represent. It is therefore worthwhile to review some of the facts about these populations.

As I have already mentioned, the total population of the territories is just over 100,000. That is not a large number, especially considering that the land mass of the territories is greater than that of Quebec, Ontario and British Columbia combined. Table 2 gives some breakdowns of that aggregate number. An interesting aspect is the variation in the Aboriginal composition across the territories. In Yukon, 25.1 percent of residents are Aboriginal people, whereas in the NWT that proportion is 50.3 percent, and in Nunavut it is 85 percent. However, the most surprising statistic is that almost all of the non-Aboriginal residents were not born in the territories; they moved there from elsewhere in Canada or from other countries. The third row of table 2 reports that more than 60 percent of the residents of Yukon were from elsewhere, and the corresponding figure for the NWT is almost 50 percent (the figure for Nunavut is not available because before 1999 that territory was part of the NWT). Moreover, assuming that practically all Aboriginal people living in the territories were born there, this information implies that almost all the non-Aboriginal people were born else-where. Calculations based on the assumption that all Aboriginal people residing in the North were born there are presented in the fourth row of table 2: about 83 percent of the non-Aboriginal population of Yukon moved there from elsewhere, and the figure for the NWT is almost 95 percent. This phenomenon of relatively few locally born non-Aboriginal people reflects high rates of in- and out-migration.[24]

Almost half of the territorial population lives in the three territorial capitals, and each capital is its territory's largest population centre. Therefore, it is worthwhile to determine whether circumstances in each capital are different from

Table 2
Population Composition of the Territories, 2006

	Yukon	Northwest Territories	Nunavut
Total population (N)	30,195	41,055	29,325
Aboriginal people as proportion of total (%)	25.1	50.3	85.0
People born elsewhere as proportion of total (%)	62.1	47.0	n/a[1]
People born elsewhere as proportion of non-Aboriginal population (%)	82.9	94.5	n/a[1]

[1] Figures for Nunavut are not available, as Nunavut was part of the Northwest Territories before 1999.
Source: Statistics Canada (2006b).

those in the rest of the territory. Table 3 highlights a few of the differences. In terms of population mix, the Aboriginal population is smaller in each capital than it is in the territory as a whole. The economic statistics for the capitals — as is typical with larger centres — are better than those for the entire jurisdiction. As the table shows, each capital has a higher median family income and a lower unemployment rate than the territory overall.

Perhaps most notable about table 3 is its indication of the prosperity of Yellowknife. The NWT's 2005 median income for census families was $86,132, which is high, but it was an astonishing $110,135 in Yellowknife. The comparable figure for Canada for the same year was $63,866, which means that median family income in Yellowknife was about 72 percent higher (Statistics Canada 2006b). Of course, the cost of living in the North is significantly higher than the Canadian average. According to a survey conducted in 2005, the cost of a basket of consumer goods and services in Yellowknife was 15 to 20 percent higher than it was in Edmonton (National Joint Council 2006). Thus, even allowing for that somewhat higher cost of living, the residents of Yellowknife are faring particularly well.

At the other end of the spectrum is Nunavut. As reported in table 3, it had a 2005 median family income of just $49,270, which was well below the Canadian figure. While exact indicators are difficult to obtain, it is widely accepted that the cost of living in Nunavut is substantially higher than it is in the other territories; thus, the real gap between the Nunavut median family income and the national one is even more serious than the simple difference between the two numbers implies. Even the higher income in the capital, Iqaluit, is not so impressive when we take the very high cost of living into account; and one might speculate that this figure is largely accounted for by the premiums that must be paid to induce people with specialized skills to move to the territory — for example, federal civil servants, and education and health professionals.

While tables 2 and 3 give us some perspective on the people and circumstances of the territories, they omit a great deal. For instance, there are huge costs involved in providing public infrastructure as well as social, educational and health services. Perhaps more importantly, the tables imply, but do not fully reflect, the social and economic problems faced by the territories' Aboriginal inhabitants. Those problems are especially acute in Nunavut, as attested to by the findings of the Expert Panel on Equalization and Territorial Formula Financing (2006) and the report by Paul Mayer (2007). In the other two territories, those problems are less severe, but still serious; and Aboriginal governments and institutions are working to ensure that their communities participate more fully in economic activity.

In a nutshell, only about 100,000 people reside in the three separate territorial jurisdictions. Half of these are Aboriginal people with deep roots, while the overwhelming majority of the other half have come from elsewhere and tend to have a high turnover rate; half the population lives in the three capitals, which are all located south of the Arctic Circle and contain a disproportionately large share of the non-Aboriginal population; and economic and social circumstances are considerably different across the three territories and between Aboriginal and non-Aboriginal residents.

The devolution question is about how much control and authority over Canada's northern lands and oceans, and what amount of fiscal benefit, the federal government ought to turn over to the three territorial governments. The answer is not obvious, because in addition to the 100,000 people who live in the territories, there are about 32 million other Canadians. It is reasonable to permit northern residents control over the public and social services that affect their lives; it is also reasonable to give them a meaningful role in the exploitation of the natural resources and in the sustainable development of the regions in which they live. However,

Table 3
Population, Unemployment and Income in the Three Territories and Their Capitals, 2006

	Whitehorse, Yukon	Yellowknife, Northwest Territories	Iqaluit, Nunavut
Capital's share of territory's population (%)	67.4	45.1	21.0
Non-Aboriginal share of capital's population (%)	81.4	77.8	40.1
Capital's unemployment rate	7.3	5.8	7.8
Territory's unemployment rate	9.4	10.4	15.6
Capital's median family income (2005) ($)	81,331	110,135	92,123
Territory's median family income (2005) ($)	75,251	86,132	49,270

Source: Statistics Canada (2006b).

those regions are federal territory; they are not provinces. And there are issues in
the North — especially in the Arctic Ocean and the Far North — that are of substantial national importance. The next section highlights some of those issues.

Some   Unresolved   Issues

THE QUESTION OF NFB IS AT THE HEART OF DEVOLUTION POLICY, BUT THERE ARE
other matters that are intimately connected with it and with one another. All
have national implications that deserve more scrutiny from Canadians.

Needs, Fairness and Net Fiscal Benefits

Each of the territorial governments is in a state of fiscal need. That is to say, their
capacity to generate own-source revenue is such that by applying reasonable tax
rates they cannot raise enough to pay for social and public services comparable
to those available in the provinces. Table 1 illustrates the size of that fiscal gap;
TFF grants support from 65 percent to more than 80 percent of territorial spending. Natural resource devolution, by giving territories access to royalties and related revenues, offers them the opportunity to decrease or even eliminate this fiscal
dependency. A crucial question is how much of a net increase in revenue a territorial government should receive — that is, how big the NFB should be.

One approach to answering that question is to consider how much more
revenue a territory needs. If the TFF grant is fully adequate, then it could be
argued that as natural resource revenues accrue to a territory, the grant should be
reduced by an equal amount. However, this is a rather extreme position for two
reasons. First, the devolution of natural resource responsibilities would require a
territorial government to build a management and administrative capacity; that
alone would entail more costs for the territorial government and savings for the
federal government. Second, even though the federal government followed the
advice of the Expert Panel on Equalization and Territorial Formula Financing by
revising the TFF grant formula and increasing its generosity, the territories still do
not have enough budgetary revenue to meet the challenges they face.[25]

On the other side of the coin, beyond allowances for the costs of managing natural resources, one may argue for a limit to the NFB. Given the territories'
small resident population, it is conceivable that even a moderate resource boom

would produce very large per capita revenues. For example, if natural resources were to generate $600 million annually in a territory with 30,000 residents, that would be $20,000 per capita. Even if the TFF grant were reduced by 50 cents for each dollar of this revenue, the territorial government would gain $10,000 per person. Outside observers might view this as too generous, especially if the territory already had a very high average personal income and a low unemployment rate as compared to national levels. Many taxpayers elsewhere in Canada would feel that such a sizable NFB was unfair in such circumstances.

This equity question would be even trickier if a resource boom resulted in royalty revenue well in excess of the TFF grant. The grant can be cut to zero, but no further. Continuing with the example of a territory with 30,000 residents, suppose that the territory had royalty revenues of $2.1 billion and its TFF grant was $0.9 billion prior to adjustment for resource revenues. Then, even with a dollar-for-dollar reduction of the TFF grant, the NFB to the territory would be $1.2 billion — a net gain of $40,000 per capita.[26] While these figures are purely hypothetical and perhaps very optimistic, they are not implausible in the long term. Devolution agreements should anticipate such situations.

In short, while most people might agree that there should be a positive NFB from devolution for territorial governments, there is a lot of scope to argue over how large it should be and whether it should have an upper limit.

Capturing Natural Resource Rents

Most economists advise that whatever level of government is responsible for natural resources, it should employ a royalty regime that captures the resources' economic rent. That rent may be defined as the difference between the value of the harvested resource and the cost of labour, capital and other inputs used in harvesting the resource, factoring in due allowance for risk and a competitive rate of return.

Whether the federal government or a territorial government would be better at designing the appropriate royalty regime is an open question. Two recent studies maintain that the federal government has a poor track record in this regard. Cizek argues that federal royalties on resources in the NWT have been much too low and have resulted in "hyper-profits" for resource developers (2005). However, implicit in that analysis is the assumption that extraction costs, risks and resource quality in the NWT are comparable to those in Alberta and British Columbia. In a study that actually incorporates the cost side of the picture, Taylor et al. come to similar, but less extreme, conclusions with respect to a number of Canadian jurisdictions, including Yukon and the NWT (2004). Based on the findings of the latter study, Irlbacher-Fox and Mills concur that the federal royalty regime has been lax and recommend higher royalties. They also recommend that all levels of government contribute to the regime's design and suggest that it be more focused on the long-run sustainable development of the North (2007).[27]

If the territorial government designed the royalty regime, then presumably different forces would be at play. Some might favour a low-royalty regime to attract new investment and thus generate local jobs and business opportunities. Others might favour a regime that would generate more public resource revenues, even if it meant a slower pace of investment. Their motives might be to collect sufficient revenues to fund public programs, to ensure that there would be more natural resource revenue for Aboriginal organizations to share, or to establish an endowment fund.

Also, the design of the royalty regime would be influenced by NFB considerations. If royalty revenues were clawed back on a dollar-for-dollar basis, then a territorial government would have less incentive to adopt an appropriate royalty regime. It might decide to delay or halt resource-related development if there were no NFB. On the other hand, it might react in a completely opposite fashion and adopt a low-royalty regime so as to obtain local benefits by encouraging even greater investment in natural resources.

So it is not clear which level of government would design the better royalty regime. This suggests that it might be worthwhile to embody the principle of an efficient royalty regime within devolution agreements. Territorial governments would have the right to set royalties, but with limitations implied by such a principle and within certain agreed-upon parameters such as environmental considerations. In broad terms, such a regime would be one that maximized royalty revenue over the productive life of the resource while not being onerous to the point of making the venture commercially unattractive or inducing the developer to cease operations prematurely.

The Nature and Sustainability of Development

The royalty regime is an important consideration, but it is not the sole determinant of natural resource development and production activities. The regulatory authority of the federal government also determines the nature and rate of development. Devolution means delegating that authority to the territorial governments. As with the choice of a royalty regime, there would likely be varying local opinion about the choice of an appropriate development policy.

Some people might be more growth-oriented and prefer large-scale immediate development with the brisk economic activity that is associated with resource booms. Others might want a slower pace of development that would place particular emphasis on environmental effects and take into account existing infrastructure and labour market capacity. They would argue that slower development would allow more Aboriginal people to acquire the skills necessary to participate; however, some Aboriginal groups might prefer to create immediate opportunities to improve their employment and business prospects.

Some communities might welcome the prospect of a booming economy sustained by a large influx of people from elsewhere. Others might see that as part of the boom-and-bust cycle and prefer smaller inflows and a reliance on fly-in workers, which would put less pressure on local public services and the environment. Such nonresident workers are sometimes seen in negative terms, because they do not spend much of their income locally. However, they are beneficial in that they do not bring with them family members who would require local social, health and public services; and their own use of such services is limited due to their absences. They also meet spikes in labour demand and fill skill gaps until local workers are fully trained. Moreover, if communities want to obtain more benefit from fly-in labour, they have the option of applying a payroll tax — territorial governments have the authority to impose such a tax on employers.[28]

More generally, an inflow of people due to economic growth could also change the political equilibrium in the North by reducing the Aboriginal proportion of the population. As the general population base is small, it would not take a large in-migration to have this effect. At the same time, there is a need to include more Aboriginal people in economic activity. For instance, in the NWT, the 2007 employment rate for Aboriginal people was 55.3 percent, compared to 86.9 percent for non-Aboriginal people (Government of the Northwest Territories 2008b, table 5.4). Making a greater effort to address the underlying causes of that large gap might be a better way of meeting the growing demand for workers.

National considerations also come into the picture. Even if far-reaching natural resource devolution occurs, the federal government still has northern responsibilities. It must still fund the TFF grant. If development results in population growth and a greater need for social, health and public services, then the cost to the Canadian taxpayer will increase. Furthermore, Canadians are now more environmentally conscious. Many see the North as a place where the federal government needs to be more vigilant with respect to the environment and resource development.

What about the Offshore Area?
Another unresolved matter is how to handle the offshore area. This is a completely open question. The Yukon devolution agreement excludes the offshore area adjacent to that territory. The NWT negotiation framework agreement explicitly limits the negotiations to onshore areas. As for Nunavut, judging from the Mayer Report, the federal government's position to date is that offshore areas are off the table. However, the Nunavut government is adamant that the territory's internal waters be included in the discussions (see Okalik 2006; Mayer 2007). The internal waters of Nunavut are those that lie between the territory's many islands — essentially, they encompass practically all of Canada's Arctic Ocean east of the Beaufort Sea.

In 1993, with the Canada-Yukon Oil and Gas Accord, the federal government did agree to negotiate a Beaufort Sea offshore management and revenue-sharing arrangement jointly with Yukon and the NWT. Yet much has changed since then — for example, oil and gas prices rose substantially until the sharp drop experienced at the end of 2008, and environmental sensitivities are even stronger. The federal perspectives that were embodied in that accord may have changed.

While we have no precise numbers, large reserves of oil and gas may lie under Canada's eastern Arctic waters and the Beaufort Sea. There has not been much exploration in the east, but the Beaufort is a different story. During the 1970s and 1980s, there was a great deal of exploration there; after that there was a lull, but interest has rebounded since 2000. In 2007, the federal government awarded an exploration licence to Imperial Oil and ExxonMobil Canada, and those two partners committed to spending $585 million on exploration. In 2008, BP acquired exploration leases that entailed a $1.2-billion expenditure plan. Such levels of expenditure indicate high expectations and suggest that large-scale petroleum development in the Beaufort Sea is possible within the next several years.

Many Canadians share concerns over the environmental health of the Arctic's oceans, the Canadian government's efforts to assert its sovereignty in the Arctic and the consequences of global warming for the region. In fact, in the October 2007 Throne Speech, the federal government drew attention to northern issues and made important commitments related to asserting Canadian sovereignty in the Arctic Ocean — for example, it promised to map the Arctic seabed and to provide new Arctic patrol ships as well as aerial surveillance of the Far North and the Northwest Passage (Government of Canada 2007).[29]

Nevertheless, very few Canadians have even heard of the idea of devolution of these waters to territorial governments. Of course, devolution would not make the federal government any less responsible for Arctic Ocean sovereignty or for its general commitments related to Canada's other ocean areas. For instance, section 16 of the 1993 Canada-Yukon Oil and Gas Accord recognizes continuing federal responsibilities in such areas. Indeed, it would seem that only the federal government has the capacity to conduct many important, and costly, activities — from monitoring travel through Arctic waters, to conducting Arctic research, to maintaining bases in the High Arctic, to addressing environmental disasters.

The fundamental question here is: What does devolution or shared management of the offshore mean? One can envision a range of responses. It could be a joint administrative board that allows territorial governments and Aboriginal representatives to have some formal input into offshore management, although final decisions would remain under federal authority. Alternatively, it could entail far-reaching control exerted from the territorial capitals — each territorial government, despite its limited capacity, would have authority, responsibility and key decision-making power over a particular wedge of the offshore area. Similarly, one might conjecture very different outcomes for revenue sharing: on the one hand, most revenue could go to the federal government in consideration of the fact that it has responsibilities in the Arctic and the region's resources belong to all Canadians; on the other hand, most revenue could go to the territories because of their proximity to the resource.

Conclusion

THERE IS A COMPELLING CASE TO BE MADE THAT PEOPLE IN ANY JURISDICTION SHOULD have a say in local public policy matters and the fiscal self-reliance to support public services at adequate levels. In the territories, such fiscal self-reliance could probably come only from natural resource devolution. However — and depending on how resource development proceeds in the long term as well as how the federal government might adjust its TFF grants — natural resource devolution could either enrich the territories beyond any reasonable notion of fiscal need or result in little net fiscal benefit. Also, devolution could affect the rate and magnitude of resource development in the North, which raises questions about social, demographic and environmental impacts. In light of these considerations, the process of natural resource devolution ought to have a projected end point — that is to say, the degree of devolution should be decided within a framework that reflects a long-term perspective on the North. To date, that has not been done.

Nevertheless, natural resource devolution in the North is happening. It is proceeding at different rates across the territories, but so far progress has been very slow. Only Yukon has been delegated jurisdiction, but it is limited to onshore resources, and the associated revenue-sharing arrangements are quite ungenerous. Despite years of talks, natural resource devolution still seems less than imminent for the NWT, and even further off for Nunavut. Yet the territorial governments are pursuing the matter, and the federal government has committed itself to allowing devolution, so the process seems destined to continue.

What is not clear is how it will end. In that regard, there are many issues related to devolution (some of which I have highlighted here) that need to be addressed. If we are to do that effectively, we must reach a greater consensus on the long-term future of the North. The territories encompass over 40 percent of Canada's land mass, but only one-third of 1 percent of Canadians reside there. The Arctic Ocean not only offers enormous natural resource potential but also creates environmental responsibilities, and these ought to be of concern to all Canadians. Therefore, any consensus on the North should be a national one, but one that gives due consideration to northern residents — especially those with deep roots in the region.

The key parties need to strike a balance between the interests of northern residents and those of Canada as a whole. That may not be easy, because we cannot presume that all northerners have common objectives. Their interests may vary according to which territory they inhabit, where they reside within that territory, whether they are of Aboriginal heritage or not, and whether they are advocates of growth or of a slower rate of development. As for national interests, they tend to increase as one moves northward to the Arctic Ocean and the nearly unpopulated islands of the Far North. In that vast area, far from territorial capitals, national concerns over sovereignty are at play, global environmental concerns are more acute, and offshore resources (especially oil and gas) may turn out to be of great national value. And Canadians can generally be expected to hold diverse views on how the North, especially its more remote areas and waters, ought to be managed, developed and protected.

A final and general conclusion is in order. Few Canadians know anything about northern devolution. It is not the sort of northern subject that captures the attention of the media, either — unlike Arctic sovereignty or melting ice caps. Devolution is much too dry a topic, and it produces no interesting visuals. Even among those who specialize in policy analysis, few know much about what is happening. Somehow, that must change. More analysts, journalists, opinion leaders and concerned citizens need to be engaged in a matter that will have far-reaching national implications.

Notes

1   Helpful comments from Thomas Courchene and France St-Hilaire are gratefully acknowledged. The author is solely responsible for any remaining errors.

2   Great Britain retained a portion of the High Arctic until 1880, at which time that area was also transferred to Canada and incorporated into federal territory.

3   In 1870, Manitoba was very small compared to its present size. Over time, the federal government transferred territory to it, enlarging it for the last time in 1912. That year, the last transfer of federal territory to Ontario and Quebec also took place (see Natural Resources Canada 2004).

4   That amendment was included as section 50 in the *Constitution Act, 1982*.

5   The preamble of this agreement states that it was guided by the principles of the Devolution Protocol Accord of 1998, which was signed by the two governments as well as by representatives of Yukon Aboriginal peoples. The inclusion of the latter reflects the success that Aboriginal peoples of the territories have had in demarginalizing their political and legal status since the 1970s.

6   For highlights of this agreement, see Indian and Northern Affairs Canada (2004).

7   This payment is subject to a cap. The per capita shared royalty revenue of Aboriginal recipients cannot exceed Canadian per capita income.

8   The distribution among those 11 Yukon First Nations is determined according to proportions stated in schedule A of the Agreement.

9   In May 2008, the Alaska government announced that the pipeline proposal submitted by TransCanada Alaska ranked highest in an assessment of options for the development of Alaska's North Slope natural gas resources (see "Palin Recommends" 2008).

10 Statistics Canada, CANSIM, tables 0384-0002 (GDP) and 051-000 (population).

11 The Aboriginal Summit consisted of representative organizations from the territory.

12 These are the Gwich'in, the Sahtu Dene and Métis, and the Tlicho agreements (see Indian and Northern Affairs Canada 2007).

13 The trust also received settlement payments from the federal government of $1.1 billion, which were issued between 1993 and 2007 (see Nunavut Trust 2007).

14 The territorial governments also receive the Canada Health Transfer and the Canada Social Transfer from the federal government, and they do so on the same basis as the provincial governments.

15 There is also a parallel here with Aboriginal self-governments that have financial transfer agreements with the federal government. As these self-governments receive revenues from their own natural resources or share in territorial or federal natural resource revenues, the federal government may reduce the amount of its financial transfer to them.

16 This assumes that any increase in spending required to manage devolution has been taken into account.

17 See Feehan (2006) for a review of the panel's report on TFF.

18 For instance, governments might decide not to permit new natural resource development if there is no scope to increase net revenues. These disincentive effects and the debates about dollar-for-dollar losses associated with natural resources are the same as those related to Equalization payments to the provinces (Feehan 2005).

19 Criticisms of the double clawback were made to the panel (see Expert Panel on Equalization and Territorial Formula Financing 2006, 36; Feehan 2005, 4).

20 This approach is generally consistent with the new Equalization formula for grants to provincial governments with weak fiscal capacity. Also, Zuker and Robinson recommend a 50 percent reduction, although they would implement it within the formula (2005, 35).

21 The economic rent of a natural resource is the remaining market value of the resource

after the costs of labour, capital and other inputs are subtracted, taking into account risk and other relevant factors.

22   The resource-revenue-sharing agreement in principle was with the Inuvialuit Regional Corporation, the Gwich'in Tribal Council, the Sahtu Secretariat Incorporated and the Northwest Territory Métis Nation. It allows the other three Aboriginal representative bodies in the territory to become parties to the agreement in the future.

23   Inuit do not receive this money directly: the payments are made to the Nunavut Trust, which is responsible for allocating the money for the benefit of Inuit.

24   For instance, according to CANSIM table 051-0012, in 2005-06 some 3,557 people left the NWT and 2,230 moved there from elsewhere in Canada (Statistics Canada 2006a). These figures, which are generally consistent with those of previous years, represent a large proportion of the population. If most movers are non-Aboriginal people, then this suggests quite a large turnover of population.

25   Some think otherwise: for example, public choice theorists and critics of big government often argue that governments and bureaucracies will always seek to increase their budgets, regardless of the merits of doing so.

26   Such a windfall could also have the unwanted side effect of inducing a huge in-migration of people whose sole motivation would be to gain from the fiscal surplus.

27   The Irlbacher-Fox and Mills study was commissioned as input into the 2007 Northern Policy Forum, which was convened by the Walter and Duncan Gordon Foundation. For a report on that forum, see Hodge, Stauch and Taggart (2007).

28   Local employers would be subject to a tax on their total payments to workers, regardless of where those workers actually resided. Exemptions and adjustments could be made for small local employers as well as for certain sectors.

29   For more discussion on the question of sovereignty and international conflict and cooperation in the Arctic, see Rob Huebert's chapter in this volume.

References

Cizek, Petr. 2005. *Plundering the North for Hyper-Profits: Non-renewable Resource Extraction and Royalties in the Northwest Territories 1998-2004*, November 29. Yellowknife: Canadian Arctic Resources Committee. Accessed September 17, 2008. http://www.carc.org/2005/royalties%20and %20hyper-profits%2005.12.15.pdf

Expert Panel on Equalization and Territorial Formula Financing. 2006. *Achieving a National Purpose: Putting Equalization Back on Track*. Ottawa: Finance Canada.

Feehan, James P. 2005. "Summary Report: The Expert Panel Roundtable held at Yellowknife." Accessed October 17, 2008. www.eqtff-pfft.ca/english/documents/ FinalReport-Yellowknife.pdf

_____. 2006. "Territorial Formula Financing." In *A Fine Canadian Compromise: Perspectives on the Report of the Expert Panel on Equalization and Territorial Funding Financing*, edited by Paul Boothe and François Vaillancourt. Edmonton: Institute for Public Economics, University of Alberta; Montreal: Centre for Interuniversity Research and Analysis on Organizations (CIRANO). Accessed September 17, 2008. http://www.cirano. qc.ca/pdf/Perequation_07.pdf

Finance Canada. 2007. *The Budget Plan 2007: Aspire to a Stronger, Safer, Better Canada*, March 19. Accessed September 17, 2008. http://www.budget.gc.ca/2007/pdf/bp2007e.pdf

_____.2008. "Federal Transfers to Provinces and Territories." Accessed October 10, 2008. http://www.fin.gc.ca/FEDPROV/tffe.html

Government of Canada. 2007. *Strong Leadership. A Better Canada. Speech from the Throne, October 16, 2007*, 39th Parliament, 2nd sess. Ottawa: Government of Canada. Accessed September 17, 2008. http://www.sft-ddt.gc.ca/grfx/docs/ sftddt-e.pdf

Government of the Northwest Territories. 2008a. *Budget Address 2008-2009, Northwest Territories: Budget Papers.* Yellowknife: Department of Finance, Government of the Northwest Territories. Accessed September 15, 2008. http://www.fin.gov.nt.ca/Documents/2008-09%20Budget%20Address%20and%20Papers.pdf

———. 2008b. *NWT Socio-economic Scan, Statistical Supplement.* Yellowknife: Bureau of Statistics, Government of the Northwest Territories. Accessed September 15, 2008. http://www.stats.gov.nt.ca/Statinfo/Generalstats/Scan/scan.html

Government of Nunavut. 2008. *Nunavut Budget 2008-2009.* Iqaluit: Department of Finance, Government of Nunavut. Accessed September 17, 2008. http://www.gov.nu.ca/finance/mainbudgets/2008.shtml

Government of Yukon. 2006. *Yukon Bureau of Statistics Gross Domestic Product by Industry, 2006.* Executive Council Office, Bureau of Statistics Information Sheet 65.13, December. Whitehorse: Executive Council Office, Bureau of Statistics, Government of Yukon. Accessed September 15, 2008. http://www.eco.gov.yk.ca/stats/pdf/gdp_2006.pdf

———. 2007. *Yukon Oil and Gas: A Northern Investment Opportunity, 2007.* Whitehorse: Energy, Mines and Resources, Government of Yukon. Accessed September 15, 2008. http://www.emr.gov.yk.ca/oilandgas/pdf/o_and_g_investment_opportunities2007.pdf

———. 2008a. *An Energy Strategy for Yukon: Draft for Public Consultation,* May. Whitehorse: Energy, Mines and Resources, Government of Yukon. Accessed September 15, 2008. http://www.nrgsc.yk.ca/pdf/energy_strategy_for_yukon_draft_for_public_consultation_may2008.pdf

———. 2008b. *Budget Highlights: A Better Quality of Life,* March. Whitehorse: Department of Finance, Government of Yukon. Accessed September 15, 2008. http://www.finance.gov.yk.ca/pdf/budget/2008_09_highlights_e.pdf

———. 2008c. *2008-2009 Financial Information.* Whitehorse: Department of Finance, Government of Yukon. Accessed September 15, 2008. http://www.finance.gov.yk.ca/pdf/budget/2008_09_fininfo_e.pdf

Hodge, R. Anthony, James Stauch, and Ingrid Taggart. 2007. *Freedom to Choose: Natural Resource Revenues and the Future of Northern Communities. Report of the 2007 Northern Policy Forum.* Toronto: Walter and Duncan Gordon Foundation. Accessed September 22, 2008. http://www.gordonfn.org/resfiles/FREEDOM_TO_CHOOSE.pdf

Indian and Northern Affairs Canada (INAC). 2004. *Umbrella Final Agreement.* Ottawa: INAC. Accessed September 15, 2008. http://www.ainc-inac.gc.ca/pr/agr/ykn/umb_e.html

———. 2007. *General Briefing Note on the Comprehensive Land Claims Policy of Canada and the Status of Claims.* Ottawa: INAC. Accessed September 12, 2008. http://www.ainc-inac.gc.ca/ps/clm/gbn/index_e.html

Irlbacher-Fox, Stephanie, and Stephen J. Mills. 2007. *Devolution and Resource Revenue Sharing in the Canadian North: Achieving Fairness across Generations.* Toronto: Walter and Duncan Gordon Foundation. Accessed September 22, 2008. http://www.gordonfn.org/resfiles/Forum_DiscussionPaper.pdf

Mayer, Paul. 2007. *Mayer Report on Nunavut Devolution,* June. Ottawa: Indian and Northern Affairs Canada. Accessed September 12, 2008. http://www.ainc-inac.net/nr/prs/m-a2007/2-2891-m_rprt-eng.pdf

National Energy Board. 2008. *2007 Annual Report to Parliament.* Calgary: National Energy Board. Accessed September 24, 2008. http://www.neb.gc.ca/clf-nsi/rpblctn/rprt/nnlrprt/2007/nnlrprt2007-eng.pdf

National Joint Council (NJC). 2006. *Living Cost Differential (LCD) Adjustments — Yellowknife and Rae, NWT.* Ottawa: NJC. Accessed September 18, 2008. http://www.njc-cnm.gc.ca/doc.php?did=283&lang=en

Natural Resources Canada. 2004. "Territorial Evolution." Ottawa: Natural Resources

Canada. Accessed September 12, 2008.
http://atlas.nrcan.gc.ca/site/english/maps/
historical/territorialevolution/1

Nunavut Trust. 2007. "What Is the Mandate of
Nunavut Trust?" *The Trust Fund*. Ottawa:
Nunavut Trust. Accessed September 17,
2008. http://www.nunavuttrust.ca/trust.htm

Okalik, Paul. 2006. "Devolution and Nation
Building in Canada's North." Speech to the
Public Policy Forum Seminar "Economic
Transformation North of 60," December 13,
Ottawa. Accessed September 17, 2008.
http://www.ppforum.com/common/assets/
arctic/paul_okalik.pdf

"Palin Recommends TransCanada for AGIA."
2008. *News and Announcements* 08-078.
Juneau: Office of the Governor of Alaska.
Accessed September 15, 2008.
http://gov.state.ak.us/news.php?id=1173

Statistics Canada. 2006a. *CANSIM Table
Directory*, June 30. Ottawa: Statistics
Canada. Accessed September 19, 2008.
http://estat.statcan.ca/MIS/Directory/
Estat_Table_Directory.pdf

———. 2006b. *2006 Community Profiles*. Cat.
no. 92-591-XWE. Ottawa: Statistics
Canada. Accessed September 18, 2008.
http://www.statcan.ca/bsolc/english/bsolc?
catno=92-591-XWE

Taylor, Amy, Chris Severson-Baker, Mark
Winfield, Dan Woynillowicz, and Mary
Griffiths. 2004. *When the Government Is the
Landlord: Economic Rent, Non-renewable
Permanent Funds, and Environmental Impacts
Related to Oil and Gas Developments in
Canada*, July. Edmonton: Pembina Institute
for Appropriate Development. Accessed
September 22, 2008. http://pubs.pembina.
org/reports/GovtisLLMainAug17.pdf

Zuker, Richard C., and T. Russell Robinson. 2005.
"Fixing Territorial Formula Financing."
Unpublished paper prepared for the Expert
Panel on Equalization and Territorial
Formula Financing. Accessed September 24,
2008. http://www.eqtff-pfft.ca/submissions/
ZukerandRobinson.pdf

ECONOMIC DEVELOPMENT

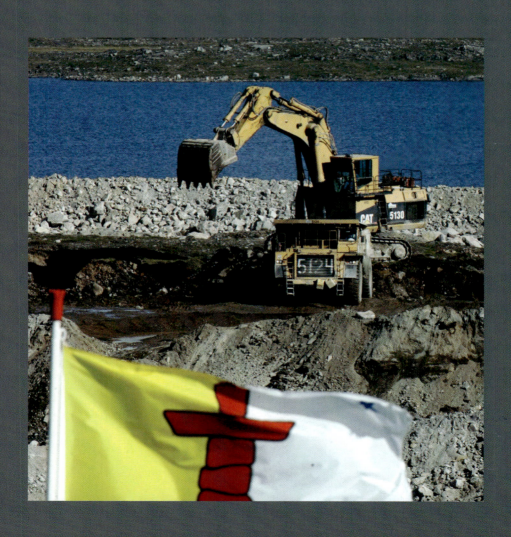

Economic Development
in Northern Canada:
Challenges and
Opportunities

N UMEROUS COMMENTATORS AND OBSERVERS SUGGEST THAT NORTHERN CANADA'S
hydrocarbon and mineral resources will, inevitably, be developed in the
name of the national interest, although just when significant exploitation will
commence remains unclear. This general view underlay Prime Minister John
Diefenbaker's "Roads to Resources" strategy of almost 50 years ago and now
informs Prime Minister Stephen Harper's view of Canada's emergence as an "energy superpower." Natural gas from Canada's Beaufort Sea and Mackenzie Valley
regions may be used, for example, to fuel the extraction of oil from northern
Alberta's tar sands, enabling nationally and internationally important oil exports
to the United States.

Developing the North's natural resources is even characterized as a means
to bolster Canada's Arctic sovereignty, a theme high on the agenda of the Harper
government. When Prime Minister Harper announced plans in July 2007 to construct ice-strengthened navy patrol vessels to assert Canada's presence in the
Northwest Passage, he said we have to use the Arctic or lose it. This was not a
recognition of the age-old and ongoing hunting, fishing and trapping economy of
the Arctic's indigenous peoples but of the need for Canada to exert a more politically visible, technological presence in the region by supporting the exploration
and development of nonrenewable resources, among other things.

Grand economic and northern development visions can be politically
important and beguiling, but they can also be beside the point. Who, for example,
would have predicted in the mid to late 1980s that northern Canada would become
a world-class producer of gem diamonds a decade later? In late 2008, the best-laid
economic development policies and plans of governments and corporations, both

big and small, melted away like snow in spring as a result of worldwide turmoil in stock markets, the fiscal and credit crisis, and a widening recession. These events serve as an important reminder of the boom-and-bust nature of economic development based on natural resource exports, which is driven by world prices and exacerbated by northern circumstances — harsh climate, expansive geography, poor infrastructure, complex regulatory system and scarce qualified labour.

The North's Underground Riches

D ISCUSSION ON NORTHERN DEVELOPMENT OFTEN GROUPS YUKON, THE NORTHWEST Territories (NWT) and Nunavut together, reflecting their shared constitutional status as territories and the province-type responsibilities exercised in the latter two territories by the Government of Canada (as a result of devolution, Yukon has since 2003 exercised responsibility for most province-type functions). All three territories also rely heavily on fiscal transfers from Ottawa. In reality, however, there are significant environmental, economic, ethnic, cultural, political and resource endowment differences between and within the three territories — which comprise approximately 40 percent of Canada's land mass — that should be reflected in public policies to promote economic development. In short, there are many "Norths" in northern Canada. Diversity, not uniformity, is the backdrop to northern economic development.

That being said, research suggests that northern Canada and the circumpolar world hold huge reserves of oil and gas. Discovered resources in northern Canada are presented in table 1 below. The United States Geological Survey estimates undiscovered conventional oil and gas reserves in the Arctic to be in the order of 90 billion barrels of oil, 1,670 trillion cubic feet (Tcf) of gas and 44 billion barrels of natural gas liquids (Bird et al. 2008). We still have much to learn about the geology of the circumpolar world and its inventory of recoverable oil, gas and minerals, particularly in northern Canada. Nevertheless, the results of a comprehensive review undertaken for Indian and Northern Affairs Canada (INAC) suggest that 33 percent of Canada's remaining conventionally recoverable resources of natural gas and 25 percent of its remaining recoverable light crude oil are located in the Northwest Territories, Nunavut and the offshore Arctic.

Table 1
Discovered Resources Inventory in Northern Canada, 2008

Region	Crude oil (millions of barrels)	Natural gas (trillions of cubic feet)
Northwest Territories (and offshore)[1]	1,597	12.2
Nunavut (and offshore)	324	19.2
Total	1,929	31.4

Source: Adapted from Indian and Northern Affairs Canada (2008, 11).
[1] Data for the NWT include the Beaufort Sea.

Estimates of potential natural gas resources are similar in magnitude for the NWT (82 Tcf) and Nunavut (71 Tcf), whereas the ultimate potential for crude oil is estimated at 5.7 billion barrels for the NWT and 2.7 billion barrels for Nunavut (INAC 2008, 9).[1]

In his preface to the 2007 *Northern Oil and Gas Annual Report*, the Minister of Indian Affairs and Northern Development concluded:

> Now, more than ever, the enormous resource potential of the North is being unlocked…Last year, we saw seven new oil and gas exploration licences issued in the Mackenzie Valley and in the Mackenzie Delta-Beaufort Sea Basin…Four significant new discoveries were declared…All of this activity demonstrates that industry partners recognize the potential that lies beneath the surface of the North's land and waters…The Government of Canada is convinced that this potential can drive the sustained economic activity needed to help provide wealth and employment to Northerners and, in turn, build strong and healthy Northern communities. A strong and prosperous North means a stronger and more prosperous Canada. That is why we are determined to move farther and faster to prepare for the challenges and opportunities these development represent, and why our Government is implementing an integrated Northern Strategy to ensure the North is ready for them. (INAC 2008)

In that vein, the Prime Minister announced in August 2008 that $100-million would be added to the $34 million allocated in the 2008 budget for the geo-mapping program to identify the location of mineral deposits across the Far North, citing the unprecedented opportunities associated with these untapped resources in the context of surging global demand for energy and minerals.

Development Prospects:
A Complex Interplay of
Factors

THE LIKELY SCALE AND PACE OF FUTURE DEVELOPMENT OF HYDROCARBONS AND minerals in northern Canada, however, are much more than a matter of deposits and reserves, and will be determined by a variety of factors. Four of these factors stand out from the rest:

1. A world demand and high prices for energy and minerals. Northern Canada is a high-cost environment in which to explore for and develop nonrenewable resources, and it usually takes several years to bring large projects from concept to reality. In recent years, rising world demand and buoyant prices for energy and minerals have encouraged investment in the northern world but, as the economic and financial turmoil that began in 2008 has shown, such conditions can fluctuate quickly and dramatically. For example, 2008 witnessed quite extraordinary volatility in the world price of oil: from a summer peak of more than US$145 for a barrel of light crude, the price fell some months later to less than US$50. Northern energy projects that made economic sense at the former world price may be completely uneconomic at the latter world price.

2. A supportive infrastructure. It has long been received wisdom among industry representatives that northern Canada is an infrastructure-poor as well as a high-cost environment, and that this combination is a significant disincentive to investment and development. This reality is well illustrated by the ongoing debate over the need for public investment to construct a port at Bathurst Inlet in Nunavut and an all-weather road from the port southward to make it economically feasible to develop base and precious metal deposits in the Slave Geological Province in Nunavut and the Northwest Territories. Ongoing feasibility studies to assess the case for an all-weather road to link Gimli and Churchill in northern Manitoba with Rankin Inlet and perhaps even Chesterfield Inlet in Nunavut in order to stimulate mineral development in the Kivalliq region are a similar case in point.

3. A stable political and public policy environment. Investors favour stable and predictable political and public policy environments that provide secure property rights, simple and straightforward regulatory systems, and lenient royalty and taxation regimes. As the chapters on governance in this volume indicate, these factors are complex, and they continue to evolve rapidly in the North.

4. A skilled, educated and motivated workforce. High unemployment and low rates of full-time employment persist in most parts of northern Canada. The local workforce, in many places largely Aboriginal, is not educated to the level commonly found further south, although significant attempts are being made by the federal, territorial and Aboriginal governments to close education and skills gaps. Continued investment in social, educational and training infrastructure is needed to develop a northern-based workforce that can take advantage of economic development opportunities as they arise.

Governments in Canada have very limited influence over the first factor, but their influence over the second, third and fourth is potentially considerable. Geography, distance and expense significantly constrain Canada's performance in relation to the second factor. No communities in Nunavut, for example, are linked by road to southern Canada. Proposed development projects in the North inevitably prompt debate about the role of governments and the provision of public money for physical infrastructure to support development. In relation to the development of base and precious metals, the Government of Canada has put in place a lenient royalty and taxation regime as an incentive to developers and, perhaps, to compensate for the lack of infrastructure. But pressure on the federal government to be more active on the infrastructure front in order to expand development opportunities is likely to persist. As for factors 3 and 4, it is important that they be fully addressed by policy-makers not only for the purpose of attracting private investment but also to ensure that resulting resource development is environmentally and socially sustainable. Ecologically, northern Canada is fragile and vulnerable. In political and cultural terms, it is important to acknowledge that the three territories are home to Aboriginal peoples, who account for 85 percent of the population of Nunavut, are a slight majority in the NWT and a sizable minority in Yukon.

The Reality and Implications of Climate Change

T HERE IS A GROWING RECOGNITION AMONG POLICY-MAKERS IN FEDERAL AND territorial agencies and members of Aboriginal governments that climate warming, which is amplified in high latitudes, is altering the natural environment, and that this has significant social and economic implications. The 2004 Arctic Climate Impact Assessment (ACIA 2005), prepared by the eight-nation Arctic Council, and the northern chapter of Canada's 2008 national climate assessment (Lemmen et al. 2008) project an increase in the speed and magnitude of climate change, with accompanying environmental, social and economic impacts, both good and bad. Climate warming is changing the context in which northern economic development will occur. According to the ACIA, the projected impacts include loss of hunting culture, decline in food security, human health problems, wildlife herd impacts, expansion of marine shipping, increase in access to resources, enhancement of marine fisheries, disruption of land transport, decline in northern freshwater fisheries and enhancement of agriculture and forestry.

Importantly, the economic development implications of climate warming seem to vary considerably between the marine and terrestrial environments. Continued thinning and ablation of sea ice is projected to leave the Arctic Ocean, including the channels of the Arctic Archipelago, free of ice in late summer, although when this will become the norm rather than the exception remains unclear. Recent research by NASA scientist Jay Zwally suggests this will be the case within five to ten years — likely within the planning horizon of nonrenewable resource development projects ("Global Warming" 2008). By easing and promoting access by ship to the region's proven and inferred hydrocarbons and minerals in the offshore and coastal regions, and by reducing the cost of exploration and development operations, the ACIA concludes that climate change is emerging as a key driver of economic development in the circumpolar world.

At a strategic level, informed observers suggest that use of the Northwest Passage for transcontinental shipping between industrial areas in Asia, Europe and North America is likely, although increased use of the Northeast Passage or even the Northern Sea Route across the Arctic Ocean may occur first. The Arctic Marine Shipping Assessment (AMSA), to be considered by Arctic Council ministers in April 2009, foresees a significant increase in tourism and destination shipping in the Arctic to supply communities and service development projects, but little increase in trans-Arctic shipping (Arctic Council 2008). Nevertheless, the geopolitical, sovereignty and economic development implications in the Canadian North of a summer-sea-ice-free Arctic Ocean are profound. On the basis of the ACIA's "big picture," which prompted resolutions in 2003 and 2008 of the Governing Council of the United Nations Environment Programme, it appears that the circumpolar region will experience development of global significance in coming decades.

The prospect of easier access by sea to the Arctic's energy and mineral resources is prompting interest worldwide. China and South Korea, for example, recently joined the eight-nation Arctic Council as official observers (seven European states already enjoy this status). In November 2008, the European Commission released its long-awaited "Arctic communication" — essentially a comprehensive policy that, among other things, seeks greater access to the region's oil, gas and minerals by Europe-based corporations.

On land, however, the picture is different. Climate change may make northern resource development more difficult and expensive. Estimates recently published in Alaska suggest that billions of dollars may be required to repair and/or replace infrastructure damaged as a result of climate warming. This issue is addressed in Tom Hoefer's commentary in this volume on the development of the Diavik diamond mine northeast of Yellowknife. The Tibbitt-to-Contwoyto ice road, developed years ago to support the currently inoperative Lupin gold mine, is used to supply virtually everything required for Diavik and other diamond mines on the tundra. Shorter ice-road seasons necessitate expensive supplemental air transportation.

Evolving Governance and Regulatory Regimes

ALL THREE TERRITORIES HAVE BEEN "MODERNIZING" SINCE THE SECOND WORLD WAR and integrating psychologically as well as economically with Canada and the broader world. Territorial residents have had no choice but to adjust to externally induced change. Representative and responsible government has taken root — Ottawa no longer appoints people to run the North — and, since the adoption by the Government of Canada in 1995 of the Inherent Right of Self-Government Policy, Aboriginal self-government has become an institutional reality in Yukon and the NWT. Reflecting the fact that Inuit form 85 percent of the population of the eastern Arctic, the Inuit of Nunavut chose to establish a public government in 1999 pursuant to the 1993 Nunavut Land Claims Agreement. With the exception of the claims related to the southern portion of the Mackenzie Valley, the land claims of Aboriginal peoples have essentially been settled. Canadian Inuit now own more land in fee simple than any other Aboriginal people or nongovernmental organization in the world, and they are keen to promote development in the Nunavut territory and on their own land.

These political and constitutional accommodations between Canada and its North have largely removed ideological and land-claims-based opposition to resource development. Modern treaties essentially guarantee local Aboriginal people benefits — jobs, training, royalty shares, equity participation and so on — from development projects in their traditional territories. Politically savvy companies embrace such arrangements as "good business" and "legacy building." The politics of protest that surrounded proposed major northern development projects in the 1970s and 1980s has been replaced by the politics of partnerships — a major, if unheralded, achievement by the Government of Canada and northerners, both Aboriginal and non-Aboriginal. Decisions on resource development can now be made largely if not solely on a project's economic merits and social and environmental effects — a key message of Hoefer's commentary.

The most striking political and constitutional difference between northern and southern Canada lies in comprehensive land claims agreements — modern treaties — that apply to all of northern Canada, with the exception of the southern portion of the Mackenzie Valley. Implementation of these agreements has had a huge impact on economic development in the territorial North. Unlike the nineteenth-century treaties, modern agreements are detailed, complex and broad in ambit. The rights they define are protected under Canada's constitution, which means that they can be amended only with the consent of the Aboriginal party concerned.

As a result of the 1986 Comprehensive Land Claims Policy, under which most modern treaties in the North have been concluded, these agreements effectively set the regulatory environment for resource development.[2] Under these agreements, northern Aboriginal peoples gained undisputed surface title to approximately 10 to 25 percent of their historic territory and smaller percentages of the subsurface;

rights to be represented on boards, commissions and other institutions that manage land, water, wildlife and oceans, that assess the impacts of development, and that address access by third parties to Crown land; cash compensation; a share of rents and royalties on development of Crown land; consultation on development of sub-surface resources on federal Crown land; various economic development opportunities, such as the right of first refusal on construction of tourist facilities and preferential access to government contracts; and much more.

Since 1995, modern treaties have also addressed institutions, funding and jurisdiction of Aboriginal self-government. Many provisions of modern treaties have been implemented well, particularly one-off, relatively simple provisions such as transferring cash or title over specific parcels of land from the Crown to Aboriginal peoples. Provisions that require cooperation and coordination among and between federal agencies have been less well implemented. In this regard, the modern treaty organizations formed a coalition in 2003 to press the Government of Canada to live up to obligations defined in agreements and to achieve their broad objectives. The coalition's critique of the questionable performance of the Government of Canada in implementing modern treaties has been supported by the Auditor General of Canada and the Senate Committee on Aboriginal Peoples. Coalition members report a range of funding problems, including lack of funding for boards and other institutions to regulate and manage development.

To bring about its goal of increased industrial development in the North, the Harper government indicated it was committed to simplifying and speeding up regulation and permitting procedures. In response to the April 2007 Cabinet Directive on Streamlining Regulation, Neil McCrank was appointed by the Minister of Indian Affairs and Northern Development to examine the nonrenewable resource regulatory system in northern Canada and to recommend improvements. His report focused on the NWT and recommended simplifying and streamlining the regulatory system, including amalgamating the land-use-permitting and water-licensing functions under a single board for the Mackenzie Valley. McCrank also outlined, but did not recommend, a more radical restructuring and institutional simplification option that would require amendment of modern treaties (2008). He clearly understood that, as a result of the constitutional status of modern treaties through which boards have been established, the reform agenda depends upon dialogue between the Government of Canada and the Aboriginal peoples who are party to these agreements.

The Government of Canada no longer has the ability to unilaterally reform the northern regulatory system, even if it has the political will to do so. Indeed, the regulatory reform agenda is now part and parcel of the coalition's broader agenda of implementing modern treaties, although it remains to be seen whether the current government will embrace this agenda. In short, it will be difficult and time-consuming to make substantive changes to the regulatory environment.

Human Resources Development

I F THE NORTH IS NOW OPEN FOR BUSINESS, THERE REMAIN MANY DIFFICULTIES AND disincentives associated with the fourth factor, outlined earlier. On the international stage, Canada portrays itself, and is broadly seen to be, a mature democracy with wide-ranging social, cultural, educational and research infrastructure. But what is true in Toronto, Montreal, Vancouver and other southern urban areas is not true in rural northern Canada. Remarkably — and it is alone in this among the eight Arctic states — Canada does not even have a university in its portion of the Arctic. A very limited number of vocational programs, such as nursing, are available in the North, but otherwise northerners have to go south to get a degree (see Greg Poelzer's chapter in this volume).

Moreover, primary and secondary education in the territorial North, particularly in Nunavut, is mired in a chronic crisis resulting in part from widespread social pathologies, including spousal assault, drug and alcohol abuse, and family breakdown (see Einarsson et al. 2004; Poppel et al. 2007). That these social pathologies are also a consequence of very significant overcrowding and poor housing was one of the conclusions of former justice Thomas Berger in his review of implementation of the Nunavut Land Claims Agreement (Berger 2006). The high dropout rates and generally low skills levels of graduating students in northern secondary schools (reflected in literacy scores) are not conducive to the sort of high-quality workforce that would-be developers seek.

Until primary and secondary education can be improved and opportunities for tertiary education expanded, the lack of a suitable and skilled workforce in the North will require companies to mount significant on-the-job training and/or to import portions of their workforce from the south — both expensive propositions. It is important to add that capacity is a factor at many levels; inadequate education sometimes hinders effective decision-making by members of the boards, commissions and institutions established by land claims agreements. Informed commentators have also questioned the capability of the Government of Canada, particularly Indian and Northern Affairs Canada, to develop and implement appropriate northern policies and programs. The basic point is that social, cultural and educational policy — primarily the jurisdiction of the territorial and/or Aboriginal governments — will, in part, determine the achievement of economic development goals and objectives promoted by the Government of Canada. Clearly, economic and social policies in northern Canada need to fit hand in glove.

In its 20-year Nunavut Economic Outlook, the Conference Board of Canada recommended that the Government of Nunavut develop human capital as a precursor to and vehicle for economic development, enabling the population to take advantage of economic opportunities as they arise (Vail and Clinton 2001). In broad terms, this advice seems appropriate across the territorial North. Nellie Cournoyea says as much in her commentary in this volume when she also urges the Government of Canada to "attend to its responsibilities in the North" and to treat northern economic development "more seriously and [address it] at a more senior level in the bureaucracy and in government."

Economic Development Perspectives

THE THREE COMMENTARIES THAT FOLLOW IN THIS SECTION — BY A SITTING politician, a diamond miner and a consultant to the oil and gas industry — reflect quite different perspectives on economic development issues and opportunities. Each nonetheless helps us significantly in piecing together the northern economic development jigsaw puzzle. A central theme of these commentaries is the ability of the North to accommodate the additional development that many believe is on the near horizon.

Nellie Cournoyea, Chair and Chief Executive Officer of the Inuvialuit Regional Corporation, suggests that Inuvialuit have been on the "pointy end" of resource development issues in the region for many years, using the 1984

Inuvialuit Final Agreement to build local capacity to take advantage of economic development opportunities and to negotiate "terms of engagement" with would-be developers of the region's oil and gas resources. She points out that the "Great Eye of Ottawa" only periodically looks north and argues that the Government of Canada should upgrade its attention to the North and strive for policy "coherence" in the development of new institutions and processes, in law-making and in strategic planning. Cournoyea argues convincingly that Ottawa and Yellowknife need to accept and act upon their responsibilities to provide public goods to ease the path to sustainable economic development. She notes that reflection and planning are rare in the "hectic atmosphere of Ottawa spin rooms." Hers is a plea for policy, planning, vision and action at the centre to benefit the Beaufort Sea region.

If Cournoyea's picture is from the North looking out, then Gordon Erlandson's picture is of the North looking in — from the perspective of a company coming into the region. Having represented the Minister of Indian Affairs and Northern Development in the review process for the Mackenzie Gas Project, Erlandson has a well-informed viewpoint. He draws on his many years of experience documenting and assessing the efficiency and effectiveness of regulatory processes north of 60 in relation to resource industry activities and reminds us of some important economic basics, including the manner in which companies evaluate and manage risks in their quest to generate wealth and profits. He notes the central importance of the Mackenzie Gas Project to the economic future of the Beaufort Sea and Mackenzie Valley regions and dispels any assumption that development is inevitable if and when this project receives regulatory approval. Erlandson offers trenchant comments on the "complexity" of the northern regulatory system as a disincentive to investment. He does not pull punches. As far as he is concerned, it does not work — at least, not in relation to the business cycle for oil and gas development. In supporting Nellie Cournoyea's plea for policy coherence, Erlandson suggests to northerners that they think about changing the regulatory system to make it more efficient and effective.

Tom Hoefer, formerly manager of communications and external relations with Diavik Diamond Mines Inc., offers a detailed and informative case study of the development of the Diavik mine, which he uses as a platform to make informed comments on the future of mineral development in the North. His commentary outlines the history of exploration for diamonds in the Slave Geological Province and beyond, and it gives pertinent details of the plan to develop the

Diavik mine with emphasis on the negotiations with local communities to provide jobs, training, business opportunities and other benefits. He provides facts and figures to support his view that modern mines like Diavik can contribute markedly to improving the North's economy.

Moving to the bigger picture, Hoefer discusses policy and program needs to sustain and enlarge diamond mining in northern Canada, focusing on rising mining costs, the capacity of the Tibbitt-to-Contwoyto ice road in the context of climate change and the need to promote exploration in order to find new deposits and to make it economically viable to develop lower-value deposits. While Hoefer focuses less than Cournoyea and Erlandson on the regulatory environment, he also recognizes the need for government agencies to plan ahead and to adopt mining-friendly policies and programs.

All three authors refer to the commitment by the Government of Canada in the 2007 Speech from the Throne to develop an integrated northern strategy. While this intent was broadly supported, some commentators at the Northern Exposure conference struck a note of caution, citing a similar but unfulfilled promise made by Prime Minister Paul Martin in late 2004. Others referred to Ottawa's growing fatigue with financial transfers to the North and suggested that a cap on, or slowing down of, such transfers might further encourage acceptance in the North of additional development of natural resources as a means to strengthen local and regional tax bases. Finally, while both the 2008 and 2009 budgets contained a number of measures confirming ongoing interest and commitment to create and pursue economic opportunities in the North — including establishing a stand-alone agency to promote northern development — it remains to be seen whether these efforts will be sustained in the context of the current global recession.

Notwithstanding the hazards of prediction in uncertain economic and fiscal times, it seems safe to suggest that in the long term, significant economic change will take place in northern Canada and elsewhere in the circumpolar Arctic. The worldwide interest in the region's hydrocarbons and minerals and the prospect of rising world prices for both when the recession ends will more than likely guarantee a place for the Arctic in the investment plans of many transnational corporations. The key challenge facing Canada is to be ready and equipped in political, policy, governance and programmatic terms when global economic conditions improve. The commentaries in this volume suggest that much has to be done to ensure that this happens.

Notes

1   In terms of "ultimate potential," the Canadian Association of Petroleum Producers (CAPP) estimates that the Mackenzie Delta-Beaufort Sea region holds 61 Tcf; the Arctic Islands, 45 Tcf; and the mainland NWT and Yukon, 17 Tcf (CAPP 2008).

2   It is also important to note, largely because it is rarely appreciated, that these agreements provide for the involvement of Aboriginal peoples in certain foreign policy negotiations undertaken by the Government of Canada when these negotiations impact on modern treaty rights.

References

Arctic Climate Impact Assessment. 2005. *Arctic Climate Impact Assessment*. New York: Cambridge University Press. Accessed February 24, 2009. http://www.acia.uaf.edu/pages/scientific.html

Arctic Council. 2008. "Arctic Marine Shipping Assessment: Presentation for Arctic Issues Workshop." Naval War College, April 23, Newport, RI. Accessed February 25, 2009. http://www.nwc.navy.mil/cnws/wardept/documents/Arctic%20Marine%20Shipping%20Assessment%20(USCGA).pdf

Berger, Thomas R. 2006. *"The Nunavut Project." Nunavut Land Claims Agreement. Implementation Contract Negotiations for the Second Planning Period 2003-2013. Conciliator's Final Report*, March 1. Ottawa: Indian and Northern Affairs Canada. Accessed February 27, 2009. http://www.ainc-inac.gc.ca/pr/agr/u/lca/nlc_e.pdf

Bird, Kenneth J., Ronald R. Charpentier, Donald L. Gautier, David W. Houseknecht, et al. 2008. "Circum-Arctic Resource Appraisal: Estimates of Undiscovered Oil and Gas North of the Arctic Circle." Reston, VA: United States Geological Survey. Accessed February 27, 2009. http://pubs.usgs.gov/fs/2008/3049/fs2008-3049.pdf

Canadian Association of Petroleum Producers (CAPP). 2008. *Canada's Oil and Gas*, April. Calgary: CAPP. Accessed February 27, 2009. http://www.capp.ca/GetDoc.aspx?DocID=134421&dt=PDF

Einarsson, Niels, Joan Nymand Larsen, Annika Nilsson, and Oran R. Young, editors. 2004. *Arctic Human Development Report*. Akureyri, Iceland: Stefansson Arctic Institute.

"Global Warming 'Tipping Point': Arctic Sea Ice Drops to 2nd Lowest Level." 2008. *New York Daily News*, August 28. Accessed February 23, 2009. http://www.nydailynews.com/news/us_world/2008/08/28/2008-08-28_global_warming_tipping_point_arctic_sea_.html

Indian and Northern Affairs Canada. 2008. *Northern Oil and Gas Annual Report 2007*. Ottawa: Minister of Public Works and Government Services Canada. Accessed February 24, 2009. http://www.ainc-inac.gc.ca/nth/og/pubs/ann/ann2007/ann2007-eng.pdf

Lemmen, Donald S., Fiona J. Warren, Jacinthe Lacroix, and Elizabeth Bush, editors. 2008. *From Impacts to Adaptation: Canada in a Changing Climate, 2007*. Ottawa: Natural Resources Canada. Accessed February 27, 2009. http://adaptation.nrcan.gc.ca/assess/2007/toc_e.php

McCrank, Neil. 2008. *The Road to Improvement: The Review of the Regulatory Systems across the North*. Ottawa: Indian and Northern Affairs Canada. Accessed February 27, 2009. http://www.ainc-inac.gc.ca/ai/mr/nr/m-a2008/ri08-eng.asp

Poppel, Birger, Jack Kruse, Gérard Duhaime, and Larissa Abryutina. 2007. "International Polar Year: Survey of Living Conditions in the Arctic Results Workshop." Presentation to the SLICA Results Workshop, University of Alaska Anchorage, March 22.

Vail, Stephen, and Graeme Clinton. 2001. *Nunavut Economic Outlook: An Examination of the Nunavut Economy. Economic Performance and Trends*, May. Ottawa: Conference Board of Canada. Accessed February 26, 2009. http://www.nu.e-association.ca/cim/dbf/Nunavut_Economic_Outlook.pdf?im_id=3&si_id=305

Navigating and
Managing Economic,
Environmental and
Social Change in the
Inuvialuit Settlement
Region

I AM PLEASED TO HAVE THE OPPORTUNITY TO OFFER THE INUVIALUIT PERSPECTIVE ON
the very present challenges of navigating and managing economic, environmental and social change that accompany resource development. This has been a
top-of-mind issue for Inuvialuit for more than 40 years, since the initial round of
petroleum exploration in the 1960s. You could say that Inuvialuit have taken the
lead in maintaining community sustainability by reconciling life on the land with
the increasingly prevalent wage-based economy, the boom-and-bust nature of
resource development and the negotiation of a role in government.

The debate over northern economic development and the role of the
Inuvialuit in the northern economy and government has occupied the people of
the Inuvialuit Settlement Region (ISR) for nearly all of my lifetime. This issue
drove the negotiation of our land claim settlement — the 1984 Inuvialuit Final
Agreement (IFA), the first settlement concluded north of 60. Concern about
potential impacts motivated rapid implementation of the IFA and the development of the institutions of environmental and wildlife comanagement that would
enable us to access opportunities and manage change.

The Mackenzie gas pipeline, part of the Mackenzie Gas Project (MGP), cat-
alyzed activity on several fronts. The Inuvialuit and First Peoples along the route of
the pipeline mobilized and formed the Aboriginal Pipeline Group (APG) to negotiate a stake in the project. The Inuvialuit Regional Corporation has been working to
build local economic capacity to take advantage of the work opportunities the project will bring. We have also undertaken in the past three years a major effort to
assess our communities' social capacity to deal with the changes and stresses ahead.
That effort identified key deficits in social programming, determined ways of

improving social conditions, and created an agenda and work plan to improve programs and services and address impacts. We ultimately persuaded the federal government to establish a social improvement and impact fund to get a head start on dealing with the deficits before the project gears up. The government will not release the funds until significant progress is made on the MGP; this delay will reduce our ability to manage the impact of the project and improve our social conditions.

This has been a long road for Inuvialuit. Preparing to meet the modern economy by negotiating the terms of engagement has been continuous, in contrast with the occasional, very intense attention when international events draw the Great Eye of Ottawa to the North. Whether it's the DEW (Distant Early Warning) Line development, the price shock and superdepletion of resources, the Roads to Resources program or the Berger Inquiry — every now and then we are caught in Ottawa's spotlight. Today, global warming and its effects on the Northwest Passage and Canadian sovereignty are catching the limelight.

It's not that we do not appreciate the interest, but in the many years between these events and issues it is very difficult to get Ottawa's attention. And we are here. We do not slip off to Ottawa or Houston or Calgary or Yellowknife when federal or corporate interest flits away. The capacity building Inuvialuit need in order to be full participants in the northern economy, as envisioned in the IFA, must go on, even in the quiet times, to equip each generation with the tools they need to get on with their lives, to be productive and to manage change.

So we firmly endorse the government's "fresh" northern priorities. In particular, we would like to be part of the strategy to strengthen sustainable northern communities. Today, communities are only marginally sustainable, and they are unable to keep their young people. This could change if there were a viable northern economy — and that would require northern resource development.

Northern resource development — and at the moment that means a natural gas pipeline to southern markets — looks quite different from the perspective of the Arctic coast. Although the National Energy Board contends that there are plentiful gas resources here, these resources can create wealth for us only if they are marketed. The Mackenzie gas pipeline is therefore needed to open the basin: without it, the resources of the ISR will be stranded. There is no other option, so we are faced with a very big project that carries big risks for companies and the APG and that could also have negative social impacts on our communities. Yet, as big as it is, the project is dependent on market forces far removed from the realities of northern communities.

Northern Exposure: Peoples, Powers and
Prospects in Canada's North

What actions would I recommend be taken to support northern economic
development? Broadly speaking, the federal government should attend to its responsibilities in the North. Although there is a territorial government in the Northwest
Territories, Ottawa has a much larger role here than it does south of 60. Northern
economic development needs to be taken more seriously and addressed at a more
senior level in the bureaucracy and in government. My specific recommendations are
that actions be taken to improve coherence, capacity and infrastructure.

Coherence

WE HEAR COMPLAINTS ABOUT HOW COMPLICATED NORTHERN REGULATORY SYSTEMS
have become. Much of the complexity comes from the requirements of
legislation and institutions, mainly federal, that are layered on top of those of the
ISR, and which were not designed to be coordinated with each other. It is just as
difficult for us to deal with all the legislative authorities involved in reviewing
development applications. However, in the ISR we have spent 20 years putting
our system in place and making it work. This has resulted in strong partnerships
and coordination among Inuvialuit, government and industry. We continue to
work together to improve our regulatory system and our capacity to effectively
participate in the development of the economy and social conditions.

Coherence requires strong partnerships and working relations at all levels
of government, and it is needed in several areas:

- In the development of new institutions and processes: We have participated in multi-stakeholder/government processes and developed action
  plans that recommend a comprehensive set of actions to improve and
  prepare for resource development and to manage the region and the
  Beaufort Sea. It is very important that these recommendations be implemented now rather than in two or three years, when we will have many
  more development applications and increased global warming.
- In law-making and policy development: We must be secure in what we
  are doing and ensure that legislation, regulations and policies are in
  place to enforce our common directions.
- In strategic planning for Canada's broad priorities: Again, Canada must
  continue to be assertive in implementing strategic plans for the Arctic

and ensure that Inuit are full participants in the development and implementation of plans.

Capacity

I NUVIALUIT ARE A PROUD AND ADAPTABLE PEOPLE. WE WOULDN'T HAVE LASTED FOR SO many generations on the Arctic coast if we weren't. Inuvialuit have also taken action early to anticipate development and assess and develop our own capacity. While there is still more for us to do, it is urgent that the territorial and federal governments accept responsibility for investing in public services such as health, education and social services. If the only investment in capacity is in reaction to development after the fact, it will come too late.

Infrastructure

A PROJECT ON THE SCALE OF THE MACKENZIE PIPELINE BRINGS INTO SHARP RELIEF THE lack of infrastructure of every sort. This deficit puts a burden on the project and limits the ability of local businesses to provide services. Officials at all levels of government are concerned about this problem, and they have made their views known to federal leaders. We must remember that the North is at a different stage of development from southern Canada. The provinces benefit from infrastructure built long ago — such as roads, railways and airports. Many publicly financed projects either were initiated in pursuit of resource wealth, or — as in Sudbury, Ontario, and Canmore, Alberta — were actual new resources discovered and developed by government.

So, yes, more money is needed — money to invest in the capacity of individuals and communities to make the most of economic development, and money to invest in physical infrastructure. These investments, provided they are directed thoughtfully, would be genuine, and they would strengthen the North for generations. An example of forward thinking is, in my opinion, evident in the federal government's recent announcement of the establishment of an Arctic research centre to assemble and reinforce expertise in our region. We strongly encourage the physical placement of the centre and its expertise where it needs to be, close to its subject — in Inuvik, on the Arctic coast.

My last point is that it is not just about money, another line in the budget, but about putting serious time and effort into appreciating the realities of the North by working with the Inuvialuit and northerners and acting to serve their long-term best interests. In the hectic atmosphere of Ottawa spin rooms, such reflection and planning are rare, but if Canada is serious about its northern priorities, it must act — and soon.

Diamond Mining in the
Northwest Territories:
An Industry Perspective
on Making the Most of
Northern Resource
Development

O F THE THEMES INITIALLY PROPOSED BY THE ORGANIZERS OF THE IRPP CONFERENCE
on which this volume is based I selected "making the most of northern
resource development." I believe that new diamond mining in northern Canada
has initiated a process that could accomplish just that.

I work for the Diavik diamond mine, a joint venture between two companies:
the Harry Winston Diamond Corporation of Toronto (formerly known as the Aber
Diamond Corporation), which holds 40 percent; and Rio Tinto of London, which
holds 60 percent through its 100-percent-owned Canadian company, Diavik
Diamond Mines Inc. As manager of the project, Diavik Diamond Mines operates
under safety, environmental protection and local beneficiation policies developed and
mandated by its parent, Rio Tinto, one of the largest mining companies in the world.

Diavik was built around four diamond deposits with an estimated in-
ground value (in diamonds) of C$10 billion. In 2006, Diavik was Canada's top dia-
mond producer, extracting nearly 10 million carats of diamonds from two of its
three ore bodies.[1] The mine's infrastructure occupies about 9 square kilometres of
a 20-square-kilometre island in Lac de Gras, 300 kilometres northeast of
Yellowknife in the Northwest Territories (NWT). The nearest Dene community is
Gamètì, a Tlicho settlement approximately 160 kilometres to the west-southwest
of the mine. Access to the remote Diavik mine site is by air and by an ice road,
which must be reconstructed annually and which is usable only for approximately two months. Along this narrow ribbon of ice — the Tibbitt-to-Contwoyto road
— Diavik and other mines must bring in virtually all of their construction materials, as well as an entire year's inventory of consumables. Lack of all-weather road
access also requires Diavik to construct and maintain fuel and other storage

facilities needed to house virtually an entire year's inventory of operating supplies, an expense that most mines in southern Canada do not have to shoulder.

The Diavik plant site is fairly compact. Up close, it bears a resemblance to many northern communities, with its diesel-powered generators to supply electricity; its airstrip to support the movement of workers and freight when the ice road is unavailable; its local road network; its water and sewage treatment facilities; and its other support infrastructure, including fuel and other storage facilities. Diavik turns its similarity to remote northern communities to its advantage, spinning off a significant portion of its site work to a local Aboriginal company. As I will explain, Diavik is creating significant new socio-economic benefits for local and Aboriginal communities in particular.[2]

The Significance of Diamonds

WHY SHOULD WE CARE ABOUT NORTHERN DIAMONDS? THERE ARE TWO GOOD reasons for us to take notice of this fledgling industry. First, the Canadian diamond industry has quickly become a player in global circles. In 2006, Canada reached third place by value in global diamond production (figure 1). This is especially impressive when one realizes that its quick rise is the result of the production of only two mines — both world-class deposits. These are the Ekati and Diavik mines. Ten years ago, there was no Canadian slice of the international diamond pie.

Second, the wealth of the industry has translated into major local benefits. Since 2004, diamond mining has accounted for nearly half of the value of the NWT's gross domestic product. This represents a fundamental change in the economy of the NWT, as this primary wealth generator becomes the largest slice of the economic pie (Impact Economics 2008).[3]

A History of Diamonds in the North

THE SEAT OF THIS NEW DIAMOND WEALTH IS AN AREA OF GEOLOGICAL SIGNIFICANCE called the Slave Geological Province, which extends northeast of

Figure 1
Distribution of Global Diamond Production, 2006

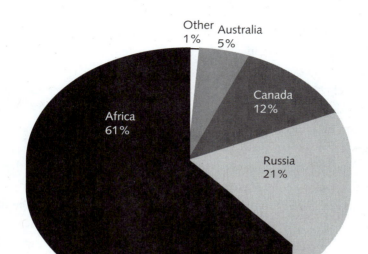

Source: Diavik Diamond Mines Inc.

Yellowknife to the Arctic coast. Two geologists, Chuck Fipke and Stu Blusson, initiated diamond fever in northern Canada in 1991 with their discovery of diamond-bearing deposits called kimberlite pipes near Lac de Gras.

The discovery of gem diamonds in the NWT launched a major staking rush, the scale of which had never before been seen in Canada — or perhaps anywhere else in the world. Over the following three years, over 50 million acres — virtually the entire Slave Geological Province — were staked in the hope that diamond-bearing deposits were hidden beneath them. As luck would have it, or perhaps due to the fecundity of the Slave Geological Province, the diamond discoveries came quickly, and within five years there were several notable finds, three of which (at the time of writing) were mines.

There are many similarities in the approaches taken by the mines, but here I will describe that taken by Diavik. In 1994 and 1995, Diavik's project geologists discovered four kimberlite pipes, the remains of ancient volcanoes that host most of the world's diamond deposits. They hoped that these would contain sufficient diamonds for mining. Because the deposits were located just offshore from what the geologists informally called "east island" and under Lac de Gras, developing a mine posed a major challenge over and above the other challenges that arise in a remote, cold and undeveloped region. Over the next several years, extensive engineering studies were conducted to determine whether it would be possible to mine the underwater deposits. At the same time, the Diavik team conducted environmental baseline studies and mounted a program of community consultations likely unprecedented in northern Canada.

The communities with an interest in Lac de Gras are home to five indigenous groups: three Dene, one Métis and one Inuit. These communities span a region stretching nearly 600 kilometres north from Great Slave Lake to the Arctic coast. When the population figures of these communities are added to those of communities with large proportions of non-Aboriginal inhabitants, the combined population of Diavik's (and the diamond industry's) drawing area is over 30,000 — well over half the population of the territory (see map on following page).

In the course of hundreds of meetings with community and government representatives, stakeholders were able to develop a common understanding of each other's needs and determine the path forward. To confirm its commitments, Diavik negotiated special agreements with the five local indigenous groups that traditionally use the Lac de Gras region: the Tlicho (formerly the Dogrib Dene First Nation), with their communities of Behchokò (formerly Rae-Edzo), Whatì, Gamètì and Wekweètì; the Yellowknives Dene First Nation, with their communities of N'dilo and Dettah; the Lutsel K'e Dene First Nation, with their community of Lutsel K'e; the North Slave Métis Alliance, with a membership living mainly in Behchokò and Yellowknife; and the Kitikmeot Inuit Association, in particular the community of Kugluktuk, downstream of Diavik.

The Diavik Mine Plan

AFTER UNDERTAKING SIGNIFICANT COMMUNITY CONSULTATION, COMPREHENSIVE environmental studies and innovative engineering work, Diavik developed a plan to build an entire mine on an island. Dikes would be built to hold back the lake water so that the ore bodies could be mined.[4] The Diavik plan also included a robust environmental management system, including measures to

Diavik's Community Focus

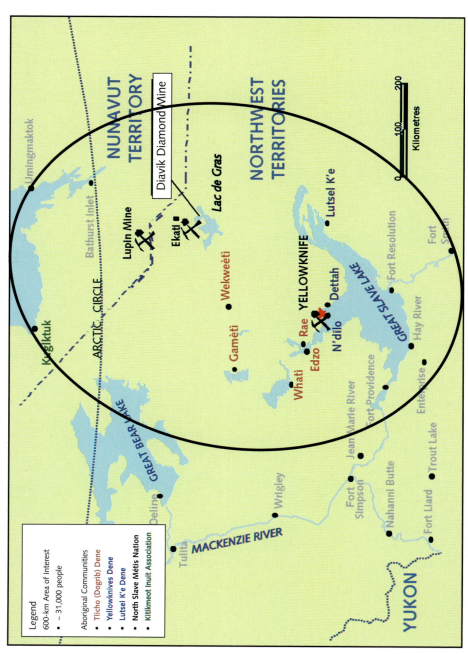

Source: Diavik Diamond Mines Inc.

close and reclaim the mine area.[5] This was a marked departure from the traditional practice, which was to wait until mining was well under way or even approaching closure before beginning the reclamation planning. By planning early, before construction started, Diavik was able to ensure progressive reclamation during mining operations. An important objective of the closure and reclamation plan was to return areas of the mine to productive fish habitat, thus meeting the Canadian government's "no net loss of fish habitat" policy.

A Robust Communities Plan

Through community consultations, Diavik developed a plan that included a range of goals designed to achieve socio-economic benefits. During the construction phase, Diavik would employ at least 40 percent of its workforce locally and would ensure that at least 38 percent of its business went to local providers. For mining operations, Diavik set as objectives that at least 66 percent of its workforce be composed of northerners, 40 percent of its workforce be made up of Aboriginal northerners, 70 percent of its business go to northern companies, and between 8 and 18 apprentices be maintained annually.

The company formalized its community plan through several agreements. It signed a socio-economic monitoring agreement with the Government of the Northwest Territories, which was endorsed by the five indigenous groups and which formalized the socio-economic commitments Diavik had made during the public approval process for the project. It also negotiated an environmental agreement with the federal and territorial governments and the five indigenous groups that addressed commitments the company had made to establish environmental management and monitoring plans, annual reporting and reclamation security. Finally, Diavik forged participation agreements[6] with each of the five Aboriginal groups; these agreements formalized their relationships and laid out the way in which Diavik would work individually with the groups, largely on socio-economic initiatives.

Several new advisory structures were established under the agreements to create a high level of Aboriginal community transparency, something new for northern Canada. The Diavik Communities Advisory Board (DCAB) is composed of representatives of nine Aboriginal communities, the Government of the Northwest Territories (GNWT) and Diavik itself; DCAB is cofunded by the GNWT and Diavik. The Environmental Monitoring Advisory Board (EMAB) includes representatives from the five Aboriginal groups; Diavik; and the

Governments of the NWT, Nunavut and Canada. EMAB receives the majority of its funding from Diavik, and it has some government support. The individual participation agreement implementation committees include representatives from Diavik and each Aboriginal group; Diavik finances these committees. These structures have given Aboriginal communities an unprecedented opportunity to provide input into Diavik's work and to help make the project effective from their own perspective.

Making the Project a Reality

Diavik submitted its project plan to the federal government in March 1998, triggering the environmental assessment, the first step toward making the project a reality. For two and a half years, the plan and its proponents were subjected to intense public and regulatory scrutiny before the permits and authorizations required to construct and operate the mine were issued. These, along with the results of the feasibility study, provided investors with the certainty they required to proceed with constructing the mine in December 2000. This, in turn, cleared the way for Diavik to begin bringing into effect the environmental agreement, the socio-economic monitoring agreement and the five Aboriginal participation agreements.

To construct the mine, Diavik needed to transport over 8,000 truckloads of fuel, equipment and construction materials to the site via the ice road. Quite coincidentally, the site lay almost directly on the historic ice-road route to mines in the Barren Lands. Without this road, constructing and operating the Diavik mine would have been impossible. The road's ability to withstand the pressure of increased traffic and a warming climate is of growing interest to communities, investors, policy-makers and regulators alike.

The Diavik diamond mine went into commercial production in 2003.

Implementing the Communities Plan

Diavik's commitment to a bold and creative communities plan would also require an ambitious implementation strategy. Upon receiving approval to proceed with construction and hiring numerous contractors, Diavik began a northern recruitment program. It also put in place a variety of training programs intended to open more employment opportunities at the mine to people in the Aboriginal communities whose skills required upgrading. These included an innovative community-based program to train trades helpers, which was built on partnerships between government, communities, contractors and the company. Offered in a number of communities, the training was given in the context of a real project chosen by the community; upon completion, the program thus left the community with a useful product. These community-based training programs, supported by various partners (see Diavik Diamond Mines 2002), produced 234 graduates, the majority of whom went on to work for Diavik and other companies. Some graduates passed trades entrance exams, and this opened up more opportunities for them.

Other training programs were offered through the NWT's Aurora College. In the past, the college had focused mainly on providing training and education programs for government, but when Diavik rejuvenated interest in mining-related training, Aurora joined the community-based partnership and expanded into process plant operator and instrumentation training, as well as apprentice training.

To provide its workers with opportunities to raise their education levels, Diavik also established, during construction, a workplace learning centre at the mine site. Staffed by two adult educators, the centre offers career counselling and education support to company employees on a continuous basis.

This commitment to training remains strong, and five years into operations, Diavik is still building on the programs established during construction. By mid-2008, Diavik had 19 apprentices, all northern residents, the majority of whom were of Aboriginal heritage (Diavik Diamond Mines 2008b). To provide promising Aboriginal workers with the skills to qualify for supervisory positions, Diavik has also established an Aboriginal leadership development program in partnership with SAIT Polytechnic, which is based, in part, on the polytechnic's management certificate program.

To enhance recruitment, Diavik launched (and continues to support) a number of initiatives. These include school career fairs to promote opportunities in mining, scholarships to support continued education (Diavik had invested over $1 million in scholarships by the end of 2006), a summer student program to provide hands-on work experience and to support post-secondary education, support for prevocational trades programs in high schools, a community awareness program, cultural awareness training, a policy of contracting work to Aboriginal firms, and attractive compensation programs to both draw and retain workers.

A Unique Local Business Approach

ARGUABLY, DIAVIK'S MOST IMPORTANT STRATEGY FOR ENHANCING NORTHERN AND Aboriginal employment was its decision to contract much of its construction and operations work to local — and, in particular, Aboriginal — firms. Before construction was approved, Diavik developed a northern business participation policy, which would prove important to the company's success. Diavik then hired an experienced business development specialist to find and even help create local business opportunities for the company. This was a challenge, since prior to the arrival of Diavik, there were virtually no Aboriginal mining businesses in the Northwest Territories.

To establish business opportunities for local communities, Diavik had to enact a number of measures. It had to create a northern vendors database in order to maintain a list of available local services, give northern companies advance notice of opportunities by publishing business opportunities profiles, identify potential opportunities for Aboriginal businesses, facilitate new joint venture partnerships and develop alliances with economic development agencies to help capitalize Aboriginal businesses. Its most significant move, however, was to contract local companies to perform much of the work at the mine site. This enabled individuals and local firms to acquire valuable business management knowledge and experience. Today, about half the work of the mine is outsourced, most of it to Aboriginal

Aboriginal Mine Contractors

- Site services – Tlicho Logistics
  - Tlicho First Nation
- Mining operators – I&D Management Services
  - 3 Dene/1 Inuit Partners
- Catering/accommodation – Ekati Services
  - Yellowknives Dene First Nation
- Security – SecureCheck
  - Kitikmeot Corporation (Inuit)
- Explosives – Western Denesoline Explosives
  - Lutsel K'e Dene First Nation

firms (see box). Using local companies has the added benefit of allowing Diavik to share its community plan commitments with local companies well positioned to help meet them. By building local businesses, Diavik is also creating a positive legacy. In addition, Diavik purchases services and supplies from many other northern and Aboriginal firms, among them the Tlicho group of companies — a success story. Tlicho Logistics won the Prospectors and Developers Association of Canada's (PDAC) second ever Skookum Jim Award on February 27, 2009, in recognition of its Aboriginal achievement in the minerals industry. Started in 1999, Tlicho Logistics provides site services and fuel resupply at the Diavik and Snap Lake mines and site management and care and maintenance services at the Colomac mine (which is currently undergoing federal government remediation). As of September 2007, Tlicho Logistics had 340 employees, of whom 60 percent were northerners (41 percent northern Aboriginal peoples, and 34 percent Tlicho) and over $50 million in revenue.

Diavik has also taken some innovative community investment approaches, including support for the construction of community infrastructure — such as an arena in Yellowknife in 2006; and, also in Yellowknife, a men's transition home in 2008 (City of Yellowknife 2008), and most recently (April 2008) with its announcement that it will manage a territorial dementia facility project (Diavik Diamond Mines 2008b). Rather than donating cash, Diavik has opted to assist governments by expediting construction of these community facilities using its project management expertise. Finally, Diavik also invests in the community through more conventional methods, including donations, sponsorships and scholarships.

Measuring Success

DIAVIK'S FOCUS ON PROVIDING OPPORTUNITIES FOR COMMUNITIES TO BENEFIT FROM the mine has been yielding significant results. In 2007, Diavik created operations jobs for an average of 785 workers. Northerners occupied 524 of these positions (or 67 percent), and approximately half (257) were filled by Aboriginal people. The same year, the company had $727 million in combined capital and operations expenditures, of which $521 million (or 72 percent) went to northern firms (Diavik Diamond Mines 2007a) (see box on following page).

So How Did We Do?

- ◆ Construction workforce: 800 workers
  - – Aboriginal: 20%
  - – Northern: 44%
- ◆ Construction contracts: C$1.2 billion
  - – Aboriginal: 50%
  - – Northern: 74%
- ◆ Operations workforce: 785 workers
  - – Aboriginal: 33%
  - – Northern: 67%
- ◆ Capital and operations expenditures: C$727 million (2007)
  - – Aboriginal: 38%
  - – Northern: 72%

Diavik did not formally project how much it might spend through Aboriginal businesses, in large part because initially there were virtually no such businesses available to service the burgeoning diamond mining industry. However, with the encouragement of Diavik, and due to the company's proactive northern business approach, new Aboriginal businesses were created — most often in partnership with experienced, well-established firms — that could serve the company. As a result, Aboriginal business has mushroomed in northern Canada.

In 2007 alone, Diavik spent $276 million (or 38 percent of its total operations and capital expenditure) through northern Aboriginal businesses. Between the start of mine construction and the end of 2007, Diavik's total operations and capital expenditure was $3.3 billion, of which 74 percent (or just under $2.5 billion) was through northern firms; of this, nearly $1.5 billion was spent through northern Aboriginal businesses (Diavik Diamond Mines 2007a). This kind of local and Aboriginal investment marks a watershed in northern mining history. Based on a quick poll of the Canadian mining industry in 2006, it appeared that this level and type of investment had been achieved by only three companies: Syncrude, with its tar sands project in Alberta; Cameco, with its uranium mining in Saskatchewan; and now Diavik.

The Bigger Diamond
Picture

I WOULD · BE REMISS IF I DID NOT CITE THE EFFORTS MADE BY THE OTHER DIAMOND mining companies in the NWT. Diavik is one of the three major diamond mining projects that contribute to the NWT's economy. BHP Billiton began producing diamonds commercially from its Ekati mine in 1998, and De Beers officially launched production on July 25, 2008. When we combine statistics related to all three projects, we see that between 1997 and 2007 the cumulative employment generated in the North by diamond mining exceeded 11,800 person-years, with the benefits almost equally split between non-Aboriginal and Aboriginal workers, mirroring the NWT's demographics (Impact Economics 2008).

Similarly, steady growth in business from all three mines has resulted in over $5 billion being spent through northern businesses over the past 10 years; nearly half of this is through Aboriginal businesses.

Sustaining Northern
Mining Benefits

Challenges and Obstacles

T HE EVIDENCE IS THEREFORE QUITE COMPELLING THAT DIAMOND MINING — AND THAT OF Diavik, in particular (keeping in mind my declared bias, of course) — has generated significant and valuable local benefits and levels of inclusion, especially for Aboriginal communities, through training, employment and business. Furthermore, I would argue that nurturing and sustaining — and even increasing — these benefits in the years to come will be in the best interests of the NWT and its residents. The question is: How long will the current mining projects last? Given the predisposition of market forces to send natural resource projects into boom-and-bust cycles, it is difficult to say. But to maintain the viability of the projects, we must take several steps: measure the health of this important industry; recognize and understand the challenges it faces; and then develop a favourable environment in which to sustain these mines or their successors and, in turn, their socio-economic benefits.

An interesting projection of the current state of the NWT diamond mining industry's future was compiled in 2006 as part of an industry-based attempt to address climate-change-related uncertainty about the seasonal ice road. Each of the mines supplied projections of its yearly ice-road shipping requirements. Since the number of truckloads required is directly linked to production at the mines, the compiled data essentially mapped out the future of the NWT's diamond mining industry. According to the mines' trucking projections, diamond mining will peak in about 2013 and then tail off to closure by about 2030. This scenario is, of course, subject to unpredictable market forces and exploration outcomes, but the data indicate that the current diamond industry will last for about another 20 years. However, allowing the door to close on diamond mining in 20 years could lead to socio-economic problems in a context of population growth and limited employment options. If mining is not sustained, recent advances brought on by meaningful employment, training and business opportunities might be reversed. If we value the benefits that diamond mining is creating for our northern communities, then our goal should be to sustain the industry longer. South Africa has had 100 years of diamond mining. Can we not stretch our industry horizon to 50 years?

It will be difficult. The challenges and obstacles diamond mining companies face in keeping their mines viable are numerous and considerable. When the first three mines in northern Canada started operations, they practised lower-cost open pit mining. But the two largest — Ekati and Diavik — are now making the transition to more expensive underground mining; and the newest mine — Snap Lake — has only ever done underground mining. Underground mining is far more expensive than open pit mining due to the fact that it requires more expensive skilled labour, its production rates are lower, and it consumes more power in manufacturing paste backfill, heating underground air and pumping water. The increased cost of underground mining can generally be justified only for high-value ore bodies. And if no more high-value ore bodies are discovered through successful exploration, then the only alternative is to make lower-quality deposits economic by reducing costs related to large budget items such as transportation, power and labour.

Another challenge the mining companies face is linked to the Tibbitt-to-Contwoyto ice road, which has been in seasonal use for approximately 25 years. Over that period, the road has seen a growth in trucking from a few hundred truckloads annually (to supply the Lupin gold mine, which the road was first built to serve) to a record-breaking 10,900 truckloads in 2007 (to supply four diamond mines). But just how much more can the capacity of this road be increased?

A key limiting factor, at least in some years, is climate change. The ice-road study mentioned earlier looked at the trend toward warmer winters. The first time this trend had an effect on the ice road was in 2006. That year, the largest deviation from average winter temperatures in Canada occurred in the southern NWT, and it was centred on the southern portion of the Tibbitt-to-Contwoyto ice road. The road builders were confronted with thinner ice, more frequent storms and a shorter ice road season. All the road users — including three mines and one mine construction project — suffered from freight shortages and, to the extent that they could afford it, they had to fly in freight and fuel. Unexpected air expenses amounted to tens of millions of dollars.

Studies show that the warming trend in the region of the ice road will continue, with unpredictable results. It will most likely impose higher cost pressures on the mines. Their decision as to whether to maintain production as usual and absorb the added transportation costs will be influenced to a great extent by the overall economic health of their operations and current marketplace conditions. They may well be forced to scale back operations, with the consequences to the local communities of fewer jobs and less business. While the past three winters have been cold, and the high-temperature winter record set in 2006 has yet to be matched, climate studies do continue to show a warming trend.

Notwithstanding the pressures that a shorter ice-road season places on the mines, the road is already operating close to capacity. That appears to be around 11,000 truckloads, a record set in the winter of 2007 under more normal weather conditions, when new efficiencies like early plowing and additional flooding crews were used. The ice-road study indicates that future demand could reach 14,000 truckloads. This would also have important economic ramifications.

Yet another challenge to sustaining the benefits of northern mining is the fact that every mine eventually exhausts its supply of ore. It will close unless more deposits are found. Furthermore, new deposits must be found if new mines are to be constructed. This requires active exploration and the policies to support it.

When we look at all the major diamond deposits discovered to date, we see two warning signs. First, they were all discovered in the mid-1990s. The fact is that all the existing mines and those that are proposed or under construction are based on discoveries made more than 10 years ago; there are no recent high-quality discoveries. If we are to sustain mine-related benefits, then we need to explore in earnest to increase discoveries. Second, an examination of the amount of time that elapses between discovery and the start of operations highlights an alarming trend: it seems that 10 years is now the norm. We therefore need to make significant discoveries today if we are to replace those mines that are currently midway through their lifespan. Again, this will require active, even aggressive, exploration.

Many industry players say that in today's northern environment exploration is increasingly difficult. Protection arguments are keeping more geographic areas off limits to exploration; regulatory hurdles and general political uncertainty are frightening away exploration investors; there is less government mapping being done; and land claims negotiations are presenting obstacles. We need a policy environment that supports and encourages exploration and mining by initiating, for example, flow-through exploration tax incentives; improved access to land and healthy investment in geological research and mapping; measures to decrease uncertainty over unsettled land claims; and possible equity participation by Aboriginal groups. Devolution of non-renewable resource responsibilities to the NWT government may also increase support for exploration inasmuch as a local government is closer to and feels the economic consequences — positive and negative — of mineral development.

In 2008, in recognition of this situation, the federal government launched several initiatives to contribute to a more certain northern policy environment: a northern regulatory improvement initiative (Indian and Northern Affairs Canada 2008); a $100-million program of geo-mapping for energy and minerals (Natural Resources Canada 2008); and a renewal of the flow-through mineral exploration tax credit (Prospectors and Developers Association of Canada 2009).

Possible Solutions

One way to sustain the benefits of northern mining projects would be to make lower-value deposits economic. The three large mines in the NWT have ore body values ranging from $100 to $300 per tonne. No new deposits of such high quality have been found — at least, not under the current exploration regime. If we are to sustain existing mining operations beyond their projected lifespan in the absence of high-value-per-tonne discoveries, we must find — and make economical — lower-value-per-tonne deposits. A number of these lower-value deposits are known to exist, but the cost of mining them is still too high.

Support through improved infrastructure could help reduce costs. In this regard, there are three significant initiatives under study. The first is a seasonal overland road that would replace southern portions of the Tibbitt-to-Contwoyto ice road, virtually eliminating the effects of climate change. It would extend the ice road's operating season by several weeks and thus preclude the expense of flying in freight or curtailing operations during a warm winter. But preliminary engineering studies undertaken by the three NWT diamond mines indicate that the cost of the project is too great for the mines themselves to absorb.

The second initiative is a northern route: the Bathurst Inlet port and road project. The project would entail construction of a port on Bathurst Inlet, which is located in the Slave Geological Province, and a 211-kilometre all-weather road to Contwoyto Lake. While it would be constructed to facilitate the opening of new mines in Nunavut, if the project could lower freight costs to the diamond mines it could help to reduce mining costs for the entire region. The third initiative is a proposal to bring hydroelectricity from a plant on the Taltson River system south of Great Slave Lake through a 700-kilometre transmission line to the diamond mines. This project could help sustain diamond mining in the Slave Geological Province provided that the power it supplied was cheaper than that currently produced at the mines. An added benefit is that it would reduce the need for diesel fuel to power the mines' generators; it would thus also reduce freight pressure on the ice road.

In the face of diminishing diamond reserves, another area to explore in an effort to sustain northern mining benefits is to diversify into other commodities. The Slave Geological Province (which hosts the diamond mines) has great mineral potential. Gold mining is being proposed near the Coronation Gulf, and a number of significant base-metal deposits are known to exist some distance inland. Bulk land and marine transportation would be required to move the large volumes of this product to market. Beyond the Slave Geological Province are other mineral development opportunities that should be examined — including, for example, uranium potential in the Thelon and Sahtu regions

Developing such resources would increase the size of the opportunity pie in the North, providing new jobs and business opportunities not only in Nunavut but also in the neighbouring Northwest Territories, where many of those workers with mining expertise now reside thanks to the diamond mining industry's efforts. Viable Aboriginal mining support companies have now established themselves, and new mining projects stand to benefit from their presence. The benefits of the working relationships between these companies and any new mining initiatives will be passed on to the local communities. Not a bad thing.

Until recently, it appeared that the planets were aligning. Mineral commodities were commanding record prices, the Canadian government was showing an increasing interest in reinforcing Arctic sovereignty, and there was growing support from local and Aboriginal governments. However, at the time of writing, the sweeping effects of the global economic crisis were seriously retarding mineral exploration in the North and around the world. One of these effects has been a decrease in production at the northern diamond mines, with subsequent layoff of workers and contractors, and reduced spending. This emphasizes the critical need for government policy support.

Conclusion

THE DIAMOND MINING INDUSTRY IS CREATING MAJOR BENEFITS FOR ABORIGINAL AND non-Aboriginal northerners and for all Canadians. These benefits are so important to the social and economic health of the North that we must work to sustain the industry for as long as possible. In order to do so, we will require a policy environment that supports initiatives such as an improving the northern infrastructure, offering exploration tax incentives, improving geoscience and creating a more certain regulatory environment. This will necessitate the participation of all levels of government. Given the long lead time between the discovery of deposits and the start of mining operations, we need to take action now to support and encourage further exploration.

I would like to conclude by citing Diavik's credo: "For centuries, people of the North have used the resources wisely. Diavik is continuing this tradition." Supportive public policy is essential if Diavik and the mining industry in general are to be able to sustain that tradition.

For the people of the North and for Canada, I believe it will be worth it.

Notes

1   Only three of the four deposits that make up the Diavik project are currently classified as ore bodies, i.e., economical to mine.

2   The Canadian Council for Aboriginal Business has awarded Diavik a gold (top-level) certification under its Progressive Aboriginal Relations program.

3   The overall contribution of the diamond industry to the territorial economy is higher than what is recorded by Statistics Canada as mining output. While the construction of these mines has a sizable influence on the economy, Statistics Canada records this expenditure elsewhere, under construction output.

4   Diavik has developed national-engineering-award-winning dike technology that allows it to access and mine ore bodies that lie under the lake in which the island is located.

5   The mine uses processing technology that doesn't require chemicals to separate diamonds from the waste minerals and doesn't create significant adverse environmental effects. Its environmental management system is certified to the international standard (ISO) of 14001.

6   Diavik chose the term "participation agreement" rather than "impact benefits agreement" to more clearly reflect the need for the parties to work together to maximize success.

References

City of Yellowknife. 2008. "Yellowknife Homelessness Coalition Opens Doors to North's First Transition Home for Men." Press release, December 12. Accessed March 20, 2009. http://www.yellowknife.ca/News/NewsRelease_YellowknifeHomelessnessCoalitionOpensDoorstoNorth_sFirstTransitionHomeforMen.html

Diavik Diamond Mines. 2002. *Diavik's Training Partnerships: Northern Partners, Northern Success.* Yellowknife: Diavik Diamond Mines Inc. Accessed March 20, 2009. http://diavik.ca/documents/DiavikTrainingBook.pdf

_____. 2008a. *Diavik Diamond Mine Socio-Economic Monitoring Report for Operations January to December 2007: Diavik Diamond Mines Inc.* Accessed March 20, 2009. http://www.diavik.ca/documents/Diavik_2007_SEMA_Report.pdf

_____. 2008b. *Diavik Diamond Mine 2008 Mid-Year Socio Economic Monitoring Report*, December 16. Yellowknife: Diavik Diamond Mines Inc. Accessed March 20, 2009. http://diavik.ca/documents/Diavik_2008_half_year_sema_report.pdf

_____. 2008c. "Diavik Partners in Health Care Facility," media release, April 30. Accessed March 25, 2009. http://www.diavik.ca/ENG/media/1131_media_releases_1409.asp

Impact Economics. 2008. *NWT Diamonds 2008*, October. Report prepared for the NWT/Nunavut Chamber of Mines and the Mining Association of Canada. Pittsburgh: Impact Economics. Accessed March 20, 2009. http://www.mining.ca/www/media_lib/MAC_Documents/Diamond_Affairs/2009/NWT_Diamonds_2008_Final_v3.pdf

Indian and Northern Affairs Canada (INAC). 2008. "Government of Canada Releases Report on Regulatory Systems in the North." Ottawa: INAC. Accessed March 20, 2009. http://www.ainc-inac.gc.ca/ai/mr/nr/m-a2008/2-3070-eng.asp?p1=209557&p2=428300

Natural Resources Canada (NRC). 2008. "Geological Survey of Canada: GEM — Geo-mapping for Energy and Minerals." Ottawa: NRC. Accessed March 20, 2009. http://gsc.nrcan.gc.ca/gem/index_e.php

Prospectors and Developers Association of Canada. 2009. "Prospectors and Developers Association of Canada Hails the Federal Government's Plan to Invest in Geological Mapping and to Renew the Super Flow-Through Program." Press release, CNW Group, February 26. Accessed March 20, 2009. http://www.newswire.ca/en/releases/archive/February2008/26/c6429.html

Aligning Petroleum
Sector Activities with
Northern Regulatory
Requirements

M Y OBSERVATIONS RESULT FROM A DECADE WORKING IN THE NORTH WITH
governments, non-government organizations and the resource industry.
One early opportunity was to document the regulatory systems involved in
authorizing resource activities, as new systems emerged from the land claims settlement process. Most recently, I undertook a term as the federal ministerial representative to the Mackenzie Gas Project (MGP), a position designed to assist
interested and affected parties in working with northern regulatory and review
systems in relation to the application for the MGP.

Northern economic development is sometimes conceived as something that
can be managed and modulated. This perception comes easily in the industrialized
and developed parts of Canada, where production, employment and markets are
firmly rooted. It's my observation, however, that northern Canada, and not just
north of 60, experiences economic activity in a very different way, and public policy either deals with these realities or it fails. I have been asked to address this idea
specifically in the context of the wage-based economy and the petroleum sector —
while acknowledging that the land-based economy remains a significant and vital
part of northerners' lives and sense of identity.

For the past half-century, the main wage activity in the North has
been government — building it, conducting it, serving it. The federal government is active there through Indian and Northern Affairs Canada,
Environment Canada, the Canadian Wildlife Service, Fisheries and Oceans
Canada and other agencies. Territorial governments also play important
roles, and there are settlement-region-based bodies, boards, agencies, committees, regional councils and municipal governments. The fact is, however,

that while government can create economic activity, it doesn't necessarily create economic wealth.

To create wealth, one must produce something that someone else wants, get it to that market and sell it ahead of the competition. As optimistic as the Berger Commission was about the potential for renewable resource development to sustain the Mackenzie Valley, the economists got it wrong. The local population is too small, the region is too far from receptive markets, and there is too little infrastructure there to support renewable resource industry or manufacturing, or service- or knowledge-based industry. The opportunity lies in nonrenewable resources — minerals, and oil and gas. In southern Canada, we have forgotten what it was like to have an economy based on mineral wealth. Mineral deposits and petroleum accumulations don't advertise. They are where they are, however inconvenient that may be, and the reason they haven't been found already is that they are well-hidden. Diamonds have been a tremendous opportunity for the North, buffering the effect of the bust in gold mining, but the boom in diamond exploration and mining is waning: BHP Billiton's Ekati diamond mine is now scheduled to close earlier than expected.

At present, the only substantial new prospect for resource development is petroleum — specifically, natural gas. Although it may seem obvious, we need to understand that the road from speculating, in the 1970s, about resource potential based on National Energy Board calculations of sediment volumes to confirming and quantifying the reserves is a long one. It's longer still to achieving a flow of oil or gas to distant markets. Long lead times are required between initial outlays for exploration and cash in hand for the product. There will be uncertainty about whether the resource is actually there and considerable risk related to technology and market conditions. It will be necessary to make available a regular supply of exploration lands that are of interest to explorers, but the pace of development must also be controlled. Land-use plans must therefore be completed and this information must be integrated into regulatory processes.

In the time frame of the Mackenzie Valley pipeline discussions, the spot price of oil has swung from US$9 per barrel in 1990 to more than US$140 in July 2008. Natural gas has seen similar price fluctuations and has been as low as $1. It is no coincidence that the energy companies involved in exploration in the Northwest Territories (NWT) are primarily the largest companies, as they are better able to bear the costs and risks of activity in the North. But there is a divide in perceptions of industry that deeply complicates doing business in the North. While these large operators can bear high cost and high risk (and understand that the North is a high-cost environment), it is an open question whether they will choose to accept that cost and risk in the North or elsewhere, in upstream activities or in other sectors. A manager for a project in the North must actively compete for investment funds with project managers pursuing other opportunities all over the world. The boards and shareholders that the project manager must report to, in light of the costs, risks and delays of working in the North, can, with amazing speed, redirect corporate strategy and funds elsewhere.

In the late 1990s, it was very important for corporations to hear from northern governments and leaders that the NWT was open for business — ready to deal with resource activity, and more secure about its capacity to cope with and profit from that activity. Company representatives met with leaders ready to talk business and terms. While the regulatory processes in the North were unfamiliar and largely untried in the sector, a number of companies began to think that northern resource development might be within reach. This shift was significant, because the effect of a drilling moratorium in the 1970s and subsequent regulatory reviews had been to put the North off limits.[1] And so the purchase of rights, the planning process for a pipeline, and the exploration and delineation of reserves began. In particular, the Mackenzie Gas Project — through conception, definition and assessment — has demanded tremendous commitments of time and effort from northerners, proponents and governments.

Very serious efforts have been made by northerners to understand corporate issues, and by companies to appreciate the demands and aspirations of the "new North." The MGP can be seen as a catalyst for a huge undertaking that has dominated northern politics and governance for years. The project is critical to opening the Mackenzie Delta basin, and it would be a critical piece of northern Canadian infrastructure. My concern is that the MGP, as significant as it is, obscures some realities. I know that many people think the petroleum industry is back, that the developers are committed, and that all that remains is to set the terms. I would not, however, describe the industry as "back" — rather, it is "poised." You can see this in activity and investment patterns. Over the past ten years, activity has been low, especially in relation to resource potential, with a peak in 2003 of 36 wells drilled in the whole of the NWT. This may seem like a lot of wells, but consider that Alberta, with its similar remaining resource potential, saw more than 17,000 wells drilled the same year (and 20,000 wells in 2006, when the NWT saw 5). Northern activity is much slower now, although this is not immediately obvious from investment figures because of the very high cost of one or two recent wells. A decision by regulators is now projected for late 2010, and after that we must wait for the industry decision on whether to proceed. The simple point here is that there is nothing inevitable about northern economic development, even if the MGP is approved.

I do not mean this to sound threatening. I am making an observation about the way the petroleum industry makes investment decisions. All investment decisions are made, more or less, on a calculation of net return — how much an investment will bring in over costs, adjusted for the risk of failure. It is in the nature of the risk that a resource decision will differ from, for instance, a decision to build a Nike factory in the Ottawa-Montreal corridor. Oil and gas operators are a strange lot: they will accept kinds of risk that most of us would consider ridiculous. For all the technology available, exploration is never a sure thing; if it were, no unsuccessful wells would ever be drilled — there would be no dry holes costing tens of millions of dollars. Yet people involved in resource exploration get excited about rooting around thousands of metres underground, about making a drill system work in the Arctic winter night, with polar bear monitors watching their backs. While they do this, however, other employees of the companies they work for are watching the markets and pricing risks.

Managing these sorts of risk (geological risk, price risk, market risk, business risk, technological risk) is the industry's job. How well a company does this will determine whether it thrives or goes bust or gets eaten up in a corporate takeover. While resource companies take these sorts of risk in stride, they are extremely wary of other kinds of risk — specifically, regulatory and political risk that can't be quantified or managed. When resource companies are deciding whether to go ahead with a project like a pipeline, they anticipate returns from both the pipe and the resource development that will supply the pipe, after adjusting for political and regulatory risk. A key consideration, should the pipeline project get the go-ahead, will be the company's ability to get the approvals it needs to do all the other necessary work related to the project on time and under terms that will allow it to make money.

Once a resource operator has addressed all the usual risks, it turns its attention to getting the piece of paper that will allow the work to proceed — the equipment moved, the people hired and put in place. That operator will want to know what has to be done, for whom, for how much, and how long it will take. Figure 1 illustrates the range of organizations that are part of the regulatory framework for petroleum sector approvals in the NWT. It is a simplified description of an operator's process requirements because it doesn't reflect the fact that multiple authorizations may be required in some jurisdictions, or that within each of the settlement areas there are eight to ten different land statuses. Between 2000 and 2003, when I was involved in the Regulatory Roadmaps Project — an initiative to prepare comprehensive guides to regulatory approval processes for oil and natural gas exploration and production across the NWT — the documents we produced ran to a thousand pages, with dozens of charts.[2] This is because regulators required everything on the road map before they were satisfied that we were properly representing requirements.

So it's complicated. But should that pose a problem? Shouldn't it just be a matter of getting to know the system and learning how to navigate within it? It's not as though systems aren't as complicated in Alberta or British Columbia. When we wrapped up the Regulatory Roadmaps Project, both industry and government took heart from the idea that once we had all gained experience with these systems, synergies and efficiencies would evolve. The problem with northern regulatory systems, however, is not that they are complex, but that they don't work — at least, not in relation to the business cycle for oil and gas sector development. While individual regulators have implemented procedures for dealing with activities and projects, these procedures, when applied as a collective set of federal and territorial systems, do not effectively accommodate large-scale development projects that involve interdependent and sequential activities and require time-sensitive approvals for year-over-year investments. Regulatory risks increase further when projects cross jurisdictional boundaries.

Industry has not seen the improvement it had hoped for and there has been no overall assessment of the impact of new northern legislative and institutional arrangements on petroleum sector activities. Perceptions of risk have actually risen over the past 10 years. Operators say they can't count on the standards of administrative law, such as consistency, predictability and timeliness, that are taken for granted elsewhere. Whether the project involves major drilling or digging a soil pit from which to take samples for an environmental quality survey, the applicant cannot be sure when the decision will be made, what terms will be

Figure 1
Regulatory Framework for Oil and Gas Activities in the Northwest Territories

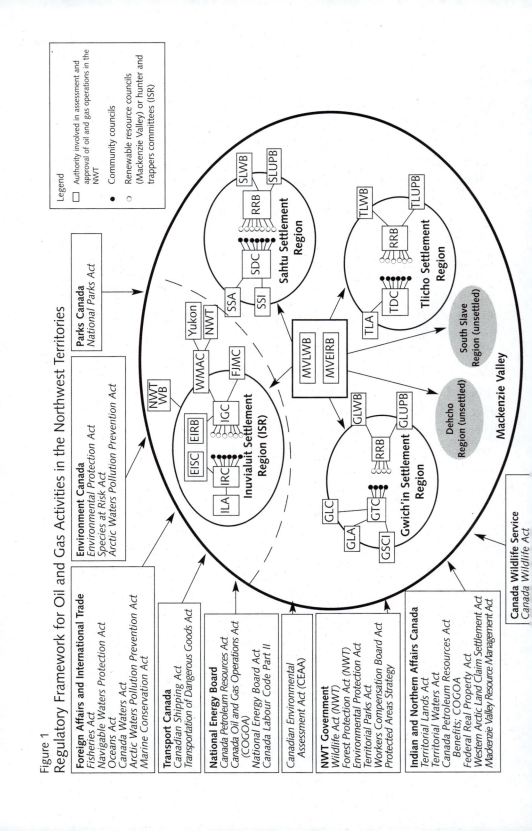

offered or even whether the project will be approved at all. And the cost of an error can be serious, given the North's brief operating season and the necessity of multi-year planning.

What is to be done? I would echo Nellie Cournoyea's call for greater coherence in northern policy and decision-making. Coherence, consistency and accountability are needed for all kinds of development, not just resource development. There is also a need for greater coordination, at a senior level, across all federal departments and agencies involved in resource management and decision-making, and an understanding of requirements at both the staff and political levels. The federal government has acknowledged regulatory risk south of 60 by establishing a major-projects office. The need is certainly as great in the North. Review and assessment of the MGP have gone ahead, but not smoothly — it has required an enormous effort on the part of all involved to keep the system moving — a level of effort that cannot be maintained. Once the pipeline decision is sorted out, there is the likelihood that all bodies will go back to business as usual. The problem is not just for major projects. Because resource activity generally proceeds in stages, a problem with a small part of a project may have serious long-term consequences. Staged processes that require assessment of components in one season can stall or stop other parts of a project planned for subsequent seasons. If processes and time frames for development and operations approvals become unpredictable, there will be less enthusiasm for further investment in exploration. This trend is already apparent in the North.

I hope that northerners will give some thought to whether changes are warranted that would make the North a more accommodating place in which to work and invest — changes that would also respect the principles of the land claims agreements and maintain very high standards for environmental and socio-economic stewardship. In November 2007, Minister of Indian Affairs and Northern Development Chuck Strahl announced a new initiative to improve the overall northern regulatory environment and appointed Neil McCrank as the minister's special representative responsible for the Northern Regulatory Improvement Initiative. McCrank's report, released in May 2008, provides strategies for system improvements aimed at achieving economic development objectives, without sacrificing environmental protections and responsibilities (McCrank 2008). Northerners should find value in system adjustments that accommodate the inherent requirements of a viable oil and gas sector while facilitating an improved management capacity, an increased efficiency in operating regulatory processes, an improved resolution process for surface rights disputes, an improved risk management process, better-structured timelines and an improved ability to capture northern knowledge.

Assessment of northern regulatory systems suggests that collective regulatory processes present a barrier to investment in the development of public oil and gas resources. Given that it is beyond the capacity or scope of any individual project to deal with this barrier effect, the efficiency and effectiveness of regulatory processes must be improved through public policy. The challenge for governments and their regulators to consider is this: "How can northern regulatory processes be adjusted to respond effectively to proposals of the scale and complexity required to develop northern petroleum resources?"

Notes

1   In the 1970s, the Government of Canada
     instituted a moratorium on the issuance of
     new exploration rights to facilitate the land
     claims process and land selection. The land
     claims settlements took two decades to
     conclude, and in that time almost all his-
     torical exploration rights lapsed. The rights
     issuance process was reintroduced after the
     settlement of land claims in the Beaufort-
     Mackenzie Basin in 1989, in the High
     Arctic in 1991 and in the mainland
     Northwest Territories in 1994.
2   Regulatory road maps for the NWT are
     available at oilandgasguides.com.

Reference

McCrank, Neil. 2008. *Road to Improvement: The
     Review of the Regulatory Systems across the
     North.* Indian and Northern Affairs
     Development Canada.

Education: A Critical
Foundation for a
Sustainable North

E DUCATION IS KEY TO FACING THE COMPLEX DUALITIES, ENORMOUS CHALLENGES AND tremendous opportunities in the contemporary Canadian North.[1] On the one hand, the North seems gripped by inexorable social and economic problems. High rates of Aboriginal unemployment, coupled with seemingly limited local economic development opportunities, declining indigenous language retention and high rates of social pathology, often grab the most academic and media attention. On the other hand, the North is the centre of much social and political innovation. The land claims agreements in Yukon, the comanagement arrangements in the Mackenzie Delta and the creation of the territory of Nunavut established Canada as an international leader in reconciling indigenous interests with contemporary governance. Resources such as oil, gas and diamonds hold the promise of a prosperous northern future. Indigenous organizations, such as the Inuit Circumpolar Conference and the Arctic Athabaskan Council, have paved the way for dynamic circumpolar cooperation. But if challenges are to be addressed and opportunities seized, the North will require a skilled population that is both confident of its place in the global community and grounded in local cultures and knowledge.

How is the Canadian North faring in meeting the challenges it faces? Viewed through the lens of education, it lags behind national and international standards. By national standards, the North is not close to being on a par with the rest of Canada in terms of its rates of literacy, high school completion and university degree attainment (table 1). By international standards, Canada lags behind all the circumpolar states in a hugely critical area: it is the only one that has no university in its Arctic region. On one level, this state of affairs is surprising, given the national

Table 1
Educational Attainment of the Labour Force, Ages 15-64, Canada, Yukon, the Northwest Territories and Nunavut, 2006 (Percent)

Highest certificate or degree attained	Canada	Yukon	Northwest Territories	Nunavut
	Total Aboriginal population 15 years and over			
No certificate, diploma or degree	43.7	41.2	54.8	68.7
High school certificate or diploma	21.8	20.6	14.3	9.5
Apprenticeship or trade certificate or diploma	11.4	11.7	10.0	6.7
College, CEGEP or other non-university certificate or diploma	14.5	19.0	16.5	12.1
University certificate or diploma below bachelor level	2.8	2.1	1.2	1.0
Bachelor's degree	4.1	3.8	2.5	1.5
University degree, certificate or diploma above bachelor level (including professional colleges, master's and doctorate)	1.7	1.4	0.6	0.5

Source: Statistics Canada (2008).

priorities of strengthening Canadian Arctic sovereignty, addressing the urgent need for climate change adaptation, building a world-class Arctic research station and developing the North's natural resources. It is also surprising given the North's pressing social and economic needs — the correlation between educational achievement and improved life outcomes is well documented. As Thomas Berger

Total non-Aboriginal population 15 years and over				Total population 15 years and over			
Canada	Yukon	Northwest Territories	Nunavut	Canada	Yukon	Northwest Territories	Nunavut
23.1	17.3	14.1	11.1	23.8	22.7	32.9	57.3
25.7	24.6	24.3	16.4	25.5	23.7	19.7	10.9
10.8	11.8	8.9	8.0	10.8	11.8	9.4	7.0
17.4	21.1	22.1	22.7	17.3	20.6	19.5	14.2
4.5	3.8	4.2	4.3	4.4	3.4	2.8	1.6
11.9	14.2	18.5	24.3	11.6	11.0	11.1	6.0
6.7	7.2	7.8	13.3	6.5	5.9	4.5	3.0

argues, "A country's education system is expected to equip its people with the skills, particularly the language skills, necessary to take up gainful employment. You can't speak of employment without speaking of education" (2006, 20).

On another level, it's no surprise at all. Notwithstanding the often-asserted platitude that the North is crucial to the Canadian identity, the region and its residents have long been neglected by both national policy-makers and the Canadian public. If the North is to emerge as a region with vibrant, sustainable communities, its people full and equal partners in building a strong Canada, this neglect will have to cease. Moreover, given the increased threat to Canadian Arctic sovereignty, it is in the national interest to have a strong, sustainable, well-governed North. In Canada we have an unprecedented opportunity to draw lessons from our own successes and failures, as well as those of our circumpolar neighbours, and to create a northern education system that will allow the North to prosper for generations to come.

Education policy is both broad and complex. In the North, it covers everything — traditional learning systems, kindergarten to grade 12 (K-12),[2] adult learning, vocational training and university studies. Within the limitations of a single chapter, it is not possible to address education policy in a systematic and comprehensive manner, so I will focus on one of these areas: post-secondary education policy, in particular, university education. I will argue that Canada requires a national policy on northern education involving federal and territorial collaboration, and that creating access to comprehensive university education should be, along with existing educational commitments, a key priority.[3] Although education falls under provincial (and arguably territorial, by extension) jurisdiction, there is still a federal fiduciary responsibility to the territorial North and to the Aboriginal peoples of Canada. The reality today is that the territorial governments deliver most of the educational programming in northern Canada.

This chapter begins with an overview of the education policy environment in the North and outlines how education is organized and funded, with particular attention to the post-secondary system; it also provides data on participation and attainment rates across the North. It then examines how policy-makers — Aboriginal, territorial and federal — view education as a policy instrument for achieving sustainable development, broadly defined. Next, I describe key education policy tensions in the North — including those related both to widespread adult literacy needs and to university education — and I discuss the imperative to address traditional knowledge, culture and language retention while providing education and skills suited to a globalized world. Within this context, the chapter highlights several key educational initiatives that may offer the means to achieve these various goals and to ensure a sustainable future for the North. I conclude with policy recommendations for building access to comprehensive university education in the Canadian North.

Education in Northern Canada: An Overview

A GENERAL DISCUSSION OF POLICY PROBLEMS, GOALS AND INSTRUMENTS SHOULD BE preceded by an overview of the learning systems, funding and formal educational attainment levels in the North.

Traditional Indigenous Learning

A crucial first step in understanding current education policy in the Canadian North is an acknowledgement of the fundamental role of indigenous learning traditions. Northern Aboriginal peoples, like all societies, have culturally rooted systems of learning. Traditional indigenous learning was fundamental to the successful adaptation of indigenous societies to the taiga and tundra regions of the North. These learning systems came under intense pressure from external forces with the expansion of European colonialism in the western hemisphere and the establishment of state policies, particularly during the twentieth century, aimed at eliminating them. However, many of the key elements of traditional learning have survived in the North, and conscious efforts have been made to ensure that traditional learning continues to thrive outside contemporary formal education systems and that indigenous knowledge and ways of learning are integrated not only into the K-12 system but also into post-secondary systems.

Traditional indigenous learning was based in everyday subsistence activities, such as hunting and gathering, and in cultural practices, such as storytelling. The transmission of knowledge from one generation to the next was largely experiential, and it was the responsibility both of families and of larger kinship groups, with elders playing a central role. Traditional indigenous learning tended to be holistic — learning about medicinal plants was as much connected to traditional ecological knowledge as it was to indigenous health and healing and spiritual beliefs. It also is important to underscore the vital role of indigenous languages as holders of the meanings and world views that defined diverse indigenous societies.

With the expansion northward of European explorers, traders, missionaries and, later, the Canadian state, traditional indigenous learning systems came under increasing pressure — and even under attack. The Dominion government, in cooperation with the Anglican, Baptist and Roman Catholic churches, established residential schools with the aim of indoctrinating Aboriginal children with the values, religion and language of the larger society. Despite the relative remoteness of many northern indigenous communities from both the Canadian state and the broader Canadian society, residential schools were established earlier in these communities than they were in First Nations and Métis communities in southern Canada. Yukon's first such school — the Carcross Indian Residential School (Forty Mile Boarding School) — was established by the Anglican Church in 1891 at Forty Mile (north of Dawson City) and was moved to Carcross in 1910. In the Northwest Territories (NWT), residential schools were established as early as 1867 at Fort Providence and Fort Resolution. The extension of the Canadian state into the eastern Arctic came later, and it opened the door to the establishment of residential schools in that part of the North. The Roman Catholic Chesterfield Inlet Indian Residential School opened in 1929. It is true that many Aboriginal children received a good formal Western education and were well treated at these institutions, but many others suffered unconscionable physical, psychological and sexual abuse. They were often forbidden to speak their own languages under threat of severe punishment, a policy that was enforced as late as the early 1970s. The removal of children from their families disrupted or permanently suspended the transmission of traditional indigenous learning systems.

There is no denying the colossal impact on Aboriginal peoples of the residential school system, but it would be inaccurate to attribute to this system all of the blame for their loss of culture and language and for the social problems that confront many Aboriginal families and communities today. Other forces have had a significant impact on traditional indigenous learning systems. Extensive natural resource development and the rise of the wage economy have had both positive and negative consequences for indigenous communities, but it is hard to overstate their impact on traditional learning systems now that individuals are increasingly choosing nontraditional economic pursuits over traditional ones. Equally important is the introduction of the welfare state, which has affected everything from traditional diet to gender roles. The introduction of new forms of governance in the North — a hierarchy of local, territorial and federal governments equipped with impersonal bureaucracies — has fundamentally changed everyday political relations. Most indigenous peoples in the Canadian North profess to be adherents of one of the main Christian denominations. Finally, it is

difficult to overestimate the impact of contemporary media on language and values in any society. Cultural globalization has enormous consequences for traditional indigenous learning systems. English-language television, music videos,
video games and Internet are the mainstays of young people not only in the
Canadian North but also in many reaches of the globe. The pervasiveness of
English in everyday life presents a difficult and, in many cases, even insurmountable challenge to indigenous languages when they are not spoken at home
or in public by the majority of community members. To lose a language is to lose
the cornerstone of a learning system.

The contemporary story of traditional indigenous learning, however, is not
without hope. Many indigenous families and communities harvest country foods,
maintain traditional cultural practices and speak their own languages fluently.
Moreover, indigenous language instruction is offered in many primary schools
across the Canadian North, though in most cases it is not nearly sufficient to
ensure that the indigenous language does not become a child's second language.
Over the past 20 years, indigenous cultural practices and oral traditions have
become an increasingly common part of the mainstream K-12 curriculum, and
community members often assist with the instruction. At the same time, a growing number of indigenous teachers — holding education degrees and immersed in
their own cultures — are powering the integration of indigenous traditional learning in mainstream schools. A number of communities run summer camps where
young people can learn traditional skills and knowledge from elders and other
community members. All of these efforts demonstrate that there is a place for traditional indigenous learning systems in the contemporary world.

The formal post-secondary education system in the Canadian North today is
organized along lines that are familiar to any educator in the post-secondary (particularly college) system in southern Canada. Post-secondary education in the territorial North has its roots in adult education and vocational training. At the end of
the 1950s, nearly 50 communities in the NWT were offering adult education in one
form or another. In 1967, Yellowknife became the capital of the Northwest
Territories and the federal government transferred some administrative control to
the NWT; responsibility for education was transferred in 1969 to the newly created Northwest Territories Department of Education. The territorial Department of
Education and the federal Department of Indian Affairs and Northern Development
engaged an external college to develop a system of community-based adult

education. The first course offered, in 1968, was to train heavy-equipment opera-tors; in 1969, the program was moved to Fort Smith, where the Adult Vocational Training Centre (AVTC) was established. By the early 1970s, the federal govern-ment had begun to fund an expansion of the training program through AVTC. In Yukon, post-secondary education emerged in the early 1960s with the founding of the Yukon Vocational and Technical Training Centre (YVTTC).

The largest transformations were to begin in the late 1970s and early 1980s. Yukon expanded its offerings through a partnership with the University of British Columbia in 1977 and began to provide university-level programs and courses. In 1983, the YVTTC and the UBC programs were merged, and Yukon College was established. In 1981, the Government of the Northwest Territories began to transform AVTC into Thebacha College. The territorial government cre-ated Arctic College from Thebacha College in 1984, with initial campuses in Fort Smith and Iqaluit; other campuses were soon established across the NWT. In 1986, the *Arctic College Act* was passed, giving the college the responsibility to deliver adult and post-secondary education. In 1992, as part of its decentraliza-tion strategy, the territorial government decided that it would create two colleges from Arctic College, closing the college's head office in Yellowknife and opening head offices in Fort Smith and Iqaluit. In 1995, Nunavut Arctic College in the eastern Arctic and Aurora College in the western Arctic were founded. Responsibility for Nunavut Arctic College was transferred to the Government of Nunavut in 1999, coinciding with the creation of Canada's newest territory.

Today, Aurora College, Nunavut Arctic College and Yukon College are the principal post-secondary institutions in the territorial North. All three offer trade and vocational training and university transfer education. All three, in partner-ship with southern universities, offer professional degrees — notably, in educa-tion, nursing and social work. Most, if not all, of the required courses can be completed through distance education, or they are taught on-site by resident instructors or by visiting instructors from southern institutions. Until recently, students in the teacher education program at Aurora College had to do their final year at the University of Saskatchewan in Saskatoon. They can now complete the program without leaving the NWT. All three colleges are funded directly by the territorial governments and, although formally at arm's length from these gov-ernments, they do not have the degree of academic autonomy enjoyed by uni-versities and many colleges in southern Canada. The presidents of Nunavut

Arctic College and Aurora College have the status of deputy minister, and they report to their respective ministers.

Education Expenditures

Education in the territorial North is funded directly by the territorial governments (as it is by provincial governments in southern Canada). However, most of this funding comes from federal government transfers to the territories. One measure of the priority a policy area holds for a government is the amount of resources the government is prepared to invest in the activities in that area. The territorial governments confront a myriad of social and economic infrastructure pressures — as well as expenses related to distance, climate and economies of scale — so it is difficult to make a direct comparison between their expenditures and those of provincial governments in the south. Both Aurora College and Nunavut Arctic College maintain regional campuses in their respective territories, which adds significant transportation costs related to administration and faculty meetings as well as community consultations. Furthermore, the political decision to decentralize the colleges has resulted in additional expenses, which absorb funds that could otherwise go to meet student program needs. The fact that neither of the college's head offices is located in the territorial capital means that significant costs are incurred for ministerial and territorial department meetings.

Table 2
Provincial and Territorial Spending on K-12 and Post-Secondary Education as a Proportion of Total Expenditures, 2007

Province or territory	Percent
Yukon	16.5
Northwest Territories	17.1
Nunavut	16.2
Saskatchewan	18.2
Alberta	25.9
Manitoba	18.0
British Columbia	21.2

Source: Statistics Canada (2006; CANSIM tables 385-002).

In terms of the overall budget, education expenditures in northern Canada are lower than they are in the neighbouring western provinces. In 2007, Nunavut spent $179 million on education, or 16.2 percent of the territorial budget; the Northwest Territories spent $242 million, or 17.1 percent; and Yukon spent $142 million, or 16.5 percent. The budget share allocated to education (K-12 and post-secondary) by each of the territorial governments appears comparable to the shares allocated by Manitoba and Saskatchewan; in each of these provinces, education represents about 18 percent of total expenditures (see table 2). However, these figures do not reflect the higher costs per student in the northern territories for the reasons outlined earlier.

In terms of specific post-secondary education funding, territorial government allocations were as follows: Nunavut, $26.5 million; the Northwest Territories, $36.1 million; and Yukon, $29.8 million (see table 3). On a per capita basis (investment in post-secondary education divided by population in the labour

Table 3
University and College Revenues and Expenditures, Nunavut, Northwest Territories and Yukon, 2007 (thousands of dollars)

	Nunavut	Northwest Territories	Yukon
Total revenues[1]	27,809	40,172	27,454
Total expenditures	26,520	36,145	29,786
Administration	8,236	7,195	4,718
Education	17,925	28,950	22,072
Supports to students	0	0	1,325
Other post-secondary education expenses	359	0	901
Special retaining services expenditures	n/a	n/a	772
Surplus or (deficit)	1,289	4,027	(2,332)

Source: Statistics Canada, CANSIM table 385-0007.

n.a. not available

[1] Includes tuition fees, grants from territorial governments and other revenues.

force), Yukon ($1,184 per person) spent more than the Northwest Territories ($1,152 per person), even though administrative costs were significantly and understandably lower in Yukon — at $4.7 million, versus $7.2 million in the NWT. Yukon has much shorter travel distances and a much better transportation network, and most of its population lives in Whitehorse and its environs. The largest per capita spender was Nunavut (at $1,370), although it had by far the greatest administrative expenditures (at $8.2 million).

Educational Attainment

Given the obvious linkages among employment, capacity-building and education, any discussion of education policy in the North — or elsewhere — will have a focus on attainment. Educational attainment levels are an important indicator of the breadth and depth of the labour pool in a region or country. But assessing these levels in the Canadian North requires more than simply looking at the aggregate Statistics Canada data. With reference to Canada, the 2004 Arctic Human Development Report notes, for instance, that "to attain an undergraduate or graduate degree, the reality for most northern students is attending southern universities. Nevertheless, one of the territories in Canada, Yukon, claims one of the most educated populations in Canada. One would thus need to survey where those people in Yukon who reported having degrees came from to get a clear idea of educational capacity in northern Canada" (Johansson, Paci, and Hovdenak 2004, 171). An exploration of educational attainment will require some discussion of rates among newcomers versus long-term residents and among Aboriginal versus non-Aboriginal residents, as well as a discussion of fields of education and training.

Yukon represents an instructive case for educational attainment in the North. One often-quoted factoid about Yukon is that the territory has the highest proportion of adults with some form of post-secondary qualification. With 63 percent of its adult population aged 25 to 64 — or nearly 54 percent of the labour force aged 15 to 64 — holding such qualification, Yukon is home to the most educated population not only in the North, but also in Canada (Statistics Canada 2006). However, many of those holding post-secondary education credentials are recent arrivals to the territory who have come to take up employment as teachers or civil servants or to work in other professional and trade areas. As Statistics Canada carefully notes, about 2,600 residents in this age group lived outside of Yukon in 2001, and nearly 70 percent of these newcomers had post-secondary

Table 4
Educational Attainment of the Labour Force, Ages 15-64, Yukon, 2006

| Highest certificate or degree attained | Non-Aboriginal population | | | | | |
| | Female | | Male | | Total | |
	N	%	N	%	N	%
Total	9,325	100.0	9,650	100.0	18,970	100.0
No certificate, diploma or degree	1,365	14.6	1,910	19.8	3,275	17.3
Certificate, diploma or degree	7,960	85.4	7,740	80.2	15,700	82.8
– High school certificate or diploma	2,535	27.2	2,135	22.1	4,675	24.6
– Apprenticeship or trade certificate or diploma	535	5.7	1,710	17.7	2,240	11.8
– College, CEGEP or other nonuniversity certificate or diploma	2,240	24.0	1,765	18.3	4,010	21.1
– University certificate or diploma below bachelor's level	475	5.1	240	2.5	715	3.8
– Bachelor's degree	1,475	15.8	1,210	12.5	2,690	14.2
– University degree, certificate or diploma above bachelor's level (including professional colleges, master's and doctorate)	690	7.4	665	6.9	1,370	7.2

Source: Statistics Canada (2008).

| | Aboriginal population | | | | |
| Female | | Male | | Total | |
N	%	N	%	N	%
2,880	100.0	2,635	100.0	5,520	100.0
1,065	37.0	1,210	45.9	2,275	41.2
1,815	63.0	1,425	54.1	3,240	58.7
670	23.3	460	17.5	1,135	20.6
210	7.3	440	16.7	645	11.7
645	22.4	405	15.4	1,050	19.0
75	2.6	40	1.5	115	2.1
160	5.6	55	2.1	210	3.8
55	1.9	35	1.3	75	1.4

Table 5
Educational Attainment of the Labour Force, Ages 15-64,
Northwest Territories, 2006

Highest certificate or degree attained	Non-Aboriginal population					
	Female		Male		Total	
	N	%	N	%	N	%
Total	7,810	100.0	8,855	100.0	16,670	100.0
No certificate, diploma or degree	955	12.2	1,390	15.7	2,345	14.1
Certificate, diploma or degree	6,855	87.8	7,470	84.4	14,325	85.9
– High school certificate or diploma	2,185	28.0	1,875	21.2	4,055	24.3
– Apprenticeship or trade certificate or diploma	0	0.0	1,210	13.7	1,490	8.9
– College, CEGEP or other nonuniversity certificate or diploma	1,760	22.5	1,925	21.7	3,685	22.1
– University certificate or diploma below bachelor's level	390	5.0	310	3.5	705	4.2
– Bachelor's degree	1,650	21.1	1,435	16.2	3,085	18.5
– University degree, certificate or diploma above bachelor's level (including professional colleges, master's and doctorate)	585	7.5	710	8.0	1,300	7.8

Source: Statistics Canada (2008).

Aboriginal population

Female		Male		Total	
N	%	N	%	N	%
7,395	100.0	7,075	100.0	14,465	100.0
3,835	51.9	4,080	57.7	7,920	54.8
3,555	48.1	2,990	42.3	6,545	45.2
1,200	16.2	875	12.4	2,070	14.3
400	5.4	1,055	14.9	1,450	10.0
1,515	20.5	865	12.2	2,380	16.5
135	1.8	50	0.7	180	1.2
245	3.3	115	1.6	365	2.5
60	0.8	45	0.6	45	0.6

Table 6
Educational Attainment of the Labour Force, Ages 15-64, Nunavut, 2006

	Non-Aboriginal population					
	Female		Male		Total	
Highest certificate or degree attained	N	%	N	%	N	%
Total	1,685	100.0	2,145	100.0	3,835	100.0
No certificate, diploma or degree	165	9.8	260	12.1	425	11.1
Certificate, diploma or degree	1,525	90.5	1,880	87.6	3,405	88.8
– High school certificate or diploma	280	16.6	350	16.3	630	16.4
– Apprenticeship or trade certificate or diploma	45	2.7	260	12.1	305	8.0
– College, CEGEP or other nonuniversity certificate or diploma	385	22.8	485	22.6	870	22.7
– University certificate or diploma below bachelor's level	90	5.3	75	3.5	165	4.3
– Bachelor's degree	485	28.8	445	20.7	930	24.3
– University degree, certificate or diploma above bachelor's level (including professional colleges, master's and doctorate)	245	14.5	260	12.1	510	13.3

Source: Statistics Canada (2008).

Aboriginal population					
Female		Male		Total	
N	%	N	%	N	%
7,725	100.0	7,785	100.0	15,505	100.0
5,345	69.2	5,310	68.2	10,655	68.7
2,375	30.7	2,475	31.8	4,855	31.3
775	10.0	705	9.1	1,480	9.5
255	3.3	785	10.1	1,045	6.7
1,060	13.7	810	10.4	1,870	12.1
75	1.0	75	1.0	150	1.0
165	2.1	65	0.8	230	1.5
50	0.6	20	0.3	75	0.5

qualifications. The data on Aboriginal versus non-Aboriginal educational attainment rates amplify the newcomer-versus-multigenerational-northerner differences, as many non-Aboriginal residents came from other parts of Canada even longer than five years ago, bringing their education credentials with them.

If we examine the percentage of Yukon residents whose highest level of educational attainment was a high school certificate or diploma, we find that the percentage of Aboriginal Yukoners was 20.6 percent and non-Aboriginal Yukoners was 24.6 percent (see table 4). Although non-Aboriginal residents fared better, the difference was reasonably close. If we look at apprenticeship or trade certificates or diplomas, the differences effectively disappear between Aboriginal (11.7 percent) and non-Aboriginal residents (11.8 percent). However, the picture changes significantly when we look at university-level education: 14.2 percent of the non-Aboriginal population held a bachelor's degree, whereas the figure for the Aboriginal population was only 3.8 percent. Moreover, gender differences were more pronounced between Aboriginal and non-Aboriginal residents. Among non-Aboriginal residents, 15.8 percent of females held a bachelor's degree, compared to 12.5 percent of males; however, among Aboriginal residents, 5.6 percent of females held a bachelor's degree, compared to only 2.1 percent of males.

The NWT displays a similar — though, in significant ways, starker — pattern (see table 5). The proportion of non-Aboriginal NWT residents (24.3 percent) who held a high school certificate or diploma was almost identical to that of non-Aboriginal Yukon residents (24.6 percent). However, the percentage of Aboriginal residents whose highest level of educational attainment was a high school certificate or diploma was considerably lower (14.3 percent) in the NWT than in Yukon (20.6 percent). In terms of their attainment rates of apprenticeship or trade certificates or diplomas, Aboriginal residents in the NWT did better than their non-Aboriginal counterparts (10.0 percent versus 8.9 percent), but the figures were again fairly close. As in Yukon, in the NWT sizable differences were evident in university-level educational attainment rates. Whereas 18.5 percent of the non-Aboriginal population held a bachelor's degree, only 2.5 percent of the Aboriginal population did. Gender differences were also evident; among Aboriginal residents, women were attaining bachelor's degrees at a rate of more than 2:1 compared to men.

Nunavut presents the third territorial case of educational attainment (see table 6). Aboriginal residents of Nunavut had lower attainment levels than Aboriginal residents of the other two territories. In the area of apprenticeships and trades, the attainment level in Nunavut was 6.7 percent, two-thirds that of the NWT; in terms of bachelor's degrees, the rate was 1.5 percent, less than half the rate of Yukon. These rates are not surprising when one looks at a high school certificate or diploma as the highest level of educational attainment. Again, Nunavut had the lowest rate (9.5 percent) of all the territories for Aboriginal residents.

The rate of high school certificate or diploma attainment (as the highest level of education achieved) for non-Aboriginal Nunavut residents was 16.4 percent; this rate was also the lowest among the three territories. This requires further explanation. Most non-Aboriginal residents of Nunavut are highly transient, and many have as their highest level of educational attainment a college diploma or university degree rather than a high school certificate or diploma. The proportion of non-Aboriginal Nunavut residents, for instance, who held a bachelor's degree (24.3 percent) was more than 70 percent greater than that of their Yukon counterparts (14.2 percent). Furthermore, the share of non-Aboriginal Nunavut residents who held a master's degree (8.5 percent) was twice that of non-Aboriginal Yukon residents (4.3 percent).

Finally, educational attainment rates need to be placed in the context of fields of study. Given the pressing need for skilled workers in the resource development and construction sector, it is not surprising that northern participation rates are higher in these areas. In Nunavut, for instance, 35 percent of adults with trade certificates held a certificate in a construction trade — the highest rate in Canada. Moreover, in terms of university education, the emphasis has overwhelmingly been placed on the areas of education and teacher training, nursing and social work. In Nunavut, among those who held a university degree, one in three was in the field of teacher education. These patterns are mirrored in other areas of the circumpolar North, where targeted trade training and specific professional programs (for example, nursing education) tend to precede the development of comprehensive postsecondary programming, particularly university education.

Policy Problems and Solutions

THE CANADIAN NORTH FACES HUGE CHALLENGES AND TREMENDOUS OPPORTUNITIES. The territorial and federal governments share the general policy goal of ensuring that the North prospers on a sustainable foundation. In their 2007 policy statement *A Northern Vision: A Stronger North and a Better Canada*, the three northern premiers identify the key elements of what a northern future should look like:

> Self-reliant individuals live in healthy, viable communities; Aboriginal rights have been successfully negotiated and implemented; Northerners are the primary beneficiaries of northern resource development; northern traditions of respect for the land and the environment are cherished; strong, responsive governments make decisions and take actions that are anchored in the principles of responsible, sustainable development; the cultural heritage of Aboriginal people is preserved, promoted and able to flourish, and...all citizens celebrate their diversity; Northern governments have the tools and authority they need to manage their own affairs; the territories are strong contributing partners in a dynamic and secure Canadian federation. (Handley, Fentie and Okalik 2007)

Currently, the Canadian North does not possess the human capacity to meet such policy goals, but it does possess the human potential. In this regard, a persuasive case could be made that the single most important instrument for achieving the broader policy goal of building a sustainable North is education. However, the lack of access to comprehensive university education stands in the way.

The problem of access has several dimensions; these are related to geography, relevance, culture, financing and preparation. The most obvious obstacle to accessing post-secondary, especially university, programming is the limited availability of university courses for northern students. Many such students, especially those from remote Aboriginal communities, are unwilling to leave family and community to travel hundreds, even thousands of kilometres to attend university in the south.[4] And, among those who do leave the North, many do not succeed in alien southern institutions because they have been separated from critical support networks. Bringing post-secondary education physically closer to where they live increases their opportunities to participate.[5]

A second, but underrecognized, obstacle to access is lack of relevance. Developing curricula that are relevant to students' experiences, lives and communities is essential to breaking down educational barriers. Even at the most basic level, a public administration course focusing on northern needs — from clearing snow to solving bear problems — would be far more relevant than one focusing on light rail transit. Moreover, curricula that integrate knowledge of traditional political culture, which continues to permeate contemporary governance, are much more meaningful than those that focus solely on the values of Anglo-American liberal democracy. Finally, the language of instruction speaks to relevance. Many post-secondary courses, in principle, could and should be taught in Inuktitut or another indigenous language. A lack of instructors capable of teaching in an indigenous language, and a lack of curricula in languages other than English or French, makes this a daunting task. But it can be done, as pioneering institutions such as the University of Greenland and Sámi University College (Norway) have demonstrated.

A third challenge is cultural, but not in the indigenous-versus-mainstream sense, which is fundamentally a relevance question. Rather, this challenge relates to the academic culture of post-secondary education. Many northern students — both Aboriginal and non-Aboriginal — are the first in their families to take a university course. The things that one requires to succeed at university (strong research and time-management skills, good study habits, the ability to participate in seminars) are often completely alien to these students. This is in sharp contrast to the upper-middle-class student with university-educated parents who enjoys full academic-cultural support. Overcoming this barrier requires cohort-based models,[6] with tutors and explicit strategies for moving from dependent learning to independent learning. These strategies will be required until the North produces significant numbers of intergenerational university graduates.[7]

A fourth challenge is financial and is faced by both individual students and territorial governments. Territorial governments have been generous in their support for northern students pursuing post-secondary education at home and in the south (all too often, students who succeed in the south do not return to the North, which does not help to build northern capacity). I should underscore the fact that many northern students are poor. For some, the cost of moving to a regional centre such as Yellowknife or Rankin Inlet, let alone to an institution in the south, even with territorial government support, is too high. This will remain a challenge, given limited personal and territorial financial resources. Perhaps even more significant is the limited territorial capacity to provide university programs on a sustainable basis. A common pattern (teacher education and nursing programs excepted) is that programs are offered on a one-off basis. Two recent examples in Nunavut are the University of Victoria law degree program and the Carleton University public service studies certificate program.

A final problem of access is what could broadly be described as preparation. Compared to two decades ago, the number of high school graduates is increasing, though these numbers lag behind those of the Canadian mainstream. There are therefore not enough high school graduates to warrant a broad range of university programming in the North. Another issue that needs to be addressed is that many of those who do have high school diplomas are not performing at levels comparable to those of their counterparts elsewhere in Canada. The Nunavut Department of Education stopped participating in national standardized tests in 2001 when it learned that just 28 percent of Nunavut 13-year-olds reached basic level skills, compared to 88 percent of those in the rest of Canada (Minogue 2006). Science and math teachers willing to work in larger centres in the provincial North, such as Prince George, British Columbia, are difficult to find; it is often impossible to recruit them to work in small, remote Aboriginal communities. How are northern students expected to succeed in science programs at the university level when they have never done a science lab or even taken a high school chemistry class?

All of these access challenges to post-secondary education in the North constitute a national problem, the resolution of which will require cooperation among northern and Aboriginal stakeholders, as well as a collaborative commitment on the part of the federal and territorial governments. I will now outline the supply-versus-demand problem arising from the lack of northerners with the requisite levels of education to occupy positions in the public and private sectors.

Supply versus Demand

THE SUPPLY-VERSUS-DEMAND PROBLEM HAS TWO DIMENSIONS: FIRST, THE INADEQUATE supply of northern residents qualified to meet the labour demand in the public and private sectors; and second, the insufficient supply of diverse educational opportunities, particularly at the bachelor's-degree level.

On March 1, 2006, Thomas Berger submitted a thoughtful yet provocative report to the minister of Indian affairs and northern development, Jim Prentice, in which he recommended new approaches to the implementation of the Nunavut Land Claims Agreement (2006). His report underscored one of the most profound ironies in contemporary northern Canada. Unemployment in Nunavut was high — ranging anywhere from 30 to 70 percent, with the more remote communities experiencing the highest rates. Yet Nunavut had a severe labour shortage. How so? Berger's report pointed out that, according to article 23 of the Nunavut Land Claims Agreement, employment in the Nunavut public service had to be representative. Given that about

85 percent of the population was Inuit, public service employees of all levels and grades should have been 85 percent Inuit, but only 45 percent of the 3,200 positions in the Government of Nunavut were occupied by Inuit persons. If one were to consider the territory's federal government positions, "there are in the vicinity of 1,500 jobs that could by claimed by Inuit had they the necessary skills" (Berger 2006, 18). This irony is not unique to Nunavut. The Northwest Territories has the highest average employment rate in Canada, at nearly 70 percent; however, the Council of Ministers of Education, Canada (CMEC) anticipates that over a 10-year period ending in 2010, there will be a 20 percent decrease in the potential labour supply, "because many workers do not have the required skills." Its report notes, "The potential labour supply is not sufficient to meet resource industry demand, let alone existing labour gaps...More than half of the available labour supply has not completed high school and three quarters does not have a post secondary education" (2007, 3).

It is important to understand the supply-versus-demand gap. It is a commonly held view that employment opportunities for northern and Aboriginal peoples in rural and remote areas are bleak at worst and limited at best. But, as Berger's report, the CMEC report and the territorial premiers' *Northern Vision* demonstrate, this is inaccurate. In fact, the North is confronting critical shortages of qualified workers in a multitude of areas. Many have argued that the North needs individuals with trade skills, not university graduates. While there is no question that expanded training programs are required for various trades in the construction, resource extraction and environmental sectors, to name but a few, there is also an urgent need for university graduates in the public sector (at the territorial, First Nations, local and federal levels), and in the fields of health, education, culture, environmental management and resource development. As global demand for northern resources increases, the effects of climate change accumulate and the challenges to Canada's Arctic sovereignty intensify, labour shortages are likely to be exacerbated. The territories will require hundreds of new northern university graduates, far in excess of the current supply. For many years, all three territorial colleges have delivered training programs in skilled trades — everything from carpentry and welding to diamond cutting and polishing — and they continue to expand their offerings. However, none is in a position to deliver regular degree programs, except for teacher training and nursing (and social work, in the case of Yukon College), and these are offered through bilateral arrangements with southern universities.

However, the solution is not simply to produce more university graduates from existing programs — particularly teacher education programs. This leads us to the second supply problem: program insufficiency. The North needs a comprehensive supply of program choices to meet its diverse needs. A university degree does provide generic skills that are transferable to a variety of occupations, but a degree in education is intended to prepare an individual to become a teacher, not a policy analyst in the territorial government. In the absence of multiple degree options, critical resources are misdirected; for example, employers requiring individuals with university degrees poach K-12 teachers from the education system because other types of degree holders are not available. While it is a common problem across Canada's entire northern region, Berger addresses the issue as it relates to Nunavut: "Some complain that many graduates of the NTEP move into positions elsewhere in government. Ooloota Maatiusi, Principal of the Nunavut Teacher Education Program at Nunavut Arctic College, when asked how to improve teacher retention, said 'Get the Government of Nunavut to stop hiring our graduates'" (2006, 52).

Policy Options

N O SINGLE POLICY INSTRUMENT WILL SOLVE THE EDUCATION CHALLENGES FACING the Canadian North. Education policy is complex, multilayered and highly interconnected with a myriad of other critical factors, such as health and well-being. Creating good education policy in the territorial North will require directing attention toward the K-12, literacy and post-secondary sectors. Considerable resources and policy attention have been directed toward the first two sectors by the territorial governments. Aurora College, for example, devotes 30 percent of its budget to basic adult education (Hodgson 2007, 55). But insufficient emphasis has been placed on post-secondary education, particularly at the university level. The territories face enormous challenges related to natural resource development, environmental management, and the building of a competent, professional civil service. Meeting these challenges will require facilitating access to university education through coherent and sustainable policy. There are three basic options available: strengthen existing university education programs, all of which have partnerships with southern institutions; expand the choices of university degree completion programs through consortium vehicles such as the University of the Arctic; or create a bricks and mortar university in the Canadian Arctic.

Bilateral Programs

There are a number of bilateral programs running in the territorial North that have a record of success. Aurora College, Nunavut Arctic College and Yukon College all partner with southern-based universities in the delivery of university programs, particularly in professional areas such as education, nursing and social work.

Teacher education programs are the longest-standing programs in the three territories. The NWT's Teacher Education Program (TEP) was launched in 1968 in Yellowknife, and it was then transferred to Fort Smith, where it has remained. The original program was diploma, not degree, based, and it focused on training teacher aides for the classroom; later, a B.Ed. program was established in partnership with the University of Saskatchewan's Indian Teacher Education Program (ITEP). The first year the full program was delivered on-site in the Northwest Territories was 2007-08; 15 students obtained their degrees through the program without having to complete their final courses in Saskatoon. Teacher education in Nunavut began prior to division. The two-year Eastern Arctic Teacher Education Program was launched in 1979 in what is now Iqaluit, and it provided teacher certification in the territory. "A partnership with McGill University in 1981 gave Inuit students access to the Certificate in Native and Northern Education. In 1986, EATEP/McGill began offering the B.Ed. degree, the only full time university program in the NWT. In 1999, with the creation of Nunavut, the program was renamed NTEP, the Nunavut Teacher Education Program" (Nunavut Department of Education and Nunavut Arctic College 2006, 19). Between 1981 and 2006, the program produced 210 graduates, 97 of whom obtained B.Ed. degrees. Today, the NTEP is delivered in partnership with the University of Regina, which also partners with Yukon College in the delivery of the Yukon Native Teacher Education Program (YNTEP). All of these programs have proven successful in producing qualified teachers for the K-12 education systems in the territories. It is anticipated that over 250 students will complete B.Ed. degrees between 2010 and 2014 in all three territories (see table 7).

Teacher education, however, is not the only type of university program offered in the territories, although it is by far the most significant. In the area of nursing, for instance, Aurora College, through the University of Victoria, offers a

Table 7
Projected Number of Graduates of Northern Teacher Education
Programs,[1] 2010-14

	2010	2011	2012	2013	2014	Total
Yukon	9	6	7	8	9	39
Nunavut	20	20	20	40	40	140
Northwest Territories	15	15	15	15	15	75
Total	44	41	42	63	64	254

Source: Yukon College, Aurora College and Nunavut Arctic College.
[1] The University of Regina delivers two teacher education programs, one in partnership with Yukon College and the other with Nunavut Arctic College; the University of Saskatchewan delivers a teacher education program in partnership with Aurora College.

BSN, and it boasted 41 graduates from the academic years 2005-06 to 2007-08. Other partnerships have included Nunavut's Akitsiraq law school program through the University of Victoria; the Nunavut public service studies certificate through Carleton University; an executive MBA program for the NWT through Queen's University; and Yukon College's master's in public administration program through the University of Alaska Southeast.

Such programs require stable and ongoing funding, otherwise they risk becoming one-off boutique programs divorced from long-term strategic planning and development. The Akitsiraq law school program was designed as a one-off, and the Nunavut public service studies program received direct incremental funding for only one cycle. The latter continues to exist, but without direct funding support from the Government of Nunavut, and it operates on a cost-recovery basis.

Consortium Models: University of the Arctic
A solution to the supply-versus-demand problem also necessitates the expansion of university programs, particularly in such fields as public policy and administration, environmental impact assessment and resource management, economic development and northern tourism. Addressing these diverse needs will require bold new approaches.

One of the most innovative models to emerge over the past decade is the University of the Arctic (UArctic). It was officially launched in 2001, and it is now a consortium of more than 100 universities, colleges and Aboriginal organizations around the circumpolar North. The primary activities of UArctic to date have been collaborating in the delivery of undergraduate programming to northern regions and facilitating student exchanges between the Arctic states.

UArctic's signature program is the undergraduate circumpolar studies program. It has two components: core courses and advanced emphases. The former consists of an introductory course and six courses in three interdisciplinary fields of study, and it provides students with a broad knowledge and understanding of the lands, peoples and critical issues of the circumpolar world as well as a solid interdisciplinary foundation for advanced studies in northern issues. The latter consists of concentrated areas of study (worth one semester of university credits) that can be delivered on a stand-alone basis to meet capacity-building and professional-development needs in the North, or they can be an integral component of a university degree completion program. Together, the UArctic's core courses and advanced emphases form the basis of the BA in northern studies offered at the University of Saskatchewan, Lakehead University and the University of Northern British Columbia.

The strategy is for students taking diploma programs from one of the three Arctic colleges to complete up to two full years of university transfer credits and then complete the remainder of a BA in northern studies (built on the UArctic core courses and an advanced emphasis) through distance and blended models of course delivery. This will allow students from the three territories to complete their degrees without having to leave the North.

Currently, the three Arctic Colleges also provide students with several different certificate and diploma programs related to administration and management. Aurora College offers natural resource technology and management studies; Nunavut Arctic College offers management studies at the Kivalliq Campus and environmental technology at the Nunatta Campus; Yukon College offers business administration and tourism management. The rates of completion in these programs can form the basis of an estimate of the number of students who could take advanced emphases and degree completion programs through UArctic (table 8). Table 9 shows the projected student enrolment in UArctic programs that build on the existing diploma programs of the three Arctic colleges.

The consortium model works. Students from the provincial North in Canada have graduated through UArctic programming with degrees in northern studies from the University of Saskatchewan and the University of Northern

Table 8
Number of Graduates of Administration and Management Programs, Arctic Colleges, 2005-08

	2005	2006	2007	2008[1]	Total
Aurora College	35	47	29	35	146
Nunavut College	8	7	0	17	32
Yukon College	12	25	29	33	99
Total	55	79	58	85	277

Source: UArctic, Fundraising Report, 2007.
[1] The figures for 2008 are estimates provided by the three Arctic colleges.

British Columbia. In the fall of 2008, degree program offerings commenced in the territories with a concentration in Aboriginal public administration. The model has major advantages. Program delivery can be done in a much more cost-effective manner than it can with go-it-alone approaches. No single southern Canadian partner can fulfill the varied and sometimes regionally specific needs of the three territories. A single affiliation model, particularly involving a large research university, invites a power relationship in which the larger institution may dominate and dictate rather than collaborate and respond.

Despite the success of the University of the Arctic, funding remains tenuous. The primary funders have been the governments of Norway, Finland and Canada. In Canada, UArctic was flagged by the Liberal government as an important activity under the Northern Dimension policy, and member institutions of UArctic were led to believe that appropriate levels of funding for the initiative were forthcoming. However, although UArctic undertook significant fundraising efforts, the Liberal government was unable to provide anywhere near the amount necessary to ensure program development, let alone delivery. In 2006, when the Conservatives came to power, the funding for UArctic was doubled to its current level of about $700,000. Other funding sources in Canada include the Government of Saskatchewan, at $200,000 annually, and First Nations of northern Saskatchewan, at more than $200,000. Universities, colleges and indigenous organizations also make significant contributions in cash and in kind — about $1.9 million in 2007-08. However, funding for UArctic has been on a year-by-year basis. Without sustained funding, it is unlikely to survive, and certainly not as an institution capable of meeting northern education supply needs.

Table 9
Projected Enrolment in Selected Programs,[1] University of the Arctic,
2010-14

	2010	2011	2012	2013	2014	Total
Aboriginal public administration						
Yukon	8	12	14	16	18	68
Nunavut	0	0	0	0	0	0
Northwest Territories	8	10	12	14	16	60
Total enrolment	16	22	26	30	34	128
Environmental impact assessment						
Yukon	8	10	15	20	25	78
Nunavut	4	10	15	20	25	74
Northwest Territories	4	10	15	20	25	74
Total enrolment	16	30	45	60	75	226
Northern policy and governance						
Yukon	0	10	15	20	25	70
Nunavut	0	10	15	20	25	70
Northwest Territories	0	10	15	20	25	70
Total enrolment	0	30	45	60	75	210
Arctic climate change adaptation						
Yukon	0	10	15	20	25	70
Nunavut	0	10	15	20	25	70
Northwest Territories	0	10	15	20	25	70
Total enrolment	0	30	45	60	75	210

Source: UArctic, Fundraising Report, 2007.
[1] Under current funding levels.

Building a Bricks and Mortar University in the Canadian Arctic

In the long term, a major part of the post-secondary education solution in northern Canada is to build a university in the territorial North. The evidence of the impact that access to university education can have on educational attainment levels, economic development and retention of a skilled labour force is overwhelming. In Canada, for instance, those with less than a high school education recently had an unemployment rate of 12.1 percent; those with a high school education had a rate of 6.4 percent; while those with a university education had a rate of only 3.7 percent (Statistics Canada 2007). Numerous studies, including those conducted by the Organisation for Economic Co-operation and Development (OCED), outline the importance of universities for regional development and innovation in an increasingly competitive global economy (see OECD 2007, 2008). However, university education has broader social goals than simply employment and economic development. As Hodgson points out, we must ensure that our education programming is not driven simply by megadevelopment projects (2007). Universities play a vital role in the social development of individuals and communities. Among other things, every country and region needs its own historians to record its history, its own political scientists to provide commentary on its public policy, its own language specialists to ensure that its literary and oral traditions survive and thrive.

A university in the North is likely to be unconventional by southern standards, and northerners, not southerners, need to determine the goals and priorities of such an institution. The question of whether there should be three separate universities, one for each territory, or a pan-territorial institution with multiple campuses will no doubt be hotly debated. Programming is likely to focus on northern priorities and involve professional training (education, nursing, business); environmental and resource management; and language and culture. There is likely to be a greater emphasis on internships and cooperative education, as well as on laddering[8] diploma programs and integrating skills-based training with theoretical education. And there will likely be a greater role for traditional knowledge in curriculum design. Such an initiative will hardly be precedent setting, as international examples such as Sámi University College in Norway demonstrate. This institution, established in 1989 in the Sámi community of Kautokeino, has about 250 students and 50 staff (30 academic and 20 administrative), and it serves Sámi students from Norway, Sweden, Finland and Russia. It offers programs in teacher education, language and culture, and sustainable development and biodiversity. Most of the instruction is in the Sámi language, and most of the students and staff are bilingual. In Canada, the University of Northern British Columbia is an outstanding example of an unconventional university strongly rooted in a northern region, guided by northern priorities and boasting an impressive record of research intensity and teaching excellence.

The Nordic countries have invested considerably in northern university education, and many of their northern universities are well known for targeting regional development needs. The sizes of these universities vary greatly. The University of Greenland (Ilisimatusarfik), for instance, founded in Nuuk in 1987, is the smallest, with a student body of about 120 and an academic faculty complement of 18 in 2007. As might be expected, its programming is limited, but it offers degrees at the bachelor's and master's levels. At the other end of the scale, Umeå University (Umeå, Sweden), founded in 1965, is a comprehensive institution offering programs in, among other fields, engineering and medicine; it has 27,000 students and some 2,400 academic faculty. There are also midsized institutions, such as the University of Tromsø (Tromsø, Norway), founded in 1972, which has extensive graduate programming and many research centres. To draw a comparison, the University of Tromsø is located in the county of Troms, which has a population of only about 150,000 — close to the population size of Canada's territorial North (just over 100,000). However, the University of Tromsø had a 2007 student population of approximately 6,500, 70 percent of whom were from the North, and an annual budget of 1.4 billion kroner (or about $300 million).

These universities did attract some criticism, but all have ultimately proven to be success stories. On its Web site, the University of Tromsø explains:

> The establishment of a university so far north has been called a gigantic experiment in regional policy. There was no lack of warning voices against the establishment of a university in Northern Norway. Recruitment of both staff and students was predicted to be so poor that it seemed that neither the standard of education nor enrolment levels would be sufficient to warrant the effort. When Parliament nevertheless approved the plan in the face of this strong opposition, it was done in order to create greater geographic equality and a sharing of opportunity between the Northern Region and the rest of the country. The aim was to provide the youth of the region with better educational opportunities and to ensure the recruitment of professional expertise to the region. The University of Tromsø today is a prime motor in the development of the region. The experiment was, and is, successful. The University of Tromsø has become one of Norway's main centres of learning and research. (University of Tromsø 2008)

The building of university capacity is not just occurring in the Nordic countries. Russia, beginning in the Soviet period and continuing past it, has built an extensive network of universities, polytechnical institutes and research centres across its northern region and Siberia. And, although Canadians may see themselves as inhabiting the kinder, gentler nation on the North American continent, the US has built the University of Alaska system, which is an impressive centre for world-class teaching and research. It consists of three separately accredited, more traditional-style universities — the University of Alaska Anchorage, the University of Alaska Fairbanks and the University of Alaska Southeast (in Juneau) — with a dozen community campuses offering university transfer programs as well as trade and vocational training. The Fairbanks campus is the strongest in research, and it is internationally renowned for its northern scholarships in the social and natural sciences. In 2006, the State of Alaska had a population of about 670,000, of which approximately 15.4 percent were Native persons (US Census Bureau 2007). In 1997, Native persons constituted 11 percent of those in the University of Alaska system; by 2004, however, the figure had increased to 14 percent. This is all the more noteworthy when we consider that in 1997 Alaska's Native population accounted for more than one-fifth of the state population, and by 2004 the proportion was about one-sixth. Between 1997 and 2004, the University of Alaska system conferred 10,300 bachelor's degrees, 3,300 master's degrees and 200 doctorates (University of Alaska 2004). This is not to say that Alaska faces no challenges related to literacy, high school completion and university degree completion. However, it does suggest that access to university education does facilitate participation rates.

Closer to home, in the provincial North, the creation of universities has had a positive impact on sustainable development. Programs in, for example, natural resource management, First Nations public administration, teacher education, nursing and business offered by such institutions as Lakehead University and the University of Northern British Columbia contribute directly to meeting labour market needs in the North by training northerners. Moreover, ongoing research at provincial northern institutions in areas such as silviculture and social work contributes to economic and social development in the regions. The provincial North, like the territorial North, has historically had a transient workforce — skilled tradespeople and professionals come from the south to work for a few years and then return home. However, since the creation of the University of Northern British Columbia, more than 70 percent of students educated in the North stay in the North. This not only helps to fill labour market needs, but it also reduces the turnover rates in skilled and professional positions. Having workers, including managers, in a variety of sectors with institutional memory and networks is a huge asset for long-term sustainability.

Why hasn't anyone thought of aiming for this in the Canadian territorial North? The idea is hardly new: it has resurfaced often over the past four decades. Amanda Graham provides an excellent historical overview of the attempt to build a university in the territorial North nearly four decades ago (1994). The University of Canada North, for many of the reasons discussed here, was viewed as important to the development of the territorial North and, more broadly, to the development of Canada's Arctic research capacity. More than 30 years ago, the Science Council of Canada observed that the role of Canadian universities in northern research and development was in decline (Science Council of Canada 1977). Graham notes that "to counter this trend, the Council proposed the creation of an 'unorthodox' northern university" (1994, 117). The idea of the University of Canada North was debated seriously in the 1970s and 1980s, but for a variety of reasons it never took hold.

The project would require much consultation and planning, and the cost would be high, but the price that northerners are paying for not having a northern university is far greater. The territories could not build such an institution themselves, so the project would require substantial and ongoing investment on the part of the federal government. But with the Arctic the site of a potential race for resources, and with Arctic sovereignty issues intensifying, can Canada really afford not to have a well-educated northern population? Even if all parties were to agree today to build a university north of 60, it would take nearly a decade to complete it, and Canada is already at least four decades behind Alaska, Russia and the Nordic states in this regard.

Obstacles to Implementation

M ANY OBSERVERS WOULD AGREE THAT EXPANDING UNIVERSITY ACCESS FOR NORTHENERS is both desirable and necessary. Some would even argue that investment in building northern education capacity is no different than historic investments that have been made in southern Canada, such as building a railway from sea to sea. Like the builders of Canada's national railway, who encountered obstacles of geography, politics and finance, those who would build a university in the Canadian North would confront some formidable obstacles.

Literacy is a huge problem in the territorial North — a problem of increasing significance as one moves from west to east. There is extreme pressure on territorial governments to address it ahead of all other issues. However, there is a tendency to frame the problem as an either/or proposition when it comes to post-secondary education. The argument goes like this: "Why should we invest in post-secondary education when so many of our people cannot even read or write?" But, the problem of literacy notwithstanding, many northerners are completing high school and entering post-secondary educational institutions, particularly the three Arctic colleges. The need for post-secondary training, including university education, is increasing at a rapid rate, and investment in this training must be made along with investment in adult literacy.

The differences between traditional and contemporary learning systems sometimes become the subject of a debate that inhibits discussion of expanding university education. The North faces a complex of cultural, economic, political and environmental challenges not generally found in southern Canada. The dominant cultures in the south, both French and English, are secure. Southern Canadians take for granted the accessibility of English- or French-language education through their K-12 and post-secondary systems; these languages are also those of the mainstream media, government services and everyday life. For the most part, the economic life of southern Canadians is directly linked with the global economy. And, while Canada does endure some constitutional roller-coaster rides, the basic institutions and values of its Westminster-style liberal democracy are widely supported and operate reasonably well, certainly by global standards. Environmental issues are becoming an increasingly important part of federal and provincial policy agendas, but the reality is that environmental problems for most Canadians are not a top-of-mind issue.

All of this stands in sharp contrast with the situation in much of the North. First, many Aboriginal communities face serious challenges in retaining their indigenous languages. Even among the Inuit of Nunavut, whose language retention rate is quite high (in the 2006 Census, 83 percent identified Inuktitut as their mother tongue, and 91 percent indicated that they could converse in Inuktitut), there is great pressure to ensure that Inuktitut remains a strong, vibrant presence in both private and public life. Second, the North has three major economies — traditional, market and transfer — each with unique (albeit interrelated) challenges. Traditional skills and knowledge are profoundly important to these economies and to the integrity of indigenous cultures. Moreover, traditional ecological knowledge is vitally important to northern communities, not only in relation to traditional activities on the land, but also to ensure the future health and well-being of inhabitants as they are affected by resource development. Environmental issues are top-of-mind in the North: they have an impact on the survival of peoples and cultures.

The argument that traditional indigenous learning systems are incompatible with contemporary Western educational institutions has two sides. On one side, some insist that university education would undermine indigenous systems of learning and should be approached with caution and skepticism. On the other side, some argue that traditional knowledge is not "scientific" and therefore has no place in the academy. Neither position is tenable or productive. There are examples of indigenous and Western learning systems not only coexisting successfully, but also enriching each other. In fact, it is increasingly common to find indigenous language courses in which a university-trained linguist works alongside community elders, wildlife management courses that utilize both scientific methodology and traditional knowledge, and public administration courses that integrate standard political science approaches with indigenous governance systems. Objections to the coexistence of learning systems have decreased over the past decade, but they remain obstacles that must be addressed.

Another obstacle to be overcome involves social funding priorities. The old guns-versus-butter debate has been transformed into a books-versus-butter debate. Education is not cheap, and the territories face critical social problems. When the need for investment in university education is raised, a common response is, "Why should we invest in university education when we don't even have basic housing?" It may seem hard to refute such reasoning — education does appear to be a luxury item when compared to food, clothing and shelter. However, the long-term ability of territorial governments and communities to provide constituents with the basics of life depends upon the existence of a well-educated population with the skills to govern and build strong economies. This debate needs to be reframed, although it is sad that in a country as prosperous as Canada it should have to occur at all.

Finally, the proposition to develop a university system based in the North raises the question of the role of the federal government. Over the past two decades, devolution has been the driving dynamic in federal-territorial relations. The degree of devolution across the three territories varies, but all three territorial governments deliver the lion's share of educational services. However, the federal government does make major contributions to education through transfer payments and continues to have a fiduciary responsibility for the North. And it is difficult to see how the federal government could make a massive investment in post-secondary education without undertaking a leading partnership role. It is in our national interest for the territories to become more economically self-sufficient, though it is quite unlikely that they will ever become fully self-sufficient. Unfortunately, it is possible that the federal and/or territorial governments could choose not to cooperate in the creation of a university in Canada's Arctic region. The federal government could wash its hands of the project on the grounds that it is a territorial responsibility; a territorial government could object to the federal government's role in the undertaking on the grounds that Ottawa might use it as an opportunity to interfere in territorial affairs.

Conclusion

FOR ABOUT HALF A CENTURY, CANADA HAS CONSIDERED THE ARCTIC A NATIONAL priority. The emphasis on Arctic sovereignty, northern research, climate change and resource development is understandable. But none of Canada's northern policy goals can be achieved without strong, vibrant, sustainable northern governments, communities and peoples. As the federal government continues to build the social or human dimension of its integrated northern strategy, it must commit significant attention and resources to developing the skills, knowledge and capacity northerners need to manage their own affairs and define their own futures. The current government is on the right track, for instance, with its goal of building a world-class Arctic research centre (or centres) in the North that would be available to Canadian and international researchers. However, there needs to be an equal commitment to developing northern post-secondary education, especially at the university level. How ironic it would be if Canada were to invest hundreds of millions of dollars in a northern research institution that only international researchers could utilize because northern Canadians had no access to the necessary training. Canada has an opportunity to become a world leader in northern education. The various bilateral, consortium, and bricks and mortar university models outlined in this chapter suggest that such an investment would contribute significantly to building strong and effective northern territorial and Aboriginal governments and dynamic, competitive northern economies. The development of sustainable access to university education in the North is an important policy, that federal and territorial governments should pursue at the beginning of the twenty-first century.

Notes

1   I have many people to thank for helping me with this chapter. However, I would like to give special thanks to Nadine Zettl, my research assistant, who did excellent work in finding reports and other materials, mining Statistics Canada data and assembling the tables. I would also like to extend warm thanks to Ken Coates, Andrew Hodgson, Margaret Imrie, Cam McGregor, Linda Pemik and Glenys Plunz, who commented on this chapter at various stages and provided important insights and corrections. And I would like to thank the reviewers at IRPP, especially Leslie Seidle, Frances Abele and France St-Hilaire, who were extremely generous, helpful and thorough — this was collegiality and professionalism at its very best. Any errors or shortcomings are, of course, mine alone.

2   Publicly supported kindergarten-through-grade-12 education.

3   Although developing university capacity across the three territories is a priority, this does not imply that the need for literacy programs, basic adult education and trade education is being met. Investment needs to be strengthened in these other areas, as they are critical to a sustainable future for the North. However, in contrast to university education, these forms of education currently receive both significant public policy attention and substantial, if inadequate, funding. Moreover, the combination of increasing devolution, demand for resources and need for environmental management makes access to university education, along with other forms of education, all the more urgent if northerners are to control their own futures.

4   See Frenette for an excellent overview of this issue (2007).

5   Mendelson identifies a similar set of issues (2006).

6   The cohort model of program delivery is based on a group of students (the cohort) who start and finish a program at the same time and who take classes together. This model provides not only efficient delivery, but also, and more importantly, strong peer support.

7   This observation is based on my nearly 20 years of post-secondary teaching and many discussions with college and university teachers across northern Canada.

8   "Laddering" is a process whereby a student completes a sequence of a certificate (a program of study worth one year of university credits) and/or a diploma (a program of study worth two years of university credits that can be transferred in whole or in part to an undergraduate university degree program). Typically, a diploma graduate requires two more years of senior undergraduate courses to complete a university degree.

References

Berger, Thomas R. 2006. *"The Nunavut Project."* *Nunavut Land Claims Agreement.* *Implementation Contract Negotiations for the Second Planning Period 2003-2013.* *Conciliator's Final Report*, March 1. Ottawa: Indian and Northern Affairs Canada. Accessed January 14, 2009. http://www.ainc-inac.gc.ca/pr/agr/nu/lca/nlc_e.pdf

Council of Ministers of Education, Canada (CMEC). 2007. "OECD Activity on Recognition of Non-formal and Informal Learning, Northwest Territories Report." In *Recognition of Non-formal and Informal Learning (RNFIL)*, November. Toronto: CMEC. Accessed January 23, 2009. http://www.cmec.ca/postsec/rnfil/07-northwestterritories_canada_oecd_web_rnfil_en.pdf

Frenette, Marc. 2007. *Do Universities Benefit Local Youth? Evidence from University and College Participation, and Graduate Earnings Following the Creation of a New University.* Analytical Studies Branch Research Paper 2006283e. Ottawa: Statistics Canada.

Graham, Amanda. 1994. "The University That Wasn't: The University of Canada North." Master's thesis, Lakehead University.

Accessed January 23, 2009.
http://www.yukoncollege.yk.ca/~agraham/
papers/ucn.pdf

Handley, Joseph, Dennis Fentie, and Paul Okalik.
2007. *A Northern Vision: A Stronger North
and a Better Canada*. Whitehorse: Premier's
Office, Government of Yukon; Premier's
Office, Government of the Northwest
Territories; Premier's Office, Government of
Nunavut. Accessed January 16, 2009.
http://www.anorthernvision.ca/pdf/
newvision_english.pdf

Hodgson, Andrew. 2007. "Implications of Mega-
project Development for Adult Education
in the Northwest Territories." Master's
thesis, University of Alberta.

Johansson, Gunilla, Chris Paci, and Sylvi
Stenersen Hovdenak. 2004. "Education." In
Arctic Human Development Report, edited by
Niels Einarsson, Joan Nymand Larsen,
Annika Nilsson, and Oran R. Young.
Akureyri, Iceland: Stefansson Arctic
Institute.

Mendelson, Mark. 2006. *Aboriginal Peoples and
Postsecondary Education in Canada*. Ottawa:
Caledon Institute of Social Policy.

Minogue, Sara. 2006. "Iqaluit Students Lacking
Basic Skills." *Globe and Mail*, April 17.

Nunavut Department of Education and Nunavut
Arctic College. 2006. *Qalattuq — 10-Year
Educator Training Strategy, 2006-2016*.
Iqaluit: Government of Nunavut.

Organisation for Economic Co-operation and
Development (OECD). 2007. *Higher
Education and Regions: Globally Competitive,
Locally Engaged*. Paris: OECD.

————. 2008. "Higher Education and Regional
Development." Special issue, *Higher
Education Management and Policy* 20 (2).

Science Council of Canada. 1977. *Northward
Looking: A Strategy and a Science Policy for
Northern Development*. Science Council of
Canada Report 26. Ottawa: Science Council
of Canada.

Statistics Canada. 2006. "Provincial and
Territorial Highlights: Yukon Territory."
Educational Portrait of Canada, 2006 Census:
Findings. Cat. no. 97-560-XWE2006001.
Ottawa: Statistics Canada. Accessed
February 6, 2009. http://www12.statcan.ca/
english/census06/analysis/education/index.cfm

————. 2007. Unemployment Rate by Level of
Education, Canada, 1990-2006. Table E3.1.
In *Education Indicators in Canada: Handbook
for the Report of the Pan-Canadian Education
Indicators Program 2007*. Ottawa: Statistics
Canada.

————. 2008. *Labour, 2006 Census*. Cat. no.
97-559-XWE2006019. Accessed February
6, 2009. http://www.statcan.gc.ca/bsolc/
olc-cel/olc-cel?lang=eng&catno=97-559-
X2006019

University of Alaska. 2004. "University of Alaska
Student Enrollment Summary: A Review of
the Enrollment Changes 1997 to 2004, and
a Listing of Current Student Enrollment
Statistics." Fairbanks: University of Alaska.

University of Tromsø. 2008. Accessed August 15,
2008. http://www2.uit.no/startsida

US Census Bureau. 2007. "State and County
Quick Facts: Alaska." Washington, DC: US
Census Bureau. Accessed January 21, 2009.
http://quickfacts.census.gov/qfd/states/
02000.html

Toward   More   Effective,
Evidence-Based   Suicide
Prevention   in   Nunavut

> If the populations of "mainland" Canada, Denmark and the United States had
> suicide rates comparable to those of their Inuit populations, national emergen-
> cies would be declared.
>
> — Upaluk Poppel, Inuit Circumpolar Youth Council, May 18, 2005

T HE WORLD'S INUIT POPULATION HAS NOT ALWAYS SUFFERED FROM THE TRAGICALLY
high rates of suicide that it now experiences. The 150,000 Inuit alive
today are an indigenous people inhabiting the Arctic regions of the Chukotka
Peninsula in the Russian far east, Alaska, Canada and Greenland. A maritime
people, Inuit traditionally relied on fish, marine mammals and land animals for
food, clothing, transport, shelter, warmth, light and tools. Until fairly recently,
there was a remarkable cultural homogeneity across their homelands, but that
began to change as the four states in which Inuit now find themselves[1] consol-
idated their grip over their Arctic regions.

Suicide was not unknown in historical Inuit culture. This might seem
obvious — has there ever been a society in which no one took his or her own life?
— but the CBC Digital Archives Web site tells its readers that "the concept of suicide was unknown to the Inuit before they made contact with colonizers"
("Linking School" 1991). Franz Boas, however, famously wrote that "suicide is
not of rare occurrence, as according to the religious ideas of the Eskimo the souls
of those who die by violence go to Qudlivun, the happy land. For the same reason it is considered lawful for a man to kill his aged parents. In suicide death is
generally brought about by hanging." (1888, 615).

In his book *The Intellectual Culture of the Iglulik Eskimos* (1929), Knud
Rasmussen documented several suicides in what we know today as the Kivalliq

region of Nunavut. Rasmussen's Fifth Thule Expedition also investigated Inuit
spiritual beliefs relevant to the taking of one's own life:

> The Moon Spirit is one of the great regulating powers of the universe which
> is not feared. Knowing the view of the East Greenlanders, who regard the
> Moon Spirit as the most terrible of the punitive deities watching over the
> deeds of men, I enquired particularly about this point, but was everywhere
> informed that no one feared the Moon Spirit, only the Sea Spirit was to be
> feared, and especially her father. The Moon Spirit, on the other hand, is the
> only good and well-intentioned spirit known, and when he does intervene,
> it is often more for guidance than for punishment. People in danger can
> often hear him calling out: "Come, come to me! It is not painful to die. It is
> only a brief moment of dizziness. It does not hurt to kill yourself."
> (Rasmussen 1929)

John Steckley has questioned the evidence supporting what he terms the
"simulacrum" (intellectual commodity) of Inuit frequently abandoning their
elders to perish when the survival of the entire family group was in peril, and he
points out that many of the accounts of Inuit elder suicide that appear in sociology texts are entirely fictional. The final sentences in this "account" suggest that
all Inuit elders died by assisted suicide:

> Shantu and Wishta fondly kissed their children and grandchildren
> farewell. Then sadly, but with resignation at the sacrifice they knew they
> had to make for their family, they slowly climbed onto the ice floe. The
> goodbyes were painfully made as the large slab of ice inched into the
> ocean currents. Shantu and Wishta would now starve. But they were old,
> and their death was necessary, for it reduced the demand on the small
> group's scarce food supply. As the younger relatives watched Shantu and
> Wishta recede into the distance, each knew that their turn to make this
> sacrifice would come. Each hoped that they would face it as courageous-
> ly. (Steckley 2003)

The simulacrum of high rates of Inuit elder suicide is so strong that when
a medical student in Alaska submitted a letter to the *Journal of the American
Medical Association* in 2000 in which he spoke of witnessing a 97-year-old Yup'ik
patient saying goodbye to his family, walking onto the sea ice and "vanishing into
the early morning fog," no one at the very prestigious and professional journal
doubted it, and the letter was published. The author's supervising physician in
the village in question wrote to *JAMA* informing the editors that the story was just
that — a fiction (Swenson 2000).

We are now seeing a new simulacrum that exaggerates the rate of youth
suicide among Inuit. Writing on the liberal news Web site and aggregated Weblog

the *Huffington Post* in 2007, the man who has been executive director of the Sierra Club for 15 years observed:

> The cemetery at Illulissat seems surprisingly large for a town of its size — the cold Arctic air preserves the wooden crosses, and the flowers are, unsurprisingly, plastic, so they too last and magnify the visual marker of the graveyard. But this March the cemetery grew in a tragic, stunning sign of how global warming and globalization are combining to take human lives.
>
> In a village which 20 years ago supported itself hunting marine mammals on the sea ice, fathers taught their sons the skills of the hunt. The sea ice has now vanished and the hunt along with it, so fathers no longer teach their sons. There is new employment in Illulissat — tourism, oil exploration, commercial fishing — but the collapse of the traditional subsistence culture has left despair and hopelessness among the young.
>
> This March, in a town of only 5,000 people, 14 teenage boys took their lives. (Pope 2007)

No evidence was offered to substantiate the claim that "the collapse of the traditional subsistence culture" had resulted in high rates of suicide because it had created "despair and hopelessness among the young."

Fourteen teenage suicides in a single month in a town of 5,000 would, without a doubt, be a tragedy of unbelievable proportion. But in reality, there was one suicide in Illulissat in all of 2007.[2] There is no need to exaggerate the seriousness of what is happening with regard to suicide in Inuit societies — the facts speak for themselves.

A Statistical Portrait of Death by Suicide in Inuit Societies

THE EVIDENCE SUGGESTS THAT UNTIL QUITE RECENTLY, INUIT SOCIETIES HAD A QUITE *low* rate of death by suicide. The earliest existing data on suicide among Inuit come from Greenland. Writing in 1935, Alfred Berthelsen calculated a suicide rate of just 3.0 per annum per 100,000 population for the period 1900 to 1930.[3] He concluded that the few suicides occurring in Greenland at that time were all the result of serious mental illnesses. As late as 1960, there was still the occasional year when no suicides by Greenlanders were recorded.

If the coroners' records from the predivision Northwest Territories are complete, then in the area we know today as Nunavut there was just one suicide

Figure 1
Number of Deaths By Suicide in Nunavut, 1960-2006

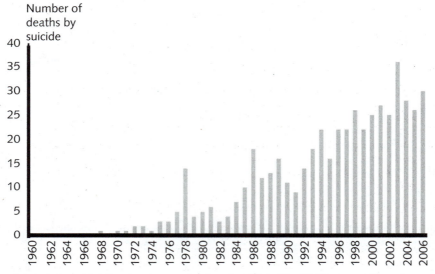

Source: Author's tabulations based on raw data from the Office of the Chief Coroner of Nunavut.

Figure 2
Potential Years of Life Lost Due to Death by Suicide among Men in Canada, by Province and Territory, 2003 (per 100,000 population)

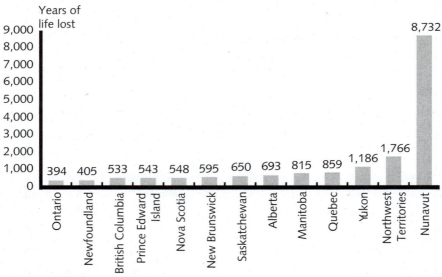

Source: Statistics Canada, CANSIM table 102-0110.

in the entire decade of the 1960s (figure 1). As recently as 1971, the rate of death by suicide among Inuit in Canada was close to that of the non-Aboriginal population of the country. And in Alaska, Kraus and Buffler found that during the 1950s, Alaska Native peoples had a rate of death by suicide that was considerably *lower* than that of the non-Native residents of the state (1979). Today, however, - Inuit-dominated regions of Canada have suicide rates that far exceed those of other parts of the country (figure 2; the use of "potential years of life lost" highlights the young median age of suicide among Inuit). The quality of data available on the four Inuit regions of Canada varies considerably, but there are sufficient basic data to tell us that Inuit in the different regions have quite different rates of death by suicide (figure 3).

Beginning in the 1950s, governments across the Arctic subjected Inuit lifeways to intense disruption. The details varied considerably across the Arctic, but the fundamental economic, political and social processes of incorporation and sedentarization[4] were similar. These processes also took place at somewhat different times in different parts of the Arctic, and they had somewhat divergent outcomes (Csonka 2005).

The transition from the historical pattern of suicide among Inuit to the present-day pattern was first documented in northern Alaska by psychiatrist Robert Kraus. In a paper he presented at a 1971 conference, he noted:

> In the traditional pattern, middle-aged or older men were involved; motivation for suicide involved sickness, old age, or bereavement; the suicide was undertaken after sober reflection and, at times, consultation with family members who might condone or participate in the act; and suicide was positively sanctioned in the culture. In the emergent pattern, the individuals involved are young; the motivation is obscure and often related to intense and unbearable affective states; the behaviour appears in an abrupt, fit-like, unexpected manner without much warning, often in association with alcohol intoxication; and, unlike the traditional pattern, the emergent pattern is negatively sanctioned in the culture. (Kraus 1971)

This suicide transition among Inuit was experienced first in northern Alaska in the late 1960s, then in Greenland in the 1970s and early 1980s, and then again in Canada's eastern Arctic in the late 1980s and through the 1990s.[5] Each time the transition occurred, it resulted in a higher overall rate of death by suicide (figure 4).

The temporal sequence in which the "regional suicide transitions" occurred is noteworthy, as it mirrors — roughly one generation later — the processes of active colonialism at the community level described earlier.[6] We can use the decline

Figure 3
Average Annual Rates of Death by Suicide among Inuit, by Region and in Canada, 1999-2003

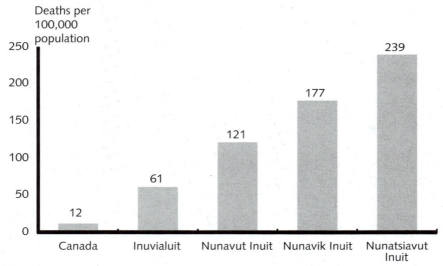

Source: Author's tabulations based on raw data from the coroners' offices in the various jurisdictions and on demographic data from national statistical agencies.

Figure 4
Rates of Death by Suicide among Alaska Natives, Greenlanders and Eastern Arctic Inuit,[1] 1960-2001

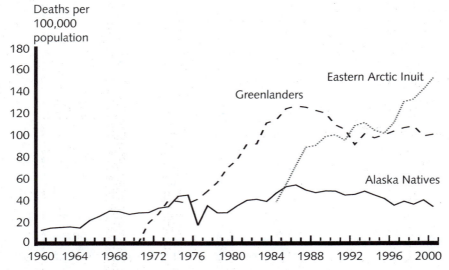

Sources: Greenland: Bjerregaard and Lynge (2006); Alaska: Personal communication, Matthew Berman, University of Alaska-Anchorage; Eastern Arctic Inuit: author's tabulations based on coroners' records from the various jurisdictions and demographic data from Statistics Canada.
[1] Three-year rolling averages; eastern Arctic is Nunavik and the Qikiqtani region of Nunavut.

Northern Exposure: Peoples, Powers and
Prospects in Canada's North

in the incidence of tuberculosis as a historical marker of the early years of "active colonialism at the community level." The historical sequence in which Inuit infectious disease rates fell (as a result of the introduction of Western medicine) was the same order in which Inuit rates of death by suicide later rose across the Arctic.

Interpreting the Statistical Evidence

E VEN THOUGH THE EXISTING DATA ON SUICIDE AMONG INUIT ARE QUITE LIMITED, THE basic statistics we do have can tell us a fair amount about what has happened and what is happening. In each jurisdiction for which data are available,[7] suicides first increased dramatically among young men. In Greenland, as Peter Bjerregaard has shown, suicide began to increase among young men born after 1950, the very year in which the Danish state initiated an intensive program to turn the island into a "modern welfare society" — a process in which only a few Greenlanders had any say (figure 5).

Figure 5
Rates of Death by Suicide among Greenlanders, by Gender and Year of Birth, 1950-78

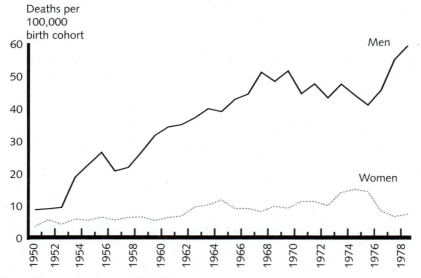

Source: Bjerregaard and Lynge (2006, 213).

Today, suicide rates are several times higher among young Inuit men than they are among Inuit women of the same age and older Inuit men and women; and the rates for these young men are many times higher than they are for their peers in mainland Denmark and southern Canada and the US. It is difficult to find words to describe the suicide-related pain and trauma that has been suffered in Inuit communities in recent years.

During the first nine years of Nunavut's existence (April 1, 1999, to March 31, 2008), there were 247 suicides. All but three were by Inuit. Of the 244 suicides by Nunavut Inuit, 201 (82 percent) were by men and 43 (18 percent) were by women. The rate of death by suicide among Nunavut Inuit more than tripled during the 20 years beginning in 1983, and it is currently just over 120 per 100,000 population. Fifty-six percent of suicides in Nunavut are by men younger than 25, compared to 7 percent Canada-wide (figures 6 and 7). Seventy-seven percent of suicides by men are by hanging; 20 percent are done with firearms (which are very common in Nunavut communities); 86 percent of suicides by women are by hanging; only a few are done by firearms or overdose.

Figure 6
Average Annual Rates of Death by Suicide among Nunavut Inuit, by Sex and by Age Cohort, 1999-2003

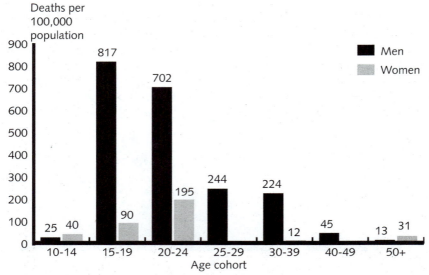

Source: Author's tabulations based on raw data from the Office of the Chief Coroner of Nunavut and on demographic data from Statistics Canada.

Figure 7

Average Annual Rates of Death by Suicide among Inuit Men in Nunavut, 1999-2003, and All Men in Canada, 1998, by Age Cohort

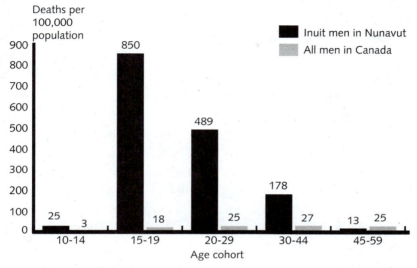

Sources: All men in Canada: Langlois and Morrison (2002, 15); Inuit men in Nunavut: author's tabulations based on raw data from the Office of the Chief Coroner of Nunavut and demographic data from Statistics Canada.

Figure 8

Average Annual Rates of Death by Suicide among Nunavut Inuit by Age Cohort in Three Time Periods, 1980-2003

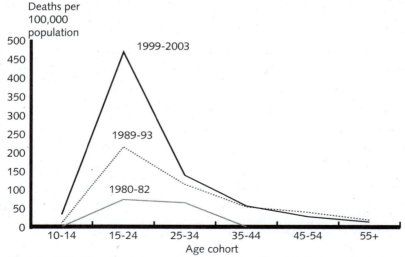

Source: Author's tabulations based on raw data from the Office of the Chief Coroner of Nunavut and on demographic data from Statistics Canada.

The rise in Nunavut's rate of death by suicide is almost entirely the result of an increased number of suicides by Inuit younger than 25. The rate of death by suicide among Nunavut Inuit aged 15 to 24 has increased more than sixfold since the early 1980s (figure 8).

Of the 11 communities with the highest rates of death by suicide, 10 are located in the Qikiqtani (formerly Baffin) region — the exception being Kugluktuk, in the Kitikmeot region (figure 9). By "home community," I mean the community in which the person who died by suicide grew up. This is usually the community in which he or she died, but a number of people who grew up in other communities have taken their lives in Iqaluit, after having been in the capital for only a few months, or even days.

In each Inuit jurisdiction, there are subregions that developed and sustained far higher rates of suicide than others did. In Alaska, the Northwest Coast has by far the highest rates. In Greenland, the suicide rate among young Inuit men peaked first in the capital city Nuuk in the early 1980s, then along the rest of the west coast in the late 1980s, and finally on the east coast in the early 1990s. Suicide among young men in East Greenland reached a rate of 1,500 per annum per 100,000 population — surely one of the highest suicide rates ever recorded anywhere on Earth — before it finally began to decline (figure 10).

In Nunavik (the Inuit part of northern Quebec), the Hudson coast has suffered from a much higher suicide rate than the Ungava coast; while in Nunavut, the Qikiqtani region has a markedly higher suicide rate than the two mainland regions (figures 11 and 12).

There are also similarities in terms of where the suicide rates are decreasing — those subregions of the Inuit world that have experienced the most development in recent decades. In Greenland, suicide rates among young men in Nuuk have declined significantly over the past 25 years, while they have remained stable on the rest of the west coast and risen considerably in East Greenland. A similar shift appears to be under way in Alaska: the suicide rate of Alaska Native peoples residing in urban Alaska[8] (14.5 per 100,000 population) is now less than a third of that of Alaska Native peoples residing in bush Alaska (53 per 100,000 population). Any serious attempt to explain suicidal behaviour among Inuit in recent decades would therefore include consideration of the difference in rates between men and women, between age cohorts and between regions and subregions, as well as changes in all of these rates over time.

Figure 9

Average Annual Rates of Death by Suicide among Nunavut Inuit, by Home Community, 1999-2003

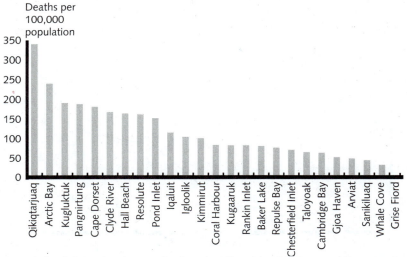

Source: Author's tabulations based on raw data from the Office of the Chief Coroner of Nunavut and on demographic data from Statistics Canada.

Figure 10

Average Annual Rates of Death by Suicide among Men Aged 15 to 29, in Nuuk,[1] West Greenland and East Greenland, 1970-99

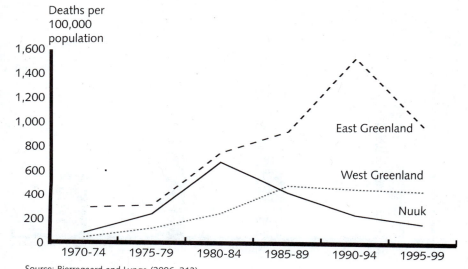

Source: Bjerregaard and Lynge (2006, 212).
[1] Nuuk is the capital of Greenland.

Figure 11
Deaths by Suicide among Nunavik Inuit, by Coast, 1974-2003

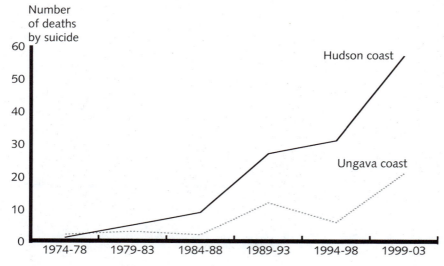

Source: Kativik Regional Health and Social Services Board.

Figure 12
Average Annual Rates of Death by Suicide among Nunavut Inuit, by Gender and by Home Community, 1999-2003

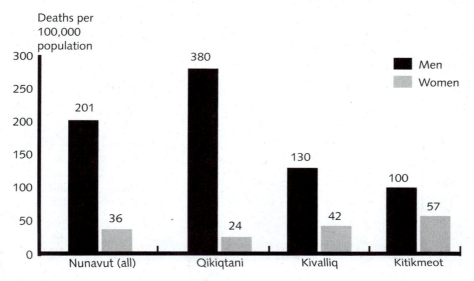

Source: Author's tabulations based on raw data from the Office of the Chief Coroner of Nunavut and on demographic data from Statistics Canada.

Identifying Root Causes
to Effect Change

T HESE STATISTICS ARE REALLY NOTHING MORE THAN BODY COUNTS. THEY TELL US very little about why these people chose to end their lives. In order to develop more effective suicide prevention strategies, we need to know much more.

There is an important body of research on mental health in Greenland. Inge Lynge, the first psychiatrist on the island, made an unparalleled contribution to our understanding of the mental health of Inuit during the second half of the twentieth century.[9] In a recent article, Lynge and another leading figure in Greenland health research in recent decades, Peter Bjerregaard, added the observation that "suicidal thoughts occur more often in young people who grew up in homes with a poor emotional environment, alcohol problems and violence…The socioeconomic and structural features of the home were less important than the emotional environment for the development of personality disorders. A logical sequence of transgenerational events would be that modernization leads to dysfunctional homes due to poor parental behavior (alcohol and violence). This in turn results in suicidal thoughts, suicides and also substance abuse among the children of those parents" (Bjerregaard and Lynge 2006). These conclusions are entirely consistent with the results of research on suicidal behaviour elsewhere in the world.[10]

The Ph.D. project of Dutch researcher Markus Leineweber also makes an important contribution to our understanding of suicide in Greenland. Leineweber worked with death certificates and police reports for deaths occurring between 1993 and 1995 that were deemed by the authorities to have been suicides; and, where possible, he obtained limited amounts of additional data on the deceased. He concluded that frequent conflict with family and friends, a recent life-threatening experience, the expression of suicidal intentions and the acute abuse of alcohol are the most common characteristics of Greenlanders who take their own lives (Leineweber 2000).

An equally important body of research has been accumulated in Nunavik by Laurence Kirmayer and his colleagues at McGill University. Kirmayer's observation that "among the Inuit, greater familiarity with the problem and expectations for recovery are more important determinants of attitudes towards a person with deviant behaviour than are specific labels or causal attributes" helps us understand the importance of conducting public education about problematic behaviours and the effectiveness of various treatment options (Kirmayer 1997 et al.).

While there are no psychiatrists living in Nunavut as permanent residents — psychiatric services are provided on a fly-in basis from the south, with some patients being sent south for treatment — one psychiatrist who lived and practised in Iqaluit for a year recently published an insightful reflection on the clinical and social characteristics of the 110 Nunavummiut he was asked to see during a 12-month period: "Interpersonal and socio-environmental stressors were found to be unusually extensive and the primary precipitators of psychiatric crises such as suicide attempts. Negative health determinants such as unemployment, overcrowding, domestic violence, substance abuse, and legal charges were also prevalent. Psychiatric issues in the Arctic appear deeply interwoven with interpersonal, socioeconomic, and societal changes; effective community mental health services must address a broad spectrum of psychosocial issues beyond the medical model" (Law and Hutton 2007).

Research on the association of suicidal ideation (suicidal thoughts) and behaviour with depression, anxiety and alcohol abuse in a Nunavut community found very high rates of both suicidal ideation and suicide attempts (table 1).

We need to learn much more about the Nunavummiut who take their own lives, who attempt to do so, and who contemplate doing so: their rates and patterns of family history and early childhood experiences; mental disorders; medical history; education history; work history; relationship history; substance use/abuse; engagement with the justice system; access to and use of health care services; and other factors that may have played a role in their suicidal behaviour. We would also like to know about the presence or

Table 1
Suicidal Thoughts and Suicide Attempts in One Nunavut Community (Percent)

Suicidal thoughts (past week) (N = 110)		Suicide attempts (past 6 months) (N = 110)	
None	56.4	Never	70.0
Sometimes	40.0	Once	14.0
Very often	3.6	Several	13.0
All the time	0.0	Many	3.0

Source: Haggarty et al. (2008).

Northern Exposure: Peoples, Powers and Prospects in Canada's North

absence of a number of protective factors. There is an accepted methodology for obtaining these much richer data: the suicide follow-back study (or psychological autopsy), by which researchers collect the detailed information they need to reconstruct the social, psychological and psychiatric history of persons who have died by suicide. This is accomplished through detailed, semistructured interviews with family members and others who knew the deceased well, plus a review of administrative data (for example, medical charts). This kind of comprehensive analysis has contributed much to our understanding of suicidal behaviour generally. The results have been summarized in two meta-analyses (Cavanagh et al. 2003; Arsenault-Lapierre, Kim, and Turecki 2004).

Considerably more will be known about the risk and protective factors specific to suicide in Nunavut in 2010, when the suicide follow-back study Qaujivallianiq Inuusirijauvalauqtunik (Learning from Lives That Have Been Lived) is completed. This study is being conducted by the McGill Group for Suicide Studies in partnership with a range of organizations in Nunavut. It is reviewing in great detail the lives of the 120 Inuit who died by suicide in Nunavut from 2003 to 2006, matched with case controls selected by community, sex and nearest date of birth.

The Impact of Adverse Childhood Experiences

THERE IS ALSO A VAST ARRAY OF RESEARCH ON MENTAL HEALTH THAT IS OF relevance to Inuit insofar as Inuit are people like everyone else, in addition to being members of a specific indigenous group. Of particular relevance to the Arctic at this moment in history is the literature on the negative impact of what are sometimes termed "adverse childhood experiences" — for example, emotional, physical and sexual abuse; neglectful or otherwise problematic parenting; substance abuse within the family; and violence within the family. In short, early childhood experiences — both positive and negative — can have a significant impact on the physical, mental, behavioural and economic well-being of the child and of the adolescent and adult he or she grows up to be.

The most important body of work in this field is the Christchurch Health and Development Study, which has

> followed the health, education and life progress of a group of 1,265 children born in the Christchurch (New Zealand) urban region during mid 1977. This cohort has now been studied from infancy into childhood, adolescence and adulthood. The data gathered over the course of the study now comprises some 50 million characters of information describing the life history of this cohort. The Study has published over 300 scientific papers, books and book chapters describing the 30 year life history of the CHDS cohort. (CHDS n.d.)[11]

It is impossible to summarize the wealth of findings from this study in a few paragraphs, but given that we are discussing a population with high rates of cannabis use in their early teenage years, we might note the findings of one of the most recent papers, on cannabis use and later-life outcomes:

> Increasing cannabis use in late adolescence and early adulthood is associated with a range of adverse outcomes in later life. High levels of cannabis use are related to poorer educational outcomes, lower income, greater welfare dependence and unemployment, and lower relationship and life satisfaction. The findings add to a growing body of knowledge regarding the adverse consequences of heavy cannabis use. (Fergusson and Boden 2008)

The work of Robert F. Anda and his collaborators has also documented the profound impact that adverse childhood experiences can have on a person's mental and emotional health as an adult. They found a "strong, graded relationship" between adverse childhood experiences and an array of negative outcomes later in life, meaning that having a range of such negative experiences has a cumulative effect that makes it much more likely that a range of mental and emotional problems will arise (Anda et al. 2006; Chapman et al. 2004; Dube et al. 2001).[12]

The Centers for Disease Control's Adverse Childhood Experiences Study has also documented the profound impact that adverse childhood experiences can have on a person's mental and emotional health as an adult: "The public health impact of childhood adversity is evident in the very strong association between childhood adversity and depressive symptoms, antisocial behavior, and drug use during the early transition to adulthood" (Schilling, Aseltine, and Gore 2007). On a happier note, a range of early childhood intervention programs have been evaluated, and some have been shown to provide at-risk children with a better start in life and better mental health outcomes later on.

Social Determinants:
Adapting to a New Life
Script

A USTRALIAN PSYCHIATRIST ROBERT GOLDNEY HAS SUGGESTED THAT ALL HUMAN SOCIETIES
are likely to have a "base rate" of suicide in the range of 5 to 10 per annum
per 100,000 population as a result of biological and other factors that are simply
a part of the human condition (Goldney 2003; Turecki and Lalovic 2005). The
differences between the base rate and rates that are significantly higher than the
base rate are, Goldney believes, primarily the result of social determinants.[13]

The only logical explanation for the dramatic increase in suicide rates
among Inuit living in different regions of the Arctic — with similar outcomes
among the sexes and age groups, at different and distinct time periods — is that a
similar basket of social determinants has impacted heavily on Inuit societies at different times across the different regions and subregions. The experiences that Inuit
in different regions of the Arctic had several decades ago may have had significant
impacts upon the mental health of their children — the next generation of young
Inuit, who, in some cases, were the first Inuit to grow up in settled communities.
The fact that suicide rates among young Inuit men residing in urban areas of
Greenland and Alaska have fallen in recent decades suggests that this basket of
social determinants is still at work, and that it continues to change over time.

It may be that young men who have grown up under these new conditions get
a better start in life and have a greater chance of becoming happy, successful adults. In
effect, a new "life script" may have come into existence in urban areas across the Inuit
world. In the old days, boys grew up seeing the adult men around them being busy
and productive, being good husbands and parents, and taking pride in their accomplishments. The opportunity to grow up seeing — and being parented by — adult men
who are happy and successful is not uncommon in the Arctic, but socio-economic circumstances create a greater opportunity for it in some places than in others. The young
Inuit men at greatest risk appear to be those who are situated somewhere between the
historical Inuit life script and the emerging urban Inuit life script in communities and
families where unemployment and social dysfunction are more common.

We are also living in a time of increasing social differentiation among Inuit,
a process that has a mental health component. Some young Inuit in Nunavut find
themselves living in a world of almost limitless opportunity, but the daily reality

of other young Inuit is one of historical traumas transmitted through family and community, overcrowded housing, a weak school system with a 75 percent dropout rate, limited employment opportunities, socio-cultural oppression (Sullivan and Brems 1997) and teenage years spent stoned on marijuana.

And while the settlement of Inuit land claims and the establishment of regional public governments that Inuit effectively control have gone a long way to redress the power imbalance that scarred several generations of Inuit, that kind of healing doesn't happen overnight. "There is still a lot of bitterness toward the government here," the mayor of a Nunavut community was recently quoted as saying. "It's passed down from generation to generation" (Belkin 2007). That bitterness is primarily directed toward the federal government.

If we accept Robert Goldney's suggestion that any society's suicide rate is a combination of a "base rate" and an incremental rate resulting from the social determinants specific to that society, then we can develop a clearer picture of what has been happening in Inuit society and what might be done to positively affect that society's mental health outcomes. Inuit take their lives for the same reasons other people do, but they also take their lives for other reasons specific to Inuit societies as they exist today. The challenge of suicide prevention in the Inuit regions, then, can be seen as the same challenge faced by all peoples on the planet, compounded by the unique social determinants underlying elevated rates of suicide among Inuit youth. Among those determinants may be the legacy of the adverse childhood experiences borne by the generation of Inuit who first began to display elevated rates of suicidal behaviour — people who grew up at a time when communities were raw and rough, when substance abuse was just beginning to ravage families and when discrimination was an everyday fact of life. Some families had the coping skills and resiliency required to protect their children from these social forces, but others did not.

Similarly, some people who suffered during those years have since healed, but many others are passing their historical trauma on to their children. If one were to pose the fundamental question "Why are Inuit societies generating such a high proportion of suicidal young people?" among the answers would have to be "Because they have high rates of adverse childhood experiences." For 50 years now, the Arctic has been a rough place to be a child. Many (but by no means all) children in the region have had (and continue to have) a much higher number of adverse childhood experiences of various kinds than do their peers in southern Canada.

Northern Exposure: Peoples, Powers and
Prospects in Canada's North

An Overview of
Prevention Strategies

W E KNOW QUITE A LOT BUT BY NO MEANS ENOUGH ABOUT THE EFFECTIVENESS of different suicide prevention strategies (Beautrais et al. 2007; Hawton 2005; Mann et al. 2006). There is a voluminous quantity of literature available to the medical/academic researcher, the government program manager and the average person who wants to help make a difference. The Web sites of the World Health Organization, the public health authorities in different countries and myriad suicide prevention organizations all share hard-won insights. Examples of "good practice" abound. One is the community development process that has taken place in the Aboriginal Australian community of Yarrabah, which appears to have significantly lowered the rate of suicidal behaviour there (Mitchell 2002). We cannot hope to prevent all suicides, but there is abundant evidence that we can prevent some suicides — perhaps even many suicides.

Given the severity of the suicide crisis in Inuit communities today and the fact that it has been developing for several decades, it is both remarkable and appalling how little the public governments in the Arctic have attempted in the way of suicide prevention. Alaska took the lead with a report issued by a special committee of the Alaska Senate (chaired by Iñupiat senator Willie Hensley), a granting program to provide communities with the resources and support they needed for community-based projects they believed would make a difference, a program to train mental health paraprofessionals to work in their home villages, a multisectoral statewide suicide prevention council and, most recently, the Alaska Suicide Prevention Plan.

Greenland, however, didn't begin to take suicide prevention seriously until 2003, when Health Minister Asii Chemnitz Narup saw the need to move beyond scattered interventions and develop a coherent strategy along the lines recommended by the World Health Organization. And, after forming the multisectoral Isaksimagit Inuusirmi Katujjiqatigiit (Embrace Life Council), based loosely on the Alaskan model, the fledgling Government of Nunavut publicly committed itself in 2004 to preparing "a suicide prevention strategy with a focus on wellness." However, no work was done to develop such a plan until January of 2007, when *Nunatsiaq News*, the more serious of the territory's two weekly newspapers, began asking embarrassing questions about the government's failure to deliver on its promise. A bland, safe, and utterly uninspired "strategy" was quickly whipped up;[14] it contained a modest to-do list of measures that would already have been enacted if the government had begun its work back in 2004.

Far more can and should be done to prevent suicidal behaviour in Inuit communities. The spokesperson for the Inuit Circumpolar Youth Council, whom I quoted at the beginning of this chapter, told the United Nation's Permanent Forum on Indigenous Issues that "mainland" Canada, Denmark and the United States would declare "national emergencies" if they had "suicide rates comparable to those of their Inuit populations." The situation would be considered intolerable. It is high time that public health emergencies are declared in and by the Inuit regions themselves. All levels of government in those jurisdictions should aspire to become world leaders in culturally appropriate suicide prevention.

Seven Working Hypotheses

1. Suicide among Inuit is every bit as complex a phenomenon as suicide among non-Inuit, and it should be treated as such. I avoid the term "Inuit suicide" because it suggests that there is something uniquely Inuit about what is happening. "Suicide among Inuit" puts the emphasis where I believe it belongs — on a universal problem occurring in a specific context.

2. We should resist explanations of elevated rates of suicide among Inuit that are simplistic and/or that externalize causality and responsibility. Examples of the first type of explanation are boredom, demonic possession and the cycles of the moon. An example of the second type of explanation is a polemic that blames the state (e.g. Tester and McNicoll 2004). While historical colonialism and ongoing internal colonialism are, in my opinion, important contributing factors to suicide among Inuit, we must not reduce it to a problem brought about entirely by outsiders. Historic oppression is a fact, but so is the internalization of oppression by the oppressed. Simply blaming the state is fundamentally disempowering. How does such an approach help communities, families and individuals figure out how best to heal themselves?

3. We need to challenge the simulacra that have developed around suicide among Inuit. Not all historic suicide among Inuit was of the type "a sick and/or older person ends his or her life so as not to be a burden to the group." One of the earliest records of a suicide by an Inuk is a Greenlandic narrative that can be dated to between 1787 and 1789.[15] It is the story of Savannguaq, a young wife and mother who drowned herself after enduring psychological abuse from an old woman who shared a house with her and her husband, who was away hunting. The husband and his father later learned of the circumstances that had led to Savannguaq's suicide and took revenge on the woman. The story could have been written by Shakespeare; there is nothing uniquely Inuit about it. Similarly, not all present-day suicides by Inuit in Nunavut are by young men who have recently suffered the breakup of a relationship. There are also suicides by teenaged girls; men and women in their thirties, forties, fifties and sixties (and, in Greenland, in their seventies and eighties); and people with serious mental illnesses — as there are in all human societies.

4. Social determinants are the only logical explanation for the pattern of suicide transition that occurred across the Inuit world beginning in Alaska in the 1960s. A significant social determinant of elevated rates of suicide among Inuit is the intergenerational transmission of historical trauma, much of which is rooted in processes and events that occurred (or were particularly intense) during the initial period of active colonialism at the community level. The temporal sequence in which these internal colonial processes affected Inuit across the Arctic was replicated some years later by rapid and significant increases in suicidal behaviour, particularly among young men. The higher rates of suicide in some subregions of the Inuit world can be attributed, at least in part, to the higher levels of unresolved historical trauma existing in those subregions as a result of actions by the state, such as coerced sedentarization and the imposition of colonial education systems. That being said, we must keep in mind the caution expressed by Laurence Kirmayer and his colleagues: "The location of the origins of trauma in past events may divert attention from the realities of a constricted present and murky future, which are the oppressive realities for many aboriginal young people living in chaotic and demoralized communities" (Kirmayer, Simpson, and Cargo 2003).

5. Living conditions in Nunavut communities today are important social determinants of elevated rates of suicide. The high rate of suicide among Inuit in Nunavut is not a stand-alone problem but a part of the widespread social suf-

fering that prevails in Inuit communities today. Nunavut's high suicide rate should not be viewed in isolation. It should be seen as a symptom of a society experiencing rapid and difficult social, cultural and economic change under specific historical and political conditions. This is a society that is suffering from high levels of violence and abuse; high rates of unemployment; high levels of unresolved trauma of various types; high rates of substance abuse; a 75 percent school dropout rate; and widespread poverty (80 percent of the Inuit population of Igloolik received income support at some point in 2006). One important mode of intergenerational transmission of historical trauma is family dysfunction, which impacts the social and emotional well-being of children in many, but by no means all, families through high rates of adverse childhood experiences.

6. We must learn from the hard-earned lessons that have come out of research conducted elsewhere in the world:

- Suicidal behaviour cannot be understood in isolation from its social context.
- Suicide is a complex, multicausal phenomenon.
- There is a wide range of possible risk factors — for example, biological issues; bullying; depression; emotional, physical and sexual abuse; mental disorders; and substance use.
- Comorbidity (multiple risk factors operating simultaneously) significantly increases risk.
- It is possible to identify risk and protective factors that are significant for a specific population or subpopulation.
- A sense of hopelessness is present in almost all suicides, regardless of any other factors that may be present.

7. We must learn from research that has been conducted on suicide prevention. Beautrais and colleagues found that "there is relatively little strong evidence for the efficacy of many existing suicide prevention initiatives, and this area has frequently been captured by strong claims about the effectiveness of programmes that have not been adequately evaluated" (2007). But after reviewing the various credible evaluations that have been made, they were able to develop "a four-fold classification of suicide prevention initiatives based on an evidence hierarchy":

> Initiatives for which *strong evidence* of effectiveness exists — Initiatives evaluated using a randomised trial design and there is consistent evidence of programme efficacy.

Initiatives that appear *promising* — Some evidence of programme effectiveness exists, but this evidence is not sufficient or consistent enough to classify
the findings as strong.

Initiatives for which no evidence of effectiveness exists but which *may be beneficial* in suicide prevention — These initiatives span a range of macrosocial,
mental health, family support, and related programmes that are believed to be
beneficial in suicide prevention by providing a context for encouraging positive health and wellbeing, but for which no direct evidence of suicide-specific
programme effectiveness exists.

Initiatives for which evidence of *harmful* effects exist — Concerns have been raised
regarding their safety and there is reason to believe that they may risk increasing
(rather than decreasing) rates of suicidal behaviour. (Beautrais et al. 2007)

Beautrais' team listed three areas in which strong evidence of effectiveness
exists: training for medical practitioners; restriction of suicide methods; and
"gatekeeper" education (suicide alertness and intervention training).

Initiatives that appear promising include providing support after suicide
attempts; pharmacotherapy for mental illness; psychotherapy and psychosocial
interventions for mental illness; public awareness education and mental health
literacy; screening for depression and suicide risk; crisis centres and crisis counselling; school-based competency-promoting and skill-enhancing programs; and
support for family, extended family and friends bereaved by suicide.

Initiatives for which no evidence of effectiveness exists but that may be
beneficial in suicide prevention include improving control of alcohol; community-based mental health services and support services; and family support for families facing stress and difficulty.

Initiatives for which evidence of harmful effects exist include school-based
programs that focus on raising awareness about suicide; public health messages
about suicide and media coverage of suicide issues; no-harm and no-suicide contracts; and recovered or repressed memory therapies.

Beautrais and colleagues concluded,

While many national policies for suicide prevention are undertaken as public
health campaigns with an explicit focus on universal, population-wide interventions, our current knowledge about suicide causation and prevention suggests that perhaps the most effective approach to reducing suicide may be
highly targeted interventions that focus on those who have made suicide
attempts who have a long term elevated risk of further suicidal behaviour, and
a range of poor psychosocial and mental health outcomes which are likely to
precipitate further suicide attempts. (2007)

Conclusions

I HAVE FIVE TENTATIVE CONCLUSIONS. THE FIRST IS THAT UNLESS APPROPRIATE AND concerted efforts are made, it is entirely possible that suicide rates in Nunavut will remain at or near their current levels for the foreseeable future. After peaking in 1986, Greenland's overall suicide rate has remained very high for the last 20 years. There is so much accumulated loss, pain and trauma in Nunavut communities already — it is hard to imagine what these communities would be like after 20 more years of tragically high rates of suicides.

Second, experience from elsewhere in the world tells us that effective suicide intervention and prevention are possible. The World Health Organization believes that developing a comprehensive suicide prevention strategy is an essential first step, and it has formulated a set of guidelines for the preparation of such strategies. Canada, however, lags behind the Nordic countries, the United States[16] and other countries (Australia,[17] New Zealand,[18] Scotland[19] and Wales,[20] among others) in putting a national suicide prevention strategy in place. It took decades for the governments of Alaska and Greenland to develop and implement their suicide prevention strategies. Despite Nunavut's high suicide rate, the government led by Premier Paul Okalik failed to deliver a promised suicide prevention strategy until shamed into doing so by the media; and it was a far weaker document than those of Alaska and Greenland. It was developed in isolation (that is, without consultation with Inuit representative organizations or the Embrace Life Council), it made no effort to apply the lessons learned by researchers and other jurisdictions, and it lacked a coherent focus.

Third, Canada is a world leader in acknowledging and addressing the intergenerational transmission of historical trauma in indigenous communities — the legacy of the residential schools. As a result of research conducted by (and recommendations made by) the Royal Commission on Aboriginal Peoples, the federal government created and funded the Aboriginal Healing Foundation (AHF) to address the historical trauma resulting from residential schools. Healing programs funded by the AHF have made a tremendous difference to indigenous peoples living in communities from coast to coast. Nunavut needs programs to heal the historical trauma resulting from sedentarization and community formation.

Fourth, immediate action needs to be taken to reduce poverty and improve living conditions in Nunavut communities. No society whose school system fails 75 percent of the students who enter it can expect to have a low rate of suicide among its marginalized young people.

My final conclusion is that there is cause for optimism. There is no reason why Nunavummiut and other Inuit should suffer decades of elevated rates of suicide among their young men — it *is* possible to break the cycle of transmission of historical trauma. We must quickly apply suicide prevention lessons learned in other jurisdictions to Nunavut, starting with an aggressive program of gatekeeper education (suicide alertness and intervention training). The fledgling Nunavut government, with its limited resources, may not be capable of solving the problem on its own. There is an urgent need for the Government of Canada to acknowledge the nature and scope of the problems and to commit the resources required to address them. In a rich country like Canada, the state is quite capable of significantly influencing the social determinants of mental health if it chooses to do so. It is high time that it did.

Notes

1 Russia, in the case of the Inuit of Chukotka; the United States, in the case of the Inuit of Alaska; Canada, in the case of Inuit ranging from the Inuvialuit of the Mackenzie Delta right across to the Inuit of the Labrador coast; and Denmark, in the case of the Greenlanders.

2 Efforts by the Greenland Home Rule government failed to convince either Pope or the *Huffington Post* to acknowledge this egregious factual error.

3 By comparison, the most recent suicide rate per 100,000 for Denmark is 13.6 (2001); for Canada, 11.3 (2004); and for the US, 11.0 (2005) (see World Health Organization, http://www.who.int/mental_health/prevention/suicide/country_reports/en/index.html (accessed March 29, 2009).

4 "The settlement of a nomadic people in a permanent place of habitation" (*Shorter Oxford English Dictionary* 2002).

5 Most of the statistical data on rates of death by suicide among Greenlanders used here were developed by Peter Bjerregaard of Denmark's National Institute of Public Health from raw data obtained from Greenland's Embedslægeinstitutionen (chief medical officer) and Statistics Greenland. The statistical data on rates of death by suicide among "Alaska Natives" were obtained from the Alaska state government's Division of Vital Statistics. It is unfortunately not possible to unpack statistics aggregated for Alaska Natives to obtain data specific to the state's Iñupiat and Yu'pik populations. The statistical data on rates of death by suicide among Inuit in the different regions of Arctic Canada were developed by the author from raw data obtained from a variety of official sources.

6 We need to differentiate between "active" and "passive" colonialism, as some Inuit populations had been colonized for several generations. However, in such cases the colonial powers had not attempted to substantially reorganize Inuit society because they (e.g., the Danes) depended on the persistence of the communal mode of production to ensure a supply of oils from marine mammal products and other products harvested from the land and the sea.

7 No reliable data are available for the Inuit of Chukotka.

8 "Urban Alaska" is defined as Anchorage, Kenai Peninsula Borough, Mat-Su Borough, Fairbanks Borough and Juneau.

9 See Lynge (2000) for a summary of her many contributions to medical journals.

10 That being said, it should be noted that different people take their lives for different reasons. Just as some children who grow up in deeply dysfunctional homes survive and thrive later in life, others who grow up in stable and happy homes and who have few adverse childhood experiences later die by suicide. It is important to keep this in mind when discussing suicide in societies like that of Inuit, who have been deeply traumatized by several decades of high suicide rates.

11 See the publications link on the left-hand side of the study's home page (http://www.chmeds.ac.nz/research/chds/) for a list of the journal articles that CHDS has produced.

12 Their data come from about as non-Inuit a source as one can imagine: a retrospective cohort study of 9,460 adult health maintenance organization members in a primary care clinic in San Diego, California (Centers for Disease Control and Prevention 2005). The members of the HMO completed a survey addressing a variety of health-related concerns, which included standardized assessments of lifetime and recent depressive disorders, childhood abuse and household dysfunction — but there's no reason to suspect that the findings don't apply to Inuit as much as they do to any other population.

13 We should, however, keep in mind that all suicides occur within both a medical context (that is, the complex biological interactions taking place within the brain of the victim) and the social context within which the victim developed and then lived his or her life.

14   No suicide prevention strategy in Nunavut
      should be taken seriously if it fails to
      include an evaluation of the counselling
      resources available to the residents of
      Nunavut communities and of the support
      provided by the territorial government to
      the grassroots suicide prevention commit-
      tees that exist in many communities.

15   "The Cute Savannguaq Who Was Exposed
      to a Pressure That Led to Her Suicide, and
      When Habakuk Met an Umiaq with
      Starving People from the South," a narrative
      recorded by the merchant Jens Kreutzmann
      (1828-99) and published in Thisted (1997).

16   See US Department of Health and Human
      Services (2001) and Centers for Disease
      Control (http://www.cdc.gov/ncipc/dvp/
      Suicide/) for the country as a whole; and
      Suicide Prevention Resource Center
      (http://www.sprc.org/stateinformation/plans
      .asp) for the individual states.

17   See Australian Government Department of
      Health and Aging, "Living is for Everyone"
      (www.livingisforeveryone.com.au/) and
      "Beyondblue: The National Depression
      Initiative" (www.beyondblue.org.au).

18   See New Zealand Ministry of Health, "Suicide
      Prevention in New Zealand" (www.moh.govt.
      nz/suicideprevention.

19   See NHS Health Scotland "Choose Life"
      (www.chooselife.net/home/Home.asp and
      www.chooselife.net/Evidence/ResearchandE
      valuation.asp).

20   See Welsh Assembly Government (2008)
      (http://new.wales.gov.uk/consultations/healt
      hsocialcare/talktome/?lang=en).

References

Anda, Robert F., Vincent J. Felitti, J. Douglas
      Bremner, John D. Walker, et al. 2006. "The
      Enduring Effects of Abuse and Related
      Adverse Experiences in Childhood:
      Convergence of Evidence from
      Neurobiology and Epidemiology." *European
      Archives of Psychiatry and Clinical
      Neuroscience* 256 (3): 174-86.

Arsenault-Lapierre, Geneviève, Caroline Kim,
      and Gustavo Turecki. 2004. "Psychiatric
      Diagnoses in 3,275 Suicides: A Meta-analy-
      sis." *BMC Psychiatry* 4:37.

Beautrais, Annette, David M. Fergusson, Carolyn
      Coggan, Catherine Collings, et al. 2007.
      "Effective Strategies for Suicide Prevention
      in New Zealand: A Review of the Evidence."
      New Zealand Medical Journal 120:1251.

Belkin, Douglas. 2007. "Dissenters in Canada's
      Arctic: Government Move to Beef up
      Military Makes Inuit Wary." *Wall Street
      Journal*, October 12.

Berthelsen, Alfred. 1935. "Grønlandsk medicinsk
      statistik og nosografi I: Grønlands befolknings-
      statistik 1901-30." *Meddelelser om Grønland*
      117 (1): 1-83.

Bjerregaard, Peter, and Inge Lynge. 2006. "Suicide:
      A Challenge in Modern Greenland." *Archives
      of Suicide Research* 10 (2): 209-20.

Boas, Franz. 1888. "The Central Eskimo." In
      *Sixth Annual Report of the Bureau of
      Ethnology to the Secretary of the Smithsonian
      Institution*, by J.W. Powell. Elibron Classics
      Replica ed. Boston: Adamant Media
      Corporation, 2006.

Cavanagh, Jonathon T.O., A. Carson, M. Sharpe, and
      S.M. Lawrie. 2003. "Psychological Autopsy
      Studies of Suicide: A Systematic Review."
      Psychological Medicine 33 (3): 395-405.

Centers for Disease Control and Prevention.
      2005. "Adverse Childhood Experiences
      Study." Collaboration between the Centers
      for Disease Control, and Prevention and
      Kaiser Permanente's Health Appraisal
      Clinic. US Department of Health and
      Human Services. http://www.cdc.gov/
      nccdphp/ACE/index.htm

Chapman, Daniel P., Charles L. Whitfield, Vincent
      J. Felitti, Shanta R. Dube, et al. 2004.
      "Adverse Childhood Experiences and the
      Risk of Depressive Disorders in Adulthood."
      Journal of Affective Disorders 82 (2): 217-25.

Christchurch Health and Development Study
      (CHDS). n.d. "Christchurch Health and
      Development Study: Introduction."
      Christchurch: CHDS, University of Otago.
      Accessed February 17, 2009.
      http://www.chmeds.ac.nz/research/chds/

Csonka, Yvon. 2005. "Changing Inuit Historicities in West Greenland and Nunavut." *History and Anthropology* 16 (3): 321-34.

Dube, Shanta R., Robert F. Anda, Vincent J. Felitti, Daniel P. Chapman, et al. 2001. "Childhood Abuse, Household Dysfunction, and the Risk of Attempted Suicide throughout the Life Span." *Journal of the American Medical Association* 286 (24): 3089-96.

Fergusson, David M., and Joseph M. Boden. 2008. "Cannabis Use and Later Life Outcomes." *Addiction* 103 (6): 969-76.

Goldney, Robert W. 2003. "A Novel Integrated Knowledge Explanation of Factors Leading to Suicide." *New Ideas in Psychology* 21:141-6.

Haggarty, John M., Zack Cernovsky, Michel Bedard, and Harold Merskey. 2008. "Suicidality in a Sample of Arctic Households." *Suicide and Life-Threatening Behavior* 38 (6): 678-96.

Hawton, Keith, ed. 2005. *Prevention and Treatment of Suicidal Behaviour: From Science to Practice.* Oxford: Oxford University Press.

Kirmayer, Laurence J., Christopher M. Fletcher, and Lucy J. Boothroyd. 1997. "Inuit Attitudes toward Deviant Behaviour: A Vignette Study." *Journal of Nervous and Mental Disease* 185 (2): 78-86.

Kirmayer, Laurence J., C. Simpson, and M. Cargo. 2003. "Healing Traditions: Culture, Community and Mental Health Promotion with Canadian Aboriginal Peoples." *Australasian Psychiatry* 11:15-23.

Kraus, Robert F. 1971. "Changing Patterns of Suicidal Behaviour in North Alaska Eskimo." *Transcultural Psychiatric Research Review* 9:69-71.

Kraus, Robert F., and Patricia A. Buffler. 1979. "Sociocultural Stress and the American Native in Alaska: An Analysis of Changing Patterns of Psychiatric Illness and Alcohol Abuse among Alaska Natives." *Culture, Medicine and Psychiatry* 3 (2): 111-51.

Langlois, Stéphanie, and Peter Morrison. 2002. "Suicide Deaths and Suicide Attempts." *Health Reports* 13 (2): 9-22.

Law, Samuel F., and E. Miles Hutton. 2007. "Community Psychiatry in the Canadian Arctic: Reflections from a 1-Year Continuous Consultation Series in Iqaluit, Nunavut." *Canadian Journal of Community Mental Health* 26 (2): 123-40.

Leineweber, Markus. 2000. "Modernization and Mental Health: Suicide among the Inuit in Greenland." Ph.D. diss., University of Nijmegen.

"Linking School and Suicide: Did You Know?" 1991. *The Journal.* CBC.ca, CBC Digital Archives, broadcast date September 17. Toronto: CBC. Accessed February 13, 2009. http://archives.cbc.ca/society/education/clips/2675/

Lynge, Inge. 2000. *Psykiske lidelser i det grønlandske samfund [Psychological Suffering in Greenlandic Society].* Århus: Psykiatrisk Hospital i Århus, Institut for Psykiatrisk Grundforskning.

Mann, J. John, Alan Apter, José M. Bertolote, Annette L. Beautrais, et al. 2006. "Suicide Prevention Strategies: A Systematic Review." *Journal of the American Medical Association* 294 (16): 2064-74.

Mitchell, Penny. 2002. "Yarrabah: A Success Story in Community Empowerment." *Youth Suicide Prevention Bulletin* 4:16-23.

Pope, Carl. 2007. "A Tale of Three Arctics." *Huffington Post*, September 10.

Rasmussen, Knud. 1929. *The Intellectual Culture of the Iglulik Eskimos.* Vol. 7, pt. 1 of *Report of the Fifth Thule Expedition, 1921-24.* Copenhagen: Gyldensalske Boghandel, Nordisk Forlag.

Schilling, Elizabeth A., Robert H. Aseltine, and Susan Gore. 2007. "Adverse Childhood Experiences and Mental Health in Young Adults." *BMC Public Health* 7:30.

Steckley, John L. 2003. "Aboriginal Voices and the Politics of Representation in Canadian Introductory Sociology Textbooks." Ed.D. diss., University of Toronto.

Sullivan, Alice, and Christine Brems. 1997. "The Psychological Repercussions of the Sociocultural Oppression of Alaska Native Peoples." *Genetic, Social, and General Psychology Monographs* 123 (4): 411-40.

Swenson, Michael D. 2001. "A Story about
    Suicide in the Arctic." *Journal of the
    American Medical Association* 286 (8): 919.

Tester, Frank J., and Paule McNicoll. 2004.
    "Isumagijaksaq: Mindful of the State: Social
    Constructions of Inuit Suicide." *Social
    Science & Medicine* 58 (12): 2625-36.

Thisted, Kirsten, ed. 1997. *Fortællinger &
    akvareller [Narratives and Watercolours]*.
    Nuuk: Atuakkiorfik.

Turecki, Gustavo, and Aleksandra Lalovic. 2005.
    "The Biology and Genetics of Suicidality." In
    Biology of Depression, edited by Julio Licinio.
    Weinheim: Wiley-VCH Verlag GmbH.

US Department of Health and Human Services.
    2001. *National Strategy for Suicide
    Prevention: Goals and Objectives for Action*.
    Accessed March 28, 2009. http://down
    load.ncadi.samhsa.gov/ken/pdf/SMA01-
    3517/SMA01-3517.pdf

Welsh Assembly Government. 2008. *Talk to Me:
    A National Action Plan to Reduce Suicide and
    Self Harm in Wales 2008-2013*. Accessed
    March 28, 2009. http://www.wales.nhs.uk/
    documents/talktomee%5B1%5D.pdf

The Next Generation

C ANADA'S NORTH IS FACING GREAT CHALLENGES AS A RESULT OF GEOPOLITICAL, environmental, economic and social trends. A very large majority of the North's population is made up of youth. It might be more fitting to refer to them as the "next" generation.

The generation before ours — our parents, our aunts and our uncles — worked tirelessly to negotiate land claims and treaties across the North. We are the next generation, the generation that has inherited these agreements, treaties and transformed governments. We are the generation that is expected to do something with what our leaders achieved for their grandchildren and for us.

We are expected to find ways to make these agreements, governments and governance models work for us, work for them and work for their grandchildren.

We are the generation after the one that was born in igloos and tents; the generation after the one that moved away from a nomadic and land-based economy.

The authors representing the next generation, whose contributions can be read in this section of the volume, come from all regions of the North — Nunavut, Nunatsiavut, Nunavik, the Northwest Territories and Yukon. We come from very different backgrounds, ethnic origins and experiences — in the private sector, the nonprofit sector, government and environmental organizations.

The authors of these contributions are very accomplished individuals for such young ages. They are all role models. But the most important achievement I would like to highlight is their commitment to their communities and regions.

Our comments are to be tied not to the regions we represent or the organizations we work for, but to our dreams and aspirations. We only hope that our presentations are a reflection of what our leaders have envisioned for us: leaders like Mary Simon, Nellie Cournoyea and Sheila Watt-Cloutier. We look up to them and use their guidance as means and ways of achieving our goals for the future and for the future of our communities.

With our dreams for the North, we recognize and embrace challenges and adversity. The greatest challenge is trying to hold on to our past, our cultures, our language and our identities.

Nonetheless, northerners are very adaptive by nature. Northerners are seasoned adapters. Many have gone from igloos to the Internet in one generation. The challenge now is to determine how to maintain the social fabric of decision-making and community processes in a new world of land claims agreements, treaties, cultural and geographical distinctions, and cash-based economies.

Our vision for the future is based on finding a balance — one that enforces old practices and effectively introduces new ones; one that uses the tools passed down from past generations to serve and empower "the collective." In the past, this meant that successes were shared and challenges met on the basis of adaptability.

Our youth envision a future not much different from that envisioned by our leaders: a future where fundamental beliefs are cherished and stand the test of time and change. This includes the preservation of language, education, culture and the environment. These fundamental beliefs must be used as anchors when developing public policy. Public policy and policy-makers must embrace these pillars with the same respect and humility as northerners have embraced change. Policies need to be adaptive and flexible, something that moves and breathes with the land and the people.

We must base public policy not simply on putting out fires and dealing with statistics about our communities, but on what our leaders envisioned for the North: the preservation of and respect for our language, education, culture and land.

Arctic Indigenous
Peoples and the
Reconciliation of Past
and Present

L IVING IN THE ARCTIC POSES STRONG CHALLENGES FOR INDIGENOUS PEOPLES TODAY.
We have a very rich history of cultural practices, identity and oral traditional knowledge that spans thousands of years. These types of knowledge are known
to be deeply embedded in our environments. Our teachings are from a time
where there was the concept of a creation period. Our belief is that we as a people have always been here, living off the land that was given us to survive as
human beings in these harsh lands of the Arctic.

However, today there is conflict and the uncertainty of trying to find a balance between living in the present and maintaining the traditional cultural practices of our ancestors in the past. I find it difficult to live in both worlds. I come
from a generation where it was essential for us to leave our homes, ignore our culture and leave our families to gain a higher education in order to survive in modern society. Although I do not live a nomadic lifestyle as my ancestors did, I do
make time within my life and with my family to go out and make use of the land
for cultural purposes. I would say that I don't choose to do it; I feel a need to do
it for my own well-being.

The issue of cultural preservation is one of the most delicate struggles
within the Arctic. It is also certainly one of the ways that we, as individuals, can
help enforce accountability on the part of local leadership for community well-
being. What that entails for me, as an indigenous woman and a Teetl'it Gwich'in,
is that for my culture, my ideology, my language, we as peoples must be able to
move forward in the future for the wellness of generations to follow. We need
those teachings and the knowledge of our traditions and all the elements of our
past existence as a people in order to continue in the future.

What has inspired me in my life experiences and work is the land my family and culture come from — land that continues to this day to sustain me and my cultural identity. It was the teachings of my parents and their knowledge that taught me who I am. A big factor also is the teachings of the forms of traditional and spiritual knowledge from my elders and those before them. We are very lucky in this day and age to still be able to have those teachings and that knowledge with us today. Some of that traditional knowledge has been lost by people in other areas of the world who are less fortunate.

I came to realize through my work for my people that the land and our environment is only one part of our well-being as a living and breathing culture. We also need to look at all the other social indicators within our community-based systems to identify the reasons for our cultural and social crisis. It certainly does not take a rocket scientist to know that we simply cannot be healthy without our land base, our culture, our language and our basic freedoms to exist as indigenous peoples of the North. The solutions that we are trying to develop involve our own cultural, individual responsibility to take initiative to strengthen our languages, our practices and our traditional forms of governance. The issue of cultural practices and language is the foundation of our northern ideologies and the survival of our knowledge as indigenous peoples of the Arctic.

One of the most important indicators that I have observed is the issue evolving around language and cultural changes in our communities. I will refer to this as a cultural "moulding" that we are seeing among our indigenous youth today. Our youth who cannot speak the language or perhaps are not around it for various reasons come up with their own form of language or communication; this is sometimes called broken English in our communities. I can speak from experience when I say that it was a challenge for me to be educated to read and write in the English language. There was a fine line between living in the past and trying to live in the present. I am living proof on this subject and wish to focus interest on cultural survival and what it means for other First Nations youth today. We are at a stage of adverse cultural changes and immense language loss among many First Nations groups in the Arctic.

According to the Gwich'in language Web site, "The Dinjii Zhu' Ginjik (Gwich'in language) is one of the most endangered Aboriginal languages in Canada. It is the most endangered Athapaskan (Dene) language in the NWT" (http://www.gwichin.ca/Language/language.html). It is known that within my language group the Teetl'it Gwich'in dialect is spoken by less than 5 percent of community members. The Web site also states, "Statistics provided in 1998 by the Government of the Northwest Territories bear witness to the seriousness of the situation. Of the 2,397 Gwich'in beneficiaries in the NWT, only 40 people (2%) spoke the language in their home and only 312 (13%) reported they could speak the language." If this staggering decrease continues, it will take only a few generations for our language to be completely wiped out; this might even happen in my own generation.

Languages and culture are interconnected and are always evolving within their environment. This means that we need to focus on ensuring that some form of our cultural identity, our knowledge and our own words are carried on for us to survive culturally today and for the future. There has to be a realization of the intergenerational effects of colonization and how it continues to influence and overwhelm our cultural and spiritual needs. How can we move forward culturally? If we do not understand our own past and current challenges, then how can we identify the roles we all play within our community to carry on those cultural needs? I personally feel that our own leadership really needs to focus on the importance of and the need for protection of our languages and to practise them. The languages also have to be spoken in the home to be brought to life in the everyday life of the community and the people it supports.

Another way of enhancing the protection of various forms of our cultural knowledge would be to integrate them with the influences of modern society. Not only do we need to develop curricula based on our culture and language in the school systems, we also need to implement alternative forms of outreach and media resources. The broadcasting and print media can be a powerful way to influence community members to be actively involved. As long as we keep in mind our strong communication and traditional knowledge protocols, media can be a means to help keep the culture and languages from being lost. Other technological means such as the Internet, video and filmmaking, and more developed traditional arts programs are means to maintain in communities not only the interest but also the opportunity for cultural revitalizing. We need to create programs that will integrate youth and/or other community members. Forming a link between cultural awareness and language revitalization can be a way to involve these community members.

The issue of environmental health and the role it plays in our lives and communities is another large subject area for the future of indigenous peoples in the Arctic. I have always found the saying "You are what you eat" quite interesting and very true, because it makes me think about the challenges it presents for us and for me as an indigenous woman in the Arctic today. We are considered the carriers of the next generation of our cultures. If we do not have direct access to our traditional means of sustenance, pollutant free and in varied abundance, we will not be able to have healthy individuals, families and therefore communities. Indigenous women are the social and health indicators of our peoples in the Arctic, of our communities, and of our nation(s). We must be concerned about the ongoing and increasingly serious issue of biological risk factors such as persistent organic pollutants that enter the food chain and that slowly poison our bodies and our unborn children, and jeopardize our very future. What future do we then have if our people are not strong and healthy?

The land is considered to be the foundation of our cultural identity and practice. Without healthy land and food resources there will be no healthy, spiritually and culturally minded individuals. There is a need to strike a balance between making a living on the land and having a reliable job in the cash-based economy. Pollution is just one of the ways that environmental health is changing and decreasing access to our sources of food for the people in our communities.

There is also the strong influence of globalization on the North and the Western world — an influence that has affected us for several generations. What is being done to enhance and celebrate our cultural or language practices, practices that will determine the survival of many cultural groups and their identity in the future? There is the knowledge that the land and our perception of spirituality are one. I hope that more people can be given the opportunity to think about and view the land as it is — an integral part of ourselves and our well-being, and not as an exterior reference and simply a source of natural resources as it is commonly viewed in the Western world.

What I feel will be important for the future of the North is that there be more culturally and spiritually minded individuals who focus on balancing the culture, land and economic needs of the people in our communities. There is a need for more people to enforce those demands and practices. Although there are a few who are fighting for that locally, we need to show the current disconnect with our traditional values and to be at the forefront of challenging our leaders in order to keep our cultures alive. The biggest disconnect I have observed in my community is the lack of balance in leadership roles and the lack of equality and rights for women at the community level. We must bring back our matriarchal systems and the concepts of governance that our ancestors used in the past. We are seeing such a great loss of spirituality and traditional protocols. The continued influences of the colonial state are separating our cultural and spiritual needs and practices as a people. We must make a shift in our way of leading the people and decolonize our views, lifestyles and government structures to benefit Arctic indigenous peoples in a new framework. These are my ideas to contribute to positive movement forward for the future.

What I envision the North to be in the future is a wide doorway for opportunities and growth for the indigenous peoples of the Arctic. Our world has changed drastically and will continue to change in the future. What I dearly hope is that my children and their children's children will have the same cultural opportunities as I had growing up in my community. We need to look at all areas of policy to ensure and enforce the cultural and spiritual enhancements of the community. We need this so we can continue to exist as indigenous peoples and to practise our most fundamental rights to protect the lands through our culture and be self-determined and sovereign.

As a generation we have to ensure that our leaders are responsible and will make positive decisions based on the spiritual and cultural needs of the peoples they represent. We need ways of improving overall well-being that have the support of community members and that follow a grassroots model of governance that meets the needs of the people. There is and will continue to be an ever-growing need for more of our people to be educated and to know how to find solutions to national and international issues that affect us on a daily basis, such as global warming, climate change and transboundary pollution. There needs to be responsibility and sustainability based on traditional laws that will not contribute to the ongoing harm of our environment and our lands that is weakening the cultural and spiritual fabric of our communities. It is a matter of reconnecting with what we have, culturally and spiritually, as individuals. Sometimes, all it takes is one person to make all the difference, to share and generate ideas within the people for change.

We Inuit Must Unlock
Our Success Instinct

L IKE MANY OF THE ELECTED LEADERS IN THE NORTH, I LIVE VARIOUS LIVES. TODAY I could be camouflaged by putting on a suit and tie, and tomorrow afternoon I could be skinning and cutting up caribou. This is just one manifestation of the many pressures pulling us northerners and Inuit to be successful in the varied societies of Canada and the world. I admire some of our Inuit leaders who have done it in a very genuine, personal and professional manner. I'd like to acknowledge Sheila Watt-Cloutier and Mary May Simon, who I am very proud of and who both happen to be my relatives.

The basic priority of our past has been survival, and survive we did. We lived in a traditional economy where everyone was very accountable to each other. When you lived a thousand miles from the nearest tree and you found a piece of driftwood on the shoreline, you took care of that driftwood. One day it could be a tent pole, part of a kayak frame or a paddle. And that simple piece of wood was something that might have saved a family or made a family perish. So you didn't break it, you were accountable, and your role as a member of the community was to be always trying to figure out ways to help the community survive.

Our priorities are presently changing. We were a semi-socialist and cooperative society, and today we've become hybrid capitalists. Our economy was based on sharing and cooperation, a lot like many other cultures around the world, but we are changing. This sometimes creates a struggle within our own population. Our companies are growing, we are benefiting very well, and some Inuit are becoming businessmen and businesswomen.

It is a balancing act that we're trying to do — trying to balance the cash-based economy with the traditional economy. And I think that it is time to unlock the success instinct we have as Inuit. We have done very well in terms of survival, we are still here, but now it is time to focus more clearly on how to succeed.

There are dilemmas that we're facing, though. It is as if many Inuit don't think our own people have the right to become successful. We have to get rid of this "successophobia." These are attitudes within our own group: our own people say, "How dare you succeed?" When you lived in a traditional economy, if someone got one seal, everyone had a part of that seal. Now the time has come where we're getting more seals than we need to survive.

There are other things that are hurting our people. One is rampant violence: verbal, physical and psychological lashing-out within our own people. I think this is one of the challenges we have to overcome during the transition from a survival-based society to a success-based society. Another is the geographical discrimination in the North. There are people in the Nunatsiavut government, from the Nunatsiavut lands in the north of Labrador, and there are areas within Nunavik that are not considered part of the North in terms of federal policies because they happen to fall south of the 60th parallel, and that hurts. This is not discrimination against a people, but it is geographical discrimination. How far north do you have to live to be a northerner? I think policy developers must really consider that when they are making policies.

As we know, dormant cultures can die, but we are extremely adaptable as a culture. We are a dynamic and proactive people who do not stand still waiting for life to happen.

Global Warming and the
Threat to Inuit Culture

FIRST OF ALL I WOULD LIKE TO TALK A LITTLE BIT ABOUT MY BACKGROUND. I WAS raised by my older grandparents, unlike my mother, who grew up in the residential school system. The main language used in my home was Inuktitut. The first encounter I had with the English language was when I attended primary school. You can recall the Charlie Brown scenario when the teacher is talking but he cannot understand the teacher's words – all he hears is a muffling sound. That is like my first encounter with the English language. All I could hear was a strange muffling sound. Another early life experience was when my grandparents told me I was a grandchild and that I was not their biological child. I did not understand this, nor did I comprehend that my skin tone was lighter than my aunts' and uncles'. I say this to point out that the Inuit culture is very adaptive and very accepting of other cultures.

There are two main points I would like to make about public policy. The first is on the environment. I live on the coast of Hudson Bay about a thousand miles from Churchill, Manitoba, on the Kivalliq coast. Climate change is a concern here, especially when polar bears depend on the formation of the ice to hunt on the sea. If global warming continues, polar bears will become an endangered species. I am not an animal rights advocate, nor do I condone hunting of polar bears. However, if polar bears no longer exist for hunting, then my sons are in danger of losing their culture. Hunting wild game is part of our culture. My great-grandfather hunted the polar bear with a team of dogs and a knife. I want my sons to be able to understand their culture and to experience the hunt. Global warming is going to affect the Inuit culture and our lifestyle. Our culture, which is primarily based on the harvesting of wild game, is in danger of becoming extinct. Policy-makers must look at ways to prevent global warming and reduce greenhouse gases.

The second topic I would like to discuss is the Inuktitut language. In order for our first language to survive it must be spoken not only in the home, it must be spoken as the first language in our workforce. If it is, Inuktitut has a higher chance of survival as a language. Our government needs to make this a top priority. If we don't have our language and our culture, then who are we?

Inuit Values and the
Implementation of Land
Claims Agreements

T HE INUIT PERSPECTIVE IS FOUNDED ON THE COLLECTIVE. THE INUIT POLITICAL representational movement, which resulted in the land claims process, is based on a collective approach to ownership, governance and decision-making. Since the early 1970s, Inuit leaders, on behalf of the collective, have achieved many historic political, economic and culture-related accomplishments. Inuit have negotiated and settled four comprehensive land claims agreements and are now in the process of implementing them. Inuit have created wealth through business development and own and control vast amounts of capital. Although we are only 55,000 in number, Inuit have been able to develop strong political representational structures that ensure the Inuit perspective is incorporated in all levels of government.

We have the control and the resources we need to improve our communities. We have self-government in Nunatsiavut and public government in Nunavik and Nunavut. Inuit control billions of dollars of assets through land holdings, natural resource rights, business ventures and funds from land claims settlements.

Despite this dramatic increase in power, socio-economic conditions for most Inuit have not improved. To fulfill the vision behind the land claims process, to implement this dream, the collective must be empowered. We must leverage our political and economic assets to strengthen our language and culture, make our communities healthy and strong, and provide a better foundation for success to our young people.

The implementation of land claims agreements has been a slow and frustrating process. Youth can easily be discouraged by this seemingly endless process and sometimes view land claims agreements as a barrier to success instead of an agent of change. Regardless of these frustrations over implementation, success can happen only when we work within the framework we have been handed by our parents' generation. Our generation cannot patiently wait for solutions from outside our society — we must force change on society from within, using the tools our parents gave us, to reform the way our communities function and how we utilize the assets we hold in trust for the collective.

Currently, young Inuit succeed in spite of the society we live in, not because of it. Some of us become successful through academic proficiency and end up in excellent jobs, living much like southern middle-class people or families. Some of us become successful because our families have instilled in us Inuit cultural, linguistic and societal values, when most families did not. This status quo is not acceptable. We need radical changes in the way our society functions, and if our communities are to be empowered by 2020, many things must be accomplished — by Inuit and by our partners.

Land claims implementation is a responsibility shared among the federal government, Inuit and the province or territory in which the claim has been settled. It is the link between theory and practice, design and delivery. Too often the federal government has not meaningfully engaged in land claims implementation, deciding instead to restrict its efforts only to actions it is legally responsible to perform, as per the provisions of an agreement. Thus, the vision of the land claims process and in the end its overall success are compromised by this legalistic, minimalist perspective.

To compound this problem, the federal government's human resources philosophy encourages key staff to shuffle through jobs on an annual or biennial basis, creating a form of institutional amnesia that requires Inuit to constantly remind the federal government about the meaning and intent of land claims provisions. Sometimes it seems federal officials last long enough to participate in only one Nunavut trip, defeating the purpose of spending thousands of dollars to orient the official to the Inuit reality. Without continuity, money is wasted and key initiatives are in constant flux.

By 2020, the federal government should be an active partner in land claims implementation, acting in good faith for the best interests of Inuit communities and Inuit society instead of acting as an adversary of its land claims partners. Land claims provisions must be thoughtfully implemented, or the end results will be shoddy and ineffective. The federal government must learn how to coordinate its actions across departments, despite political change and attrition among federal bureaucrats.

Inuit live in a rapidly changing society, but that does not mean we need to change our ideology to be successful. Our organizations were created to ensure our beliefs and customs are considered in the development of governance models, legislation, public policy and programs that affect us. As land claims implementation has replaced land claims negotiation, these Inuit organizations are now also tasked with investing, managing and controlling Inuit assets. But these organizations have not become the efficient structures they were created to be, and in some regions they have regressed into unstructured, financially wasteful and unaccountable organizations. The collective is losing faith in these structures, and this faith must be restored. Inuit organizations must find a way to address community issues efficiently and respond to them in a timely manner. Inuit organizations must also stay true to the idea of the collective.

One of the first resolutions passed by the Labrador Inuit Association board of directors, after the members of the association overwhelmingly voted to ratify our land claim agreement, was to award $5,000 in cash to each member over the age of 16. This example illustrates an enormous shift in the philosophy of the administrative structures created to manage the settlement, and it undermines the very premise of land claims. If this is how our Inuit organizations act when money and resources are finally in our control, then how long will our collective hold? Inuit organizations must become more responsible and find ways to involve and empower the majority of beneficiaries. The current models of communication and information transfer are ineffective in relaying information, as much of the legal, policy and program work is not well understood by most Inuit. We must be informed and we must understand our assets, our governance model and how the activities of our organizations fulfill the mandate and ideals of our society.

Provinces and territories play pivotal roles as partners or delivery agents. They can either help or hinder Inuit goals at the community level, and this is most often seen in jurisdictional policies on accreditation, academic standards and funding for delivery of services. As an example, accreditation standards limit many competent Inuit from becoming teachers, and inflexible provincial/territorial curriculum standards are cited as the reason why the education system cannot be more Inuit-specific in its design and delivery. This must change. To be successful, school systems in Inuit regions must operate from the Inuit perspective, instead of the current reality where Inuit society and culture are considered add-ons to the curriculum and even a barrier to success. Discussions concerning instruction in the Inuit language follow a similar path, as non-Inuit still struggle to grasp the relevance of using the mother tongue as the foundation for curriculum delivery throughout the education system.

Provincial and territorial barriers to training, education and employment must be removed. Standards often protect those who are already empowered instead of ensuring the quality of the results. Inuit must be afforded the opportunity to succeed, and presently this is not always the case.

Inuit society is still feeling the effects of tremendous change and upheaval. Despite this, from Labrador to the Northwest Territories, Inuit are very clear about what we value and what we want for our society. We want to maintain and enrich our Inuit culture through an Inuit-specific education system, administered and delivered primarily in the Inuit language. We want to implement our land claims agreements in partnership with all signatories, in good faith. We want better living conditions through improved delivery of services and programs that are administered and staffed by Inuit and will result in healthy communities. We want to respect and care for our lands and waters. We want our representational organizations to mature into financially sustainable, focused and fully accountable structures that are run by morally sound political leaders.

As my generation ascends to leadership roles, we must be grounded in the idea of the collective. We have all the tools we need to create a functioning and productive Inuit society without abandoning Inuit values and ideology. We will inherit unprecedented political and financial control, and must use it wisely. We will also depend upon the support of our primary partners to fully implement land claims. I believe this can happen in our generation, and I look forward to participating in making our dreams a reality.

Climate Change and Sustainable Management of Yukon Forest Resources

I AM PLEASED THAT IRPP HAS PROVIDED AN OPPORTUNITY FOR YOUTH TO PRESENT THEIR perspectives on the North and the path to furthering its development. This is important, given the critical role young people have in shaping the future and the fact that they will also live in a future that is shaped by decisions that are made today. My perspective is as a member of this generation, a generation that will play an increasingly large role in northern affairs as we move toward the year 2020.

In the post-land-claims northern context, much of my work has been involved with the implementation of a vision that has been developed through a consultative process or conducting research on approaches to achieving this vision. My own vision is not something I often sit down to formulate or contribute, so this has required a bit of a mental flip to prepare.

The vision I would like to present comes from my doctoral research on climate change adaptation in the forest sector in Yukon (Ogden 2007; Ogden and Innes 2007a,b; Ogden and Innes 2008a,b; Ogden and Innes, forthcoming). While the focus of this commentary is on a resource development sector in which I have some direct experience, I believe that elements of the approach I will present may be broadly applicable to other sectors.

My vision is for northern resource management plans to be well adapted to climate change. Specifically, my commentary will focus on Yukon forest management plans.

By well adapted, I mean that forest management planning processes should reflect community goals and aspirations, that the goals and objectives of forest management plans are achievable in light of climate change, and that forest management plans incorporate measures to reduce vulnerability to changes that may arise in forest ecosystems because of climate change to ensure that community aspirations are realized (Ogden and Innes 2007a).

The challenges facing the forest sector and forest-based communities in addressing climate change are many. Evidence of the high sensitivity of northern forested ecosystems to climate change is ever increasing. In recent decades, relatively minor climate changes (minor in comparison to what is projected to take place over the next century) have triggered significant ecological responses (Parmesean and Yohe 2003, Juday et al. 2005, Scholze et al. 2006). Climate-associated impacts such as drought, wildfires, insects and outbreaks of diseases are projected to become more frequent and severe across the boreal forest, affecting forest productivity, ecosystem functioning and habitat values (Juday et al. 2005, Bhatti et al. 2003). Northern forest-dependent communities are expected to be significantly affected by these ecological changes because of their strong connections to forested ecosystems (Davidson, Williamson, and Parkins 2003; Ogden 2007). While the challenges posed by climate change are great, I do not believe they are insurmountable. However, without near-term action, it will become increasingly difficult to develop resilient forest management plans and policies.

First, let me quickly review why forests are managed. They are generally managed to meet certain objectives (Ogden and Innes 2007a). In Yukon, these objectives are established through planning processes that are undertaken at the level of a First Nations traditional territory. Some of the objectives that have emerged from these planning processes include providing economic opportunities, reducing the risks to communities from fire, sustaining traditional land uses, protecting soil and water resources, conserving wildlife and protecting wildlife habitat, producing timber, harvesting fuel wood and preserving recreational opportunities. The balance and mix of objectives varies from region to region across Yukon, and the different regions are at different stages in the planning process (Ogden and Innes 2008a).

However, forest management planning processes in Yukon have not yet directly grappled with climate change (Ogden and Innes 2008a). I believe it is essential to overcome any barriers to achieving this and to mainstream adaptation to climate change into forest management planning.

The key to successful adaptation is to be proactive and to embrace the uncertain future in our decision-making. By being proactive, I mean that we need to proactively identify actions to reduce vulnerabilities and manage risks in anticipation of change. By embracing uncertainty, I mean that we need to identify management practices and policies that have a higher likelihood of achieving management objectives, across a wide range of potential climate futures.

A useful framework to mainstream adaptation considerations is structured decision-making. The steps in this approach are the development of comprehensive objectives, the consideration of reasonable alternatives and the evaluation of these alternatives against objectives (Ohlson, McKinnon, and Hirsch 2005). Let me be a bit more specific about the application of structured decision-making.

First and foremost, a vision for the future is needed. Before making a decision on how to adapt to climate change, it is first essential that management objectives be clearly established. For example, what direction has been set by the community for the management of forest resources? A clear statement of goals and objectives will increase our ability to address long-term concerns within short-term decisions. Without a clear vision, it is impossible to evaluate alternative approaches. Once it is clear what the vision is for the future of a particular land base, an assessment of how to adapt current policies and practices to achieve this vision in light of climate change can be undertaken.

A recent review identified over 80 forest management adaptation options that have been suggested by researchers for the forest sector (Ogden and Innes 2007a). The difficulties involved in making a decision when faced with such a large number of choices can easily result in no choice being made and the status quo being maintained.

It may be appropriate to implement some of these adaptation measures in some areas but not in others. Management objectives differ from place to place, and so do other factors such as the magnitude and rate of climate change, vulnerability to climate change and the social acceptability or economic feasibility of these options. Correspondingly, the choice of adaptation measures to implement may also vary. Adaptation is not a one-size-fits-all approach.

Since the choice of adaptation options may vary from place to place it is important to evaluate options within a specific geographical context, such as a planning unit with defined management objectives and identified values (Ogden and Innes 2007b; Ogden and Innes 2008b).

There are different ways of characterizing this long list of options. For example, some options involve facilitating "natural" ecosystem responses to climate change, while others are akin to engineering resistance to ecological change;

some options adapt social and economic systems to ecological change, while others adapt ecosystems to meet social and economic needs.

With this in mind, I propose five conceptual approaches to adaptation in the forest sector. The first approach is to allow ecological responses to climate change to proceed with minimal human interference. A second approach is to facilitate adaptation of forest ecosystems to future climate conditions through active management. A third approach is to engineer resistance to changing climate conditions. This approach acknowledges that special or unique habitat features, wildlife populations, timber harvesting opportunities or cultural/heritage sites may be so highly valued by the local community that extraordinary efforts to preserve them are warranted. A fourth approach is to focus efforts on building socio-economic resilience to changing climate conditions. In the forestry context, this entails enhancing the capacity of local communities and economies to deal with changes in forest ecosystems that may arise because of climate change. The last approach is to not make any changes to current management policies and practices. There are perfectly valid reasons why a local forestry planning process may involve this choice. The key is for there to be a deliberate choice, as not making a choice and not carrying out an evaluation may expose a region to undesirable and avoidable climate-associated risks. These five approaches are not necessarily complementary. Their appropriateness depends on the vision for the future forest, on local values and aspirations for the future and, of course, on management objectives.

There is absolutely no doubt in my mind that an evaluation to determine where, when and how to adapt forest management plans and policies to address climate change should be a local exercise. Local values, local experiences and the implications of decision-making about adaptation to climate change for local futures make it essential that these choices be made locally. It is essential that those involved in resource management and planning begin to gain experience in evaluating alternative adaptation options and strategies.

Because of the uncertainty associated with climate change, adaptation will be a moving target. Therefore, it is essential that the performance of adaptation efforts in enabling management objectives to be achieved be evaluated on an ongoing basis. Indicators can be used to gauge the effectiveness of management activities in achieving management objectives. When indicators are used alongside clear targets and thresholds, established through a community process, they can signal when an alternative management response is warranted or when the management objectives themselves need to be revisited (Ogden 2007).

I do not believe it is possible to identify one right approach to climate change adaptation in forest management plans. Each region has its own unique combination of environmental, social, economic and cultural characteristics; vulnerabilities; and visions for the future. Instead, it would be better to evaluate adaptation options and strategies for a specific area within a specific decision-making context.

The Umbrella Final Agreement legally established a strong role for community and local knowledge and participation in how lands and resources are managed in Yukon. Living in Yukon — where people now have a unique opportunity, and a legal right, to be directly involved in the decision-making that affects them, their families and their communities — has shaped the vision and path that I have presented today. The combination of scientific, community and government knowledge and priorities that is becoming more common in decision-making in Yukon provides the foundation for Yukoners to make decisions that will allow us to not only adapt to regional and global pressures but also provide an example to other areas of Canada and the world of a new way of governing and managing lands and resources.

In conclusion, in the future the North will be influenced to a great extent by the decisions that are made today. Our collective success in taking long-term considerations into account in near-term decisions will shape that future. There are many challenges to come; we need to ensure management policies and practices are flexible and can be adapted, that they embrace uncertainty and are proactive in how they address the future.

References

Bhatti, J.S., G.C. Van Kooten, M.J. Apps, L.D. Laird, I.D. Campbell, C. Campbell, M.R. Turetsky, Z. Yu, and E. Banfield. 2003. "Carbon Balance and Climate Change in Boreal Forests." In *Towards Sustainable Management of the Boreal Forest*, edited by P.J. Burton, C. Messier, D.W. Smith, and W.L. Adamowicz. Ottawa: National Research Council of Canada.

Davidson, D.J., T. Williamson, and J.R. Parkins. 2003. "Understanding Climate Change Risk and Vulnerability in Northern Forest-Based Communities." *Canadian Journal of Forest Research* 33: 2252-61.

Juday, G.P., V. Barber, P. Duffy, H. Linderhorm, S. Rupp, S. Sparrow, E. Vaganov, and J. Yarie. 2005. "Forests, Land Management and Agriculture." In *Arctic Climate Impact Assessment: Scientific Report*, 781-862. Cambridge, UK: Cambridge University Press.

Ogden, A.E. 2007. "Forest Management in a Changing Climate: Building the Environmental Information Base for Southwest Yukon." *Forestry Chronicle* 83 (6): 806-09.

Ogden, A.E., and J.L. Innes. 2007a. "Incorporating Climate Change Adaptation Considerations into Forest Management Planning in the Boreal Forest." *International Forestry Reviews* 9 (3): 713-33.

_____. 2007b. "Perspectives of Forest Practitioners on Climate Change Adaptation in the Yukon and Northwest Territories of Canada." *Forestry Chronicle* 83 (4): 557-69.

_____. 2008a. "Climate Change Adaptation and Regional Forest Planning in Southern Yukon, Canada." *Mitigation and Adaptation Strategies for Global Change 13* (8). Accessed February 10, 2009. http://www.springer-link.com/content/m5v68317w3285282/?p=df0848d0637547468d3c44b09f0f091e&pi=6

_____. 2008b. "Application of Structured Decision Making to an Assessment of Climate Change Vulnerabilities and Adaptation Options for Sustainable Forest Management." *Ecology and Society* 14(1). Accessed February 10, 2009. http://ecologyandsociety.org/vol14/iss1/art11/

_____. Forthcoming. "Adapting to Climate Change in the Southwest Yukon: Locally Identified Research and Monitoring Needs to Support Decision Making on Sustainable Forest Management." *Arctic* 62(2).

Ohlson, D.W., G.A. McKinnon, and K.G.Hirsch. 2005. "A Structured Decision-Making Approach to Climate Change Adaptation in the Forest Sector." *Forestry Chronicle* 81 (1): 97-103.

Parmesean, C., and G. Yohe. 2003. "A Globally Coherent Fingerprint of Climate Change Impacts across Natural Systems." *Nature* 421: 37-42.

Scholze, M., W. Knorr, N.W. Arnell, and I.C. Prentice. 2006. "A Climate Change Risk Analysis for World Ecosystems." *Proceedings of the National Academy of Sciences of the United States of America* 103 (35): 12116-13120.

LOOKING FORWARD: NORTHERN POLICY IN CANADA

Climate Change,
Sovereignty and
Partnership with
the Inuit

T HE MAIN PURPOSE OF MY COMMENTARY IS TO IDENTIFY FACTORS THAT I THINK
should be the drivers in shaping Canada's policy-making for the Arctic in
the coming years. None of these will come as a surprise. Each was a topic of discussion at the Northern Exposure conference. Interestingly, each has been a topic
in previous northern domestic and international policy-making initiatives.

When I was Canada's ambassador for circumpolar affairs, one of my proud-
est achievements was developing and producing the Northern Dimension of
Canada's Foreign Policy. This initiative had four objectives: to enhance the security and prosperity of Canadians, especially northerners and Aboriginal peoples;
to assert and ensure the preservation of Canada's sovereignty in the Arctic; to
establish the circumpolar region as a vibrant geopolitical entity integrated into a
rules-based international system; and to promote the human security of northerners and the sustainable development of the Arctic. Forgive me a hint of cyni-
cism, but what goes around comes around! Here we are, almost 10 years later,
facing the same challenges. The difference is that we now have an increased sense
of urgency. The clock is ticking on climate change. Our collective responsibility
is to do something about it. Our response to the reality of climate change needs
to go way beyond comforting policy statements. We must act. We must hold governments accountable.

Canada's claim to sovereignty in the Arctic is under serious assault. Russia's
recent activities; President Bush's clear position, stated at the 2007 meeting of leaders on the Security and Prosperity Partnership of North America; and the Hans
Island incident have finally caused the federal government to sit up and take
notice. An argument can also be made that the global hydrocarbon demand has a

direct bearing on both climate change and sovereignty. Sustainable and equitable development of our natural resources must also drive policy development.

Many of us are children of the 1960s and '70s, and we recall the heated discussions over the sale of our raw natural resources to foreign interests. Our Arctic was described by a senior Canadian politician at the time as "a frozen treasure chest." But there is a big difference between even 10 years ago and today. And that is that land claims and new governance structures in the Arctic set out the rights of Inuit and other Aboriginal peoples to work in concert with governments. Inuit are no longer "knocking at the door." Implementing land claims and ensuring that Canada fulfills its commitments to creating new governance structures in the Arctic must underpin all policy development — be it domestic or international.

My current responsibilities as president of Inuit Tapiriit Kanatami (ITK) include ensuring that Inuit are at the table whenever these matters are being discussed. Coherent policy-making for Canada's Arctic entails acknowledging the central requirement for enduring and constructive partnerships with Aboriginal peoples. At some point, sensible federal government policy-making will have to consciously ground itself on two basic demographic, sociological and political propositions: first, the Arctic is not open for homesteading, and the Aboriginal presence is not going to fade to the margins; second, it's better to work with this fact than to ignore or resent it.

All sorts of policies need to be shaped around these two propositions, ranging from policies governing how the federal government devolves natural resource management powers to northern governments and shares development benefits and risks, to fisheries allocation policies, to policies related to the use of federal spending power to make major near-term investments in education and training and infrastructure to facilitate the adaptation of Aboriginal peoples to modern economies and circumstances. Put another way, it is the vocation of Aboriginal peoples living in the Arctic to run the Canadian Arctic on behalf of Canada, and it is in the best interest of Canada to accept this. This is the new northern policy universe.

Let me expand on two policy areas for Inuit. One is front and centre: climate change. And the other needs to be brought to the forefront: education and language preservation. Recently, the Government of Canada made several announcements that relate to its commitment to address climate change. Four new initiatives, funded at $71 million collectively and spanning four federal departments, were announced. The four projects include: improved climate change scenarios, within Environment Canada; regional adaptation work programs, under Natural Resources Canada; programs to assess key vulnerabilities in northern and Aboriginal communities, within Indian and Northern Affairs Canada; and programs to address health adaptation in northern and Inuit communities, under the First Nations and Inuit Health Branch of Health Canada. The government has also announced an integrated northern strategy focused on strengthening Canada's sovereignty, protecting our environmental heritage, promoting economic and social development, and improving and devolving governance, so that northerners will have greater control over their destinies. And it has promised to build a world-class Arctic research station that will be on the cutting edge of Arctic issues, including environmental science and resource development.

The key here is to make sure that each of these announced northern initiatives, first of all, clearly includes and addresses Arctic and Inuit issues; and, second, that each is developed with Inuit as full and active partners in the management and direction of its programs. We have had much experience working with the federal government to promote partnerships that ensure Inuit needs and issues are addressed.

The effects of climate change in the Arctic are wide-reaching — they affect the health of Inuit and of wildlife and ecosystems, and they disrupt the already fragile economies of our communities. At ITK, we recognized these interrelationships, and we restructured our organization to address the fact that communities and regions were saying our health and environment are crucially linked. We combined our departments in order to ensure that we approached issues, including climate change, in a more holistic manner.

We would like to hold this up as an example for what the government needs to consider: decreasing the stovepiping of this issue with Environment Canada, Health Canada, Natural Resources Canada, and Indian and Northern Affairs Canada. We are advocating that the recently announced programs bring all parties together, including Inuit, to coordinate initiatives and actions and improve collaboration. By contributing their observations and knowledge, Inuit have a lot to offer the world in terms of understanding some of the changes that are occurring in the Arctic. Inuit hunters are keen observers of the environment on a daily basis; they see the climate-induced changes in permafrost, sea ice, lake ice and snow cover that are expected to have significant implications for infrastructure maintenance and design.

According to a recent report on climate change impacts in Canada's North, climate-related changes will result in shifts in species availability, accessibility and quality, with consequences for biodiversity and the human populations that rely on these resources. The increased navigability of Arctic marine waters and the expansion of land-based transportation will bring both opportunities for economic growth and challenges related to culture, security and the environment. As a result, maintaining and protecting traditional and subsistence ways of life in many Arctic Aboriginal communities could become more difficult (Furgal and Prowse 2008). This issue impacts on every facet of our life in the Arctic and deeply impacts on the wellness not only of individuals, but also of communities and cultures.

Let me switch gears to address an issue that must be moved to the front burner: education and the preservation of the Inuit language. In 2005, the United Nations Permanent Forum on Indigenous Issues (UNPFII) published an expert paper on indigenous children's education and languages. Five international experts on indigenous studies examined the published research on indigenous children receiving their education in schools where the language of instruction was a dominant one — such as English. Their main conclusion after examining all the research was that "the greatest predictor of long-term success in school for indigenous children is how long they receive instruction through their first language. The length of mother tongue medium education is more important than any other factor (including socio-economic status) in predicting the educational success of bilingual students. The worst results…are with students in programmes where the students' mother tongues are not supported at all or where they are only taught as subjects" (Magga et al. 2005).

The authors also noted that two major United Nations agreements — both of which Canada has been signatory to — recognize the right of all children to education. They go on to say, "Given what we know about the effects of enforced dominant language medium education policies, which tend to result not only in considerably poorer performance results but also higher levels of non-completion [of school], the pursuit of such policies could be said to be contrary to the right of indigenous children to an education" (Magga et al. 2005). In other words, if the model of education chosen for a school does not allow indigenous children to be educated in a language they understand, then they are effectively denied access to their right to an education. We should be viewing access to education in Inuktitut as a human right.

It is also interesting to note that the United Nations Committee on the Rights of the Child (UNCRC) has recommended that parties to the agreement — Canada is one — take these four steps: implement indigenous children's right to be taught to read and write in their own language; undertake measures to effectively address the higher dropout rate; take effective measures to increase the number of teachers from indigenous communities and provide them with appropriate training; and allocate sufficient financial, material and human resources to implement these programs and policies effectively (UNCRC 2003, 4). So, as you can see, in many ways the timing is right for a major new initiative in Inuit education.[1]

Whether we are tackling the issue of our time — climate change — or asserting Canadian sovereignty in the Arctic or improving Inuit education and language, it is legitimate for Inuit to expect a full partnership role in the development of Arctic public policy. It is also legitimate to expect that public investments will be made to address glaring economic and social disparities and inequities with the rest of Canada (the sad mistake of the derailed Kelowna Accord notwithstanding). I am optimistic. In my career, I have always tried to find diplomatic and negotiated solutions to the many challenges facing Inuit and the Arctic region. I will continue to do so.

Note

1   The Inuit Education Accord, developed by
Inuit Tapiriit Kanatami and a number of
other parties, was signed in April 2009.
Fourteen Inuit and public government bodies, and Chuck Strahl, the Minister of
Indian Affairs and Northern Development,
signed the Accord, which, among other
things, will supportInuit-friendly cur ricula.

References

Furgal, Chris, and Prowse, Terry D. 2008.
"Northern Canada." In *From Impacts to
Adaptation: Canada in a Changing Climate
2007*, edited by D.S. Lemmen, F.J. Warren,
J. Lacroix, and E. Bush. Ottawa: Natural
Resources Canada.

Magga, Ole Henrik, Ida Nicolaisen, Mililani
Trask, Tove Skutnabb-Kangas, and Robert
Dunbar. 2005. "Indigenous Children's
Education and Indigenous Languages."
Expert paper written for the United Nations
Permanent Forum on Indigenous Issues.

United Nations Committee on the Rights of the
Child. 2003. *Day of General Discussion on
the Rights of Indigenous Children:
Recommendations*, October 3, 34th session.
New York: Office of the United Nations
High Commissioner for Human Rights.
Accessed October 6, 2008.
http://www2.ohchr.org/english/bodies/crc/
docs/discussion/indigenouschildren.pdf

Challenges and
Expectations in the
Canadian North

C ANADA'S NORTH PRESENTS GOVERNANCE CHALLENGES WELL BEYOND THOSE found elsewhere in Canada. It also presents great opportunities for its inhabitants and for those who would contribute to its future. In consequence of these opportunities, it is subject to a set of expectations that are high indeed, but that, because of the unique challenges that face northern institutions, may also be quite unrealistic. After all, fewer than one in three thousand Canadians lives in Canada's northern territories. The combined population of Yukon, the Northwest Territories and Nunavut is just over 101,000 — considerably less than the population of Prince Edward Island — yet nearly 40 percent of Canada's land mass lies within their boundaries. That tiny population is responsible for three territorial governments, which handle most of the responsibilities managed by vastly larger provincial governments south of 60, as well as a host of indigenous governments. And it must do all this in a social and physical environment that would deeply challenge the most competent of provincial governments.

Other contributions to this volume detail many of these challenges and expectations. My aim in this commentary is to draw some of them together in order to help us appreciate better the enormity of the task faced by northern governments and peoples and to make some suggestions as to how they might be dealt with, both by northerners and by those in the south who hope to help. I will concentrate on the three northern territories of Yukon, the Northwest Territories and Nunavut, but those responsible for governance in Labrador and northern Quebec face most of the same challenges, albeit in the context of a provincial regime rather than a more independent territorial regime.

Challenges in the North

Climate Change

P ERHAPS THE MOST WIDELY RECOGNIZED CHALLENGE IS THAT POSED BY CLIMATE
change. A general conclusion of most climate change models is that northern regions will warm more quickly than southern ones. Much of northern
Canada is projected to face warming of five degrees Celsius or more by the end
of this century, but the impacts will be far from even. Observed temperature
changes over the half century to 2002 were greater than 1.5 degrees Celsius in
the western Arctic and about 0.5 degrees in the central regions, but there were
temperature declines in the far eastern regions, and the waters off the coast of
Labrador are projected to cool. Dramatic declines in sea ice in the central Arctic
in the summer of 2007 highlighted just how quickly effects can occur.

Uncertainty and variability reinforce the difficulty of dealing with climate
change. So does the recentness of our recognition of the problem. Fifteen years
ago, it dawned on us that we faced major problems with climate change, but,
aside from occasionally expressing concerns that the melting of permafrost might
threaten northern structures, particularly pipelines, we paid little attention to the
issue until the last decade.

What is clear is that due to a combination of social factors and the very large
climate changes that seem likely to occur, global warming poses challenges for
northern peoples that greatly exceed those faced by most Canadians living in the
south. A substantial portion of northern Aboriginal peoples still live traditional
lifestyles. They rely for much of their food, particularly protein, on the land and
the sea. They travel over land and water on snow and ice for many months of each
year, and it is often easier in winter than in summer. The majority of communities
in many parts of the North, and all of them in Nunavut, lack any road structure
outside of community boundaries, so access to alternative means of overland travel in predictable conditions is essential. And a quick glance at the map of Nunavut
reveals that, with the exception of Baker Lake, every permanent community is
coastal, so the impact of rising sea levels could be very great indeed.

While there may be some beneficial effects of climate change in the North
— lower heating costs and, possibly, some new agricultural opportunities, for
example — these are either highly uncertain or likely to occur only in the distant
future. Meanwhile, the caribou herds are shrinking and their migration patterns are

Northern Exposure: Peoples, Powers and
Prospects in Canada's North

changing. The permafrost that supports current buildings is melting. Elders note that weather patterns have already become less predictable. The negative effects are immediate. Potential problems for southerners who will have time to adjust are real problems for northerners today, or they will be in the very near future.

Young Governments

Northern governments are young governments. Significant devolution of powers to the Northwest Territories (NWT), including the area that has become Nunavut, did not begin until 1967, and until 1985, the federal commissioner, a federal public servant appointed by the minister responsible for the North, chaired the executive council and effectively controlled the territorial administration. While the Yukon Territory was created in 1898, it was not until 1979 that a legislative assembly with a cabinet and an elected government leader was established. And, of course, the Government of Nunavut was created only in 1999.

Territorial governments are responsible for the delivery of education, health and social services, and they have to deliver those services under extremely difficult circumstances. In addition to tackling the problems created by sheer distance — they are responsible for delivering reasonably full services in many small communities — they must operate with severe human resource limitations and without benefit of the long experience enjoyed by provincial governments. This is particularly true in Nunavut, where the combination of many small communities, an almost complete lack of infrastructure and an acute shortage of an educated indigenous labour force able to deliver professional services creates an extremely difficult situation for a young and inevitably inexperienced government.

There is, or should be, no lack of agreement on the ultimate objective with respect to territorial governments: full provincial powers and seats of completely equal status at the table of Confederation. But, even allowing for the considerable differences among territorial governments, we should also have no illusions about how great the distance is that they must travel to achieve that objective and how much support they will need from Canadians everywhere.

Human Resources and Education

The Government of Nunavut is committed to ensuring that Inuit are represented in government employment in the same proportion as in the population, which currently means that 85 percent of jobs should be held by Inuit. Other territorial governments have similar commitments but serve proportionally smaller Aboriginal populations. In all cases, however, there is a lack of available human resources with a level of education commensurate with the requirements of such employment, and there is great competition among government agencies and claims management organizations for those people who are qualified.

Given the strong commitment of all northern governments to employing Aboriginal people and the current lack of qualified individuals, the hope for the future lies in education. But if the Aboriginal peoples of the North are to preserve their cultural heritage yet still be ready to participate in the modern workplace, this education must be provided in ways more complex than those familiar to southern Canadians. Native languages must be retained, yet students must also learn to operate in English or French. And if cultural practices such as living off the land are to live on, then the expectation that students will be regularly and reliably in school five days a week, every week, may not be appropriate. Of course, hiring qualified Inuit and First Nations teachers would make these objectives easier to attain, but such teachers are in critically short supply.

As Frances Abele has pointed out elsewhere in this volume, the mixed economy of many outlying communities is essential to their cultural and economic survival, yet the mixed economy does not always fit well with the world of work as it exists in the south, and it does not always fit well with the requirements of employment in modern government bureaucracies. The challenge, then, is for territorial governments to find ways to deliver necessary public services, often in remote communities, using the indigenous workforce, which will often have less than ideal qualifications. In addition, they must increase levels of education in a culturally suitable way and with an inadequate number of Aboriginal teachers. This would be an immense challenge for a large provincial government, let alone for a small territorial administration.

Economic Development and Infrastructure

Outside of the major centres of Whitehorse, Inuvik, Yellowknife and Iqaluit, infrastructure in the North is underdeveloped, and it becomes more so as one moves from west to east. While most remote communities have an airstrip and a few roads within community boundaries, as well as a school and a nursing station, there is little else. There are no deepwater ports in the Canadian North, and the only road connections to the south are the Alaska and Dempster highway system, which serves the western Arctic to Inuvik, and the Frontier highway system, which runs north from Alberta to Yellowknife. Winter roads serve many communities in the NWT but are obviously unavailable for much of the year. The inception of diamond mining in the NWT has led to substantial improvement in the air and winter road links to those few parts with mining operations, but there is little else, and the construction of regular roads is prohibitively expensive where it is possible at all.

The great hope for economic development across much of the North lies in resource extraction, but one consequence of this is the disruption of parts of the environment necessary for the practice of traditional ways of life. And, of course, resource extraction is notoriously cyclical, as the stop-start history of base-metal mining in Yukon so amply illustrates. In consequence, much of the employment in the North is public sector employment, and the northern economy is far more dependent on this than are southern economies. In Yukon and the NWT, approximately 40 percent of the labour force is in the public sector. In Nunavut, this rises to 55 percent. In Canada as a whole, public sector employment accounts for less than 20 percent of the labour force.

While overall employment rates in Yukon and the NWT appear high by Canadian standards, in fact all the northern territories share low levels of Aboriginal employment, particularly in the more remote communities (Indian and Northern Affairs Canada [INAC] 2007, 27). In both Yukon and the NWT, the employment rate for Aboriginal people is 52 to 55 percent, while for non-Aboriginal people it is 75 percent in Yukon and 80 percent in the NWT. In Nunavut, the rate for non-Aboriginal people is also 80 percent, but among Inuit, only 45 percent of those of working age are employed in the regular labour force.

Cultural Diversity and Culture Shock

While southern Canadians have grown accustomed to thinking of themselves as highly diverse both ethnically and culturally, many have no concept of the cultural diversity of the North. The Government of the Northwest Territories recognizes, and translates its territorial assembly proceedings into, nine official Aboriginal languages — three Inuit and six First Nations — as well as English and French. The Yukon government uses only English and French as official languages, but there are 10 Aboriginal languages spoken within the territory — some of them dangerously near extinction. Nunavut is more homogeneous, with its preponderantly Inuit population, but here, too, there are two Inuit languages spoken and used as official languages; regional dialects introduce a further linguistic complication.

The culture shock faced by many Aboriginal northerners is immense. In many northern communities, the current or immediately preceding generation is the first one not raised almost entirely on the land. While some contact with European culture has occurred in most northern communities over the last 80 years, in many cases the contact has been quite limited and not always beneficial, and in many communities the residential schools policy has removed much of the cultural heritage that provides continuity between generations.

Social Pathologies

In consequence of the culture shock and the cultural gap faced by many northern Aboriginal people, northern governments face a number of social pathologies. They must deal with these in a difficult physical and economic environment with the help of workers who are themselves stressed by the workloads and by the same cultural difficulties that beset their clients.

Crime rates across the northern territories are far higher than those in southern Canada. For example, in the whole of Canada in 2005, there were 78 criminal code offences per 1,000 people. Comparable figures for Yukon, the NWT and Nunavut were, respectively, 224, 412 and 328 per 1,000. Violent crime rates are three times higher in Yukon than in Canada as a whole, and they are seven times higher in the NWT and Nunavut. The suicide rate in Canada in 2001 was 11.3 per 100,000 people; in Yukon the rate was 18.5, in the NWT it was 20.8 and in Nunavut it was 80.3 (INAC 2007, 17).

The tragically high suicide rate in Nunavut is eloquently outlined in a report on Nunavut devolution prepared by Paul Mayer for the federal minister of Indian affairs and northern development in 2007:

> Twenty-nine people in the territory took their lives in 2006, the second-worst year on record. Young men between 15 and 24 years of age in Nunavut are about 40 times more likely to commit suicide than the average Canadian in that same age group...The phenomenon is a relatively new one that defies simple explanation, especially since it does not stand alone. The high suicide rate is a symptom of the current social malaise in Nunavut society caused by, among other things, rapid social change, high drop-out rates, poverty, unemployment and dysfunctional families (INAC 2007).

Mayer goes on to emphasize that the Government of Nunavut "has yet to honour its 2004 commitment to implement a suicide prevention strategy" (2007, 10).

The people of all the northern territories, particularly outside Whitehorse and Yellowknife, suffer from chronically overcrowded housing, poorer access to health care, higher overall mortality rates, lower levels of education and far fewer employment opportunities than those enjoyed by other Canadians — problems they share with First Nations peoples living on reserves even in the south of Canada.

Population Growth and Age Distribution

Population growth in some areas is extremely rapid, and the fastest growth is concentrated in the more remote areas. In all the northern territories, the birth rate is above the Canadian average. In 2005, the Yukon birth rate was marginally higher than that of the rest of Canada, but the NWT rate was 1.6 times the Canadian average and the Nunavut rate was 2.5 times that of Canada as a whole. In consequence, the population age distribution, particularly in Nunavut and the NWT, is radically different than that in the rest of Canada. In Nunavut, approximately 45 percent of the population is under 19, compared to 24 percent in the rest of Canada. This — combined with the lack of adequate housing, the difficulty in finding teachers and the cultural problems outlined earlier and in other contributions to this volume — means that the challenges facing young northern governments are very great indeed.

Dependency

Given the lack of private sector economic development in the North, northern territorial governments are deeply dependent on the federal government for the funds they need to provide services to their citizens. Territorial budgets indicate that in 2007-08, grants and transfers from the federal government accounted for 69.5 percent of the revenues of the Yukon government, 72 percent of those of the NWT government and almost 90 percent of the revenues of the Nunavut government.

Land Claims Settlements

Land claims settlements across the North present both a challenge and an opportunity. In the quarter century from 1975 to 2000, comprehensive land claims settlements were signed covering northern Quebec, more than four-fifths of the

NWT, all of Yukon and Nunavut, and part of Labrador. These settlements — modern treaties — are constitutionally protected arrangements that clarify the nature of land and resource ownership and responsibility, and they codify much of the relationship between Aboriginal peoples and public governments in the North.

Claims settlements are very complex, and implementing them has been a difficult and protracted intergovernmental process (I will return to this point). They are expensive in terms of dollars and in the human effort needed to implement and manage them. Because they are so broad and so important, they are often the source of conflict, particularly between Aboriginal groups and the federal government. They require Aboriginal groups to participate in myriad boards and agencies, a process that is beneficial to these groups because it allows them to participate in the protection of the rights of the people they represent. But it also poses difficulties for them because the procedures these bodies follow are most often those of non-Aboriginal governments, and their working languages (English or French) may be second or third languages for Aboriginal participants. The difficulties are compounded by the fact that effective participation may require a level of formal education that the Aboriginal participants lack.

Land claims settlements have brought hundreds of millions of dollars to Aboriginal-owned corporations to be managed or invested for the land claims beneficiaries. On the whole, these funds have been managed well and with the appropriate level of accountability. They have produced some remarkable commercial successes, as well as many employment opportunities and financial benefits. But they are also a burden because they require careful management, which should, as far as possible, be handled by the beneficiaries themselves, and that draws talented Aboriginal people away from other valuable activities. Once again, we see a familiar story: opportunities are accompanied by heavy obligations, which bear upon groups that do not always have the resources to manage them.

Land claims settlements should improve economic opportunities across Canada's North and help clarify and improve relations between Aboriginal and non-Aboriginal Canadians. They should help Aboriginal people find a balance between traditional and modern ways of life. But they must be implemented in an environment where economic and social challenges abound, and those challenges weigh particularly heavily on Aboriginal northerners.

Northern Exposure: Peoples, Powers and Prospects in Canada's North

Lack of Knowledge

While the readers of this volume will have a substantial interest in and knowledge of Canada's North, most Canadians do not. To southern Canadians, the North, while an integral part of our nation and our national identity, remains unknown. Most southern Canadians would be sympathetic to the concerns and needs of northern Canadians if they knew what they were. Yet southerners' expectations of northerners and northerners' expectations of themselves and their governments are immense.

Expectations

WHILE WE WHO LIVE IN THE SOUTH MAY RECOGNIZE IN A SOMEWHAT ABSTRACT way the challenges faced by northerners and their governments, we still seem to believe that northerners can simultaneously take a lead role in dealing with climate change, not just in the North but also internationally; act as leading partners in the protection of Canadian Arctic sovereignty; protect their own cultures; participate in literally dozens of management boards and commissions, most of which operate according to southern rules; manage huge amounts of money in land claims settlement corporations; interact constantly with much better resourced southern governments and industries; deliver a full range of services to a scattered population that suffers from considerable social pathologies; and develop government structures and procedures — in effect, build a car while the wheels are moving.

So, What Now?

OBVIOUSLY, THERE IS A SIGNIFICANT GAP BETWEEN THE EXPECTATIONS FOR NORTHERN peoples and governments and the challenges under which they labour. While the potential of the North is great, and while with the right mix of policies (and some luck) the future could be bright, we should not underestimate these challenges. So, what to do? The answer is certainly not to stand back and ask northerners to do it all themselves. As the great dependency of northern governments on financial transfers from Ottawa well demonstrates, that has never been a viable answer, and it will not become one in the foreseeable future. We in the south must actively help Aboriginal and non-Aboriginal northerners to cope and to develop, but we have to begin by defining our objectives correctly. And we must ensure that the actions we take are not patronizing, demeaning, colonizing — or excessive.

If northern governments are united in any one thing, it is probably in the belief that transfer payments from Ottawa are far from excessive. Given the high cost of service delivery and the limited access that territorial governments have to own-source revenues, they may well be right. But a budgetary flood is at least as destabilizing as budgetary stringency, and considerably less likely. Thus the issue is not only how to provide support but also how much support to provide.

We must therefore ensure that support is provided in ways that permit territorial governments to make their own decisions and take full responsibility for them, while at the same time encouraging these governments to do everything possible to increase their own-source revenues and economic development. To some degree, the federal government has done this by making changes to Territorial Formula Financing (TFF) in the 2007 budget — changes that exclude 30 percent of territories' own-source revenues from the offsets used to calculate federal transfers. However, the formula is based on provincial rates of spending and, more particularly, on provincial rates of increase applied to an expenditure base intended to take account of higher service delivery costs in the North. Whether expenditure increases south of 60 are applicable in the North is always debatable.

The issue of how to ensure adequate revenues in an appropriate form for northern governments becomes most pointed when we look at the devolution of resource management and revenues to the territorial governments. Resources certainly offer the best opportunity for increasing territorial own-source revenues — if territorial governments gain access to those resources through devolution. The devolution of resource management to the Yukon government is complete, but devolution to the two other territorial governments has a long history of frustration and failure. The issue is a matter of both trust and fear — fear on the part of the federal government and the resource industries that territorial governments will not manage the resources responsibly and for the benefit of all Canadians as well as themselves. And fear, too, on the part of the territorial governments that they will be saddled with large management costs and see little revenue, and that the federal government will adjust TFF payments in a way that effectively preempts them from achieving any real economic benefit from their resources.

Northern Exposure: Peoples, Powers and
Prospects in Canada's North

In the end, the federal government and the resource industries will simply have to develop trust in the territorial governments' ability to manage resources. But they can help ensure an acceptable management regime by adopting a supportive, nonconfrontational attitude and by ensuring that there is adequate initial financial support for the territorial governments to acquire the appropriate resource management expertise before the resource revenues begin to flow. As for the territorial governments, they should not expect devolution to entail a transfer of all revenues but no corresponding offset in TFF payments. They must also trust that the federal government will not unilaterally alter the rules of the game, although that trust is understandably hard for them to offer, given the federal government's long history of changing the rules of intergovernmental transfers whenever it perceives the need for financial stringency. But, equally, the federal government cannot expect that the offsets will be anything like 100 percent, and it must anticipate and truly guarantee a long phase-in period for both the assumption of the costs of management and any offsets for revenues.

The Yukon Northern Affairs Program Devolution Transfer Agreement, signed in 2001, already provides for the transfer to the Yukon government expenditure base for TFF purposes of the full amount budgeted by the northern program for resource management in Yukon in 2001-02, plus assorted transitional payments; and then it excludes up to $3 million from Yukon government revenue offsets for federal TFF transfers. While this formula has been acceptable in Yukon, which has very limited potential revenues from oil and gas exploitation, it has not proven attractive to either the NWT or Nunavut. In their cases, the magnitude of future expenditures and revenues with respect to resource exploitation is a great unknown; the formula must be made to reflect this, but a strategy for doing so has thus far eluded federal and territorial negotiators.

On another front, extra financial support to send more human resources to the North, particularly to Nunavut, sounds appealing and would provide some real assistance now, when it is most needed. But Nunavut is, quite properly, committed to developing the capacity of Inuit to participate fully in the management of government, and too much help for too long a time would not encourage that. At times, however, the government of Nunavut has been too refractory in resisting outside help. For instance, the failure of the Baffin Regional Hospital in Iqaluit to attain accreditation is largely the result of a lack of skilled personnel. Resistance to bringing personnel from the south, assuming they are available, will not help to resolve such problems. Similarly, an insistence on employment equity in an environment where there is an undersupply of skilled workers simply encourages raiding and salary escalation without improving the real employment prospects of the targeted group or services to the public.

The role of the federal and provincial governments in mitigating climate change through emissions reduction is far greater than that of the territorial governments and northern peoples. But even if we were to sharply reduce carbon emissions today, the world climate would continue to warm, and with a greater effect in the North than elsewhere. The federal government will have to recognize that it must provide support to help northerners cope with inevitable changes. And the territorial governments must recognize that if they do not formulate appropriate policies in this area, they will weaken their ability to get the help they need, and they will use whatever support is provided in a less than optimal fashion.

We have not yet defined a rational division of responsibilities between the territorial governments and the federal government. Perhaps the greatest current lack in the North is infrastructure. Protection of our Arctic sovereignty, not to mention the economic and social development of the North, will depend on it. There is no way that territorial governments can provide the requisite infrastructure. If it is to be built at all, it will have to be built largely by the federal government. The same is true of northern housing. A fundamental root of the pathologies that afflict the North is inadequate housing. Yet building costs in Nunavut and other remote areas in the North are at least three times those in the south. While the delivery of programs by the Nunavut Housing Corporation, which is operated by the Government of Nunavut, is appropriate, it remains highly questionable whether the federal government is providing as much support as it should in this area.[1]

One area where the division of responsibilities has become extremely vexed is the sharing of costs and responsibilities for claims implementation. Given the importance of claims implementation to northern development, it is sad indeed to see the claims implementation bodies and the federal government at such loggerheads that they have become involved in a major court case. Claims implementation has always been contentious — as the 30-year fight between the Cree (and to some extent Inuit) of northern Quebec and the federal government illustrates only too well — and we do not seem to be learning how to avoid such conflicts as we move along. Claims organizations and even northern governments have sometimes blamed INAC, charging that the department is either uninterested in delivering what is required or unable to do so. While it is not true that INAC is uninterested, there is certainly some merit in the assertion that it has difficulty rallying other departments to deliver on obligations that are in fact government-wide.

One solution that has been put forward is to create a special section in a central agency — possibly the Privy Council Office — to manage the process, but this solution is strenuously resisted inside the federal government, since central agencies are not set up to manage programs or budgets involving external clientele. A more realistic approach might be to mandate the publication of a biennial review of implementation, possibly by an external commission, or even an internal body, but with the participation of claims organizations. Sporadic reviews by the auditor general, while of value, are not regular enough to handle the ongoing issues produced by such large agreements. Certainly court cases are not the answer.

It is also important for all parties to recognize that while claims settlements are often characterized as final agreements, they are anything but; we cannot expect them to be immutable. While they all have some provision for formal amendment, the procedures, like those for other forms of constitutional amendment, are far too cumbersome to be used with any frequency. All parties must therefore accept that implementation will be a process of ongoing mutual accommodation. A great deal of frustration can be avoided if settlements are seen as processes, not immutable structures.

Finally, we must recognize the encouraging signs while also acknowledging that patience is necessary. Education is often identified as the greatest hope for the future, and, in spite of some difficulties, there are certainly encouraging signs in this area. In 1997, just 66 of all 230 secondary school graduates (that is, 29 percent) in the NWT were Aboriginal people. By 2005, 168 of 343 graduates (49 percent) were Aboriginal people — not far off the Aboriginal share of the total population (INAC 2007, 13-16). To move from 66 to 168 graduates over an eight-year period is a remarkable achievement. In Nunavut, the rate of increase has been slower, but the education system there, outside of a few large communities, is actually a very new one. And over 900 students will graduate from high school in Nunavut between 2007 and 2012, most of them Inuit, thus adding greatly to the human resource capacities of Inuit in Nunavut.

While this rate of progress can seem frustratingly slow, we often forget how long it took those of us in the south to reach our current levels of education. For example, in 1871, less than 55 percent of people aged 5 to 19 in Canada were enrolled in school, and average daily attendance was 45 percent.[2] By 1921, enrolment had risen to 66 percent, but average daily attendance was still only 72 percent, and it did not rise to 90 percent (essentially what it is today) until the mid-1950s. In the south, then, it took the better part of a century for enrolment in primary and secondary schools to rise to current levels. There are a number of reasons for this — ranging from a lack of infrastructure and transportation, to the fact that many families needed their children to help out at home, to the length of time it took for a cultural and economic shift to occur that would place greater value on education. All of these factors still apply in the more remote areas of the North, and although it took us so long to overcome them ourselves, we expect northern Aboriginal people to do so in just a few years.

But neither should the need for patience vitiate the need to press ahead with both social and physical projects. In doing so, we will sometimes face urgent situations that will be very difficult to manage. The epidemic of suicides in Nunavut is one example; certain aspects of the delivery of health care services provide other examples. When pressing social problems arise, we can argue that the federal government has a duty to step in, even if its intervention is not particularly welcome to the territorial governments. In the end, people matter more than the sensitivities of governments.

Conclusion

THE CANADIAN NORTH IS AN ONGOING STORY, RICH IN OPPORTUNITIES AND RIFE WITH challenges. A rapidly changing set of circumstances faces people who have lived on the land and sea for thousands of years; it also faces those who have chosen to join them in developing a new way of life in a difficult environment. We in the south can and must help, but in the end it will be northerners themselves who decide their own futures.

Notes

1   Although the additional $500 million that
     was announced in the 2008 and 2009 fed-
     eral budgets is certainly welcome.

2   It was necessary to use the somewhat awk-
     ward age category of 5 to 19 in order to
     construct a historically consistent series
     back to the mid-nineteenth century. The
     data used for this are adapted from
     Statistics Canada's *Historical Statistics of
     Canada*, particularly table W67-93
     (Wisenthal 1983).

References

Indian and Northern Affairs Canada (INAC).
     2007. *Northern Indicators 2006*, March.
     Ottawa: First Nations and Northern
     Statistics Section, Strategic Research and
     Analysis Directorate, INAC. Accessed April
     20, 2009. http://dsp-psd.pwgsc. gc.ca/col-
     lection_2007/inac-ainc/R1-24-2006E.pdf

Mayer, Paul. 2007. *Mayer Report on Nunavut
     Devolution*, June. Ottawa: Indian and
     Northern Affairs Canada. Accessed
     September 8, 2008. http://www.ainc-
     inac.net/nr/prs/m-a2007/2-2891-
     m_rprt-eng.pdf

Wisenthal, M. 1983. "Section W: Education."
     Historical Statistics of Canada, edited by F.H.
     Leacy. Cat no. 11-516-XWE. Ottawa:
     Statistics Canada. Accessed September 10,
     2008. http://www.statcan.ca/english/
     freepub/11-516-XIE/final_pdf/english/
     seriesw.pdf

A Fog Hangs over
Arctic Waters

> Four strong winds that blow lonely
> Seven seas that run high
> All those things that don't change
> Come what may
> — "Four Strong Winds," Ian Tyson (1964)

F OR OVER A CENTURY, WINDS OF CHANGE HAVE SWEPT THE CANADIAN NORTH. THOSE winds have blown cold and warm, hard and soft, and the changes have come from all four directions.

East

W INDS FROM THE EAST BROUGHT EUROPEANS AND NORTH AMERICANS OF EUROPEAN ancestry: explorers, whalers, traders, trappers, miners, preachers and teachers arrived in the Canadian North. Some came to get rich quick; others came to spread the word of God or to confidently bring the benefits of European enlightenment and English law.

For much of the twentieth century, Indian agents and colonial governors, called "commissioners," ruled Yukon and the Northwest Territories. The commissioners reported to a Great White Father in Ottawa, also known as the minister of Indian affairs and northern development. Even until the year 1970, this minister acted as the ultimate arbiter of disputes in the affairs of Aboriginal and non-Aboriginal northerners. As a result, the residents of the Indian villages and mining towns, the "homeland" and the "frontier" in the Mackenzie and Yukon watersheds (Berger 1977), had little need to truly get to know their neighbours. Over the next three decades, Aboriginal land claims — or, more particularly, land claims negotiations — changed all that.

Since the eighteenth century, the European powers had been making treaties with the continent's First Nations. For as long as Aboriginal people were the majority in North America, the Europeans negotiated military, trade and peace treaties with them. During the nineteenth century, when European immigration reduced the Aboriginal population to minority status, Britain, then Canada, made land surrender treaties with First Nations. The ceremonies attending negotiations for these treaties — for example, those for Treaty 6 at Fort Carlton in 1876 — still observed international conventions. However, the government party clearly held an unapologetically colonial view of these arrangements — one demonstrated by the passage the same year of the *Indian Act*, which made Aboriginal people wards of the federal state rather than partners bound by nation-to-nation covenants. Of course, the Crown's purpose in signing Treaty 6 and the other numbered treaties was to clear Aboriginal title to make way for a transcontinental railway and, ultimately, the settlement of European farmers — farmers who would not "waste" agricultural lands as Indian hunters were alleged to have done.

By the twentieth century, especially after the signing of Treaty 11 in 1921, governments were tending to regard treaties largely as ancient history. But many major economic projects still required the surrender of Aboriginal title to the lands slated for development. In turn, projects such as Hydro-Québec's James Bay dams, the Beaufort Sea oil development and the Alaska Highway gas pipeline through Yukon brought treaty makers back to the table. Encompassing Aboriginal ownership of tens of thousands of square kilometres of land, hundreds of millions of dollars and quasi-provincial powers for Aboriginal governments, the treaties negotiated across the Canadian North in the late twentieth century are huge improvements over the numbered treaties. Moreover, in 1982, Canada adopted a new constitution that recognizes existing Aboriginal rights. It is the first country in the world to do so.

In his chapter in this volume, Graham White compares the 40-page Inuvialuit treaty of 1984 with the 300-page Nunavut treaty of 1993, which created a new eastern Arctic territory with an Inuit majority. The Inuvialuit text profited stylistically from having only two principal authors. The 1993 Yukon treaty, which is covered with the fingerprints of dozens of lawyers, is longer than the New Testament, but broke new ground by including nonstatus Indians as beneficiaries, establishing third-order Aboriginal governance and making the territorial govern-ment a signatory. In 1999, the Nisga'a treaty in northwestern British Columbia gave constitutional protection to its self-government provisions. Because the Nisga'a agreement is largely based on Yukon precedents, it counts as a northern treaty.

These northern modern treaties represent significant nation-building achievements for Canada, but they are far from being instruments of perfect rec-onciliation for the Aboriginal and settler communities in the region. When the federal government wanted to get a project done quickly, it moved with remark-able speed; to expedite Hydro-Québec's massive hydroelectric power project, it negotiated the James Bay and Northern Quebec Agreement in about two years. Other modern treaties typically took 20 years of tiring talks. This endless talking led some observers to question whether Ottawa's policy objective was treaty set-tlements or just treaty negotiations. A Finance Canada official once justified end-less negotiations by noting that it was cheaper to negotiate treaties than to settle them, but a former Indian and Northern Affairs Canada (INAC) deputy minister doubted the wisdom of this penny-wise approach: "We have capped the costs of the claims, but not of negotiations."[1]

As Inuit Tapiriit Kanatami president Mary Simon observed at the Northern Exposure conference, land claims treaties should be respected as living, breathing documents. Certainly, treaty-making processes could be greatly improved, espe-cially at the implementation stage. The United Nations special rapporteur on treaties concluded in 1999 that, though treaties are honourable instruments with a long history, the greatest disappointment for the indigenous parties was the con-sistent failure of settler governments to faithfully implement what had been nego-tiated (Martinez 1999).

Reporting in 2003 on the implementation of the Gwich'in and Nunavut treaties, Auditor General of Canada Sheila Fraser echoed this critique, pointing out that INAC's "performance on both counts has left considerable room for improvement." Fraser also reflected on the department's failure to reorganize itself to reflect its evolving role in the North following the completion of Aboriginal treaties, self-government agreements and the devolution of province-like pro-grams to territorial governments (Auditor General of Canada 2003).

Aboriginal rights are made meaningful by implementation, Stephanie Irlbacher-Fox and Stephen Mills argue in their chapter in this volume. The suc-cessful implementation of treaties requires government-to-government partnerships and mutual learning. Almost every Aboriginal party to the northern treaties has complaints about the federal failure to fairly and fully implement the provisions of their signed agreements. In 2003, modern treaty organizations representing Aboriginal peoples in northern British Columbia, Yukon, Northwest Territories (NWT), Nunavut, northern Quebec and Labrador formed the Land Claims Agreement Coalition to press their implementation grievances and to urge the Government of Canada to live up to its treaty obligations.

Many implementation issues concerned funding, but inconsistent federal policies provoked other complaints. Because Finance Canada officials refused to respect the arbitration provisions of the Nunavut treaty's dispute resolution chapter, the Inuit political organization Nunavut Tunngavik Incorporated (NTI) threatened to sue. When federal officials left subsequent negotiations, NTI launched a lawsuit. Doug McArthur notes in his chapter in this volume that even after the federal government had acceded to a similar request from the Tlicho nation in the NWT, Yukon First Nations were still trying to gain the section 35 constitutional protection for their self-government agreements that their land claims settlements enjoyed.

Yet federal officials continue to ignore such complaints, including urgent ones concerning implementation funding. Reflecting perhaps the centrally controlled nature of the Harper government, officials now refuse to speak frankly — even on matters about which they hold strong feelings. As former NWT premier George Braden has observed,[2] the Government of Canada may be unhappy with some of the boards and agencies created by land claims agreements to manage environmental or project approval processes, but its representatives have not said as much. Even more bizarre, Canada has so far declined to sit down with the Land Claims Agreement Coalition to work out their differences.[3] Since the "honour of the Crown" is at stake, one hopes that Ottawa will someday mandate somebody to speak plainly not for Indian Affairs or Finance or Justice but for the federal Crown and the Canadian people, on whose behalf the treaties were signed.

For the territories, the introduction of formula financing in 1985 was a truly liberating event. No longer did Yukon and NWT government leaders have to beg for capital expenditure dollars on the streets of Ottawa. The early years of Territorial Formula Financing (TFF) enabled the Yukon government to spend a quarter of its total budget on much-needed infrastructure: roads, schools and colleges. The TFF transfers also provided the means to construct more energy-efficient buildings and reduce operating costs, despite the "perversity" element, which reduced the amount of the transfer by more than a dollar for each dollar of new territorial revenue raised. Because it seemed to discourage economic development, Ottawa has removed this perversity element. That aside, the TFF's hidden genius was that it allowed territorial governments to build their capacities according to their own priorities and their own schedules.

Yukoners were less charmed by federal language policies. It was one thing to make Canada officially bilingual; it was quite another to impose bilingualism in a region where the two solitudes were Aboriginal and non-Aboriginal rather than English and French. After many years of misunderstanding, the federal government and the Yukon territorial government eventually agreed to practical arrangements by which equivalent sums were spent on Aboriginal-language services and French-language ones (Smyth 1996). The NWT legislature agreed to official bilingualism but also gave legal recognition to nine Aboriginal languages. Yet, as Udloriak Hanson and Natan Obed emphasize in their commentaries in this volume, the teaching and honouring of indigenous languages in educational and governmental institutions remain urgent priorities. According to Mary Simon, access to education in Inuktitut is a human rights issue.

The recognition of "existing" Aboriginal rights in the Constitution made northerners proud to call themselves Canadian, and territorial governments willingly contributed to the work of defining those Aboriginal rights. Then, in 1987, just as territorial residents began to contemplate their future as inhabitants of provinces and full partners in Confederation, there came a rude surprise: the Meech Lake Accord. No northerner resisted the notion that Quebec should be reconciled to the new constitution of Canada, which that province's government had refused to sign in 1982. At the same time, no northerner could imagine that through the Meech Lake Accord, Quebec — or any other province — would aspire to a veto power over the creation of new provinces in the North. From here on, the territories' constitutional future would seem cloudy.

West

WITH THE END OF THE COLD WAR, THERE WERE SUDDENLY FRESH BREEZES FROM the west. For northerners who feared being frozen out of Confederation by federal-provincial plans, this presented a wonderful opportunity. Faced with chilly blustering from Canada's provinces, northerners began to believe that warm new friendships with circumpolar cousins would present interesting possibilities. Numerous regional organizations emerged to give expression to this idea.

The Inuit Circumpolar Conference reconnected with its constituents in Russia. The Gwich'in in Alaska, NWT and Yukon found common cause in protecting the Porcupine caribou herd. A NWT contractor built an entire town in Russia, and Russians taught the NWT how to build better ice bridges.[4] Territorial education ministers sat at conference tables in Kiruna and Oslo with ministers from the Nordic nations. Regional governments in the Arctic and sub-Arctic formed the Northern Forum. Northern colleges created a virtual educational entity: the University of the Arctic. Eight nation-states created the Arctic Council, and for the first time an international body invited northern Aboriginal organizations to become permanent participants. These emerging institutions still seem rich with potential.

In political and geopolitical terms, the Arctic is in a period of massive transformation. In the face of ongoing Arctic border and resource disputes, promoting Canadian interests and values will require interaction with all our northern neighbours, as Rob Huebert suggests in his chapter of this book. Moreover, core interests may have to be sacrificed. For example, Canada's disagreement with the United States over the maritime boundary between Alaska and Yukon might be resolved by a joint oil and gas management regime. In his chapter in this volume, Franklyn Griffiths favours a broader approach that is less focused on sovereignty narrowly defined. Debates about policy directions will no doubt heat up as the consequences of climate change become more apparent in the Far North.

North

B Y REPUTE, THE NORTH WIND (TO AGAIN QUOTE IAN TYSON) "SURE CAN BLOW COLD way out there." Northerlies bring winter weather — cold fronts, heavy snowstorms and subzero temperatures. For thousands of years, north winds swept across the Arctic seas, making the ice cap an enduring reality. In recent summers, though, more ice has melted than has been created during the preceding winters. In the summer of 2007, way ahead of scientific projections, the ice cap turned into open water. Northerners saw the effects of this aspect of climatic change in the behaviour of wildlife populations, in the undermining of communities and in the overheated political rhetoric accompanying challenges to Canada's Arctic sovereignty.

Russia, in pursuit of a questionable claim to Arctic resource wealth, had crew members of one of its submarines plant a titanium flag on the ocean floor under the North Pole the same summer. That September, scientists confirmed that Arctic sea ice had shrunk to the smallest area ever recorded. For the first time, it might be possible to open the Northwest Passage to commercial shipping. Canada seemed unready to face any of these challenges.

Even New Yorkers seem to know that polar bear populations are in decline (Yaeger 2007), but, based on traditional knowledge, Inuit hunters question scientists' numbers. Writing in the *New York Times* on January 5, 2008, Alaska governor Sarah Palin also cast doubt on the scientific basis for listing polar bears as an endangered species (2008). Still, environmentalists fear that Alaska and the American oil industry resist listing polar bears mainly because that decision might curtail oil drilling within the bears' habitat on land or at sea. What cannot be questioned is that the ice pack from which the bears hunt and breed is shrinking.

World media have turned their cameras on the polar bears, but many in the North wish that journalists would focus more on the impacts of climate change on the area's humans. Both on- and offshore, oil exploration could disrupt caribou migrations and therefore the Gwich'in way of life. Pacific salmon are appearing in Arctic char streams like the Firth River. Coastal communities are at serious risk as warmer waters erode the shore ice that once functioned as a natural breakwater against pounding waves during winter storms. From Alaska to Nunavut, ongoing erosion threatens coastal infrastructure, the marine economy and Inuit cultures. In her commentary in this volume, Sheila Watt-Cloutier calls this an "environmental disaster." In other locations, melting permafrost has destabilized buildings and made long-standing communities unsustainable. Forced relocation could turn their inhabitants into "climate refugees" (Matthiessen 2007).

These events bolster the case for considering scientific research and traditional knowledge as necessary foundations for solid public policy. In his chapter for this collection, Michael Bravo sees the need for a new Arctic science "social contract" between science and its stakeholders. Recognition of northern voices and traditional knowledge, along with higher standards of consent, has brought scientists to accept their responsibility to contribute to dialogues on self-determination and nation building. Canada needs to view research as investment, not as expenditure. Front and centre should be capacity building to address knowledge deficits. For example, no existing body audits either the positive or the negative impacts of northern science. At the Northern Exposure conference, Violet Ford noted that NGOs could misuse science — sometimes to the disadvantage of the Inuit. Everybody needs to ask questions about the relationship between scientists, southern expectations, Inuit governments and Inuit traditional knowledge, she argues.

With the Northwest Passage potentially open to summer shipping, Canada finds itself unable to even monitor traffic through those straits. Nunavut encompasses two-thirds of our country's coastline but lacks active harbours. In fact, Canada is the only Arctic nation without a deepwater port from which to access the northern seas. We have no capacity to respond to a military threat, and at least three neighbours have challenged our sovereignty. As Terry Fenge explains in a *Policy Options* article, "The nightmare of many Inuit is to see a rusty, convenience-flagged, single-hulled, inadequately crewed oil tanker laboriously navigating the Northwest Passage" (2007). However, Griffiths thinks Canada has little to fear from "a few tramp ships or rust-bucket tankers, even a single rogue ship," and mocks "academic purveyors of polar peril." Still, he might not dismiss Fenge's thought that Arctic residents would sleep more peacefully were Canada to fully exercise its sovereignty and jurisdiction over the waters of the Canadian Arctic Archipelago. A key component of that exercise would be the faithful implementation of the Nunavut Land Claims Agreement. Provisions of the Agreement that have not yet been implemented, such as the creation of a Nunavut marine council, would, once enacted, assure Inuit that muscular environmental and safety regimes do apply to ships navigating the Northwest Passage.

South

IRONICALLY, ARCTIC WARMING — CAUSED BY THE HUMAN HUNGER FOR SCARCE ENERGY resources — is fuelling a new southern rush to tap the oil and gas buried beneath northern lands and waters. Climate change is opening up previously inaccessible areas for exploitation, at the same time exposing Arctic communities to greater risk of environmental degradation. Though they have contributed very little to global warming, Arctic residents are among the earliest victims of climate change. They may receive little in the way of benefits from the extraction of energy riches from their homelands, and faulty public policy choices could saddle them with a ruined environment, uprooted communities and extreme cultural alienation.

In the interests of economic justice, environmental sanity and Canadian sovereignty, it would make strategic sense to devolve responsibility for mineral and energy resources to northern governments. In the simplest of terms, territories seek the powers that provinces enjoy. They want control — jurisdiction and management — of the natural resources beneath the lands and waters within their political boundaries. Only this kind of control will win them a major share of the revenues that flow from resource development.

Territories do *not* want the routine management of existing INAC programs transferred to them, any more than First Nations desired only the delegation of *Indian Act* powers. The administrative transfer of the underfunded, poorly staffed programs, which now manage the northern minerals paperwork but which do not effectively manage northern lands, would only frustrate Nunavut. Mere as-is/where-is program dumping could bankrupt the territory. Inuit control of oil and gas resource revenues, however, would spur the development of Nunavut's private sector and give the territory's children and grandchildren access to private sector employment and business opportunities. Indeed, this is Nunavut's best hope for prosperity beyond the days of federal transfers and federal dependency. Nunavummiut (the citizens of Nunavut) do not want to be clerks in a federal storehouse. They want to own the store.

Regrettably, big question marks punctuate most statements about federal intentions for devolution. Before becoming prime minister, Stephen Harper promised that the northern territories would be the primary beneficiaries of northern natural resource revenues in any devolution deal with a Conservative government. After the election, like the winter sun, that promise quickly sank from sight.

Article 23 of the Nunavut Land Claims Agreement obliges both the federal and the territorial governments to build a representative public service in the Nunavut territory. Eighty-five percent of Nunavut's people are Inuit, many of them children. The territorial government has so far recruited 51 percent of its employees from the Inuit community. At less than 35 percent Inuit employment, the federal government offices in Nunavut have done less well. In fact, a recent communication from the Director General of INAC's Implementation Branch shows things going from bad to worse.[5] This situation will amplify appeals for federal financing of the recommendations in Thomas Berger's report for an over-haul of the territory's education and training systems (2006).

Every senior official in the territorial government understands that only a massive investment in training can produce the number of accountants, geologists, engineers, managers and technicians Nunavut needs to properly manage a north-ern minerals, oil and gas program. Nobody seems to know how much the federal government really cares about the capacity question; federal officials talk about it a lot, but mainly in terms of supposed Inuit inadequacies. Inuit incapacity is even used to justify the federal refusal to negotiate jurisdiction over oil and gas beneath Nunavut's internal waters — a management responsibility that the territory has offered to contract back to the National Energy Board, as did the Yukon Territory. Nevertheless, the Government of Nunavut and Nunavut Tunngavik Incorporated have both indicated a readiness to negotiate a capacity-building agreement, including funding commitments, with the federal government.

Few Canadians realize how solidly Canada bases its sovereignty claims to the Arctic on thousands of years of Inuit occupancy and use of Arctic lands, waters and sea ice. In his expansive *Policy Options* piece, Fenge argues that the Inuit in general, and the Nunavut Land Claims Agreement in particular, are the bedrock of the country's claims (he also notes that in 2006, nobody could have predicted that Arctic sovereignty would be at the top of the government's agenda in the October 2007 Speech from the Throne) (2007). On taking office, Stephen Harper echoed some of John Diefenbaker's romanticism about northern develop-ment while replaying Reaganite fantasies of warrior potency, but he showed little of Brian Mulroney's Main Street pragmatism. The idea of armed icebreakers might appeal to people in denial about global warming. But ports and roads work best in locations where they can help mineral development and where not just the military and industry but also local populations can use them ("New Arctic" 2007). As the child of a northern company town, Mulroney knew that develop-ment was primarily about people. Before leaving office in 1993, his government settled the Yukon and Nunavut treaties. The Inuit have documented their con-tinuous utilization of 3.8 million square kilometres of land and ocean, including the eastern portion of the Northwest Passage, an area the United States views as an "international strait."[6] Yet when Prime Minister Stephen Harper uses the slo-gan "Use it or lose it" in relation to Arctic sovereignty, he seems to forget the very people who have used the area for centuries. Harper's government has yet to discover the wisdom of invoking the Nunavut Land Claims Agreement to defend our Arctic sovereignty.

Regardless, northerners cheered Harper's promises to defend Canada's Arctic sovereignty, as they did those of leaders who responded to previous challenges. When Americans sailed the *Polar Sea* through the Northwest Passage in 1985, protesters dropped leaflets onto the vessel from a chartered aircraft. In response to the *Polar Sea* challenge and an Inuit claim to lands and waters based on use and occupancy studies published in 1977, Canada redrew its boundaries to enclose the Arctic Archipelago and its internal waters. As stated at the time by Minister of External Relations Joe Clark, "Canada's sovereignty in the Arctic is indivisible. It embraces land, sea and ice. It extends without interruption to the seaward-facing coasts of the Arctic Islands. These islands are joined and not divided by the waters between them."[7]

All three territorial governments champion Canada's Arctic assertions. Nunavummiut strongly believe that devolving responsibility for managing northern resources to the territory would reinforce the country's sovereignty claims. Yet the Inuit have been forced to sue the federal government for its failure to implement their hard-won treaty. As Mary Simon has said, "Sovereignty begins at home."[8] Federal-territorial-Aboriginal cooperation could help Canada secure an international treaty to protect the Arctic environment — especially if that treaty guaranteed international acceptance of high standards for energy exploration and development, along with a mandated role for Arctic communities in social and environmental impact monitoring. To serve the greater good of fighting climate change, some issues, such as the Canada-United States contretemps over the status of the Northwest Passage, could be settled on an "agree-to-disagree" basis (to quote Griffiths in this volume).

Despite frequent announcements about development and sovereignty, the federal government still hides its ultimate intentions toward the people of the North. Two views about Ottawa's designs have currency. The first is that certain federal officials have a hidden agenda to correct a historical error in the drawing of Nunavut's political boundaries at the land claims negotiation table before 1993. They would make this "correction" by resisting territorial claims to jurisdiction and the right to manage mineral resources beneath the oil-rich waters within Nunavut's "provincial" boundaries. In this scenario, national security, economic necessity or the public interest might provide the justification. Nevertheless, as former Nunavut premier Paul Okalik has indicated, Canada established the Nunavut territory by way of a constitutionally protected treaty and an act of Parliament.[9] Some officials at INAC may be infected by deeply colonial attitudes, but it is too harsh to brand every diligent INAC official an agent of an evil empire.

The second, and more credible, view is that the federal government is truly undecided. Arguably, few federal officials truly understand the internal-waters argument as articulated by the Nunavut government. Of those, very few understand the argument well enough to appreciate its potential value in supporting Canada's Arctic sovereignty cause. This small group of officials may understand that Canada does not want to create a precedent in Nunavut that might complicate relations with coastal jurisdictions among the provinces. Canada will not concede territorial or provincial jurisdiction over lands beyond the low-water mark anywhere in the country until a court says it must. This tiny federal elite might even favour the kind of comanagement and revenue-sharing arrangements negotiated between Ottawa and Newfoundland and Nova Scotia as models applicable to the Northwest Territories or Nunavut. Skeptics would respond by pointing out that Ottawa has floated nothing like these models in negotiations at Yellowknife or Iqaluit.

Because not enough senior people understand the issue and too few view it as nationally significant, there may be no internal-waters negotiations in the near term in either the Northwest Territories or Nunavut. (Yukon already has a devolution deal.) What this might mean for the policy coherence of Canada's Arctic strategies, one can only guess. Rather than a policy wall, there exists today a policy void. What from a distance looks like a mammoth iceberg may be just a thick policy fog up close.

Nunavut is not looking for a definitive answer from Ottawa to the marine-areas or internal-waters questions, only a commitment to negotiate. Federal officials suggest that the Nunavut government must take baby steps toward improved administrative capacity before Ottawa will seriously discuss its jurisdictional case. But administrative capacity cannot trump jurisdictional rights. Nunavut may be willing to negotiate cooperative administrative structures, but it will not abandon its jurisdictional cause before negotiations even begin. After the Meech Lake experience, to do so would be utterly foolish. The country could use an honest discussion about territorial hopes and federal fears. What Ottawa's officials propose instead sounds exactly like the kind of paternalism Prime Minister Harper has promised to end.

For Nunavut, the land claim settlement was the first step toward what George Berthe, in his presentation at the 2007 Montebello conference referred to as "decolonization." The second step was the creation of the territorial government. Devolution should be the third step, but fears abound that Ottawa may not show the political will to deal honourably with oil and gas management issues related to Nunavut's internal waters. Because federal mandates are shrouded in mysterious mists, devolution negotiations could "go south."

In his chapter, McArthur argues very persuasively that the North has achieved a de facto constitutional settlement, one that includes federal caps on resource revenue sharing. Yet uncertainties about the territories' constitutional future, triggered by the Meech Lake Accord, are exacerbated by disputes over implementation of northern land claims and by Ottawa's refusal to enter into negotiations about the energy resources in Nunavut's internal waters. As Jack Hicks pointed out at the conference, devolution might be the only prospect the territory has for building a private sector and for ensuring prosperity, physical health and mental health for future generations. If that's all there is — if devolution is the constitutional endgame for the territories — then northerners must be extremely careful about their next moves.

When the world has taken the last of the North's diamonds, oil and ice, what will be left for the people there? Will they have heritage funds or holes in the ground? Northerners heard the 2007 Speech from the Throne. Now they wonder if the federal government, in writing its Integrated Northern Strategy, will listen to them. One thing is sure: no northern strategy worthy of the name can ignore the legitimate aspirations of northern peoples. In order to make such a strategy effective, the federal government must take these steps:

- Develop the Integrated Northern Strategy in a dialogue with territorial citizens.
- Fully implement northern land claims agreements and self-government agreements, for these treaties are the cornerstones of the North's future societies.
- Negotiate devolution agreements based on the legal boundaries of the territories, the right of citizens to enjoy the benefits of resource revenues earned from their lands and waters, and the benefits to Canada of building capacity through jurisdictional transfers and cooperative management regimes.

- Recognize that fully implementing the northern treaties and fairly negotiating devolution of province-like powers over resources would strengthen Canada's Arctic sovereignty claims.
- Realize that cooperation with other Arctic nations and with territorial and Aboriginal governments can assist in the struggles against climate change and for environmental protection.
- Clearly state federal intentions with respect to the future of the northern territories as partners in Confederation.
- Reorganize INAC to reflect the department's emerging roles as facilitator and funder of treaty implementation and devolved programs.
- Finally acknowledge that to uphold the honour of the Crown, the Prime Minister, not INAC, must join the other parties in resolving outstanding northern treaty implementation issues.

Four strong winds blow back and forth across the Arctic, but an icy fog hangs over Nunavut's internal waters. The North needs some sunshine to burn the fog away, and, as Yukoners are ever ready to concede, the weather — or, at least, Environment Canada — is a federal responsibility.

Notes

1   Steve Penikett, Kenn Borek Air Limited, con-
    versation with the author, January 29, 2008
    (Penikett 2006).
2   Comment made at the Montebello confer-
    ence on which this volume is based, in
    October 2007.
3   Terry Fenge commented on this point at
    the 2007 Montebello conference.
4   Dennis Patterson, e-mail to the author,
    December 3, 2007.
5   Terry Sewell, letter to David Akoak, Charlie
    Evalik and John Merritt, November 19,
    2007.
6   Fenge also made this point in 2007; see note 3.
7   Joe Clark, *Edited Hansard,* September 10,
    1985, p. 6463.
8   Mary Simon made this comment at the
    2007 Montebello conference on which this
    volume is based.
9   Paul Okalik made this comment at the
    2007 Montebello conference on which this
    volume is based.

References

Auditor General of Canada. 2003. "Indian and
    Northern Affairs Canada: Transferring
    Federal Responsibilities to the North."
    Chap. 8 of *2003 Report of the Auditor
    General of Canada,* November. Ottawa:
    Office of the Auditor General of Canada.

Berger, Thomas. 1977. *Northern Frontier, Northern
    Homeland: The Report of the Mackenzie Valley
    Pipeline Inquiry.* 2 vols. Ottawa: Ministry of
    Supply and Services Canada.

————. 2006. *Conciliator's Final Report:
    Nunavut Land Claims Agreement
    Implementation.* Ottawa: Indian and
    Northern Affairs Canada. Accessed April 7,
    2008. http://www.ainc-inac.gc.ca/pr/agr/
    nu/lca/index_e.html

Fenge, Terry. 2007. "Inuit and the Nunavut Land
    Claims Agreement: Supporting Canada's
    Arctic Sovereignty." *Policy Options* 29 (1):
    84-8. Montreal: IRPP.

Martinez, Miguel Alfonso. 1999. *Study on Treaties,
    Agreements and Other Constructive
    Arrangements between States and Indigenous
    Populations: Final Report,* June 22, 51st ses-
    sion, provisional agenda item 7. New York:
    United Nations Economic and Social
    Council Sub-commission on Prevention of
    Discrimination and Protection of
    Minorities. Accessed April 9, 2008.
    http://www.unhchr.ch/Huridocda/Huridoca.
    nsf/0/696c51cf6f20b8bc802567c4003793
    ec?Opendocument

Matthiessen, Peter. 2007. "Alaska: Big Oil and
    the Inupiat-Americans." *New York Review of
    Books,* November 22.

"New Arctic Army Facility, Navy Port Support
    Battle for the North." 2007. *Edmonton Sun,*
    August 10. Accessed April 9, 2008.
    http://www.edmontonsun.com/News/Canada/
    2007/08/10/4408489.html

Palin, Sarah. 2008. "Bearing Up." *New York
    Times,* January 5. Accessed April 9, 2008.
    http://www.nytimes.com/2008/01/05/
    opinion/05palin.html?_r=1&oref=slogin

Penikett, Tony. 2006. *Reconciliation: First Nations
    Treaty Making in British Columbia.*
    Vancouver: Douglas and McIntyre.

Smyth, Steven. 1996. "Colonialism and Language
    in Canada's North: A Yukon Case Study."
    Arctic 49 (2): 155-61. Accessed April 9,
    2008. http://pubs.aina.ucalgary.ca/
    arctic/Arctic49-2-155.pdf

Yaeger, Lynn. 2007. "Drowning Polar Bears: The
    New Lumps of Coal." *Village Voice,*
    November 27. Accessed April 9, 2008.
    http://www.villagevoice.com/nyclife/0748,
    yaeger,78483,15.html

The New Northern

Policy Universe

The Arctic is an essential part of Canada's history. One of our Fathers of
Confederation, D'Arcy McGee, spoke of Canada as a northern nation, bounded by
the blue rim of the ocean. Canadians see in our North an expression of our deep-
est aspirations: our sense of exploration, the beauty and the bounty of our land,
and our limitless potential...But the North needs new attention. New opportunities are emerging across the Arctic, and new challenges from other shores.

Speech from the Throne, 2007

W HILE CANADA'S NORTH HAS INDEED LONG HELD A SPECIAL PLACE IN OUR
country's narrative, its presence on governments' policy agenda has tended to ebb and flow over time according to domestic political and economic circumstances (see Frances Abele's chapter in this volume). The reasons behind the
current surge of interest and renewed attention, however, are clearly global in
nature. As Rob Huebert has observed elsewhere, "The Arctic is facing a transformation of epic proportions at almost every level. Furthermore the rate of change
is accelerating in ways that are not yet understood. There are three main factors
that are contributing to this change: 1) climate change; 2) resource development;
and 3) geopolitical transformations" (Huebert 2008, 19).

The effects of climate change can already be seen in all circumpolar
regions. Beyond their impact on ecological, economic and human systems, they
give rise to significant global strategic issues, as previously remote and inaccessible areas are poised to become less so. For Canada, the increase in marine traffic
and access that is likely to occur with the opening of the Northwest Passage has
enormous economic and geopolitical implications, especially given the passage's
unresolved status as internal waters or an international strait. With the prospect
of vast (discovered and undiscovered) reserves of oil, natural gas and minerals in

the Arctic, the whole region is fast becoming a focal point for claims from a number of countries with Arctic shorelines, as Huebert points out in this volume.[1]

No matter how they play out, these forces of change will have a significant impact on Canada's northern communities. Northerners will inevitably be faced with complex and unprecedented challenges that, depending on how they are managed, will present either threats or opportunities for the region's inhabitants. This dimension often receives insufficient attention in federal government policy statements and expert analyses of strategic interests. This is unfortunate, because sound public policy for Canada's North needs to address the ways in which the potential transformation of the region, which has a population of just under 115,000,[2] will affect residents' daily lives.

The 2007 Speech from the Throne included the following commitment: "Our Government will bring forward an integrated northern strategy focused on strengthening Canada's sovereignty, protecting our environmental heritage, promoting economic and social development, and improving and devolving governance, so that northerners have greater control over their destinies" (Government of Canada 2007). Although the federal government has yet to issue a policy statement outlining the strategy, it has made several announcements and significant budget commitments related to each of the four objectives set out in the Speech from the Throne (see appendix). While Ottawa's efforts so far seem to be more focused on addressing sovereignty concerns and fostering future economic development, one of the overarching messages to come out of the research and commentary in this volume is the central importance of the other two objectives. As many of our contributors reiterated, environmental protection will be essential to preserve ecosystems, human health and quality of life (including maintaining Aboriginal customs and traditions) in the context of climate change. As for social development and improved governance, we believe these constitute the true prerequisites for northerners to "have greater control over their destinies." Northerners and their governments must be better equipped to benefit from any future resource and other development that may occur. They also need to have the capacity to play an active part in shaping and adapting the Arctic of the future, the benefits of which should be broadly shared.

A truly integrated northern strategy is what is needed — one that takes into account the global forces that are affecting life in the North and its prospects, and that also places a particular focus on the well-being of its communities and residents. Put another way, what is required is a new northern policy universe that, with the full participation of northerners, will lead to changes that will strengthen the economic, social and human capital of the region.

The main purposes of this concluding chapter are to identify the key elements of this policy universe and to offer a number of observations about potential actions. As policy-makers look to the medium and longer terms, they will face important and complex challenges, such as how to improve the life chances of northerners (particularly Aboriginal peoples), address inadequacies in treaty implementation and the entanglement of jurisdictions (notably in the regulatory field) and find more equitable ways of sharing resource revenues. We will address these interrelated issues later in the chapter. However, before presenting our analysis, we look briefly at the three overarching factors of climate change, sovereignty and resource development.

<h1 style="text-align:center">Climate Change,
Sovereignty and
Resource Development</h1>

Climate Change

I N JANUARY 2009, AS THIS VOLUME WAS BEING COMPLETED, A NATIONAL ROUND TABLE on the polar bear was held in Winnipeg. This unprecedented event followed predictions that two-thirds of the world's polar bears (more than half of which live in Canada) would disappear by the middle of this century (Amstrup, Marcot, and Douglas 2007, 36). The main cause is the disruption of their habitat, notably the shrinking of the polar ice cap as a result of climate change.[3] There are good reasons why the polar bear has become the poster animal of the campaign against climate change, beyond its iconic character. Because the Arctic is extremely exposed and sensitive to climate-related change, that is where concrete evidence of the far-reaching implications of this worldwide phenomenon is first manifesting itself.[4]

The phenomenon of shrinking Arctic ice has been explained as follows: "Melting ice leaves behind open ocean water that has a much lower reflectivity (or albedo) than that of ice. Open ocean water absorbs about 80 percent more solar radiation than sea ice does. And so as the sun warms the ocean, even more ice melts, in a vicious circle" (Homer-Dixon 2007). Although this process is far from linear, it is occurring at a faster rate than previously anticipated. In September 2008, the extent of sea ice in the Arctic region as a whole was 34 percent smaller than the long-term average from 1979 (when satellite measurements began) to 2000 (although it was 9 percent larger than the record for the smallest area, set in 2007). Perennial sea ice, the year-round layer that remains even when the surrounding seasonal ice melts, has been shrinking rapidly from year to year: it used to cover 50 to 60 percent of the Arctic, but in March 2008 it covered less than 30 percent of the region. Based on current estimates of the thickness and extent of the ice cap, scientists have predicted that the Canadian Arctic will be free of seasonal ice by 2015 or even 2013.[5]

The most important consequence of these changes is the increased navigability of Arctic marine waters, which will provide greater access to the region. In mid-September 2007, the main channel of the Northwest Passage (Lancaster Sound to M'Clure Strait – see map in Franklyn Griffiths's chapter) had been open (nearly ice free) for about five weeks. Researchers, political commentators and other observers predict that these trends will expand intra-Arctic access as well as south-to-Arctic shipping for resource exploration and development, commercial and tourism activities, and a myriad of government functions (for example, security and environmental monitoring).

On the important matter of shipping, once the Northwest Passage through the Parry Channel becomes ice free, it will provide a shipping route that is considerably shorter than those used at present. For instance, it is 15,930 kilometres by sea from London to Yokohama through the Northwest Passage, compared to 23,300 kilometres via the Panama Canal (Lasserre 2007, 39). However, some have questioned the imminence of a new marine highway. For example, Frédéric Lasserre has pointed out that the Northwest Passage could not accommodate the largest cargo ships now being built. In addition, the Northern Sea Route (north of Siberia) presents a viable alternative, in part because sea ice in the Russian Arctic has been shrinking more rapidly than in the Canadian Arctic (40). In light of this, Griffiths suggests that a marked increase in commercial shipping between the Atlantic and Pacific oceans through the Northwest Passage should not be expected in the near term.

Looking beyond the potential for expanded shipping and passage within Canadian Arctic waters, climate change is already having an enormous impact on the lives of northerners. A recent report on the impacts of and adaptation to climate change documents some of the profound consequences of climate-induced changes in permafrost, sea ice, lake ice and snow cover on infrastructure maintenance and design as well as the biodiversity issues and effects on humans resulting from shifts in species availability, accessibility and quality (Furgal and Prowse 2008 and Huebert in this volume). As Mary Simon notes in her commentary, "The effects of climate change in the Arctic are wide-reaching — they affect the health of Inuit and of wildlife and ecosystems, and they disrupt the already fragile economies of our communities." Hunting and travel have been affected by shorter ice-road seasons, and there are reports of sightings of insects and birds never seen before in the region. Those pursuing traditional and subsistence-based ways of life in the more remote Aboriginal communities may be most vulnerable to these effects (Furgal and Prowse 2008).

Much of the vast research program undertaken for the 2007-08 International Polar Year (IPY) was intended to lead to a better understanding of these complex changes and their implications. As Hanne Petersen suggests in this volume, the participating countries need to sustain the momentum of research activity the IPY helped trigger, and make use of these results to guide their future policies. However, the years ahead will also require concrete action in a range of sectors, in collaboration with northerners, aimed at mitigating the effects of climate change and helping them adapt to its inevitable impact.

Sovereignty

On the geopolitical front, the major powers will obviously be interested in the Arctic for economic and strategic reasons. Russia in particular has made clear its intention to become considerably more active in the area along its northern shores. Russia's assertions of its Arctic interests — such as its planting of a Russian flag on the North Pole sea floor in 2007 and militarily "testing" Canadian Arctic boundaries in 2009 — certainly caught the world's attention, as has its announcement that it intends to rebuild its submarine force to be stationed in its northern naval bases. But the United States, Denmark and Canada have also become more actively engaged in this new global "hot spot" that is the Arctic — a magnetic epicentre where melting polar ice is engaging global environmental, economic and strategic forces and players.

As Franklyn Griffiths and Rob Huebert demonstrate in their chapters, this nexus of interests explains the heightened attention paid by the Government of

Canada and others to safeguarding their Arctic sovereignty. Huebert provides a thorough survey of issues that have arisen related to Canada's claims in the region.[6] Some are minor, such as the dispute with Denmark over tiny Hans Island. Others, related to potential economic development, are more significant. One of these is the disagreement between Canada and the United States over a portion of the Beaufort Sea where there may be extensive oil and gas reserves. But the most politically salient issue concerns sovereignty over the Northwest Passage, which Canada claims as part of its historic internal waters, giving it authority to pass legislation and impose regulations on all Canadians and foreigners on the passage's ice and waters. The United States has long disagreed with Canada's claim, arguing that the passage is an international strait, a position that was reiterated in a presidential directive on Arctic region policy issued during the Bush administration's final weeks (Bush 2009).

Several of the Harper government's initiatives since 2007 have — wisely we believe — avoided pursuing legal resolution of its claim over the Northwest Passage. Huebert notes that it is not certain the International Court of Justice would actually side with Canada. Rather, the federal government is concentrating on establishing a heightened presence and a monitoring role in the Arctic. Increased military surveillance is to be bolstered by enhanced scientific knowledge (for example, completing the geological mapping of the continental shelf off Canada's northern coasts and building a world-class Arctic research station). In August 2008, it was announced that the *Arctic Waters Pollution Prevention Act* would be amended to allow the Canadian government to regulate all shipping and enforce environmental laws in zones up to 200 nautical miles (an increase from the present 100 nautical miles) offshore (see appendix).

The Harper government's emphasis on heightened surveillance and regulation is a sound policy stance, although it remains to be seen whether Canada's material capacity and presence on the ground will increase enough to turn the government's promises into reality. In this context, Griffiths proposes an alternative approach. He argues that Canada needs to move beyond military presence and surveillance to embrace a much broader agenda based on Arctic stewardship. Such an agenda would entail using "existing and new institutions to address a host of matters relating to the Arctic environment, health, social and economic development, human resources and circumpolar affairs." Along the same lines, in this volume Sheila Watt-Cloutier advocates "respectful stewardship of the land through natural resource comanagement bodies."

Looking at Arctic sovereignty more broadly, we believe that two directions deserve particular attention. First, it will be important to work much more closely with other Arctic countries to improve knowledge and develop joint approaches on climate change, pollution and sustainable development. As Huebert notes, the Cold War inhibited the development of multilateral cooperation in the North. Now there are forums through which this multilateral cooperation can take place, such as the Arctic Council, established in the 1990s with Canadian leadership. There is nevertheless clear potential for more concerted action that is not unduly focused on differences about legal claims.[7] In their article for *Policy Options*, Terry Fenge and Tony Penikett call on Canada to play a more assertive role in the Arctic Council's sustainable development activities (2009). There have recently been some signs that the federal government intends to do just that as Canada prepares to assume chairmanship of the Arctic Council in 2013.[8]

A second direction concerns the role of northern residents in safeguarding Canada's Arctic sovereignty. Griffiths notes that the 1993 Nunavut Land Claims Agreement called for a marine council to provide advice to government agencies on marine matters in the settlement area covered by the Agreement. He suggests that if the council were enlarged to include representation from the Beaufort Sea-Mackenzie Delta area, it could become a key forum "for priority setting and analytical input into federal government policy on High Arctic issues."

In our view, suggestions along the lines of those made by Griffiths and Watt-Cloutier merit serious consideration. So do other avenues that draw on the knowledge and perspectives of indigenous peoples living in the Canadian Arctic and give northerners a larger say in decisions that will affect their immediate communities.

Resource Development

The 2008 United States Geological Survey estimated that the Arctic as a whole contains more than one-fifth of undiscovered, recoverable oil and natural gas resources. A recent review undertaken for Indian and Northern Affairs Canada (INAC) suggests that 33 percent of Canada's conventionally recoverable resources of natural gas and 25 percent of its recoverable light crude oil are located in the NWT, Nunavut and the Arctic offshore (INAC 2008, 9). This explains why the prospect of a more accessible Arctic has led to a flurry of activity on the part of multinational oil companies. For instance, Royal Dutch Shell spent more than US$2 billion in 2008 to acquire drilling leases in Alaska's Chukchi Sea. In 2007,

Exxon Mobil and Canada's Imperial Oil bid nearly US$600 million for a large exploration block in the Beaufort Sea. Such developments strengthen the perception of the Arctic as the new frontier. And much like the resource-rich frontiers of previous eras, this one is subject to the boom-and-bust nature of resource development, but even more so due to the very high costs and uncertainty associated with exploration and operating in the North (see Terry Fenge's commentary in this volume). The sudden halt, slowdown and postponement of some development activities in the North in the last few months of 2008, just as a worldwide economic recession and financial crisis took hold, attest to that.

Looking to the longer term, the 2008 report of the Arctic Council's Protection of the Arctic Marine Environment Working Group presents four development scenarios based on greater or lesser resource demand, on the one hand, and greater or lesser stability in governance, on the other:

> Arctic race: High demand and unstable governance set the stage for a "no holds barred" rush for Arctic wealth and resources.
> Arctic saga: High demand and stable governance lead to a healthy rate of development that includes concern for the preservation of Arctic ecosystems and cultures.
> Polar lows: Low demand and unstable governance lead to a murky and under-developed future for the Arctic.
> Polar preserve: Low demand and stable governance slow development while introducing an extensive Arctic eco-preserve with stringent "no-shipping zones." (Arctic Council 2008)

Despite current low energy and resource prices, it is reasonable to assume that as global economic growth resumes, the demand for the Arctic's resources will rebound and prices will recover. This means that the most probable scenarios will be "Arctic race" or "Arctic saga," or some combination of the two. Moreover, the resource players in the circumpolar North will likely go beyond the Arctic states to include China, Japan and others.

It is nevertheless unlikely that resource development will proceed as quickly as some had anticipated. The cost of exploiting nonrenewable resources in the North is very high, and the drop in oil prices since mid-2008 has already dampened exploration activities. Regardless of the pace at which development ultimately proceeds, oil, gas and mining activity can provide significant benefits for northern residents. As Tom Hoefer notes in this volume, Aboriginal workers have been a significant part of the labour force at the Diavik diamond mine since it opened. Larger projects such as these provide training and employment opportunities for workers and start-up momentum for new local businesses as well as direct and indirect benefits for local suppliers and neighbouring communities. On the other hand, they may also bring environmental and social disruption and, in the case of certain resources such as uranium, concern about the long-term consequences.

We now turn to the elements of a new northern policy universe that takes account of the global forces just discussed and is founded on a broader view of balanced and participatory development.

Northerners and Their Communities: Winning the Battle to Lose the War?

M ANY COMMUNITIES IN NORTHERN CANADA ARE LOCATED IN SOME OF THE MOST spectacular landscapes on the planet, with abundant fresh air and water and ready access to healthy foods from the land and sea, as well as quiet and solitude in good measure. They benefit from the neighbourliness and community solidarity that is characteristic of the North's indigenous societies, reinforced by the tendency of all people living in small places to get to know each other and to readily offer mutual aid.

If the North has many advantages as a healthy place to live, it also has major social challenges that must be addressed. As Jack Hicks shows in his chapter, the suicide rate in Nunavut is alarmingly high compared to all other jurisdictions in Canada, and young Inuit men are most in danger. While Nunavut has the highest suicide rate, it is a fact that all over northern Canada, Aboriginal young people, especially young men, are far more likely to kill themselves than are their non-Aboriginal peers. As Hicks argues, no simple generalizations should be made about why this long-term human disaster continues to unfold. It seems possible, though, that it is related to the stresses of the rapid changes that have visited northern societies in the last half century and, perhaps, to certain structural features of the new communities that have been created.

It is also clear that these high suicide rates are a manifestation of a number of interrelated social problems. Among these, rates of alcohol and drug abuse

Frances Abele, Thomas J. Courchene,   570
F. Leslie Seidle and France St-Hilaire

and associated violent crime are already high in some places and growing in others. As in the rest of Canada, literacy, education and employment levels are lower for Aboriginal people than for non-Aboriginal people.[9] While in many parts of the North Aboriginal languages, cultures and traditions remain strong, there are some worrying signs. Only three northern Aboriginal languages are considered endangered but for all of them, to varying degrees, there is reason to be concerned about their future vitality.[10] There is also a pronounced disparity, almost everywhere in the North, between incomes and employment opportunities in the few regional centres (such as the capital cities) and those in the more than 100 small, predominantly Aboriginal communities. There is some early indication of a drain of young people from these communities to the regional centres and the south. In short, a pattern of uneven development may be emerging.

Southern and northern Canadian society benefits from the existence of viable and healthy communities in all parts of the North. Canada's national purposes have long been served by the presence of the northern indigenous peoples, as their communities provide support to Canadian sovereignty claims, members for the resident militia who have monitored the northern boundary and, of course, destinations for tourists and bases for mineral explorers who wish to share in the North's bounty. More important, northern communities are home to various indigenous peoples whose members choose to remain close to the land and who keep their cultures, languages and practices alive through their harvesting, artistic and recreational uses of the land, ice and sea. Concerns about the future of this traditional culture and its importance are eloquently expressed by our contributors in the section "Voices of the New Generation."

A New Approach to Sustaining Healthy Northern Communities

Clearly there is work to be done to create the conditions under which all northern individuals, families and communities will have an opportunity to live satisfying and balanced lives. While not all will choose to live in the smaller northern communities, or indeed to remain in the North at all, it is in Canada's interest that those who do are able to lead a satisfying life.

In the healthiest small communities, the connection to the land is still strong, and substantial numbers of people make their living in the mixed economy. As Frances Abele explains in her chapter, the term mixed economy, as applied to northern communities, refers to the household-based organization of

Northern Exposure: Peoples, Powers and
Prospects in Canada's North

production and sharing based upon income from a variety of sources: wages, commodity sales (art, fur, crafts), harvesting from the land and transfer payments. Where the mixed economy is able to thrive, it can foster overall community well-being in many ways: by providing people with meaningful work and an opportunity to hone and share skills and expertise; by satisfying norms of sharing and mutual aid, healthy food, recreation and spiritual satisfaction; and by offering a practical arena for the teaching and development of indigenous languages. In short, the existence of a mixed economy can be a rich store of social and human capital upon which to build the future.

The viability of the North's 20 or so larger communities, cities and towns, on the other hand, depends on wage employment and small businesses. Many of the larger centres — the territorial capitals Yellowknife and Whitehorse, for example — have origins in mining, to which has now been added a very substantial public sector. Others, such as Iqaluit, the newest territorial capital, owe their present form and size almost entirely to their role as government and administrative centres. In the wage centres, home to the majority of the northern population in almost every region, economic vitality thus depends upon resource development and public expenditures. Larger communities tend to have a higher proportion of non-Aboriginal people (and transients), as well as higher labour force participation and lower unemployment rates.

It seems clear that Aboriginal, provincial, territorial and federal governments must be able to develop economic development strategies that create the conditions under which both the small, mixed-economy communities and the larger wage centres can develop in a balanced way. This means taking into account the greater vulnerability of more remote communities to climate-related changes and, more broadly, the potentially disruptive social and environmental effects of resource development. It also means having the social infrastructure in place to ensure the resident population is educated, healthy and capable of taking advantage of the economic opportunities that may emerge. All the governments involved need to coordinate their efforts so that decisions to promote more balanced economic development are based on knowledge about which policies are most helpful to community development. The key element, however, is that northerners and their governments be in a position to make these fundamental decisions for themselves and to take ownership of their futures.

Some Immediate Steps

What are the immediate obstacles to balanced development? Some have to do with physical infrastructure. Although the severity of the problem varies from place to place, in many parts of the North housing is inadequate.[11] Too many people live in overcrowded conditions that increase the spread of infectious diseases such as tuberculosis. Moreover, overcrowding affects young people's performance at school and the ability of all members of the household to live their lives in a balanced way. Women and children who live in violent domestic situations are particularly vulnerable, as they may literally have nowhere to escape to.

Overcrowding at home is not the only infrastructure problem that leads to lower educational attainment among Aboriginal children. The education system itself contributes to the problem. One problem is that in many small communities there is a very high turnover rate for teachers. This also relates to capacity issues overall as territorial governments — facing a lack of human resources — often recruit potential teachers for public service positions (see Greg Poelzer's chapter in this volume). In addition, curricula and school materials are still not adapted to the localities where they are used. Although the severity of the problem varies a good deal across the North, all regions could benefit from having more northern-trained educators. There are signs these problems are being more fully recognized. In April 2009 the Inuit Education Accord, developed by Inuit Tapiriit Kanatami and a number of other parties, was signed — something Mary Simon called "a milestone in Inuit education (Bell 2009).[12]

In the area of health care, problems of hard infrastructure are compounded by problems of human and social capital. There is a shortage of health care professionals at all levels, and there are very high costs involved in serving people in numerous and remote small centres. Quite often, primary medical care is still being provided by visiting practitioners from the south, with all the costs and discontinuities of care this can involve. The innovative community-based health care and North-specific illness prevention programs that have been developed in some locations are urgently needed across the North.

From the perspective of communities, all these factors converge and reinforce each other. Investment in one area, without attention to the others, is unlikely to be sufficient. Decisions about economic development, social services expenditures, health care arrangements, educational opportunities and recreational facilities have a cumulative effect in small centres. These communities are remarkably vulnerable to small changes in personnel or opportunity: an effective teacher leaves because of inadequate housing or lack of suitable health care for one of her children, and in the transition, while a new teacher is found, many children in the community fall behind; a federally funded program that supports a group of older teens to organize a music program for younger children leads to a decrease in overall drug use and fewer losses to theft in the retail co-op. These are the endemic vulnerabilities of all small places and also, of course, their strength. We believe that individual program interventions must take place within the context of a holistic approach to the health of the community, understood in the broadest sense.

If there are gathering signs of worsening social and economic conditions in northern communities, there are also reasons for optimism. The North has many assets. The permanent population is young and increasingly well educated. In general, northern residents have high expectations of their governments and there are high levels of political participation, especially when one takes into account the geographical obstacles to communication and organization. They live in small centres where community solidarity and neighbourly support are strong and where relatively modest, sustained interventions can make a large difference.

Governance: Currents of Change and Emerging Issues

CANADA'S APPROACH TO INSTITUTIONAL SELF-GOVERNMENT IN THE NORTH HAS BEEN impressive. As various authors in this volume demonstrate, extensive changes have resulted from the signing of modern treaties with Aboriginal peoples since 1975. Indeed, to quote Doug McArthur, "a new constitutional settlement is in the making." One major change has been the creation of a host of Aboriginal governing institutions, in many cases directly elected by Aboriginal residents, and land claims (beneficiary) organizations. The territories all have public governments (elected by all residents), and a new system of public government is being established in Nunavik (see Thierry Rodon and Minnie Grey's chapter in this volume). However, public government in some parts of the North differs from the Westminster-based institutions in the rest of Canada. For example, members of the Nunavut and NWT legislatures are not affiliated with parties and are responsible for selecting the cabinet.

In addition, northern leaders have gained a higher national profile. Unlike the pattern even 20 years ago, the territorial premiers are full members of the Council of the Federation and attend First Ministers' Meetings on the same footing as provincial premiers. These and other developments in the past three decades demonstrate that Canadian federalism is flexible enough to incorporate new institutions for indigenous peoples and to accommodate quite a measure of asymmetry in governance structures.

Concerns have nevertheless been raised about jurisdictional complexity in the territories. In fact, each region of the North faces similar questions of democratic development — questions set in motion by modern treaties and self-government, but not fully resolved by them. For example, in the Northwest Territories, there are now numerous and relatively well-funded regional Aboriginal organizations and governments. Will these become the prime representatives or advocates for the people living in their ambit? If so, what will be the role of the territorial government? In his commentary, George Braden (a former NWT premier) suggests that "the western North will become a balkanized collection of Aboriginal institutions competing with territorial public governments that do not have the jurisdiction or financial resources to effectively govern in the interest of all territorial residents."

In Nunavut the tensions are different, but the underlying cause is similar. Nunavut Tunngavik Incorporated (NTI), the single beneficiary organization, represents about 85 percent of the electorate and it controls and benefits from development of about 18 percent of the territory's land. What will the working relationship be between NTI and the Government of Nunavut, particularly if resource development accelerates? In light of the transformation brought about by modern treaties, it was inevitable that governance in the territories would become more complex. Aboriginal governments and land claims organizations have substantial responsibilities, and it is clear, as Graham White concludes in his chapter, that these organizations will play a key role in long-term political developments. Concerns like Braden's nevertheless need to be borne in mind, particularly in the context of economic development.

Treaty Implementation

As outlined by several of our contributors, distinctly different Aboriginal governance arrangements and intergovernmental collaborative institutions have been developed in each northern region. For example, all 11 of the agreements with First Nations in Yukon provide for self-government, but only one of the modern treaties in the Northwest Territories is of that type.[13] However, all the modern treaties entail land claims settlements and have provided for considerable cash payments to beneficiary organizations. Elsewhere in this volume, Richard Van Loon (a former associate deputy minister of Indian affairs and northern development) assesses the situation as follows:

> Land claims settlements have brought hundreds of millions of dollars to Aboriginal-owned corporations to be managed or invested for the land claims beneficiaries. On the whole, these funds have been managed well and with the appropriate level of accountability. They have produced some remarkable commercial successes, as well as many employment opportunities and financial benefits. But they are also a burden because they require careful management, which should, as far as possible, be handled by the beneficiaries themselves, and that draws talented Aboriginal people away from other valuable activities.

The implementation of modern treaties has given rise to dissatisfaction among Aboriginal peoples that goes well beyond the management questions Van Loon mentions. One set of issues concerns the position of the Department of Indian Affairs and Northern Development (DIAND). First, the department is charged with coordinating overall federal responsibility in Indian and northern affairs, which means that the mandate of the small Northern Affairs Program — the principal federal institution focused on the North — is to fulfill the government's wide-ranging constitutional responsibilities in the North, a task that requires an unusual degree of coordination and leverage in negotiating with other departments. Second, the department employs the modern treaty negotiators as well as the people with primary responsibility to implement the treaties (including funding and monitoring). These two functions require quite different institutional attitudes and skill sets, and it is not surprising that tensions between the two roles sometimes arise.

A number of the authors in this volume echo these concerns and describe the difficulties encountered as a result. Some even suggest that federal institutional arrangements need to be revised and brought in line with the radically altered governance landscape in the territories and the full spectrum of northern social, environmental and economic matters that need to be addressed. Tony Penikett proposes that DIAND be reorganized to better reflect its "emerging roles as facilitator and funder of treaty implementation and devolved programs." Natan Obed, one of the young leaders who attended the Northern Exposure conference, says "the federal government must learn how to coordinate its actions across departments, despite political change and attrition among federal bureaucrats." Stephanie Irlbacher-Fox and Stephen Mills suggest a deputy-minister-level committee be established, with a dedicated staff to assist relevant departments "in implementing systems or protocols." Van Loon proposes that a biennial review of implementation, prepared by an outside commission or an internal body with the participation of land claims organizations, be published. In light of the importance of this issue for the successful implementation of modern treaties within the signatory communities, these and other possible ways to encourage a stronger shared commitment and better horizontal coordination within the Government of Canada merit serious consideration.

Another source of tension concerns the capacity of Aboriginal governments to carry out their responsibilities under modern treaties. The Land Claims Agreement Coalition, founded in 2003, has called for the development of an implementation policy that would "give rise to much needed capacity building and training at all levels to ensure successful governance" and would "provide adequate resources during the pre-implementation period to ensure effective transition and ongoing implementation" (quoted in Irlbacher-Fox and Mills).[14] The coalition's position has been endorsed by the Standing Senate Committee on Aboriginal Peoples (St. Germain and Sibbeston 2008, 41).

A broader though related issue pertains to what some see as a quite rigid view of modern treaties, the terms of which are enumerated in "final agreements." While not all such treaties have been formally protected under section 35 of the *Constitution Act, 1982*, they all have legal authority. This need not, however, close the door to subsequent adjustments in their implementation. In this regard, the James Bay and Northern Quebec Agreement (JBNQA), signed with the Crees of Eeyou Istchee and the Inuit of Nunavik in 1975,[15] provides a salutary example. According to Martin Papillon, "The implementation of the JBNQA largely followed old models of state-led and state-controlled development in Aboriginal communities, and relations with governments suffered from an absence of formal dispute resolution and intergovernmental coordination mechanisms" (2008, 26).[16] Following negotiations, the Crees and the Quebec government signed the Paix des Braves agreement in 2002. Though not a new treaty, it modifies the JBNQA regime in a number of respects, in particular to clear the path for additional hydroelectric projects.[17] Drawing on this experience, Papillon concludes that governments should acknowledge that "treaties must adapt to changing realities on the ground" (26).

Northern Exposure: Peoples, Powers and
Prospects in Canada's North

While the Paix des Braves agreement reflects particular circumstances, it demonstrates that the implementation of modern treaties can be adjusted without the treaties themselves being renegotiated. In our view, Aboriginal governance needs to be seen as an ongoing and adaptable process. This means opening the door for parties to modify self-government arrangements to take into account changes in circumstances and enable communities to take the necessary steps to enhance the capacity of their members and thus secure future progress.

Toward an Arctic Economic/Regulatory Union

The vast changes in northern governance of the past three decades have, by design or happenstance, led to jurisdictional tensions and overlap — both territorial-Aboriginal and Aboriginal-Aboriginal. Of the three territories, the problem may be most pronounced in the NWT, because it has a wider diversity of Aboriginal governments, not all of which have achieved self-government. In addition, its population is split almost evenly between Aboriginal and non-Aboriginal people (the former counted for half of the population in 2006). Although there are 14 First Nations in Yukon, the fact that they all fall under the 1993 Umbrella Final Agreement makes their interface with the territorial government easier.[18] In Nunavut, where 85 percent of the population is Inuit, there is a significant overlap between the constituencies served by the territorial government and NTI, the land claims organization. Even so, there have been some notable tensions between the Nunavut government and NTI over certain policy issues, which suggests some adjustments may be required in these governance models as they evolve (Rodon forthcoming). Should the "Arctic race" scenario come to pass, the non-Aboriginal population of Nunavut could grow substantially, which could put more distance between the interests of Nunavut and NTI.

The resulting jurisdictional complexity has led some political and business leaders to claim that it is almost impossible to obtain approval for economic development projects in the territories. Gordon Erlandson addresses this issue in his commentary. Drawing on his extensive experience in the resource sector, he writes: "The problem with northern regulatory systems…is not that they are complex, but that they don't work — at least, not in relation to the business cycle for oil and gas development." The long history of attempts to build a pipeline through the Mackenzie Valley is often used as a case in point. Indeed, it served as a catalyst for the Northern Regulatory Improvement Initiative and the federal government's appointment of Neil McCrank to review and report on the possibility of streamlining the northern regulatory system.

In May 2008 McCrank presented his report to the Minister of Indian Affairs and Northern Development, Chuck Strahl. McCrank sees the regulatory challenges in the North as truly enormous. He notes, for example, that there are now more than 20 comanagement bodies in the three territories, each with its own membership, staff and advisers. The largest number of these boards is in the NWT. In this regard, McCrank writes: "I've heard from industry that it's becoming impossible to do business in the NWT — it's too complex, it's too unpredictable, it's inconsistent, there are no timelines" (McCrank 2008, 96-7). To return to the four scenarios outlined earlier in this chapter, what some see as a regulatory quagmire suggests a fifth scenario, a combination of an Arctic race and polar lows, namely high demand for resources and stalemated governance resulting in unrealized economic potential and missed opportunities.

The McCrank Report included a number of recommendations for streamlining the regulatory regimes in the North, especially in the NWT. Its first recommendation, however, was that "priority should be given to completing the Land Use Plans in all areas, and obtaining their approval from the federal Government" (McCrank 2008, 15). These plans, which are being developed by the Regional Land Use Planning Boards established by the *Mackenzie Valley Resource Management Act* (*MVRMA*), are meant to "provide for the conservation, development and use of land, water and other resources in a settlement area. Any regulatory authority issuing an authorization for the use of lands or waters, or the deposit of wastes is legally bound to abide by the approved Land Use Plans" (15). As for the approval process for the Mackenzie Gas Project, the report offers two options for consideration. The first would involve a fundamental restructuring and require all parties to agree to amend the comprehensive land claims agreements and the *MVRMA*, while the second would involve less restructuring but might still necessitate amendments to the *MVRMA*. Under both options, the unfinished land claims process would need to be completed before the regulatory process is addressed. Thus one of the major stumbling blocks on the regulatory front is not only that some land claims have not been settled, but also that land-use plans have not been approved. This complicates regulatory reform because it is difficult to assure Aboriginal groups that their as-yet-undefined rights and interests are being respected. So the intractability remains. What is also clear, as Terry Fenge points out, is that Ottawa is no longer in a position to act unilaterally to resolve this issue.

In this context, George Braden's view is that all parties need to recognize that the environment in which they operate has changed since the modern treaties were finalized and, therefore, the parties' views also need to change. In particular, Braden believes the solution will "require Aboriginal stakeholders to look beyond their individual settlements and regions and consider how they can contribute to the strength of the territory within which they reside." This broader perspective could be encouraged if, as suggested above, the other parties to modern treaties, namely governments, adopted a perspective that sees treaty implementation as an ongoing process that allows for adjustment when circumstances warrant. Contemporary governance recognizes that governments and other actors have complex, often dynamic relationships that entail new forms of collaboration and power sharing. This is certainly true in Canada's North, and one of the major challenges for the future will be to minimize the degree to which fluid relationships and the diffusion of decision-making stand in the way of ensuring the best outcomes for all northerners.

Northern Economic Development: Territorial Government Financing and Devolution

THE FINANCING OF TERRITORIAL GOVERNMENTS RAISES EQUALLY CHALLENGING governance issues. The long-standing model, which is based essentially on federal transfers, may not be up to the task in terms of the demands and the growing pressures that will be placed on territorial governments in the context of rapid resource development and economic growth. On the recommendation of the 2006 report of the Expert Panel on Equalization and Territorial Formula Financing, the 2007 federal budget made significant changes to the Territorial Formula Financing (TFF) arrangements,[19] but some of the more fundamental problems have not been resolved.

As James P. Feehan documents in his chapter, these TFF transfers are very large and represent a correspondingly large proportion of the territories' total

revenues: the per capita transfers for 2008-09 and the share of the territories' overall revenues are as follows: Yukon — $18,166 (64.5 percent), NWT — $18,704
(65.4 percent), Nunavut — $30,265 (81.2 percent). Given that the largest provin-
cial Equalization transfer is under $2,500 per capita (for Prince Edward Island), and
that Ontario's overall per capita revenues (as projected for 2008-09 in its 2008 budget) are less than $8,000, these TFF transfers are indeed large. Not surprisingly, per-
haps, this has led to concerns about whether the territories are, in effect, not much
more than fiscal wards of the federal state and whether this degree of transfer dependency is more likely to hamper rather than enable the prospects of northerners.

The concerns with respect to the magnitude of the transfers need to be examined more closely. The first point to note relates to the primary difference between
Canada's two approaches to horizontal fiscal equity — Equalization and TFF. While
both programs are conceived to address the gap between "expenditure needs" and
"revenue means," the formal Equalization Program implicitly assumes that expenditure needs are identical, in per capita terms, in all provinces. In sharp contrast, the
operating assumption of TFF is that per capita expenditure needs differ dramatically
north and south of 60 and among the territories themselves; hence the critical importance of the gross expenditure base (GEB) in determining TFF transfer payments.

The GEB is intended to reflect the level of revenues needed to provide territorial citizens with public goods and services that are reasonably comparable to those
available to people south of 60. Indeed, the first task of the Expert Panel on
Equalization and Territorial Formula Financing in assessing TFF was to address the
unique factors affecting the territorial GEBs, including faster population growth than in
the rest of Canada; greater geographical dispersion and isolation; high health care costs
and poor outcomes; important social challenges; and deficiencies in education, infrastructure and housing. The panel's conclusion was that the GEBs needed to be (and
later were legislated to be) larger for all three territories than a continuation of their historical trajectories would have delivered, and that a more in-depth analysis was needed for Nunavut in order to ensure that its GEB was adequate. All of this is consistent
with the Equalization provisions of our Constitution, namely, that access to reasonably
comparable public goods and services at reasonably comparable levels of taxation is the
right of all citizens, no matter where they may reside. These public goods and services
just happen to cost a great deal more to produce and deliver north of 60.

Second, the high levels for TFF transfers to the territories might be interpreted as indicating that they are economic laggards. However, in terms of per capita

GDP, this is certainly not the case. The result of the combination of significant mineral development, on the one hand, and a small population, on the other, is that the NWT has a per capita GDP of $97,923. This is by far the highest in Canada. Alberta comes a distant second (at $69,789), while Yukon has the third-highest ($51,154), Nunavut ranks eighth, and Prince Edward Island has the lowest ($31,278) (Statistics Canada 2007). Given the potential energy/resource endowments north of 60, under an "Arctic race" scenario the resulting per capita GDPs, especially in the NWT and Nunavut, could easily be an order of magnitude higher than that of the lowest province. And Yukon would not be far behind if offshore energy resources were assigned to it.

Third, Ottawa derives significant revenues from resource development in the territories, and these revenues would obviously escalate sharply if new large-scale projects came to fruition. In terms of per capita federal revenues and transfers by province/territory, looking at the NWT (the territory where most mineral development is occurring at present), the federal government received $16,721 per capita in revenues from the NWT for 2004. Alberta is the next largest source of revenue at $7,927 per capita, followed closely by Yukon and Ontario (West 2007). More to the point, the amount of TFF transfer received by the NWT for fiscal year 2004-05 was $678 million (Expert Panel 2006, 25), or $15,658 per capita, which is less than the $16,721 per capita that Ottawa collects in revenues from the NWT. To be sure, Ottawa transfers other monies besides the TFF to the NWT, just as it provides other payments to the provinces (for example, through the Canada Health Transfer). Nonetheless, this casts quite a different light on the true extent of transfer dependency.

The fourth point relates to what is now the obvious question: If GDP in the NWT is so large and if Ottawa gets so much money from NWT resource development, why is the TFF transfer for the NWT still so high? The reason is that territories do not have anywhere near the access to the incomes/revenues generated within their borders that the provinces or Ottawa have. This is partly because the expenses associated with northern resource enterprises (transporting workers and machinery, capital expenditures and depreciation, infrastructure spending) are very high and, therefore, reduce profits and in turn territorial corporate income taxes collected per unit of output or GDP. Moreover, because the NWT and Nunavut have not signed resource devolution agreements with Ottawa, the royalties flow to the federal government rather than to the two territories. And while much is typically made of the fact that Yukon has a resource devolution agreement, the reality, as Feehan points out, is that the agreement excludes offshore resources, and the "associated revenue-sharing arrangements are quite ungenerous."

Fifth and finally, the territories get precious little in income tax revenues from the many "fly-in" workers in the territorial resource enterprises: rather, the provincial component of these workers' personal income tax is paid to the province where they reside on December 31, and one presumes that most of the spending of these fly-in workers is also undertaken in their home provinces. Overall, since Ottawa ensures that the territories do not receive much own-source revenue from resource development, it must therefore fill the resulting gap between a territory's GEB and revenue with a correspondingly higher TFF transfer. Based on the above analysis, the level of TFF transfers reflects, to a considerable degree, the federal government's decision to constrain the territories' ability to access own-source revenues.

The existing arrangements are obviously problematic on economic grounds because the territories are not the principal fiscal beneficiaries of their economic development decisions, and on political grounds because they effectively force the territories to plead for federal dollars and thus appear to be wholly transfer dependent when they are, or certainly will be, anything but.

This should matter to the federal government on equity, efficiency and strategic grounds. The equity issue is captured by what Van Loon calls the "ultimate objective" of the territorial governments, namely, "full provincial powers and seats of completely equal status at the table of Confederation." Creative as Canada's approach to northern governance has been, there is not much evidence of equality with the provinces when it comes to natural resource devolution and other fiscal issues. For instance, given that the federal government has allowed two Atlantic provinces access to offshore resource revenues, it is hard to deny this to the territories. In this context, Nunavut is a most interesting case. For purposes of establishing Canadian sovereignty, the federal government argues that the Arctic waterways are in effect part of Nunavut's "internal" waters, while claiming at the same time that any oil and gas found in these same waters constitute "offshore" resources. Another fiscal issue relates to the question of fly-in workers. One of the possible compromises might go as follows: Since the territories are not accorded the full fiscal privileges of provinces, there is less reason that they should be bound by south-of-60 fiscal arrangements that will clearly work against them. Specifically, why not allow the territories to collect the territorial personal income taxes for fly-in workers, on the one hand, and, on the other, have Ottawa and the provinces agree that these territorial taxes will be a credit against any provincial taxes owing under the existing December 31 residence regime. This would be a much better avenue for capturing some income from the thousands of fly-in workers than the present 2 percent NWT payroll tax, which also applies to residents and thereby limits the NWT's ability to implement an appropriate territorial income tax.

As a bridge between equity and efficiency issues relating to resources, it is convenient to focus on within-territory resource revenue implications. Consider Nunavut, although what follows also has implications for the NWT. In a recent article, the Nunavut Economic Forum described the issue of the split in mining royalties between the Nunavut government and NTI as follows:

> Article 25 of the NLCA [Nunavut Land Claims Agreement] stipulates that 50 per cent of the first $2 million and 5 per cent of all additional royalties generated on Crown Land are to be transferred to Nunavut Trust. Additionally, the Mary River iron deposits, as with the deposits of all six mining prospects discussed earlier, are on land where the Inuit own subsurface rights. In these cases, NTI receives royalty payments directly under a far more lucrative schedule that amounts to 12 per cent of net profits from operations. The government of Nunavut, even under a complete devolution agreement, holds no title to these lands and therefore will receive none of the royalty revenues generated from them. (Nunavut Economic Forum 2008, 72)

The report does note that the Nunavut government would get the fiscal benefits of the wages-and-salaries and corporate-profits components of the development (subject to earlier observations on the taxation and spending of fly-in workers and the 70 percent TFF clawback of additional own-source revenues). Nonetheless, one of the key issues at stake here is the role of the public government of Nunavut, which has limited revenue capacity, in providing territorial-based public goods and services when Inuit governing bodies are becoming increasingly wealthy as a result of investing their compensation funds and receiving revenue from resource development on their lands. This challenge could be even more significant if future resource development led to a sizable migration of non-Inuit into Nunavut, a situation that could further accentuate the tensions between the Nunavut government and NTI.

The efficiency argument is straightforward. If maximizing territorial revenues associated with resource development is effectively ruled out, then the territories will seek other criteria for making decisions relating to development, such as imposing resident employment and training conditions, requiring companies to undertake major infrastructure initiatives and utilizing the regulatory process to tilt benefits in their direction. Northern economic development already faces enough challenges on the governance/regulatory front without further diverting firms from pursuing market incentives.

Finally, on the strategic front, the federal government's decision to not devolve more resource revenues to the territories may well prove very costly, especially in light of the equity and efficiency issues noted above. In particular, as the *Mayer Report on Nunavut Devolution* notes, Nunavut's demands for resource devolution go well beyond the Yukon model and comprise not only full fiscal devolution along provincial lines, but also full management and oversight of resources, including the transfer of responsibility for human resources and physical infrastructure (Mayer 2007). It might have been wise if Ottawa had embarked earlier, even unilaterally, on an initial program of resource devolution as a way to address the various equity and efficiency issues related to territorial development. The trump cards would now seem to be more in Nunavut's hand. In any event, aspects of the preceding analysis will presumably be given serious consideration by Bruce Rawson, the chief federal representative, during the review of Nunavut devolution.[20]

Looking to the Future

THE LAST GENERATION OF ABORIGINAL AND NON-ABORIGINAL NORTHERNERS WORKED hard, in collaboration with southern political leaders, to develop major constitutional and legislative changes that were subsequently adopted by Parliament and the territorial legislative assemblies. As a result, the political map of northern Canada was redrawn, traditional political institutions were linked to newer concepts of governance, new systems of land stewardship and public decision-making were invented, and standard operating procedures for resource development companies were transformed. The overall intent was to ensure a healthy and democratic way of life for all of the North's residents, commensurate with that afforded other Canadians. Moreover, all this was achieved peacefully, through compromise, focus and determination. It would be tragic indeed if, in the wake of these enormous achievements, northern communities themselves failed to flourish.

It is evident that the future of Canada's northern regions is closely tied to the well-being of its residents and the strength of its communities. The gaps in life chances between Canadians in general and many northerners, particularly Aboriginal peoples, are deeply unsettling and unacceptable. Social well-being must be an integral part of a northern policy framework. This will require, among other things, significant improvements in the stock and quality of housing and improvements to health care. Broad-based measures to reduce the alarmingly high rates of suicide, particularly among young men, are urgently needed. In addition, basic education levels must be raised and new opportunities provided for post-secondary learning. This is a daunting task that needs to be undertaken by northerners themselves but that will also require the sustained collaboration of all the government bodies involved. As Nellie J. Cournoyea reminds us in her commentary, "The North is at a different stage of development from southern Canada." Both she and Doug McArthur convincingly argue that this reality needs to be taken into account in all decisions related to northerners' efforts to build capacity and pursue self-sufficiency.

Canada is a wealthy country and we have the capacity to study and learn from our own experiences and those of other nations around the North Pole. Recent scholarship has demonstrated the value of comparative circumpolar research, although thorough analysis that can link policy interventions with social and economic outcomes has barely begun (Poppel et al. 2007). Such work would be quite valuable as northerners and the circumpolar countries of which they are a part prepare to cope with the twin pressures of global warming and accelerated industrialization of the North. To advance this type of research, dedicated international funding programs and a northern-based university system (as Poelzer recommends) are needed. In addition, research initiatives must include a human development component, as was the case in the 2007-08 International Polar Year.

Huge progress on Aboriginal self-government has been made through the host of modern treaties signed in Canada's northern regions since 1975 (see McArthur, White, and Rodon and Grey in this volume). In light of the scale of these changes, it is understandable that certain difficulties concerning implementation have emerged. A number of participants in this research project consider that it is unsatisfactory that one ministry, Indian and Northern Affairs Canada, should be almost solely responsible for treaty implementation. In their view, the federal government needs to adopt a more horizontal approach. On this, we agree.

We also believe the Government of Canada should undertake an in-depth study, supported by a consultative process, to address calls for greater flexibility and adaptation in the implementation of modern treaties; the study should explore practical measures, including a policy statement or guidelines, and the merits of companion agreements.[21]

A number of major issues will affect future economic development in Canada's North. One of these is the regulatory environment in the territories, which has become highly complex. In part this reflects the increase in the number of actors involved in various consultation and approval processes in the lead-up to the actual launch of projects. Some believe the territories' public governments do not have sufficient authority — at least in practice — to adjudicate among competing interests and chart the way forward in reasonably expeditious ways. The various governments and organizations involved must move beyond defending their particular interests in order to develop, and act on, a shared vision of sustainable development for their communities and regions.

Another major concern is the way that the benefits of northern development, particularly in the resource sector, are shared — or, rather, not adequately shared — with northern residents. As we have demonstrated here, the territories are perceived as being more dependent on transfer payments from the federal government than any of the provinces that receive equalization. While there is certainly a national interest in resource development in Canada's northernmost regions, there is a strong case, on both political and economic grounds, for allowing the territorial governments a greater capacity to raise own-source revenues than they do at present. Finding a satisfactory accommodation will not be easy, but the federal government should demonstrate a renewed commitment in this regard. A more equitable sharing of wealth with the territories would not only be consistent with the various transfers of authority that have taken place over the past three decades, but would also underpin the actions necessary to strengthen human capital and the vitality of northern communities. Finally, there is a need for a new vision of balanced economic development led by the people who live in the North. In this regard, a clear, empirically based understanding of how community economies work is needed in order to help inform an approach to development that strikes a balance between that dimension and more conventional approaches to northern economic development.

As we have underlined here, a new northern policy universe must not only take account of global environmental and geopolitical trends but also provide a broader, more comprehensive framework for action in a number of areas of public policy and governance. Above all, it should focus more closely on the future well-being of northerners and their communities and ensure they do have greater control over their destinies. While we do not claim to have presented a complete agenda for reform, we have highlighted several issues that require serious attention.

In concluding, it is appropriate to return to Rob Huebert's comment, quoted at the outset, that the Arctic is facing a transformation of epic proportions. Climate change and melting sea ice are transforming our traditional vision of the Arctic as Canada's northern frontier and its people as guardians of our northern sovereignty. Progressively, the Arctic will find itself at the crossroads of the interplay of international economic and geopolitical interests involving many of the world's political powers. Northerners' relationships with south-of-60 Canadians will likewise evolve as they become more fully engaged in new geo-economic and political realities and opportunities. We hope that this volume not only serves to document this dramatic "Northern Exposure," but also contributes to the ongoing discussion about the social, economic and governance changes required to strengthen the peoples, powers and prospects of Canada's North.

Appendix
Recent Federal Government Commitments in the North

	Schedule	Budget
Sovereignty		
Expansion of the Canadian Rangers program from approximately 4,200 to 5,000	2008-09 to 2028-29	$240 million
Acquisition of eight new Arctic/offshore patrol vessels and building of a deepwater Arctic docking and refuelling facility in Nanisivik, Nunavut	2008-09 to 2033-34	$7.4 billion
Complete mapping of the underwater continental shelf to meet 2013 United Nations Commission on the Limits of the Continental Shelf deadline	2008-09 to 2012-13	$40 million
Construction of a new Polar-class icebreaker[1]	By 2017	$720 million
Amend regulations to make reporting by ships in Arctic mandatory under NORDREG and to extend its application to-200-nautical-mile limit	2009	–
Environmental protection		
International Polar Year research focused on climate change impacts, including the human dimension	2007-08 to 2013-14	$156 million
Conducting feasibility study for the establishment of a world-class Arctic research station	2009-10	$2 million

Appendix
Recent Federal Government Commitments in the North (cont'd)

	Schedule	Budget
Land set aside to expand Nahanni National Park (Northwest Territories)	Announced August 8, 2007	–
Amending the *Arctic Waters Pollution Prevention Act* to allow Canada to regulate all shipping and enforce environmental laws up to 200 nautical miles (from the present 100 miles) offshore	Bill C-3 introduced January 28, 2009	–
Economic and social development		
Initiatives related to proposed Mackenzie Gas Project	2009-10	$37.6 million
Mackenzie Gas Project impact fund	Once project approved	$500 million
Northern Regulatory Improvement Initiative to respond to mounting development pressures	Neil McCrank submitted a report on May 20, 2008	–
Accelerating construction of a commercial fishing harbour in Pangnirtung, Nunavut, to support the emerging commercial fishery in that territory	2008-09 to 2010-11	$25 million
Geological mapping, primarily in the North, to support the exploration and development of mineral resources	2008-09 to 2010-11	$134 million
New regional economic development agency for the North	2009-10 to 2014-15	$50 million a year

Appendix
Recent Federal Government Commitments in the North (cont'd)

	Schedule	Budget
Strategic investments in northern economic development programs	2009-10 to 2014-15	$90 million
Additional funding for affordable housing in the territories	2006-07 to 2011-12	$500 million
Extending for one year the 15 percent Mineral Exploration Tax Credit to help companies raise capital for mineral exploration	2009-10	
Improving Internet/broadband service in the Northwest Territories and Nunavut	2009-12	$36 million
Infrastructure (Building Canada Plan)	2007-14	$175 million to each territory
Arctic Research Infrastructure Fund	2009-11	$85 million
Governance		
Increasing funding for Territorial Formula Financing for territorial governments	2006-07 to 2008-09	$195 million (total for three fiscal years)
Strengthening the Nunavut government's financial management capacity	2007-08	$28 million
Signing of Nunavut Protocol Agreement on devolution	September 5, 2008	–
Bruce Rawson appointed as chief federal representative for Nunavut devolution	January 15, 2009	

Source: Compiled by authors from federal budget documents (2006-09) and official announcements.
[1] Prime Minister Harper announced on August 28, 2008, that the new icebreaker, to be named after former prime minister John G. Diefenbaker, would replace the *Louis S. St-Laurent*, which is expected to be decommissioned in 2017. The new icebreaker will have greater icebreaking capabilities than any other vessel currently in the Canadian fleet.

Northern Exposure: Peoples, Powers and Prospects in Canada's North

Notes

1   One well-regarded international publication even suggested the Arctic could become the theatre for a new Cold War (*Courrier international* 2008).

2   In 2006, the aggregate population of the three territories, Nunavik and Nunatsiavut was 114,539.

3   The increased melting of sea ice means polar bears have a shorter period for feeding on the ice, particularly to catch seal pups, in order to put on fat for the months when they have to live onshore. In 2008, the United States listed the polar bear as threatened under its *Endangered Species Act*. Inuit spokespeople have noted that the polar bear population in Canada has increased from about 8,000 in the early 1970s to the current estimate of about 16,000 (Bird 2009).

4   See, in particular, the first section ("The Changing North") of Rob Huebert's chapter.

5   National Snow and Ice Data Center (2008), National American Spatial Agency (2008), National Snow and Ice Data Center (2007). T. David Barber, who participated in a 15-month Arctic scientific expedition, predicted in December 2008 that the Arctic would be free of multi-year ice in the summer by 2015 (in Séguin 2008). Research led by Wieslaw Maslowski of the Naval Postgraduate School in California has predicted that by summer 2013 there will be no ice in the Arctic other than a few outcrops on islands near Canada and Greenland (in McKie 2008).

6   See the section of Huebert's chapter titled "Current Canadian Action"; and Coates et al. (2008, 169-87).

7   In a speech in January 2009, the NATO Secretary-General, Jaap de Hoop Scheffer, called on the four NATO countries with Arctic coasts, as well as Russia, to prevent the region from becoming a source of division (Boswell 2009); see also Young (2008, 81).

8   The Minister of Foreign Affairs and International Trade recently indicated that Canada intended to play a leadership role in Arctic affairs and that he plans to meet the other members of the council "to further engage them on the challenges and opportunities unfolding in the Arctic" (Foreign Affairs and International Trade Canada 2009).

9   Young and Bjerregaard (2008); see Frances Abele's chapter in this volume for more detail.

10   The endangered languages are Tlingit (in Yukon), Kutchin-Gwich'in (Northwest Territories [NWT] and Yukon) and North Slave or Hare (NWT). A measure of the vitality of a language is its "continuity index" — a ratio that compares the number of people who speak it at home with the number of people for whom it is their mother tongue. A continuity index of under 100 is considered to indicate some decline in the strength of the language. For northern languages, the continuity index in 1996 ranged from a high of 86 for Dene and Inuktitut, to a low of 24 for Kutchin-Gwich'in (Norris 1998).

11   For example, it is estimated that Nunavut, with a population of just over 30,000, requires nearly 3,000 new housing units to approach national standards and an additional 270 new units a year to keep up with the population increase. There has been some recognition of this need in recent federal budgets, which allocated $300 million for housing in the three territories in 2006, and another $200 million over two years in 2009 (divided unequally, with Yukon and the NWT each receiving $50 million, and $100 million being transferred to Nunavut). Although substantial funding ($400 million) was earmarked for housing on reserves, there was no new money for housing in Nunatsiavut or Nunavik.

12   Fourteen Inuit and public government bodies, including Chuck Strahl, the Minister of Indian Affairs and Northern Development, signed the Inuit Education Accord, which, Simon said, would push for Inuit-friendly curricula.

13   The agreement with the Tlicho, concluded in 2003, provides for self-government.

According to Doug McArthur, the Tlicho treaty "is considered state of the art — the template for future settlements in the NWT."

14 In March 2009, the coalition released a "model national policy" on land claims agreements (Land Claims Agreement Coalition 2009).

15 In 1978, the Naskapi First Nation signed a parallel agreement and joined the institutions established by the 1975 agreement.

16 In this context, Irlbacher-Fox and Mills note that, although the dispute resolution provisions of the Yukon self-government agreements were used on one occasion, the federal government has declined to participate in the dispute resolution process provided for in the Nunavut and Gwich'in land claims agreements.

17 The agreement, valid for 50 years, provides for joint jurisdiction by the Quebec government and Cree in the seven municipalities of James Bay and surrounding territories. In exchange, the Cree gave their consent to hydroelectric development of the Eastmain and Rupert Rivers by Hydro-Québec.

18 In 2006, 25.1 percent of the Yukon population was Aboriginal (according to the Aboriginal identity measure used by Statistics Canada).

19 As Feehan notes, the reworked TFF reverted to its earlier formulation of "filling the gap" between what might be termed a territory's expenditure needs and its revenue means. The former is defined in terms of a gross expenditure base (GEB) adjusted annually for a territory's population growth rate and the average growth rate of provincial government spending. From this GEB one subtracts a territory's revenue means, defined as 70 percent of its own-source revenue capacity (where this revenue capacity is calculated on the basis of the seven largest territorial revenue sources). The difference between a territory's GEB and 70 percent of its own-source revenue capacity is its TFF transfer. This means that for every dollar of additional revenue capacity, a territory's transfer falls by 70 cents.

20 Rawson's appointment was announced on January 15, 2009 (Indian and Northern Affairs Canada 2009).

21 A companion agreement would not re-open the original treaty but, as with the Paix des Braves, would modify the application of certain of its provisions in light of changes in circumstances and needs since its signing.

References

Arctic Council. 2008. *The Future of Arctic Marine Navigation in Mid-Century: Scenario Narratives Report.* Polarmiljøsenteret, Norway: Arctic Council.

Amstrup, S.C., B.G. Marcot, and D.C. Douglas. 2007. *Forecasting the Range-wide Status of Polar Bears at Selected Times in the 21st Century.* US Geological Survey administrative report.

Bell, Jim. "Inuit Schooling goes National Under Accord." Nunatsiaz News. April 9, 2009. Accessed April 15, 2009. http://www.nunatsiaq.com/news/nunavut/90410_2055.html

Bird, John. 2009. "Minister Gives Nod to Inuit Bear Knowledge." *Nunatsiaq News,* January 30. Accessed April 2. 2009. http://www.nunatsiaq.com/archives/2009/901/90130/news/nunavut/90130_1867.html

Boswell, Randy. 2009. "NATO Chief Cautions against Arctic Divisions." Canwest News, January 29. Accessed April 2, 2009. http://www.canada.com/Technology/story.html?id=1232006

Bush, George W. 2009. "Arctic Region Policy — National Security Presidential Directive and Homeland Security Presidential Directive." Washington, DC: Government of the United States of America.

Coates, Ken, P. Whitney-Lackenbauer, Greg Poelzer, and Bill Morrison. 2008. *The Arctic Front: Defending Canada in the Far North.* Toronto: Thomas Allen Publishers.

Courrier International. 2008. "Arctique: l'autre Guerre froide." *Courrier international* 935 (October 2-8): 10-15.

Expert Panel on Equalization and Territorial Formula Financing. 2006. *Achieving a*

National Purpose: Improving Territorial Formula Financing and Strengthening Canada's Territories. Ottawa: Finance Canada.

Fenge, Terry, and Tony Penikett. 2009. "The Arctic Vacuum in Canada's Foreign Policy." *Policy Options* 30 (4): 65-70.

Foreign Affairs and International Trade Canada. 2009. "Minister Cannon Outlines Canada's Arctic Foreign Policy." News release no. 67. Accessed March 30, 2009. http://w01.inter national.gc.ca/minpub/Publication.aspx?isR edirect=True&publication_id=386927&Lan guage=E&docnumber=67

Furgal, C., and Prowse, T.D. 2008. "Northern Canada." In *From Impacts to Adaptation: Canada in a Changing Climate 2007*, edited by D.S. Lemmen, F.J. Warren, J. Lacroix, and E. Bush. Ottawa: Natural Resources Canada.

Government of Canada. 2007. *Strong Leadership. A Better Canada. Speech from the Throne*, October 16, 2007, 39th Parliament, 2nd sess. Ottawa: Government of Canada.

Homer-Dixon, Thomas. 2007. "A Swiftly Melting Planet." *New York Times,* October 4. Accessed on April 2, 2009. http://www.nytimes.com/2007/10/04/ opinion/04homer-dixon.html

Huebert, Rob. 2008. "Canadian Arctic Security: Preparing for a Changing Future." In *Canada's Arctic Interests and Responsibilities,* Behind the Headlines 65 (4): 14-26.

Indian and Northern Affairs Canada. 2008. *Northern Oil and Gas Annual Report 2007.* Ottawa: Minister of Public Works and Government Services Canada. April 2008. _____. 2009. "Government of Canada, Government of Nunavut and Nunavut Tunngavik Incorporated Set Path for Nunavut Devolution." News release 2-3088, January 15. http://www.ainc-inac.gc.ca/ai/mr/nr/ j-a2009/nr000000156-eng.asp

Land Claims Agreement Coalition. 2009. *Honour, Spirit and Intent: A Model Canadian Policy on the Full Implementation of Modern Treaties between Aboriginal Peoples and the Crown.* Land Claims Agreement Coalition.

Lasserre, Frédéric. 2007. "La souveraineté canadienne dans le Passage du Nord-Ouest." *Policy Options* 28 (5): 34-41.

Mayer, Paul. 2007. *Mayer Report on Nunavut Devolution.* Ottawa: Indian and Northern Affairs Canada.

McCrank, Neil. 2008. *Road to Improvement: The Review of the Regulatory Systems across the North.* Indian and Northern Affairs Development Canada.

McKie, Robin. 2008. "Meltdown in the Arctic Is Speeding Up." *The Observer,* August 10. Accessed on April 2, 2009. http://www.guardian.co.uk/environ ment/2008/aug/10/climatechange.arctic

National American Spatial Agency. 2008. "Researchers Say Arctic Sea Ice Still at Risk Despite Cold Winter." Accessed April 2, 2009. http://www.nasa.gov/topics/earth/ features/seaice_conditions_feature.html

National Snow and Ice Data Center. 2007. "Arctic Sea Ice News Fall 2007." Accessed April 2, 2009. http://nsidc.org/news/press/2007_ seaiceminimum/20070810_index.html _____. 2008. "Arctic Sea Ice Down to Second-Lowest Extent; Likely Record-Low Volume." Accessed April 2, 2009. http://nsidc.org/ news/press/20081002_seaice_pressrelease.html

Nunavut Economic Forum. 2008. *2008 Nunavut Economic Outlook: Our Future to Choose.* Accessed April 1, 2009. http://www.nunavu teconomicforum.ca/public/library/index.php

Norris, Mary Jane. 1998. "Canada's Aboriginal Languages." *Canadian Social Trends* (51): 8-16.

Papillon, Martin. 2008. "Aboriginal Quality of Life under a Modern Treaty: Lessons from the Experience of the Cree Nation of Eeyou Istchee and the Inuit of Nunavik. *IRPP Choices* 14 (9) Montreal: IRPP.

Poppel, Birger, Jack Kruse, Gérard Duhaime, and Larissa Abryutina. 2007. *Survey of Living Conditions in the Arctic: Results.* Anchorage: Institute of Social and Economic Research, University of Alaska Anchorage.

Rodon. Thierry. Forthcoming. "Iqqanaijaqatgiit: The Highs and Lows of Multilevel Governance in Nunavut." Montreal: IRPP.

Statistics Canada. 2007. "Gross Domestic
        Product (GDP), Expenditure-Based,
        Provincial Economic Accounts, Annual
        (dollars)," table 384-0002, and "Estimates
        of Population, by Age Group and Sex for
        July 1, Canada, Provinces and Territories,
        Annual," table 051-0001. CANSIM.

Séguin, Rhéal. 2008. "Scientists Predict Seasonal
        Ice-Free Arctic by 2015." *Globe and Mail*,
        December 12. A7.

St. Germain, the Honourable Gerry, and the
        Honourable Nick Sibbeston. 2008.
        *Honouring the Spirit of Modern Treaties:
        Closing the Loopholes.* Standing Senate
        Committee on Aboriginal Peoples. Senate of
        Canada.

United States Geological Survey. 2008. "Circum-
        Arctic Resource Appraisal: Estimates of
        Undiscovered Oil and Gas North of the
        Arctic Circle." Fact sheet 2008-3049.

West, S. 2007. "Federal Government Revenue
        and Spending by Province: A Scorecard of
        Winners and Losers in Confederation?"
        Canadian Economic Observer
        2007 (February). Statistics Canada, cat.
        no. 11-010-XIB. Acccessed April 1, 2009.
        http://www.statcan.gc.ca/pub/11-010-x/
        00207/9586-eng.htm

Young, Oran R. 2008. "Whither the Arctic?
        Conflict or Cooperation in the Circumpolar
        North." *Polar Record* 45 (232): 73-82.

Frances Abele holds a Ph.D. in political science from York University, is a professor at Carleton University's School of Public Policy and Administration and is academic director of the Carleton Centre for Community Innovation. She has been working with Aboriginal people and studying northern political and economic development for over 30 years. The author of many writings on these topics, she is currently studying the northern social economy and Aboriginal self-government and Canadian federalism.

Elaine Alexie is a member of the Teetl'it Gwich'in First Nation. She has participated in forums of the Arctic Council and of the United Nations. In 2002, she cofounded the Arctic Indigenous Alliance. In 2003, she helped to launch a national campaign called Boreal Rendezvous, which focuses on raising awareness of Canada's threatened rivers. She has been a television producer with the Inuvialuit Communications Society, GEO Graphic Productions and Northern Native Broadcasting Yukon in Whitehorse, and she recently spent time as a video journalist in the Middle East working with Palestinian and indigenous organizations in Palestine and Israel.

George Berthe has been secretary-general of Makivik Corporation since 1998. In that capacity, he is responsible for the organization's administration and day-to-day activities. He is also president of Air Inuit and a member of the boards of directors of First Air, Nunavik Arctic Foods, the Unaaq fishing enterprise, the Nunavik Tourism Association and Cruise North. He is a champion of the Ivakkak dogsled race, an event that he helped to found. Deeply involved in his community, he won the National Aboriginal Achievement Award in 1997 for his contribution to youth issues and, more recently, he was selected as one of Nunavik and Nunavut's 10 outstanding people under the age of 35 by the eastern Arctic weekly the *Nunatsiaq News*.

George Braden holds an MA in political science from Dalhousie University. From 1979 to 1983, he was a member of the Legislative Assembly of the Northwest Territories, becoming the first elected leader of the territorial cabinet. He also served as deputy minister of economic development and tourism and deputy minister of intergovernmental affairs in the Government of the Northwest Territories. From 1980 to 1984 he served as the second premier of the Northwest Territories. During the 1990s, he was a member of the Northwest Territories Commission for Constitutional Development, and he acted as an adviser to the territorial government on various national and territorial constitutional initiatives. From 2000 to 2004, he was an adviser to the Premier of the Northwest Territories as well as to the territorial cabinet and a number of government departments. He currently works as an Ottawa-based consultant.

Michael T. Bravo is an Arts and Humanities Research Council research fellow on leave from the Scott Polar Research Institute of the University of Cambridge, where he is head of the Circumpolar History and Public Policy Research Group. His academic roots are in the Cambridge history and philosophy of science department. He is joint editor of *Narrating the Arctic: A Cultural History of Nordic Scientific Practices* (2002). He was a member of the International Arctic Social Sciences Association task force that wrote the *Humanities and Social Sciences Sixth Theme* of the Scientific Framework for the International Polar Year. He is currently writing about public spaces of knowledge and governance in the Arctic.

Thomas J. Courchene is the Jarislowsky-Deutsch Professor of Economic and Financial Policy at the Queen's School of Policy Studies, Senior Scholar of the IRPP and Contributing Writer for *Policy Options*. He has published on a wide range of economic, financial, social and federal policy issues. His book *Social Canada in the Millennium* (1994) won the Doug Purvis Prize for the best contribution to Canadian economic policy, and his *From Heartland to North American Region State: The Social, Fiscal and Federal Evolution of Ontario* won the inaugural Donner Prize. He is a fellow of the Royal Society of Canada (elected 1981); he was awarded the Canada Council's 1999 Molson Prize for lifetime achievement in the social sciences and humanities; and he holds honorary doctorates from the Universities of Western Ontario, Saskatchewan and Regina. In 1999, he was inducted as an officer of the Order of Canada.

Nellie J. Cournoyea holds honorary doctorates in law from Lakehead University, Carleton University and the University of Toronto. She is the chair/CEO of the Inuvialuit Regional Corporation, which was established in 1985 with the mandate to receive the Inuvialuit lands and financial compensation resulting from the 1984 land claim settlement. Beginning in 1991, she served as premier of the Northwest Territories for four years. Representing the western Arctic riding of Nuakput from 1979 to 1995, she held a number of ministerial portfolios. She was a founding member, and later administrator and land-rights worker, of the Committee of

Original People's Entitlement. She was the first managing director of the Inuvialuit Development Corporation, she held the position of implementation coordinator for the Inuvialuit Final Agreement, and she served on the board of directors of the Inuvialuit Petroleum Corporation and Inuvialuit Arbitration Board.

Gordon Erlandson is president of Erlandson Consulting. He undertakes conflict assessments, designs public processes and multiparty negotiations, and is often engaged as a neutral third party. This work has required him to build strong relationships within governments, communities, Aboriginal organizations, public interest groups and industry. He developed the Regulatory Roadmaps Project, a series of procedural guides for oil and gas authorizations in the Northwest Territories, the Beaufort Sea and the offshore areas of Nova Scotia and Newfoundland and Labrador. From 2004 to 2007, he served as the Government of Canada's ministerial representative for the Mackenzie Gas Project.

James P. Feehan is a professor of economics at Memorial University of Newfoundland, where he is also joint director of the J.R. Smallwood Foundation for Newfoundland and Labrador Studies and the Institute for Social and Economic Research. He is a past member of the executive council of the Canadian Economics are public finance; natural resource development; the economics of public infrastructure investment; and fiscal federalism, including Equalization and Territorial Formula Financing. He has also worked extensively on public policy issues such as bulk water export, health care costs associated with smoking, and the treatment of natural resource revenues in Canada's Equalization Program.

Terry Fenge is the principal of Terry Fenge Consulting, which specializes in Aboriginal rights and interests, environmental affairs and national-international public policy in the circumpolar Arctic and beyond. He holds a master's degree in applied geography from the University of Victoria and a doctorate in regional planning and resource development from the University of Waterloo. He served as director of research and later as executive director of the Canadian Arctic Resources Committee, as well as director of research and senior negotiator for the Tunngavik Federation of Nunavut, the Inuit organization that negotiated the 1993 Nunavut Land Claims Agreement. From 1996 to 2006, he was strategic counsel to the chair of the Inuit Circumpolar Conference; he is currently senior policy adviser to the

Arctic Athabaskan Council; and since 2000 he has worked with Nunavut Tunngavik Incorporated to implement the Nunavut Land Claims Agreement. He is co-editor of *Northern Lights against POPs: Combatting Toxic Threats in the Arctic* (2003).

Violet Ford is vice-president of international affairs for the Inuit Circumpolar Conference (ICC Canada) and has represented ICC and Inuit interests at many international forums — in particular, the World Intellectual Property Organization. She has also represented the Inuit at the Conference of the Parties to the Convention on Biological Diversity and been a member of the official Canadian government delegation at the negotiations of this convention. She was appointed to the Nunavut Arbitration Board in 1994 and was reappointed in 1999. She is currently a doctor of laws candidate with a focus on international law at the University of Lapland (Province of Finland). She is the recipient of an Academy of Finland grant to conduct legal research on the Convention on Biological Diversity as it relates to Arctic indigenous peoples.

Danny Gaudet, a Sahtu Métis from Deline, Northwest Territories, has been a nego-tiator for the community's self-government agreement since 1999, achieving an agree-ment in principle in 2003. He is currently taking it through its final negotiation phase. He successfully completed negotiations with the Government of Canada related to the impact on his community of the government-owned Port Uranium radium mine. He maintains an active interest in promoting Deline's economic potential and protecting the wellness of the community's youth. He is the owner of Deline Construction.

Minnie Grey was born in Kangirsuk, Nunavik. She served as vice-president of Makivik Corporation. Later she became vice-president of the Canada office of the Inuit Circumpolar Conference and chaired the Nunavik Education Task Force. From 1991 to 2000 she was executive director of the Ungava Hospital and chair-person of the Nunavik Nutrition and Health Committee. She has served as exec-utive director of the Nunavik Regional Board of Health and Social Services, and was appointed to the Inuit Governing Committee under the National Aboriginal Health Organization. She led the implementation of the Tapiriilirniq process, a Nunavik Regional Board of Health initiative to address the issue of suicide. She is on the Circumpolar Inuit Health Steering Committee for the Inuit Circumpolar Council. Since 2002 she has been lead negotiator for Nunavik self-government.

Franklyn Griffiths is a professor emeritus of political science and George Ignatieff Chair Emeritus of Peace and Conflict Studies at the University of Toronto. His research interests centre on the Arctic and International security affairs. He is the author of *A Northern Foreign Policy* (1979), *Arctic Alternatives: Civility or Militarism in the Circumpolar North* (1992) and *Strong and Free: Canada and the New Sovereignty* (1997); he is also the editor of *Politics of the Northwest Passage* (1987). He has been director of the Centre for Russian and East European Studies at the University of Toronto, senior policy adviser for the Office of the Secretary of State for External Affairs, visiting professor at Stanford University and visiting scholar at Cambridge University's Scott Polar Research Institute. In 2008-09 he was a senior fellow of the Canadian International Council, for which he prepared a policy paper entitled *Towards a Canadian Arctic Strategy*.

Udloriak Hanson was born and raised in Iqaluit, Nunavut. She has two under-graduate degrees with honours in business and education. She started her career in the private sector, then moved to the nonprofit sector, where she works with Inuit land claims organizations to advance and promote Inuit interests. She has also served as an executive assistant to the minister of environment and sustainable develop-ment, Government of Nunavut. She is currently working on policy issues related to the Inuit and the Arctic with Nunavut Tunngavik Incorporated, which provides legal representation to the Inuit of Nunavut in treaty rights and negotiations.

Jack Hicks served as director of research for the Nunavut Implementation Commission and then, from 1999 to 2004, as the Government of Nunavut's director of evaluation and statistics. He is currently coordinating the Qaujivallianiq Inuusirijauvalauqtunik ("Learning from Lives That Have Been Lived") suicide follow-back study, and completing a Ph.D. dissertation entitled "The Social Determinants of Elevated Rates of Suicide among Inuit Youth."

Tom Hoefer was born and raised in Yellowknife and is the son of a gold miner. He is the director of mineral and petroleum resources for the federal government in Yellowknife, Northwest Territories. Formerly manager of communications and external relations at Canada's largest diamond producer, the Diavik diamond mine, he assisted in the development of the project for 11 years. He holds degrees in geology from the University of Saskatchewan and Queen's University. Before joining Diavik, he was manager of public affairs and environment at Highland Valley Copper in British Columbia. Prior to that he was general manager of the Northwest Territories Chamber of Mines, where he was responsible for promoting the mining industry to the public and to government.

Rob Huebert is an associate professor in the Department of Political Science at the University of Calgary and the associate director of the Centre for Military and Strategic Studies. He has also taught at Memorial University, Dalhousie University and the University of Manitoba. His research interests include international relations, strategic studies, the law of the sea, maritime affairs, Canadian foreign and defence policy, and circumpolar relations. He has published on the issues of Canadian Arctic security, maritime security and Canadian defence, co-authored a report for the Council for Canadian Security in the 21st Century entitled *To Secure a Nation* (2001) and co-edited *Commercial Satellite Imagery and United Nations Peacekeeping: A View from Above* (2004) and *Breaking Ice: Canadian Integrated Ocean Management in the Canadian North* (2005). He comments on Canadian security and Arctic issues in the Canadian and international media.

Stephanie Irlbacher-Fox is a Yellowknife-based political anthropologist who has spent the last decade working for indigenous peoples' organizations in the Northwest Territories, with a focus on self-government, Northwest Territories devolution and resource-revenue-sharing negotiations, and community development processes. She holds a BA and an MA in political science from the University of Alberta and a Ph.D. from Cambridge University. She works as a researcher and negotiations and political adviser to indigenous governments in the Northwest Territories. She is a research associate at the Canadian Circumpolar Institute of the University of Alberta and the Stefansson Arctic Institute, Iceland. Her latest book is *Finding Dahshaa: Self Government, Social Suffering, and Aboriginal Policy in Canada* (forthcoming).

Laura MacKenzie was born and raised in Rankin Inlet, Nunavut, and she has served her community in various capacities, working for cooperatives, nonprofit organizations and government. She was appointed vice-chairperson of the board of governors of Nunavut Arctic College and has served as chairperson of the Nunavut Research Institute. She is regional director of community operations in the Kivalliq region for the Department of Economic Development and Transportation, Government of Nunavut.

Doug McArthur is a professor of public policy in the graduate public policy program at Simon Fraser University and was a senior fellow in public policy at the University of British Columbia. He has served as deputy minister to the premier, as cabinet secretary and deputy minister of Aboriginal affairs in British Columbia; as chief land claims negotiator in the Yukon; as deputy minister of northern Saskatchewan; and deputy minister of agriculture in Saskatchewan. From 1978 to 1982, he was Saskatchewan's minister of education. He has acted as an adviser to the Tsawwassen First Nation. He was an international observer for the 2004 Ukraine elections and an adviser to members of the Afghanistan Parliament elected in 2005, and he advised Pakistan's democratic political parties on renewal. He is a graduate of the University of Saskatchewan, the University of Toronto and the University of Oxford, where he was a Rhodes Scholar.

Stephen J. Mills is a consultant with over 15 years' experience in a wide range of fields, including treaty negotiations, community economic development, business development, and socio-economic and environmental assessment. He is a member of the Vuntut Gwitchin First Nation and an active hunter and trapper. He is president of Vuntut Development Corporation, vice-president of Air North, executive member of the Yukon Environmental and Socio-economic Assessment Board, chair of the Yukon Surface Rights Board, chief negotiator for the Vuntut Gwitchin First Nation and fiscal negotiator for Deline in the Northwest Territories.

Natan Obed is an Inuk from Nain, Labrador. He is the director of social and cultural development for Nunavut Tunngavik Incorporated, the Inuit representational organization for Nunavut. He holds a BA in English and Native studies from Tufts University. He has worked as socio-economic development director for Inuit Tapiriit Kanatami, and as Voisey's Bay Project Impacts and Benefits Agreement coordinator for the Labrador Inuit Association.

Aynslie Ogden of Whitehorse, Yukon, is a senior research forester for the Government of Yukon. She recently completed a Ph.D. at the University of British Columbia. She is a registered professional forester, a registered professional biologist and a professional agrologist in British Columbia and has been working in the field of land and resource management for almost 15 years. She played a key role in establishing the Northern Climate ExChange and the northern office of the Canadian Climate Impacts and Adaptation Research Network. She developed and taught a course on climate change for Yukon College and contributed to the northern chapter of the National Climate Change Assessment.

Tony Penikett served as the MLA for Whitehorse West in the Yukon Legislative Assembly from 1978 to 1995 and he was premier of the territory from 1985 to 1992. His government negotiated an umbrella agreement for First Nations land claims and final treaty and self-government agreements with four First Nations. The government also developed pioneering education, environment and human rights legislation. Penikett later worked as a senior official in the Saskatchewan and British Columbia public services. Today he provides mediation and negotiation services through his company Tony Penikett Negotiations Inc. He wrote *Reconciliation: First Nations Treaty Making in British Columbia* (2006).

Hanne K. Petersen completed a degree in environmental biology at the University of Copenhagen. For 13 years she was the director of the Arctic Department of the Environment in the Ministry of the Environment. In 2001, she became the director of the Danish Polar Center, and in 2007 she became head of secretariat at the Danish Agency for Science, Technology and Innovation. She has participated in the Arctic Council since it was established, and for four years she chaired the working group of the council's Arctic Monitoring and Assessment Programme. She was host to the International Conference on Arctic Research Planning (ICARP) 2005 in Copenhagen and member of the steering group. She was on the board of the United Nations Environment Programme Global Resource Information Database, and she was a member of the Danish/Greenlandic Commission for Science in Greenland, the regional board of the International Arctic Science Committee and the European Polar Board executive. She serves on the Norwegian National Committee on Polar Research.

Greg Poelzer is the director of the International Centre for Governance and Development and associate professor of political studies, and an associate member of the School of Public Policy and the School of the Environment and Sustainability at the University of Saskatchewan. He was the inaugural dean of undergraduate studies at the University of the Arctic, a consortium of 110 universities, colleges, indigenous organizations and NGOs. He leads the University of the Arctic's international Northern Governance Thematic Network. His research focuses on comparative politics and policy as it relates to northern regions and to Aboriginal-state relations. He is the co-author of *Arctic Front: Defending Canada in the Far North* (2008).

Thierry Rodon is an adjunct professor at the School of Public Policy and Administration at Carleton University and at the Department of Political Science at Université Laval, and he is a member of the board of the Centre interuniversitaire d'études et de recherche autochtone. His research interests are Aboriginal governance, northern policy, Aboriginal education, participatory democracy and minority accommodation. He has designed and taught courses for the Nunavut Public Service Certificate, a program developed for the Nunavut government civil service, and he teaches at Nunavut Sivuniksavut. He is currently developing a training plan for the future Nunavik regional government.

F. Leslie Seidle is senior research associate at the IRPP, senior policy adviser with the Forum of Federations and a public policy consultant. He previously held a number of senior positions in the Government of Canada, including director general of strategic policy and research, intergovernmental affairs, in the Privy Council Office (1996-2002). He was the senior research coordinator for the Royal Commission on Electoral Reform and Party Financing (1990-91). He is the author of *Rethinking the Delivery of Public Services to Citizens* (1995) and numerous articles on electoral reform, citizen participation, constitutional reform, public management and political finance. He is also co-editor of *Belonging? Diversity, Recognition and Shared Citizenship in Canada* (2007) and the comparative study *Reforming Parliamentary Democracy* (2003).

Mary Simon is currently president of Inuit Tapiriit Kanatami. She was ambassador for circumpolar affairs at the Department of Foreign Affairs and International Trade from 1994 to 2003 and Canada's ambassador to Denmark from 1999 to 2001. Between 1997 and 2000 she was a member of the Joint Public Advisory Committee of NAFTA's Commission on Environmental Cooperation. She was the president of the Makivik Corporation and has held various positions with the Inuit Tapiriit Kanatami. Until 1994 she was executive council member, president and special envoy of the Inuit Circumpolar Conference. She was a senior Inuit negotiator in the repatriation of the Canadian Constitution, and in 1994 she was appointed first Canadian ambassador for circumpolar affairs. In 2004-05, she worked on reports for the conclusion of the April 2004 Canada-Aboriginal Peoples Round Table. She was special adviser to the Labrador Inuit Association on the 2004-05 land claims agreement and in 2006 became president of Inuit Tapiriit Kanatami. She is a member of the Order of Canada and holds honorary doctorates of law from McGill, Queen's and Trent Universities.

France St-Hilaire is vice-president, research, at the Institute for Research on Public Policy. She joined the IRPP as research director in 1992, and now oversees the institute's research agenda and coordinates projects in economic and social policy. She is the author of a number of monographs and articles on public finance, social policy and fiscal federalism, as well as co-editor of several volumes published by the IRPP, including *A Canadian Priorities Agenda: Policy Choices to Improve Economic and Social Well-Being* (2007) and *Money, Politics and Health Care: Reconstructing the Federal-Provincial Partnership* (2004). She holds a graduate degree in economics from the Université de Montréal and has worked as a researcher at the Institute for Policy Analysis at the University of Toronto and in the Department of Economics at the University of Western Ontario.

Richard J. Van Loon was appointed president and vice-chancellor of Carleton University in 1996 and reappointed for a four-year term in 2001. His career in government and academia has spanned almost 40 years, and he has held a number of senior positions in the federal government. Prior to his appointment at Carleton, he was associate deputy minister at Health Canada, a position he held for two years. He has also served as associate deputy minister of Indian affairs and northern development. He taught political studies at Queen's University, and public administration at Carleton University and the University of Ottawa. He has a Ph.D. in political studies from Queen's University and an MA in political science from Carleton University.

Sheila Watt-Cloutier is past chair of the Inuit Circumpolar Conference (ICC). From 1995 to 1998, she was corporate secretary of the Makivik Corporation. Elected as president of ICC Canada in 1995, she was re-elected in 1998. She was spokesperson for a coalition of northern indigenous peoples in the global negotiations that led to the 2001 Stockholm Convention. In 2002, she was elected international chair of the ICC and contributed to ICC Canada's Institution-Building for Northern Russian Indigenous Peoples project. For the past few years she has worked through the Inter-American Commission on Human Rights to defend Inuit human rights against climate change. She holds an honorary doctorate of law from the University of Winnipeg, and honorary degrees from the universities of Guelph, Royal Roads, McMaster, Wilfred Laurier, and INRS at Université du Québec. She is an officer of the Order of Canada, and in February 2007 she was nominated for the Nobel Peace Prize.

Graham White is a professor of political science at the University of Toronto. His main area of interest is the structures and processes of government at the provincial and territorial levels. The most recent of his 10 books is *Cabinets and First Ministers* (2006). Since the late 1980s, he has been a frequent visitor to the North, and he has written extensively about government and politics in the three territories. He is co-author of *Northern Governments in Transition: Political and Constitutional Development in the Yukon, Nunavut and the Western Northwest Territories* (1995) and the author of *Breaking the Trail to Northern Community Empowerment: The Community Transfer Initiative in Cape Dorset* (1998). He is currently finishing two books, one on the comanagement and regulatory boards established under the northern comprehensive claims and the other on the decentralization of the Nunavut government.

John B. Zoe is a member of the Tlicho First Nation and lives in Behchokò, Northwest Territories. With the help of community elders and resource persons, he has revived the ancestral canoe trip, an annual event during which elders share their stories with the young; these trips revive and deepen the meaning of traditional stories. In 1992, he became the chief negotiator for the Tlicho and assisted in the settlement of the community's land claim and in negotiating self-government with the Governments of Canada and the Northwest Territories. With the help of a team of tribal members and elder advisers, these negotiations were completed, and the agreement was approved and put into effect in August 2005. He is now the Tlicho executive officer for the recognized Tlicho government, and his major responsibility in that capacity is managing the development of governance and corporate structures.

Marquis Book Printing Inc.

Québec, Canada
2009

**Institute for
Research on
Public Policy**

*Institut de
recherche
en politiques
publiques*

FOUNDED IN 1972, THE INSTITUTE FOR RESEARCH ON Public Policy is an independent, national, nonprofit organization.

IRPP seeks to improve public policy in Canada by generating research, providing insight and sparking debate that will contribute to the public policy decision-making process and strengthen the quality of the public policy decisions made by Canadian governments, citizens, institutions and organizations.

IRPP's independence is assured by an endowment fund, to which federal and provincial governments and the private sector have contributed.

FONDÉ EN 1972, L'INSTITUT DE RECHERCHE EN politiques publiques (IRPP) est un organisme canadien, indépendant et sans but lucratif.

L'IRPP cherche à améliorer les politiques publiques canadiennes en encourageant la recherche, en mettant de l'avant de nouvelles perspectives et en suscitant des débats qui contribueront au processus décisionnel en matière de politiques publiques et qui rehausseront la qualité des décisions que prennent les gouvernements, les citoyens, les institutions et les organismes canadiens.

L'indépendance de l'IRPP est assurée par un fonds de dotation, auquel ont souscrit le gouvernement fédéral, les gouvernements provinciaux et le secteur privé.